KB123440

연희전문학교 운영보고서(Ⅱ)

－교장 · 부교장 · 학감 보고서(1915~1942)－

연희전문학교 운영보고서(Ⅱ)
–교장 · 부교장 · 학감 보고서(1915~1942)–

초판 1쇄 발행 2021년 3월 31일

편 자 | 연세대학교 국학연구원 연세학풍연구소
발행인 | 윤관백
발행처 | 도서출판 선인

등록 | 제5-77호(1998.11.4)
주소 | 서울시 마포구 마포대로 4다길 4 곶마루빌딩 1층
전화 | 02)718-6252 / 6257 팩스 | 02)718-6253
E-mail | sunin72@chol.com

정가 83,000원

ISBN 979-11-6068-468-1 94370
ISBN 978-89-5933-622-7 (세트)

연세사료총서 9

연희전문학교 운영보고서(Ⅱ)

-교장 · 부교장 · 학감 보고서(1915~1942)-

연세학풍연구소 편

▌간행사▌

연세대학교는 지난해 전 지구적인 감염병 유행으로 남 못지않은 어려움을 겪는 가운데 2035년 창립 150주년을 준비하고 도전과 선도, 창의와 혁신, 공존과 헌신의 가치를 지향할 것을 다짐하였다. 연세인들은 대학의 이념, 정신, 비전을 명확하게 인지하였든 인지하지 못하였든 간에 누대에 걸쳐 한 울타리 안에서 지내는 동안 그 본질을 감지하여 후속세대에 전수하고 시대적 여건에 맞춰 변형해왔다. 그러므로 2020년의 이런 비전도 본교 설립 정신을 창의적으로 발현한 것이라고 할 수 있다. 다만 아쉬운 점은 그 설립 정신의 본체가 무엇이고, 어떻게 전수되었으며, 한국 근현대사 속에서 어떤 의미를 주었는지를 오늘날 충분히 규명하지 못하고 있다는 것이다.

연세학풍연구소는 연세대학의 역사와 정신에 관한 자료 편찬, 연구, 교육, 홍보의 업무를 전담하도록 2017년 본교 국학연구원 산하에 설치되었다. 그 후 자료 편찬 분야에서는 연희전문학교의 제2대 교장인 에비슨(O. R. Avison)의 문서들을 모아서 발행하는 일에 주력해왔다. 본교의 설립자이자 연희전문 제1대 교장인 언더우드(H. G. Underwood)의 문서들은 본 연구소가 설립되기 전 2005~2010년간에 국학연구원에서 발간한 바 있다. 지난해에 본 연구소는 연희전문의 역대 임원들이 썼던 보고서들을 편찬해도 될 만큼 모았다고 판단하고, 1915년부터 1942년까지 역대 교장들, 부교장들, 학감들이 작성한 총 60편의 보고서들을 영인하여 발간할 계획을 세웠다. 보고서 작성자들이 학교의 운영 주체들이었기 때문에 자연스럽게 이 책에 『연희전문학교 운영보고서』란 제목을 붙이게 되었고, 연세대학교 박물관에서 2013년 『연희전문학교 운영보고서』 (上) · (下)권을 펴낸 적이 있었기 때문에 본서를 그 후속편인 'II'권으로 만들면서 국학연구원의 《연세사료총서 9》 안에 넣게 되었다.

전편인 (上)·(下)권과 후속편인 'II'권을 비교하면, 전자는 학교 차원에서 공식적으로 발행한 영문, 한글, 일문 보고서들을 엮은 것—예외적으로 교장의 연례보고서 2편 포함—이고, 후자는 운영진이 각각 직책에 따라 업무상 작성한 여러 형태의 영문 보고서들을 엮은 것이다. 또한 전자는 1923년부터 1941년까지의 문서들을 수록하고, 후자는 1915년 대학 개교 전부터 1942년까지의 문서들을 수록하고 있다. 전자는 학교 상황을 종합적으로 보여주지만, 후자는 학교 상황과 함께 운영진의 활동상과 생각 등도 보여준다.

이런 특징들로 인해 『연희전문학교 운영보고서(II)』에서는 독자들이 연희전문을 이끌었던 주요 인물들에게서 직접 보고받는 자리에 선 듯한 마음으로 그들에게 질문을 던지며 학교의 여러 면모를 더 다양하게 살펴볼 수 있다. 연희전문의 역사를 초창기부터 일제 말까지 연대기를 보듯이 개관해볼 수도 있고, 체제 확립과정, 학사 운영방식, 학풍 형성과정을 살펴볼 수도 있으며, 각 시기의 학교 현안과 학과, 교수, 학생, 졸업생, 음악·체육·종교활동, 도서관·박물관 등의 현황을 살펴볼 수도 있다. 학교의 경계를 넘어 한국근대사의 연구 자료로도 활용할 수 있음은 물론이다.

본서는 독자의 편의를 위해 각 보고서의 원문 앞에 작성자, 수신자, 작성 시기, 작성 배경, 이본의 유무 등을 설명하고 내용을 요약한 설명문을 함께 제시하고 있다. 이 보고서들은 미국 장로교와 감리교 아카이브들에서 수집하였는데, 감리교 측 자료들은 본 연구소의 전임 전문연구원인 최재건 교수께서 제공해주셨다. 이를 바탕으로 자료를 더 수집하고 보완하여 정리하고 설명문을 작성하는 일은 본 연구소의 전문연구원인 문백란 박사가 맡아서 하였다. 그리고 이 자료집의 체제 설정 및 설명문의 교정과 윤문, 전체 내용의 감수는 연세학연구소의 초대 소장인 김도형 교수께서 해주셨다. 두 분의 헌신에 진심으로 감사드린다. 학교의 정책 과제로서 이 책을 편찬할 수 있게 해준 서승환 총장께도 감사드린다. 자료를 제공해준 최재건 교수와 사진 선정·행정 업무 측면에서 편찬을 도운 본 연구소의 정운형 박사, 그리고 영인과 편집의 까다로운 작업을 감당해준 선인출판사의 편집진에 깊은 감사의 뜻을 전한다.

2021년 3월

연세대학교 국학연구원장 겸 연세학풍연구소장
김성보

▌일러두기▐

1. 번역 용어

1) 'president', 'vice-president', 'dean' 등의 직책명은 실제로 사용된 '교장', '부교장', '학감' 등으로 표기하였다.
2) 초기에 나오는 'registrar'는 '학사 기록관'을 뜻하지만, 학감이 이 직을 수행하였으므로 '학감'으로 표기하였다.
3) 'Board of managers'는 직역하면 '관리이사회'가 되고, 또 'Field Board'는 선교지 한국에 있는 대학이사회라는 의미를 지니므로, 이를 모두 '이사회'로 통칭하였다.
4) 선교사를 파송한 미국 · 캐나다 등의 교단 선교본부는 '선교부'로, 재한 선교사들의 한국 내 조직은 '선교회'로, '선교회'의 지방 거점은 '지회'로 표기하였다.

2. 보고서 소개

1) 개개의 문서 앞에 기초정보를 정리하고, 작성 배경과 이본(異本) 등을 설명하며, 내용을 요약하는 페이지를 두었다.
2) 내용 요약 부분에서 교수들의 명단이나 교육 · 연구 활동을 다룰 때는 한국인 교수들의 이름, 직급, 역할을 가능한 한 구체적으로 밝히고, 영문 이니셜로 표기된 이름을 한국명으로 옮겼다.
3) 내용 요약 부분에서 원문에 없는 내용을 첨부 · 설명할 때는 '역자주' 표기 없이 [ ]로, 원문에 있는 것을 가져와서 보충하거나 내용 요약이 힘든 명세서, 규칙, 목록 등을 소개할 때는 ( )로 표시하였다.

3. 소장처 표기

보고서들은 미국 장로교 역사연구소(Presbyterian Historical Society)와 연합감리교회 역사자료보관소(United Methodist Archives and History Center)에 소장되어 있다. 전자는 'PHS', 후자는 'UMAH'란 약어로 표기하였다. 두 곳의 문서를 비교하여, 보완되거나 이본이 있는 경우에는 자료 소개 부분에서 설명하였다.

4. 보고서 작성자 및 수신자 소개

보고서를 작성한 사람들(1~9번)과 수신한 사람들(10~13번)은 아래와 같다. 그들에 대해서는 해제에서 더 자세히 설명하였다.

1) 언더우드(Horace G. Underwood, 1859~1916): 연희전문 설립자, 초대 교장(1915~1916).
2) 에비슨(Oliver R. Avison, 1860~1956): 제2대 교장(1917~1934) 및 세브란스의학전문학교 교장.
3) 원한경(Horace H. Underwood, 1890~1951): 제3대 교장(1934~1941), 언더우드 초대 교장의 아들.
4) 베커(Arthur L. Becker, 1879~1978): 수물과 과장·학감(1915~1925), 부교장(1923~1926, 1939~1941), 교장 대리(1923~1926).
5) 빌링스(B. W. Billings, 1881~1969): 부교장(1915~1923), 문과 과장(1915~1928).
6) 로즈(Harry A. Rhodes, 1875~1965): 신과 교수 및 과장(1918~1933), 학감 대리(1919~1921).
7) 유억겸(俞億兼, 1896~1947): 상과 교수(1923~1938, 1941~), 학감(1925~1938), 부교장(1934~1938).
8) 이춘호(李春昊, 1893~1950): 수물과 교수(1922~1938, 1939~) 및 과장(1925~1938), 학감 대리(1931~1932, 1937~1938).
9) 이묘묵(李卯默, 1902~1957): 문과 교수(1934~1937, 1938~) 겸 도서관장(1934~1937, 1938), 학감 대리(1938~).
10) 이사회(Board of managers): 1915년 3월 5일 창립. 미국과 캐나다의 4개 교단을 대표하는 선교사 이사들과 한국인·일본인 선출직 이사들로 구성.

11) 북장로회 서울지회(Seoul Station of the Korea Mission of the Board of Foreign Mission of the Presbyterian Church in the U.S.A.): 재한 장로교 선교사들 다수의 반대 속에서 대학설립을 주도.

12) 합동위원회(Joint Committee on Education in Korea, 약칭 Joint Committee): 한국에서 선교하는 6개 교단(미국 북장로회 · 남장로회 · 북감리회 · 남감리회, 캐나다장로회, 호주장로회) 선교본부들이 1912년 결성한 한국 내 고등교육사업 협의기구.

13) 협력이사회(Cooperating Board for Christian Education in Chosen, 약칭 Cooperating Board): 1917년 연희전문학교와 세브란스연합의학전문학교 인가 취득 후 두 대학을 후원하기 위해 1918년 합동위원회를 확대 · 개편한 조직.

▌차 례▌

【언더우드 초대 교장 시기】

【에비슨 2대 교장 시기】

【원한경 3대 교장 시기】

▎해 제▎

1. 자료소개

1) 소장처

이 자료집은 현재까지 찾아낸 총 60개의 보고서를 수록하고 있다. 그러나 다 찾지 못하여 빠진 것이 있고, 1917년, 1924년, 1934년도는 보고서들이 모두 누락되어 있다. 이 문서들은 미국 필라델피아에 있는 장로교 역사연구소(Presbyterian Historical Society, 이하 PHS)와 뉴저지주의 드류신학교 안에 있는 연합감리교회 역사자료보관소(United Methodist Archives and History Center, 이하 UMAH)에 소장되어 있다. 특별히 이 지료집에서 소개하는 언더우드 초대 교장의 보고서들 가운데 차례 번호 1번, 3~5번, 7번 문서는 이 두 소장처에 있지만, 연세대학교 출판부에서 발행한 『언더우드 자료집』에 수록되지 않은 것들이다. 한편 1934~35년도 연례 교장보고서는 이 책에 없는 대신 연세대학교 박물관에서 펴낸 운영보고서 상권에 실려 있다.

PHS에서 제공한 'Korea Mission Records 1904~1960: Box 15 Folder 14~29'란 이름의 마이크로필름 Reel 3개에는 연희전문과 세브란스의전의 각종 보고서와 이사회 회의록만 담겨 있다. 그런데 여기에도 빠진 문서들이 있어 또 다른 마이크로필름 문서군인 'Korea Mission Records 1903~1957'과 PHS에 있는 원본 파일들에서도 몇몇 자료를 찾아냈다. 현재 'Korea Mission Records 1904~1960'은 연세대 중앙도서관에도 있고, 'Korea Mission Records 1903~1957'은 국립 중앙박물관과 연세대 중앙도서관에도 있다.

UMAH에도 두 대학의 문서들이 충실하게 소장되어 있다. 그곳에서 제공한 이미지 파일에는 'Board of Managers,' 'Underwood, Horace H. (Dr.),' 'Cooperating Board for Education in Chosen,' 'Chosen Christian College' 등의 범주, 문서 작성 연도, 작성자에 따라 이미지 파일명이 조금씩 다르게 붙여져 있다. 이 파일들은 현재 연세대 국학연구원 연세학풍연구소에 입수되어 있다.

2) 작성 기간, 작성자, 수신자

(1) 작성 기간

본 자료집은 1915년부터 1942년까지 연희전문학교의 역대 교장, 부교장, 학감이 영문으로 작성하여 제출한 보고서들을 수록하고 있다. 그 기간은 대학이 개교를 목전에 두고 있던 때로부터 제3대 교장이 조선총독부의 압력으로 사임하고 떠날 때까지이다. 따라서 이 보고서들은 대학이 개교를 준비한 때로부터 일제 말에 파행을 맞을 때까지 전체 과정을 포괄하고 있다.

(2) 작성자

보고서를 작성한 사람들은 다음과 같다.

직책	순서	이름	재임 기간
교장	1	언더우드(H. G. Underwood, 元杜尤, 1859~1916)	1915.4~1916.10
	2	에비슨(O. R. Avison, 魚丕信, 1860~1956)	1917.2~1934.10
	3	원한경(H. H. Underwood, 元漢慶, 1890~1951)	1934.10~1941.3
부교장	1	에비슨	1915.12~1917.2
	2	빌링스(B. W. Billings, 邊永瑞, 1881~1969)	1917.2~1923
	3	베커(A. L. Becker, 白雅德, 1879~1979)	1923~1926.6 1939.2~1941.2?
	4	원한경	1927.9~1934.10
	5	유억겸(俞億兼, 1896~1947)	1934.10~1938
학감	1	베커	1915.4~1919.3 1921.9~1925.9
	2	로즈(H. A. Rhodes, 魯解理, 1875~1965) (대리)	1919.3~1921.10

	3	유억겸	1925.9~1938
	4	이춘호(李春昊, 1893~1950) (대리)	1931~32, 1937~38
	5	이묘묵(李卯默, 1902~1957)	1938~?

교장의 교체는 언더우드의 죽음(1916)과 에비슨의 사임(1934)을 계기로 이루어졌고, 부교장의 교체는 위의 계기 외에 빌링스와 베커의 안식년(각각 1923, 1926)을 계기로 이루어졌다. 학감의 교체와 대리(Acting Dean) 또는 부학감((Assistant-Dean) 임명은 베커의 안식년(1919)과 업무 과다(1915, 1925), 유억겸의 안식년 미국 여행(1931)과 업무 과다(1937~38)와 흥업구락부 사건 연루(1938)를 계기로 이루어졌다.

① 교장

언더우드 제1대 교장은 내한 초기부터 의학교를 포함하는 종합대학의 설립을 주창하여 마침내 1915년 4월 12일 조선기독교대학을 개교하고 초대 교장과 이사장이 되었다. 그 후 총독부의 교육법에 따라 전문학교 인가를 받기 위해 노력하던 중 건강이 악화되어 1916년 10월 12일 미국 애틀랜틱시티에서 57세를 일기로 사망하였다.

에비슨 제2대 교장은 이사회에 의해 1915년 12월 부교장으로, 1917년 2월 교장으로 선임되었다. 그 후 총독부로부터 조선기독교대학이 연희전문학교란 교명으로 인가(1917년 4월)를 받게 하고 학교 발전의 기틀을 닦았다. 1922년 12월 열린 연희전문 이사회와 세브란스의전 이사회 연석회의의 결정으로 양교 교장의 행정업무를 부교장 이하 임원들에게 맡기고 대외활동만 하게 되었다. 연희전문에서 이 결정은 1927년 9월 철회되었는데, 에비슨은 그 사이 1924~26년 기간에 (1925~26년에는 원한경과 더불어) 미국에서 모금 활동을 펼쳤다. 이 일은 1929년 연희전문이 누적 적자를 해소하고 이후에 눈부신 발전을 이루는 효과를 내었다. 그는 1934년 10월 교장직을 사임하고 1935년 12월 한국을 떠났다.

원한경 제3대 교장은 1915년 개교 첫해부터 조선기독교대학에서 영어와 심리학을 가르쳤다. 1925년 뉴욕대학에서 박사학위를 받았고, 1927년 9월 연희전문 부교장이 되었으며, 1934년 10월 12일 3대 교장으로 취임하였다. 1941년 2월 일제의 압력으로 교장직을 사임하였고, 1941년 12월 일제의 진주만 공습 다음 날 체포 · 구금되어 1942년 6월 1일 추방되었다. 해방 후 1945년 10월 다시 내한하여 미군정청에서 고문으로 활동하고 연희전문의 재건을 도왔으며 1951년 2월 부산에서 사망하였다.

② 부교장 · 학감

빌링스는 평양 숭실학교 대학부에서 가르치다가 조선기독교대학의 창립을 도왔고, 영어와 성경을 가르치면서 1917년부터 1923년까지 부교장을, 1928년까지 문과 과장을 역임하였다. 1932년 교수직을 사임하고 감리교신학교 교장으로 부임하였다. 1940년 한국을 떠났다가 1946년 4월 다시 내한하여 구호사업을 하고 1953년 미국으로 돌아갔다.

베커는 숭실학교 대학부에서 가르치다가 1914년부터 언더우드와 함께 대학설립을 주도하였고, 개교 후 학감과 수물과 과장을 역임하였다. 1919년 봄부터 1921년 9월까지 안식년을 보내면서 미시간대학에서 물리학 박사학위를 받고 돌아온 후, 수물과 과장(~1925)과 학감(~1925)만 아니라 부교장(1923~26)까지 겸직하였고, 에비슨이 미국에 갔을 때(1924.3~1926.8)는 교장직까지 대리하였다. 1926년 6월부터 2년간 안식년을 보냈고, 1939년 2월 부교장으로 다시 선임되었으나 6월부터 안식년을 가져 부재상태에서 직책만 한동안 유지하였다. 해방 후 다시 내한하여 미군정청 고문관, 연희대학 이사로 활동하였다.

로즈는 평북 강계에서 선교활동을 하다 1918년 연희전문 교수로 부임하여 신과 과장을 역임하면서 종교교육을 전담하였다. 베커가 안식년을 보내는 1919~21년에는 그를 대신하여 학감직을 맡았다. 1925년 그로브시티대학에서 신학박사 학위를 받았고, 1933년 학교를 떠나 피어선성경학원(현 평택대학교) 교장이 되었다. 1934년과 1965년 미국북장로교 한국선교회사 2권을 저술하여 백낙준으로부터 이어지는 연세대학교의 한국교회사 연구 대열에 합류하였다.

유억겸은 개화파 인사인 유길준의 둘째 아들로 도쿄제국대학 법학부를 졸업하고 1923년 9월 연희전문 상과 교수로 부임하여 시민법과 상법을 가르쳤다. 한동안 부학감(부학감이 된 때는 미상)으로 있다가 1925년 9월 베커가 부교장과 학감을 겸직하고 미국에 간 에비슨의 교장업무까지 대신 보던 상황에서 학감이 되었고, 1931년 7월부터 1932년 3월 초까지 안식년을 얻어 미국에 다녀왔다. 1934년 원한경 부교장이 교장으로 취임할 때 부교장으로 승진하여 학감을 겸직하였고, 1937년 원한경이 미국에 다녀오는 동안에는 교장업무를 대신 보았다. 흥업구락부, 신간회 등에서도 활동하였고, 1938년 흥업구락부사건으로 체포되자 교수직을 사임하였다. 1941년 복직하여 원한경 교장 대신 윤치호가 교장이 되었을 때 학교 운영을 주도하다 1942년 사임하였다. 해방 후 재건된 연희전문학교 교장, 미군정청 문교부장, 조선체육회장을 역임하였다.

이춘호는 개성에서 태어나 오하이오 웨슬리언대학을 졸업하고 오하이오 주립대 대학원에서 한국 최초로 수학석사 학위를 받았다. 1922년 수물과 교수로 부임하여 수학과 천문학을 가르쳤고, 1925년 수물과 과장이 되었으며, 1930~31년간에 안식년을 얻어 미국에 다녀왔다. 귀국 후 유억겸 학감이 안식년을 갖게 되자 학감을 대리하였고, 1937년에도 원한경 교장이 미국에 가서 유억겸이 교장을 대리하게 되자 학감을 대리하였다. 1938년 흥업구락부사건으로 체포된 후 사임하였다가 1939년 복직하였다. 1947년 제2대 서울대 총장, 1948년 문교부 차장을 역임하였고, 1950년 전쟁 중에 납북되었다.

이묘묵은 평남 중화에서 태어나 연희전문 문과를 졸업하였고, 오하이오주 마운트유니온대학을 거쳐 뉴욕주 시라큐스대학에서 도서관학 석사학위를 받고 보스턴대학에서 역사전공으로 철학박사 학위를 받았다. 1934년 연희전문 문과 교수로 부임하여 영어를 가르쳤고, 도서관장을 맡았으며, 박물관장을 겸하기도 하였다. 1937년 동우회사건으로 체포된 후 사임하였다가 복직하여 영어와 서양사를 가르쳤다. 1938년 유억겸이 흥업구락부사건으로 체포되자 학감 대리를 거쳐 학감과 도서관장을 역임하였다. 해방 후 미군정장관 하지 중장의 통역, 주영공사 등으로 활동하였다.

그밖에 이노익(Root Lee) 수물과 조교수가 개교 후 1915년 4월 교수회에서 부학감으로 지명된 일이 있었다. 그는 네브라스카주 웨슬리언대학을 졸업하였고, 개교 후 첫 학기부터 학교 형편에 따라 수물과 또는 응용화학과에 속하여 입체기하학, 천문학, 물리학, 화학, 생리학을 가르쳤다. 그는 더 공부하기 위해 1920~21년 기간에 사임하고 1921년 초에 미국으로 떠났다.

(3) 수신자

① 이사회

이사회는 1915년 3월 5일 오전 9시 예수교서회에 모인 3개 미국 장·감 교단의 선교사 9명에 의해 창립되었다. 창립 회의는 5일과 6일 이틀간 진행되었다. 언더우드는 보고서에서 이를 '임시이사회'(provisional Board of Field Managers)라고 칭하였으나, 이사회 회의록

기록자는 'provisional'란 단어 없이 '이사회'(Board of Field Managers)란 명칭만 사용하였다. 연례회의는 연희전문의 학기가 3학기제로 4월, 9월, 1월에 시작되는 것에 맞추어 2월이나 3월에 열렸으나, 중간에 수년 동안 9월 중에 열리기도 하였다.

이사회의 구성을 보면, 한국인과 일본인 선출직 이사도 있었으나, 본교의 설립과 운영에 참여한 해외 교단들을 대표하는 선교계 이사가 계속 다수를 이룬 가운데 한국인 이사들과의 수적 차이가 점점 줄어들고 있었다. 한국인은 1917년 2월부터 신흥우를 필두로 이사진에 참가하였다. 1923년 9월부터는 조선예수교장로회 총회, 감리회 연회, 연희전문 동창회에서 파견한 대표들이 이사로 합류하였다. 그에 따라 회의가 영어로 진행되다가 이때부터 2개 언어로 진행되었고, 1942년 원한경 교장의 회고문에 따르면, 일제가 일어만 쓰도록 강제하기 전에는 한국어로 진행되었다. 이 자료집의 보고서들은 영어로 진행된 이사회 회의에 제출하기 위해서만 아니라 미국에 보내기 위해서도 영어로 작성되었다.

이사회가 개회하면 교장과 학감이 업무보고서를 제출하였고, 부교장도 때에 따라 보고서를 제출하였다. 그밖에 회계보고서와 건축보고서 등의 사안별 보고서들도 회의 때 제출되었다. 이 모든 보고서와 이사회 회의록은 그 후 미국으로 발송되어 그곳에서 보관되었다. 그리하여 연세대학교에 있는 한국어 · 일어 · 영어 문서들과 더불어 오늘날 학교 상황을 알려주는 중요한 1차 자료들이 되고 있다.

② 합동위원회 · 협력이사회

학교에서 발송한 보고서들과 회의록은 합동위원회(Joint Committee) 또는 협력이사회(Cooperating Board)의 뉴욕 사무실에서 수신하였다.

합동위원회는 한국에서 선교사업을 과점하고 있던 미국 북장로회 · 남장로회 · 북감리회 · 남감리회, 캐나다장로회, 호주장로회의 6개 교단 선교본부(이하 선교부)들이 한국에서 대학설립 문제가 부상하는 것에 대응하기 위해 1912년 뉴욕에서 언더우드가 참석한 가운데 결성한 협의체였다. 한국에서 활동하는 장로교 선교사들의 다수는 서울에 대학을 세우는 것을 반대하였지만, 합동위원회의 6개 교단 선교부 대표들은 1914년 서울에 종합대학을 세울 것을 결정하였다. 그러나 그 후에는 신설 대학의 기독교적 성격을 확실히 보장하도록 설립과정을 까다롭게 감독하여 이 일을 추진하던 언더우드를 비롯한 장로교 소수파와 감리교 선교사들의 애를 태웠다.

합동위원회는 자신들이 연합하여 후원하는 대학들이 1917년 4월과 5월에 각각 연희전문학교와 세브란스연합의학전문학교란 이름으로 인가를 받은 후에는 두 대학의 운영을 뒷받침하도록 역할을 조정할 필요를 느꼈다. 그리하여 1918년 1월 뉴욕에서 에비슨이 참석한 가운데 협력이사회(Cooperating Board)를 발족시켰다. 이 새 조직은 기존의 합동위원회 인적 구성에 언더우드(J. T. Underwood), 세브란스(J. L. Severance)를 합류시켜 연희전문과 세브란스의전을 재정적으로 후견하는 체제를 갖추었다. 이들은 두 대학의 학사업무와 교직원 인사행정에는 관여하지 않았다. 그러나 학교의 기본 재산, 경상비, 교수 봉급을 분담하고, 각종 기부금과 기부 물품을 받아서 전달하며, 두 대학과 미국 업체 간의 거래(건축가 선정, 설비 · 기기 구매 등)를 돕는 역할을 하였기 때문에 학교 운영상황에 관해 계속 보고를 받았다. 그런데 연희전문을 위해서는 애초에 협력이사회의 형성에 참여했던 6개 교단(호주장로회가 나중에 탈퇴하여 5개 교단 협력체제가 되었다) 가운데 4개 교단, 곧 미국 북장로회, 남 · 북감리회, 캐나다장로회만 후원하였다. 미국 남장로회와 호주장로회의 선교부들은 그들의 재한 선교사들이 평양 측에 동조하고 연희전문과의 연대를 반대하였기 때문에 후원하지 못하였다. 협력이사회의 양교 후원은 일제 말에 한동안 중단되었지만, 해방 후까지 이어졌다.

③ 그밖의 수신자들

연희전문의 교장들과 학감들은 이사회가 아닌 다른 곳들에도 업무보고서를 보냈다. 먼저 교장들은 때때로 서울에 있는 북장로회 선교사들에게 보고서를 보냈다. 그들은 한국에서 활동하는 장로교 선교사들 사이에서는 소수파를 이루었지만, 다수파의 강력한 반대를 무릅쓰면서 본 대학의 설립을 주도하였다. 대학설립 후에는 학교 운영을 주도하였는데, 그들 중 언더우드는 초대 교장을, 에비슨은 2대 교장을, 원한경은 3대 교장을 역임하였다. 겐소(J. F. Genso)는 초대 회계를 맡으면서 대학 자산을 그의 명의로 등기하였으며, 밀러(E. H. Miller)는 건축위원장으로 활동하였다.

그밖에도 협력이사회나 미국 북장로회 · 북감리회와 같은 개별 교단의 지도자들에게도 교장과 학감이 학교 상황을 알리는 업무보고서를 발송하였다. 물론 이 모든 후원 요청은 학교 이사회의 승인 아래 이루어졌다. 학생들의 학비와 한국사회의 기부금이 학교 수입에서 차지하는 비중이 매우 적은 형편에서 해외로부터 후원금을 얻는 것은 필수 불가결한 일이었다. 그런데 일제 말에는 학교가 폐교되지 않기를 바라는 한국인들의 후원금이 크게 늘어 국내 후원금만으로도 학교 운영이 가능해지는 상황이 빚어졌다.

2. 자료를 통해 알 수 있는 것

연희전문의 역사는 한국 근대사와 불가분의 관계를 맺고 한국사회의 중심에서 시대의 흐름을 선도하거나 영향을 받으면서 전통을 형성해왔다. 그러므로 연희전문의 기록물들은 한국 근대사의 연구를 위한 자료로 활용할 수 있다. 한국 정치사나 민족운동사만 아니라 인물사, 학술사, 건축사, 체육사, 음악사, 박물관사, 도서관사 등의 분야들에서도 자료로 활용할 수 있다. 연세대학의 역사 연구를 위한 자료가 되는 것은 말할 나위도 없다. 이 자료들을 통해 학교 역사를 개관할 수도 있고, 각 시기의 학교 규정, 정책, 현안을 알아볼 수도 있으며, 각 분야, 곧 임원과 교직원, 학생과 졸업생, 학술연구와 발표, 음악·체육·종교활동, 도서관, 박물관 등의 현황을 확인할 수도 있다. 그러나 여기에서 이 모든 것을 다룰 수는 없으므로 연희전문의 설립과 발전과정, 학사 운영방식, 학풍의 형성과정과 관련하여 살펴보고자 한다.

그런데 연희전문의 역사를 충실하게 연구하려면, 다음의 1차 자료들을 이 자료집과 함께 참고하면 더 좋을 것이다. 그 자료들에는 연희전문 이사회 회의록(미간행), 회계보고서(미간행), 연세대 박물관에서 펴낸『연희전문학교 운영보고서』상·하(선인, 2013)의 영문 일람(Bulletin)·한글 상황보고서·일문 일람, 연세대 도서관에 소장된 연희전문의 각종 학회지, 동문회보, 학생단체 간행물, 연세대 국학연구원에서 펴낸『언더우드 자료집』1~5권(2005~2010)과『에비슨 자료집』I~V(2017~2020)이 있다.

1) 학교의 설립과 발전

(1) 설립 정신

본 자료집의 보고서들은 대학의 개교가 초읽기에 들어갔을 때부터 작성되어 시종 각 시기의 실무와 현안들을 처리하는 일에 집중하고 있다. 그런 가운데서도 일정한 원칙과 지향점을 가지고 학교가 운영되었던 것을 보여주고 있다.

① 기독교주의

대학설립을 준비할 때는 동조자들과 후원자들에게 기독교 교육에 대한 확고한 의지를 보여주는 것이 가장 중요하였다. 이는 재한 선교사들의 다수가 총독부의 교육법을 반(反)기독교 법률로 여기고 대학설립을 극렬하게 반대하였기 때문이었다. 이에 1915년 4월 개교 후에 열린 이사회에서 언더우드 교장은 적은 수의 학생들로 시작하여 최고의 기독교 이상을 구현하도록 하겠다는 의지를 밝혔다(2번). 이사회는 '기독교주의'(Christian principles)에 따라 대학을 운영한다는 기본 원칙을 정관에 명기하였다. 그런데 그 '기독교주의'가 무엇을 뜻하는지를 정의하지는 않았다. 아마도 이때의 '기독교주의'는 방금 대학을 세운 미국과 캐나다 선교사들이 공유하며 현실에서 구현하기를 소망하고 있던 그 시대의 기독교적 가치관이었을 것이다. 그러나 기독교에 대한 사회적 인식과 교계 안의 해석이 많이 달라진 1920년대와 30년대를 지나는 동안에는 아마도 당대의 연희전문 사람들 안에서 초창기와는 조금 다른 형태의 기독교 이념이 되었을 것이다.

② 연합정신

연희전문은 또한 여러 교단 사람들의 합심과 노력으로 세워졌기 때문에 처음부터 연합의 정신을 존중하였다. 그러면서 이를 교파연합에 국한하지 않고 민족과 인종 간의 화합을 꾀하는 것으로 확대하였다. 베커는 1919년 3개 민족의 교수들이 저녁 시간에 교대로 집에서 모여 월례회를 갖고 하나가 되어 건설적인 정책을 세우고 있다고 보고하였다(12번). 그런데 당시에는 교육법상으로 일본인 교수의 영입이 불가피하였으므로 운영진은 기독교인만 골라서 받아들이면서 영입한 일본인들이 독실한 기독교인임을 강조하였다(4번). 그런 점에서 그들이 추구한 연합은 기본적으로 '기독교주의' 안에서의 연합을 뜻하는 것이었다.

③ 사회지도자 육성

언더우드를 비롯한 대학 설립자들은 한국 사회를 이끌 기독교인 지도자를 육성하는 것에 목표를 두었다. 그들은 이 대학의 출신들이 장차 교회에서만 아니라 한국 사회에서도 큰 역할을 하기를 기대하였다. 그에 반해 평양 중심의 다수파 선교사들은 교인 자녀에게만 컬리지 수준의 대학교육을 제공하여 교회의 지도자와 수호자를 길러내기를 원하였다. 그런 목적에서 대학을 새로 세우지 말고 평양에 이미 있는 숭실대만을 운영해가기를 원하였다. 교인이 아닌 사람들을 가르치는 일에 선교비를 많이 쓰는 것은 온당하지 않다고 여겼고, 서울은 정치적이고 온갖 악과 세속적인 유혹이 많아 종교교육을 방해하므로 교육기관을 두기에 합당하지 않다고 주장하였다(편지: S. A. Moffett to A. J. Brown, Jan. 11, 1913; W. N. Blair to A. J. Brown, Jan. 13, 1913). 그러나 서울 중심의 소수파 선교사들은 한국의 중심지인 서울에서 경쟁력 있는 교육을 제공하여 기독교의 영향력을 전방위적으로 확대하기를 원하였다(편지: Lillias Underwood to A. J. Brown, 1913. 5. 23; Noble, Bunker, Underwood, Hardie, Avison, Koons to the Joint Committee in New York, Dec. 8, 1913).

그들은 대학을 개교한 후에도 이런 뜻을 유지하였다. 에비슨 교장은 1918년 보고서에서 "한국 사회의 모든 부분에 영향을 주기 위해 6개 학과가 개설되었다"라고 말하고 "기독교 민주주의 세계의 건설을 위해" 본교에 투자해줄 것을 미국 후원자들에게 호소하였다(10번). 같은 해에 베커 학감은 좀더 구체적으로 연희전문의 교육 목표는 한국의 남학생과 여학생에게 대학교육을 제공하고 일본과 미국의 종합대학 진학을 준비시켜 한국 사회와 교육을 개선하게 하는 것이라고 밝혔다(9번). 그런 다음 총독부의 관립학교들에는 이렇게 하는 학교가 없다고 하면서 연희전문의 존재의의를 강조하였다. 실제로 연희전문 졸업생들은 처음부터 그런 기대에 부응하였다. 제1회(1919년) 졸업생들은 아직 재학 중일 때 3·1 운동을 주동하여 옥고를 치렀고(15번), 그 가운데 1명은 상해에 가서 임시정부 요원으로 활동하였다(22번). 수물과의 제1회 졸업생 3명은 미국으로 유학을 떠났다(22번). 부교장 베커가 1925년 보고서에서 제시한 통계를 보면, 졸업생 110명 가운데 20명이 미국에서, 9명이 일본에서 유학하고 있었다(27번).

④ 한국 사회와의 소통 중시

학교를 설립한 선교사들이 사회적 책임을 중시하였던 것은 한국 사회와의 소통을 중시하는 것으로도 나타났다. 베커는 1918년 보고서에서 본교는 계층과 인종과 종교를 초월하여 모두에게 고등교육을 제공할 책임이 있으며, 한국사회의 타 종교계는 본교에 관용적이고 비기독교인들은 호의적이며, 기독교인들은 본교를 기꺼이 도우려 한다고 기술하였다

(9번). 그들은 학교가 성공하려면 한국 사회의 협조를 얻어야 한다는 사실을 늘 의식하였다(1 · 2번). 그러나 처음에는 기대와 달리 학비 수입 외에 한국 사회로부터 경제적인 지원을 거의 얻지 못하였다. 예를 들면, 1917년에는 총수입 1만 달러 가운데 1천 달러를 학비 수입에서 얻었고 나머지는 모두 해외로부터 얻었다(9번).

그 후 1920~30년대를 지나는 동안 제도적인 지원과 각종 활동을 통해 연희전문과 한국 사회의 관계가 크게 돈독해졌다. 1923년부터는 협력관계의 구축을 위해 한국 장로교회와 감리교회 대표들과 연희전문 동창회 대표가 이사회 회의에 이사로 참석하기 시작하였다(25번). 또한 여러 보고서에서 밝히 설명되고 있는 것처럼, 강연회, 운동경기, 음악회, 연극공연, 웅변대회 등의 각종 행사를 주최하고 신문, 잡지에 글을 발표하거나 사회문제에 직접 관여하면서 학교가 한국 사회와 활발하게 소통하고 여러 곳에서 후원을 받았다.

⑤ 한국인의 지도력 존중

학교 설립자들의 책임 의식은 한국인의 지도력을 존중하는 것으로도 나타났다. 학교 교수진에는 첫해부터 소수이나마 한국인 교수가 있었고, 그 수는 점점 많아졌다. 개교 첫 학기의 교수 명단에는 6명의 이름(백상규, 이노익, W. J. Nah〈혹은 Noh〉, 신흥우, K. Yang, 변성옥)이 등장하였다(2 · 3번). 이들 가운데 이노익(Root Lee)은, 앞에서 설명했듯이, 1915년 4월 개교 후 교수회에 의해 부학감으로 지명되기도 하였다(3번). 1919년에는 교수진에서 선교사가 6명, 한국인이 9명, 일본인이 3명이었고(12번), 1922년에는 선교사가 8명, 한국인이 13명, 일본인이 2명이었다(22번).

학감과 과장은 1920년대 중후반부터 완전히 한국인이 맡았다. (그 내용은 다음의 '학풍 형성' 항목에서 더 자세히 설명할 것이다.) 에비슨 교장은 1924년 *The Korea Mission Field* 1월호에 발표한 "Can it be Done?"이란 글에서 한국에 있는 동료 선교사들을 향해 선교사가 할 일은 이 나라를 개종시키는 것이 아니라 기독교를 받아들인 한국인이 자생적인 활동으로 더 큰 일을 이루도록 준비시키는 것이란 점을 깨달아 한국인들에게 우리를 도우라고 요청하지 말고 우리가 그들을 돕도록 하자고 호소한 적이 있었다. 이듬해(1925년)에는 협력이사회에 제출한 보고서에서 연희전문과 세브란스의전이 자신의 지난해 발언을 실행에 옮겨 한국인 교수를 우선하여 쓰려 한다고 기술하였다(26번). 같은 해에 *All the World* 1월호에 발표한 "The Biggest Thing in Chosen"이란 기고문에서도 선교사가 할 수 있는 가장 큰 일은 선교지 사람들에게 선교사가 필요 없어지게 하는 일이고 스스로 능력을 기를 수단, 곧 종합대학을 주는 일이라고 하면서 연희전문과 세브란스의전의 한국인 교수들을 보면 한국인은 그렇게 할 지적 능력이 있다고 주장하였다. 이상의 일들과 발언들을 보면, 연희전문의 선교사 교수들은 서양인 우월의식과 오리엔탈리즘을 완전히 탈피하였다고 확언하기는 어려워도 그런 것에 대한 문제의식만큼은 분명히 가지고 있었다고 할 수 있다.

⑥ 최고 수준 지향－종합대학 설립, 모범적 캠퍼스 조성

설립자이자 초대 교장인 언더우드만 아니라 그와 뜻을 같이한 동료 선교사들도 세우고 싶어 하였던 대학은 타 대학들에 대해 경쟁력이 있는 수준 높은 종합대학이었다. 언더우드는 1910년 자신이 세우고자 하는 대학의 모습을 구체적으로 밝혔다.

> 우리는 이 나라에 있는 모든 대학의 중심이 되고 시시때때로 이 나라의 다른 지방에 있는 고등학교들과 한두 개 대학을 도울 만큼 충분히 큰 재단을 가진 초교파적인 기독교 종합대학을 기대하고 있습니다(편지: H. G. Underwood to A. J. Brown, July 18, 1910).

이 진술은 그가 여느 대학 수준의 교육기관 하나를 세우는 것으로 만족하지 않고 모든 대학의 중심에 서서 널리 영향을 끼칠 종합대학을 세우기를 원하였던 것을 알려준다. 그러나 재한 선교사들의 다수는 이 계획을 극렬히 반대하였고, 총독부도 전문학교규칙을 만들어 종합대학의 설립을 저지하였다.

종합대학의 세우려는 오랜 노력이 1917년 전문학교의 인가를 받는 것으로 귀결되었을 때 에비슨 교장은 연희전문의 6개 과 하나하나가 제각기 전문학교이기 때문에, 그 수준이 일본의 제국대학만은 못해도, 사실상 종합대학이 되는 셈이라고 하며 스스로 아쉬움을 달랬다. 그런 다음 세브란스연합의학교도 연희전문의 한 학과가 될 수 있다고 하면서 세브란스를 포함하는 종합대학 수립의 꿈을 포기하지 않는 모습을 보였다(편지: O. R. Avison to S. H. Chester, November 13, 1917).

그 후로도 학교 운영진은 종합대학의 수립을 늘 염두에 두면서 학교 발전을 도모하였다. 1918년 에비슨은 “이 대학은 한국을 위한 기독교 연합대학이자 한국 기독교 종합대학의 출발이다"(It is the Union Christian College for Korea and the beginning of the Christian University of Korea)라고 하며 미국 협력이사회에 후원을 요청하였다(10번). 1928년 유억겸 학감은 보고서에서 학과들의 상황을 설명할 때 "본 대학은 종합대학 체제를 이루고 있고, 3개 과를 운영하고 있다"(The College is organized on a university system and has three separate departments in operation)라는 말을 서두에 넣었고(36번), 이 문장은 이후의 모든 학감 보고서에 등장하는 클리셰가 되었다.

실제로 교수들은 1928년부터 종합대학을 수립할 계획을 세우고 1929년 3월 교수회의 '학교 교육정책에 관한 특별위원회'가 만든 종합대학수립계획안을 1929년 3월 13일 이사회 회의에 제출하였다(동일자 이사회 회의록; 연세대학교 박물관 편, 『연희전문학교 운영보고서(上)』, 선인, 2013). 에비슨은 1929년 이 계획안에 대해 "지난가을 본교의 향후 목적, 방법, 계획을 연구하기 위해 만든 교수회의 특별위원회가 많은 건설적인 제안을 하였다"고 간단하게 언급하였으나(37번), 이사회는 32쪽에 달하는 그 계획안에서 많은 사항을 채택하고 이후 7년 동안 대학 승격을 준비하게 하였다.

연희전문이 최고 수준의 교육을 지향하였던 것은 현실의 제약 속에서 가장 높은 수준에 이를 길을 찾게 만들었고, 이는 당시의 여건에서 제도권 안에 머물게 하는 한 요인이 되었다. 1919년 에비슨 교장은 교육법이 교육 수준을 낮추는 장애 요소가 되고 있다고 토로하였다(13번). 교수들은 이를 극복하기 위해 1920년 2년의 예과 과정을 추가하는 내용의 교육과정 변경안을 만들고 총독부에 제의하려 하였다(15번). 그 후 1922년 총독부가 학교 교육 요건을 강화한 제2차 조선교육령을 공포하였을 때 연희전문은 예과를 설치하여 교육 수준을 높일 기회가 왔다고 여겨 1923년 이 법에 따라 다시 인가를 받았다(20 · 25번).

연희전문은 또한 캠퍼스를 조성하는 일에서도 최고 수준을 지향하였다. 그들은 1915년 개교할 때부터 총독부, 동양척식회사, 개인 소유자들과 협상하면서 꾸준히 오랜 기간에 걸쳐 교지 확보를 위해 노력하였다(1 · 2 · 5 · 24 · 31 · 32 · 34 · 40 · 43번). 에비슨은 학교가 300에이커의 땅을 확보하기를 희망하였으나(10번), 1927년까지 211.5에이커(약 26만 평)를 확보하였고(34번), 그 후에도 땅을 더 샀으며, 팔기도 하였다(40 · 43 · 47번).

건축 문제에서도 신중히 계획을 세워 확실한 결과를 얻으려 하였다. 에비슨은 1917년 캠퍼스 배치도와 건축양식을 정할 때 나중에 아쉬워하지 않도록 서두르면 안 된다고 말하였다(편지: O. R. Avison to F. M. North, Jun. 20, 1917, 『에비슨 자료집』 3권, 56번). 1918년에는 학교가 향후 20년 동안 필요한 건물들을 지어 50년에서 100년 동안 수천 명의 학생을 배출하게 될 것을 바라보게 하였다(10번). 1920년에는 본교를 학문의 전당으로만 아니라 실용성과 건축학적 표현의 모델(a model both in utility and architectural expression)로도 만들기 위해 노력하고 있다고 말하였다(편지: O. R. Avison to J. T. Underwood, Jan. 5, 1920).

(2) 설립 · 발전과정

① 설립 준비

이 자료집의 보고서들은 학교의 역사가 시작한 이후의 상황을 다루고 있다. 그러므로 그 전의 설립 준비과정을 많이 알려주지는 않지만, 학교가 처음부터 잘 갖춰서 시작하지 않았던 것은 잘 알려주고 있다. 그중에서 베커 학감의 1918년 보고서는 매우 간략하게나마 설립 준비과정을 설명하고 있다(9번). 그러나 감리교 선교사들의 역할을 과도하게 부각하고 있다.

베커의 설명을 더 균형 있게 보완하여 그 과정을 다시 설명하면 대략 다음과 같다. 서울에 대학을 세울 것을 주장한 언더우드를 비롯한 서울 주재 장로교 선교사들은 다수의 지지를 받으며 반대론을 주도한 평양 측에 밀렸으나, 1912년부터 감리교 측의 가세로 대등하게 표 대결을 벌일 수 있게 되었다. 서울 측과 평양 측은 팽팽하게 맞서다 합동위원회에 결정을 의뢰하였고, 합동위원회는 1914년 1월, 서울에 대학을 짓는 것을 확정하였다. 그러자 베커의 주도로 감리교 측이 언더우드와 상의하여 1914년 4월 감리교 계열의 배재학교에 대학 예과를 개설하고 총독부에 통보하였으며, 그 후 장 · 감선교사들이 함께 총독부와 협상하며 학교설립을 준비하여 1915년 4월 예과 학생들과 장로교 계열의 경신학교 대학과 학생들을 데리고 경신학교 대학과의 인가로 종로 YMCA 건물에서 조선기독교대학을 개교하였다(김도형, 『민족문화와 대학: 연희전문학교의 학풍과 학문』, 혜안, 2018).

그런데 설립 인가 문제와 관련하여 베커의 보고서는 두 가지 사실을 알려준다. 그것은 선교사들이 총독부의 허가 아래 경신학교 대학과의 인가로 새 대학을 출범시켰고, 개교할 때부터 이후에 전문학교 인가를 받아 독자적인 법적 지위를 얻을 생각을 하고 있었다는 사실이다. 이 일에 대해 언더우드는 1915년 9월 합동위원회에 보낸 편지에서 그들이 학교설립 규정을 기한 안에 이행할 수 없어서 총독부의 동의를 받아 경신학교 대학과의 인가 아래 학교를 운영하고 있다고 설명하였다("This was because we were unable to conform entirely to the laws concerning charters, permits, etc., within the prescribed time and with the consent of the Government authorities we have been carrying on our college under the charter of our J. D. Wells' School[경신학교]." H. G. Underwood to F. M. North, Sep. 15, 1915). 이 진술을 참작하면, 개교 전 3월 24일 공포되어 4월 1일부터 시행된 〈전문학교규칙〉의 설립 조건을 갖추어 신청하고 인가받는 절차를 시행일 전에 완료하는 것은 애초에 불가능하였으므로, 다수파 선교사들의 많은 반대 속에서도 어떻게든 대학설립을 성사시키기 위해, 총독부의 동의를 받아 학교를 일단 4월에 경신학교 인가로 출범시켜놓고 이후에 독자적인 인가를 받으려 하였던 것으로 보인다. 총독부 쪽에서는 선교사들이 그렇게 해서라도 먼저 개교할 수 있게 해주면서 그들이 종합대학의 설립을 강행하지 않고 전문학교규칙을 순순히 따르도록 유인하려 하였던 것으로 보인다.

② 교장 칭호 문제

언더우드는 3월 5일 대학의 이사회가 창립된 후 이사장으로서 개교 준비상황을 뉴욕 합동위원회에 알렸고, 4월 12일 개교식을 거행한 후 4월 21일 열린 제2회 이사회 회의 때 '임시 교장'(Provisional President)으로서 학교 현황과 해결할 일을 설명하였다(1 · 2번; 제1회 이사회 회의록). 그런데 그는 '임시'라는 단어를 '교장' 앞에만 아니라 '이사회' 앞에도 붙였다(1 · 2 · 4번). 그러나 실제로 이사회 회의록들을 보면, '임시'는 '교장' 앞에만 붙어 있다. 당시에 교장의 경우에는 합동위원회 또는 소속 선교부의 승인이 필요하였다. 그런 것은 1917년 2월 17일 이사회에서 제2대 교장으로 선임된 에비슨의 경우도 마찬가지였다. 이때 이사회는 총독부에 제출할 설립인가신청서의 교장 부분에 이름을 적어넣기 위해(편지: O. R. Avison to F. M. North, Jan. 6, 1917) 교장 선출을 강행하고 '교장' 앞에 '임시'란 단어를 붙이지 않았다. 그 후 에비슨은 합동위원회로부터 1918년 3월 31일까지 1년간 교장직을 수행하도록 승인을 받았고(편지: F. M. North to O. R. Avison, Mar. 14, 1917; 『에비슨 자료집』 3권, 48번), 1919년 4월 북장로회 선교부로부터 다시 교장 승인을 받았다(편지: G. T. Scott to the Field Board of Managers of Chosen Christian College, April 12, 1919). 그런데 그 전에 그는 다음과 같은 이사회 요청사항을 선교부에 전하였다.

회의록 2항은 나를 교장으로 재선출하는 문제를 다루면서, 협력이사회에 내가 이런 자격으로 활동할 수 있도록 북장로회 선교부의 동의를 얻어주기를 요청하고 있습니다. 그들이 지난번에 요청했을 때는 일 년으로 한정하여 동의를 얻었지만, 지금은 이런 제한을 두지 말고 에비슨 박사를 실제 교장으로 생각해달라는 요청을 한다는 말을 전하라고 내게 시켰습니다. 이렇게 하는 것이 최선인지 아닌지 모르겠지만, 이사회는 나를 단순히 교장 대리로만 취급하면 안 된다고 정하는 문제를 이 학교의 이해관계가 달린 일로 여기는 것 같습니다. 그 이유는 그 자리를 채울 다른 사람을 금방 찾을 수 있을 성싶지 않기 때문입니다(편지: O. R. Avison to G. T. Scott, Feb. 18, 1919).

에비슨이 1934년까지 17년간 교장직을 수행하였던 것을 생각하면, 위의 요청은 받아들여졌던 것으로 보인다. 그러나 사실상으로 교장 앞에 '임시'를 붙이거나 떼는 일은 선교사들 내부의 업무처리 방식과 절차의 문제에 불과하였다. 개교 직후의 불안정한 시기에 언더우드는 그들 내부의 공식문서에서는 '임시 교장'으로 불렸어도 다른 문서들, 특히 총독부에 제출한 문서에서는 그냥 교장으로 불렸고, 연희전문의 역사 내내 '설립자이자 초대 교장'이란 지위를 공식적으로 인정받았다.

③ 교명 결정

연희전문의 교명은 개교한 후에 정해졌다. 영어 교명의 경우는 초창기의 보고서들에서 볼 수 있듯이 처음에 'Korea Christian College,' 'Chosen Christian College,' 'Union Christian College,' 'Union College of Seoul,' 'Union Christian College at Seoul' 등으로 불렸다. 그런데 사실은 이사회가 1915년 4월 21일 제2회 회의 때 미국 합동위원회 측에 학교 이름에 'Korea'를 붙이지 말고 'Chosen Christian College'라고 바꿔서 불러달라고 요청함으로써 영어 이름을 확정하였다(동일자 회의록).

'연희'를 교명으로 사용하는 것은 이사회가 1916년 12월 13일 결정하였다. 이 회의에서 교명 선정위원들의 제안에 따라 '연희전문학교'란 교명이 결정되었다. 교명 선정위원은 1916년 7월 13일 이사회 회의 때 한국인, 일본인, 서양 선교사 모두를 만족시킬 수 있도록 게일, 백상규, 와타나베로 구성되었다(동일자 회의록). 이때 '익교', '개명', '개도', '인교'가 교명 후보들로 제출되었으나, 12월 13일 이사회 회의 때 위원장인 게일이 '연희전문학교'란 교명을 제안하여 채택되었다. 그는 이때 '연희'가 교지에 있었던 옛 궁궐의 이름이고 복을 베푼다(Extended Blessings, 延禧)는 뜻을 지닌다고 설명하였다.

④ 학과 설치

학과의 종류도 개교 후에 확정되었다. 개교 직후에는 운영진이 문과, 수학 및 물리학과, 상과만 설치하였고, 1, 2학년 때 교양과목과 전공 기초과목을 공부하고 3, 4학년 때 각 과의 전공과목을 공부하게 하였다(3번). 그와 동시에 일본어, 영어, 성경, 농학 과목을 필수로 이수하고 타전공 과목들을 선택하게 하였다(6번).

그런 가운데 그들은 전문학교설립 인가신청서를 작성하기 위해 총독부 관리들과 학과 설치 문제를 상의하였다. 총독부의 종교교육 보장 문제로 대학설립을 반대하는 소리가 여전히 힘을 얻고 있던 상황에서 1916년 5월 총독부 내무부장 우사미(宇佐美勝夫)가 학교 측에 성경교육과, 곧 신과를 설치하여 종교교육을 무기한 보장받게 하는 안을 제시하였다. 그 후 1916년 7월 운영진은 기존의 3개 과에 신학과, 농업과, 응용화학과를 새로 더하여 6개 과를 두는 전문학교설립신청서를 작성하였다. 그 후 1917년 3월 신청서를 다시 작성하여 총독부에 제출한 후, 4월 7일 6개 과를 두는 연희전문학교 설립 인가를 받았다(「연희전문학교일람(1940)」, 『연희전문학교 운영보고서(下)』).

전문학교 인가를 받은 후에는 설립신청서에 기재한 대로 문학과(4년제), 상업과(3년제), 수학 및 물리학과(4년제), 농업과(3년제), 신학과(3년제), 응용화학과(3년제)의 6개 과를 두었다(9번). 그런데 신설된 과들은 지원자가 적었고, 특히 응용화학과는 지원자가 없어 거의 운영하지 못하였다. 또한 과들의 호칭을 '문과', '신과', '상과', '수물과' 등으로 축약하여 부르게 되었다. 1919~20년간에는 신과를 4년제로 만들고, 과마다 2년의 예과를 두며, 음악과를 신설하자는 의견을 교수들이 제기하였다(15번), 1921년에는 문과와 신과의 명칭을 바꾸거나 두 과를 합치자는 주장이 커졌다(16번). 또한 이사회가 경제적인 이유에서 입학생이 10명 미만인 과는 신입생을 받지 말도록 결정하여 이후에 학교가 문과, 상과, 수물과만 운영하게 되었다(16번). 그들은 여자학과를 설치하는 문제도 논의하기 시작하였다(16번). 신과는 학생은 없었으나 종교교육을 위해 폐과하지 않고 교수를 배치하였다. 예를 들면, 백낙준이 1927년 신과 교수로 부임하여 종교교육을 하다가 1928년 문과 과장이 되었다(34번).

그 후 1922년 공포된 제2차 조선교육령에 따라 1923년 3월 설립 인가를 다시 받았는데, '문과', '신학과', '상과'만 인가를 받았다(「연희전문학교일람(1940)」). '수물과'는 유자격 교수가 부족하여 인가를 받지 못하고 이듬해에 인가를 받았다. 1928년에는 음악과의 설치가 다시 요망 사항으로 언급되었다(35번). 교수회는 1929년 2월 22일 자체 회의 때 '교육정책에 관한 연희전문 교수회의 특별위원회 보고서'를 채택하고 종합대학으로의 승격과 함께 음악과, 농업과, 종교교육과의 신설을 건의하였다(37번; 『연희전문학교 운영보고서(上)』).

⑤ 전문학교 인가 취득

전문학교의 인가 취득은 대학을 개교할 때부터 계획되었다. 언더우드는 개교 직후의 보고서에서 총독부의 새 교육법에 따라 전문학교 법인을 만들기 위해 와타나베 판사 등의 도움을 받아 메이지 학원의 법인을 참고할 예정이고, 경신학교 허가 대신 새 허가를 받기 위해 [학무국장] 세키야의 도움을 받고 있다고 기술하였다(2번). 그는 그해 9월 보고서에서 모든 일이 잘 진행되고 있으므로 경신학교 인가로 운영하는 일은 얼마 가지 않을 것이라고 하며 전문학교 설립 허가를 곧 받게 될 것으로 예상하였다(4번).

그러나 그해 말 언더우드는 와타나베 판사의 도움으로 재단법인의 초안을 만들어 총독부 관리에게 보여주었다가 지적을 받고 허가를 받지 못하였다고 설명하였다(5번). 그는 교육법을 충족하려면 재단법인을 만들 뿐만 아니라 학교 운영을 보장할 자산을 확보하고, 교육과정 · 과목 · 수업시수 등을 기재한 신청서를 작성해야 한다고 설명하였다(7번). 대학 설립을 가로막는 다른 변수들도 발생하였다. 당시에 다수파를 대변하고 있던 교육평의회(Educational Senate, 재한 선교사들의 학교 교육 협의기구)의 회장 일행이 내무국장 우사미를 찾아가 미국의 선교부들은 일제에 순응하는 학교를 절대 지원하지 않을 것이라고 말하였고, 미국 북장로회 선교부 총무도 총독부에 직접 편지를 보내 종교교육의 자유를 요구하였다(7번). 그로 인해 총독부에서 1916년 3월 20일 설립 허가를 내주려고 하였던 것이 미뤄졌다. 그런 분위기에서 언더우드는 직접 일본으로 건너가 수상, 문부대신, 고위 관리들, 대학 총장들과 교수들, 기독교 지도자들을 만나 그들이 일본 정부에 적대적이지 않다는 점을 알리려고 노력하였다(7번).

합동위원회를 설득하는 일도 쉽지 않았다. 학교 측은 총독부에 낼 전문학교설립 인가 신청서를 1916년 7월 13일 자로 작성하였다. 미국에 간 교장 대신 부교장 에비슨과 이사회 총무인 루카스가 서명한 이 문서의 설립신청자는 언더우드 교장으로 되어 있었다. 그들은 신청서에 포함된 전문학교 재단법인의 정관을 합동위원회로부터 승인받아 총독부에 제출하기 위해 이 문서를 미국에 보냈고, 언더우드는 미국에서, 에비슨은 한국에서 합동위원회에 승인을 요청하였다. 합동위원회는 우사미가 성경교육과의 설치를 제안한 것이 사실인지, 총독부의 종교의 자유 보장 약속에 진정성이 있는지를 확인하기를 원하였다. 그 때문에 태평양을 사이에 두고 많은 편지가 오갔고, 그 사이에 언더우드가 1916년 10월 12일 미국에서 사망하였다.

합동위원회는 마침내 1917년 1월 15일 자로 연희전문과 세브란스의전의 법인설립을 승인한다는 사실을 통지하였다. 에비슨은 "오랫동안 기대하고 기다린 결과가 지연되는 것을 경험한 사람만 느낄 수 있는" 큰 기쁨으로 그 통지문을 반겼다(F. M. North, to O. R. Avison, Jan. 15, 1917; O. R. Avison to F. M. North, Mar. 8, 1917). 그리고는 즉시 이사회를 소집하였고, 이사회는 그를 교장으로, 빌링스를 부교장으로 임명하였다. 그들은 설립인가신청서를 다시 작성하여 1917년 3월 7일 경성부윤에게 신청서 3부를 제출하였고, 4월 7일 '사립연희전문학교'와 '사립연희전문학교기독교연합재단법인'의 설립을 인가받았다(O. R. Avison to F. M. North, Mar. 8, 1917).

그 후 연희전문은 총독부가 1922년 2월 제2차 조선교육령을 공포하자 일본의 사립 전문학교 수준으로 종교교육의 자유도 얻고 교육과정의 수준도 높일 수 있게 되었다고 여기고 전문학교 등록신청서를 작성하여 제출하였다(23번). 그리하여 1923년 3월 '연희전문학교'란 교명으로 설립 인가를 다시 받았다. 그러나 새 교육령에 따라 비인가 중등학교 졸업생을 받아들일 수 없게 되어 별과를 설치하였는데(25번), 그때 미션계 중등학교들에서 고등보통학교의 인가를 받은 곳은 감리교계 학교밖에 없었다. 이 문제는 1923년 4월 총독부가 지정학교 제도를 인정하여 지정학교 출신도 본과로 받을 수 있게 됨으로써 해결의 실마리를 얻었다(25번). 그 후 경신학교가 1925년 지정을 받은 것을 필두로 해서 장로교계 중등학교들이 차례로 지정학교가 되어 졸업생을 연희전문의 본과에 보낼 수 있게 되었다.

⑥ 1920년대 후반 이후의 발전과 일제 말의 수난

연희전문은 1920년대 중반부터 크게 도약하기 시작하였다(A. L. Becker, "Growing Pains: Process of Development," *The Korea Mission Field*, Vol. XXXIV, No. 8, 1938). 먼저 한국인 교수들이 학교 운영의 전면에 나서기 시작하였다. 1925년 유억겸이 학감이 되고 이순탁과 이춘호가 각각 상과와 수물과의 과장이 되었다(1925년 9월 26일 이사회 회의록). 문과에서는 이관용이 1925년 과장대리가 된 데 이어 백낙준이 1928년 문과 과장이 되었다(27 · 35번). 다음으로 경제적인 어려움에서 벗어나기 시작하였다. 1924년부터 에비슨이 미국에서 후원금을 얻기 위한 모금 활동을 시작하였고 1925년 뉴욕대에서 박사학위를 받은 원한경이 이 일에 합류하였다가 1926년 8월 함께 돌아왔다(30번). 그 후 학교가 적자를 줄이기 위해 노력한 것과 합하여, 마침내 1929년, 모금해온 기금으로 모든 적자를 해소하고 새 출발을 하였다(35 · 37번). 그뿐 아니라 학생 수도 매년 늘어났고, 학생들이 운동경기에서 많은 우승을 거두어 학교의 사기를 크게 높였다.

그런 가운데 교수들이 학술연구에 매진하면서 대학을 종합대학으로 승격시키는 계획을 세웠다. 유억겸은 1928년 9월 학감 보고서에서 교수들이 이 나라에서 최고 수준에 있고, 계속 연구하고 있으며, 이 대학을 한국문화의 중심지로 만들기 위해 도서관에서 한국 고서를 수집하고 있다고 설명하였다(36번). 에비슨은 이 해(1928년) 가을에 교수회의 특별위원회가 학교의 발전을 위해 많은 제안을 하였다고 설명하였다(37번). 교수회는 1929년 3월 특별위원회가 작성한 종합대학수립계획안을 이사회에 제출하였고(『연희전문학교 운영보고서(上)』). 이사회는 그 계획안을 검토하여 많은 사항을 채택하고 이후 7년 동안 대학 승격을 준비하게 하였다(1929년 3월 13일 이사회 회의록). 이 계획안에는 각 과에서 장차 하려고 하는 일들이 나열되어 있었는데, 그중 한 가지씩만을 소개하면, 문과는 문화 과정을 설치하여 한국문화를 특별히 강조할 계획이고, 상과는 한국의 경제 상황을 개선하는 교육을 할 계획이며, 수물과는 한국사회의 문제점을 해결하기 위한 졸업 후 교육을 할 계획이라고 밝혔다.

이상의 보고서들과 계획안은 1920년대 후반에 교수들의 연구 의욕이 높아졌고, 그런 분위기에서 조선학운동이 태동하였던 것을 보여준다. 이후 1930년대에 실로 르네상스라 할 만한 현상이 학교에서 발현하였다. 이 시기의 보고서들은 교수들의 연구 활동, 연구 결과의 학회지 · 신문 · 잡지 게재, 저서 출판, 연구실 운영, 도서관 장서 확충, 박물관 소장품 수집 사실들을 계속 소개하였다. 학생들의 종교 · 음악 · 체육 활동도 눈부신 약진을 이루었다고 설명하였다. 교수들의 학술 활동은 해외 학회와 국제회의 참가로 이어졌다(49 · 50 · 52번). 교수들은 1936년부터 시작하여 1937~1938년간에 줄지어 해외로 나갔다.

그런데 바로 그러한 때에 동우회사건(1937년), 흥업구락부사건(1938년), 경제연구회사건(1938년)이 벌어져 유억겸 학감과 이춘호, 이순탁 과장들을 비롯하여 여러 교수가 체포되고 해임되었다(52 · 53 · 54번). 이 사건들과 교수들의 해외 출타는 교수진에 큰 공백이 생기게 하였다. 원한경 교장은 "정치 상황, 질병, 출타로 학감과 과장들에 변동이 생겼고, 13명 이상의 교수가 일시적으로 자리를 비웠다"라고 설명하였다(51번). '질병'의 경우는 정인보가 병가를 낸 것이었다. 그리하여 오랫동안 안정적으로 유지되었던 학과장 체제가 무너졌고, 이묘묵을 비롯한 신진 교수들이 그 자리에 오르면서 사회적 명망까지 얻어 해방 후에 상당한 영향력을 행사하게 되었다. 그뿐 아니라 1930년대에 한껏 고조되어가던 학내의 기세가 총독부의 위력과 충돌하면서 이후에 학교가 표류하게 되었다.

일제 말 총독부는 침략전쟁의 와중에서 학교 운영을 더욱 간섭하고 억압하였다(김도형, 『민족문화와 대학: 연희전문학교의 학풍과 학문』). 교육과정을 변경하여 군사교련을 시행하고 한국어 과목을 폐지하며 일본문화 · 역사 교육을 강화하였고(55 · 56번), 창씨개명, 지원병 제도, 한국어 사용 금지와 일본어 사용을 강요하였다(60번). 더 나아가 교장을 1941년 3월 원한경에서 윤치호로 교체시켰고(57 · 58 · 59 · 60번), 1941년 12월 원한경 교장, 원일한(H. G. Underwood) 교수, 밀러(E. H. Miller) 교수를 체포하여 구류하다가 이듬해 6월 추방하였다. 이런 상황에서 신사참배 문제와 관련하여 종래에 연희전문을 후원해오던 북장로회 선교부가 공식적인 관계를 끊고 후원을 중단하였고(57번), 협력이사회도 미국 정부의 미국 내 일본자산 동결과 송금 중단 조치로 학교 운영비를 송금하지 못하였다(59번). 상황은 계속 악화하여 1942년 조선어학회 사건으로 문과 교수들이 체포 · 구금되고 이윤재가 옥사하였으며, 1942년 8월 교장이 일본인으로 바뀌고 이사회가 해체되며 재산이 적산으로 규정되어 몰수되었다. 마침내 1944년 5월 학교가 폐교되고 경성공업경영전문학교가 되었다.

2) 학사 운영

(1) 학사 운영방식

① 운영방식에 대한 오해

연희전문의 운영체제와 운영방식은 이제까지 별로 알려지지 않았고, 관심거리도 아니었다. 그런 상태에서 서구 선교사가 세운 학교라는 사실에서 기인한 선입견에 따라 운영방식을 판단하는 경우가 있었다. 그런 선입견들에는 선교사들이 학교를 임의로 운영하였다거나 한국인을 고압적, 차별적으로, 한국문화를 배타적으로 대하였다는 것 등이 있다.

음악 교육 분야에서 그 예를 들면, 먼저 연희전문에서 음악을 가르친 김영환은 한국인이었기 때문에 끝내 교수가 못 되고 떠났다는 설이 있다. 그러나 김영환은 1918년 강사로 부임하여 이듬해에 조교수가 되었고, 1925년경에 교수로 승진하여 가르치다 1929년 사임하였다(12 · 27번, 1929년 9월 20일 이사회 회의). 다음으로 음악과 설치 운동에 관해 베커 부인 또는 원한경이 김영환을 시켜 음악과 설치 제안서를 작성하게 하고 미국에 보냈는데 미국 본부에서 시기상조라는 이유로 불허하여 무산되었다는 설이 있다. 그러나 실제에 있어서 음악과 설치 제안서는 1920년 교수회의 의견을 모아 로즈 학감이 작성하여 이사회 회의 때 제출하였고, 대구에서 활동하는 블레어 이사의 동의로 이사회가 보류 결정을 내렸다(15번, 1920년 2월 21일 이사회 회의록). 그때 베커 부인은 남편과 함께 미국에서 안식년을 보내고 있었고, 그 제안서에서 교수들은 음악 과목을 담당하는 김영환의 의견을 존중하고 있었다.

이 같은 오해들은 운영방식이 알려지지 않은 데에서 비롯되었다. 그러나 이 보고서들은 각 시기에 학교가 어떻게 운영되고 있었는지를 있는 모습 그대로 보여준다.

② 규정에 따른 자율적 운영

그 운영방식을 대략 정리하면, 초창기부터 학교 이사회는 최고 의결기구의 역할을 하였고, 이사회와 교장 등의 임원들은 학내 인사 문제와 학사업무를 규정에 따라 자율적으로 처리하였다. 학교가 학칙 또는 규정을 갖추어 그것에 따라 운영하면서 학사업무를 완전히 자율적으로 처리하였던 사실은 첫 번째 보고서에서부터 입증된다. 개교 직후에 교육관으로 사용하였던 YMCA 건물도 언더우드가 YMCA 이사장이었지만 그곳을 임의로 사용하지 않고 YMCA 측과 계약서를 작성하여 임대료를 지불하고 사용하였던 것을 볼 수 있다(1 · 3번).

③ 협력과 견제

이사회가 어떻게 운영되었는지는 보고서들이 보여주고 있지 않지만, 이사회는 교단별 선교사 이사들과 한국인 · 일본인 이사들로 구성되었고, 임원은 이사장, 서기, 회계로 구성되었다. 교장이 당연이사로서 이사장을 맡았고, 나중에는 학감도 당연이사가 되었다. 서기는 오웬스(H. T. Owens), 원한경, 조병옥, 백낙준 순으로 교체되었고, 회계는 겐소(J. F.

Genso), 오웬스, 피셔(J. E. Fisher), 최순주, 스나이더(L. H. Snyder), 다시 최순주 순으로 교체되었다. 선교사 이사들은 약간의 수적 차이로 이사회 안에서 다수를 이루었는데, 그들의 수는 교단별로 후원금의 규모에 따라 차등 있게 정해졌다. 가장 많은 후원금 할당액을 내는 교단은 더 적은 할당액을 내는 교단보다 이사를 더 많이 보내 발언권을 더 많이 행사할 수 있었다. 실제로 4개 교단에서 이사를 가장 많이 보낸 교단은 북장로회와 북감리회였다(9번). 이런 사실은 학교가 후원단체들의 협력과 견제 속에서 운영되어 한 세력의 일방적, 자의적인 운영이 불가능하였음을 가리킨다. 1919~22년간에 북장로회 선교사 교수인 밀러와 로즈의 사택을 북감리회에서 낸 돈으로 짓고 북감리회 선교사 교수인 빌링스와 베커의 사택을 북장로회에서 낸 돈으로 지은 일은 협력과 견제가 이루어졌음을 입증하는 한 예가 될 것이다.

④ 한국인 중용과 책임 이양

학교 설립에 관여한 선교사들은 한국 사회와 좋은 관계를 맺기 위해 노력하는 것에 그치지 않고 한국인을 교직에 중용하였다. 위에서 설명했듯이, 개교 첫해부터 한국인 교수를 두었고, 그 수가 점차 많아져 1920년대 초부터 한국인 교수가 선교사 교수보다 많아졌으며, 중후반부터는 한국인이 학감과 과장 업무를 전담하였다. 이에 대해 에비슨은 1928년 "지금까지 한국인들이 과장과 학감 업무를 잘 수행하였으므로 좋은 결과를 얻을 것으로 기대한다"고 하였다(35번). 이처럼 연희전문은 한국인 교수를 우선으로 쓰는 것을 운영방침으로 삼았고(26번), 한국인의 내재적 발전 능력과 지도력을 인정하여 운영의 책임을 한국인에게 이양하였다.

(2) 운영의 어려움

① 적자 속의 성장 정책

보고서들은 학교 운영진의 운영행위만 아니라 결정을 내릴 때 어떤 생각을 하고 있었는지도 알려준다. 예를 들면, 베커는 1926년 6월 부교장직을 사임하면서 지난 5년간 학생 수가 2배로 늘었지만, 그런 만큼 적자를 무릅쓰며 예산을 늘려서 조달하느라 긴장과 심리적 압박도 커졌다고 회고하였다(28번). 이 발언은 그들이 적자의 확대를 감수하면서도 학교 발전에 필요한 일에는 재정을 확장하여 발전을 도모하는 정책을 썼음을 알려준다.

그들이 무조건 확장 정책만 강행하였던 것은 물론 아니었다. 예를 들면 이사회는 1921년 3월 23일 회의 때 경제적인 어려움을 덜기 위해 입학생이 10명 미만인 과는 입학생을 받지 말 것을 결정하였다(16번). 그에 따라 6개 과에서 3개(문과, 상과, 수물과)만 운영하는 역사가 시작되었다. 에비슨이 미국에서 모금 활동을 하고 돌아온 후인 1927~28년간에는 해외 후원금으로 본관 진입 계단을 놓고 장학금도 더 지급하였으나, 학교 운영을 위해서는 그간에 쌓인 적자를 줄이기 위해 긴축 재정정책을 펴면서 다른 재원으로부터도 후원을 얻기 위해 노력하였다(35번). 그 결과 1929년 에비슨은 "1927년까지 누적되어온 적자를 줄이려고 노력해오다가 이 해에 받은 기부금들로 인해 적자를 해소하고 새 출발을 할 수 있게 되었다"라고 이사회에 보고하였다(37번). 그가 이 해에 받았다고 한 기부금은 미국에서 모금 활동을 할 때 홀(Hall) 재단과 존 T. 언더우드로부터 약속받은 것이었는데, 그가 1925년 제출한 기부금들의 명세에는 전자에서 6만 달러를 후자에서 5만 달러를 약속받은 것으로 되어 있다(26번).

② 일제 말 외부 압박 대응

연희전문은 일제 말 총독부의 신사참배 강요로 인해 학교를 폐교 또는 유지하라는 상반된 압박을 받았다. 폐교를 요구한 쪽은 대다수의 장로교 선교사들이었다. 그들은 일제의 신사참배 강요를 신앙 양심의 차원에서 거부해야 한다고 생각하여, 1938년 3월 숭실학교를 폐교하고 연희전문에도 폐교를 요구하였다. 미국의 북장로회 선교부도 1939년 1월 연희전문의 소속 선교사들에게 1941년 3월 말까지 학교를 떠날 것을 지시하였다(54번). 그러나 한국교회의 대다수는 현실적인 이유에서 폐교를 반대하였고, 이로써 선교사들과 한국교회(교회 지도자들)의 오랜 밀착 관계가 깨어졌다.

이런 정황은 1938년 보고서에서 처음 드러났다(51번). 원한경 교장으로 추정되는 보고서의 작성자는 선교사들의 비판이 부당하다고 항의하면서 학교가 선교사들에게는 비판을 받아도 한국 기독교인들에게는 신뢰를 받고 있다고 주장하였다. 이처럼 연희전문은 신사참배 문제에 타협하고 학교의 유지를 선택한 일의 정당성을 주장하는 근거로 한국교회의 지지를 내세웠다. 실제로 연희전문은 1940년 미국 정부의 조치로 협력이사회의 지원금 송금이 중단된 상황에서(59번) 김성권을 비롯한 여러 한국인이 보낸 기부금으로 큰 적자를 내지 않고 지탱할 수 있었다(56 · 57번). 원한경은 1940년 2월 "이 대학이 신실하게 사역해 온 것을 자랑스럽게 여겨도 되며, 총독부가 앞으로 어떻게 할지라도 지난 25년간 해온 것처럼 어려움을 이겨나가자"라고 격려하였다(56번). 그러나 갈수록 커진 일제의 탄압 속에서 한국교회와의 관계도 끝내 결렬되었다(60번).

원한경은 총독부의 압박을 받고 자진사퇴의 형식으로 1941년 3월 10일 졸업식을 마친 후 사임하였다(59번). 그런데 그를 이어 윤치호가 교장으로 있는 동안 총독부가 원한경과 같은 날 동반 사임한 학감과 과장들의 빈자리를 일본에서 공부한 사람들로만 채우기를 원하여 교직원들의 분노를 샀다(59번). 이렇게 하여 연희전문 안에서 서양인의 영향력을 지우는 일에 동참하는 이들이 생겨나 기존의 정체성을 지키려는 이들과 충돌하였다(59 · 60번).

3) 학풍 형성

(1) 토대가 된 설립 정신

연희전문의 학풍은 매우 당연한 일로서 설립 정신의 바탕 위에서 형성되었다. 앞에서 언급한 설립 정신의 요점을 정리하면 대략 다음과 같았다.

기독교주의	대학교육의 기본 원칙으로서 최고의 기독교 이상을 구현
연합정신	기독교주의 바탕 위에서 교파, 민족, 인종을 초월한 화합 도모
사회지도자 육성	한국사회의 모든 부분에 영향을 주어 한국 사회와 교육을 개선
한국 사회와 소통	계층, 인종, 종교를 불문하고 모두에게 교육적 책임 의식을 갖고 소통
한국인의 지도력 존중	한국인의 내재적 발전 능력을 인정하고 지도력을 존중
최고 수준 지향	모든 대학의 중심이 되는 종합대학 설립, 모범적 캠퍼스 조성

(2) 학문 간 융합 도모-한국문화 존중

연희전문 사람들은 이상과 같은 설립 정신의 바탕 위에서 이 정신을 더 창의적으로 응용하여 학문 간의 융합을 도모하였다. 한 예로 에비슨 2대 교장은 1920년 이치지마(市島吉太郎)란 일본인 교수가 농과를 담임하고 있을 때 서양인 농학 교수를 구하려고 노력하였다(16 · 17번). 그는 이치지마가 동양의 농업 지식을 가르치기에는 유능하지만, "우리는 서양식 교육으로 학생들에게 유익을 끼칠 사람을 얻어 동양과 서양의 최고지식을 융합시킬 수 있기를 바라고 있습니다"라고 하였다(1920년 2월 2일 자 에비슨의 편지, 『에비슨 자료집』 V, 16번). 그런데 이 발언은 동 · 서양의 화합을 추구한 것처럼 보이기도 하지만, 일본의 농학을 위주로 농과에서 가르치는 것을 막으려고 한 것처럼 보이기도 한다.

일제하의 억압된 상황에서 동서 학문의 융합은 사실상으로 한국 학문과 서양 학문의 융합을 뜻하는 것이었다. 때마침 그해(1920년) 2월 21일 열린 이사회 회의에서 학감은 교수회의 교육과정 변경안을 보고하였다. 그 변경안에서 교수들은 과마다 예과를 설치하여 교육 수준을 총독부가 허용한 전문학교 수준 이상으로 높이고, 모든 과에서 일본어 수업 시수를 줄이며, 수신을 예과에서만 가르치고, 신과 1, 2학년 과정에 조선어 과목을 신설할 것을 요청하였다(15번). 그러나 이때는 그들이 변경안을 총독부로부터 승인받는 것은 고사하고 당장 실행에 옮길 수 있을 만한 형편에 있지도 못하였다. 이는 학교가 이제 비로소 교수진을 갖추고 학교 건물들을 짓는 일을 본격적으로 추진하는 단계에 들어섰기 때문이었다(A. L. Becker, "Growing Pains: Process of Development." 1938). 그러므로 한두 가지 사례를 가지고 학교가 이때 이미 조선학을 부흥시키면서 동서 학문의 융합을 꾀하는 화충학풍(和衷學風)을 형성하고 있었다고 말하기에는 어려운 점이 있다. 다만 그것을 꽃피울 토양을 조성하고 있었다고 할 수는 있을 것이다.

한국문화를 존중하는 태도는 1920년 2월에만 아니라 그 전 1917년 캠퍼스의 조성을 구상하고 있었을 때도 나타났다. 에비슨은 1917년 9월 교육관들의 건축에 관해 고딕 양식, 르네상스 양식, 한국식과 외국식의 혼합 양식을 제안받고 있는데, 돌아가신 언더우드는 생전에 한국의 건축술로 현재의 교육적 필요에 어떻게 맞출 수 있는지를 보여주는 최고의 실례를 영원히 남기고 싶다고 하며 한옥 양식을 강력히 주장하였다고 설명하였다(1917년 9월 3일 자 에비슨의 편지, 『에비슨 자료집』 III, 68번). 그러면서 그때는 자기가 반대하였으나 최근에 감리회 측의 이사인 웰치(H. Welch) 감독이 한옥 양식을 쓰기를 다시 주장하여 그들이 한옥 양식을 쓸 때의 장단점을 분석하였다고 설명하였다. 그들이 꼽은 장점은 선과 장식의 아름다움, 전통 양식인 점, 전통 보존심리 충족, 이질적인 외국식 교육관이 주는 교육 효과 절감 방지였고, 단점은 선례 없음, 비싼 건축비, 넓은 처마의 채광 방해, 지붕 무게로 많은 기둥 건립 필요, 2층 이상 건물 설계의 난점, 폭풍 속 누수 방지 곤란 등이었다. 그들은 이처럼 건축학적 우수성의 측면보다 전통문화를 살릴 필요성의 측면에서 한옥 양식의 활용 여부를 고심하였다.

(3) 화충학풍 형성－(1)과 (2)의 결실

연희전문은 그 후 1920년대 동안 학문을 부흥시킬 인적, 제도적, 경제적 조건들을 갖춰갔다. 우선 한문 강사로 이상재를 1919년, 김도희를 1920년 임용한 후, 정인보를 1923년 임용하고 1925년 조교수, 1930년 교수로 승급시켰다(12 · 17 · 25 · 27번, 1930년 10월 2일 이사회 회의록). 1922~23년간에 동양문학을 정규수업으로 편성한 것은 정인보의 영입과 관련 있을 것으로 짐작된다(25번). 그들은 또한 이춘호, 이순탁, 유억겸을 1923년 교수로 임용하였고, 백남운을 1925년 조교수로 임용하였다가 그해에 교수로 승급시켰으며(27번, 1923년 9월 15일 이사회 회의록, 1925년 9월 26일 이사회 회의록), 최현배를 1926년 조교수로 임용한 후, 1927년 교수로 승급시켰다(28 · 31 · 32번). 그 사이 학감과 수물과 과장을 1925년 베커에서 유억겸과 이춘호로 바꾸었고(1925년 9월 26일 이사회 회의록), 문과의 경우는 빌링스 과장 아래 이관용을 1925년 과장대리로 세웠다가 1927년 그가 교수직을 사임하고 1928년 빌링스가 과장직을 사임하자 백낙준을 과장으로 임명하였다(25 · 27 · 29 · 32 · 33 · 35번). 상과는 이순탁을 1923년 과장대리로, 1925년 과장으로 임명하였다(1923년 9월 15일 이사회 회의록, 1925년 9월 26일 이사회 회의록).

그 후 교수들은 1928년과 1929년간에 이런 인적 구성을 힘입어 연희전문을 종합대학으로 승격시켜 한국문화와 한국사회의 발전을 위한 학술연구와 교육의 구심점으로 만들 계획을 세웠다. 그와 동시에 연구에 매진하여 1929년 보고서들에서부터 연구 성과를 보여주기 시작하였다. 그런데 보고서에서 가장 먼저 거론된 이는 문과 교수들이었다. 유억겸은 1929년 보고서에서 최현배가 『우리말본』을 출판하였고 정인보도 옛 시가의 연구서를 출판할 예정이라고 보고하였다(38번). 교수들은 또한 3개 과 모두에 연구실을 설치하여 연구 자료들을 구비하고 학생들과 함께 연구에 힘썼다. 이후 1930년대 내내 풍성한 학술연구와 신문 · 잡지 게재, 출판, 강연 활동을 펼쳤다. 그러는 동안 조선학이 학술연구의 한 분야로 자리 잡게 되었고, 조선학의 발흥을 힘입어 1932년 "기독교주의 하에 동서고근사상(東西古近思想)의 화충(和衷)으로" 교육하겠다는 내용의 교육방침이 학교에서 천명되었다(「연희전문학교상황보고서」, 『연희전문학교 운영보고서(下)』, 30쪽). 조선학 연구는 이처럼 1930년대에 학교가 '동서고근사상의 화충'을 내세우는 근거가 되었고 조선학은 여기에서 동양 사상을 대표하였다. 그런 점에서 연희전문의 학풍을 상징하는 화충학풍의 토대는 '기독교주의'를 비롯한 각양의 설립 정신과 이로부터 창의적으로 발현된 학문 간 융합 정신이었지만, 화충학풍의 형성을 선도한 것은 바로 문과의 '조선학 연구'였다고 할 수 있다.

문과 교수들의 조선학 연구 운동에는 문과에서 발행한 첫 번째 영문출판물인 "A Partial Bibliography of Occidental Literature of Korea"(한국에 관한 서양문헌 서목)를 작성한 서양인인 원한경도 합류하고 있었다(43번). 선교사 교수들과 이사들은 한국문화 보존의 중요성을 인지하고 있었고 한국인 교수들의 연구 활동을 지지하였다. 그들은 한국인 교수들이 조선학을 포함하여 모든 학문 분야에서 연구 결과를 널리 발표하여 학교의 명성을 높이는 것을 기쁘게 여겼다. 1932년 9월 22일 열린 이사회 회의 때 유억겸이 학감 보고서를 발표한 후 노블(W. A. Noble) 이사는 보고서 덕분에 각 과의 연구 활동에 관해 알게 되어 기쁘다고 하면서 유억겸을 치하할 것을 이사회에 제안하였다(44번 자료소개 부분 참고).

한국인 교수들의 연구 활동은 해가 갈수록 더 활발해졌고 활동 범위도 더 넓어졌다. 1936년 정인섭은 코펜하겐에서, 1937년 백남운, 최현배, 이순탁, 최순주, 이원철은 도쿄에서 학회들에 참석하거나 연구 논문을 발표하였다(49 · 50 · 52 · 53번). 현제명은 1936년 박사 학위를 받으러 미국에 갔고, 유억겸은 1936년 YMCA 국제대회에 참석하러 인도에 갔으며, 백낙준은 1937년 출국하여 영국과 미국에서 열린 국제선교대회에 참석하였다(49 · 51번). 유억겸은 1938년 학감 보고서에서 최현배와 백남운이 저서를 출판하여 불멸의 명성을 얻었다고 말하고, 교수들이 해외에서 학술대회에 참가한 일들을 나열하였다(52번). 그러므로 이 모든 기록을 종합하면, 활발한 학문연구로 연희전문의 사회적 위상을 높이고 학풍의 형성을 주도한 이들은 다름 아닌 한국인 교수들이었음을 알 수 있다. (연세학연구소 전문연구원 문백란)

▌사 진▐

▲ 1915년 4월 본교 창립 기념사진

개교식에 참석한 교수, 하객, 학생이 다 함께 촬영하였다. 언더우드는 보고서에서 4월 12일 개교식을 거행하였음을 밝혔다. (출처: 『연희전문학교 제1회 졸업생 기념사진첩』, 1919)

▲ 이사회 이사들 (1935년 2월 15일 촬영)

3대 교장 원한경이 이사장으로서 앞줄 중앙에 앉아있다. 초창기 학교 임원들인 에비슨(왼편에서 5번째)은 명예 교장, 베커(뒷줄 맨 왼쪽)는 평교수, 빌링스(앞줄 맨 왼쪽)는 감리교신학교 교장이 되었으나 이사직은 계속 유지하였다. (출처: 연희전문 1936년 졸업앨범)

◀ 언더우드(H. G. Underwood, 1859~1916)
연세대학교의 설립자 겸 초대 교장이란 그의 지위는 연희전문 초창기부터 공식화되었다. 그는 1880년대 후반부터 의학교를 포함하는 종합대학의 설립을 꿈꾸었고, 한국에서 선교하던 장로교 일부 선교사들과 감리교 전체 선교사들, 본국 선교본부들의 지지, 그리고 그의 형 존(John T. Underwood)의 재정 지원을 힘입어 대학설립을 추진하였다.
(출처: 연희전문 제1회 1919년 졸업앨범)

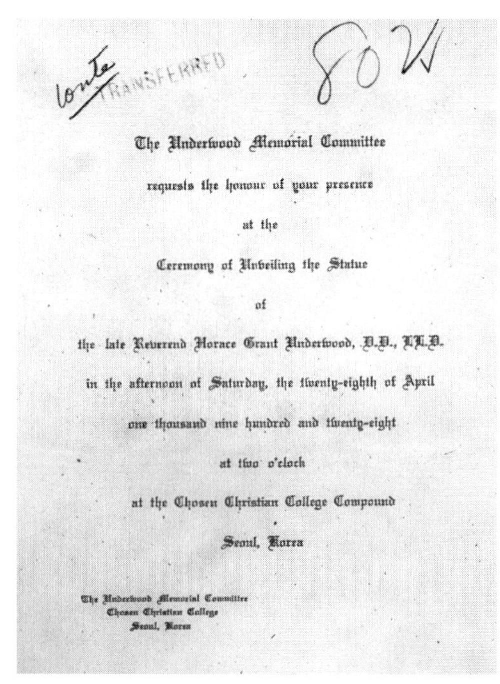

TRANSFERRED

The Underwood Memorial Committee
requests the honour of your presence
at the
Ceremony of Unveiling the Statue
of
the late Reverend Horace Grant Underwood, D.D., LL.D.
in the afternoon of Saturday, the twenty-eighth of April
one thousand nine hundred and twenty-eight
at two o'clock
at the Chosen Christian College Compound
Seoul, Korea

The Underwood Memorial Committee
Chosen Christian College
Seoul, Korea

▲ 언더우드 동상(좌)과 제막식 초청장(우)
언더우드상은 우애회(교수친목회)와 동창회의 성금으로 제작되어 1928년 4월 28일 제막되었다. 이때 언더우드의 아들과 손자들이 제막하였다. 고원두우박사동상건립위원회(Underwood Memorial Committee)는 이날 오후 2시 교정에서 거행하는 동상 제막식에 참석해달라고 하는 내용의 초청장을 만들었다.
(출처: 1937년 졸업앨범, United Methodist Archives and History Center)

◀ 에비슨(O. R. Avison, 1860~1956) 제2대 교장
세브란스의학교 교장 에비슨은 연희전문 개교 연도인 1915년 12월 이사회 회의에서 언더우드의 일본 방문으로 인한 교장의 부재 기간 발생에 대비하여 부교장으로 선임되었다. 1916년 10월 언더우드가 미국에서 사망하자 1917년 2월 교장으로 선임되었다. 이후 17년간 양교 교장을 겸임하다 1934년 은퇴하고 1935년 한국을 떠났다.
(출처: 1927년 졸업앨범)

▲ 연희전문학교 교수회 (1927~28년경)
에비슨 교장이 교수회를 주재하고 있다. 오른편 인물은 1927년 부교장이 된 원한경이다. 맨 왼편의 인물은 최현배 교수이고, 맨 오른편은 백낙준 신임 교수로 보이며, 그로부터 네 번째 인물은 조병옥 교수이다. 교수회는 조교수급 이상으로 구성되었다. (출처: 1928년 졸업앨범)

◀ 원한경(H. H. Underwood) 제3대 교장
언더우드 초대 교장의 독자로 대학 초창기부터 영어, 심리학 등을 가르쳤다. 1927년 부교장에, 1934년 교장에 취임하였다. 한국 전통문화를 깊이 연구하며 해외에 알리기 위해 노력하였고, 대학의 화충학풍 진작을 독려하였다. 1941년 일제의 압력으로 사임한 후, 1942년 추방되었다. 해방 후 미군정청 고문으로 활동하고 연희전문의 재건을 도왔다.
(출처: 1935년 졸업앨범)

◀ 원한경이 집무한 교장실
(출처: 1935년 졸업앨범)

◀ 원한경의 사택
원한경이 사비로 1927년 대지를 구입하고 건축하였다. 전쟁 때 파괴되어 복구되었으나, 위층에 다락방만 설치되었다. 연세대학에 기증되어 언더우드가 기념관으로 활용되고 있다.
(출처: Ann Avison Black 〈Douglas B. Avison 세의전 교수의 딸〉 개인 소장품)

▲ 빌링스(B. W. Billings, 1881~1969)

개교 후부터 영어를 가르치며 부교장과 문과 과장을 겸직하다가 1923년 부교장직을, 1928년 문과 과장직을 사임하였고, 1932년 학교를 떠나 감리교신학교에 교장으로 부임하였다.

▲ 베커(A. L. Becker, 1879~1979)

개교 후부터 학감과 수물과 과장을 겸하다 1925년 사임하였고, 1923부터 부교장을, 1924년부터 교장 대리까지 겸하다 1926년 사임하였다. 1939년 다시 부교장이 되었으나, 그 해에 귀국하였다.

(출처: 1919년 졸업앨범)

▲ 연희전문학교 교수회(Faculty Meeting) (1925~26년경)

베커가 교수회를 주재하고 있다. 이 회의에 참석한 20명 가운데 서양인 선교사 교수는 5인(왼편에서부터 노블, 빌링스, 베커, 히치, 로즈), 일본인 교수는 3인(왼편에서 세 번째 가토와키, 오른편에서 두 번째 히라이, 세 번째 츠바키다)이다. (출처: 1926년 졸업앨범)

▲ 로즈(H. A. Rhodes, 1875~1965)

1918년 교수로 부임하여 신과 과장으로서 채플 운영과 성경 교육을 담당하였고, 1919~21년 학감을 대리하였다. 1933년 학교를 떠나 피어선성경학원 교장을 역임하였고, 1940년 귀국하였다.

▲ 유억겸(兪億兼, 1896~1947)

동경제대 법학부를 졸업하고 1923년 상과 교수, 1925년 학감이 된 후, 1934년부터 부교장을 겸하였다. 1938년 흥업구락부사건으로 사임한 후, 1941년 복직하고 이듬해 사임하였다. 해방 후 연희전문 교장, 문교부장관을 지냈다.

(출처: 1927년 졸업앨범)

▲ 유억겸 학감 사무실 (1928~29년)

상과에서 법률을 가르치는 한편 학감과 부교장으로 일하면서 교수들의 연구와 학생 활동을 지원하였다.
(출처: 1929년 졸업앨범)

▲ 이춘호(李春昊, 1893~1950)

오하이오 주립대를 졸업하고 1922년 수물과 교수로 부임하여 1925년 과장이 되었다. 1931~32년과 1937~38년 학감을 대리하였고, 1938년 흥업구락부사건으로 사임하였다가 복직하였다. 해방 후 서울대 총장을 역임하였고, 납북되었다.

(출처: 1933년 졸업앨범)

▲ 이묘묵(李卯默, 1902~1957)

연전 문과를 졸업하고 보스턴대에서 박사학위를 받았다. 1934년 교수로 부임하여 도서관장을 역임하였고, 1937년 동우회사건으로 사임하였다가 복직하여 1938년 학감이 되었다. 해방 후 하지의 통역, 주영공사를 역임하였다.

(출처: 1936년 졸업앨범)

▲ 이춘호 교수의 미분방정식 강의 장면

(출처: 1929년 졸업앨범)

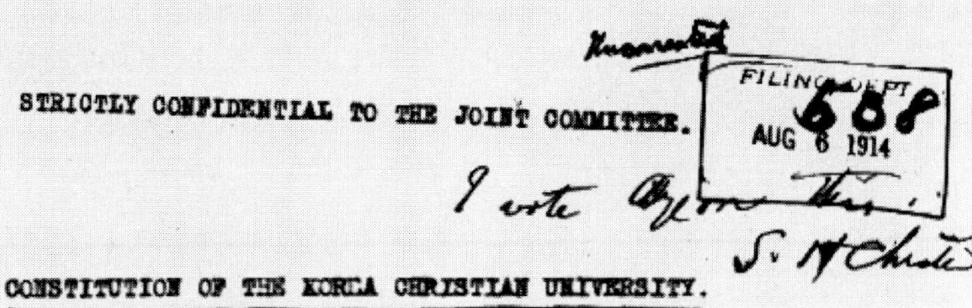

STRICTLY CONFIDENTIAL TO THE JOINT COMMITTEE.

CONSTITUTION OF THE KOREA CHRISTIAN UNIVERSITY.

PREAMBLE.

The University is organized on the basis of the union of the higher educational work in Korea of the Board of Foreign Missions of the Methodist Episcopal Church, the Board of Missions of the Methodist Episcopal Church, South, the Board of Foreign Missions of the Presbyterian Church in U.S.A., the Executive Committee of Foreign Missions of the Presbyterian Church in the U.S. (South), the Foreign Missions Committee Presbyterian Church in Canada and the Presbyterian Church of Victoria, Australia. Other incorporated missionary organizations may, at any time, be affiliated with and made constituent, trustee-electing members of the corporation of the University, by the favoring vote of the managing Board of all of its then existing such constituent bodies; and each such so added constituent body shall be entitled to choose, as its representative, or representatives, to hold for a term of three years, an additional member, or members, not exceeding three, as the vote of affiliation shall provide, of the Field Board of Managers and the Board of Trustees of the University, and to choose, each three years, a successor, or successors, to such representative manager and trustee, or managers and trustees, to hold for a like term.

The six original parties of the Union hereby adopt the following agreement and Constitution with reference to the funds and property contributed by each and the government and conduct of the University.

ARTICLE I - OBJECT.

The object of the University is to prepare Christian leaders, to provide educational advantages for the children of our Christian constituencies, and to promote higher education in Korea under Christian influences and in harmony with the Word of God.

ARTICLE II - NAME.

The name of this institution shall be The Korea Christian University.

▲ 합동위원회(Joint Committee)가 정한 신설 대학의 헌장 (1914년)

미국, 캐나다, 호주의 6개 선교부 대표들로 구성된 합동위원회가 1914년 서울에 종합대학을 세울 것을 결정하고 헌장까지 만들었다. 그들은 8쪽 분량 문서의 제1쪽에서 3개국의 6개 선교부가 연합하여 한국에 기독교 종합대학을 세울 것과 고등교육을 통한 한국 내 기독교 영향력 확대를 설립 목적으로 정했음을 밝혔다. 이 문서는 그들이 기독교인 자녀에게만 컬리지 수준의 교육을 하기 원했던 한국 내 다수파 선교사들이 아닌 서울 소수파(언더우드)의 손을 들어주었음을 입증한다.

(출처: Presbyterian Historical Society)

40 West Ninth Ave,
Columbus, Ohio,
May 10, 1922.

802

Dr. Frank M. North,
150 Fifth Ave,
New York City.

Dear Sir:

I like to ask you whether it is possible for your Board to secure a statement or a vise for me from the Japanese authorities. I might write for this matter to Bishop Welch who knows me well personally and also knows that I have no passport of any sort, but, as it takes a long time to get his reply, I could not do it on account that I have to leave for home as soon as possible. So I ask you for a favor. Bishop Welch has participated in securing the position in the Chosen Christian College, Seoul, Korea, to which I am planning to go as a teacher of mathematics and science for the coming September. In order to give you my assurance, I will quote the following words from a letter of Dean A.L. Becker, which I received a few weeks ago.

"Bishop Welch sent on your records, letters, and recommendations; and we have considered them. We would like to have you come to us as a teacher of mathematics and science.......... Can you come out so as to begin teaching in September? ....".

TRANSFERRED

After I received this letter and have consulted this matter with professor L.G. Westrate in Ohio Wesleyan University, I have decided to accept the position offered and plan to return home this summer so as to begin work from September. But I feel that, as I have no passport, I have to have some sort of statement from the Japanese authorities for my travel, and it is my conviction that your Board has more influence than a single individual like myself to try to obtain one directly from the Japanese consul, for they might have some suspicion of me, although I had or have not any connection directly or indirectly with the political movement in home as well as abroad. In order to give you a working source, I state the following information.

When I was in Korea, I had been one of the good obedient citizens, and the government did not have any suspicion or any sort on my conduct. The reason why I left Korea without having a passport from the government is a plane fact that the Japanese policies were at that time in Korea in such that the young Koreans were not allowed to go to the Western world for higher education. Before I left Korea, I once tried to obtain a passport to America but the application was rejected in the police station of my home town without having reached the general office. Then I learned through some medium that a student might be allowed to land to America for education without having a passport. I decided to try for a luck, and I had the luck.

Concerning the problem with the politics, as I have already stated above. I assure you that I have no connection at all directly or indirectly with the political movement or with the Korean politics at the present time. My sole intention has been and is that I will return home and devote myself to the educational and religious work for the Koreans, especially for the Korean students. You may assert, if you like to, to the Japanese authorities that my future work will solely lie on education and religious work.

Probably you may need the following statement in securing the vise.

Name......Choon Ho Lee.
Age....... .25.
Born.... in Songdo, Korea.
Home address..Songdo, Korea.
Left Korea in May, 1914, and arrived at San Francisco sometime in June, 1914.
Present occupation....Grad. student and teaching Fellow at Ohio State Univ.

I thank you in advance for your kind consideration for this matter.

Yours sincerely,

C. H. Lee

▲ 이춘호 수물과 교수의 부임 전 편지 (1922년 5월 10일)

오하이오 주립대에서 한국 최초로 수학석사 학위를 받은 이춘호가 연희전문 교수 초빙을 받고 1922년 9월 개강 전에 귀국하기를 원하여 북감리회 선교부에 일본 여권을 구할 수 있게 도와주기를 요청하고 있다. 그는 애초에 미국 유학을 위한 여권 발급을 일본 경찰서에 신청하였으나 거부당해 여권이 없는 채로 미국에 왔다고 설명하고 있다. 이 문제가 쉽게 해결되어 여비까지 지원받아 귀국하였다.

(출처: United Methodist Archives and History Center)

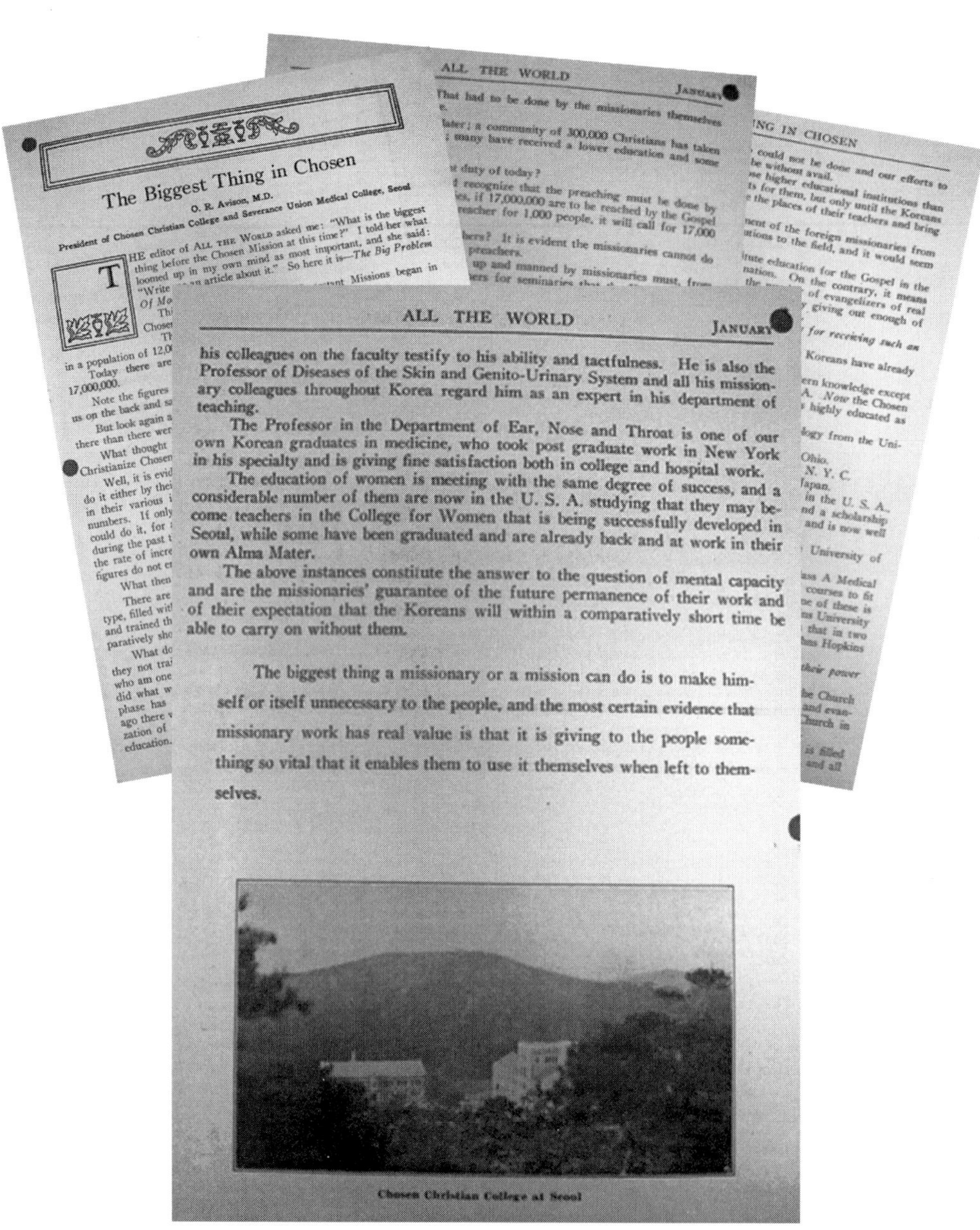

ALL THE WORLD

The Biggest Thing in Chosen

O. R. Avison, M.D.

President of Chosen Christian College and Severance Union Medical College, Seoul

ALL THE WORLD JANUARY

his colleagues on the faculty testify to his ability and tactfulness. He is also the Professor of Diseases of the Skin and Genito-Urinary System and all his missionary colleagues throughout Korea regard him as an expert in his department of teaching.

The Professor in the Department of Ear, Nose and Throat is one of our own Korean graduates in medicine, who took post graduate work in New York in his specialty and is giving fine satisfaction both in college and hospital work.

The education of women is meeting with the same degree of success, and a considerable number of them are now in the U. S. A. studying that they may become teachers in the College for Women that is being successfully developed in Seoul, while some have been graduated and are already back and at work in their own Alma Mater.

The above instances constitute the answer to the question of mental capacity and are the missionaries' guarantee of the future permanence of their work and of their expectation that the Koreans will within a comparatively short time be able to carry on without them.

The biggest thing a missionary or a mission can do is to make himself or itself unnecessary to the people, and the most certain evidence that missionary work has real value is that it is giving to the people something so vital that it enables them to use it themselves when left to themselves.

Chosen Christian College at Seoul

▲ 연희전문 후원을 호소하는 에비슨 교장의 기고문 (1925년 1월)

에비슨 교장의 기고문 "The Biggest Thing in Chosen," *All the World* (Jan., 1925)는 1924~26년간에 미국에서 어떤 논리로 후원을 호소하였는지를 알게 한다. 그는 선교사가 할 가장 큰 일이란 선교지 사람들에게 선교사가 필요 없어지게 만드는 것과 스스로 능력을 기를 수단, 곧 종합대학을 주는 것이라고 주장하였다. 한국인에게 스스로 발전할 지적 능력이 있음을 입증하는 예로 연·세전 한국인 교수들의 해외 유학 사례를 나열하였다. (출처: United Methodist Archives and History Center)

Action of the Board of Foreign Missions of the
Presbyterian Church in the U.S.A.

CHOSEN MISSION PROPOSED MINUTE FOREIGN DEPT. COM.
December 13, 1938.

Pursuant to Board action of September 19, 1938, relative to the proposals of the Chosen Mission (V.996 and V.997, 1938 Minutes) for the withdrawal of the Board and Mission from the Severance Union Medical College and the Chosen Christian College, the Board noted the statements of the Cooperating Board for Christian Education in Chosen replying to the notice given to them by the Acting Secretary for Chosen in accordance with the instructions of the Board. The reply is as follows:

"The Cooperating Board for Christian Education in Chosen has learned with regret of the action taken on September 19, 1938, by the Board of Foreign Missions of the Presbyterian Church in the U. S. A. relating to higher education in Chosen.

"We recall the initiative and sacrificial leadership of Presbyterian missionaries and the Presbyterian Board in establishing Severance Union Medical College and Chosen Christian College and also in inspiring other denominations to join in this program. We are grateful for that leadership and for the years of enjoyable cooperation.

"We would respectfully point out to the Presbyterian Board that great harm would be wrought to the interests of the other Boards of Foreign Missions concerned, as well as to the cause of Christian higher education in Chosen, if the Board adopts the recommendation of the Chosen Mission calling for withdrawal from the institutions by March 31, 1939. The Cooperating Board needs considerable time for consulting Boards of Foreign Missions located as far apart as Toronto, Canada, and Nashville, Tennessee. We, therefore, express the earnest hope that the Presbyterian Board will find it possible to extend that time by at least one year, preferably two, in order to allow the Cooperating Board and the denominations to explore ways of conserving the Christian interests involved."

In view of the expressed statement of the Cooperating Board and in line with the usual procedure in such cases, it was voted to set the date of Mission and Board withdrawal from the two schools as of March 31, 1941. It was understood the Board and Mission would continue in full cooperation with the schools until this time, and that the question of the terms of withdrawal will be taken up before that date.

▲ 연 · 세전과의 관계 절연을 결정한 미국 북장로회 선교부의 통지문 (1938년)

북장로회 선교부는 일제의 신사참배 강요에 맞서 1938년 9월 19일 회의를 열고 1941년 3월 말 이후에는 연희전문, 세브란스의전과의 관계를 끊을 것을 결정하였다. 그들은 이 사실을 협력이사회에 1938년 12월 통지하였고, 학교에는 1939년 1월 통지하였다. 그러나 그 후에 소속 선교사가 개인적으로 학교를 위해 일하는 것은 묵인하였다. (출처: United Methodist Archives and History Center)

CHICAGO OFFICE—77 W. WASHINGTON STREET

SAN FRANCISCO OFFICE—228 MCALLISTER STREET

THE BOARD OF FOREIGN MISSIONS
OF THE PRESBYTERIAN CHURCH IN THE
UNITED STATES OF AMERICA
156 FIFTH AVENUE
NEW YORK

DIVISION OF SPECIAL GIFTS AND ANNUITIES
MISS RUTH ELLIOTT, DIRECTOR
HORACE H. UNDERWOOD
ACTING DIRECTOR

December [illegible]

RECEIVED BY
DEC 29 1942

Dr.George Sutherland
The M.E.Board of Foreign Missions
150 Fifth Avenue
New York City.

My dear Dr.Sutherland:

You will remember that I prepared a report for the Cooperating Board for Christian Education in Chosen which was presented at the luncheon meeting which you so kindly arranged. In addition to this, I have prepared and sent out to quite a number of individuals a letter and personal report for 1940-42. This second report was not purely on college business but quite a large section of it, of course, dealt with the Chosen Christian College, and it was mailed to a large number of individuals who, I thought, might be interested in the work of the college. The mimeographing of these two came to a total of $19.30. In addition to this there was postage and a number of other expenses which I have not itemized but which it seems to me could legitimately be considered a charge against the college and its work. Including the mimeographing mentioned above, I have expended a total of approximately $30.00 (possibly a little more). If you consider this a legitimate expenditure and properly chargeable to the college, I would greatly appreciate a check to cover this expenditure. I do not know if it is necessary for this to be passed on by any committee or not, but if you will in any case take up the matter and if it is approved send me a check for $30.00, I will greatly appreciate it.

Thanking you for your attention to this, and with best wishes to you all for the Christmas season,

I am

Yours very sincerely,

Horace H. Underwood

Horace H.Underwood

HHU/EC

(Dictated but not signed.)

▲ 원한경이 미국에서 협력이사회 회계에게 보낸 편지 (1942년 12월 28일)

원한경이 일제에 의해 추방되어(1942년 6월) 미국에 도착한 후 쓴 편지이다. 이 편지는 원한경이 본 자료집에 실린 마지막 두 보고서를 언제 누구에게 제출하였는지를 짐작할 수 있게 한다. 첫 번째 보고서는 협력이사회 이사들에게, 두 번째 보고서는 불특정의 다수에게 제출하였다. 그는 이런 사실을 설명하면서 두 문서의 발행비와 발송비를 협력이사회 회계에게 청구하고 있다.

(출처: United Methodist Archives and History Center)

교장 · 부교장 · 학감 보고서

1915~1942

1. 언더우드 이사장의 합동위원회 제출 개교 준비 보고서

문서 제목	Letter of Horace Grant Underwood to George Heber Jones
문서 종류	이사장 보고서
제출 시기	1915년 3월 26일
작성 장소	서울
제 출 자	H. G. Underwood
수 신 자	합동위원회 (G. H. Jones, 위원장 권한대행)
페이지 수	4
출 처	Scan 1789 Chosen Christian College: Underwood, Horace., (Dr.) (Rev.) 1912~1916 (UMAH)

자료 소개

이사회가 창립된 후 언더우드가 이사장의 자격으로 1915년 3월 26일 미국 합동위원회(Joint Committee)에 개교 준비상황을 알린 편지 형식의 보고서이다. 이사회는 1915년 3월 5일 예수교서회에서 3개(미국 북장로회, 남 · 북감리회) 선교회의 선교사 9명이 창립하였다. 언더우드는 이 이사회를 '임시이사회'(provisional Board of Field Managers)라고 불렀다. 그러나 창립회의 회의록은 이사회 명칭 앞의 'provisional'이란 수식어를 붙이지 않고 있다.

보고서를 받은 존스는 북감리회 선교본부(이하 선교부)의 보조 총무로, 1915년 전반에 노스(F. M. North) 합동위원회 위원장의 권한대행이었다. 합동위원회는 한국에서 선교하는 주요 6개 교단의 선교부들이 고등교육사업을 위해 결성한 것이다. 1914년 서울에 'university'를 세우기로 결의하고, 이후에 조선기독교대학의 설립 과정을 감독하였다.

수신처는 뉴욕 5번가 156번지에 있는 북장로회 선교부이다. 언더우드가 이 편지를 인근의 5번가 150번지의 북감리회 선교부로 곧장 보내지 않은 것은 합동위원회의 일원이자 자신의 소속기관인 북장로회 측도 이 서신을 참조하게 하기 위함이었던 것으로 짐작된다. 합동위원회의 사무실이 그곳에 있었기 때문이었을 수도 있다.

이 문서는 보고서(1~2쪽)와 첨부 문서(3~4쪽)로 구성된다. 보고서는 개교 준비상황과 운영 계획 등을 설명하고 있고, 첨부 문서는 예산명세서와 학생선발 규정을 제시하고 있다.

내용 요약

◩ 보고서

이미 통보한 대로 임시이사회가 3개[북장로회, 남 · 북감리회] 선교회에 의해 결성되었다. 이제 며칠 내로 학교를 개교하여, YMCA 건물을 연 1,380.00원에 임대하고 교실 5개, 도서관, 사무실을 얻을 작정이다. 또한 YMCA 건물 꼭대기를 기숙사로 고쳐 쓰는 것을 허락받았다.

한국인과 일본인 교수를 몇 명 쓰기를 원하고 있다. 첫해에는 예과, 1학년, 2학년 학생들만 입학시킬 것이고, 예과는 2년 안에 폐지하려 한다.

한 해의 수입과 지출 예산서를 함께 보내니, 이사회의 정관에 따라 위의 3개 선교회가 $6,000(또는 ¥12,000)을 지급해주기를 희망한다.

현재 캠퍼스용 대지를 매입하고 정규 이사회를 재단법인으로 만들기 위해 노력하고 있다.

◩ 첨부 문서

(예산〈지출 · 수입〉 명세, 입학요건, 입학시험 과목, 입학 자격조건, 입학금 규정 등을 제시하고 있다.)

H. G. UNDERWOOD,
Seoul, Korea.

Seoul, Korea, March 26, 1915

Rev. Dr. George Heber Jones,

156 Fifth Avenue, New York City

My dear Dr. Jones:

I presume that you have already heard that the representatives of three Missions met in Seoul, and organized a provisional Board of Field Managers, and suggested a certain changes in the provisional Constitution.

I have been told that you are now the Chairman of Joint Committee in America and I am writing at the present time let you know what our plans are.

We expect to open in a few days and have succeeded in securing five class-rooms, library room, and office-room in the Y.M.C.A. building at an annual rental of Yen 1,380.00 This is only 60 Yen more than what the Y.M.C.A. rented their two office-rooms.

We have also made arrangement with them whereby we are allowed to fit up the top-floor of the new Y. M/ C/A. building for dormitory. We have to put in partitions and floors, which will give us room enough for 60 or 70 students. For this we are we are to pay for the cost of same, which is to go as two years' rental. This will give very compact and handy quarters, with the School all under one roof and properly cared for.

At the start we are looking to use a few Japanese and Korean professors and during the first year we expect only to take in men for a preparatory grade and Freshman and Sophomore work.

The preparatory grade is simply for men who are not advanced in English and Japanese.

In a couple of years we expect to drop this preparatory

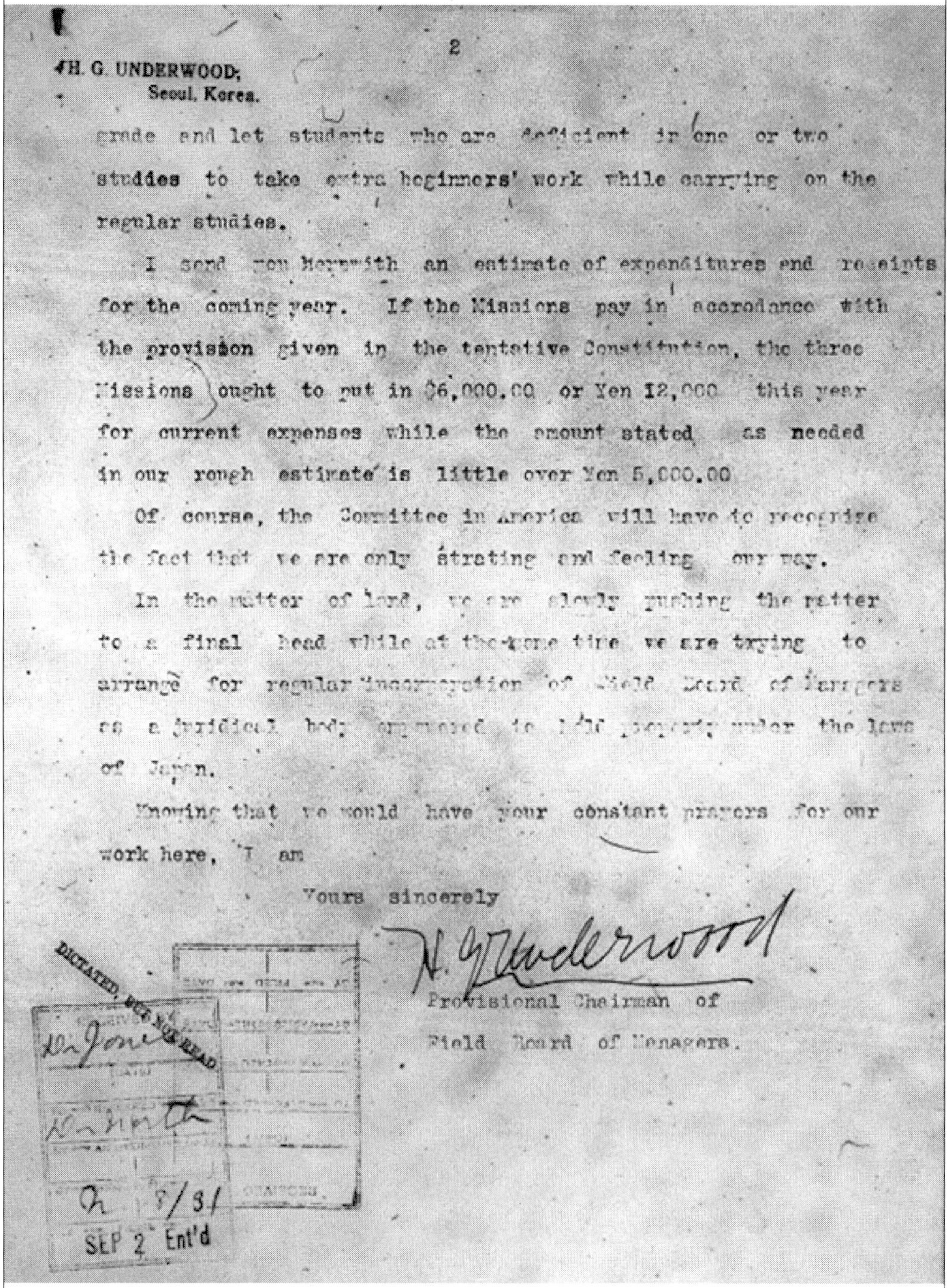

2

H. G. UNDERWOOD,
Seoul, Korea.

grade and let students who are deficient in one or two studies to take extra beginners' work while carrying on the regular studies.

I send you herewith an estimate of expenditures and receipts for the coming year. If the Missions pay in accordance with the provision given in the tentative Constitution, the three Missions ought to put in $6,000.00 or Yen 12,000 this year for current expenses while the amount stated as needed in our rough estimate is little over Yen 5,000.00

Of course, the Committee in America will have to recognize the fact that we are only strating and feeling our way.

In the matter of land, we are slowly pushing the matter to a final head while at the same time we are trying to arrange for regular incorporation of Field Board of Managers as a juridical body empowered to hold property under the laws of Japan.

Knowing that we would have your constant prayers for our work here, I am

Yours sincerely

H. G. Underwood

Provisional Chairman of

Field Board of Managers.

DICTATED, BUT NOT READ

Dr Jones

Dr North

Ch 8/31

SEP 2 Ent'd

I

KOREAN CHRISTIAN COLLEGE (Seoul)

Budget, Estimate.

I Expenditures

(I) Rental School rooms, office (I2 mo. @II5.00)--¥1380.00

(2) Dormitory heated and lighted (I2 Mo. @75.00)-- 900.00

(3) Dining room (I2 mo. @I0.00)------------------ I20.00

(4) Japanese Professors (I2 mo. @200.00)--------- 2400.00

(5) One Korean Instructor (I2 mo. 50.00)--------- 600.00

(6) One Korean Instructor (Agriculture specially)- 420.00

(7) Laboratory Assistants------------------------ 720.00

(8) Office and Library Assistants (Students)------ 216.00

(9) Stenographer and typist----------------------

(I0) Telephone---------------------------------- 72.00

(II) Janitor- --------------------------------- I44.00

(I2) Reference books for Library---------------- 200.00

(I3) Miscellaneous, Laboratory expenses---------- 500.00

Total----------- 7,672.00

2 Income Estimated

(I) Students, dormitory fees (50. @I0.00)--------- 500.00

(2) " Matriculation fees (50. @4.00)--------- 200.00

(3) " Tuition (50. @I2.00)----------------- 600.00

(4) " Laboratory fees----------------------- 400.00

(5) Co-operating Missions three missions, each ¥4,000 or ¥12,000.00 – 3

Total----------

Passed by the Executive Committee of Field Board of Managers.

2

KOREAN CHRISTIAN COLLEGE (Seoul)

Entrance Requirements

TRANSFERRED

English------------------8 hrs.
Janpanese--------------24 hrs.
Chinese-----------------12 hrs.
Algebra-----------------8 hrs.
Plain Geom.------------ 5 hrs.
Solid Geom.------------ 2 hrs.
Physics----------------- 5 hrs.
Chemistry--------------- 5 hrs.
Phys. Geog. and Botany--- 3 hrs.
Zoology and physiology-- 3 hrs.
History----------------- 9 hrs.
Booking Keeping--------- 3 hrs.
Ethics------------------ 3 hrs.

Examinations

Japanese-----(Must read and speak Japanese)
Chinese------(Should read easy Chinese readily)
English------(Should have finished Step 4th)
Math.--------(Should be ready in all general operation in Algebra and Geometry)
Physics and Chem.------- A definite knowledge of Elementary Theory and Experience is requird
Botany Zoology and Physiology.--------General knowledg of facts required.
History-------- A knowledge of important events of General History.
Ethics-------- A knowledge of the Gospels.

1. Students must have recommendation of character and Church standing.

2. A guarantee from parent or guardian.

3. Pass a physical examination.

4. Must pass examinations as above and be able to take at least ten hours work in Freshman class.

Fees

Matriculation---------¥ 4.00
Term fee (in advance) 4.00
Laboratory fee (in Chem. and Physics)--¥ 3.00
Dormitory fee--------- 1.00 per mo.

2. 언더우드 교장의 이사회 제출 개교보고서

문서 제목	Provisional President's report of the initial steps thus far taken in connection with the inauguration of the Chosen Christian College
문서 종류	교장 보고서
제출 시기	1915년 4월 21일
작성 장소	서울
제 출 자	H. G. Underwood
수 신 자	이사회
페이지 수	11
출 처	① Korea Mission Records 1903~1957, Series 3, Roll 20 (PHS) ② Scan 0790 Chosen Christian College: Underwood, Horace H. (Dr.) October 1913-December 1923 (UMAH) ③ 2114-5-2: 06 Board of Managers 1915~1922 (UMAH)

자료 소개

언더우드 교장이 1915년 4월 21일 열린 제2회 이사회 회의에 제출한 보고서이다. 여기에서 그는 자신을 '임시 교장'(Provisional President)이라 칭하였는데, 이사회 2회 회의록에도 '임시 교장'으로 기록되어 있다. 이 보고서는 3가지 형태로 남아 있다. PHS에 1가지, UMAH에 2가지가 소장되어 있는데, PHS의 ①번 문서는 제목의 "President's"에서 소유격을 가리키는 작은따옴표가 빠져 있고, UMAH의 ②번 문서는 개교일인 "12th" 부분이 "1wth"로 되어 오타를 보이고 있으며, ③번 문서는 다른 두 문서와 달리 9쪽 분량이다. 수록된 원문은 ①번 문서이다.

이 보고서는 서언과 아래의 항목들로 구성되어 있다.

I. 임시교육관, II, 교수, III. 이사회, IV. 학생, V. 캠퍼스 부지, VI. 법인,

VII. 총독부 설립인가, VIII. 실행위원회, IX. 전망.

내용 요약

서언: 4월 12일 서울 YMCA 건물에 마련한 임시교육관에서 조선기독교대학의 개교식이

거행되었음을 보고하게 되어 감사한다.

I. YMCA 건물의 방 8개를 임대받았는데, YMCA 수공부에서 의자와 책상을 만들어주었다. 맨 위층의 새 체육관을 칸막이하여 기숙사로 쓰도록 타협이 이루어졌다. 이달 셋째 주쯤에는 기숙사에 입주할 수 있을 것이다.

II. 현재 선교사 교수 8명, 한국인 교수 5명(백상규, 이노익, W. J. Nah, 신흥우, 양주삼)이 교수진을 이루고 있고, 일본인 목사 3명과 그밖에 몇 사람이 교수로 합류하였다.

III. 이사회는 동양인 기독교인들의 도움을 받아야 한다. 정관에서 교장이 당연이사로 규정되어있어서 나의 북장로회 측 이사 자리를 교회 장로인 와타나베 판사[고등법원장]에게 넘겼다. 남장로회 측이 편지를 보내와 한국 내의 6개 선교회 가운데 5개 선교회가 이 대학의 운영에 협력해야 자신들도 협력하겠다는 유보적인 입장을 다시 밝혔다.

IV. 현재 상황에서는 학생을 많이 수용할 수 없는데도 예상보다 많게 61명이 입학을 지원하였다. 적은 수로 시작하여 최고의 기독교 이상을 구현하도록 하겠다.

V. 캠퍼스 부지를 마련하기 위해 1차 임시이사회에서 위촉된 캠퍼스 부지위원 3인이 고마츠[조선총독부 외사국장]와 부지 구입 협상을 벌이기 시작하였다.

VI. 총독부의 새 교육법에 따라 전문학교 법인을 만들기 위해 와타나베 판사 등의 도움을 받아 메이지 학원의 법인을 참고할 예정이다,

VII. 조선기독교대학의 설립 근거가 되는 기존의 경신학교 인가 대신 새 인가를 받기 위해 세키야[학무국장]의 도움을 받고 있다.

VIII. 실행위원회가 승인한 예산을 이 회의에 제출한다. 경상비를 얻기 위해 이 예산을 각 선교회에 알릴 필요가 있다.

IX. 선교사 교수 3인(E. H. Miller, B. W. Billings, H. H. Underwood)이 봄학기가 끝나면 미국에 가야 하므로 일본인을 영입해야 하고, 총독부와 좋은 관계를 유지하면서 건축을 준비해야 한다.

H. G. UNDERWOOD,
Seoul, Korea.

R. S. Underwood
Report

FILING DEPT.
1426
MAY 8 1916
SECRETARIES

Provisional Presidents report of the initial steps thus far taken in connection with the inauguration of the Chosen Christian College.

To the Field Board of Managers.

It is with feelings of thankfulness to Gof for His guidance that I find myself able to report that the opening exercises of the Chosen Christian College were held on April 12th in the temporary quarters that have been secured from the Y.M.C.A. of Seoul.

There are many things to report on at this first time that I must condense a good deal.

1. Temporary Quarters.

In accordance with the authorization of the Field Board of Managers, we secured from the Y.M.C.A. eight rooms, and they were willing to rent to us at what we might call a nominal rent. Two of the rooms had been rented for Yen 110.00 per month, and they were willing to let us have all the rooms for Yen 115.00 with the understanding that the classrooms with the College equipment were open to the use of the Y.M.C.A. for their night school.

The laboratory and office rooms, of course, do not come unde this head.

It seems to me that a vote of thanks is due to them for their generous treatment of the College.

Still further are we indebted to them for the energetic way in which Mr Gregg pushed forward the work in the Y.M.C.A. Industrial Department on our seats and benches, so that we were enabled to begin our work on April 12th, although this was little more than a month after the order had been placed with them for the work.

The desks are models of neatness, strength, and cheapness. They are a credit to the institution that has made them for us.

Arrangements have also been made with the same institution whereby the top-floor of the new gymnasium has been divided into rooms and will be used for our dormitory. This has been handed over to us for a mere payment of the cost of partitions and flooring, which is to cover the rent for two years. Some members of the Board of Directors of the Y.M.C.A. seriously questioned whether it was doing justice to the Y.M.C.A. interestes to let this whole floor go at this nominal rental, but it was passed because of the interest which we are mutually serving.

A special arrangement has been made for all College students living in this dormitory concerning membership in the Y.M.C.A. and the privileges of the Y.M.C.A, baths, gymnasium, reading-room etc.

The dormitory is not quite furnished but we expect to have it occupied about the third week of this month.

11. The Faculty.

At the present time, a Faculty consists of the following gentlemen:

Messrs. A.L.Becker, B.W.Billings, J.L.Gerdine, Dr R.A.Hardie. Messrs. E.H.Miller, R.G.Mills, H.H.Underwood and H.G.Underwood, as sent by the co-operating Missions.

In addition to the above gentlemen, we have secured the services of theb following gentlemen: (U. of South Cal)

(Ph. B. Brown) (...) (Grad. ... Tokyo)

Messrs. S.Pack, Root Yi, W.J.Nah, H.H.Cynn, and K.Yang. (B.S. Yale)

Mr Foster Beck has kindly agreed to act as physical directer. It was early detirmined to secure from Japan one or two Japanese professors, but the time has been too short and when we opened the College we found ourselves minus some important factors in our College work.

I am very glad to report that this time we are ably helped by Japanese Pastors of the city, in the following manner:

Rev. Kiyoshi Fujioka has charge of the Japanese History.

Rev. Yamamoto has charge of the Occidental History.

Rev. Inoguchi has charge of the Oriental History.

A special vote of thanks was passed by the Faculty for the kindness of these gentlemen, but it seems to me that our Field Board of Managers should take notice of this and the Secretary of the Board should be instructed to send them a formal vote of thanks.

In the Department of the Japanese Language, we have temporarily secured the service of Mr Niiyama who is professor of the Japanese Language in the Pierson Memorial Bible School and the Methodist Theological Seminary in this city.

111. Personnel of Field Board of Managers.

It was early felt by me that we ought to have the assistance of Oriental Christians on our Field Board of Managers and noting that the Constitution provided that the President of the College was ex-officio, the Chairman of the Field Board of Managers, I tended my resignation as one of the representatives on the Field Board of

H. G. UNDERWOOD,
Seoul, Korea.

4.

Managers of the Presbyterian Church in U.S.A. and nominated Judge Watanabe of the Supreme Court of Korea, and an elder in the Presbyterian CHurch, Seoul. He was duly elected and we are in great hopes that he will consent to serve us although we know that he has hands already more than full.

There has been nno other change in the Field Board of Managers.

Receiving a telegram from Chun Ju asking that a statement concerning what has been done thus far be sent to the Southern Presbyterian AdInterim Committee, I replied telling them of what had been done and invited their co_operation and I received the following letter in reply:

Rev. H.G.Underwood, D.D.

Seoul Chosen.

Dear Dr Underwood,

The following if the action of our AdInterim Committee, which as you perhaps know has full power of the Mission, and whose actions are reported to the Mission for information only:

" With regatd to the communication concerning the Union College, we reiterate the action of our last Annual Meeting as to the co-operation of Five-sixths of the Mission in the proposed Union College, and again call attention to the minimum request of our Mission as to Field control of the College (see 1914 Minutes, page 55)

"We dirct that the proposed constitution, with suggested changes be sent to the various Stations for review and suggestion, pending next Annual Meeting and that the attention of our Executive Committee at Nashville be directed to the said proposed constitution and our objections thereto"

Also the following:

"Mr Parker was moved to Mokpo, after the close ~~of the June~~

H. G. UNDERWOOD,
Seoul, Korea.

of the June term at Pyeng Yang, and put in charge of the Mokpo Boys School"

Trusting that our action is clear to you from the above extract from the Minutes, and that it is satisfactory,
I beg to remain,

Faithfully yours

(signed) M.L.Swineheart
Mission Secretary.

Kwangju, Korea, April 7th 1915.

Copies to
Moffett
Holdcroft
Adams
Miller

The Paragraph in the Minutes referred to above is as as follows;

" We restate the position of our Mission on the College question as follows:

1. That there should be but one Union Christian College for all Korea.
2. That we regatd the question of location as of secondary importance, and are willing to unite in any plane where a Union College for the whole country can be established.
3. That in view of the action of the home Boards through the Joint Committee locating the one Union Christian College for all Korea in Seoul, in reply to the 1st request of the Educational Senate at its meeting of June 13th, 1914, we hereby officially state our purpose to co-operate in the establishment of the Union Christian College for all Korea at Seoul in case five of the operatung constituent missions concur.
4. That in reply to the 2nd request of the Educational Senate at its meeting of June 13th, 1914, we notify the General Secretary of the Senate of the election of the following three officiale representatives, to act only in case four other missions decide to co-operate Messrs Preston, Bell, and Mc Cutcheon.

"We recommend that the proposed constitution for the one Union Christian College for all Korea" sent out by the Joint Committee, be referred for criticism and suggestion to the committee of three official representatives named in Recomendation IX Section 4. This Constitution with proposed changes, shall be circulated among the Stations for vote. Further in response to the invitation of the Joint Committee to the Missions for criticism and suggestion on their proposed constitution for the Union College for Korea, resolved that we respectively submit that it is the sense of this Mission.

First: That full control of the College, as to the selection of President and professors should be vested in the Field Board of Managers.

Second: That the home Boards of Trustees have charge only of such matters as collecting and investing endowment adopting for the Boards the annual budget.

IV. The Students.

Under existing circumstances, we hardly deemed it wise to strive to secure a large body of students and therefore we planned to have a quiet opening with whoever came up to the requirements ~~and reply.~~

~~that~~ The fact ~~that~~ we were to open at the Spring term be in generally known throughout the missionary body and among Christians we sent to all applicants and to all enquirers a statement as to the requirements for admission and time of opening. We were greatly surprised at the number replying and opened with an enrollment of 61 applicants with some others who are still applying. It is our desire to hold the College down to a comparative small number at first, so that the spirit of the College can be moulded and the highest Christain ideals can be maintained.

V. Permanent Site.

At the first meeting of the Field Board of Managers, Messrs. Noble, Cram and Underwood were selected as a

Committee for the site and were instructed to proceed with the purchase of the site concerning which Dr Goucher had opened negotiations with the Government. The following day we made an appointment with Mr Komatsu and called upon him and told him our desire to secure not simply the land belonging to the Forestry Depaatment but also that portion of land immediately surrounding the plot belonging to the Treasuery Department and consistang of farming land.

Mr Komatsu promised to take the matter up at once and at his request I called on him the following day and he informed me that the Govebnment had decided that we should be allowed to purchase not simply the forestry land but also whatever awable land we desired in the neighbourhood that belonged to the Government.

The forestry land amounts to 72 Cho, 8 Pan, 5 Bo, a total of about 186 acres and theb price of the land itself is Yen 18,829,10. but the land is covered with timber which has been estimated very generously by the Government, making a total to the Forestry Department Yen 45,806,98.

In addition to this there is a considerable tract of arable land that is to be purchased and when the whole is obtained we shall have a fairly symmetrical, oblong valley, finely wooded on the hills with rich farming lands in the valley with a total acrage of possibly 300 acres.

It is our expectation to purchase to the stream on the South West and down to the straight line running from "A" to "B".

The boundary lines will then be as marked by "ABCD" etc.

C enquiry we found that certain little patches are owned by private individuals, and we have started to purchase these for farming lands. Thus far the average price has been about 45 Japanese sen per tsubo (86 By 6 feet square) which at the present time for land at this section is considered as a very moderate price.

We expect to offer the Government an average price for their farm land 35 or 40 sen per tsubo.

We are glad to report that we are progressing as satisfactorily as this and that we will be in legal possession of the whole site at no distant date.

The thanks of the Board are due to the Governor-General for his generosity in granting our request andb specially to Mr Komatsu for the trouble to which he has put himself in assisting us at this time.

VI. Juridical Body.

The new law that went into effect on April 1st made it necessary that Special Schools under which Colleges are classed, shall beb under the care of a juridical body. As soon as this was known, we took em immediate step to have the Field Board of Ma gers incorporated as a juridical body.

In this connection we have had the kind help and assistance of Judge Watanabe and Mr Niwa of the Japanese Y.M.C.A.

We secured the English and Japanese copies of the Articles of Incorporation of Meiji Gakkiun of Tokyo, and have modelled our application on them. The final draft is not yet ready, but the copy as finally presented to Judge Watanabe for suggestion and criticism is submitted herewith.

We had considerable fears as to the length of time it would take to secure incorporation, but I am glad to be able to report that Messrs. Komatsu and Sekiya have kindly promised to assist with suggestions so that at the time of making our application everything may be in order, and I have been assured that in this way the matter can be put through in a few weeks.

VII. Government Permit.

In regard to the matter of permit to Special Schools, the new regulations are definite and precise, and it was with very evident that we could not secure all the necessary papers for a new permit before the date on which we desired to open our College work.

We talked the matter over with Mr Sekiya and it was suggested that as the John, D, Wells School had still its old permit we do College work, under it we should begin on that permit and this suggestion met with Mr Sekiya's hearty approval.

In this connection I want to express my hearty thanks to Mr Sekiya for the kind thought and consideration that he has given to our plans. He has not only kindly consented to go over the Article of Incorporation but has also carefully considered our curriculum and has given his assent to the same.

VIII. The Executive Committee.

The Executive Committee duly met and passed on the budget a copy of which is presented herewith.

The President would suggest that the representatives of the various Missions notify their Treasures of the need of appropriations for current expenses. None of the Boards except one has been heard from in this practical and necessary manner.

IX. The Future.

a. Certain difficulties will have to be met at the close of this term. Mr E.H.Miller, who has charge of the Chemistry Department not only finds his furlough due but also owing to the health of Mrs Miller finds it necessary to take the furlough at the time when it is due.

Mr W.B.Billings also will be returning immediately after the Spring for a furlough and Mr H.H.Underwood's present term of service ends at the same time.

Suggestion has been made that these two gentlemen should stay over for a year, but circumstances are such that thus far the suggest has not been feasible to either. It behoves that some arrangements must be made by the Field Board of Managers for filling in these gaps

b. In regard to the Japanese professors, it is our aim to secure from Japan, men who already have a national reputation and to do this, it behooves us to go at it a little slowly and secure the right kind of men. We want to secure if possible men who hold the degrees from the Imperial University of Japan and who by their work have won their laurels and are willing to come here for the sake of the greatness of the work they will be doing.

c. We expect to secure the services of Japanese surveyors and have a topographical map of our property made. With such a map on hand, we would be able to offer the opportunity to certain firms to compete for the general lay-out of the buildings and ground. Having secured

H. G. UNDERWOOD,
Seoul, Korea.

11.

this it is thought that we can commence next Spring the erection of our Industrial Buildings and that it will be best to here carry on our work temporarily while the main buildings are builded.

D. We hope the present cordial relations between ourselves and the Government authorities will be maintained. It has been our experience that the Government officials in the Educational and other Departments most heartily welcome every effort for the development of the people of this land.

In this connection, we desire that this institution in all its departments shall go hand in hand with the Government and shall see to it that the Government policy so well outlined by the Educational Department of the training of hands and brain at the same time shall be fully maintained by us.

For this purpose, we hope to practically demonstrate the proper developement of farming and all its branches. Here also we hope to have some of the most accurate carpenter shops and at the same time we expect to have practical brick-making work going on.

The ground we are purchasing, we are glad to report, provides both timber for oue carpenter shop and clay for our brick works and we hope to find stones for the trimming of our buildings.

Asking from the church you represent youe earnest prayers for the success of the work and bespeaking the hearty corporation of the whole Field Board of Managers, we respectfully submit this report.

April 21/15 H G Underwood

3. 베커 학감의 이사회 제출 보고서

문서 제목	Report of Registrar
문서 종류	학감 보고서
제출 시기	1915년 4월 21일
작성 장소	서울
제 출 자	Arthur L. Becker
수 신 자	이사회
페이지 수	5
출 처	2114-5-2: 06 Board of Managers 1915~1922 (UMAH)

자료 소개

베커 학감이 1915년 4월 21일 열린 제2회 임시이사회 회의 때 제출한 보고서이다. 보고자의 직책이 'Registrar'로 표기되어 있는데, 내용을 보면 1918년 문서에서부터 표기되는 '학감'(Dean)의 보고서에 해당하고, 이 두 가지 호칭의 직책을 동일 인물이 맡고 있었으므로, 'Registrar'는 사실상 학감을 뜻한 것이었다고 생각된다. 이 문서에 작성자의 서명은 없지만, 'Registrar' 직을 맡고 있던 사람은 바로 베커였다. 베커는 북감리교 선교사로 1914년부터 언더우드와 함께 이 대학의 설립을 주도하였다.

이 보고서는 아래의 11개 항목으로 구성되어 있다. 번호가 12번까지 붙여졌으나, 6번 항목이 빠져서 사실상 모두 11개 항목이고, 7번 항목이 맨 뒤로 돌려져 있다.

1. 교육과정, 2. 교육과정 규정, 졸업 규정, 입학 규정, 3. 입학금 규정, 학비 규정, 4. 기숙사 규정, 5. 학생지원부 규정, 8. 대학과 YMCA의 합의, 9. 장비 구입과 보수 비용, 10. 1915~16학년도 예산, 11. 봄학기 개교 때 주목할 점, 12. 일본인 교수, 학생지원 규정, 7. 봄학기 수업계획

내용 요약

1. 문과, 수학 및 물리학과, 상과의 학생들은 1,2학년 때 교양과목과 전공 기초과목들을 이수하고, 3,4학년 때 각 과의 전공을 몇 개로 세분하여 전공과목을 공부한다.

2. 교육과정 · 졸업 · 입학에 관해 전교생은 입학시험, 신체검사, 필수과목과 선택과목의 수업시수 등을 정한 6가지 규정을 따른다.

3. 입학금과 학비에 관해 입학금은 4원, 학비는 한 학기에 4원, 물리학과 화학 실험비는 한 학기에 3원, 기숙사비는 월 1원으로 정한다.

4. 기숙사의 모든 학생은 4가지 규정을 따른다.

5. 학생지원부는 예산을 책정하여 가난한 학생 2명에게 근로장학금을 주고, 선교회들의 기부로 이 기금을 마련하도록 한다.

8. 대학과 YMCA가 YMCA 방들을 2년 기한으로 임대받아 쓰고 떠나기로 합의하였다. [이 부분에서는 제목만 붙이고, 10번 예산 항목 다음에 합의서를 첨부하고 있다.]

9. (실험 장비, 학교 가구, 비품의 마련과 보수에 필요한 예산과 보유 자금 현황을 제시하고 있다.)

10. (1915년 4월 1일~1916년 4월 1일의 지출과 수입 예산 명세를 제시하고 있다.)

11. 등록생 70명 가운데 평양에서와 감리교 특별반[1914년 개교한 대학 예과]에서 온 학생 25명은 이전에 취득한 학점을 인정받아 2학년에 진급하였다. 등록 학생의 수는 문과 31명, 수물과 13명, 상과 2명이었다. 전교생에게 토요일에 농업 교육을 하기로 하였다. 교수회가 이노익을 부학감으로 지명하였다.

12. 일본인 교수 3인에게 감사를 표한다. 근로장학생들은 반드시 기숙사에 입소하고 맡은 일을 즐겁게 할 것 등의 4가지 규정을 준수해야 한다.

7. (봄학기에 강의를 맡은 17명의 교수 명단과 과목의 명단을 나열하고 있다.) 한국인은 백상규, 이노익(Root Yi), 신흥우(Hugh Cynn), 노(Noh, 위의 교장 보고서에서는 'W. J. Nah'라고 표기됨), 변성옥(S. O. Pynn)이다.

TRANSFERRED 802 A

Report of Registrar.

I. Outline of Corriculum.

1st year.	Literary Course	Scientific Course	Commercial.
	Philosophy	Physics I/	Business
	History	Chemistry.	Shorthand.
	Language	Mathematics	Industries.
	Literature	Languages	Languages

2nd Year; Same as above, advanced work.
(Student must elect one of these courses and put in 45 hours work in the course during the year 15 hours work must be selected in another course.

3rd and 4th year; it is suggested that the Literary Course branch out into special work along the line of Theology, Educational Medical Law or Philosophy. Scientific Course branch out into Special work along the line (practical) of Chemistry Engineering Electrical, Mechanical Mining or Civil Engineering. Commercial Course take up special work in Banking Agriculture forestry fishery and Commerce.

2. Some general rules regarding Corriculum and graduation and entry.

I. Every student must pass examinations H.S. subjects and be able to take at least 70 hours work in the College before he can enroll.

2. Every student must take a physical examination.

3. Every student must have clear recommendation.

4. Every student must take one of these courses, Literary Scientific or Commercial and must take 90 hours in the selected course and 45 hours in the other courses before he is elegible to enroll as a Jr student and must also have worked off all the conditions of entry before he can become a Jr.

5. The student must have 240 hours before he is elegible for graduation(this is an average of 20 hours per term for 12 terms.)

6. No student can take more than 25 hours work per term

3. Fees and Tuition.

I. The Matriculation fee is ¥4.00 paid on entry.

2. The term tuition fee is ¥4.00 paid in advance on the opening of the term.

3. The Physics and Chemistry Laboratory fees are ¥3.00 each term paid in advance.

4. The Dormitory fee is ¥1.00 per month paid in advance.

4. Dormitory regulations and assignments.

I. All students whose homes are not in Seoul must reside

Registrar's Report

4-21-15

2.

2. All dormitory students outside of scholl hours are in the charge of the dormitory Director.

3. Any student disobeying orders regarding study hours sleeping hours, eating hours, visitors and smoking in the dormitory etc, are liable to fines or expulsion by the faculty.

4. The dormitory students shall form a club and hire their own cook who shall be responsible directly to the officers of that club.

5. Students Aid Department.

It is planned that a small amount of money be contribute by each Mission and some separate in the budget for the aid of needy students for the Spring term;-

I. On the budget Yen 160.00, to be contributed on II students who shall serve as secretaries, janitors errand boys and librarian and job assistants.

2. Contributed funds Y100.00. each from each co-operating Mission.

We still have to provide teachers for Agriculture, Industries, Rapid Calculation, Shorthand and typewriting.

8. Memorandum of Agreement made between "The College" and the Y.M.C.A?

(Separate Sheet)

9. Equipment and repairs.

I. About Y6000.00 of Physical Apparatus is onhand or or
2. " " 450.00. " Chemical " " " " " " "
3. " " 1600.00. " furniture " " " " " " "
4. " " 250.00. " School supplies are on hand.
Total Y8300.00. for permanent equipment expended.

5. About 450.00. will be spent on alterations and rep
6. " " 250.00. " " " " " floor covering.
7. " " 200.00. " " " " " dormitory equipment

About Y300.00. will be the outlay outside Regular Budget.

10. Budget for school year April 1st 1915 to April 1st 1916.

Expenses.

I. Rental of Y.M.C.A. rooms, as per contract Y1200.00.
2. " " " Dormitory(pay 1200.00. in 15 960.00.
3. " " " Eating house 120.00.
4. Salaries of Japanese teacher or teachers 2400.00.

3.

5. Salaries of Assistant teachers Y1800.00.
6. Student work as Janitors secretaries errand boys" 480.00.
7. Reference Books Library 200.00.
8. Laboratory expenses 400.00.
9. Telephone. 72.00.
Y 7532.00.

Memorandum of Agreement made this day of 1915

between the

Union Christian College hereinafter known as "The College"

on the one part and the Young Men's Christian

Association hereinafter known as the Y.M.C.A.

on the other part.

1st The Y.M.C.A. hereby leases the western portion of the Third Floor of their property at Chong No, Seoul known as the part above the gymnasium, for a period of two years or less, at a rent of Y1200.00. payable in advance. It is mutually understood that the Y.M.C.A. in doing this is not seeking revinue, but is an act of service and in order that it may use the rent in fixing up the property. It is also mutually agreed that this does not entail the right to the College to sub-rent all or any part of this portion of the building.

2nd. It is mutually understood that the Y.M.C.A. reserves the two rooms for its photographic work in the above mentioned portion of the building.

3rd. The Y.M.C.A. hereby leases two of its front rooms in the eastern portion of the building, a laboratory and four class rooms to the College at a rent of Y1[illegible]0.00. per calander month, to be paid monthly. Thisrent is also based upon the fact of service and it is mutually understood that the Y.M.C.A. reserves the right to use four class rooms at night for its Night School.

4th. The Y.M.C.A. hereby leases the small Korean house upon its compound at a rent of Y10.00 per month, payable monthly.

5th. It is mutually understood that all necessary changes and adaptions are to be made at the expense of the College.

6th. The installation of radiators, lamps and dormitory fixtures are to be made at the expense of the College with the understanding that these may be taken over by the Y.M.C.A. at cost price, less wear and tear, if they so desire

7th. It is mutually understood that the Y.M.C.A. shall have the privilege of requesting and securing the dismissal from the dormitory of any resident or residents who may be found engaged in practices considered by the Y.M.C.A. derogatory to the cause of Christ.

4/21/15

6.

8th. It is mutually understood that lighting, water and heating are to be extra.

9th. It is mutuall understood that the College is to leave the aforesaid premises in as good a condition as they are now in, reasonable wear, accidental fire and avoidable causes excepted.

10th. It is mutually understood that the College have the option of giving up the two front rooms, the laboratory the four class rooms and Korean building at any time by giving three months notice in writing.

Representing the College. Representing the Y.M.C.

* *

Income:-

Student fees (approximated)	Y1652.00.
From co-operating Missions	Y2000.00
	Y 13652.00.

II. <u>Noteworthy facts at the opening of the Spring term.</u>

1. We had over 70 applicants for enrollment in the College.
2. We have now enrolled 47 under our regulations.
3. Of the 47 enrolled all but are graduates of Christian High Schools.
4. About 25 of the above have advanced credits from the PYI. College and the Special Methodist Class so are nearly of Sophomore grade.
5. The examination revealed the fact that some of the preparatory work was not thoroughly done.
6. We had applications for entry to a preparatory Department but did not interview them.
7. About 21 are enrolled in the Literary Department, 13 in the Scientific Course and 5 in the Commercial.
8. We have decided that all students should take Agricultural training on Saturday.
9. Mr Noot Rhee was nominated by the faculty as Assistant Registrar.
10. Students well recommended, were enrolled in the Students Help Department list.
11. Bishops Lewis and Harris, Dr Goucher all gave inspiring messages to the students in our opening days.

6.

4/21/15

12. We are very grateful to the three pastors Messrs Inoguchi, Yamamoto and Kiyoshi for offering their services.

The students that receive aid from this department must;-

I. Reside in the dormitory, students living in the city are not helped.

2. Sign a contract to do cheerfully and well anything they are told to do, and report receipt and expenditure of all funds received from home or friends.

3. Work and give good service for money received.

4. Understand that aid is according to value of service rendered and this will range from Y1.00. to 6.00.

The officers of the Faculty are superintending this special work.

7. Schedule for Spring term.

Dr Underwood	teaches	Psychology 3 hrs and Hist; of Ed 2hrs
Rev. E. H. Miller	" "	Elementary Chemistory 2hrs, chem; 5hr Algebra 5hrs.
Rev. A. L. Becker	"	Physics I 5hrs Electricity 5hrs Surveying 2hrs Civil Geom; 5hrs.
Rev. B. W. Billings	"	Ethics I 5hrs English 5hrs Eng II 5hrs
Rev. R. A. Hardie	" "	Ethics II 3hrs.
Rev. J. L. Gerdine	" "	English A 5 hrs.
Mr. H. H. Underwood	" "	English I. 5 hrs.
" G. [illegible]	"	Logic 2 hrs, Pol; Econ; 3 hrs, Book keeping 3 hrs.
" [illegible]	" "	Solid Geom; 2 hrs, Astronomy 2 hrs, Physiology 2 hrs.
" [illegible]	" "	Principles of Education 2 hrs, and Sociology 2 hrs.
" [illegible]	" "	Biology 3 hrs.
" [illegible]	" "	Music and in Dormitory director
" F. [illegible]	" "	Athletics.
" [illegible]	" "	Japanese 3 hrs.
" Inoguchi	" "	Oriental History 2 hrs.
" Yamamoto	" "	Occidental History 2 hrs.
" Fugioka.	" "	Japanese History 2 hrs.

4. 언더우드 교장의 북장로회 서울지회 제출 보고서

문서 제목	To the Seoul Station of the Presbyterian Mission
문서 종류	교장 보고서
제출 시기	1915년 9월 4일
작성 장소	서울
제 출 자	H. G. Underwood
수 신 자	서울 주재 북장로회 선교사회(Seoul Station, Korea Mission, PCUSA)
페이지 수	4
출 처	Korea Mission Records, 1904~1960, Box 15, Folder 18 (PHS)

자료 소개

언더우드 교장이 본교의 설립을 지원한 서울 주재 북장로회 선교사회에 1915년 9월 4일 제출한 보고서이다. 교장이 그들에게 보고서를 제출한 것은 이후에 관례가 되었다. 세브란스에서도 교장이 정례적으로 그들에게 보고서를 제출하였다. 언더우드는 "I present herewith my first report as Provisional President to the Board of Trustees"라고 하여 이 보고서를 받는 서울의 북장로교 선교사들을 '재단이사회'라 칭하였다. 그렇게 부른 이유를 정확히 알 수는 없지만, 조선기독교대학과 세브란스의학교 및 병원의 자산이 본교 이사회의 회계를 맡은 북장로교 선교사에게 등기되어 있었고, 두 대학의 가장 큰 독지가인 존 T. 언더우드와 존 L. 세브란스가 모두 북장로회 소속의 인물들이었다. 언더우드는 또한 학교를 "Union College of Seoul, known as the Chosen Christian College"라고 칭하여 영어 교명이 아직 여러 가지로 불리고 있음을 나타내었다. 'Chosen Christian College'란 교명은 1915년 4월 21일 제2회 이사회 회의 때 확정되었다. 이사회는 처음에 'Korea Christian College'와 'Union Christian College of Korea'란 명칭을 썼으나 이날 회의 때 이같이 바꿀 것을 결정하였다. 언더우드가 'Union College' 뒤에 'Seoul'이란 지역명을 붙인 것은 평양의 'Union College'(숭실대)와 구별하기 위해서였다. 숭실대는 그 학교를 함께 운영하던 남·북감리교 선교사들이 서울의 조선기독교대학 설립을 위해 빠져나감으로써 4개 장로교단 선교사들만의 연합학교로 운영되었다.

언더우드는 이 보고서에서 항목 설정 없이 아래의 사항들을 다루었다.

대학설립 인가 문제, 첫 학기 현황, YMCA 건물의 교육환경, 학생들의 학력 수준, 교재, 교직원 보강, 교지 확보.

내용 요약

대학설립 인가 문제: 학교가 현재 경신학교의 인가 아래 경신학교의 대학과로 운영되고 있으나, 모든 일이 잘 진행되고 있으므로, 이 인가로 운영하는 일은 얼마 가지 않을 것이다. [경신학교 대학과의 인가로 새 대학을 개교한 것은 임의로 한 것이 아니라 총독부의 허가를 받아서 한 것이었다. 이 진술은 언더우드가 이때까지만 해도 개교 전 3월 24일 공포된 총독부의 전문학교규칙에 따른 설립 인가를 수월하게 받을 줄로 여기고 있었음을 알 수 있다.]

첫 학기 현황: 첫 사분기는 매우 성공적이고 유망하였다. 첫 학기에 거의 70명이 신청하였으나 입학시험으로 두 학년에 60명가량을 선발하였고, 그 후에도 지원자들이 많이 오고 있으나 받지 않고 있다.

YMCA 건물: YMCA의 수공부에서 마련해준 비품이 매우 만족스럽다. 실험 장비들을 들여와 학생들이 활용하고 있으며, 기숙사와 식당도 잘 갖춰져 아주 잘 활용되고 있다. 학생들은 거의 다 YMCA 회원이고 시내의 다른 학교 학생들을 위해 특별 활동을 벌이고 있다.

학생들의 학력: 학년말 시험[1914년 개교한 대학 예과의 학년말 시험]을 치르면서 학생들의 기초실력이 부족한 것을 알게 되었다.

교재: 교재 문제는 점차 해결될 것이다.

교직원 보강: 일본 제국대학 출신의 독실한 기독교인인 다카이(M. Takai)를 영입하여 역사와 일본어를 가르치게 하고 삿포로 제국대학 출신[K. Ichijima, 市島吉太郎]에게 농과를 맡기기를 희망하고 있다. 루퍼스(W. C. Rufus) 교수가 다시 오고 미국에서 유학한 한국인들이 올 가능성도 크다. [이들의 부임은 다음번 학감 보고서에서 상세하게 설명된다.]

교지 확보: 이미 많은 부분을 확보하였지만, 나머지 땅을 확보하기 위해 총독부와 협상하고 있다.

The Rev. Dr. H. G. Underwood

FILING DEPT.
MAR 6 1916
21 — 2
SECRETARIES

H. G. UNDERWOOD,
Seoul, Korea.

RECEIVED
OCT 22 1915
Dr. Brown.

Noted but not copied

September 4th, 1915.

To the Seoul Station of the
Presbyterian Mission.

It becomes my duty at this time to report for the Union College of Seoul, known as the Chosen Christian College. In this connection I present herewith my first report as Provisional President to the Board of Trustees in connection with the inauguration of the same.

A perusal of the will show you that we are at the present time working under the charter of the John D. Wells school and are really the collegiate department of that institution. How long we will continue under this it is not yet settled but everything is going along very nicely and we have reason to believe that at least for some little while we will continue under this charter.

The conditions are very much the same now that they were when I made my report, which is attached hereto. We have had a very successful and very promising first quarter. We had a large number of applicants. As stated before we had almost seventy applicants these, however, were considerably reduced when it came to entrance examinations and as a result we had about sixty students in the two classes during the first term.

The number of applications that we are receiving for entrance later from students in other institutions is rather larger than we would care for. We have been writing to them urging them to stay in the institutions in which they are and to pursue their studies there if possible. However, it is very evident that we shall be compelled to receive more and our capacity in the Y.M.C.A. building will be taxed to the utmost. The equipment at the Y.M.C.A. as provided by the Industrial Department there is very satisfactory. The apparatus has been installed in the laboratory and the students are doing individual work. It is somewhat crowded but the simplest and best of apparatus is there and they are all of them taking an intense interest in the practical laboratory work that each and every individual student is compelled to do.

The dormitory has been fixed up very nicely and with the dining room on the same compound and everything is working out very nicely indeed.

I am glad to be able to report that there is a very strong Y.M.C.A. among the college students and in fact every member of the college body is a member of the Y.M.C.A. and all of them are taking an intense interest in this work. They seem to feel that the being college students it is their place to be in the lead in Christian activities and Christian work. They seem also to feel in an especial manner that being students in an Educational Institution of this grade it is their place to take the lead of Christian men in the giving of the Gospel to the other students of the city. They have been having a number of special services for other students, inviting students of other institutions to special meetings in connection with the Y.M.C.A. The Y.M.C.A. of course, have only been too glad to allow the use of any of their rooms and a good work is going on in these lines.

When it came to the examination at the end of the year, it was found that the provision for study has not been all that we had hoped and in certain of the studies it was very evident that quite a few of the students would have to take the re-examination.

The old plan which has been vogue of counting the number of hours studied and not so much the amount of work covered has had its effect here and we find that it is absolutely essential to let the students know that a certain amount of ground must be covered before he can be considered as having passed.

The difficulty of text-books is, of course, before us at the present time but these will gradually be overcome.

We are in the process of securing before the fall comes a man who is very highly recommended to us from Japan, Professor H. Takai. He is a graduate of the Imperial University, has made history a specialty and comes very highly recommended as an earnest Christian worker and a man who is willing to come to Korea because he believes that there is a work that he will have to do in bringing the Gospel also to Koreans. We are in great hopes that his taking charge of the care of history and at least temporarily of the care of Japanese language a literature will very materially strengthen our Institution here. We are also making arrangements for the securing from the Imperial University of Sapporo one of the graduates in their agricultural department to take charge of the agricultural department of the college here. The personal of teachers has somewhat changed but we are glad to be able to report that the prospects are that Prof. Rufus will be with us again as well as several graduate Koreans from America. The prospects of the fall are very bright.

In the matter of the site, a goodly portion of the same has already been obtained and we are now continuing to carry on our negotiations with the Government concerning the balance of the site.

- 4 -

Commending the Institution to your prayers and praying God's richest blessing upon the same.

Respectfully submitted,

H. G. Underwood

5. 언더우드 교장의 이사회 제출 보고서

문서 제목	To the Board of Managers of the Chosen Christian College
문서 종류	교장 보고서 (추정)
제출 시기	1915년 12월 28일 (추정)
작성 장소	서울
제 출 자	H. G. Underwood (추정)
수 신 자	이사회
페이지 수	11
출 처	Chosen Christian College, President's Report 1914~1941. F TU74 C 456pre (PHS)

자료 소개

언더우드 교장이 1915년 12월 28일에 열렸을 것으로 추정되는 대학이사회 회의에 제출한 보고서이다. 이 보고서에 작성자와 일자 표시가 없지만, 학감이 이 자료집 차례 6번의 보고서를 제출했던 이사회 회의일과 같은 날에 언더우드 교장이 이 보고서를 제출하였던 것으로 추정된다. 그 이유는 보고자가 이 문서를 본인이 소집한 이사회에 내는 보고서로서 가을학기 말의 "semi-annual report"이자 세 학기 중의 두 학기에 대한 보고서라고 규정하고 있고, 그 내용도 총독부와의 교섭, 학교 재정 등을 다루어 학사업무만을 다룬 학감 보고서와는 다른 면을 보이고 있기 때문이다. 당시에는 3학기제를 실시하면서 4월에 첫째 학기를, 9월에 둘째 학기를, 이듬해 1월에 셋째 학기를 시작하였다.

보고자는 이 보고서를 번호 없이 아래의 5개 항목으로 구성하였다.

개교와 설립, 자산, 대학 운영, 교수, 재정.

내용 요약

개교 · 설립: 총독부 학무국의 도움으로 학교의 조직화에 성공하였으나, 와타나베 판사의 도움으로 재단법인의 초안을 만들어 총독부 관리에게 보여주었다가 지적을 받고 아직 경신학교 대학과(collegiate department of the John D. Wells' School) 단계에 머물러 있다. 이 학교가 속히 인가를 받고 재단법인을 만들게 되기를 바란다.

자산: 예정지 주변의 개인 소유지들을 대부분 확보하였으나, 부지를 확보하는 일은 지체되고 있다. 부지 주변의 농지를 살 것을 권고하고, 그곳의 지형도를 속히 얻어 구획하기를 희망한다. 또한 부지 안에 벽돌가마를 설치하여 임시 교실과 기숙사로 활용할 농업교육용 벽돌 건물들을 이듬해 봄에는 짓도록 하고, 캠퍼스 건물들의 건축 규정과 표준을 정하고 교수들의 집을 지을 준비를 해야 한다.

대학 운영: 가을학기의 학생은 67명이었다. 세브란스의전에 입학할 수 있도록 과학, 영어, 일본어 공부가 더 필요한 학생들을 위해 별과를 만들 예정이다.

교수: 다카이와 이치지마(제국대), 루퍼스(미시간대 Ph.D.), 김득수(T. S. Kim, 컬럼비아대학)가 새로 왔다. 교수들의 직급을 정하여 백상규를 정교수로, 김득수와 이노익(Root Lee)을 조교수로 임명하였다. 로즈(Harry A. Rhodes)의 영입 승인을 북장로회 선교회에 요청해달라고 이사회에 제의한다. 봄학기를 마치고 미국에 갔던 밀러, 원한경 등은 내년에 돌아올 것이다.

재정: 내가 [존 T. 언더우드에게서] 받은 $50,000은 학교시설을 위한 것이다. 그러므로 학교 운영비는 협력하는 선교회들에서 충당해주기를 희망한다. 재단법인을 만들려면 총독부에 보여줄 조선은행 잔고가 있어야 한다.

F
Tu74
C456pac

TO THE BOARD OF MANAGERS OF THE CHOSEN CHRISTIAN COLLEGE.

It becomes once more my privilege to render a report to you concerning the work that the Chosen Christian College is doing though at this time it is only what might be termed a semi-annual report. It seemed best to call this meeting at the end of the Fall term rather than at the begining, so that at the present time as to actual work we are two-thirds through another year instead of being simply a merely half year and as a consequence the report really is for two terms out of three.

Inauguration and establishment.

In connection with this report, I will turn first to those things that concern the inauguration and establishment of the College. As out lined in my previous report, through the kind assistance of the educational department and of the Government here we have succeeded in carrying on our organization thus far and with the able assistance of Judge Watanabe, a member of our Board, the charter for our Zaidan, or property holding body, has been duly drawn up. This took some time to translate and after it was translated it seems to have, through some errors of typists, been somewhat mistranslated. It was handed over in an unofficial way to members of the Government and they have returned the same with suggestions and queries and criticisms and the document is still in process of settlement. No settlement has as yet been arrived at and the consequence is that we have no charter of our own as the Chosen Christian College but we are still continuing to run as previously as the collegiate department of the John D. Well's School. This is satisfactory as a temporary expedient but as soon as possinle we are desirous of coming under the charter and under the regular rules that would pertain to an Institution of our own. There are varous little things that have come in from time to time that has shown us that this would be better for us and better for the John D. Well's School and it looks to us as though there will be very little difficulty in bringing this about somewhat speedily now. The various small details concerning the adjustment I think can easily be make and I am in hopes that in a very short time the matter of the Zaidan and our incorporation can be settled and than the other matter concerning our obtaining the proper College charter from the Government will go forward.

Property

In regard to the property, we have secured most of the private property in the immediate neighbourhood of the lot proposed and we hope soon to be able to report that the money for the entire plot has been paid over and that the property id ours. There have been delays in this, delays that were unexpected and that we thought would not have arisen but we have to report that the delays did arise, One thing and another has brought about delay. They have not all of them been understandable but we have been assured by The Government authorities that there is no need for further delay and we are looking forward to the Government seeing to it, as they have said they would, that we early securing a proper title piece to our property.

Recommends. Your President would recommend that we also endeavour to purchase a piece of property in the immediate vicinity adjoining this consisting almost entirely of rice and fields arabke up lands that will be absolutely invaluable to us part of our experiment and training station. It is a very fine tract and can be had at the present time at a low price. It is good land, has a good yield and can be secured now at a price lower than any farm land that we have thus far been purchasing. Your President would recommend the purchase of these added fields of land. The cosr of the same will be about

Topographical map. In regard to the site itself we have been in great hopes that a complete topographical map of the site would have been in hand some time before this. OUr surveying band has been out there on several occasions and have made the beginings of this but it is not yet ready to hand over to those who could use it and lay out the land as we had hoped. We are in hpoes that they will be able now to push this matter forward and let us have a map as soon as possible so that we can have some general lay-out of the property and be preared to go ahead. Just exactly what to do in this road we are at a loss to know.

Present property inadequate. The present property occupied temporarily by us is at the present time inadequate. The in-coming cladd when it comes in next spring will make it more inadequate and if we are to ahve anything ready for us by next fall, which we certainly ought to do, we ought to be begining in the spring.

My suggestion would be that there in one point where we have excellent land for brick building. It is on the site that will be on the further side of the railroad track. It is low ground. It would be furthest from our regular buildings where the main buildings ought to be. It would be the point that would be least objectionable in the matter of having buildings that might at any time be termed unsightly. It seems to me the point at which, if we are to have a brick kiln and brick works, we ought to have our brick kiln and brick works. It comes at the lowest point and at the end of the present fields which are to be used for agricultural purposes and it seems to me that here we might next spring erect some temporary buildings, (I do not mean "temporary" in the sense of the buildings themselves, but buildings that might be used temporarily) for class rooms and class work but which are to be our permanent Industrial Buildings, erected in a simple, cheap way, without lathand plaster, with hollow brick walls which will leave the brick shewing on the inside, such brick eventually to be painted or simply coloured or left natural and these buildings might be used temporarilyfor class rooms and possibly dormitory rooms for thestudents and sheds erectd to carry on the brick works, a kiln might be put up here, temporary sheds for the rougher kinds of farm work that is to be done and eventually these sheds to be pulled down and these buildings erected there would be used as the industrial plant of the Institution. In this way we will be able without waiting too long, to have some buildings that we

Next spring temporary buildings.

can occupy in the meantime and at the same time have our general plan wait until we have x come to some definite decisions as to rules and standards for the general buildings on the place. It is absolutely essential that our buildings should be uniform, those at least that are grouped on the College campus, but these buildings down in one corner need not necessarily be exactly the same wspecially as they will be entirely detached, and off on one side and will not be seen at the same time. If this is done behove us to provide some means of locomotion for a goodly number of our professors because it will be impossible for us to ahave professors house out there ready by the fall of next year. I do think that the college work itself, the w ak that they are to do, ~~dddd~~ demands that we shall plan to have our men on the ground and wosking they year from this past fall . If this is to be done we must plan for the temporary buildings to be building during the coming year and to be begun in the spring.

College. Work.

In regard to the college itself and the work there. The student boy has been 67 during they the past term. There have benn applicants for admission but we do hot desire to take in new students at the present time and it looks as though we have a body of students there that in all probability w ll remain with us during the full course. We ~~ams~~ are in hopes that they will. During the past year we were asked by the Severance Medical College to take charge of the students who had graduated from the ordinary middle-school and needed some extra wosk in the sciences and in

6

English and Japanese for their medical preparation . We found last year that this would entail the necessity of our carrying on work somewhat differently in the College and declined at that time to undertake the work. During the coming year, however, we will have an extra class going on at the same time so that the classes will be going on and it looks as though we shall be ready to allow these special students to take whatever course they can, as far as time will allow to be crowded in during the one year on which they expect to work in their preparation. This, of course, will crowd our class rooms more than ever. What we are to do next year with the incoming class is also at the present time a conundrum. The dormitory is fairly crowded but it will be possible for us to use the large room, that is used also as a dormitory we might be able to crowd twenty or a few more students in but that is as many as the dormitory will hold. To have, therefore, come to our practical dormitory capacity after we take in twenty more students. The class room capacity will also be a difficulty with us but we can possibly secure an extra room from the Y. M. C. A. and we can get the privilege of having our General Assembly in the chapel upstairs. This is the only thing for us to do but these will simply be temporary expedients and the way in which we are being crowded shows more and more the necessity of our having some building of our own as speedily as possible.

The faculty.

Before I spoke of the student body, I should have spoken of the faculty and of the work that is being done. We have secued several additions during the part year. Notably, Dr. Rufus has come back to us. He is one of those who was elected as a professor to take charge of mathematics and astronomy at our first meeting. Then in addition xt to that, we have secured the services of Professor N. Takai, a graduate of the Imperial University of Japan, who is to take charge of the Deapartment of History and temporarily will have charge of the Department of Japanese Language and Literature. Professor Ichijima, of the Imperial University of Agriculture, of Sapore, Japan, is also with us and he will temporarily take charge of the Department of Agriculture and will, we hope, introduce a good many good things is this department, Mr. Kim Tuk-su, a graduate of Ohio-Westlyn University and who has taken post-graduate work in Columbia University, New York, is also to stop with us and will help us in biology. We have, therefore, to recommend as far as professors are concerned:

That Rev. J. R. Gerdine be elected professor of the Dep rtment of Ethics; That Mr. Paok Sang Kui be elected to a full professorship in charge of the Department of Commerce; That Mr. Takai be elected a full professorship in charge of the Department of History and temporarily in charge of the Department of Japanese Language and Literature; That Professor Ichijima be elected as an associate professor temporarily in charge of the Department of Agrcultural; That Professor Kim Tuk Soo be elected Associate Professor in the Department of Biology; That professor Root Ye be elected Associate Professor in the Department of Chemistry.

Another recommendation H.A.Rhodes.

I have another recommendation to make, and looking toward the future and knowing the needs that we will have in the future, I would recommend at the present time xkxx that the Board of Managers ask the Board of Foreign Missions of the Presbyterian Church in the United States of America to set aside Rev. Harry A. Rhodes to college work here and that he be especially asked to give his attention to some post-graduate work while he is home in America looking towards his assistance in the Department of Psycology and Philosophy.

Number of instructors.

At the present time we have a number of instructors that are helping us very ably and for whose assistance we are exxpremely thankful. They are Mr. Pyun Sung Ok, who assists in music; Mr. Im yung pil, in physics; Mr. Weller, in mechanical drawing and architecture; Mrs. Weller in typewriting; Mrs. Becker in instrumental music; Mr. Cynn in sociology and Mr. Oh Sung Kun in Oriental History as well as assisting me in the care of psychology.

When Professor E. H. Miller will be returning we do not yet know.

Mr. H. H. Underwood will be reutrning home to America in all probably at the end of the spring term of college work and, of course, his place will have to be filled but with this corps of teachers and instructors and the looking forward to the coming of others, as we shall naturally do, I think we are prepared for pretty solid work and with all of us uniting in this work I feel confident that we can look forward to a future for this college that willbe a credit to the cause of Christ and to the education in the Far East.

The next subject upon which I want to touch in this report is the matter of finances. A practical $50,000 or about ¥100,000 has been turned over to my hand but this was entirely for the plant and the establishing of the Institution and was hardly to be used for running expenses. I regret to have to report, as you will judge from the treasurer's report to that will be later handed in, that on the matter of running expenses there appeared as if there will be a shortage. We had expected that there would have been at least three Institutions coming in at the start on full corporation. At the present time, only two Institutions have come in on full corporation and these two have neither of them paid over the amount of the promise inthe conditions concerning full membership. Not only is it necessary that this amount from each of the Mission shall be in ~~xxx~~ hand to cover our running expenses but unless more than two Missions come in we shall have to secure a somewhat larger annual grant from each of the Missions. The next matter t hat comes in finances, is the fact that thus far nothing but the $50,000 and some few small other sums have been handed in in concerning with the original amount promised by the various bodies and this will interfere very materially indeed with the establishment of our property holding Zaidan. I am definitely told that for the establishment of the property holding Zaidan, not only must the appropriation be make but the money itself must be in the bank and proof of ~~the~~ its existance in the bank to the credit of the college authorities must be given to the Government. In that very connection, not only is it necessary for me to show them the bank-book of the Bank of Chosen here but they tell me that I must secure from America a statement from the bank there that the balance of the $50,000 gold is at this time in the ~~xxx~~ bank in America. The Government authorities say that in the establishment of these property holding Zaidans the Government cannot give a Zaidan unless they themselves are legally cognigant of the actual existence of the money in the hands of those representing the Zaidan. This also will have to be true concerning the appropriation promised from the Methodist Mission. It is absolutely necessary then to secure the funds as actual funds have been promised and at the same time we see the added necessity because of the necessary development of the work of securing added appropriation and added funds for the other buildings. With the $104,000 in hand we have sufficient money to purchase the main part of the site and put up our first Industrial building and secure in all probability a certain amount of

11

machinery for the begining of our industry and for the begining of our farming. Beyond this, at the present time, we have nothing until the other appropriations are in. This is a matter that it behaves the Borad of Managers and the Board of Trustees in America to take into account and consider very seriously.

6. 베커 학감의 이사회 제출 보고서

문서 제목	Report of Registrar of Chosen Christian College, Seoul, Korea
문서 종류	학감 보고서
제출 시기	1915년 12월 28일
작성 장소	서울
제 출 자	A. L. Becker
수 신 자	이사회
페이지 수	9
출 처	①·② Scan 0790 Chosen Christian College: Underwood, Horace H. (Dr.) October 1913-December 1923 (UMAH) ② 2114-5-2: 06 Board of Managers 1915~1922 (UMAH) ② Chosen Christian College, Registrar's Report F TU74 C 456rer (PHS)

자료 소개

베커 학감이 1915년 12월 28일 열린 이사회에 제출한 보고서이다. 첫 장 제목의 바로 위에 손글씨로 "Covering the First Term of School"이란 문구가 적혀 있고, 제목 아래에 "To the Board of Managers of C.C.C."이란 문구가 적혀 있어 이 문서가 대학 설립연도의 학사 업무를 개관한 것이고 이사회 회의 때 제출된 것임을 알려주고 있다. 이 보고서는 네 곳에서 두 가지 종류로 소장되어 있다. UMAH의 한 파일에는 약간의 차이를 보이는 ①·② 번 문서가 연이어 배치되어있고, 다른 파일에는 ②번 문서가 있다. PHS에도 ②번 문서가 있다. 이 가운데 ①번 문서에만 작성자인 베커의 친필 서명이 있으므로 ①번이 원본일 것으로 생각된다.

베커는 이 보고서를 번호 없이 아래의 6가지 항목을 담고 있다.

학생등록, 교육과정, 학과, 학생 자조부, 비품과 설비, 기숙사와 식당.

내용 요약

학생등록: 봄학기 등록생 60명 중 57명이 6월 25일 기말시험을 치렀고, 가을학기는 9월 2일 시작하여 등록생 62명 중 59명이 기말시험을 치렀다.

교육과정: 신입생에게 문과, 수학 및 물리학과, 상과 중에서 전공을 선택하게 하였다. 전체 학생에게 일본어와 영어 습득이 필수적임을 주지시켰고, 성경, 농학 과목도 필수로 이수하고 타전공 과목들도 선택하도록 하였다. 문과에 40명, 수학 및 물리학과에 20명, 상과에 2명이 있다. 문과가 가장 많은 것은 한국의 교육 전통 안에서 놀랄 일이 아니다.

학과: 다카이, 이치지마, 김득수, 루퍼스 교수가 와서 학과들이 더 확실한 모습을 갖추게 되었다. 11개 과목을 담당한 교수들 가운데 한국인은 밀러와 함께 화학을 가르치는 이노익, 상과를 이끌고 있는 백상규, 베커 부인과 함께 음악을 가르치는 변성옥, 밀즈 의사와 함께 생물학을 가르치는 김득수이다.

학생 자조부: 지방의 가난한 학생들을 돕기 위해 학생지원기금을 마련하여 1인당 월평균 6원을 지급하고 있다. 가을학기에 여러 방면에서 일한 근로 장학 학생에게 총 ¥1,350.00을 지급하였는데, 그 재원들은 표로 제시한다.

비품 · 설비: 초창기에 마련한 5가지 비품과 나중에 마련한 비품들의 종류와 가격의 명세를 제시한다.

기숙사 · 식당: 가을학기에 7개의 큰방에서 47명의 학생이 지내고 있고, 식당에서는 월 ¥4.30에 깨끗하고 건강에 좋은 음식을 제공하고 있다.

Covering the First Term of School.

1915
46

Report of Registrar of Chosen Christian College.
Seoul, Korea.

To The Board of Managers of C.C.C. Dec. 28th, 1915.

Typed page 112

STUDENTS ENROLLMENT.

Out of the sixty students who enrolled in the spring 57 took the examinations at the close of the spring term, June 25th. Altho we made no announcements nor offered any inducements for the students, when the Fall term opened on Sept. 2nd we has 17 applicants and after examination 16 of this were received on trial; many are taking preparatory studies, it being our rule that, if an applicant cannot pass the entrance examinations which we are making strict in order to standardize the course, he must take the work in a preparatory class. The total enrollment for the Fall term was 62; of this 59 took the examinations.

COURSES OF STUDY.

When a student enters he has been asked to state his preference for one of three courses; v.s. -Literary, Scientific, or Commercial, in which he will specialize. But in selecting studies he has been made to understand that a good knowledge of Japanese and English was fundamental in every course and that any failure in preparatory work would disqualify for full college work. Also it has been understood that every student is to take the Bible instruction given. Ariculture has been required of all the students. 25 recitation periods in one week was the limit so requirements were met within this amount. Even tho the student, can specialize as above, he must take one third of his work in the otehr courses. After two full years of standard college work (it will take most students three years because of a lack of preparatory training) a student may take the specialized courses of Medicine, Pedegogy or Liberal Arts. The Science students may enter courses in either Industrial Chemistry or Electrical En-

gineering. The Commercial students can enter courses in Agriculture or Commerce. This specializing work will be taken either in our own school or in Affilizted Schools. 40 students are working in the literary course; 20 students are in the Science course and 2 are in the Commercial work. You will notice that the largest number are enrolled in the Literary work, and this is not surprising considering the ancestry of the Korean students and also his previous training; not only are the larger number temperamentally and intellectually incapable of appreciating scientific or industrial training but they could not qualify for this kind of study, if they should wish to do so. The smaller number in the Scientific and Commercial courses really represent a larger proportional initiative, mental compacity and willingness for hard work. Of course this does not mean that most of the others will not make good in their chosen line, for I certainly have reason to believe that they will; many are good lingists and are making great progress in English and Japanese; many are developing capacity for church and public work.

typed page # 103

DEPARTMENTS.

With the arrival of Prof. Takai, and Mr. Ichijima, Mr. T.S.Kim and Dr. W.C.Rufus our departments have assumed a more definite form; the departments as we have arranged to date are:-

1. Dept. of Philosophy - H. G. Underwood Lld.
2. Dept. of History and Japanese Literature - N. Takai
3. Dept. of Ethics - J. L. Gerdine
4. Dept. of Physics - A. L. Becker
5. Dept. of English - B. W. Billings and H. H. Underwood
6. Dept. of Chemistry - E. H. Miller and Root Lee
7. Dept. of Math. & Astronomy - W. C. Rufus

8. Dept. of Commerce - Mr. Pack and Mrs. G. A. Weller

9. Dept. of Agriculture - Mr. Ichijima

10. Dept. of Music - Mrs. A. L. Becker and Mr. Pyen

11. Dept. of Biology - Dr. Mills and Mr. T. S. Kim

Beside the Mr. Weller is teaching Mechanical Drawing preparatory to applied Science work, Several other teachers have been temporarily employed.

Of course, the different departments have not yet thoroughly organized their work but this is proceeding rapidly.

Prof. Takai since his arrival in Oct. has taken up his teaching of History and Japanese with enthusiasm and has shown that he was just the man we needed. The students like him and he is a good teacher. As he does all his teaching in Japanese he found that a portion of his students were slow is taking instruction but this has not dampened his ardor and he has been teaching Japanese Language out side his regular work to correct this weakness in the students and he has said that he was much gratified to see the great advance in the use of Japanese made by the students even in the two months of this Fall term. Typed page # 114

Mr. Ichijima has been with us about half the term and has been teaching Botany; Zoology, Japanese Language and Agriculture, all in Japanese; and Agriculture is required of all students we were able to find out though Mr. Ichijima just how many of the students were able to take instruction in Japanese; those who were not able to stand this test were put back into preparatory Japanese Classes. Mr. IChijima has proven himself thoroughly trained and capable as well as tactful with students; altho he has been with us so short a time we feel confident that he is the right man for the teaching of agri-

culture. He is a strong Christian teacher and we are glad he has joined our ranks.

We are glad to welcome W.C.Rufus back from the University of Michigan where he has won his Ph.D. He is already at work on his course in Math. and Astronomy and as he has a reputation as a mathematician is Chosen, we are sure the work in his department will soon be a great factor in our institution. He has had a chance to test out some of our boys is their advanced Math. and is greatly pleased with their ability. Indeed I would like to say that I don't believe there is any better material any where than the five boys in the Aual. Geom. Class. There is a fine bunch of 10 boys in a trig. Class which Mr. Rufus will take in charge.

Mr. T. S. Kim who, after rearly finishing a college course in Pyeng Yang (he was in our church schools in Pyeng Yang about 12 years; one of Dr. Noble's pupils about 17 years ago) graduated at Ohio Weslayan University and then took his M. A. at Columbia University, has just returned and will take up our Biological Dept. work for which he has specialized. As Mr. Kim is as inthusiastic Christian worker as well as a good teacher and speaker we know that he will have a large share in building up our school.

As Mr. Billings is on Furlough Mr. H. H. Underwood is in entire charge of the Dept. of English. Besides Literary English he has taught Commercial Geography in English to a group of boys who were ready to take instruction in English. The way in which these boys have taken this work under Mr. Underwood has show us that there is great hope of our being able to give at least a part of our advance work in English. The good progress make by the boys in the five divisions of English, which has been taught in a rather haphazzard way

-5-

because of a lack of teaching force, makes us feel that when we get into operation the systematic course being worked out by a committee of the faculty, the students aught to make very marked development is the use of English. We believe that a good knowledge of English is fundamental to a complete course of study so we are planning to give a committee examination to every student, who desires to enter the more specialized course after having had at least four years preparatory work in this subject. I might say that at college entrance we required at least two years of English: (and unless one is qualified to take instruction in the Japanese Language he is conditioned on entrance requirements until he makes this up.

During Mr. Miller's absence I am temporalily in charge of the Chemistry department work with Mr. Root Lee of Nebraska Wesleyan University as my assistant. There are two classes; a preparatory class and one in General Chemistry. The latter has two hours of lecture and six hours of laberatory work per week; it goes thru the year and covers as much as a Fresham Course in the Universities in U.S.A. There are 14 boys taking this and most are showing real inthusiasm and ability only one being laggard on account of poor preparation. Practically all of these boys have taken a year preparatory Chemistry after leaving the H.S. The High Schools have not up to date prepared their students well in either chemistry of physics; we are expecting to put all applicants for these course thru a year preparatory course, so that our course may retain its standard equal to college or universities in other countries. Typed page #145

In the Physics Dept. we are now running three classes - Prep. Physics, a class in Mechanics and Heat, and a class in Electricity and Magentism. The first has three hours instruction the other six hours of Lab. and two lectures, each per week. In this work we are

-6- typed page #115 (50)

putting great stress upon the student being able to work out experiments and practical problems in the laboratory and these who are taking these courses are beginning to develope a scientific attitude of mind and much initiative and enthusiasm in getting proper, accurate results in all the physical measurements; thus, we feel that we are adding something important to the Korean character when a student will spent days patiently working to find a small error in his experimental data.

Mr. Gerdine was appointed to the school and came to us a little late in the term so that it was difficult to arrange his classes at first but he finnally arranged to teach two classes in Bible and one in English. We wanted all the ~~staten~~-students to enroll in either one of these two classes but, as Mr. Gerdine has work at the Theological Semminary and the Union Bible School, he could give us only a limited portion of his time and, as some students could not be at school at these hours, not all students could take the Bible this last term but there is evidence to show that Mr. Gerdine's instruction has been inspirational to many of the students. We hope to make it possible for all the students to have Bible instruction this next term.

One of our most efficent teachers is Mr. Pack who is proposed as head of the Commercial department work. He has received thorough training at Borwn University, U.S.A. and in Europe and is one of the most competent, conscientious, Korean teachers I have ever had the fortune to be associated with. He taught Political Economy and Logic ~~fortune to be associated with. He taught Political Economy and~~ as well as commercial work his classes were the largest in the school (30 in one, 31 in another), yet the students were not only thoroughly instructed but the subject matter was covered in the same time us-

typed -7- (51)

ually given to these subjects abroad, this necessitated a most careful preparation of each lesson; miniographed translations were made and every minute of the alloted time was utilized. The most that I can say is that Mr. Pack is a fine Christian teacher and the institution is most fortunate to have him in its faculty. He says.

"I am convinced that, of various subjects taught in a modern College. Logic is one of the most essential studies, as now-a-days an educated man, whether he be that of the West or of the East, is expected to know something of the logical processes of thinking and the modern scientific methods. This is more so with the Korean people, inasmuch as the Korean mind is by no means a logical one. Furthermore, in a transition period like the present, one of things most needed by the Korean people is a clear and wholesome thinking, and the study of logic will help our boys to be broad-minded in their points of view, to use an exact language and to discriminate the fallacious from the logical.

Considering all these, the writer ventures to suggest that hereafter Logic be made one of the compulsory studies for all students in the Chosen Christian College."

The institution appreciates very much the services of Mrs. Weller in training a class of boys in the use of the typewriter as this will help the students in self support.

STUDENT HELP DEPARTMENT. typed page# 116

A very necessary adjunct of a Mission school is a Student Aid Dept. as the most of our best and most promising students are from poor homes in the country. As was reported before we have formed a student aid fund from which we distribute aid to worthy students in return for specified service to the school. Each student sends in his request at the beginning of each term with recommendations and credentials and after each case have been examined carefully a card settling amount of aid per month, kind of work and number of hours work per day is given the student, the average help is ¥6:00 per month, for which the student gives two to three hours service per day depending on the kind of work. Some scrub the floors of the school room and offices once a day, other clean apparatus in the Laboratories, others spend their Saturdays washing windows; a few act as secretaries in office and library, some act as errand boys still others help in dormitory and dining hall. Some do translating and mimiograph work. Some of the older students act as assistants in Laboratory and preparatory classes. Eight of the students help as teachers in primary schools of the city, some act as language teachers to Missionaries, one is a teacher in Pai Chai and one is a teacher in Ewha.

We have helped students during the Fall term to the amount of ¥1350:00

The sources of this fund has been a follow:

College budget for janitors, office sec. work, etc. . . ¥280:00
Dr. Underwood 100:00
Paid in to Dept. From Local sources for Student work . .268:00
M.E.Mission 160:00
Friends have Contributed 542:00

APPARATUS AND EQUIPMENT.

For beginning work we have a fair amount of apparatus and equipment:-

1. Physical and Chemical Equipment. ¥9030.35
2. Library books and Equipment. 1289.00
3. Office Equipment and Teachers room. 560.00
4. Class room Equipment 725.00
5. Biology 200.00
Total 11804.35

Of course this represents but a beginning yet every peice is

-9-

in full use and soon must be added to if we wish to approach the high standard of practical up-to-date instruction at which we are aiming; ¥7686.66 worth of the above has been bought by funds secured by Dr. Underwood and ¥4117.69 worth has been provided by the Methodist Mission.

Physical apparatus bought in U. S. A.	¥2906.68
Books from all source, ...	930.00
Chemical and Physical apparatus bought in Japan.	4078.52
Made by Y. M. C. A. and others.	2357.15
Bought at Local dealers.	530.00
Total	11804.35

DORMITORY AND EATING HOUSE.

The schools has provided a dormitory in which all out of town students are supposed to stay. An upper story at the Y.M.C.A. has been rented. There are seven large fooms and during the Fall 47 students have been provided for. The rooms are heated by steam and lighted by Electricity. These rooms are well lighted, large airy and as they are kept clean and sanitary the health of the students has been remarkable; there has been no serious illness among any of these students during the Fall.

The eating house has provided clean wholesome food well served at ¥4.30 per month and the students have seemed to be well nourished.

Night heating of the dormitories during the winter months has pro[illegible] unexpected expense but the faculty after discussing the matter thoroughly voted that as, very few students had more than one blan[illegible], steam heat must be provided.

Yours Respectfully

A. J. Becker

7. 언더우드 교장의 이사회 제출 보고서

문서 제목	Provisional President's Report to the Spring Meeting of the Board of Managers of the Chosen Christian College
문서 종류	교장 보고서
제출 시기	1916년 3월 27일
작성 장소	서울
제 출 자	H. G. Underwood
수 신 자	이사회
페이지 수	4
출 처	2114-5-2: 06 Board of Managers 1915~1922 (UMAH)

자료 소개

언더우드 교장이 1916년 3월 27일 열린 이사회 회의를 주재하는 가운데 제출한 보고서이다. 건강이 악화된 언더우드가 미국으로 떠나기에 전에 마지막으로 이사회에 제출한 보고서이기도 하다.

이 보고서에서 언더우드는 재단법인과 학교설립을 인가받기 위해 학교 측이 총독부와 어떻게 힘들게 교섭하였고, 그 자신은 1915년 12월 말과 1916년 3월 사이에 일본에 가서 어떻게 많은 사람을 만났는지를 설명하였다. 이 설명에서 인가 취득을 방해한 쪽은 오히려 선교계 인사들이었던 것으로 묘사되고 있다. 이 문제는 총독부가 1915년 4월 1일부터 개정사립학교규칙을 시행하면서 벌어진 논란을 염두에 두고 볼 필요가 있다. 재한 선교사들의 다수는 총독부가 사립학교의 종교 교육을 정규 교과 안에서 금지한 것을 기독교 탄압이라 규정하고 그런 법령에 따라 대학설립을 인가받는 것은 기독교 탄압에 굴복하는 것이라고 주장하였다. 미국에 있는 선교 지도자들도 총독부에 여러 차례 편지를 보내 서구 국가들의 경우에 비추어 일본의 종교와 교육 분리 방침은 부당하다고 주장하였다.

이 보고서에서 언더우드는 항목의 분류 없이 아래의 사항들을 설명하였다.

총독부의 새 교육법 아래에서의 재단법인과 학교설립 인가 취득 문제, 설립 인가 지연, 언더우드의 일본 활동, 그의 건강 악화로 미국에 가야 할 필요성.

내용 요약

설립 인가: 새 교육법 아래에서 이사회는 세 가지 과제를 안고 있다. 그것은 첫째로 재단법인을 설립하고, 둘째로 학교 운영을 보장할 일정한 자산을 확보하며, 셋째로 교육과정, 과목, 수업시수 등을 기재한 신청서를 작성하여 대학설립 인가를 받는 것이다.

인가 지연: 교육평의회(Educational Senate, 재한 선교사들의 학교 교육 협의기구) 사람들이 우사미[내무부장]를 찾아가 자신들을 재한 선교사들의 대표라고 내세우며 미국의 본부들은 체제에 순응하는 교육기관을 결코 지원하지 않을 것이라고 말하여 우사미가 대학설립의 후과를 우려하게 하였다. 나(언더우드)는 해리스(M. C. Harris, 감리교 선교사) 등을 통해 선교계의 상황을 설명하여 협상이 재개되게 하였다. 그 결과 총독부에서 내가 일본에서 돌아온 후인 3월 20일 설립 인가를 내주려고 하였으나, 브라운(A. J. Brown, 북장로회 선교부 총무)이 보낸 편지를 고마츠[외사국장]가 받으면서 그 일이 다시 미뤄졌다.

언더우드의 일본 활동: 나는 일본에서 대학 문제를 위해 오쿠라 수상과 문부대신 다카다를 비롯한 일본 고위관리들, 와세다대와 게이오대 총장들과 교수들, 제국대학 교수들, 일본 기독교 지도자들을 만났다. 이 만남을 통해 재한 선교사들이 일본 정부에 적대적이지 않다는 점을 알리는 데에 적지 않게 성공하였다. 그렇지만 노스(F. M. North, 북감리회 선교부 총무이자 합동위원회 위원장)가 자금 지급을 방해하면서 인가 취득을 또 지연시킬 가능성이 있다. 그런 상황에서 우사미는 종교학과를 설치하는 방안을 조언하여 대학이 기독교적 성격을 더 확고히 할 수 있게 하였다.

언더우드의 미국행: 내가 의사의 지시로 미국에 가야 할 형편이 되었지만, 건강을 속히 되찾아 한국을 위해 많은 가치 있는 역할을 할 이 학교의 완성을 위해 다시 일하게 되기를 희망한다.

TRANSFERRED 3/27/16

Provisional President's Report to the Spring Meeting of the Board of Managers of the Chosen Christian College.

March 27, 1916.

......

Your President at the present time is glad to be able to report progress along all lines that the College is making. At the immediate present what we are especially after is the proper incorporation of the institution and for this we find that our work runs along three different lines, but that these three different lines must be carried on simultaneously according to the rules of the Government General of Chosen. According to the kind that we propose we must have a juridical person or body on which to lean and must be based on what is known as either a Shadan Hogin or Zidan Hogin. It has been decided for us that our juridical person must be in the nature of a deed of trust or Zidan Hogin and that this must be duly incorporated according to the laws of the country. As up to the present time no such Zidan Hogins have been incorporated there are no existing laws that will guide us in the drawing up of our charter and consequently it takes a good deal longer to bring this to perfection than were we in a position where we had a model on which to go.

In the second place, in accordance with the same rules and regulations, there must be a certain amount of property, both real and movable, that will insure the proper carrying out of the work of the school. In this connection the Government has, as you well know, offered to sell us at a very reasonable rate, property that is well adapted to our needs and is finely located and well suited in every way. Concerning the requirements of this property too, various stipulations have to be entered into and these negotiations are not completed.

The third thing that an institution like this requires is what might be called the charter or permit for the College. This too, must follow certain stipulated rules and regulations and at this point we are the better prepared for our work because the Government General has prepared a form for the filing of applications for such charters. Here again the matter of the courses to be taught, the subjects under the courses, the hours assigned to each individual subject and the total resultant, all have to be brought under the consideration of the officials of the Educational Department and this is being done. It seems almost as though neither one nor other of these can be carried to perfection alone, that they must all go simultaneously and that when the three things are done then everything will be ready for the proper signing of the documents. We had felt that everything was under way for a speedy settlement and Dr. Speer's visit here had helped not a little to clear away any difficulties, but just after Dr. Speer left a committee of the Educational Senate of Korea called on Mr. Yusumi and attempted to tell him that the missionary Boards at home would never support a conforming institution and raised no few doubts in their minds as to what would be the result even after the charter had been given. It was a great surprise to me to find the slowness of progress that was being made in all the three things that we were trying to obtain until I was informed by one of the heads of the Government here that it was very evident that a misunderstanding had been arrived at, that the representatives of the Senate having gone to Mr. Yusami as representatives of the Senate and announced that they were the legal representatives of all the bodies in Korea doing educational work, Mr. Yusami naturally concluded that their statements were authoritative. With the assistance of Mr. Smith and Bishop Harris I was able to show Mr. Yusami how matters stood and to practically re-open negotiations and since then the difficulties that seemed to exist have all been overcome. As you will hear later from Dr. Avison's report as Vice President, the draft of the Zidon Hogin charter is practically completed and they are ready to sign the same. Mr. Komatzu has informed me that as far as the property is concerned everything is now ready to be turned over to the Zidon Hogin as soon as they are ready to take the same, and Mr. Becker's report, which you will duly hear, will show you plainly that everything is completed now for the turning over to the institution of a charter as a college. I had heard that everything was ready in Japan and supposed that immediately on arriving here the papers would be duly handed over and, in fact, I was told that the Department was expecting to give us our regular charter on March the 20th, which was the date set because it was known that it would be after my return from Japan, but in the meantime the action of the Joint Committee has reached us and Dr. Brown's letter has been sent to Mr. Komatsu and while this may not cause a breaking off of negotiations, it will naturally hinder our completing them to the fullest extent and this will have to be done after further consultation with America and after the Board of Managers have decided what steps shall be taken.

During my stay in Japan I was constantly engaged in the interests of education and of the college here. I was enabled while there to have most cordial interviews with the Japanese officials, professional men and Christians and did my best to enlist them all in our work. I had a most cordial reception from the Premier, Count Okuma, who was extremely kind and gracious in stating that it was his desire that if we had anything to speak of that we should bring it direct to him. He spoke about the necessity of the proper assimilation of the two peoples and it was interesting to note how he referred to the similarities in the grammatical structure of the language as well as of the philological affinity of the people which he said was a sign of the real unity of the two peoples. I had a long and interesting chat in the Department of Education with the Minister of Education, Dr. Takata, the Director of Education, Professor Tadokoro and a counselor of the Educational Department, the Hon. Mr. Koyama. They talked at considerable length of the educational future of Japan and her colonies and they all tried to impress upon me the fact that while at the present time there might be differences in the system of education as carried out in the colonies and in the Mother Country, the tendency will be for all to coincide with that of the Mother Country and that we ought to look forward to this in our plans, while at the present time making our system coincide with that of the colony of Chosen. I had very interesting conferences with professors in the Imperial University of Japan and with the presidents and professors of Waseda and Keyo Universities. The discussions were very largely on the same line. In addition to the above it was my privilege to meet a large number of Christian educators and we talked quite freely on the trend of things in Korea and in Japan and they all told me that the trend was universally towards a more liberal interpretation of the relations between private and Government schools and that whatever might be said at the present time we might be assured that we might always look forward to a steadily increasing liberal attitude of the authorities in Japan towards the religious workers throughout the Empire. The general idea, however, that I found prevailing very largely among the bulk of the people in Japan was that the missionaries in Korea, as far as the Government was concerned, were "Antis" and I did my best to dispel this idea and I think succeeded in no small way.

Now the Christian pastors and leaders are with us and will do all they can to help us in our efforts. The leading educators of Japan I think, are also with us and in connection with our college and its development here I think we can count on the moral support and assistance of men like Professors Nitobe, Anesaki, Nanagi, President Komada, etc., etc., and at the same time we have the definite promise of kind assistance and help from the Minister of Education Dr. Takata, from the Director of Education Dr. Todoka and from the Counselor Mr. Koyama. The changes that are contemplated in Japan proper in their educational system are all of them towards a granting of greater liberties to the provate institutions and will all of them be a help to us. The four years college course, making the system of Japan quite nearly coincide with that of America, having been advocated by the Minister of Education will, it seems to me, without doubt prevail and, in fact, it looks as though the prevailing of this plan in the Cabinet and elsewhere will be pushed to such an extent that if it is not agreed to there may be a change of Cabinet. The Minister of Education is very confident that it will carry through. Having gone thus far in Japan and having heard all that had been done here I naturally was looking forward to the definite agreement being signed with the Government for our new charter at the present time and to start for America with this being settled. Dr. North's letter, however, will hinder us very materially from the spending of money and we will have to get a delay of time for the payment for the site, but conferences with Mr. Yusami since the reception of Dr. Brown's letter by Mr. Komatz have led them to offer to us the added privilege of a Religious Department in the University and this, together with the privileges already granted, certainly make the Christian character of the institution an assured fact. This was what the Board was after and those with whom I have talked, both Seoul collegeites and anti Seoul collegeites have said that they do not see what more can be asked. Under these circumstances I would suggest that the Executive Committee be authorized to go ahead with their negotiations to secure a charter for the Zidon Hogin and a charter for the college and to report the terms of the same to the Board in New York. I regret to say that my health is such that the doctors have ordered my return to America and consequently an

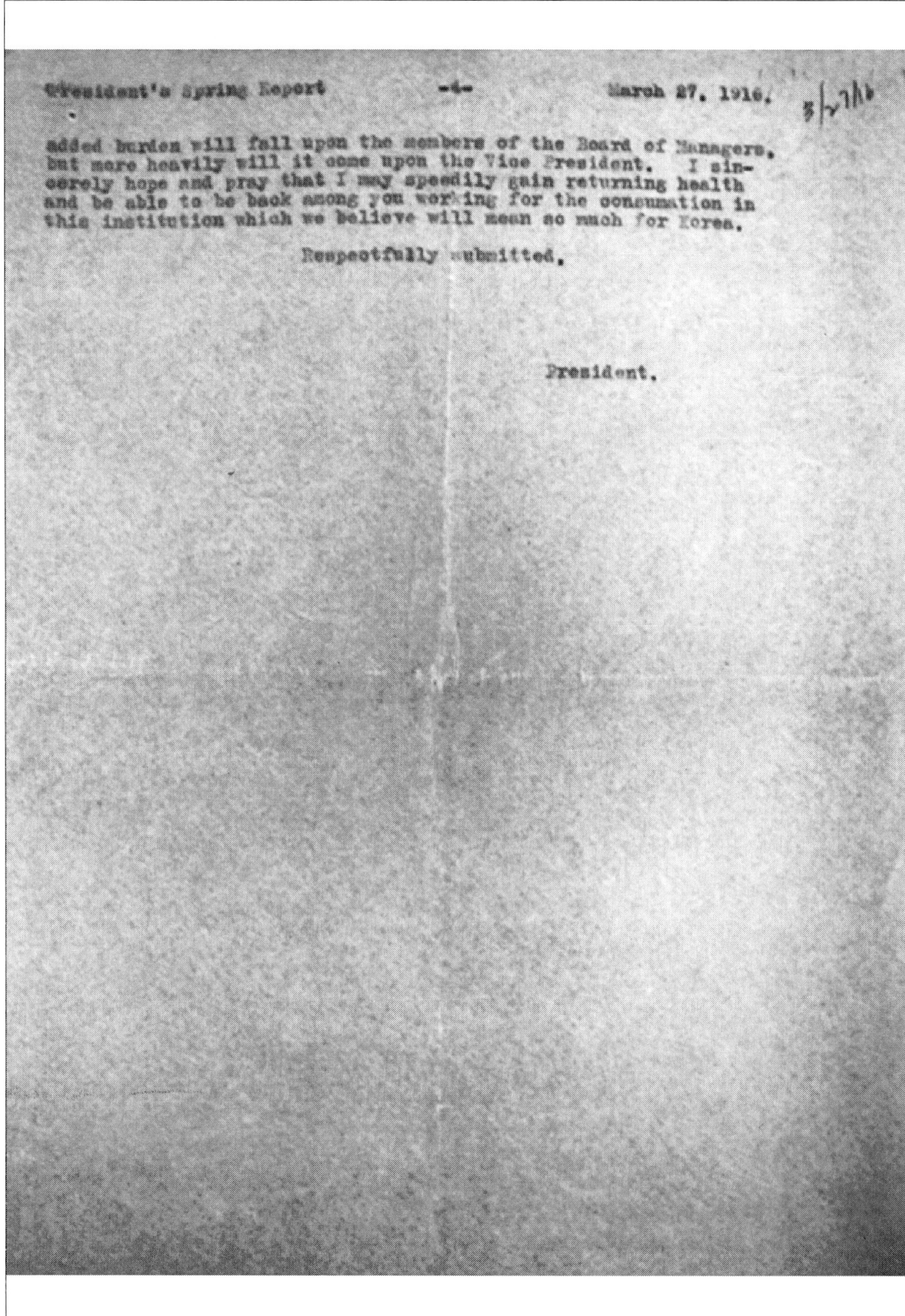

President's Spring Report -4- March 27, 1916.

added burden will fall upon the members of the Board of Managers, but more heavily will it come upon the Vice President. I sincerely hope and pray that I may speedily gain returning health and be able to be back among you working for the consumation in this institution which we believe will mean so much for Korea.

Respectfully submitted,

President.

8. 베커 학감의 이사회 제출 보고서

문서 제목	Report of Registrar for 1916
문서 종류	학감 보고서
제출 시기	1916년 12월 13일 (추정)
작성 장소	서울
제 출 자	A. L. Becker
수 신 자	이사회 (추정)
페이지 수	20
출 처	2114-5-2: 06 Board of Managers 1915~1922 (UMAH)

자료 소개

베커 학감이 1916년 연말에 제출한 보고서이다. 이 보고서는 연도만 표시하고 있지만, 맨 첫 줄의 "the year of 1916 has almost passed"란 문구를 통해 연말에 제출되었음을 알려준다. 그러므로 12월 13일에 열린 이사회 회의 때 제출되었을 것으로 짐작된다. 이 문서의 오른편 상단에 필기된 "12/31/16"이 무엇을 가리키는지는 알 수 없다. 13일의 회의에서 교명선정위원 3인(게일, 백상규, 와타나베)의 제안에 따라 '연희전문학교'란 교명이 결정되었다. 이 보고서는 언더우드 교장의 죽음(10월 12일)과 설립 인가의 지연으로 학교 관계자들이 애를 태우고 있던 상황에서 작성되었다.

이 보고서에는 학감의 보고서와 부서들의 보고서가 함께 편집되어 있다.

1. 학감 보고서는 서언과 아래의 7가지 항목으로 이루어져 있다.
   학생과 교육과정, 교수, 기숙사, 체육, 음악, 학생지원, 시설.
2. 부서들의 보고서는 아래 8개 분야의 교육 활동 상황을 설명하고 있다.
   YMCA, 수학, 농학 · 생물학, 공학, 영어, 상업 · 경제학, 성경, 역사 · 일본어.

내용 요약

◩ 학감 보고서

학생과 교육과정: 학교가 한 해 동안 원하는 것을 다 이루지 못하였고 언더우드 교장의

죽음으로 심한 고통을 당하였지만, 실망스러운 일들은 제쳐두고 진전을 이룬 것들에만 집중하도록 하겠다. 등록생은 총 104명이고, 교육과정은 공학, 문학, 성경, 상업-농업, 의학 예과로 나뉘어 있다.

교수: 교수는 총 10명(한국인 교수는 백상규, 이노익, 김득수)이다. 전임강사는 4명이고, 조수는 3명(임용필, 장세운, 백남석)이다. 가을학기에는 김득수와 원한경이 가르치지 못하였지만, 빌링스가 돌아와 빈틈을 메꾸어주었다. 밀러와 원한경이 돌아오기를 기대한다. 모두 서로 도우며 시련을 지탱해내었다.

기숙사: YMCA 건물 3층을 기숙사로 계속 쓸 수 없게 되어 서울 북쪽의 100칸짜리 한옥을 임대하여 기숙사로 쓰고 있다.

체육: 운동장과 체육 교사가 없지만, 야구, 배구, 테니스 장비를 사서 가르치고 있다.

음악: 루퍼스(W. C. Rufus) 교수 부인이 밴드를 결성하였고, 베커 교수 부인이 올갠과 피아노를 가르쳐 좋은 성과를 얻었다.

학생지원: 27명의 학생이 매일 3시간씩 일하여 월 ¥5.30을 받고 있고 25명은 학교 밖에서 돈을 벌고 있다.

(시설들과 시설들의 가격을 제시하고 있다.)

◩ 부서들의 보고서

대학 YMCA: (노준탁 보고) 1915년 10월 29일 24명으로 조직되어 영·지·체의 개발을 위해 꾸준히 노력하였다.

수학 교육: (루퍼스와 조수 장세운 보고) 수학 교육에 어려움이 큰데, 이는 암기 위주의 동양식 교육 방법에서 비롯되었다.

농학과 생물학 교육: (이치지마 보고) 대학의 농지에서 발전된 농법을 가르치고 실증하였으며, 생물학, 일어도 가르쳤다.

공학 교육: (베커와 조수 임용필 보고) 실용적인 응용과학의 발전을 희망하면서 화학, 물리학, 건축학을 가르쳤다.

영어 교육: (빌링스 보고) 영어를 배울 필요성을 강조하고 영어 회화를 숙련하도록 노력하였다.

상업과 경제학 교육: (백상규 보고) 경제학, 재정학, 부기, 타자, 논리학 등 이론과 실용

교육을 겸비하여 가르쳤다.

성경 교육: (저다인 보고) 3학년 학생들만 주 2시간씩 수업하였고 나머지는 주 3시간씩 수업하였다.

역사와 일본어 교육: (다카이 보고) 일본사, 중국사, 서양 로마사를 가르쳤고 일본어도 가르쳤는데, 학생들의 일본어 학습 진도가 빠르다.

12/31 16

ANSFERRED

REPORT OF REGISTRAR FOR 1916.

The year of 1916 has almost passed and we have made progress but we have not gained as much as we had hoped and have suffered a severe loss in the death of our beloved President, Dr. H. G. Underwood, but setting aside the things which have been discouraging, I propose to confine myself to the things in which I feel we have advanced:-

(1) Students and courses of study. The total enrollment has been 104; in the spring term we enrolled 42 new students and this fall we enrolled 7 more; with a very few exceptions the students are all graduates of christian High Schools. We have been very fortunate in the personal of our present student body; they are without exception e studious, well-believed and obdient. We have not yet adopted the authorized courses of study, still the studies and grade as well as courses of this proposed cariculum have been approximated and the students devided in four main courses:-Engineering, Literary and Bible course and Commercial-Agriculture course and Medical preparatory course. Of those who finished the years work, 14 students are in the Engineering course, 10 are in Commercial-Agriculture course, about 46 are in Literary and Bible course and 13 are taking the Medical preparatory course. We have been teaching full courses in the Freshman and Sophomore years but only a few studies in the Junior year, as only a few students were qualified for that work; a few students has been given preparatory work in Science, Mathemetics, Japanese and English, so that they could make up any deficiency in their previous training and pass, without any entrance conditions, on a equal basis, into the Freshman course. The full number of hours work per week according to the new courses of study average 30 hours, but the students who must spent a part of their time at work are allowed to take only portion of this amount, the minimum allowed is 10 hours per

-4-

week. Our school motto has been "thoroughness and efficiency" and the most of our students are now imbued with a desire to do all their work well even tho it may mean a longer period in school. The ambition to merely pass up the grodes in due order and final graduate is distructive of good work in school, so this has been discouraged by establishing certain standards of efficiency in each kind of work which standard must be attained before the student is allowed to pass on; we have thus developed a few real students of whom we are very proud and hopeful. We believe that the student body as a whole are fairly happy in their work and share, very closely, with the faculty and Board the hopes of a great future for Chosen Christian College.

The working faculty of the years been:-

Rev. J.L. Jerdine----------	teacher of	Bible.
Prof. Takai--------------	" "	History and National language.
Prof. S. Pack------------	" "	Commerce, Economics, Logic and Public Finance.
Dr. W.C. Rufus------------	" "	Mathemetics and Astronomy.
Rev. B.W. Billings---------	" "	Bible and English.
Prof. Ichijima-----------	" "	Agriculture, Botany, Zoology, and National Language.
Rev. A.L. Becker-----------	" "	Physics and Chemistry.
Mr. Root Lee-------------	" "	Laboratory Chemistry.
Mr. H.H. Underwood---------	" "	English.
Mr. T.S. Kim-------------	" "	Physiology and Biology.

Besides the above we have had the following instructors in the various Departments:-

Mr. O. A. Weller---------	teacher of	Mechanical Drawing.
Mrs. O. A. Weller---------	" "	Typewriting.
Mrs. A. L. Becker---------	" "	Organ, Piano and Vocal Music.
Mrs. W. C. Rufus----------	" "	the College Band.

Also we have had the follow assistant teachers:-

Mr. Im Yong Pil----------	teacher of	Laboratory Physics.
Mr. Chang Sae Woon-------	" "	Mathemetics.
Mr. Pack Nam Sok---------	" "	Music and English.

Altho Mr. Kim Tuk Soo and Mr. H. H. Underwood could not teach in the fall term the return of Prof. Billings helped us to bridge over their the gap. Perhaps our greatest loss in the teaching force has been that of Dr. Underwood who tought Psychology Sociology and Philosophy during 1915: We have had no one this year who could take up his work so these subjects have not been tought. One of our urgent needs is a teacher for this department. The departure of Dr. Underwood and his son has left the school without any teacher from the Presbyterians but we are in hope, with the return of Prof. E. H. Miller and H. H. Underwood and the possible appointment of another teacher by the Presbyterian Board very early in 1917, that we may have our faculty sufficiently enlarged to meet the demands of the additional classes of the 3rd years work in the several courses. Our teachers without exception have labored loyally and faithfully this year and there has been the utmost scooperation and "Spirit de Corps" as well as and exceptional close sympathetic brotherliness in the faculty in spite of the fact that it includes three different nationalities. All have been mutually helped and sustained in the trials and labours of the year. As Registrar, I wish to thank the other members of the faculty for their hearty cooperation. All our teachers desirve special mention for their excellent and wholly satisfactory work; I think I may say that no Christian School in Korea has had up to the present such an excellent corps of workers, each a specialist of high educational qualifications yet all enthusiastic Christian workers and exerting the highest influence on the students. Our student body has been exceptional but our faculty have commanded their fullest respect and loyal devotion: and so there has been a porpor- general advance in behavior, morals and Christian Character as well as intellectual capacity much exceeding that of any period of my 11 years teaching experience in Chosen. The students have not been burdened by school regulations and have been allowed much liberty by the faculty and the result has been a more manly self-assertion and a development of initiative what has been highly gratifying to us who are primarly working for development of strong character in the students. Recently the students gave the faculty a "reception" which showed not only their good well but a real feeling of affection for all the members of the faculty.

The college Dormitory. Our College Dormitory is considered by us as one of the most important features of the college work for we fully understand that unless class room work is backed up by proper dormitory conditions then we must waste much of our efforts; thus under the necessity of providing a dormitory which would be cheap, clean, healthy yet have all the essentials of heat, light, space, beauty and comparative quietness. We found that it was impossible to remain in the 3rd story of the Y.M.C.A. building and after much effort secured an exceptionally fine Korean house of over 100 Kan in the northern part of the city at the most reasonable rent of 65 yen per month. The faculty decided that as the building was larger than necessary for the requirements of the college students alont that other students of good character might be received and thus provide a Christian Hostel for a few others. This was a large venture but having a couple of fine young men to as managers we have made a fine start and have 35 college students and 25 other students making a total of 60. The Board is ¥5.00 per month and a dormitory fee of ¥1.00 per month is charged. The average room has two students per Kan. Altho it is impossible to satisfy students regarding food and we have had to try three diferent "Chu-ins" yet we are now satisfied that the food is clean and wholesome as well as cheaper than in other places. Inevery other way the conditions disired for a Korean Dormitory seems to be met so well that the students are healthy, happy and studeous. We have had no serious illness in the dormitory yet, where lost year there was much sickness at the Y.M.C.A. dormitory and much discomport and dissatisfaction as well as a lack of quietness Prof. Billings was elected by the faculty to be the Evangelistic director of the dormitory and he has done much for the spiritual tone of the place by personally conducting weekly services there. The dormitory committee has also profited very much by the advise of Prof. S. Pack who is a member of this committee. This dormitory could well take the whole time of one teacher and be developed to meet a great need felt in the city for a good Christian "Hostel".

Athletics. As the school has no athletic field and no physical director we have been hampered very much in developing a taste for proper enercise. However by offering to duplicate any amount raised the students for athletic goods, the faculty arroused so much interest that they had to subscribe over 50 yen; thus about 100 yen was spent on base ball outfits, basket and volley balls and tennis, and can get the Y.M.C.A. or dormitory to throw balls, etc. Mr. Barnhart of the Y.M.C.A. has been teaching a large numger of the students in a Gymnasium class which meets twice a week. However I sincerely hope that we may soon be able to get out our own athletic field and have our own direcetor; I would like to recommend to the Board the appointment of a Japanese teacher as director athletics and the students have since been taking advantage of every space they

17/31/16

-6-

national language teacher.

College Music. I could largely make a statement of progress without speaking of our "Band. Mrs. W. C. Rufus has undertaken the difficult task of starting and training a band for the college and after many discouragements has developed the uncleus of players who are very promising and we expect to hear great things in the near future.

Mrs. A. L. Becker has been able to give more attention to Organ and Piano teaching this year, so that many students are showing proficiency along this line. We need a piano very much.

Student Help Department. As was reported last year a student help department was or anized in order to give some aid to promising students who were needy; all the cooperating missions were asked to contribute for this perpose and 6.00 yen was declared the Maximum aid per student permonth. Of course in the absence of an industrial department in the school, thus is our only course and as yet absolutely essential to the life of the school as we are not yet in a position to appeal to well-to-do students.

The department has three functions:

(a) Give direct help under difinite rules.
(b) Indeavors to find employment for students.
(c) Destributes and checks up aid given for the use of certain students.

(a) An average of 27 students were given direct aid under the rules of the student help department, and the average aid was ¥5.30 per month. So that the total amount for the year will approximate closely to ¥1430.00: to meet thus we have received the following contributions:-

Special Gifts secured thru M. E. Mission---------------¥950.00
On College Budget for Janitors,Assistants, etc.---------¥240.00
Received from M. E. Mission South----------------------¥200.00

12/31/16

Each student is required to give an average of 3 hours service per day for the above aid; their work was approximately as follows:-

In Primary Schools of Seoul	8
College office errant boys	1
Laboratory worker	2
Mimiograph work of the college	2
Janitor work of School rooms	2
" " " dormitory	2
Carpenter work repairs of school and dormitory	2
Translating and coppying	3
Office Typewriting	1
Library work	2
Assistant Secretary, School records	1
Total	27

Of the above, 12 were Northern Methodists, 10 were Northern Presbyterian, 3 were Southern Methodists and 2 were Canadian Presbyterian. Over 200 letters of appeal for scholarship aid were sent to U. S. A. during the year by this department.

(b) The department secured outside employment for an average of 25 students as language teachers, secretaries, typists etc and with a no exceptions all seem to be giving complete satisfaction.

Mr. Billings and Dr. Rufus have helped to carry the burdens of this department and owing to their efforts we hope to close the year without a deficit and thus has been attained in spite of the lack of Dr. Underwood's liberal contributions of last year and an increased list of students helped.

Equipment. The value of our equipment, up to date, at cost price is:

Physical and Chemistry Equipment	¥9299.02
Library books and equipment	¥1780.95
Office and teachers room	¥651.84
Class room equipment	¥748.80
Biology, Botany	¥298.00
Band instruments	¥325.00
Dormitory equipment	¥292.83
Agriculture implements	¥90.00
Total value	¥13486.44

The addition of Equipment in 1916 is valued at ¥1682.09

12/31/16

THE COLLEGE YOUNG MEN'S
CHRISTIAN ASSOCIATION.
(President) Ko Chun Tack in charge.

With the usual purpose of furthering our spiritual, intellectual and physical welfare by constantly holding devotional services, and carrying on social, literary, and athletic activities, this organization came into its being on October 29, 1915 with twenty-four charter members. To accomplish our ends in view we found it necessary to organize the following three departments, the nature of whose activities I describe herewith.

(1) Religious Department.

The activities of this department may well to divided into the following.:

A. We conduct a bible class every Sunday.

B. We hold devotional services under the leadership of some noted preachers twice or thrice a week.

C. In conjunction with the other school Y.M.C.A.'s we hold prayer meetings twice a month at the Seoul Y.M.C.A.

D. We carry on a Children's Sunday School at Jeh Tong.

E. During the summer vacation we are intending to organize and sent out a Preaching Band to do some evangelistic work in the country.

(2) Literary Department.

Under the auspices of this department we give to our members such privileges as of hearing some noted persons' lectures, of participating in debating exercises, and of reading up-to-date magazines.

(3) Physical Department.

In order to keep our members in fine physical condition, we

play various sorts of games: Base-ball, Tennis, Ping-Pong and Volley-ball etc.
Thanks to the generosity of the faculty and students we were able to raise a large sum of money to purchase a complete base-ball outfit and we have fine materials to get up a splendid base-ball team but we are very much handicapped on account of lack of athletic field.

We

We have now 46 members and total receipts for the past twelve month. was ¥224.55 out of which we spent yen 184.685.

DEPARTMENT OF MATHEMATICS. W. C. Rufus in charge.
Assistant S. W. Chang.

During the past year instruction in mathematics has been given in preparatory Algebra, First year Algebra and Trigonometry, Second year Analytical Geometry, and Third Calculus.

Candidates for admission to the college show a marked dificiency in ability to apply the formulas and principles of elementary mathematics and to carry out independently any logical processes. This is chiefly due, we believe, not to native inability, but to the Oriental method of teaching in vogue in the Higher Common Schools; which is a method of communication and demonstration by the teacher, and does not stimulate nor develop individual work on the part of the student. How centruies of memory training at the expense of the reason have left more than a vestigial convolution of gray matter is a problem for the evolutionary psychologist.

Early in our course of study an attempt is made to remedy this deficiency. Students, who show the greatest lack, are given a course in preparatory algebra conducted by Mr. Chang Sae Woon. In this class it is necessary repeatedly to inquire concerning the amount of work actually done by the students; and to insist that the ambitious instructor shall not monopolize for himself all the benefit of the course.

Japanese text books are used in all the classes. Among the texts examined up to date we have been unable to find a satisfactory book for Freshman Algebra. There appears to be a hietus between the ordinary elementary Algebra on the on side, and translations of Crystal or similar theoritical works and elaborate monographs on the other. During the spring term we tried to give the Freshman an insight into algebraic processes from a more generalized standpoint, and Mr. Chang ahas carried on the work during the fall term.

In trigonometry insistance is also placed upon ap lication, but the teacher has to do his full share of the work, as the text lacks a sufficient member of satisfactory problems.

The text in Analytics is based upon the works of Smith and of Puckle, which guarantees not only the rogidity of the theory of the old English school but also the lack of suitable application, last year the class was able to complete plane analytics, including point, line, circle, parabola, ellipse, and hyperbola, using both rectangular and polar coordinates. This year we expect to be able to include also the elementary principles of Solid Analytics.

In Calculus we areable to supplement the text with references to American works for purposes of application and practical problems.

as the boys read English quite readily. The students in this class, four in member, show greater ability in applying principles, as they have had a longer course of training, where the teacher is not the chief performer and the students passive auditors. This is the first extensive course in Calculus, five hours per week for one year, that has ever been given in Korea, and the results so far are very satisfactory. One of the boys has real mathematical ability. He surpasses the average American College student in directness of attack and ingenuity in the solution of difficult problems. Another one is a close second in perseverance and accuracy of results. The object of the course is not merely to acquaint the students with the technique of differentiation and integration, but to give them an intelligent appreciation of the methods of the infinitesimal calculus as a means to approach the problems of modern science.

In fact this statement fairly represents the spirit of all the mathematical courses given. The government regulations place special emphasis upon vocational subjects, and pure science finds its only justification in its invaluable contribution to the subjects which function in Korean life.

DEPARTMENT OF AGRICUL-
TURE & BIOLOGICAL.
Ichijima in Charge.

In the Agriculture Department, I am teaching two classes in General Agriculture, each has an hour lecture and two hours farm practice every saturday afternoon. There are w37 students taking this course.

Most of them taking much interest in learning new methods of cultivation and scientific knowledge of Agriculture and are showing real enthusiasm.

In the begining of the spring term, we bought some farming tools, seeds and fertilizers for begining field work, and these cost about 90 yen and I chose and acre of about 600 Pyon(about half an acre) in the college fields for the boys' farm practice. We cultivated eight kinds of crops as experiement work, wish the help of a Korean farmer, and had a good harvest in the fall. The students, apprehending that there are many things to be improved in the old Korean methods of cultivation, took up their farm practice wish much interest, altho it was hard work for them to walk two miles from the school and to work in the field 2 hours in each time.

By this year's experimental cultivation, I found out that the college fields are the most firtile in the locality.

I am also temporarily in charge of the Biology Department and teaching Higher Botany and Zoology the standard of which are almost the same as that of college preparatory course in the Imperial University of Japan. There are four classes, two classes in Botany and two classes in Zoology; each has two hours of lecture and one hour of demonstration work per week.

40 students are taking Botany and 45 students Zoology. Most of them have no preparatory. knowledge of these subjects, I tried, therefore one hour's demonstration per week in order to make them understand the lectures more clearly, and I have prepared mimeographed outlines of the lecture for them.

8 students are studying in the class of Geology, in all of these classes, most of the students are quite enthusiastic and show ability in the study of these natural sciences, altho I could not give them Laboratory Work and show them specimens owing to the lacking of apparatus

To be able to teach in the Korean Language I have taught entering in the National Language yet the students have able to make very good progress in my department.

National Language Work: There are 24 boys in my Elementary Japanese Language class. I have been teaching three hours per week. When I began my class in the fall of last year, only few students could use the Japanese well, but after one year now most of them understand Japanese very well. I am very glad to see the great advance in the use of Japanese made by the students.

DEPARTMENT OF ENGINEERING.M A. L. Becker in charge.
Assistant Im Yong Pil.

Per-haps the name of this department sounds ambitious but it is because we hope to develope along the line of practical applied science that we use it; of course our present courses are but the basis of the more technical studies to follow in the 3rd & 4th years if we can carry out our plans. In chemistry we are giving the Freshmen the students the lecture course as outlined in Smith's General Chemistry for colleges, twice a week and along with this the correlated, laboratory course using as a text "A laboratory Manual of General Chemistry by Smith & Hole" in 3 double hour periods per week, the students have made excellent progress. The medical preparatory students have taken this course in an extra devision. An advanced laboratory course in analytical Chemistry was carried for a part of the year and Mr. Root Lee has also taught a course in Elementary Chemistry using the High School Text. The department has carried on

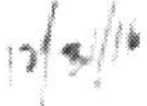

four classes in Physics.-

1. An elementary course 3hours per week taught by Mr. Im.
2. A special course of 6 hours Laboratory work and three hours lecture work for Medical students by Mesors Becker and Im.
3. A Freshman course of 6 hours laboratory work by Im and 2 hours lecture work by MrL Becker.
4. A sophomore Course in Electricity consisisting of 6 hours laboratory work and 2 hours lecture, by Mesors Becker and Sae-Oon Chang.

Mr. O. A. Weller has taught two classes:-

1. Mechanical Drawing 4 hours per week.
2. Building & Construction 4 hours per week.

As we have sufficient equipment for the work we have been doing so far and the teachers have had considerable experience in Laboratory work, we are fairly well pleased with the records of work done. In every class we have made a great advance on the quality and quantity of work done and this year for the first time we seem to have students that bid fair to become specialists; a real scientific spirit of investigation is becoming evident.

ENGLISH DEPARTMENT. B. W. Billings in charge.

Teachers:-
H.H.Underwood, Root Lee,
N. S. Pack and S. Pack.

As many of our students come with little or no training in English we still find it necessary to conduct three preparatory classes in English where the pupils are pushed as rapidly as possible to get them ready for the college classes. These have been taught by Mr. N. S. Pack, Root Lee, and Mr. S. Pack.

The three English classes in the college are now being taught by Mr. Billings. The reading work has been given in the New National Reader No. 4 for 1st year, No. 5 for the 2nd year and Orison Swett Morder's Winning Out for the 3rd year. As the work advances English is more and more used in the class-room until we are confident that we shall soon be able to produce students who have a fairly good working knowledge of English. In all these classes we have drills in use of English conversation but to give a larger opportunity for those who wish to speak as well as read English, we have a class in English conversation which meets two hours a week and practices sentences on some subject of interest to the students. This course is elective and the students are therefore doing good work.

Aside from the Bible, the English Language seems to as the most valuable thing which we foreigners are permitted to teach this people at this time. With so few good books in the Korean Language a knowledge of Japanese and English are absolutely essential for any youwng man who wishes to occupy any large place of usefulness in the future development of this people. The students seem to realize this and have given themselves to the study of English with an enthusiasm that has made it a real pleasure to teach them.

DEPARTMENT OF COMMERCE & ECONOMICS.

S. Pack in Charge.

This department offered the following courses during the term just ended: Economics II, Public Finance, Bookkeeping II, Bookkeeping 3, and Typewriting.

Economics II:

This was the continuation of Economics I given in the previous term. The principal topics under discussion were: Division of Labor; theories on Population; Population and its Relation to the

Economic well being of a Nation: Nature, Forms, Formation and Functions of Capital; Savings and Savings Institutions; Effect of Use of Machinery on Modern Industrial Life; Organization of Industry, Rise of Corporate Forms of Production; Trust and combinations; the concept of Value; Theory of Prices; Nature and Functions of Money, etc.

This was strictly an advanced class in economic theories, as a large majority of the students had taken the Waseda University correspondence course in Económics in addition to their High School work and judging from the fact that not a few of the last year's best students came in as auditors and stayed throughout the term, the writer is gratified to say that he did not burn the midnight oil to no purpose.

Public Finance II:

We used the writer's own text-book and dealt with the Nature of Public Needs; Forms of Public Revenues; Principles of Taxation; Forms of Taxes and its Effect on Industry; Shifting and Incidence of Taxation, etc., always with particular reference to Korean conditions. Works of a large number of German, English and American writers such as Wagner, Cohn, Bastable, Adams and Daniels were consulted(as all of these are in Japanese translation) and discussed.

Bookkeeping II:

This is both a theoritical and practical course in double entry. The class met twice a week for lectures and the students were required to do a large amount of outside work in Journalizing, in entering items in the Ledger, in the use of Most up-to-date forms of Cash Book; in the matter of closing the accounts; they were also trained to make Trial Balances, Financial and Business Reports, etc.

In fact the aim of them was to make it as much practical as to be of much practical value and at the same time as much theortical as to be worthy of a College Course.

Bookkeeping B:

This was an elementary class to meet the need of thosewho did not have Bookkeeping in the High School work as well as to prepare them to take up Bookkeeping I next year. We met twice a week and chief emphasis was laid in the matter of Journalizing and entering items in the Ledger. In spite of the inconvoinence of the hour we met (at 5.10-6.00)P.M.) the attendance has been very large and satisfactory.

Typewriting:

The department of Commerce is very furtunate in having the able service of Mrs. Weller in this important branch. Of the twelve students enrolled all of them are now very proficient in this art and several of them have been rendering very acceptable service in their spare hours. The registrar will kindly remember that his office assistant of whose work he spoke very highly was no other than one of these twelve.

- ....

In addition to the courses mentioned above I took charge of a class in Logic and an English class.

LogicII:

We met twice a week for lectures and we used my own text book and the amount of work we did during the term may practically be covered by chapters IX-XVIII inclusive in Hyslop's "ELEMENTS OF LOGIC" (6th edition) dealing with the Nature Deductive and Inductive inferences, Syllogism, Various Forms of Fallacies etc. My aim has

12/13/16

been as in the previous year to make it as realy an equivalent course as given in any of the leading American Universities.

English C:

(see Professor Billings' report re same)

BIBLE DEPARTMENT. Rev. J. L. Jerdine in charge.

During the year 1916 I have taught the 2nd & 3rd year classes in Bible. Each class has had three study periods a week, except that during the present term the 3rd year class has had only two periods, by reason of the difficulty of in arranging the schedule so as to provide for three periods.

The course we are using is in Old Testment History and Prophesy and is arranged to cover a period of two years. In includes 1st & 2nd Samuel, 1 & 2 Kings Daniel, Ezra and Nehemioh with a member of the minor prophests introduced in their historical setting. In addition to a study of the text, our endeavor is to relate the period under consideration to the earlier and later history of Israel in such a way as to give an orderly and comprehensive view of the main points in bible history and doctrine.

Each class has had an average enrollment of about twelve. The interest of the pupils has been, as a rule, goodand they shown considerable advancement after the years work.

If it is contemplated that this course attract students from other departments and that a large number of such students take this as an optional course. I am of the opinion that the method of teaching must be changed to that of the lecture system. If a teacher can be obtained for this department, who will be free to give his first

12/31/16

attention to the preparation and delivery of such a lecture course on the Bible, it might be made so popular as to attract the entire student body. This would, I believe, be the best and most feasible way to insure Bible instruction for the general student body. Since my main work is necessarily in other fields, I trust that the Board will be able to secure a teacher for this department, who will be able to build it up on the line suggested.

Rev. B. W. Billings has taught the first year's work and Reports as follows:-

For the work in Ethics for the first year during the past term. We have used the "Imprisonment Epistles of St. Paul". Though we have tried to give a careful exposition of these as well as the setting in which they belong, we have not tried to duplicate work done in other schools but to create a love for the Bible and a desire to conform the life of each student to its teachings.

DEPARTMENT OF HISTORY AND
NATIONAL LANGUAGE. N. Takai in charge.

Three courses of lectures on history have been given regulary since April of this year and they were attended alike by the students.

According to the carriculum lectures on "Japanese History" were delivered to the first year class covering the period from mythical age to the end of the Nara deparasity (A.D. 7th century) through the 1st and the 2nd term, two hours a week, while the course of Chinese History has come down to the epoch of Sangoku (Three countries period A.D. 4th century) since her begining.

In Western History Rome was the subject of the lectures during the first term; this class were mostly third year students, as a continuation of the previous year's work and we have come to the "Effect of the Crusade" at the end of the year.

The students seem to enjoy the lectures of these different countries and the lecturerfinds they are becomming more and more skillful in copying the lectures in Japanese and so there are few hindrances to lecturing in the class-recom in Japanese.

As to the Japanese Language study, Koto readers Vol. I and II were used in the first year class as the text book and we have finished this at the ends of the 2nd term, while the Sekai Tokuhon (Globe reader) was read, following the previous year in the 2nd year's work in the first term, after which the Fairy Tale of "Momotaro" were read in the 2nd term, Koto reader Vol. VII and the Life of Socrates were altarnately used in the 3rd year course, though the latter was rather difficult to understand still with some hardship we have gone through half of that.

The students are making very rapid progress in language study because of their enthusiastic spirit in getting into the heart of the new language and so the teaches feels himself very happy in finding his pupils are trying to overcome the difficulties before them.

9. 베커 학감의 북감리회 미국 선교부 제출 특별 보고서

문서 제목	Memorendum for Dr. North
문서 종류	학감 보고서
작성 시기	1918년 2월 이전
작성 장소	서울
작 성 자	A. L. Becker
수 신 자	Frank M. North
페이지 수	26
출 처	Scan 0791 Chosen Christian College: Underwood, Horace H. (Dr.) October 1913 -December 1923 (continued) (UMAH)

자료 소개

베커 학감이 북감리회 측의 후원자들에게 학교를 소개하기 위해 1918년 2월 이전에 특별히 작성한 보고서이다. 표지의 '1918년 12월 6일'이란 일자는 이 문서가 북감리회 선교부 총무 노스(North)에게 전달된 날짜이다. 실제 작성 시기는, 2쪽과 19쪽의 일자 표시에 따르면, 2월 이전이다. 2쪽에는 베커가 1918년 2월에 이하 18쪽까지를 수정하였다는 기록이 있고, 19쪽에는 2월에 그 이하를 작성하였다는 기록이 있다. 조선기독교대학 운영진은 새로 설립 인가를 받기 전에 그들이 준비한 설립신청서를 총독부에만 아니라 미국 선교부들의 합동위원회에도 보여주고 승인을 받아야 하였다. 그런데 합동위원회의 위원장이었던 노스는 총독부가 종교교육을 보장하지 않을 것을 염려하여 재단법인의 정관을 만드는 일에 매우 신중한 자세를 취하여 일을 지연시키기도 하였지만, 전문학교 인가가 난 후에는 연희전문을 착실히 후원하였다.

베커가 이 문서를 작성하였을 때 에비슨은 미국에 있었다. 에비슨은 연희전문과 세브란스의전이 1917년 4월과 5월에 인가를 받은 후 미국에 가서 합동위원회(1912년 결성된 6개 교단 선교부가 협의체)가 협력이사회로 개편될 때(1918년 1월 18일) 그 자리에 있었다. 이 기구는 한국에서의 기독교 교육 문제를 포괄적으로 다루는 것을 표방하였지만, 실제로는 연희전문과 세브란스의전의 재정을 후원하였다. 협력이사회가 1월에 결성된 사실을 참작하면, 이 문서는 베커 학감이 협력이사회의 출범을 기하여 여기에 가담한 북감리회 측 관계자들에게 연희전문에 대한 후원을 독려하기 위해 작성하였을 것으로 추측할 수 있다. 그러나 2월에 작성된 문서가 12월에야 다른 사람을 통해 전달된 까닭은 알 수 없다.

이 보고서는 세 부분으로 구성되어 있다. 1. 연희전문에 관한 기본 정보, 2. 연희전문의 현재 상태, 3. 연희전문학교의 발전사이다.

1. 연희전문에 관한 기본 정보 부분은 아래의 17개 항목으로 구성되어 있다.

   I. 명칭과 등급, II. 위치, III. 협력 기관, IV. 본교의 영향권과 종교적 배경, V. 본교에 대한 현지 각계의 태도, VI. 시설, VII. 교직원, VIII. 교육과정, IX. 등록생, X. 재정 수입, XI. 대학이사회, XII. 학생 활동, XIII. 한국 북감리회와 동 교단의 미션학교, XIV. 교육 목표, XV. 본교에 대한 한국인의 후원과 책임, XVI. 한국 내 타 교단의 학교 교육, XVII. 필요와 요구 사항.

2. 연희전문의 현재 상태 부분은 이 학교의 상대적인 우월성을 부각하고 있다.
3. 연희전문학교의 발전사 부분은 감리교 측의 활약을 중심으로 꾸며져 있다.

내용 요약

◪ 연희전문에 관한 기본 정보

I · II. 본교의 명칭과 수준은 Union Christian College 또는 Chosen Christian College이고, 한국, 서울에 있다.

III. 한국에 있는 북장로회, 남감리회, 캐나다장로회의 선교회들이 북감리회 선교회와 연대하여 그들의 대표를 본교에 이사와 교수로 파견하고 있고, 본국의 선교부들도 본교를 후원하고 있다.

IV. 본교는 천사백만에서 6백만 명의 인구와 모든 계층에게 고등교육을 제공하려 한다.

V. 총독부, 한국 기독교인과 비기독교인, 타 종교계는 본교에 호의적이거나 관용적이다.

VI. 본교에 아직 건물이 없지만, 곧 설계도를 노스(North) 박사에게 보낼 것이다.

VII. 선교사 교원은 8명, 한국인 교원은 5명이고, 그밖에 10명이 있다.

VIII · IX. 문과(4년), 상과(3년), 수물과(4년), 농과(3년), 신과(3년), 응용화학과(3년)의 6개 과가 있다. 1917~18년 등록생은 총 92명인데, 현재 1학년과 2학년만 있다.

X. 1917년의 총수입은 $10,000.00, 1918년의 총수입은 $5,000.00이었는데, 학비 수입은 1917년에 $1,000, 1918년에 $500이었고, 나머지는 모두 해외에서 왔다.

XI. 이사 14명 중 선교사 이사(10명)가 2/3이고, 한국인(2명)과 일본인(2명)이 1/3이다.

XII · XIII. 졸업생은 없고, 학생들은 모두 교회에서 활동하고 있다. (한국 감리교회의 교인수와 교회 관할 학교들의 현황에 대해 설명하고 있다.)

XIV · XV · XVI. 교육 목표는 한국의 남학생과 여학생에게 대학 교육을 제공하고, 일본과 미국의 종합대학 진학을 준비시키며, 사회와 교육을 개선하게 하는 것이다. 관립학교들에는 이렇게 하는 학교가 없다. 학비 외에 한국 사회에서 받는 지원금은 없지만, 본교는 교회와 국민(nation)을 위한 지도자 배출을 목표로 하고 있다. 본교에 필적할 학교가 한국에 없고 본교는 모든 한국인에 대해 책임감을 갖고 있다.

XVII. (필요한 건물들의 명단과 예상 건축비를 제시하고 있다.)

◪ 연희전문의 현재 상태

미션학교들이 관립학교들보다 여러 가지로 열등한 수준에 있지만, 본교는 관립 고등보통학교의 졸업생들도 입학을 지원할 만큼 높은 수준을 인정받고 있고, 한국 사회와 교회를 발전시키고 필요를 채우며 토대를 놓는 교육을 하는 점에서 비인가 학교인 평양의 숭실대학보다 우월하다.

◪ 연희전문학교의 발전사

1912년 감리교 선교사들이 하나의 교파연합대학을 세울 때가 되었다고 판단하고 이 일을 추진하기 시작하였고, 1914년 베커의 지도와 언더우드의 협력 아래 감리교 선교사들이 배재학교에서 대학 예과를 개설하였으며, 총독부의 허가를 받아 경신학교 대학과의 인가로 1915년 대학을 개교하였고, 1916년 언더우드를 잃는 고통을 당하였으나, 1917년 총독부의 인가를 받은 후 서울 근교에 땅을 사서 캠퍼스를 조성할 준비를 하고 있다.

802

December 6,1918.

Memorandum for Dr. North.

Attached herewith is material relating to Chosen Christian College as follows:

I. A write-up of the Institution.

Under Topic XVII you will find the itemized needs and askings.

2. Explanation of the Status of the Chosen Christian College.

3. History of the Evolution of the Chosen Christian College.

William B. Tower.

Chosen Christian College.
Seoul District
Korea Conference.

As Amended by Arthur L.Becker.
February 1918.

I. **Name and Grade:**

The Union Christian College at Seoul is also called the Chosen Christian College.

II. **Location:**

The Chosen Christian College is in the city of Seoul, Korea.

Chosen Christian College
Seoul District.
Korea Conference.

111. Co-operation and Union:

1. With other denominations:

(1) The denominational grouping in the government of the Institution.

(2) Co-operation and Union as related to the educational program of the Mission.

2. With W. F. M. S.

1. & 2.

The Presbyterian Church, North of U.S.A. The M.E. Church, South and the Canadian Presbyterian Missions, are not only associated with the Methodist Episcopal Church both in the local controlling Board and the Faculty of the Chosen Christian College but the Boards of the Churches in U.S.A. are associated together in active support of the institution.

The institution has no relation to the W.F.M.S.

Chosen Christian College,
Seoul District
Korea Conference.

IV. Population of Area which Institution Serves:

1. The total population which the institution serves is from fourteen to sixteen millions.

2. Estimate number of Methodism's responsibility:

About two million.

3. Among what castes, classes, races and religions does this responsibility lie:

Among all kinds of Koreans but our special task will be to furnish higher Education to the poorer class. There is no caste.

As to religion there are a few Buddists and Confucianist, but the major part are controlled by a superstitious fear of Evil Spirits or Ancestral Spirits.

Chosen Christian College
Seoul District
Korea Conference.

V. <u>Attitudes Toward the Institution:</u>

1. Of the Government.

Very favorable under present Constitution.

2. Of the official representatives of the non-Christian Religions.

Tolerant.

3. Of non-Christians - friendly.

4. Of Christians

Willing and ready to support all they can.

Chosen Christian College
Seoul District
Korea Conference.

VI. Plant:

1. Buildings:

(1) Kinds — As yet we have no buildings. Plans of building will soon be in the hands of Dr. North.

(2) Number

(3) Estimated value

2. Estimated value of Equipment and Furniture $10,000.00

Chosen Christian College
Seoul District
Korea Conference

VII. **Staff**:

1. Missionaries 8
2. Native teachers 5
3. Others 10

Chosen Christian College
Seoul District
Korea Conference.

VIII. <u>Curriculum;</u>

The curriculum is that of a College.

The College has six Courses

1.	A literary	course	of	4	years
2.	A Commercial	"	"	3	"
3.	" Engineering	"	"	4	"
4.	" Agriculture	"	"	3	"
5.	" Bible	"	"	3	"
6.	" Chemistry	"	"	3	"

Chosen Christian College
Seoul District
Korea Conference.

1X. Enrollment:

For 1917 & 1918 we have a total enrollment in all courses of 92 (but we are only teaching freshman and sophomore grades)

Chosen Christian College
Seoul District
Korea Conference.

X. Support-Budget Receipts:

1. Total receipts

About $10,000.00 for 1917
5,000.00 " 1918

2. From students, tuition fees, etc.

About 1,000.00 for 1917
500.00 " 1918

3. From local sources --- in area of institution

None

4. From Home Base

4,500.00
9,000.00 from several boards

5. From Board of Foreign Missions

2,000.00 from Methodist Episcopal Board.

6. From other sources

None.

Chosen Christian College
Seoul District
Korea Conference.

XI. Local Governing Body:

1. Number

Legal Board of Control consisting of fourteen. Two thirds of body Missionary and one third native, Japanese and Koreans.

2. Composition

(1) Missionary - 4 Missionaries of M. E. Board
4 " " Presbyterian Board N.
1 " " M.E.Church South
1 " " Canadian Presbyterian

(2) Native

4 - 2 Koreans
2 Japanese

Chosen Christian College
Seoul District
Korea Conference.

XII. Graduates and Non-Graduates:

1. Total

(1) Graduates

No graduates up to the present.

(2) Non-graduates

Between 40 or 50 have attended and now are at work or in other schools in Japan or America.

2. Occupation

Up to the present our students are mostly in church occupations (schools and churches)

3. General Influence:

There is no other missionary college in Seoul and no Government Institution of the kind. It is doing a splendid work.

Chosen Christian College
Seoul District
Korea Conference.

XIII. <u>Constituency</u>:

1. Statistics.

(1) Estimated number of Methodist Christians from which to draw

About 50,000

(2) Estimated number of boys or girls of school age in (1).

At least 10,000 boys and girls.

(3) Estimated number of Christians from which it draws.

Has students from every part of Chosen Methodists as in (1).

(4) Estimated number of boys or girls of school age in (3).

No Material.

2. Problems involved in reaching this Constituency.

The greatest problem we have is to prove to our Christians that our school can give a better training than the other competing schools. It is a problem of proper building equipment and staff. If we can prove our efficiency we can get more capable students than we can take care of easily. As yet our school can not appeal to those who have money because we can not be compared to good schools in Japan or America. The Japanese Government is placing so much stress on education that we must show that we are "up-to-date" and fully qualified to train the youth or we might as well close the doors.

Chosen Christian College
Seoul District
Korea Conference.

XIV. Purpose, Place and Service of this Institution:

1. Purpose: Its aim is to give a college education to the boys and girls of Korea.

2. Place in the educational program of the Mission:

(1) It draws from the Higher Schools.

(2) For what institutions does it prepare.

It is a finishing institution but graduate students can enter the Universities of Japan and America.

3. The social life and educational life are made better by the insitution.

4. There is no Government school of this kind.

Chosen Christian College.
Seoul District
Korea Conference.

XV. **Creating and Developing Native Responsibility:**

1. There are 5 native teachers.

2. For Financial Budget.

(1) Student fees.

Regular fees (12 yen) $6.00 per year per student. Matriculation fee of $2.00. Laboratory fees extra.

(2) Native Support.

As yet there is no native support.

3. For Governing Body

1/3 of the Board of Control are Natives.

4. For Christian Leadership in the Church and Nation.

The aim of the school is to produce leaders for the dhurch and the nation; and already many of our students are in positions of responsibility.

Choson Christian College
Seoul District
Korea Conference

XVI. Institutions of Other Denominations:

1. There are no other institutions of this grade in the territory.

2. This institution is responsible for practically all the Koreans.

3. There can be no overlapping.

Chosen Christian College
Seoul District
Korea Conference

XVII: **Needs and Askings:**

The following are the plans for a permanent plant for the Chosen Christian College:-

I. To be provided at once:

Grounds	$40,000
Main Building	45,000
Dormitory & Dining Hall (100)	15,000
Power Plant, Heating, Lighting	25,000
Astronomical Building	10,000
Four Missionary Residences	12,000
Three Residences for Japanese teachers	3,000
Three Residences for Korean teachers	3,000
Industrial Building and Equipments	20,000

II. Additional Buildings:

Gymnasium and Athletic field	20,000
Library	25,000
Chapel and Theological Building	20,000
Engineering Building	50,000
Chemical Building	50,000
Agricultural Building	25,000
Dormitories	15,000
4 Residences	12,000
10 Assistant Teacher's Residences	10,000

III. Endowment (Invest in adjacent fields for permanent income: 50,000

450,000

The Methodist Episcopal Church should raise one-third or $150,000.

Four (4) native teachers are needed in 1918, two (2) in 1919, 1920 1921, 1922. A missionary teacher is needed in 1921,1922.

The institution would be complete and able to do excellent work with that equipment.

A. W.

-1-

Explanation of the Status of the
Chosen Christian College

By Arthur L. Becker
February, 1918.

The Government provides (a) Lower Common School of 4 years in which only pupils 8 years of age, able to read and write Korean are allowed to enroll (so below this there is the Kindergarten or unclassified Elementary Schools (Keul Bange) which give one or two years training), (b) A Higher Common School of 4 years into which only the Lower Common School graduates are enrolled.

In these schools:-

(a) The quality of the students is of the best (selected by entrance examination).

(b) Only the best trained teachers are employed.

(c) The buildings are up to date, sanitary, and built so as to be fully serviceable for school work.

(d) The equipment is very complete; in fact, there seems to be a superabundance.

(e) The discipline is strict, in fact, almost military, yet it gets good results.

(f) The methods of teaching are intensive and most effective for training the Korean character.

(g) The school work requires the attendance of the pupil six hours per day for about 11 months per year; this would naturally tend to shorten the years of the course necessary to finish a given curriculum.

Some of the Mission Schools which are still on the old basis give about 10 years to the work given in the Government Schools in

8 years, but all these Mission Schools are handicapped by the following conditions:-

1. Inferior quality of pupils as they must (or do) take any who apply.
2. A lower grade of poorly paid, mostly untrained teachers.
3. Poorly equipped school buildings; many places without even proper buildings, let alone equipment.
4. Poor discipline.
5. 'Hit or miss' methods, as many schools are managed by those who know very little about the training of children or the young.
6. Intensive training almost altogether lacking.
7. Usually the curriculum calls for a shorter number of hours per day and only 9 or 10 months per year.
8. They are working on a system which is contrary to the wishes of the Government, hence can get no assistance from this quarter.

Looking at the above, it will not be difficult to understand why students applying for entrance to the Seoul College are all put on the same basis and expected to take the same entrance examination whether the applicant is a graduate from the so-called 'Mission High School' or the Government standardized Higher Common School, and the Chosen Christian College has found out in the last two years that quite as many High School graduates fail to pass the entrance examinations as those from the Government Higher Common Schools; among those enrolled in our present Freshman Class which numbers (37), (18) are from High Common Schools, (13) are from Mission High Schools, (5) are from Special Schools, and (1) is from a Government Agricultural College. No advance credit could be allowed any candidates on enrollment.

The educational Department of Chosen considers that their Higher Common Schools give better training than any Mission High School and the quality and ability of students in the college classes have led us to the same opinion. It is unthinkable that any graduate of a Government Higher School would go to any Mission High School, existing in Korea today, to take a two years' finishing course.

The Seoul Chosen Christian College has four highly specialized courses in which about half of the time is given to special subjects which would not appear in an Arts College course, and in these courses only three years is required; in two courses, four years is required; one is a regular Arts College course, and one is an Electrical Engineering Course. If any one will study the subjects given in any one of these courses, they must concede that the curriculum gives a full college training along the special line of the course. We calculate that it would take at least 12 years for any student to finish all the different courses in the school. Advanced students in certain departments have changed to other courses and been reduced one or two years in their courses; a graduate of a Government Agriculture College is now studying as a Freshman in the Bible Department. Of course, one cannot compare the Departments, one with another, because the work in each is so different, but the standard of the work in each course is college work.

Of course, the subjects and the number of years named in a

curriculum do not determine the standard of the institution, the ability of the teachers, equipment, etc. does much more to determine this. This we realize, and have obtained (or expect to obtain in the near future) highly trained specialized teachers for every qualification and special departments,

1. B. W. Billings, M.A., English and Bible.
2. A. L. Becker, M. A., Physics and Mathematics.
3. ?. A. Weller, (Elec. Engineer, Ohio) Elec. Engineering.
4. H. H. Underwood, M. A., English and Psychology.
5. S. Paik, (Brown Univ.) B. A., Commercial Department.
6. Root Lee, (Nebraska Univ.) B. A., Chemistry.
7. N. Wakai, (Imperial Univ.) History and Language.
8. K. Ichijima, (Imperial Univ., Japan) Agricultural Department.
9. Yamamoto, (Higher Normal, Tokyo) Language.
10. J. L. Gerdine, Bible.

Those expected in the near future are:-

1. An Imperial University Graduate (Japanese) for Law and Commerce.
2. A Missionary appointed by the Presbyterian Board for the Bible Department.
3. E. H. Miller for the Chemistry Department.
4. Mr.................for English (Missionary teacher appointed by the Canadian Presbyterian Board).

We are rapidly equipping our School and now have about $15 000 worth of apparatus and equipment; sufficient apparatus to carry on the grades we are teaching at present (we are only teaching the beginning grades in each department).

The college at Pyeng Yang cannot give specialized training on its present curriculum and even though it gives 4 or 5 years, it cannot give a practical training which can be compared to that of the specialized technical courses of 3 or 4 years given in the Chosen Christian College.

We feel with reason that we can with our Force, Equipment and Present Status do, to say the least, just as high standard work as that done at the Pyeng Yang College. We should within the next few years, be able to turn out graduates that ought to be even better equipped for the Actual problems of developing Korea and the Church.

And one other thing must not be forgotten, the present Mission School system still adhered to in Pyeng Yang and in some other places clearly and definitely, is only temporary and limited and it can be only carried on at present under the sufferance of the Government; and it is a system which is out of touch with the whole political, social, and industrial training of the Korea people which is being worked out carefully, comprehensively and thoroughly by the Government-General of Chosen. So nothing of a permanent nature in Christian Education in Chosen can be built on this sand of uncertainty.

On the other hand, the college at Seoul is building on Bed-Rock with the cordial sympathy and hearty cooperation of all those who are thoroughly in touch with the needs of Korea whether such ones be Foreigners, Japanese, or Koreans. The students are satisfied that they are being given the best, and although (52) of our present students are graduates of Mission High Schools, yet they are fully satisfied that they are getting all that is coming to them and their classification on the basis of College work. There are two boys from Southern Presbyterian territory in the college, both graduates of Mission High Schools; they have had nothing to say about the low standard of the work done here in the Chosen Christian College of Seoul.

History of the Evolution of the
Chosen Christian College

By Authur L. Becker,
February 1918.

In 1912 the M. E. Mission reviewed the Educational Situation in Chosen and decided that the time had come to establishment "One Union College" for all Korea and invited the other Missions to cooperate at Seoul. The matter was brought up in the 'Educational Senate (in which all missions were then represented) but, as it was difficult for the missions to agree on the location the Senate refered the matter to the Joint Committee of the Boards in America. This body, after getting considerable correspondence from all sections of Korea, finally rendered a decision in favor of Seoul As soon as this decision was rendered the M. E. Mission authorized the beginning of a preparatory college class in the Pai Chai High School Building in Seoul under the direction of A. L. Becker; Dr. H. G. Underwood, cooperated as far as possible altho his mission did not accept the Joint Committee's decision as final and decided to continue the college work at Pyeng Yang.

In 1914 Union College was started under the direction of a Provisional Committee consisting of members of the M. E. Mission, the M. E. Mission South and members of the Presbyterian Mission of Seoul: Dr. Underwood was elected Provisional President. Every effort was made to get the cooperation of the other missions but there was such a strong prejudice in favor of the Pyeng Yang College that a complete Union could not be affected. Until a proper registeration and a legal status could obtained, permission was granted by the Government to begin college work under an old charter of the J.P.

Noble's training school. The actual school work was begun in rented rooms at the Y. M. C. A. building and during 1914, 1915 and 1916 an average of 70 students were in attendance and the course of study approximated that of the American College. Dr. Underwood secured money by which we were enabled to buy about $5000.00 worth of equipment and during this time we secured the services of two Japanese teachers both graduates of Imperial University of Japan and these with the five Missionary teachers and two Korean teachers, graduates of American Colleges, made up the faculty.

In 1916, the school suffered the severe loss of Dr. Underwood who died in America; Dr. O. R. Avison was elected to fill his place as President.

In April 1917 we were enabled by the Government to open school as a Registered College of six Departments:-

1. Bible Course.
2. Electrical Engineering Course.
3. Commercial Course.
4. Agricultural Course.
5. Chemical and Technological Course.
6. Literary Course.

The teachers are as follows:-

1. B. W. Billings, M. A. English and Bible (Vice President).
2. A. L. Becker, M. A., Physics and Mathematics (Dean).
3. C. A. Keller, (Elec. Engineer, Ohio) Elec. Engineering.
4. H. H. Underwood, M. A., English and Psychology.
5. S. Pack, (Brown Univ.) Ph. B., Commercial Department.
6. Root Lee, (Nebraska Univ.) B. A., Chemistry.
7. N. Takai, (Imperial Univ. Japan) History and Language.
8. K. Ichijima, (Imperial Univ. Japan) Agricultural Department.
9. Yamagata, (Higher Normal, Tokyo) Japanese.
10. M. Jack, M.A., B. D., English (Canadian Presbyterian)

During 1917 school has been held as formerly in the Y. M. C. A. but over 200 acres of beautifully wooded land has been purchased near the city and the architect's plans for the "lay out" are nearing completion and a temporary building will be built early in 1918 so that from 1918 the Chosen Christian College Work can be carried on in its own building.

Contributions aotaling $125000.00 have already been secured and the President, Dr. Avison, is now in America in order to get a more complete cooperation with home Boards and Churches.

Four Mission Boards are now actually cooperating in the college Methodist Episcopal Board, the Presbyterian Board, the Canadian Presbyterian Board and the Board of the M. E. Mission South.

All interested in this institution believe that it is destined to be one of the greatest factors in the Development of Korea, and see the "Hand of God" in the establishment of the Chosen Christian College in Seoul the capital and largest city of Korea.

10. 에비슨 교장의 협력이사회 제출 특별 보고서

문서 제목	Chosen Christian College at Seoul Korea
문서 종류	교장 보고서
작성 시기	1918년 4~7월 사이
작성 장소	뉴욕 (추정)
작 성 자	Oliver R. Avison
수 신 자	협력이사회(Cooperating Board, 뉴욕)의 일부 회원들 (추정)
페이지 수	6
출 처	Korea Mission Records, 1904~1960, Box 15, Folder 19 (PHS)

자료 소개

에비슨 2대 교장이 학교에 대한 후원을 요청할 목적으로 미국에서 1918년 4~7월 사이에 작성한 학교 현황 보고서이다. 에비슨은 조선기독교대학의 부교장으로 있다가 1916년 10월 언더우드가 사망하자 1917년 2월 이사회에서 교장으로 선임되었다. 그는 언더우드의 뒤를 이어 총독부의 새 교육법에 따라 대학설립 인가를 새로 받기 위해 노력하여 그해 4월 7일 '사립연희전문학교'와 재단법인 설립 허가를 받았다. 그 후에는 캠퍼스의 조성에 주력하였는데, 이 일에 많은 자금이 필요하여 협력이사회(Cooperating Board)에 지원을 요청하기 위해 보고서를 작성하였다. 그 내용과 마지막 서명 부분("Issued by O. R. Avison President")은 이 보고서가 건축 문제를 위한 회의자료로 작성된 것임을 짐작할 수 있게 한다.

이 문서에 연도와 일자가 나타나 있지는 않지만, 북장로회 선교부가 이 문서를 보관 처리할 때 찍은 1쪽 오른편 상단 도장의 일자가 "1918년 7월 8일"로 되어있어 그 전에 작성되었음을 알 수 있다. 5쪽에는 임시교육관으로 쓰는 건물(치원관)이 있다는 내용이 들어있어, 이 글이 치원관이 완공된 4월 이후에 작성되었음을 알 수 있다. 그러므로 작성 시기는 4월에서 7월 사이가 된다.

에비슨은 연희전문과 세브란스의전을 위한 후원금 모금 등의 여러 문제를 해결하기 위해 미국에 가서 1917년 11월 말부터 1918년 8월 말까지 서울을 떠나 있었다. 그는 뉴욕에서 5월 10일 자로 뉴욕에 있는 북감리회 선교부의 총무인 노스(Frank M. North)에게 보낸 편지에서 "당신이 내일 받을 서류에서 보게 되겠지만"이라고 하면서 연희전문의 건축 문제를 언급하였다. 그는 이 편지를 보내고 나서 그 "다음 주 월요일"(5월 13일) 언더우드의 형(John T. Underwood)의 사무실에서 어떤 "중요한 회의"(에비슨, 노스, 언더우드 외의 참석자들은 미상)를 하였고, 이 회의에서 존 T. 언더우드가 언더우드관의 건축비를 기부하기로 약속하였다. 에비슨이 만일 이 회의에 제출하기 위해 이 문서를 작성하였다고 가정한다면, 작성 장소는 뉴욕이고 작성 시기는 5월이 된다.

이 보고서는 서언과 아래의 8가지 항목들로 구성되어 있다.

협력이사회 구성, 캠퍼스 부지, 학과, 대학이사회, 교지 배치도, 필요 자금, 학교 현황, 교수, 결어.

내용 요약

서언: 이 대학은 '한국을 위한 기독교 연합대학'(Union Christian College for Korea)이자 '한국 기독교 종합대학의 출발'(the beginning of the Christian University of Korea)이다. [에비슨은 첫 문장에서 이같이 선언하여 1914년 합동위원회가 이 대학을 'University'로 세우기로 결의하였던 사실을 유념하도록 압박하려 하였던 것 같다.]

협력이사회: 협력이사회의 이사장은 존 T. 언더우드, 총무는 스코트, 자산 · 재정위원장은 세브란스, 실행위원장은 존스이다.

캠퍼스 부지: 서울에서 3마일 떨어진 거의 300에이커의 땅에 산과 계곡과 아름다운 숲과 풍부한 화강암이 있다.

학과: 학생들의 기독교적 인격을 함양하고 한국사회의 모든 부분에 영향을 주기 위해 6개 학과가 개설되었는데, 의과는 세브란스의전이 있으므로 만들 필요가 없다.

대학이사회: 이사회는 선교사 11명, 한국인 2명, 일본인 2명으로 구성되어 있고, 등록생은 94명이다.

교지 배치도: 캠퍼스의 숲이 우거진 산들 사이에 지금과 향후 20년 동안 필요한 건물들을 짓고 향후 50년에서 100년 동안 발전해가면서 수천 명의 학생을 배출할 넉넉한 경사지가 있다. 넓은 운동장 터, 기숙사들과 교수 사택들을 짓게 될 숲이 우거진 산지, 50평 이상의 농지, 접근성을 높이는 부지 남쪽의 철로와 기차역, 급수시설로 활용될 산속 샘들, 12,000그루 이상의 큰 소나무들이 있다.

건물 배치도의 1호에는 행정용 건물로서 교장실, 학감실, 회계사무실, 집회실, 도서관, 사무실, 신과 교실이 들어갈 것이다. 2호에는 이학관[아펜젤러관]으로 실험실, 강의실, 과학교육 기자재실, 박물관이 들어갈 것이다. 3호에는 문과와 다른 과들의 교실, 강의실이 들어가고 지하에는 전체 캠퍼스의 중앙난방, 조명, 전력 시설이 설치될 것이다.

조혼 풍습으로 많은 기혼 학생이 수학 기간에 부인과 수년간 별거하다가 돌아가는 문제가 발생하고 있다. 이런 문제를 해결하기 위해 기숙사의 일부를 기혼 학생 부부가 사는 한국인 마을, 곧 '모범촌'(model village)으로 만들려고 한다.

(캠퍼스 조성과 학교 운영에 필요한 비용의 명세를 제시하고 있다.)

학교 현황: 예상 부지의 절반 이상을 구입하였고, 교육관으로 쓰는 농업관용 건물[치원관]을 하나 지어놓고 있다. 스팀슨관 건축을 1918년 가을에 시작할 예정이고[실제로는 1919년 4월에 건축 시작], 학관[언더우드관], 이학관, 교수 사택들, 기숙사들을 짓기를 희망하고 있다.

교수: 선교사 교수는 7명인데, 곧 10명으로 늘어날 것이다. 일본인 교수는 2명이고 한국인 교수는 1명이다. 한국인 조교수가 2명이고, 전임강사로 일본인 2명과 한국인 몇 명이 있고, 그밖에 파트타임 강사들이 있다. [명단은 없이 숫자만 개괄하고 있다.]

결어: 기독교 민주주의 세계의 건설을 위해 협력 이사들이 개인적으로나 선교부 또는 협력이사회를 통해 투자해주기를 요청한다.

O R Avison 1918?

CHOSEN CHRISTIAN COLLEGE
AT SEOUL KOREA

It is the Union Christian College for Korea, the beginning of the Christian University of Korea.

AFFILIATIONS:

The Foreign Mission Boards of the following churches cooperate in it through a representative Board known as The Cooperating Board for Christian Education in Chosen.

Presbyterian Church in the U.S.A.
Mr. John T. Underwood, President of the Cooperating Board.
Mr. John L. Severance, Chairman of the Com. on Property and Finance
Rev. Dr. Arthur J. Brown, Sec. Board of Foreign Missions
Rev. George T. Scott, Secretary, Assoc. Sec. Bd. of Foreign Missions.

Methodist Episcopal Church
Rev. Dr. Frank Mason North, Sec. Bd. of Foreign Missions
Rev. Dr. Geo. Heber Jones, Chairman of Exec. Com., Assoc. Sec. of Board of Foreign Missions.
Rev. Dr. John D. Goucher
Mr. Charles Gibson, Albany, N.Y.

Presbyterian Church in the U.S.A., South
Rev. Dr. S. H. Chester, Sec. Exec. Com. for Foreign Missions

Methodist Episcopal Church, South
Rev. Dr. W. W. Pinson, Sec. Board of Missions
Rev. E. H. Rawlings, Sec. Board of Foreign Missions

Presbyterian Church of Canada
Rev. Dr. R. P. Mackay, Sec. Board of Foreign Missions
Rev. Dr. A. Gandier, Principal Knox College (Seminary)

Governmental Relations:

It has a Charter from the Government General of Korea which guarantees its Christian character and places it permanently under the direction of a Board of Managers and Faculty every member of which must be Christian.

Site:

Consists of nearly 300 acres of hills and valleys, beautifully wooded, situated about three miles from the center of the capital of the country, Seoul.
On this site is an abundance of granite which will be used in the college buildings.

Departments:

It is planned to develop Christian Character in its students and to influence every phase of Korean life and to this end offers courses in the following departments:-

Liberal Arts, Bible, Agriculture, Commerce, Applied Mathematics and Applied Chemistry and Physics, other courses to be added later on as evelopment proceeds.

(The already developed Severance Union Medical College made it unnecessary to provide a medical department)

Board of Managers:

Consists of eleven missionaries representing the cooperating missions and four Japanese subjects, two of whom are Japanese and two Korean.

President	Dr. O. R. Avison
Vice-President	Mr. B. W. Billings
Secretary	Mr. H. H. Underwood
Treasurer	Mr. J. F. Genso

The College is now in its fourth year and has 94 regular students enrolled, - 49 of whom are Freshmen chosen from a large group of applicants.

Judging by the number who apply for admission, it is evident the opportunity for giving a Christian training to the young men of Korea is great. Up to the present, all our students have been Christians at the time of their admission. Though we are not averse to admitting a certain proportion of others, the number of Christian applicants has been so large that we have preferred to give them the first opportunity for study in the College.

We send with this the following:

1. Diagram of the Site. This shows in a general way how the site is being laid out, although, since this drawing was made, several changes have been determined on, such as locating the dormitories on the hill to the left and the residences on the hills to the right and some others.

Special Features:

The beautiful campus away up amongst the wooded hills on natural terraces, with space not only for the buildings needed now and during the next twenty years, but for whatever may be required for even several thousands of students if the developments of the next 50 or even 100 years should produce them.

The extensive Athletic Fields, sufficiently large for many games at one time.
The fine wooded hills on one side for dormitories and on the other for teachers' residences.
The 50 acres or more of agricultural fields of such variety that students in that department can be trained in every variety of farming, afforestation, fruit raising, stock raising and dairying.
The main line of railway through the country will pass through the lower end of our property and a station will afford easy access to the college from every part of the land.
A series of springs on the hills far above the campus will afford a supply of water for all purposes.
There are more than 12,000 large pine trees on the hills.

2. Bird'-eye view of the Campus showing some of the college buildings nestling amongst the pineclad hills.

Our plan is to begin with the buildings marked 1, 2, and 3, which will constitute an attractive group from almost the very start and these will also afford sufficient accommodation for several hundreds of students.

No. 1 will be the Administration Building and will contain the offices of President, Dean and Treasurer, an Assembly Hall, a Library and the offices and classrooms of the Biblical Department.

No. 2 will be Science Hall in which will be all the necessary Laboratories, Lecture Rooms and Accessory Rooms for teaching Chemistry, Physics and Biology, together with rooms for the Museums for those subjects.

No. 3 will house the Class Rooms, Lecture Rooms and all the facilities for teaching the Liberal Arts and developing all the other departments until they grow to require special buildings.
A sub-basement in this building will house the Central Heating, Lighting and Power Plant for the whole Campus.

Nos. 3,4,& 5 are perspective elevations of the three buildings described above.
3 and 4 will each be 114 ft. long by 41 ft. broad, while 5 will be 200 ft. long and about the same width as the others or perhaps slightly wider.
No.5 will have an open archway of sufficient width going right through it to open up a vista of the buildings and hills beyond.

Unique Feature;

One of the sad and unfortunate side results of our educational work in the Orient has been the fact that our schools have been planned for the education of young men without reference to whether they are married or single and for only unmarried young women, and, as practically all the young men are married at an early age, the result has been to leave the young wives of our students without any education so that after a separation of years the educated young men go home to ignorant wives and the equilibrium of the home is greatly distrubed. This will be the case during all the years to come until the custom of marrying so early in life is gradually changed as it probably will be, though not soon.

To overcome this great disability, we propose to break away in part from the usual dormitory sustem so far as to replace part of our dormitories with a group of small Korean homex which will constitute a Korean village in which married students who desire to dos o may rent a house and bring their families with them so as to obviate the separation and in this village to have a school for students' wives where the wives may receive as much education as may be possible under the circumstances so that when the husbands have completed their courses they may have wives who will be companions for them and helpers in whatever life work they may enter and so we hope to offset, in some measure, the serious results of former methods.

We further propose to make this village a "model village" and an object lesson to the studnets in many ways of which the following are now in mind;-

Proper methods of laying out a small town
" " " constructing streets that can be kept drained and clean
Best methods of draining and sanitation that can be adapted to Korean conditions in various parts of the country.
Improved methods of constructing their houses so as to make them easier to ventilate, to keep free from vermin, etc.
Planning and construction of a Primary School Building.
Model Korean Church, the architecture of which may be suggestive to the students when they go out into their several fields.
Methods of municipal government as applied to towns and villages and in accord with the laws governing the country.

In brief the whole plan of the Institution will be to train young men and women to make the best use of their lives in connection with their home conditions and to enable them to gradually introduce into the life of Korea such improvements as will elevate the mass of the people and promote the development of the highest type of manhood and womanhood.

While not neglecting the solid foundation of an education through the liberal arts and sciences, we shall lay great stress upon a training in industry and all the practical things of Korean life so that the graduates will go out prepared to meet the conditions that will face them and not be separated from the real life of Korea by long years of mere book study.

Needs.

The immediate needs are as follows;

1. Fund of $25,000 to $30,000 for the erection and equipment of the Science Building.

2. Several sums of $4500 to $5000 each to erect residences for the missionary teachers who must live out there from the earliest possible moment so as to be most helpful to the students.

3. Several sums of $2500 each for the erection of residences for the Japanese and Korean professors.

4. Several sums of $1500 each for residences for Associate Professors.

5. Several sums of $1000 each for residences for Korean Instructors.

6. Fund of $15,000 to $20,000 for the upbuilding of the Model Village.

7. Several sums of $7500 each for the erection of Dormitory U nits.

Other projects which must have early attention;

Athletic Field and Gymnasium, Building for Chapel, Y.M.C.A. and Students' Activities, Observatory, Central Heating, Lighting and Power Plant, Water Supply, Drainage System.

8. A very pressing need felt from the beginning will be a fund for meeting the current expenses which will inevitably increase year by year during the first few years especially.

The increased amounts to be raised over and above the present revenues are estimated as

1919-20	$6000
1920-21	7000
1921-22	10000
1922-23	11000

These increases will be caused by

1. Increased cost of service, heat, etc., as the new buildings are erected.
2. Increased number of teachers as the students increase in number and the several departments get into full swing.

Present Status;

Land;

More than half of the site has been bought and paid for and the rest is in process of being purchased.

Buildings;

One building has been erected on the agricultural side of the site which will eventually be used in connection with the agricultural work but is now being used as a Recitation Hall and will continue to be so used until the first permanent building (the Charles Stimson Building) has been erected and equipped, which we hope to accomplish by September, 1919.

The Charles Stimson Building will be begun in the Fall of 1918. It is to be the Administration Building as described above but will have to be used as a class room building in part until a second has been erected.

As mentioned above, we hope to follow the erection of this building at once with the Liberal Arts Building and the Science Hall, both of which should be completed not later than 1921 or 1922.

A fund for residences has been started but it is insufficient for even the first group which should consist of the following:

4	residences	at	$4500	each
4	"	"	2500	"
4	"	"	1500	"
2	"	"	1000	"
			$38000	Total

Dormitories are just as urgent as residences for without them the students must either walk the three miles from the city every morning and evening or be housed in the far from clean village houses scattered more or less near the College Site.

Faculty;

Seven Missionary Professors are now teaching and we expect that number will be increased to ten within a short time. These men give all their time to the work of the institution. Two Japanese full professors and one Korean full professor give all their time also. Two Korean Associate professors are also on the faculty as full time workers. Two other Japanese and some Koreans rank as Instructors and several other missionaries and Koreans give part time as Instructors in special subjects.

-6-

The above is a brief outline of the present standing and immediately future development of the Chosen Christian College, and, if it interests you as an opportunity for the investment of some of the funds you wish to use in the building up of the worldwide Christian Democracy which is the only world state which we can look forward to with complacency, you may give either through your own church's Foreign Mission Board which is the preferable method, or directly to the Cooperating Board, of which the Secretary and Treasurer is Rev. George T. Scott, 156 Fifth Avenue, New York City.

Issued by

O. R. Avison
President

11. 에비슨 교장의 이사회 제출 연례보고서

문서 제목	Chosen Christian College, President's Annual Report to Field Board of Managers
문서 종류	교장 보고서
제출 시기	1919년 2월 14일
작성 장소	서울
제 출 자	Oliver R. Avison
수 신 자	이사회
페이지 수	3
출 처	Korea Mission Records, 1904~1960, Box 15, Folder 17 (PHS) 2114-5-2: 06 Board of Managers 1915~1922 (UMAH)

자료 소개

에비슨 교장이 1919년 2월 14일 열린 이사회 연례회의에 제출한 보고서이다. PHS와 UMAH, 두 곳의 문서가 모두 똑같은 모습을 보인다. 둘 다 끝부분에 서명이 없고, 2쪽과 3쪽의 왼쪽 상단에 "C.C.C. Pres.'s Annual Report 2/14/19'라는 머리말이 있다.

당시에는 학년이 4월 1일에 시작되었으므로 2월에 열린 이사회 회의는 한 해의 학교 운영과 교육 활동을 종합 정리하는 시간이었다. 이 보고서에서 에비슨은 지난 일과 현안을 함께 다루는 가운데 학교의 건축계획이 본격적 이행되기 시작하는 모습을 보여주었다.

에비슨은 이 보고서에서 항목 설정 없이 아래의 사항들을 설명하였다.

모범촌 부지확보, 급수시설 설치, 학교 홍보 팸플릿 준비, 학교 진입로 학보, 건축감독 선정, 도서 구입, 문과와 신과 통합, 북감리회에서 제공한 자본금 사용, 스팀슨관 건축을 위한 건축업자 계약 체결, 교과서 구입 기금 마련, 존 언더우드의 건축기금과 언더우드관 건축비 1차 분할금 지급, 협력이사회 회의록 내용.

내용 요약

모범촌 부지: 지난 이사회 회의에서 한옥 마을[모범촌]의 일부가 될 한옥들을 몇 채 지어 학생들을 수용하는 문제를 논의하고 동남쪽 땅을 부지로 선정하였다. [그곳은 지금의 의대 자리로 추정된다.] 이에 우리 땅 남쪽에 있는 동양척식회사의 땅을 살 필요가 생겨

매입을 시도하였으나, 동척 측이 그곳은 철도의 제방을 쌓는 흙을 파낼 땅이라는 이유로 팔기를 거절하였다. 우리가 흙을 파내기에 좋은 학교 땅과 바꾸자고 제의했으나, 그들이 역시 거절하였다. [모범촌은 이 자료집 10번 보고서에서 설명된 것과 같이 기혼 학생이 많았던 당시 상황에 대처하는 방안으로, 학생 부부가 재학 중에 장기간 별거하다가 가정이 깨지는 것을 막고 학생들이 마을 공동체를 스스로 운영하는 체험을 하여 사회 발전을 도모할 역량을 기르기 위해 조성하는 주택 단지였다. 그들은 그러는 한편으로 한국인 교수들의 사택을 그 근처에 지어 학생들을 감독하게 하려 하였다.]

급수시설: 이사회의 결정에 따라 급수시설을 일부 설치하였다.

홍보 팸플릿: 학교 홍보 팸플릿을 신과 교수 로즈(Harry A. Rhodes)가 만들어 배부하였다.

캠퍼스 진입로: 철로 가설공사가 캠퍼스 진입로의 확보를 방해하여 우리가 이 문제의 해결을 위해 노력하고 있다.

건축감독: 머피 앤 다나(Murphy & Dana) 건축회사가 만든 주요 건물들의 설계도와 시방서에 따라 건축을 진행하도록 건축가 베이커(Norman Baker)에게 건축감독을 맡기는 문제를 검토하고 있다. [실제로는 1919년 베이커가 아닌 루카스(A. E. Lucas)가 부임하여 건축을 감독하고 건축학을 강의하였다.]

도서 구입: 교수회가 도서 구입 목록을 만들었으므로, 이 일의 집행을 위해 이사회가 그들과 상의해주기를 바란다.

문과 · 신과 통합: 지난 이사회에서 제기되었던 문과와 신과의 통합 문제를 교수회가 검토하고 부정적인 결론을 내렸는데, 이에 대해 이사회가 의견을 내주기를 바란다.

북감리회 자본금: 북감리회 선교부가 학교에 주기로 약속했던 $52,000을 현재 조성하고 있다. 우리는 그 기금을 캠퍼스 조성에 필요한 각종 기초공사를 위해 쓰기를 원하고 있다.

건축업자 계약: 스팀슨관 건축을 위해 건축업자인 해리 장(Henry Chang)['Henry'는 'Harry'의 오타이다]과 계약을 체결하였다.

교과서 구입: 졸업반 학생들이 교과서를 마련할 기부금을 요청하여 학교 예산에서 그 비용을 책정할 계획이다.

존 언더우드의 건축기금: 존 언더우드가 현재 진행 중인 건축공사를 위해 $5,000을 보낸 데 이어 언더우드관 건축비의 첫 번째 분할금을 보내기로 하였다.

협력이사회 회의록: 협력이사회에서 보낸 그들의 회의록을 여러분께 제출한다. 그 안에 연희전문의 경상예산을 증액하는 데에 필요 자금을 확보하는 계획을 세우기로 한 내용이 있다.

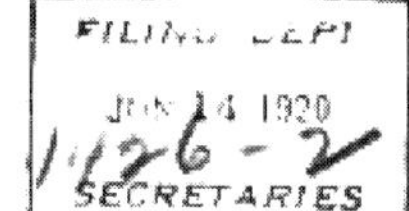

CHOSEN CHRISTIAN COLLEGE

PRESIDENT'S ANNUAL REPORT TO FIELD BOARD OF MANAGERS

February 14, 1919.

One of the matters stressed at the last meeting of the Board was the housing of students, and at that time the Building Committee was directed to proceed at once with the erection of certain Korean houses which would be part of the Korean village.

The first step towards this was the selection of the site for the village. It had been directed that a Committee consisting of those members of the Board who could visit the site immediately after the last Board meeting should have authority to determine upon the entire layout of the site. This Committee selected the south-east section of the site, where the village would be on a gentle slope facing the south and the new railway station, and backed by the hills upon which the residences of the Korean professors and teachers might be built so as to form an integral part of the village. We all think the choice a very happy one.

It seemed necessary in order to plan out the village in anything like an ideal way to purchase certain lots of land lying to the south of our property and owned by the Oriental Development Company. We took steps to purchase this land but were met by a refusal on the part of the Company, the Manager of which stated that those fields had been promised to the Engineering Company engaged in the construction of the railway as locations from which to obtain earth for the embankments. After much effort we secured an interview with the Superintendent of the Engineering Company and arranged to trade locations with them, we to have the lower slopes and they to get the required amount of earth from the hill to the east of the proposed village site. We were then met by a statement from the Oriental Development Company that they themselves had other plans for using those lots, and up to this time we have been unable to come to an agreement with them.

The negotiations in the fall hindered the carrying out of the plan to begin this village before cold weather came on, but a plan for it has been drawn up by Mr. Miller and approved by the Building Committee. This plan, however, was made with the expectation that we could secure the fields referred to above, andif proceeded with before the fields are obtained will have to be somewhat modified, I think. As the Board is now meeting, we would like to submit this plan to the consideration of the Board and get suggestions before going on with it as we hope to do as soon as the weather permits.

We were also directed by the Board to proceed at once with a plan for a water supply. This has been worked out somewhat definitely by Mr. Miller, and I will ask him to report on that matter directly to you.

Mr. Rhodes was appointed a Committee to get up a pamphlet giving briefly such information as could be given about the progress of the Institution. That pamphlet has already been put in your hands, and it is a pleasure to me to be able to say that it has been very well received and has won friends for the Institution.

The construction of the embankment for the railroad has gone on, as you will see if you visit the site, and it has brought with it problems concerning the entrances to our site which have not yet been adjusted to our full satisfaction. The map is here for you to examine, and I shall ask Mr. Miller to explain to you the problems the railroad has brought us and how far we have succeeded in meeting them.

Before Mr. Murphy left the city we discussed the question of a Building Superintendent, and it was decided to investigate as to the advisability of securing Mr. Norman Baker, an architect in New York City, as a member of the faculty, possibly under the Methodist Episcopal Board, to give certain types of instruction in the College and to supervise the erection of the buildings according to the plans and specifications given us by Messrs. Murphy & Dana. No definite word has come to us from New York concerning this matter as yet, but I hope the matter will be arranged in the way indicated, as this would give us a competent Building Superintendent as well as a teacher and missionary.

At a recent meeting of the Faculty, a Faculty Library Committee was appointed to make a list of books which it would be well to purchase, this Committee to work in conjunction with the Library Committee of the Board so as to make the work more effective. I would suggest that the Board's Committee be instructed to confer cordially with the Faculty Committee in making its selection.

The Faculty was instructed by the last Board meeting to consider and report on the question of uniting the Literary and Bible courses in one. The Faculty appointed a Committee of its own to consider the matter, and, if thought advisable, to devise a plan for carrying this out. That Committee, after very careful consideration, reported to the Faculty that such a union would not be in the best interests of the College or of the students. The Faculty adopted their report, and will make certain suggestions to the Board concerning some modifications.

This Board at its last meeting passed a resolution making certain recommendations as to the use of the $52,000 to beprovided by the Methodist Episcopal Board on capital account, and the recommendations were forwarded both to the Methodist Episcopal Board and to the Cooperating Board in New York, I understand that the Methodist Mission here also entered into correspondence with their Board, urging that the funds be appropriated in accordance with the wish of the Field Board. I understand that in the meantime Dr. North had been pushing the Church proposition and has secured pledges for sums aggregating $30,000 for it, and that it was not practicable to accede to the request of this Board and of the Methodist Mission. I regret that Bishop Welch is not here to state the case for the Methodist Board, but in conference with me he suggested that we do not press this matter any further but rather urge the Methodist Board to increase its contribution to the capital funds by adding to the amounts available for foundation work. I am very happy, therefore, to recommend that we ask the Methodist Mission here to cooperate with us in requesting the M. E. Board to appropriate the balance of the $52,000 left after deducting the $30,000 for the Church, and the amount already appropriated towards buildings. This would total $22,000. And that we also ask them for a further sum of money to be usedin the foundational work of the Institution.

We were directed by this Board to sign a contract with Mr. Henry Chang for the erection of the Stimson Building on the basis of the figures reported to the Board at itslast meeting. On going into these figures more carefully, it became evident that some of the amounts estimated by Mr. Murphy for building materials andequipment were too small, and it became necessary to go carefully into the items of the estimate made by Mr. Chang. We therefore informed Mr. Chang that the contract would go to him on the basis of the figures he had given, less certain savings which we hoped to make after mutual conference, Mr. Chang went down with the "Flu" followed by pneumonia, which prevented us from taking matters up with him in detail for many weeks; and since then Mr. Chang has been getting out stone and having stone trim out so as to be ready to go on with the building in the early spring. In the meantime, certain definite figure s were obtainedfor the items which had been merely estimated by Mr. Murphy, and a contract has been entered into with Mr. Chang. The details will be reported by the Property Committee. The Property Committee will also report upon residence sites and roadways to these, and upon other matters it has been working on in the interval.

I have asked the Dean to report upon certain matters concerning the Faculty, graduations, etc. The present graduating class sent in a request to the Faculty for a contribution towards the cost of preparing a class book, and the Faculty asked me to bring the matter to the attention of the Board. The request is for a sum of Fifty Yen from the Budget of the College. Further reference to this will be made in the report of the Executive Committee.

Correspondence from Mr. Underwood, together with a letter from Mr. Scott, Secretary of the Cooperating Board, informs me that Mr. Underwood has paid over the sum of $5,000 to cover the cost of the present building, and that in January he would turn over to the Board the first instalment of the money for the erection of Underwood Hall. With reference to the $5,000 referred to, it will not quite cover the cost of the building for which it is intended at the present rate of exchange, but will do so if the rate drops to 52, which is likely to occur by the time the appropriation reaches us.

I lay before you the Minutes of the recent meeting of the Cooperating Board, together with a letter from the Secretary, Mr. Scott, which I am sure will prove of great interest to you. One of the mostpleasant items to me isthe one reporting that the Finance Committee had been directed to formulate plans for securing increased amounts for the current budget. This to my mind is one of the most important matters as we add new buildings and so increase our opportunities.

12. 베커 학감의 이사회 제출 연례보고서

문서 제목	Chosen Christian College, Dean's Annual Report, February 1919
문서 종류	학감 보고서
제출 시기	1919년 2월 15일
작성 장소	서울
제 출 자	A. L. Becker
수 신 자	이사회
페이지 수	5
출 처	Korea Mission Records, 1904~1960, Box 15, Folder 15 (PHS) 2114-5-2: 06 Board of Managers 1915~1922 (UMAH)

자료 소개

베커 학감이 1919년 2월 14 · 15 · 17일 열린 대학이사회 연례회의의 둘째 날에 제출한 보고서이다. 이 보고서는 제출 시기를 연월만 밝히고 있으나, 이사회 회의록에서 15일 오후에 제출된 사실을 확인할 수 있다.

베커는 이 보고서를 번호 없이 아래의 5개 항목으로 구성하여, 1918년 4월부터 시작된 1년간의 교육 활동을 정리하였다.

등록생, 교육 시설, 교수진, 학과 운영, 졸업생, 기독교 활동.

내용 요약

등록생: 1918년 4월에 48명이 지원하여 40명이 시험에 합격하였는데, 문과 8명, 농과 9명, 수물과 6명, 상과 13명, 신과 4명이다. 2학년 이상으로 올라간 학생들은 총 45명으로 문과 17명(4학년 8명), 수물과 7명(4학년 3명), 상과 16명, 신과 5명이다. 문과, 신과, 상과에서 진급에 실패한 학생들도 있으므로, 전체 학생 수는 95명이다.

시설: 새 학년의 시작에 맞추어 힘들게 마련한 임시교육관이 비좁아져서 크게 불편하지만, 시설은 어느 곳보다 좋다. 기숙사와 교수 사택이 없어 모든 이가 학교와 서울 사이의 2마일 거리를 걸어서 오가고 있다. 소나무 숲의 신선한 공기와 아름다운 경관이 이상적인 교육환경을 제공하지만, 겨울에는 난방을 해도 추위를 막지 못한다.

교수진: 올해에 최고 수준의 교수들이 불편한 환경 속에서 성실하게 가르쳤다. 쓰다(Tsuda), 사무라(Samura), 김영환[원문에서는 'Mr. Kim'으로만 표기되어 있다]이 새로 왔다. 3개 민족[한국인, 일본인, 서양인]의 교수들이 저녁 시간에 교대로 집에 모여 월례회를 갖고 하나가 되어 건설적인 정책을 세우고 있다.

학과: 문과의 교육 목표는 일본어와 영어를 능숙하게 구사하는 학교 교사와 교회 사역자를 길러내는 것이다. 8명이 가르치고 있고, 한국인은 조교수 김영환(음악)과 이노익(생리학), 그리고 이상재(한문)[직급 표시 없음]가 있다. 수물과는 물리학과 수학을 가르쳐서 전기기사와 측량기사로 일하게 하는 것이 목표이고, 이 과정이 매우 어려워 소수의 학생만 이수하므로 졸업생이 앞으로 시간이 갈수록 중요한 자리를 차지하게 될 것이다. 6명이 가르치고 있고, 한국인은 조교수 임용필(물리학), 장세운(삼각법, 전기), 이원철(수학)이 있다. 신과는 교회 사역 지망생들이 신학 수업을 하도록 준비시키는 것이 목표이고, 다음 학기(1919년 봄)부터는 3학년까지 있게 될 것이다. 상과는 훌륭한 재정가, 정확한 회계사, 법의 옹호자, 최상급 비서가 될 기독교인을 양성하는 것과 상인들과 은행가들에게 기독교의 이상을 심어주는 것이 목표이다. 교수 백상규(재정 경제학), 강사 김상옥(상업), 교사 이범일(타자), 일본일 조교수 쓰다(법률)가 가르치고 있다. 농과는 이 나라의 농법이 옛날식인 까닭에 매우 필요한 영감 있는 지도자를 배출하는 것이 목표이고, 학교 캠퍼스를 가꾸는 것도 이들의 일이 될 것이다. 이치지마가 올해 처음으로 학생들을 받아 가르쳤고, 교장의 교지 구입업무를 도왔다.

첫 번째 졸업생을 내는 것을 자랑스럽게 여기고 앞으로 큰 역할을 하게 될 그들을 격려해주자. 졸업생은 김동익, 김한영, 노준탁, 유기준, 전처선, 최상현, 최치완, 홍기원, 강헌집, 김병석, 김원벽, 김형주, 이범일, 문승찬, 박동걸, 정순규, 전종린, 최순탁, 이원철, 임용필, 장세운으로 총 21명이고, 문과생 8명, 상과생 10명, 수물과 3명이다.

학생들의 도덕적, 영적 발전을 위해 신과, 채플 예배, 학생 YMCA, 학생 신앙지도 사역자를 두고 있고, 로즈(H. A. Rhodes)가 1918년 9월부터 신과에서 일하고 있다. 6시간의 정규수업 후에 채플 시간을 갖는데, 모든 학생이 완전히 자유롭게 채플에 오고 있고, 절반 이상 참석하고 있다.

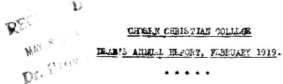

CHOSEN CHRISTIAN COLLEGE

DEAN'S ANNUAL REPORT, FEBRUARY 1919.

* * * * *

Enrollment, April 1918.

48 applicants took the entrance examinations and on faculty recommendation 40 were enrolled; 8 in the Literary Department, 7 in Agriculture Department, 6 in the Engineering Department 15 in the Commercial Department and 4 in the Bible Department. Of those enrolled, 4 were graduates of Pai Chai, 10 were graduates of Methodist Higher Common School of Pyeng Yang, 4 were graduates of Pyeng Yang Soong Sill, 3 were graduates of Su Won Agriculture School.

There were 17 Methodists and 18 Presbyterians. Of the Old Students on faculty action, the advancements in grades were as follows:

Departments	Into 2nd	Into 3rd	Into 4th
Literary	7	2	8
Engineering	3	1	3
Commercial	6	10	
Bible	5		

Two Juniors of the Literary Department were held up and asked to spend a year in making up deficiencies, 3 Sophomores and 2 Freshmen were held back in the same grade. In the Bible Department one Freshman failed to pass. In the Commercial Department three fialed to pass into 2nd grade.
(Total number of Students, 95)

Teaching Equipment

By strenuous effort we managed to get a temporary building ready for use at the opening of the school year. We found that the building was barely sufficient for the actual work of carrying on instructions in several departments and the lack of room for the various activities of the college has made a considerable inconvenience, to say the least, however, the building accommodations were better than could have been possible elsewhere. The fact that we had no dormitories and no residences for teachers on the site, made it necessary for teachers and most of the students to cover a distance of 2 miles from the city at least twice a day. At first the students were dismayed at the prospect of walking this distance each day in all kinds of weather but the good example of the teachers who loyally uncomplaining went back and forth mostly on foot inspired the students so that practically no complaint has been heard and in fact on the other hand many have said that the exercise has made them stronger and better students.

In the spring and fall the delightful pure air filtered through the pine trees and the beauty as well as the quietness of the site was a great help to school work and none of us could go from the dirt and noise of Seoul out to the site without feeling that we were almost in another world in which conditions for study were at least in part ideal; and so we have become more and more and hopeful of a great future for the school in such inspiring surroundings. However, the winter term introduced the problem of heating which could at best only be partially solved and all have had to put up with uncomfortable rooms yet there has been no complaints, for all recognized that for this year this condition was unavoidable.

When we entered the new building, desks, tables, blackboards and cabinets to the value of Yen 606 were provided as teaching equipment for the building. We have added very little new apparatus to the laboratories only Yen 345 worth in all as we have felt that we had no rooms for expansion. We have added Yen 451 worth of well selected books to the library. A small number of maps have been provided.

Teaching Force

We have had by far the best teaching force this yearthat we ever had and the curriculum for the school year has been carried thru with some unimportant exceptions exactly as planned; every teacher has carried out faithfully his allotted share even at considerable inconvience. Mr. Tsuda and Mr. Samura and Mr. Kim all began their work this year. They took up their work so earnestly that they were soon bearing all the varied responsibility of the school as naturally as the older members of the faculty.

In our monthly faculty meetings, which met in the evening and rotated around the homes of the faculty; the three nationalities were merged into one and altho sometimes it took time to get together on some projects, yet we have invariably presented a united front to the students and the policies adopted always proved constructive; I think that there has been no faculty action of 1918 that we need regret. I believe our faculty is exceptional both i n Christian character and ability. We were unfortunate in losing Mr. and Mrs. Weller from our teaching force just as they were making plans to take up full college work but as they left just as the year's work was being planned, we were able to get their work provided for, temporarily, we hope theMethodist Board will soon send a substitute.

DEPARTMENT WORK

1. The Literary Department, This Department gives a "Liberal Arts" course and aims to train school teachers and church workers, who will be especially efficient in the use of the Japanese and English languages. The work of this Department has been carried during the past year as follows:

Prof. B. W. Billings, English (Freshman and Sophomore)
Prof. Milton Jack, English (Juniors & Seniors)
Prof. H. H. Underwood, Phsycology, Sociology, Pedagogy, Ethics
Assistant Yamagata, History & Japanese Literature
Assistant Kim, Vocal and Instrumental Music.
Assistant Root Lee, Physiology
Mr. Lee Sang Chai, Chinese Literature.
Mr. Samura, Japanese & Exercise.

After Prof. Tokai's death, Mr. Yamagata has acceptably carried on the teaching of history and has shown himself able and efficient in school work so that I would like to recommend that Mr. Yamagata be advanced to the rank of Associate Professor. We have tried hard during the year to get a substitute for Prof. Takai but havebeen so far unsuccessful; as this department needs Japanese teacher of the highest qualifications, I hope that our President or the Board of Managers will not relax their efforts to get such a man, even though at this present time we are able to get along with the present teaching force.

There is a feeling among the teachers of the Department that the number of hours given to the study of English is insufficient and I would suggest that some

Our plan is to begin with the buildings marked 1, 2, and 3, which will constitute an attractive group from almost the very start and these will also afford sufficient accommodation for several hundreds of students.

No. 1 will be the Administration Building and will contain the offices of President, Dean and Treasurer, an Assembly Hall, a Library and the offices and classrooms of the Biblical Department.

No. 2 will be Science Hall in which will be all the necessary Laboratories, Lecture Rooms and Accessory Rooms for teaching Chemistry, Physics and Biology, together with rooms for the Museums for those subjects.

No. 3 will house the Class Rooms, Lecture Rooms and all the facilities for teaching the Liberal Arts and developing all the other departments until they grow to require special buildings.

A sub-basement in this building will house the Central Heating, Lighting and Power Plant for the whole Campus.

Nos. 3,4,& 5 are perspective elevations of the three buildings described above.

3 and 4 will each be 114 ft. long by 41 ft. broad, while 5 will be 200 ft. long and about the same width as the others or perhaps slightly wider.

No.5 will have an open archway of sufficient width going right through it to open up a vista of the buildings and hills beyond.

Unique Feature;

One of the sad and unfortunate side results of our educational work in the Orient has been the fact that our schools have been planned for the education of young men without reference to whether they are married or single and for only unmarried young women, and, as practically all the young men are married at an early age, the result has been to leave the young wives of our students without any education so that after a separation of years the educated youhg men go home to ignorant wives and the equilibrium of the home is greatly distrubed. This will be the case during all the years to come until the custom of marrying so early in life is gradually changed as it probably will be, though not soon.

To overcome this great disability, we propose to break away in part from the usual dormitory sustem so far as to replace part of our dormitories with a group of small Korean homex which will constitute a Korean village in which married students who desire to dos o may rent a house and bring their families with them so as to obviate the separation and in this village to have a school for students' wives where the wives may receive as much education as may be possible under the circumstances so that when the husbands have completed their courses they may have wives who will be companions for them and helpers in whatever life work they may enter and so we hope to offset, in some measure, the serious results of formar methods.

We further propose to make this village a "model village" and an object lesson to the studnets in many ways of which the following are now in mind;-

high-class secretaries, as well as furnish merchants and Bankers who have Christian edeals. The work of the department has been carried on the past year by; Prof. S. K. Pack, Head Professor Teacher of Finance Economics and Bookkeeping. T. Tsuda, Associated Professor teacher of Law subjects. Kim Sang Ok, Lecturer, Com. Geography, Commercial Practice. Rhee Pum Yil, teacher of typewriter.

This department needs equipment and more regular teachers and I would recommend that during the coming years efforts be made to add to the two professors above, -

(a) A Foreign Professor to teach Com. English, typewriting.
(b) A Native " " " Commerce, Commercial Geography
Commercial Japanese.

5. Agriculture Department: This department has a great field of activity in that Chosen is as yet an agriculture country of the old type and is greatly in need of inspirational leadership along this line; and along with this larger duty, the care and development of the college site will naturally fall upon this department. The aim is not to produce just mechanical farmers but to fill the students with a vision of the possibilities of development of "the most direct God-given means of livelihood" and happiness.

The department took in its first class of students this year so that Prof. Ichijima, head of this department, has been able to carry the work alone. Besides this teaching Mr. Ivhijima hastaken charge of the site property and helped the president in his purchases of land. The care and use of the 20000 pine trees on the site has been no small part of the responsibility of this department. A small farm was developed on the site during the year by the aid of the agriculture students and the sale of the produce was so gratifying that we look forward to this becoming the best market-garden of the city during the year. The teachers of the college were especially glad to get fine strawberries and celery from this garden. Mr. Ichijima spent the entire summer personally looking after this college farm while the rest of the faculty were resting. We owe him our thanks.

As this new year will add a new class and new responsibilities to this department it is imperative that an assistant teacher be added to the faculty and I would recommend that an appropriate man be employed immediately. I would like also to recommend that Prof. Jack be also asked to prepare for work in this department.

GRADUATES

This is our first graduating class; the first fruit of five years of college work in Seoul and we can be proud of everyone of them for they have been tested and drilled as no college students in Chosen have been trained before. We believe that they will all make good and do much for future Chosen. At least 1/3 have very exceptional ability and character and have been trusted with considerable responsibility already. Let us help and encourage them all we can because the conduct of these men in the next ensuing years will mean much for the reputation of the college. They are listed below:-

C.C.C. Dean's Annual Report Feb. 1919. -5-

Name	Department	Age	Yrs. in College	Probable Occupation 1919
Kim Tong Yik	Literary	22	5	School Work
Kim Han Yung	"	29	5	" "
Noh Chun Taik	"	35	5	Secretary
Ryu Keui Choon	"	25	5	Y.M.C.A. or Church
Chun Cho Son	"	29	5	School Work
Choi Song Hyun	"	29	5	Church work or study
Choi Chi Wan	"	25	5	School work
Hong Keui Won	"	24	5	Study in Japan or U.S.
Kang Heun Chip	Commercial	26	5	Secretary and Typist
Kim Pyung Suk	"	23	5	Business
Kim Won Pyuk	"	26	5	School or Church
Kim Hyung Choo	"	31	5	School Work
Rhee Pom Yil	"	23	5	Secretary & Typist
Moon Seung Chan	"	26	5	Interpreter
Pak Tong Kol	"	24	5	School or Church
Cheung Soon Kyu	"	24	5	School Work
Chun Chong Lin	"	30	5	Business or School
Choi Soon Taik	"	24	5	Bank Business
Reigh Won Chul	Engineering	22	5	School Work (College)
Yim Yong Pill	"	28	5	" " "
Chung See Woon	"	26	5	" " "

CHRISTIAN ACTIVITIES

As a Christian institution we have several activities aimed to the moral and spiritual development of the students; these are; the Bible department, the chapel services, the student Y.M.C.A. and a special worker who does "personal work" with the students. As Mr. Rhodes did not get into the work before September last the work of his department was not fully developed during the year but since Mr. Rhodes' arrival he has enthusiastically taken up plans for making his department a means to the spiritual development of the whole student body and hopes to use his assistant this coming year so as to keep in personal touch with every student.

At the chapel services Mr. Billings has had a difficult task to draw students who were not only tired after 6 hours study, but largely employed after school hours in various tasks; it has been up hill business but, in spite of the obstacles and the fact that every student was absolutely at liberty to come or to stay away, Mr. Billings is to be congratulated that the average attendance at the chapel service has been considerably more than half the enrollment. And owing to the very fact that only those who wish to do so come, the ones who did come listened attentively to the earnest exhortations of Mr. Billings and the other teachers; so that the chapel exercises habe been a decided help to the spiritual life of the school.

The Y.M.C.A. of the college has been an outlet for the spiritual and social aspirations of the students and nothing but a decided good has come out of their meetings and work; and many of the leaders have taken their responsibility very seriously and have done their best to lift up the ideals of the student body. This organization has petitioned the college Board of Managers to help them employ a regular secretary and I commend this to your attention. There can be no doubt of the value of this Christian organization for it appeals strongly to the students.

(The complete catalogue of students' names, addresses, ages, affiliations, etc., is omitted in this copy.)

13. 에비슨 교장의 북장로회 미국 선교부 제출 특별 보고서

문서 제목	Information Blank of Higher Educational Institutions Related to the Board of Foreign Missions of the Presbyterian Church in the U.S.A.
문서 종류	교장 보고서
제출 시기	1919년 10월 30일
작성 장소	서울
제 출 자	O. R. Avison
수 신 자	이사회
페이지 수	5
출 처	Korea Mission Records, 1904~1960, Box 15, Folder 17 (PHS)

자료 소개

에비슨 교장이 1919년 10월 30일 북장로회 선교부에 제출한 질의응답서였을 것으로 추정된다. 문서만 보아서는 그 목적과 용도를 알 수 없으나, 비슷한 시기에 오간 다른 문서들을 통해 짐작할 수 있다. 북장로회 선교부의 보조 총무인 스코트는 1919년 4월 24일 자로 세브란스의전의 이사들에게 편지를 보내 세계교회협력운동(Interchurch World Movement) 수죄 측의 질의서를 발송하겠다고 공지하였다. 세계교회협력운동은 북장로회가 1차 대전 후의 세계선교를 위해 미국의 여러 교단을 초청하여 개최함으로써 1919년 1월부터 1921년 4월까지 진행된 초교파적인 선교 캠페인이었다. 북장로회 선교부는 이 대회에서 모금한 돈을 세브란스의전과 연희전문에도 지원해줄 생각에서 두 학교에 질의서를 보내 학교에 필요한 것을 알려달라고 하였다. 이에 세브란스의전 이사회는 9월 회의 때 운동 주최 측에 1만 불의 기부를 요청하자는 의견을 나누고 한센병과 결핵 치료사업을 사용처 항목에 넣기로 결의하였다. 그 후 에비슨은 북장로회 선교부에 보낸 10월 3일 자 편지에서 세브란스의전은 질의서 작성을 마무리하고 있다고 설명하였다. 연희전문 측은 $599,100의 자본금과 $500,000의 기본재산을 제공해주도록 요청하였다(차례 번호 14번 에비슨이 1920년 2월 21일에 쓴 글 참조). 이후의 일은 알 수 없지만, 이런 일이 있었던 사실을 고려하면, 이 보고서는 세계교회협력운동 측이 작성해달라고 요청한 질의서에 연희전문 측이 응답한 문서로 보인다.

또한 이 보고서는 '고등교육에 관한 내용을 빈칸에 적어서 북장로회 선교부에 내는 서류'라는 막연한 제목을 붙이고 있지만, 일자 표기 하단에서 연희전문학교(Chosen Christian College)에 관한 것임을 밝히고 있다.

이 문서는 로마자 번호를 매긴 아래의 8개 항목으로 구성되어 있는데, 각 항목에서 요점만 제시하고 항목 끝에 질의응답 문장을 두어 내용을 보충하고 있다.

I. 운영, II. 자산, III. 교직원, IV. 재정, V. 학과와 학생, VI. 졸업생, VII. 출판물, VIII. 총론.

내용 요약

I. 교장은 에비슨, 학교와 이사회의 회계는 겐소(J. F. Genso), 이사회의 총무는 오웬스(H. T. Owens), 뉴욕에 있는 협력이사회의 총무는 스코트(G. T. Scott)이고, 후원하는 협력선교부들은 북장로회, 북감리회, 남감리회, 캐나다장로회이다.

II. 캠퍼스 부지의 전체 면적은 196,117에이커이고, 가격은 원가로 $35,000(시가는 $150,000)인데, 300에이커를 채우려면 더 많은 돈이 필요하다. 주요 두 건물과 사택 2채의 원가는 총 $42,500이고, 시설의 가격 총액은 $8,500이다.

III. 교수들 가운데 풀타임은 선교사 8명, 본토인(한국인과 일본인) 11명이고, 파트타임은 선교사 9명, 본토인 1명이다. 선교사 교수들은 북장로회 3명, 북감리회 2명, 남감리회 1명, 캐나다장로회 1명이다.

IV. 협력 선교부들의 지급금이 경상비를 다 채우지 못하고 학비 수입은 소액에 불과하므로 '자본금'을 위한 별도의 기부금이 필요하다. '활용할 수 있는 자금'인 선교부들의 연례 지급금은 $19,000인데, 이 가운데 $14,000이 선교사 후원비로, $5,000이 다른 경비로 사용되고 있다. 한국에서 거두는 학비와 기부금은 1918~19년 수입의 7.6%를 차지하고 있다.

V. 1918~1919년간[1918년 4월부터 1919년 3월까지]에는 학생 수가 신과 11명, 농과 10명, 문과 25명, 상과 34명, 수물과와 응용화학과가 14명이지만, 3 · 1운동 이후의 정국에서 20명만 출석하고 있다. 정규수업 후의 채플과 성경 수업에는 학생의 50%가 자발적으로 참석하고 있다.

VI. 10명의 졸업생이 모두 교직에 진출하였다.

VII. 학교에서 발행하는 정규 출판물은 없다. 사진과 좋은 책을 보내주기를 요청한다.

VIII. 학교에서 각종 기록의 관리를 철저히 하고 있고, 지역사회와 소통할 준비를 하고 있으며, 총독부로부터 재단법인 설립 인가를 받았으나, 1920년 4월 1일부터 수업 시간에 일본어를 사용하게 한 법령이 철회되지 않고 있고, 신과 외에서는 종교교육이 제한되고 있으며, 교육법의 입학요건이 낮아 교육 수준을 낮추는 문제점이 있다.

FILING DEPT.
DEC 6 1919
SECRETARIES
1426

INFORMATION BLANK OF HIGHER EDUCATIONAL INSTITUTIONS

Related to

The Board of Foreign Missions of the Presbyterian Church in the U.S.A.

RECEIVED
NOV 26 1919
Answered
Dec 5

Date October 30, 1919.

Institution -- CHOSEN CHRISTIAN COLLEGE Address SEOUL, Korea.

I. ADMINISTRATION

Name.		Address
Pres. of Institution	Dr. O. R. Avison	Seoul
Treas. of Institution	J. F. Genso	"
Secy. of Field Board	H. T. Owens	"
Treasurer of Field Board	J. F. Genso	"

Co-operating Board for Christian Education in Chosen New York

Secretary Rev. Geo. T. Scott 156 Fifth Avenue, N.Y.

Sustaining Home Boards 1. Presbyterian in U.S.A. 2. Meth. Episcopal in U.S.A.
3. Methodist Episcopal, South
4. Canadian Presbyterian

II. Property

A. LAND.

Holdings:
Size in acres 196.117 Cost $35,000 Market Value $150,000

Askings: Additional land needed for
(1) Present work: Size 50 acres Cost $30,000 Explain For agricultural development
(2) Early development: Size 2nd 50 acres Cost $30,000 Explain For agricultural development and Model Village development
(3) Ultimate Goal -- Size 300 acres Cost Probably As above

Where can detailed information regarding land be found ? Field Treasurer has deeds, also Secretary of Co-operating Board in New York has full information.

2.

B. BUILDINGS

Holdings:

Number of Principal Buildings	One	Cost $20,000	Value $40,000 (Rise in prices)
Number of secondary Buildings	One	Cost $ 5,000	Value $ 8,000 (do.)
Number of Residences	Two	Cost $12,500	Value $12,500
Total number of Buildings	Four	Cost $42,500	

Askings: Additional Buildings needed for (See Statement appended)

What New Buildings are promised by Sustaining Boards ? Science Hall by Methodist Episcopal or Methodist Episcopal South; Underwood Hall, by Northern Presbyterian; Chapel and Y.M.C.A. by Methodist Episcopal Board; three residences Northern Presbyterian, one residence Southern Methodist, one residence, Canadian Presbyterian.

Where can detailed information regarding buildings be found ? Murphy & Dana's plans, and house plans (on field); and from Secretary of Co-operating Board in New York.

(Enclose a rough, ink Ground Plan of Campus and Buildings, dotting the outlines of proposed Buildings)

C. EQUIPMENT

Holdings:
Approximate cost (or value) of total present equipment $8500.

Askings: See statement appended.

Where can detailed information regarding equipment be found ? From Rev. A. L. Becker, Dean, Seoul, Korea.

III. STAFF

Holdings:

Missionaries,	Full time 8 (incl. President)	Natives, Full time	11
"	Part time None	" Part time	1
"	supported by Pres. Board 3 and President		
"	supported by M. E. Board 2	Natives, professing Christians ..	All
"	supported by M.E. South 1		
"	supported by Can. Presby. 1		

Askings:
Additional Missionaries needed for
(1) Present work 4 Northern Presbyterian share 0.
Explain: For Mathematics, Commerce, Industrial, Building and Grounds Superintendent.
(2) Early Development 1 Northern Presbyterian share 0
Explain: Woman Community worker
(3) Ultimate Goal Total 16 Northern Presbyterian share 1

What vacancies are there in quota promised by Sustaining Boards ? One, Methodist Episcopal Board (Prof. Weller resigned, not replaced yet) Southern Methodist Board has promised a second man out of Centenary Funds.
Where can detailed information regarding staff be obtained ? Booklet herewith.

IV. FINANCES

A. CAPITAL FUND.

Should your Institution be separately endowed ? Yes. Why ? Because ordinary revenues of Mission Boards appear to be unable to meet the increasing expense budget, and fees from students are only a small part of the cost of the institution.

Holdings:
Amount of Endowment None

Askings of Capital Sums of Endowment for
(1) Present Needs $100,000 Northern Presbyterian share ...
(2) Early Development $100,000 per year for the next five years.
(3) Ultimate Growth $1,000,000. Northern Presbyterian Share $250,000
Explain: The shares may be as follows eventually: Northern Presbyterian 25%; Northern Methodist 25%; Southern Methodist 18¾%; Canadian Presbyterian 12½%; Southern Presbyterian 12½%; Australian Presbyterian 6¼%.
What percentage of Endowment Askings could be secured locally on the field ? Present conditions make an estimate impossible now.

B. CURRENT FUNDS.

Annual Receipts:
From Boards $19,000, of which $14,000 is for Missionaries' support and $5,000 for other expenses.

From Student Fees Fiscal year ending March 31, 1919 Yen 827.oo
Present Fees $6.oo per year: to be increased from April, 1920.
From Room and Board: No dormitory revenues as yet. Dormitories will probably be built in 1920.
From Local Gifts: None as yet
Fees and Gifts on field constituted 7.6% of total current receipts in 1918-19.
What is being done to increase this percentage ? The natural growth of the College will increase this percentage as soon as political conditions become more stable, and also we may expect gifts from Koreans under other conditions than those that exist now.

Where can Details be found regarding Finances ? In the Treasurer's Annual Reports in hands of Secretary and Treasurer of Co-operating Board in New York, Rev. Geo. T. Scott, 156 Fifth Avenue, and Mr. Geo. F. Sutherland., 150 Fifth Avenue.

V. DEPARTMENTS AND STUDENTS.

Name of Dept.	No. of Students 1918-19 Enrolm't	No. Graduating this year	Total No. of Graduates
(1) Bible	11		First Class graduated April, 1919, as shown
(2) Agriculture	10		
(3) Arts	25	8	
(4) Commerce	34	10	
(5) Applied Chemistry) (6) Applied Physics & Mathematics)	14	3	

Cannot report properly on number of present students now because of disturbed conditions. Only 20 in attendance now.

Religious Training:
In the Curriculum Bible Department
Outside the Curriculum Voluntary chapel exercises daily: over 50 per cent. of students attended during year 1918-19.
In voluntary Bible Classes 50%.

What community service is done by Students ? Sunday-school Teaching and Preaching.

Religious Affiliation of Students: 1. Christian 100%; Methodist 65%; Presbyterian 35%.

Average number of Students to unite with Church during last three years All were Christians from admission.
Seven Students receive aid through the Selfhelp department of the College. Of these, some are given scholarships which they are not expected to repay. Some students receive help from individual missionaries, or possibly from Missions, but as this is in the nature of private arrangements the College has no exact data at the present time.

Where can Details be found regarding departments, courses, student body, Christian Service, Self-help, etc. Copy of Curriculum attached.

VI. GRADUATES.

Total Graduates from Higher Departments 21 of whom 100% are Christians.

Of those who enter first year, how many graduate. Too early in College life to know. As this class was our first, we cannot supply information yet.

Graduates are engaged in following pursuits:
1. Preaching 0 (Other questions all blank)
2. Teaching 10
In Christian Schools 10
In other Schools 0

How does Demand for Graduates' Services compare with supply ? Unable to answer yet as this year is our first graduation.

What is attitude of Graduates toward entering Christian Service ? Of first graduating class, ten are teaching in Mission schools.

How do preparation and Purpose of Graduates relate to Fundamental Needs of their Home Communities and Nations ? See list of students in Departments.

What would increase graduates' usefulness as Christian Promoters of Human Welfare ? Greater devotion to Christ and ahigher sense of service for their fellowmen.

VII. PUBLICATIONS.

Are regular publications issued ? No.

5.

What special publications issued ? Notes on Chosen Christian College
Circulation Given out as seems desirable.

Please send some interesting photographs First Class Book now in mail.

VIII. General.

Your system of records cover what matter ? Very complete covering grades finances, examinations, facts about students, textbooks used, rules and regulations, etc.

In what ways is your institution a community center ? Too near its beginning yet, but arrangements are being made for summer schools and conferences in 1920. Also see plan for Model Village.

What relationship has your institution to the Local and National Government ? An incorporated body with Government charter.

Mention your great outstanding Educational problems ? (1) As yet unrepealed Ordinance to teach all subjects in the Japanese language from April 1, 1920.
(2) The restriction of religious teaching as a part of the regular curriculum except in the Biblical Department.
(3) Low standard of matriculation requirement and consequent low grade of work during course. This is according to Government ordinance.

Signature O R Avison

Position in Institution, President

Address Seoul, Korea

Rev. George T. Scott,
156 Fifth Avenue,
New York, N.Y.

14. 에비슨 교장의 이사회 제출 연례보고서

문서 제목	Chosen Christian College, President's Report to Field Board of Managers
문서 종류	교장 보고서
제출 시기	1920년 2월 21일
작성 장소	서울
제 출 자	O. R. Avison
수 신 자	이사회
페이지 수	4
출 처	Korea Mission Records, 1904~1960, Box 15, Folder 17 (PHS) 2114-5-2: 06 Board of Managers 1915~1922 (UMAH)

자료 소개

에비슨 교장이 1920년 2월 21일 열린 이사회 연례회의 때 제출한 보고서이다. 이 문서도 PHS와 UMAH에서 같은 문서로 보관하고 있다.

이 보고서는 서언과 아래의 7가지 항목으로 구성되어 있다.

1. 토지매입 현황, 2. 가우처의 방문, 3. 스코트의 방문, 4. 제1회 졸업앨범 발행, 5. 재정 적사 대책, 6. 교수진의 변농, 7. 협력 선교부들에 대한 후원 요청.

내용 요약

이사들의 사임, 사망 등으로 재선출이 필요하다.

1. 지난 회의 후에 120평을 사서 197에이커가량을 소유하게 되었다. 지가 상승과 동양척식회사와의 토지 협상에 대응하기 위해 향후의 토지매입 전략을 의논할 필요가 있다. 철도 건설회사 측과 조율하여 모범촌의 부지를 확보하였으나, 동척의 농지가 그 안에 들어가게 되어 그 땅을 사야 하고, 철도가 캠퍼스에 접근하는 것을 막기 위해 치원관 서남쪽의 땅도 사야 한다.

2. 뉴욕 협력이사회의 이사인 가우처(John F. Goucher)가 스팀슨관의 건축 상황과 캠퍼스를 둘러보았고, 산지에 다양한 나무를 심어 계절마다 더 아름다운 경관을 갖게 하라고 제안하고 총독에게도 직접 말하여 총독이 삼림 전문가들을 보냈다.

3. 협력이사회의 총무인 스코트(Geo. T. Scott)가 미국으로 돌아가는 길에 다시 방문하여 학교를 돌아보았다.

4. 첫 번째 졸업앨범이 1919년 가을에 발행되어 미주 선교부들에 발송하고 감사 인사를 받았다.

5. 이번 회계연도의 적자는 ¥10,093이고 지금까지의 적자 총액은 ¥2,317.58인데, 앞으로 적자가 더 심해질 것이 예상되므로 협력이사회에 추가 지원을 촉구해야 한다.

6. 건축감독으로 루카스(A. E. Lucas)를 고용하여 1920년 1월 1일부터 반년간 일하게 되었고, 캐나다에서 맥켄지(McKenzie)가 농과 교수로 올 뜻이 있음을 알려왔으며, 문과 교수 잭(Jack)이 농과 과목을 맡기를 거부하였다. 피셔(J. E. Fisher)가 1919년 10월 한국에 도착하였는데, 심리학을 가르치도록 초청받았으나 과목을 조정하여 원한경(H. H. Underwood)이 심리학을 맡고 피셔는 교육학을 맡기로 하였으며, 상과 교수 백상규가 한성은행에서 일하게 되어 전임교수 직을 내려놓고 무급으로 가르치게 되었다.

7. 북감리회 선교부가 약정금 $52,000에서 $22,000(금화)을 협력이사회 회계에 넘겼고, 강당[채플] 건축비 $30,000을 학교에서 요청하면 주기로 하였다. 남감리회 한국 선교회는 피셔의 주택 건축비 $5,000(금)을 주면서 본국 선교부에도 더 많은 자본금을 본교에 보내도록 요청하였다. 캐나다장로회 한국 선교회가 본국 선교부에 선교 캠페인 모금액의 지출 예산에 본교 지원금을 책정해달라고 요청하여 선교부가 $35,000을 책정하였다. 우리는 세계교회협력운동(Interchurch World Movement) 측에 자본금과 기본재산을 요청하고 선교사 교수 5명의 파송을 요청하였다.

RE[illegible] SCOTT

President's report

APR-2 1920

Ansd.

FILING DEPT.
1426-2
APR 14 1920
SECRETARIES

CHOSEN CHRISTIAN COLLEGE

PRESIDENT'S REPORT TO FIELD BOARD OF MANAGERS -- FEB. 21, 1920

1920

Since the last meeting the Board has sustained the loss of Mr. Sakaide and Dr. Sharrocks, the former by resignation due to his leaving Korea and the latter by death, as you already know. On the retirement of Mr. Sakaide I wrote a letter of appreciation of the services he had rendered to our College, and having asked for suggestions as to a successor Mr. H. Kawae, Manager of the Construction Department of the Railway Department of the Government, and Mr. Hoshino, chief of the Investigation Bureau of the Bank of Chosen, were highly recommended to me for the position, and I sent out voting papers, as a result of which Mr. Kawae was elected. Dr. Sharrocks' place is still unfilled, and careful consideration is being given to the question of a successor.

The following members of the Board retire at the close of this meeting -- Messrs. Noble, Gale, Rhodes, Hitch and Watanabe -- and I would ask you to give careful consideration to the filling of their places, either by re-election of these men or of others.

I wish to direct your attention to the following matters:

1. The state of land purchases. We have purchased only one lot of land since the last meeting, consisting of certain fields which run deeply into the forest reservation purchased from the Government between the site occupied by Mr. Rhodes' house and the one proposed for the President. These total 1201 tsubo, and were purchased at the rate of ¥1.90 per tsubo. This is considerably higher than they could have been purchased for a year or two earlier. At one time these lots were valued at only 80 sen per tsubo, and when Dr. Goucher was here he strongly advised us to purchase even at this higher figure. The amount of land now owned by the institution is therefore 197.18 acres. The map which I lay before you will indicate what we now own and the parts which we had planned to purchase. You will notice that some of these fields are owned by the Oriental Development Co. which first declined to consider any proposition to sell them to us. They now, however, have stated that they will exchange them for other lots, but they will accept only ricefields even for uplands, which are of course cheaper than ricefields, and then they demand a premium of ten per cent. more in area. As all lands in this vicinity have greatly advanced in price, and ricelands as I said are more expensive than uplands, this means that we must either do without these fields or pay a larger sum than had entered into our first estimates. A somewhat recent letter from the Chairman of the Cooperating Board in New York, Mr. Underwood, suggested that perhaps we had better go slow in the purchase of more land, and I wish to get your instructions as to how much we should plan to purchase in view of our plans for development and the present prices asked. The total amount expended for land to this time is ¥69988.55 / Our original estimate was ¥80,000 which estimate was raised afterwards to ¥100,000 † If we are to proceed with the enlargement of the site as originally intended, it will be necessary to secure special funds immediately for this purpose. All the property so far purchased has been registered so that there will be no question as to legal ownership.

We have been negotiating with the owner of certain ricefields in the next valley west of our property which would be convenient for exchange with the Oriental Development Company. The price asked is ¥ 2.00 per tsubo which would mean a cost of ¥ 20,000 for the valley which runs into our residence section.

† In the Interchurch World Movement estimates the amount for land is increased to ¥130,000

I want to draw your attention also to the location decided upon for the Model Village. The part of the hill which formerly ran out like a promontory by arrangement with the railway contractors has been used as borrow for railway purposes and has been cut down, so that we have now a location suitable for the erection of the village buildings. But you will notice that the Oriental Development Company's fields run up into this section, and it is very desirable for us to secure at least certain of these fields, to which I now direct your attention.

There are also certain fields connected with the farming lands to the southwest of the present agricultural building which we should get as soon as possible. The original plan had been to secure the section south of the railway as far as the point of the southwestern hills which we own. I think we should at this time come to some understanding as to whether we are to make any effort to carry out the original plan, or if not to what extent it ought to be modified.

The report of the Building Committee will show the present condition of the Building Program and make recommendations along this line for the coming summer, so that I will not at this time refer to them in detail.

3. Since our last meeting we have had a visit from Rev. John F. Goucher, D.D., a member of the Cooperating Board in New York. He was deeply interested in the development that has already taken place. He was much pleased with the appearance and inside plans of the Stimson Building, while his opinion of the campus in general and the progress we are making is most commendatory. He was very enthusiastic over a plan which he proposed for the planting out of different kinds of trees in groups on the various hillsides, so as still more to beautify the appearance of the site at different seasons, his idea being that there should be a definite color scheme. He talked with the Governor General on this subject, and asked his assistance and that of the Forestry experts in the development of the scheme, and the Governor General sent his experts to the site to confer with Mr. Ichijima on the subject. As I said above, Dr. Goucher strongly urged the purchase of certain fields and the purchase was carried out while he was still here.

3. We also had a return visit from Rev. Geo. T. Scott, Secretary of the Cooperating Board, on his way to America. This visit was very brief, but Mr. Scott saw the school in operation and the progress of construction.

4. In the fall the first class book of the College was published, and copies sent to America. Acknowledgments have been received from Dr. Mackay and Mr. Armstrong of the Canadian Board, and from Dr. Chester of the Southern Presbyterian Executive Committee.

5. The Budget for 1921-22 shows an estimated deficit of ¥11,806, compared with ¥10,092 for the coming fiscal year. The estimated deficit for the current year was ¥1501, and the Treasurer's report shows that this has already been exceeded and the year has still more than a month to run. The deficit to date is ¥1209.93 with ¥1047.65 from the previous year, making a total deficit to date of ¥2257.58 We should urge upon the Cooperating Board the necessity of providing additional sums for the budget so that we would not be under the constant anxiety concerning funds that we are at present. Our deficits at present are carried by the Building Fund, but this will not always be the case.

6. In pursuance of the authority granted at our last meeting, Mr. Lucas was engaged to work on the building program for a period of six months from January 1st. At the end of this period, if matters are

mutually satisfactory, Mr. Lucas would like to return to serve in such capacity as may be decided upon. The Y.M.C.A. are giving Mr. Lucas half furlough allowance, we understand.

I was informed that a Mr. Ross, a brother-in-law of Dr. Rogers of Soonchun, who is a civil engineer, has some thought of coming to Korea and I at once wrote the Boards interested to get in touch with him. At the same time, I learned that Mr. Lilly, a brother of Mrs. Hitch, also a civil engineer, had the same intention, and his name was also forwarded to the home Boards. These names are mentioned in connection with the vacant chair of Mathematics. I have also had mentioned the possibility of securing Mr. K. C. Fowie, B.Sc., a member of the Canadian Mission in Formosa, who is a graduate of McGill University in architecture, and whose services might be useful during the absence of Mr. Lucas in America on the building program and who could also probably take the chair of Mathematics. Among these three applicants, one may be secured for the vacancy.

I have also received a communication from a Mr. McKenzie, of the British Columbia College of Agriculture, who seems to be thinking of coming to Korea to do work in agriculture. Mr. McKenzie asks whether he should specialize in animal husbandry. It may be that in view of Mr. Jack's withdrawal from the proposed appointment to the Agricultural Department Mr. McKenzie might be kept in mind. He has one or two years more work before graduating apparently.

Mr. Jack's time for furlough has arrived, and that brings up the question of his permanent appointment to the Faculty. By former action of the Board we had looked forward to his taking up the subject of Agriculture, but further consideration had led him to ask for a change, and after a good deal of consideration the Faculty recommended that that action be rescinded.

Mr. J. E. Fisher, the representative of the Southern Methodist Mission on the Faculty, arrived in October. The former action of the Board invited Mr. Fisher to come out as Professor of Psychology and allied subjects, but when the matter was again discussed that decision was modified so that the matter should be finally decided after Mr. Fisher's arrival on the field. A conference between Mr. Fisher and Mr. Underwood resulted in an arrangement by which Mr. Underwood will continue his work in Psychology, while Mr. Fisher main assignment would be Pedagogy and Education, and both will assist in the Department of English.

Mr. Paek, who has been in charge of the Commercial Department, has become associated with the Hanseung Bank, and is no longer a full time member of the Faculty. He is continuing in charge of the department and lecturing on certain subjects without salary.

7. Progress is being made in the realization of cooperation on the part of the Boards and Missions behind this enterprise. The Northern Methodist Board has turned over to the Cooperating Board Treasurer the $32,000 gold due on their pledge of $52,000, and have in hand the $20,000 for the auditorium when it shall be called for. It is my understanding that in the Centenary budget the askings will bring the Northern Methodist total up to $100,000.

4.

I had a conference with the Southern Methodist Mission during the visit of Dr. Rawlings to Seoul. This Mission has appropriated $5,000 gold for a residence for Mr. Fisher, and have asked their home Board to make available $21,000 in 1922 and $14,000 in 1923 for capital funds. This action brings this Mission into full cooperation as defined in the Act of Endowment. In 1921, this Mission will contribute to current budget at the rate of $2,000 gold.

The Canadian Presbyterian Mission at their last Annual Meeting asked their Board to include $20,000 in the Forward Movement Campaign. and the Board has put $35,000 in it's Forward Movement Budget.

Our askings from the Interchurch World Movement for capital funds total $599,100, and $500,000 for endowment. We request 5 foreign workers, and anticipate an increase in native staff to 27 within the next five years.

Respectfully submitted,

O.R. Avison

15. 로즈 학감 대리의 이사회 제출 연례보고서

문서 제목	Dean's Report to the Board of Managers Chosen Christian College
문서 종류	학감 보고서
제출 시기	1920년 2월 21일
작성 장소	서울
제 출 자	Harry A. Rhodes
수 신 자	이사회
페이지 수	15 (학감 보고서 6, 학감이 제출한 교수회 요청서 9)
출 처	① Korea Mission Records, 1904~1960, Box 15, Folder 15 (PHS) ② Korea Mission Records, 1904~1960, Box 15, Folder 20 (PHS) ③ 2114-5-2: 06 Board of Managers 1915~1922 (UMAH) ④ Scan 0791 Chosen Christian College: Underwood, Horace H. (Dr.) October 1913-December 1923 (continued) (UMAH)

자료 소개

로즈 학감 대리가 1920년 2월 21일 열린 이사회 연례회의에 제출한 보고서이다. 로즈 신과 교수는 베커 학감이 1919년 봄 안식년을 보내기 위해 미국에 가면서 학감을 대리하였다.

이 문서는 보고서와 첨부된 두 가지 요청서로 구분된다. 요청서들은 ⓐ 교육과정 변경 요청서 ⓑ 음악과 설치 요청서인데, PHS 문서 ①에는 보고서만 있고, ②에는 ⓑ 요청서만 있으며, UMAH 문서 ③에는 학감 보고서와 두 요청서가 다 있고, ④에는 보고서의 1쪽만 있다.

학감 보고서는 번호를 매긴 5가지 항목과 학감의 권고안으로 구성되어 있는데, 5가지 항목은 아래와 같다. 그 뒤에 첨부된 요청서들은 교수회가 작성하여 로즈 학감 대리가 대표로 이사회에 제출한 것이다.

I. 등록과 학생, II. 교수, III. 학과, IV. 교육과정 변경 요구, V. 필요한 것과 문제점.

내용 요약

◩ 보고서

I. 학교가 정치적 혼란[3 · 1운동]으로 3월 15일 수업을 중단하였고 학생들이 3월 1일부터 출석하지 않았다. 8월 27일 개학한 가을학기 동안 학생은 16명이었고, 평균 연령은 23세였으며, 7명이 기혼이었다. 졸업생 21명 가운데 2명이 감옥에 있고, 이들을 포함하여 학생 15명이 몇 개월간 감옥에 있었으며, 이 가운데 1명이 감옥에서 죽었다.

II. 교수진에 조수를 포함하여 23명이 있고, 베커가 미국 앤아버[미시간대]에서 공부하고 있으며, 백상규가 무급으로 상과를 이끌고 있고, 루카스가 와서 건축 업무를 맡고 있다.

III. 문과는 피셔가 와서 원한경과 담당 과목을 조정하였는데, 문과의 교육과정이 충분히 전문화되지 않아 한국인들에게 만족스럽지 못한 것이 분명해졌다. 신과는 4년제로 만들자는 요청안을 총독부에 제출하였다. 수물과는 베커가 부재하여 그에게서 배운 조수들(이원철, 김술근, 장세운)이 과를 이끌었고, 현재는 이 과에 학생이 없어 그들이 다른 과들에서 수학과 물리학을 가르치고 있으며, 이원철과 장세운은 경신학교와 정신여학교에서도 몇 개월간 오후에 가르쳤다. 응용화학과는 밀러와 이노익이 있으나 아직 운영되지 않고 있고, 밀러는 건축 업무로 극히 바쁘다. 농과는 이치지마가 혼자 이끌고 있다. 그는 캠퍼스의 농지와 삼림을 돌보고, 이 대학을 대표하여 총독부를 상대하고 있다. 상과는 백상규가 담당 과목들의 강의를 대부분 중단하여 운영에 어려움을 겪었다. 사무실의 업무는 거의 전적으로 노준탁이 이끌어왔고, 근로장학생들이 타이프를 치고 등사를 하였다.

IV. 지난 몇 개월 동안 교수회 회의 때마다 교육과정을 변경하는 문제를 토론하였는데, 이는 총독부의 교육법이 바뀌는 시기에 중요하고 시의적절한 일이었다. [이 논의를 뒷받침하는 교육과정 변경 요청서가 7~14쪽에 첨부되어 있다.]

V. 한국인과 일본인 교수들의 사택과 학생 기숙사 마련이 가장 시급하다.

◩ 보고서에 있는 로즈의 '권고안'

1. 문과 4학년 박태원과 김재련을 1920년 3월 말에 졸업시킨다. 2. 1920년 4월 1일까지 문과, 농과, 상과의 한국인과 일본인 교수들을 당장 확보한다. 3. 농과, 상과, 수물과의 교수와 건축감독을 1명씩 임명해주도록 협력이사회에 요청한다. 4. 스팀슨관을 최대한 빨리

완공하고, 한국인과 일본인 교수 사택들, 최소 100명을 수용할 기숙사들을 최대한 빨리 마련한다. 5. 음악과의 설치를 위해 총독부에 승인을 요청한다. 6. 교육과정 변경안을 총독부에 제출한다. 7. 1920~21년과 1921~22년 예산이 부족해질 수 있다는 점을 주목하고 협력이사회에 요청한다. 8. 사무실의 서기이자 회계인 노준탁에게 50원의 사례비를 준다. 9. 미국에서 자동차와 차고 기금을 구할 특별위원들을 위촉한다. 10. 베커 부부에게 편지를 써서 피아노를 구해오게 한다.

◪ 교수회의 '교육과정 변경 요청서'

10개 요청안: 1. 2년의 예비과정을 둘 것. 2. 처음부터 전공을 선택하게 하지 말 것. 3. 전체 학생이 음악을 최소한 일 년간 주 2시간씩 수강하게 할 것. 4. 베커가 돌아올 때까지는 수물과를 급격히 바꾸지 말 것. 5. 별도의 음악과를 설치할 것. 6. 채플 시간을 매일 두고 채플 참석을 필수로 할 것. 7. 일어, 영어, 한국어로 가르치는 것을 허용받을 것. 8. 전체 학생이 성경 과목을 매년 최소 주 2시간씩 수강할 것. 9. 어떤 과들의 선택과목을 허용할 것. 10. 농학 과목과 그 밖의 과목들을 다른 과에서 선택하게 할 것. [교육과정 변경안은 이사회에서 총독부 학무국에 제출하기 전에 학무국과 미리 상의해보도록 결정되었다(1920년 2월 21일 이사회 회의록).]

각 과의 과목 변경안: [예과 2년의 추가를 가정하고 있다.]

문과(Literary Dept.)는 역사 · 지리, 교육학 시간을 늘리고 일어를 줄인다. 과학개론, 동양 문학, 철학, 사회학, 성경, 작문을 신설한다. 음악은 선택에서 필수로 옮긴다. 식물학, 물리학, 화학은 폐지한다. 수학, 한문, 수신은 예과에서만 가르친다. 과학을 1학년 선택과목으로 둔다. 영어, 심리학, 경제학, 부기, 논리학, 윤리학, 체육은 기존과 같고, 영어, 체육은 예과에서도 가르친다.

신과(Biblical Dept.)는 일어를 줄이고, 한문을 예과로 옮기며, 조선어(Korean Lang.), 사회학, 경제학, 웅변을 신설한다. 역사 · 지리, 수학, 과학개론, 부기, 수신은 예과에서만 가르친다. 영어, 성경, 체육은 기존과 같고, 예과에서도 가르친다. 음악은 각 학년의 수업시수를 서로 바꾼다.

수물과('Scientific and Applied Chem. Course'로 표기되어 있다)는 일어, 역사 · 지리, 수학, 물리학, 화학, 부기를 예과에서만 가르친다. 대수, 삼각법, 미분방정식, 물리화학, 전기화학, 건축학, 천문학을 폐지한다. 대신 각 학년에서 6~8가지씩 서로 다른 과학 과목을 배운다. 외국어(Foreign Lang.)를 신설한다. 영어, 기하, 계산, 체육은 기존과 같고, 예과에서도 가르친다.

상과(Commercial Dept.)는 상업 영어, 상업 일어, 법률, 사회학, 성경, 타자, 상업 수학을 신설한다. 일어, 역사 · 지리, 수신을 예과로 옮기고, 수학, 물리 · 화학, 한문을 예과에 신설한다. 상업, 부기, 경제학은 시간을 늘린다. 영어, 재정, 상업 실습, 성경, 체육은 기존과 같고, 영어, 성경, 체육은 예과에서도 가르친다.

(응용화학과와 농과의 변경 과목은 원문의 표를 참고.)

◪ 교수회의 '음악과 설치 요청서'

3년제 음악과를 설치하고, 조교수를 1명 더 뽑으며, 피아노와 올갠과 각종 관현악기를 구입하고, 음악관을 지을 것을 요청한다. [이 요청서는 학감의 권고안 5항의 첨부 문서이고, 1920년 2월 12일 작성되었다. 음악과 설치 건은 이사회에서 심의를 보류하였다(위의 이사회 회의록).]

Deans Report Duplicate

DEAN'S REPORT
to the
BOARD OF MANAGERS CHOSEN CHRISTIAN COLLEGE
Feb. 21st, 1920

I. ENROLLMENT AND STUDENTS.

As the members of the Board are aware, owing to political disturbances. We were compelled to declare school closed about Mar 15th., 1919, the students having absented themselves from the first of that month.

This was before the end of the school year; consequently no final examinations nor commencement exercises were held. In accordance with the practice in other schools, the faculty voted to grant promotions and diplomas upon satisfactory term work having been done. Although, in this way a class of 21 were officially graduated, they have to date not availed themselves of the opportunity to receive their diplomas.

In a series of faculty meetings during the spring of 1919, it was decided that it would be useless to attempt to open school at that time.

However, announcements were sent out during the Summer and the new School year formally began on Aug. 27th, Since then, we have been in session contionnously with the exception of the holiday vacation.

Although we had many inquires from prospective new students from all parts of the country, only 24 reported. Of which 17 took the entrance examinations. Of these 15 were admitted; but only [illegible] continued to study till the end of the Fall term. When school closed in March, 1919, aside from the graduating class, we had 36 students; of these 13 reported when school opened, but only 7 continued their studies. So that our student body during the Fall term numbered 16: according to department they were enrolled as follows: Literary 4th.,2; 2nd.,1; 1st.,5; Commercial 2nd.,1; 1st.,4; Agriculture 2nd.,3; It will be seen then that no students were admitted to the Biblical, Applied Chemistry, or Mathematics and Physics Depts, although we had one applicant for each of these.

According to denominations these 16 students were listed as follows; Methodist Episcopal, 7; Methodist Episcopal South, 6 Presbyterian, 3. Their average age was 23 years; they came from ten different provinces; 7 of them married; both parents of ten are living; more than half of them were engaged actively in some Christian work in connection with the churches of the city and community. Of these 16, two did not return for the Winter term but 3 others were admitted as special students so that our student body at present numbers 17.

Of the 21 graduates, 14 are teaching and all, except one in Christian schools; 2 are in secretarial positions; 2 are in business; 1 is in a news paper office; and two are in prison.

Including the two graduates, 15 of our students were in prison for some months. Finally, 2 were released; 5 were let out on bail and afterwards sentenced to six months imprisonment but with the sentence suspended for three years (one of these has been in school since last Fall but was taken again recently by the police for examination); 4 were sentenced to six months hard labor. (of these, one died in prison and the other three have been released having served their sentence);

- 2 -

The Methodist Episcopal Board sent us a special contribution of $1,000 to be applied to the reduction of the deficit debt which was thus reduced to Y22,223.19. We heartily wish this could be wiped out in toto.

Teaching Staff

Even while we were doing this we improved our teaching staff materially and were able to carry on even though Professors Miller and Fisher, Becker, and Hitch were still in America. During the year Dr. E. H. Miller returned and a new Korean professor from America joined us, viz. Dr. L. G. Paik, while still others, graduates of Japanese Universities, were added. Dr. Fisher rejoined us at the beginning of this school year and Dr. Becker has informed us he will return next September.

During the year we made strenuous efforts to secure from the Educational Bureau the recognition of graduates of the Literary Department as teachers of History (Occidental and Oriental) and some other subjects in addition to English, formerly granted, but we have so far failed to obtain those privileges.

This year, for the first time since the Government's recognition of our Science Department, on the high standard, we had a graduating class in Science and the question of qualification for those graduates as teachers was a very burning one. At our invitation the Educational Bureau sent out three inspectors to examine the status of the equipment, the standing of the teachers and the scholarship of the classes. They spent an entire day doing this, giving written examinations. We were much gratified when they reported that the results of the examinations were excellent, the teachers satisfactory and the equipment good, the graduates would have qualification to teach Mathematics, Physics and Chemistry. They told us they seldom gave qualification to one school for more than one subject, or at most two, but, being so well pleased, they were stretching a point to give us three.

In regard to our teaching Staff, the Bureau required that at least two-thirds of the teachers shall have full qualification. This means that we can carry on with that proportion though it is considered a mark of weakness to have even that proportion non-qualified. This Spring the Government recognized the full qualification of four of those who had been in the unqualified group and gave temporary qualification to five others so that our proportion of qualified teachers is now 87% which is considered very satisfactory.

In regard to Christian standing, all the teachers are rated as Christians though of course some are less stalwart than others. During the year some of them have shown marked growth in Christian character.

3.

Biblical.

According to a former dicision, our request to make this a four years course was granted by the Government. Twenty hours a week in Bible and related subjects were substituted for certain subjects in science; otherwise the course stands much the same as the Literary course. The subjects in Bible were selected after a years study, the examinations of many college catalogues, and extensiv correspondence with missionaries in Korea,-an account of which you will find in the Korea field for September, 1919, we are not assured however that this course will be attractive to any considerable number of students for the reason that it will neither take the place of, nor shorten their theological course, and for the additional reason that a student from any other department could enter the seminary as well.

While Mr.Choi the assistant in this department has not done any actual teaching, he has done some pastoral work among the students, has helped in preparing courses to teach in the future, and in translation work.

As has been stated before the purpose of this department is to prepare students for the theological seminary, and for leadership in the church as Sunday School Workers, Church officers, evangelists ect.

3. Mathematics and Physical Course. In the absence of Mr. Becker the work in connection with this department has been carried on by the assistants whom he trained, and who have been working during the year under the superision of Mr. Miller, while there are no students in this department at present, it has been caring for the Math. and Physics in connection with the other departments. Mr.W.C.Lee has been giving much of his time to the Library and Messers. Im and Chang have helped with the surveying of roads and building sites, and with the drawing of building plans,-all under the direction of Mr. Miller. An arrangement was made by which Messers W. C. Lee and Chang were loaned to teach certain afternoons each week for several months in the John D. Wells Training School and in the Gir's Acodemy at Yundong, thus reimbursing our treasury to some extent for the salaries of these two teachers.

4. Applied Chemistry. This department has not been put into operation yet, although with Messers Miller and Root Lee both at work, we are well propared to receive students. We had one application and there are indications that with the opening of the new school year there will be more. Mr. Miller however has been exceedingly busy in superintending building operations, in supervising the laying out of roads and in the installation of the initial water system. Indeed it is hard to see how we ever could have gotten along without him in our building and site development program this last year. Mr. Lee has taught the Chemistry in connection with the other departments and has helped with other teaching.

5. Agriculture. Mr. Ichijima has been carrying this department alone, an assistant for him not having been employed as yet. For this reason we could not admit an entering class in the department last Fall although we had two or three applicants. As formerly, much of Mr. Ichijima's time has been taken up in supervising the campus, fields and forest, and in representing the college to the Goverment.

4.

1..., Commercial.

With Mr. Pack's resignation from most of the subjects he taught formerly, we have had difficulty in caring for this department. Mr. S. O. Kim, could assist only a part of the time and then only for one day a week which in some cases required the same subject to be taught twice on the same day, which is not satisfactory. This department promises to popular among the students but it is evident that we must have an associate professor and an assistant before the new school year opens.

7. The Office. The office work has been carried on almost entirely by Mr. Noh. In addition he has supervised the care of the building. and the boys in the self help department who do typewriting and mimeographing. He has ordered fuel and supplied, and acted as treasurer. He willingly consented to get along without an assistant for the time being and concurred in the attempt to get along with one janitor instead of two as heretofore. In every way his work has been very satisfactory. When the new school year opens, if we have any considerable number of students, I would recommend that he be given an assistant again, and that he himself be assigned to a few hours teaching each week and be regarded as an assistant in the Literary department.

IV. PROPOSED REQUEST FOR CHANGES IN THE COURSES OF STUDY

This subject has occupied much of Faculty's attention, and of the Dean's time in particular, during the last few months. it has been the main topic of discussion in recent faculty meetings and has required many committee meetings. The report on the subject will be presented to the Board separate from this report.

Even though the request for changes are not granted, the discussion has crystallized the ideas of both faculty and students, and caused us to consider anew as to just what the real purposed of the college are. We trust that the members of the Board also will go thoroughly into the whole matter, in the initial stages of the college and at a time of change in the Government's educational ordinances, it is a very important and timely question to consider.

V. NEEDS AND PROBLEMS.

In my judgment the most urgent need for the develoment of the college is to provide at the earliest possible moment, residences for Japanese and Korean professors and teachers, and dormitory provisions for the students. As soon as Stimson Hall is complited, almost everything else could be dropped in order to rush forward these two items on the building program. Students and teachers are scattered and paying exhorbitant prices for Board and rent.

There can be no esprit de corps, no intensified work, no proper superision of students until these residences and dormitories are provided. The dicision of the Board last year to provide for the students by erecting Model Village houses first, is probably the wisest thing to do. As the dormitory question is a difficult one, dormitories should be erected only after thorough investigation as to types and a careful study of the problem.

6.

In view of the probable absence of dormitory accommodations by the end of August this year, it does not seem wise to go ahead and plan for a Summer Conference for Korean Church leaders per your recommendation at your last meeting. The holding of such a conference is very desirable in every way and personally I give up the idea for this coming Summer with great reluctance; but undoubtedly the success of such a movement depends much upon having satisfactory rooming and boarding accommodations for these who come.

The matter of industrial work, scholarships, and a selfhelp department which were referred back to the Faculty by the Board of Managers has been under discussion from time to time.

A, somewhat comprehensive questionnairre on the subject was sent out; many answer have been received, but not all; the committee has not been able to report to the Faculty as yet so that we will have to delay reporting to the Board upon this important matter until you next meeting.

I will append to this report certain recommendations for your consideration. Many others might well be included. But in these first years of the growth of the college it will be necessary to confine ourselves to the most urgent matters first, keeping in mind of course the completed structure so far as we can the end from the beginning.

Respectfully submitted,

Harry A. Rhodes

6.

DEAN'S REPORT.........RECOMMENDATIONS.

1. That Pak Taiwon and Kim Chairyun of the 4th. Literary Dept. be gradtatted at the end of March, 1920, if their grades are satisfactory.

2. That steps be taken at once to secure the following Japanese and Korean teachers by April 1st., 1920;-

(a) Literary Dept.,-
A professor of Japanese History and Literature.
An Assistant to teach Chinese.

(b) Agricultural Dept. An Assistant or an Associate professor.
(This necessary before another class in this department can be admitted.)

(c) Commercial Dept.
An Associate professor.
An Assistant. (both necessary in order to carry on the work of this department)

3. That strong representation be made to the Cooperating Board for the following additional missionary professors;-

(a) One for the Agricultural Dept.(in case Mr. Jacks assignment is changed)

(b) One for the Commercial Dept.

(c) One for architecture, superintendence of building, industrial work, development of site, etc.(or possibly two men)

(d) One for Mathematics.

4. That the Board take immediate and intensive measures to provide at the earliest possible moment the completion of Stimson Hall, residences for Japanese and Korean professors, and dormitory accommodations for at least 100 students. (If necessary hold up other building operations until these buildings are erected)

5. That request be made to Government that we be allowed to have a Music Dept. in the College.(See separate report)

6. That the request to the Government for proposed changes in the cirric ula be made, together with certain allied requests.(see separate report)

7. That in considering the budgets for 1920-21 and 1921-22, the Board take notice of a probable shortage of 10,000 and 15,000 yen resepectively, and make request to the Cooperating Board on the same. (Also a probable deficit of 3,000 yen for the year 1919-20.)

8. That an honorarium of 50 yen be granted to Mr.Noh.Office Secretary and Treasurer, because of special responsibilities well carried, and that he be assigned some teaching work.

9. That a special committee in America be appointed to secure the amount already approved for motor bus and garage.

10. That Mr.Mrs. Becker be written to at once to secure if possible a piano for the college, and $500.for immediate music equipment.

Course of Study-Literary Dept.

Subject	present 1st.	present 2nd.	present 3rd.	present 4th.	proposed p-1.	proposed p-2.	proposed 1st.	proposed 2nd.	proposed 3rd.	proposed 4th.
Required										
English (Lang & Lit.)	5.	5.	5.	5.	10.	10.	10.	10.	10.	10.
Japanese (" ")	5.	5.	5.	5.	3.	3.	2.	2.	2.	
History & Geo.	3.	3.	3.	2.	3.	3.	3.	3.		3.
Math.	3.				2.	2.				
General Science					5.	5.				
Botany & Zoology	4.									
Physics & Chemistry		3.								
Education & Pedagogy				2.				2.	2.	
Chinese			3.	3.	2.	2.				
Literature (Oriental)							3.	2.	3.	
Psychology			3.				3.			
Philosophy								2.	3.	3.
Logic			2.					2.		
Ethics				3.						3.
Economics		3.							3.	
Sociology										3.
Bookkeeping			2.			2.				
Music							1.	1.		
Bible					2.	2.	2.	2.	2.	2.
Chemistry		3.								
Composition and Argument & Debate								2.	2.	2.
Moral Teaching	1.	1.	1.	1.	1.	1.				
Exercise	1.	1.	1.	1.	& 1.	1.	1.	1.	1.	1.
					29.	31.	25.	29.	28.	27.
Elective 1 Science							3.			
Geology	2.									
Astronomy				3.						
Physics										
Chemistry										
Music	3.	3.	1.	1.						
Agruculture	3.	3.	3.	3.						
Social Institution		1.								
Sanitary Science		2.								
Total	30.	31.	29.	29.	29.	31.	28.	29.	28.	27.

Chosen Christian College Biblical Dept. course of study.

Subject	present				proposed					
Required	1st.	2nd.	3rd.	4th.	p-1.	p-2.	1st.	2nd.	3rd.	4th.
English	5.	5.	5.	5.	10.	10.	5.	5.	5.	5.
Japanese	5.	5.	5.	5.	3.	3.	2.	2.		
Chinese			3.	3.	2.	2.				
Korean Lang.							2.	2.		
History & Geography	3.	3.	3.	3.	3.	3.				
Math.(H.Alg.S.Geom. Trig.					3.	2.				
General Science					5.	5.				
Botany & Zoology	4.									
Physics										
Chemistry										
Bookkeeping		2.				2.				
Education & Pedagogy				2.				2.	2.	
Economics									3.	
Psychology		3.					3.			
Philosophy								2.		
Logic				2.				2.		
Ethics			3.							3.
Sociology										3.
Bible	3.	3.	3.	3.	2.	2.	3.	3.	3.	3.
Moral Teaching	1.	1.	1.	1.	1.	1.				
Music	3.	2.	2.	1.			1.	1.	2.	2.
Publics Speaking								2.	2.	
Exercise	1.	1.	1.	1.	1.	1.	1.	1.	1.	1.
					30.	31.	17.	22.	18.	17.
Electives from Group I.II.III.IV.							10.	6.	8.	10.
Agriculture	3.	3.	3.							
Christian Evidences & other subjects (now elective)	2.	2.	2.	4.						
	30.	31.	31.	30.	30.	31.	27.	28.	26.	27.

Chosen Christian College Scientifdo and Applied Chem.Course

Subject	present				proposed					
Required.	1st;	2nd;	3rd;	4th;	p-1,	p-2;	1st;	2nd;	3rd;	4th;
English	5.	5.	5.	5:	5:	5:	5.	5.	5.	5.
Japanese	5:	5.	5.	5.	3:	3:				
History & Geog.	3:				3:	3:				
Math(Solid Geom.)	1:				3.	3.				
Algebra	2.									
Trigonometry	3.									
Analyst.Geom.		5.					5.			
Calculus			5.					5.		
Differen Equ.				2.						
Physical Chemistry		2.								
Physics	6.	6.			5.					
Chemistry	3.					5.				
Science(One of Groups Below)							5.	5:	5.	5.
Foreign Lang.							3.	3.		
Bookkeéping						2.				
Bible					2.	2.	2.	2.	2.	2.
Moral Teaching	1.	1.	1.	1.	1.	1.				
Exercise	1.	1:	1,	1.	1.	1:	1:	1.	1.	1:
Analyst Chem.		5.			23.	25.	21.	21.	13.	13.
Suveying			3.		Electives				8:	8:
Dynamics			3.		For Lang.				3.	3.
Electro Chem				2;	Congnato					
Elect Eng.			5,	6:	Science				8.	8.
Kinematics				3.	(From Groups Below)					
Building			2.							
Workshop Appliance				2.						
Astronomy				3.						
Mechan Draw		2:			Groups 5hrs a week each.					
	30.	30.	30;	30.						

Groups 1st.	2nd.	3rd.	4th.
1.Chem.Inorg.	Chem.Analyst	Chem.Organic	Chém.Electro
2.Physics Sound	Ph. Heat. Light.	Ph.Meg.Elec.	Ph.Adv.Lab.Wk.
3.Biology	Biol.	Biol.	Biol;
4.Geol Dynamic	Geol;Historic	Geol Miner.	Geol.Miner Econ.
5.Math.H.Alg.	Math.	Math.	Math.

Applied Chemistry Required

Chem.Inorg. 5.	Analyst. Quant. 5:	Ind.Chem. 3.	Indust.Lab. 5.
	Organic 3.	Preparat. 2.	Preparat 2.
		Organ.Lab. 2.	
5.	8.	7.	7.
Plus Totals Above			
16.	16.	8.	8.
Elect.Fr.Groups		5.	5.
Totals for Appl.Chem.			
21.	24.	20.	20.

7/21/20

Chosen Christian Course Applied Chemistry Course

Subject Required	present 1st.	2nd.	3rd.	proposed p-1.	p-2.	1st.	2nd.	3rd.	4th.
English	5.	5.	5.	10.	10.	5.	5.	5.	5.
Bookkeeping					2.				
Japanese	5.	5.	5.	3.	3.				
Chem. Tech. Pract.			10.						
History & Geog.	3.			3.	3.				
Chinese				2.	2.				
Minerology		4.							
Math. H. Alg. S. Geom & Trig.	6.			3.	2.				
Analyst Geom.						5.			
Calculus							5.		
Geology		2.							
General Science. Phy. Chem. Bot. Zool.				5.	5.				
Phys. Chem.	8.								
Physical Chem.		2.							
Chem. Organic						5.			
Analyst Grant.							5.		
Chem. Organic		6.					3.		
Analyst. Chem		3.						3.	
Ind. Chem.								2.	
Preparat.								2.	
Organ Lab.			5.						
Chemical Teach									5.
Indust. Lab.									2
Electrical Che.			2.						
Elect. from Group. Below								5.	5.
Bible				2.	2.	2.	2.	2.	2.
Moral Teaching	1.	1.	1.	1.	1.				
Exercise	1.	1.	1.	1.	1.	1.	1.	1.	1.
Music						2.			
For Lang.						3.	3.		
	29.	29.	29.	30.	31.	24.	24.	20.	20.

Notice that this course is change to a 4 years course.

Groups	1st.	2nd.	3rd.	4th. (Thrs)
(1)	Phys. Sound.	Ph. Heat. Light.	Ph. Mag. Elec.	Ph. Adv. Lab Wk.-each
(2)	Geology Dyn	Geol Historic.	Geol Miner	Geol. Miner. Econ.
(3)	Math.	Math.	Math.	Math.
(4)			For Lang. 3 hrs.	For Lang. 3 hrs.

Chosen Chfistian Course Applied Chemistry Course

Subject	present			proposed					
Required	1st.	2nd.	3rd.	p-1.	p-2.	1st.	2nd.	3rd.	4th.
English	5.	5.	5.	10.	10.	5.	5.	5.	5.
Bookkeeping					2.				
Jápnese	5.	5.	5.	3.	3.				
Chem. Tech. Pract.			10.						
History & Geog.	3.			3.	3.				
Chinese				2.	2.				
Minerology		4.							
Math. H. Alg. S. Geom & Trig.	6.			3.	2.				
Analyst Geom.						5.			
Calculus							5.		
Geology		2.							
General Science. Phy. Chem. Bot. Zool.				5.	5.				
Phys. Chem.	8.								
Physical Chem.		2.							
Chem. Organic						5.			
Analyst Grant.							5.		
Chem. Organic		6.					3.		
Analyst. Chem		3.						3.	
Ind. Chem.								2.	
Preparat.								2.	
Organ Lab.			5.						
Chemical Teach									5.
Indust. Lab.									2
Electrical Che.			2.						
Elect. from Group. Below								5.	5.
Bible				2.	2.	2.	2.	2.	2.
Moral Teaching	1.	1.	1.	1.	1.				
Exercise	1.	1.	1.	1.	1.	11	1.	1.	1.
Music						2.			
For Lang.						3.	3.		
	29.	29.	29.	30.	31.	24.	24.	20.	20.

Notice that this course is change to a 4 years course.

Groups	1st.	2nd.	3nd.	4th. Hrs
(1) Phys. Sound.	Ph. Heat. Light.	Ph. Mag. Elec.		Ph. Adv. Lab Wk. each
(2) Geology Dyn	Geol Historic.	Geol Miner		Geol. Miner. Econ.
(3) Math.	Math.	Math.		Math.
(4)		For Lang. 3 hrs.		For Lang. 3 hrs.

Chosen Christian College Biblical Dept.

Course of Study Elective Group.

Subject	1.	2.	3.	4.
Group I. Lang. Hist				
English Literature	5.	5.	6.	5.
Japanese	2.	2.	2.	
Oriental Literature	3.	2.	3.	
History	3.	3.		3.
Typewriting	2.			

Subject	1.	2.	3.	4.
Group II. Theo. Preparatory				
Psychology		3.		
philosophy			3.	3.
Relig. Education			2.	
Hisrory of Religeon	2.			
(Greek or Bible Relat. Subject)	2.	2.	2.	2.
Chur. Hist.	2.			
S.S. Bib. Geog.		2.		
Christian Ev.			2.	
Ch. Workers Trol.				2.
Fund of Faith				2.
Pedagogy.			2.	
Teaching of Jesus.	2.			
Comparative Relig.		1.		
History of Missions.	1.			
The poetical Books.			2.	
Agrament & Debate.				2.

Subject	1.	2.	3.	4.
Group III. Social Science & Agric				
Horticulture		2.	3.	
Crops	2.	2.	2.	
Soil & Fertiliz	4.			
Entomol-Plant Path	2.		2.	
Cattle Feed. & Dair.		2.	2.	
Sericulture		2.	2.	
Forestry				3.
Pomology				2.
Bee Keeping				1.
Com. Veg. Gardening.				2.
Law-Introductory	3.			
Civil		4.		
International				1.
Sanitary Science	2.			

Subject	1.	2.	3.	4.
Group IV. Science and Math				
Surveying. . 6.				3.
Astronomy				3.
Biology	5.	5.	5.	5.
Physics	6.	6.		
Mechan Drawing			2.	
Building				2.
Chemistru	3.			
Physical Chemistry		2.		
Analytical Chem.			3.	
Electro-Chemistry				2.
Geology		3.		

2/21/20

Chosen Christian College Agricultural Dept. Course of Study

Subject	present.			proposed.				
	1st.	2nd.	3rd.	p-1.	p-2.	1st.	2nd.	3rd.
Required								
English	5.	5.	5.	10.	10.	5.	5.	
Japanese	5.	5.	5.	3.	3.	2.	2.	
History-Geography	3.							
Math.(H.Alg. & S. Geom.)				2.	2.			
Math.(Trig.& Surveying)						3.	3.	
Geology		2.				3.		
Botany&Zoology	4.			2.	2.			
Physics Chemistry	3.	3.		3.	3.			
Sanitary Science		2.				2.		
Crops	2.					2.	2.	2.
Horticulture	2.	2.					2.	3.
Soil & Fertilizers	2.	2.				4.		
Entomol.-Plant.Path.		1.	2.			2.		2.
Agric.Tech.& Dairyiny			4.					2.
Cattle Feeding			2.				2.	
Sericulture			2.				2.	2.
Commerce		1.						
Forestry			3.					3.
Agric.Practice	4.	4.	4.					
Agric.Economics			1.				2.	2.
Bookkeeping		2.			2.			1.
Moral Teaching	1.	1.	1.	1.	1.			
Bible				2.	2.	2.	2.	2.
Exercise	1.	1.	1.	1.	1.	1.	1.	1.
Plant Physiology						2.		
Animal Physiology						2.		
Agric.Engineering						2.	2.	
Heredity-Appl.Mychology							2.	
Bio Chemistry							1.	
Horticulture								2.
Plant Breeding								2.
Zootechny								1.
Meteorology				1.				
	32.	31.	30.	25.	26.	32.	28.	25.
Optional								
Pomology								2.
Com.Veg.Gardening								2.
Bee Keeping.								1.

Chosen Christian College Commercial Dept. Course of Study

Subject	present			proposed				
Required	1st.	2nd.	3rd.	p-1.	p-2.	1st.	2nd.	3rd.
English	5.	5.	5.	10.	10.	5.	5.	5.
Japanese	5.	5.	5.	3.	3.			
History & Geography	3.	3.	2.	3.	3.			
Commercial English	3.	3.	3.			5.	5.	5.
Commercial Japanese		2.	2.			2.	2.	2.
Law-Introductory	3.					3.		
Civil		3.					3.	
Commercial			5.					4.
International			1.				1.	
Criminal		2.						
Finance		2.					2.	
Money-Banking-Insure.			2.	(Inclosed under Eco.)				
Commerce	2.					3.	2.	2.
Bookkeeping	2.	2.	2.		2.	3.	2.	2.
Economics	3.					3.	2.	2.
Commercial Practice			2.				2.	
Math. H.Alg. S.Geom.				2.	2.			
Physics-Chemistry				3.	3.			
Sociology								3.
Chinese				2.	2.			
Bible				2.	2.	2.	2.	2.
Moral Teaching	1.	1.	1.	1.	1.			
Exercise	1.	1.	1.	1.	1.	1.	1.	1.
Typewriting						2.		
Business Math.						2.		
	28.	29.	31.	27.	29.	31.	29.	30.

Henry A. Rhodes
Music Department

FILING DEPT
APR 14 1920
SECRETARIES

Ansd.______ Seoul, Chosen, Feb. I2th., 1920

To the Board of Managers of the
Chosen Christian College
Seoul, Chosen

Dear Sirs,-The Faculty of the College have voted to ask the Board to establish a Music Department in Cinnection with the College, the reasons being the great need of development along the line of music among the Korean people requiring specially trained leaders, and the additional reason that a music department will insure a lively Interest among the students in all kinds of music,-singing,glee clubs, orchestra,musicales,concerts,school songs,etc.,making all our religious services more attractive and enliven an interest in music among the young married women of the model village under the direction of the foreign ladies. It was voted also in the Faculty theat in case the establishment of a Music Dept. is granted by the Board of managers "that the course of study be made out in correspondence with Mrs.Becker with the thought that it may be necessary to wait until her return before making request to the Government that this department be established.

If such a department is established it will be necessary to two teachers-a professor and his associate-one for instrumental and one for vocal music.

Prof.Kim has submitted a suggested three year course of study. In addition to this there would be according to the proposed new courses of study the teaching of all the student body in music for the equivalent of two hours a week for one year plus some special training to ge given to the students of the Biblical department.

As to equipment prof.Kim had submitted the following:-

2 Practice Pianos..........	¥1440.	
I Better Grade Piano.......	I760.	
3 Piano Stools.............	75.	3275
2 Practice Organs..........	230.	
I Better Grade Organ.......	250.	
3 Organ Stools.............	I8.	598
5 Violins..................	226.	
I Cello....................	200.	
2 Clarinets................	I90.	
I Flute....................	40.	
I Oboe.....................	60.	
I French Horn..............	I00.	
3 Cornets..................	200.	
Music Stands,etc...........	II5.	II30 Total 5003 yen.

In addition to the above the question as to whether a new building for this department alone would be necessary or not would have to be considered.Hoping this matter will receive your favorable consideration. I am

Sincerely yours,
Henry A. Rhodes

16. 에비슨 교장의 이사회 제출 연례보고서

문서 제목	Chosen Christian College Annual Meeting-March 23, 1921, Report of President
문서 종류	교장 보고서
제출 시기	1921년 3월 23일
작성 장소	서울
제 출 자	O. R. Avison
수 신 자	이사회
페이지 수	5
출 처	Korea Mission Records, 1904~1960, Box 15, Folder 17 (PHS) 2114-5-2: 06 Board of Managers 1915~1922 (UMAH)

자료 소개

에비슨 교장이 1921년 3월 23일 열린 이사회의 연례회의에서 제출한 보고서이다. 그는 미국에서 돌아온 지 얼마 지나지 않았을 때 이사회에 참석하여 이 보고서를 제출하였다. (1920년 4월에 도미하여 1921년 3월 15일 서울에 돌아왔다.) 이 문서는 두 곳에서 발견되는데, 문장 전체는 똑같지만, 서로 다른 부분에서 오타를 수정하고 있다. 두 문서의 맨 뒤에 있는 에비슨의 서명은 에비슨 대신 그의 비서이자 연희전문 이사회의 서기인 오웬스(H. T. Owens)로 추정되는 인물이 쓴 것이다.

에비슨은 이 보고서에서 항목 구분 없이 아래의 사항들을 다루었다.

건축 문제에 관해 협력이사회와 상의한 내용, 남감리회 선교회의 기부, 서울과 학교 간 셔틀 자동차 구입, 교수 사택 건축, 난방 · 조명 · 전력 시설, 학교 홍보요원 고용, 대학 등록, 학과 수 축소, 홍보 팸플릿 발행, 농학, 수학 담당 선교사 교수 구하기, 루카스 건축감독의 귀임, 여자학과 설립.

내용 요약

건축 · 기부금: 1월에 열린 협력이사회 회의에 내(에비슨)가 참석하여 학교의 건축 상황을 보고하였고, 캐나다장로회가 학교의 자본금에 대한 후원금을 증액하였다. 남감리회 선교회가 $40,000의 기부를 약속하였고, 피츠필드(Pittsfield Church)의 감리교회가 이학관[아펜젤러관]의 건축비를 대기로 결정하였다.

셔틀 자동차: 대학과 서울을 오가며 사람들을 실어 나를 차를 빨리 구입해야 한다.

사택: 남감리회 기금으로 피셔의 집을 짓고 북장로회의 기금으로 북감리회 교수들의 사택을 짓는 일을 서둘러야 한다. 사택 설계도는 건축위원회가 작성해야 한다. [북장로회 교수들의 집은 북감리회의 기금으로 1919년부터 짓기 시작하여 건축을 거의 끝내고 있었다.]

시설: 내가 미국에서 중앙집중적인 난방, 조명, 전력 시설의 문제를 언더우드, 루카스와 함께 논의한 후, 뉴욕에 있는 최고 수준의 난방기술자 회사를 선정하여 부지 전체를 위한 계획을 세우기로 하였다.

학교 홍보: 협력이사회 회의 때 미국에서 연희전문을 홍보해줄 대리인을 고용하는 일을 논의하였다.

대학 등록: 인가받은 학교의 특권을 유지하기 위해 총독부에 대학을 등록하는 문제를 검토해주도록 이사회에 요청한다.

학과 수: 학과를 6개 대신 2개 정도로 줄이는 것이 좋을지의 여부를 검토해주도록 이사회에 요청한다. [이사회는 이날의 회의에서 경제적인 이유로 입학생이 10명 미만인 과는 입학생을 받지 말 것을 결정하였다.]

홍보 팸플릿: 내가 미국에 가기 전부터 홍보용 팸플릿을 준비하기 시작하였다가 미국에 있는 동안 한국 근대교육의 발전과정 속에서 연희전문의 존재를 부각시키는 형식으로 팸플릿을 꾸미는 방안을 구상하였으나 완성하지 못하였다.

교수: 농학 교수를 캐나다에서 구하려고 노력하였으나 성과가 없었고, 수학 교수도 미국에서 구하지 못하였다.

건축감독: [건축감독으로 근무하다 미국에 갔던] 루카스가 여름에 복귀하면 존 T. 언더우드가 그의 봉급을 지급할 것이고, 루카스가 오면 근로장학생[산업부 또는 근로부]을 돕는 방법을 찾을 것이다. 농과를 활용하여 농업 방면에서 근로장학생이 일할 곳을 찾는 것도 좋을 듯하다. [루카스는 2020년 6월부터 컬럼비아대학에서 1년간 공부하고 2021년 9월 돌아왔다.]

여자학과: 내가 미국에서 본교에 여자학과를 설치하라는 권고를 받았는데, 이는 여자대학을 연희전문 근처에 두려는 계획[이화여전 설립계획]에서 비롯되었다. 이 일에 세 가지

실행방법이 있는데, 그것은 ① 예정된 부지를 사서 건물을 짓고 연전의 교수진을 활용, ② 연전 캠퍼스에 여자대학 기숙사를 짓고 연전의 교수진을 활용, ③ 남녀공학으로 하여 같은 교실에서 가르치되 기숙사는 완전히 분리 등이다. 이 세 방법에 각각 장단점이 있다.

CHOSEN CHRISTIAN COLLEGE

Annual Meeting -- March 23, 1921.

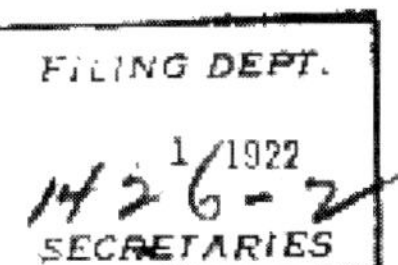
FILING DEPT.
1/1922
1426-2
SECRETARIES

Report of President.

The Vice President will doubtless report upon all matters of interest which have taken place on the field since the meeting of the Board in November last, so that my own report will be confined to occurrences in America after October 21, 1920, when Mr. Billings quoted from my letter of that date.

With regard to the building procedures: at a meeting of the Cooperating Board on January 21 I presented to that Board a review of the present building situation, when I outlined the order in which I thought the buildings ought to be undertaken. In view of the promise of the Canadian Presbyterian Board to increase their contribution to capital funds to $40,000 and to make it available for use between the spring of 1921 and the same period in 1922, out of which they would like to have $22,500 used in building a dormitory and accompanying dining hall, $2500 in residence for Korean professor and teacher, enough of balance for a foreign residence and any remainder to go towards the general fund I suggest that their desire be acceded to and the above buildings be started as soon as contracts can be made for them.

With regard to the sum of $40,000 being contributed by the Southern Methodist Mission, Dr. Rawlings assured us that we could depend upon receiving $23,000 between May 1st, 1921, and the same period of 1922, the balance of $17,000 to be paid over during the ensuing year. He also assured us that there would be no string on the use of these funds. The Field Board of Managers to be left free to use them for whatever purposes they deem most important. I therefore suggest that we proceed at once to the erection of at least one Japanese residence, several houses for Korean teachers and several students' residences in the Model Village. At the same time I feel it would be the part of wisdom to go on at once with the erection of the Science Building and the Underwood Hall because funds have been provided for those buildings which cannot be used elsewhere, and their erection will not in any way interfere with the carrying out of the preceding plans. I do not know how fast the funds for Science building will come in, but we have $10,000 now in hand and I know that something like $9,000 are in the hands of Mr. Sutherland, the Treasurer of the Cooperating Board in New York, which can be sent out at any time. The Pittsfield Church is greatly interested in the erection of this building, and we cannot afford to risk the loss of this interest by delaying the erection of the building. The official Board of the Church passed a resolution in my presence last fall that when the building had been completed and paid for they would devote their foreign missionary contributions each year towards the support of the work to be carried on in the building. I think it would also be well to look forward to the erection of a second dormitory, if the funds already mentioned prove sufficient, but I think grants from those funds should be made for additional work in grading the main campus, and making certain other improvements on the site, such as improving the roadways and putting in permanent bridges.

Another very important need is the working out of a plan for transportation of teachers and others between the College and the city, and I recommend that a fund be set aside from the general funds for the purchase of an auto for this purpose, and that the proper committee should be directed to carry this out at the earliest possible moment. A resid-

2.

ence for Mr. Fisher should be at once built, and this I think should be the first charge on the funds given by the Southern MethodistsBoard. Residences should also be built this summer for Professors Billings and Becker from the funds given by the Women's Board of the Presbyterian Church north.

In regard to the location of these buildings I would suggest that the Building Committee be asked to consider carefully the proposition made by Mr. Lucas, and that if the Property Committee and the Executive Committees can agree as to the acceptance or rejection of this plan the power to decide be lodged in those two committees combined. I would further suggest that plans for residences should be drawn up by the Building Committee which shall be average houses without necessarily waiting for the approval of individual members of the staff who are likely to occupy them. I mention this particularly because one member of the staff who is xxx recently resigned was very anxious to have a residence which was so different from in its design from those generally planned that it would not likely have suited anyone else. The fact that his resignation took place before the house could be built indicates the undesirability of endeavoring to follow too closely the desires of individuals, although of course these desires could not be entirely ignored. Although Mr. Billings will soon go on furlough and Mr. Becker will not be back until next fall, it is my opinion that we should proceed with these houses at once so that there may be as little delay as possible in getting teachers out to the site.

The question of central heating light and power plant was discussedin America, especially between Dr. Underwood, Mr. Lucas and myself, and it was finally decided to consult an architect friend accustomed to the designing of large buildings in New York City and elsewhere, as to the best way to find out how to proceed in getting good advice on this subject. This architect Mr. Lucas and I had a conference with before I left New York on my return trip and by agreement with Mr. Underwood it was finally left to this architect to recommend a firm of heating engineers to go into the matter, and I received a letter from Mr. Lucas when I reached San Francisco stating that one of the best firms of heating engineers in New York had been selected who had agreed to lay out a plan for the whole site which would include heating, lighting and power, water supply, drainage and all mechanical equipment which might be needed, that their bill would be based upon a xxx-xxx multiple of three times their actual outlay for drawing, blue-prints, specifications and all work actually done, but that it would be guaranteed that this bill would not exceed $3,000. I wrote to Mr. Lucas saying that Mr. Underwood had stated he would be willing to abide by the decision of this architect, and that he should now consult with Mr. Underwood and bring the matter to a conclusion. It was also thought that the best way to provide for this central plant would be to assess each building with its proportion of the expense and thus make it unnecessary to provide a special fund for this work. The matter of the budget for current expenses is very pressing because the Treasurer now reports a deficit of xxxxx about Y10,000 which has been borrowed from capital accounts, and it is impossible to carry on our work xxxxxx on a smaller budget than we now have, and indeed unless we xxxxxx decide to concentrate upon a smaller number of departments the present budget will have to be increased so that we must either increase our deficit and our borrowings from capital funds or else find some way of getting larger contributions for the budget. I succeeded in getting a promise from xxx one of the Trustees of the Hall Estate that they would contribute $50,000 towards an endowment fund provided we would secure an equal amount from some other source. This condition was made because they felt that the College was not yet providing as much for this purpose as it ought to do. I was unable before leaving America to secure any part of this $50,000 but if by any means it can be secured the $100,000 would produce an added income of not less than $5,000. As already reported the Cooperating Board asked the four Boards now interested in the institution to increase their contributions by the sum of $5,000, and if this could be done the College would have a total budget income of not less than $15,000. I present this matter to you as one of great urgency, and would ask you to consider some plan for realizing it. In one of my letters from America I urged that something be done to interest Koreans in providing funds for the College, and I would like now to ask what your judgment would be upon the securing here of someone who would promote this interest by personal work amongst Koreans who might be able to donate funds for these purposes.

At the last meeting of the Cooperating Board the proposition was discussed for the employment in America of a promotional agent, and it was generally felt that it would be wise to secure such a man if the right type of man could be found. I am not sure but what it would be equally wise to have such a man in this country. Of course it would be necessary that he should be a Korean, a man of some influence and one interested in the education of the Korean people.

Referring again to the desirability or otherwise of reducing for the present the scope of our work I would ask you to consider whether we should not confine our efforts for the present to perhaps two departments instead of the six that we have had in hand.

I would like to ask you to give consideration to the question of registration of the College, whether we should continue as we are or proceed to unregister in view of the present status of the regulations for private schools. I brought the matter to the attention of the Cooperating Board. The matter was discussed with considerable interest, but it was decided to express no opinion until the Board here had acted and made some recommendation on the subject. I may say that all who took part in the discussion including members from all the different Boards said they felt it might be wise to go somewhat slowly in view of the transition stage through which the laws on education in this country are now going. I do not know that we can at this time formulate any wise recommendation on this very important subject. I am sure we all feel that we would like to get rid of all the restrictions upon religious teaching which hamper us, but at the same time it may be wise for us to wait and see what further changes will be proposed by the Investigating Commission which has been recently appointed. On my way through Japan I discussed this matter with Bishop Welch and he expressed this same opinion. I am aware that a considerable number of missionaries would like to see the College unregister and I greatly sympathize with this view, but it may be well for us to be patient a little longer lest we endanger the privileges we now have.

Before I left America I began the preparation of a publicity pamphlet, planned on the basis of a statement showing the very beginnings of educational mission work in the early days and the improvements made since then up to the establishment of the Chosen Christian College. Each phase of this work is illustrated by a photo, so that the interest of the reader will be thoroughly aroused in still further carrying on the development of education to its higher stages. This method of preparing the pamphlet was strongly approved by the authorities in New York, and I had hoped to get it in good shape before I left but was compelled for lack of time to bring it with me unfinished, but I hope to complete it soon and would like to have it reviewed by a committee of the Board and such changes made as the collective wisdom of the Committee might determine. I have copies of pamphlets issued by several Mission colleges in China but none of them have followed this method. They are all profusely illustrated but deal entirely with the situation of to-day so that they lack the advantage of comparison with the meagre facilities of the earlier days and the stimulus that comes from observing the process of development.

Additional foreign teachers. You already know of the resignation of Mr. Jack. I made considerable effort to get an agricultural man in Canada but up to the time I left neither of two men who had been somewhat prominently before me had been actually secured. A young man in the University of British Columbia Agricultural Department is very anxious to come to us as soon as he completes his course and followed it up with special preparation along the line of his choice, namely animal husbandry. The young man belongs to a good family and is enthusiastic about his profession and in his desire to come to Korea; but we are not yet in a position to begin on Animal Husbandry. However, by the time he is ready to come we may be in such a situation that we can ask him to come and take a couple of years in preparation here by language study and study of the needs of the country so as to be fully prepared for his work when we are ready to open the department. In the meantime while the Canadian Presbyterian Board is looking for a successor to Mr. Jack they will pay to us the sum of $2,000 per year in lieu of his services. ~~Thex~~ I have advised the Canadian Board that a ~~manxf~~ teacher for the Commercial Department would be equally acceptable if they cannot secure an agricultural man. At the present time a great deal of emphasis is being laid upon agricultural missions and the Board of Missionary Preparation is taking much interest in this phase of work. While I was in New York a conference was held of all those who were interested in agricultural missions, which was very successful in its attendance and very interesting, and I trust that in due time we shall have a thoroughly practical department of agriculture, and that the demand for it on the part of students will steadily grow. Until we can equip it and man it better than it is at the present time I fear it is scarcely worth the cost we are putting into it.

We thought at one time that the Northern Methodist ~~Presbyterian~~ Board had secured a teacher of Mathematics, but the negotiations fell through. When I was leaving New York the Candidate Secretary of that Board told me they had about three different men in view and that he hoped they would soon have their third man on the staff. The Southern Methodist Board are prepared to appoint a second man as soon as one is found. Mr. Lucas expects to return here during the coming summer. His salary will be paid by Mr. Underwood, so will not be a tax on any of the Boards, nor will it come out of the building funds as we had at one time thought. He is taking special courses in Columbia University and says that he is able to get exactly the kind of instruction that he needed.

Industrial Department. I see no way of even beginning this work until after Mr. Lucas's return when he hopes to study the situation still more carefully and introduce gradually such things as the conditions here most urgently call for. A good deal was said at the agricultural conference in favor of using the agricultural department as the basis for industrial education by introducing such types of industrial work as naturally are called for by the development of agriculture, such as blacksmithing, wagon-making and other things which will suggest themselves to any one who knows anything about farm work.

While I was in America it was reported to me that the Executive Committee had recommended to the Board the establishment of a department for Women in connection with the College, but the report was not definite as to the form that this should take. I told Miss Appenzeller of this recommendation and she seemed to be not averse to considering it. I shall be glad to hear more details concerning the plan that was in the mind of the members of the Executive Committee. Taking it for granted that the suggestion arose

5.

from the scheme previously conceived of having the Women's College on the hill near the C.C.C., ~~and~~ I can think of two or three different ways in which effective cooperation could be carried out. We must naturally take it for granted that the disadvantages arising from cooperation under the conditions of life in Korea can be more than offset by the method if it is to be put into execution, and these advantages will be either on lines of financial economy or a better type of teaching. It would seem to me that in order to make the cooperation effective from the economical standpoint there must ~~either~~ be a saving either in the purchase of the site, in the erection of school buildings and purchase of equipment or the employment of teachers. One plan might be to purchase the proposed site and erect buildings on it, and then try to utilize the same teaching staff to a considerable extent. Another plan would be to do away with the purchase of this site and erect dormitories on the C.C.C. site, using the same school buildings as the men, but at different hours, and utilizing the same staff as much as possible. A third plan would be that of coeducation, the young women attending the same classes as the men but having their dormitories entirely separate and in different parts of the grounds. Each one of these plans might have certain advantages and certain disadvantages. As I said above I should be glad to know just what was in the minds of those who made the suggestions.

Other subjects than those I have mentioned will come before you under the reports of Committees and the Dean's report and the report of the Vice President. We seem to be at a somewhat critical stage but if we hold on persistently, believe in the institution with conviction, and work with enthusiasm, all difficulties can be overcome, as many have already been conquered. We shall miss from our Board meetings some familiar faces, that of Mr. Rhodes and that of Mr. Blair but we welcome their successors and I feel confident that you will all continue to work zealously for the success of the institution.

(Sgd) O R Avison
President

17. 로즈 학감의 이사회 제출 보고서

문서 제목	Chosen Christian College, Seoul, Korea, Synopsis of Dean's Report, April 1, 1920 -March 31, 1921
문서 종류	학감 보고서
제출 시기	1921년 3월 23일 (추정)
작성 장소	서울
제 출 자	Harry A. Rhodes
수 신 자	이사회
페이지 수	5
출 처	Korea Mission Records, 1904~1960, Box 15, Folder 15 (PHS) 2114-5-2: 06 Board of Managers 1915~1922 (UMAH)

자료 소개

로즈 학감 대리가 1921년 3월 23일 열린 이사회에 제출한 보고서로 보인다. 신과 교수인 그는 안식년을 보내는 베커 학감을 대리하고 있었다. 제목의 일자 표시는 이 보고서가 1921년 3월 31일에 끝나는 한 해의 교육 활동을 종합 정리한 것임을 알게 한다. 그런데 이사회의 연례회의는 3월 23일에 열렸고, 이사회 회의록에는 학감이 이날 보고서를 제출한 것으로 기록되어 있다. 이 문서의 제목이 '학감의 보고서 요약본'인 사실을 참작하면, 이 보고서는 학감 대리가 이사회 때 발표한 보고서를 이후에 어떠한 목적에서(어쩌면 미국에 보내기 전에 더 정리된 형태로 만들기 위해) 요약한 것으로 추정할 수 있다.

이 보고서는 크게 세 부분으로 나뉜다.

학생, 교수, 학과, 졸업생.

(1) 이사회 결정 사항, (2) 교수회 권고안, (3) 또 다른 필요와 변화.

새 학년에 대한 전망

내용 요약

학생: 1920년 새 학기에 56명을 선발하여 학생 수가 총 72명이 되었고, 가을학기에 학생을 더 뽑아 83명이 되었다가 탈락한 학생들이 있어 마지막에는 55명이 되었다.

교수: 이치지마 농과 교수를 포함하여 4명이 사임하였고, 상과 교수로 원달호, 송필만을, 농과 교수로 H. R. Yim을, 한문 교수로 김도희를, 농과 강사로 김술근, C. E. Chung을 영입하였다.

학과: 문과는 학생들과 교수들 사이에서 과의 성격을 규정하는 일로 이견이 있다. 일본어 교수가 필요하고, 2학년과 3학년의 일본어 수업시수가 줄어들었다. 신과는 5명이 등록했다가 3명이 탈락하고 1명이 전과하여 1명만 남았다. '신학과'라는 명칭은 학생들에게 신학을 배울 것을 기대하게 하므로 잘못되었다. 학생들이 성경만 배우려고 이 과를 선택할지 의문이 있다. 수물과는 학생이 7명이고, 그중 3명이 새 학기에 세브란스의전에 입학할 예정이다. 응용화학과는 지원자가 별로 없고, 밀러 교수는 건축일과 치원관을 기숙사로 바꾸는 일로 바쁘다. 상과는 학생이 가장 많고, 백상규가 무급으로 가르치고 있다. 두 명의 한국인 교수를 영입하였지만, 학생들은 백상규의 강의 축소에 불만을 품고 외국인 교수를 요구하고 있다. 농과는 지원자가 별로 없고, 졸업을 앞둔 3학년 3명만 데리고 있으며, 이치지마가 사임한 대신 3명의 한국인 교수와 강사를 구하였다.

졸업생: 이 해에 졸업할 학생을 포함하여 총 26명의 졸업생이 교사, 진학, 기자, 사업, 투옥, 무직 등의 상태에 있다.

(1) 전에 이사회가 결정하였던 일을 아직 실행하지 않고 있다. 학교와 서울 간에 학생과 교수와 방문객을 운송할 셔틀 차량을 마련하지 못한 것, 장학금을 조성하지 않은 것, 피아노가 절실히 필요한 것, 여러 과목의 교수들이 필요한 것 등이다.

(2) 교수회는 다음의 사항들을 권고한다. 각 과의 과장을 임명할 것, '문과'의 이름을 '문예과'로 바꿀 것, '신과'의 이름을 '성문과' 또는 '문겸신과'로 바꿀 것, 대학을 비인가로 되돌리자는 의견을 불허할 것, 학생 자조부(근로장학)를 유지할 것, 고정된 장학금을 확보할 것, 운동 장비를 마련하기 위해 예산을 책정할 것, 전교생이 30분씩 성경을 배우고 매일 20분(10:40~11:00 AM)씩 채플 예배에 참석하게 할 것 등이다.

(3) 새로 마련하거나 바꿔야 할 것들이 더 있다. 교수들의 사택을 부지 안에 마련할 것, 한국인 교수들의 안정적인 교육을 위해 봉급을 조정할 것, 교수들의 직급 구분을 바꿀 것, 기숙사 시설을 속히 확보할 것, 적자가 커지고 있으니 입학금을 더 올릴 것, 한국인과의 협력을 증대하여 재정 지원을 받을 것 등이다.

전망: 입학시험을 일주일 앞두고 벌써 34명이 지원하였다. 10개 교실에 150명의 학생을 받아들일 수용 능력이 있으므로 많은 학생이 오기를 희망한다.

CHOSEN CHRISTIAN COLLEGE
Seoul, Korea

Synopsis of Dean's Report

April 1, 1920 - March 31, 1921

Students.

There were 103 applications for entrance examinations at the beginning of the school year. Of the 90 who came to be examined four were admitted without examination, and fifty-two more were successful, making 56 new students admitted. The applicants came from every Province and Manchuria. Twenty-six middle schools were represented, the largest number of applicants from any one school being ten. In addition to the 56 new students, sixteen second and third year students reported, making 72 in all. Last fall, 11 more were admitted, making a total of 83 registered during the year. Twenty-eight dropped out, so that at the end of the year the registration was 55. In departments and classes they are registered as follows:

	Literary	Bible	Commerce	Agriculture	Math & Physics
1st year	13	1	16	...	7
2nd year	9	...	3	...	...
3rd year	4	...	...	3	...

Of the number now in school, one-half are married, which is about the usual proportion. Denominationally, they are as follows:--

Meth. Episcopal 25 Presbyterian 19 M. E. South 11

Fourteen of the 55 are under 20 years of age, the youngest being 17; only three are above 25 years of age, the oldest being 28. During the year, seven students were allowed to change from one course to another. At the close of the year about thirty of the students were in the dormitory; 16 came out from the city daily, while the others found rooms in the vicinity of the College.

Faculty.

The changes during the year were as follows: Messrs. K. Ichijima and H. C. Lee resigned from the Agricultural Dept., Mr. T. Tsuda from the Commercial Dept., and Mr. Root Lee from the Chemistry Dept.

We have secured new teachers as follows: Mr. T. H. Won and Mr. S. P. Song for the Commercial Dept., Mr. H. R. Kim for the Agricultural Dept., Mr. T. H. Kim as teacher of Chinese; Mr. S. K. Kim and Mr. C. K. Chung as instructors in the Agricultural Dept.

Departments:

Literary Department: The Korean name (Moon Kwa) is misleading. The students like the name and have asked for a strictly literary course which the Faculty does not favor. The only course contemplated for this department is a liberal arts course with special emphasis on English. After much consideration the Faculty recommends a change of name which will be referred to later. During the year extra-curriculum courses in this Department in English and Chinese have been given. Geology could not be taught for lack of a suitable textbook. We greatly need a second Japanese teacher, as Mr. Samura has carried all the Japanese language classes, Oriental history, Geography, Moral Teaching and Exercise. Second year Japanese work has been reduced from five hours a week to three and the third year work to two hours without formal permission from, but on an understanding with, the educational authorities.

Bible Department. During the year five students registered; three dropped out; one changed to Literary Department; so only one is left. The name "Theological" (Sin Kwa) for this department is very misleading and causes dissatisfaction. Students come expecting a theological course which was not intended to be furnished in this department. It is doubtful if any considerable number of students will elect to take a college course with Bible in it unless it is made a specialized course in theology.

Mathematics & Physics Department. Of the seven students who continued in this department until the end of the year, at least three expect to enter Severance Union Medical College this spring.

Applied Chemistry. There were not enough applicants to warrant taking in a class in this course. Mr. Miller's time, however, was mainly devoted to the building program, supervising coverting of the Agricultural Building into a dormitory, etc.

Commercial Dept. This department has the largest single class in the school -- 15 in number. Mr. Paek continued to give generously of his time without salary, teaching five hours a week and directing the department. It is a matter of great regret that he could not be persuaded to give all of his time at full salary according to the action of the Board of Managers a year ago. The major part of Mr. Underwood's teaching for the present is given to this Department. In spite of this, and of the fact that we have two new and acceptable teachers, Messrs. Won and Song, the students have been somewhat dissatisfied largely because of not having all of Mr. Paek's time. Also they make request that a foreign teacher be secured.

Agricultural Dept. There were not enough applicants to warrant taking in an entrance class in this department, so the efforts of the deparment were devoted to carrying the three third year men who graduated this year. It was a great disappointment to lose Mr. Ichijima whose continued ill health caused him to resign. Mr. H. C. Lee also resigned, as he did not feel he was qualified to continue teaching without more preparation. He was succeeded by Mr. H. R. Rim, and we also employed Messrs. S. K. Kim and K. S. Chung as instructors, and in view of the fact that there were only three students in the department it was carried at considerable expense. Out site is preeminently suited for agricultural work, but the fact that we have not yet been able to properly man and equip the department has prevented us carrying it on with sufficient efficiency to attract any large number of students. We hope in the near future that this can be done.

Graduates.

Including this year's graduates our graduate roll numbers 26. Two have died, eleven are teachers in Christian schools; two are ~~studying~~ carrying on further studies; three are in secretarial work; one is a magazine writer; one is in business; one is in prison for political offences; and two are unemployed; and three graduating this year have not reported their posts. The graduations by departments are as follows: Literary 10; Commercial 10; Mathematics & Physics 3; Agriculture 3.

In concluding this report the Board's attention should be called (1) to certain actions of the Board that have not yet been carried out; (2) to a number of Faculty recommendations to the Board; and (3) to certain other needs and changes, all of which bear directly upon the organization and running of the College from the standpoint of students and Faculty.

(1) Former Board actions:

1. Transportation. Only the Faculty and students perhaps realise fully the handicap of three miles' distance from the city without adequate transportation facilities. If these could be provided this handicap could be turned into a great advantage. The new railroad station, when erected, will give some relief. The problem will not be solved, however without a college automobile. It may not be self-sustaining but it is necessary. Students, faculty members in the city, visitors, the families living at the College, and especially the children going back and forth to school, all need better transportation facilities.

2. A temporary Scholarship Fund. You voted to secure, if possible, $1,000 for immediate use. We will need at least ¥600. for this coming year. Unless the Board can find some money at once for this purpose we will have to discontinue all scholarships for this coming school year and have so announced to the students.

3. Piano. The Board has taken favorable action on this item and once or twice Mr. and Mrs. Becker have been written to and urged to secure a piano by special gifts from friends. If they are unable to do so the Board should adopt other measures. A piano is very much needed by the music teacher. Some very gifted musicians are now living in Seoul who might contribute largely to the efficiency of the Music Department had we one or more pianos.

4. New Teachers: These should be secured as soon as possible and somewhat in the following order:
(a) A Japanese Professor for the Literary Department
(b) a foreign teacher of Mathematics
(c) A foreign Professor for the Commercial Department
(d) A foreign Professor for the Agricultural Department
(e) A Korean or Japanese Professor for the Commercial Department
(f) A Korean Professor of Chemistry
(g) A Professor of Philosophy & kindred subjects
(h) A short term Foreign teacher of English

(2) Faculty Recommendations:

1. A request that the Board appoint heads of Departments.

2. A request that the name of the Literary Department (Moonkwa) be changed to Literary and Arts Course (Moon Yei Kwa). At first the Faculty recommended that the new name be the Arts Course (Hak Yei Kwa) but this did not satisfy the students and Alumni. They would prefer a strictly Literary couse but at least want the name "Moon" to be retained. They are not satisfied with an Arts Course under the name Literary.

3. Both the English and Chinese names for the Theological Department are unfortunate. The Faculty has discussed the matter several times but the Korean members have not been able to agree upon a Chinese term. In English the name Literary and Biblical Course would be satisfactory. For Chinese equivalents the names Sung Moon Kwa and Moon Kyum Sin Kwa have been suggested. It is hoped that the Board can agree upon a suitable name.

4. The possibility and advisability of the College reverting to the nonregistered state should be considered by the Board. This matter was discussed by Faculty and a straw vote taken. One voted against a change, three did not vote desiring more information, and the rest voted in favor.

At the request of the Faculty Mr. Ichijima interviewed the Educational Department, and reported that a change could be made, but was advised against making it. He was told that while at present the advantages of registered schools are not particularly apparent they will become more so as time goes on. On the other hand the disadvantages under the present system for a Mission Christian college are many and serious.

5. More than a year ago the Board turned back to the Faculty for further consideration the advisability of organizing a self-help department. A carefully prepared questionnaire was sent to all the Mission Schools in Korea and to some in other Mission lands. The questions dealt with self-help, scholarships and trade schools. Answers were received from Japan, China, India, South America, Syria as well as Korea -- 35 in all. The recommendation of the Faculty, after careful consideration, is submitted separately from this report. During the year we have been able to give work to ten students on an average. Constant enquiries have come from missionaries and Korean leaders asking if students can be given work. As it is, about half of our students (including all second and third year students) are receiving aid either from work given, or scholarships, or mission funds, or missionaries.

6. Also the Faculty presents a recommendation on a plan for a permanent scholarship fund. The Faculty assumes that such a fund will be necessary and will be provided by the Board. In this connection the desirability of a few of our teachers training in America is often mentioned by those interested in the College.

7. We have been handicapped in not having in the budget an item for Athletics. A gift of Y100.oo, together with personal subscriptions by members of the Faculty, helped to tide us over. The athletic fee from students has been doubled, and we are including an item in the budget for athletic supplies.

8. Another Faculty recommendation looks forward to providing a half-hour period of Bible study for all students. The plan is to follow a 20-minute daily chapel service (10:40-11 A.M.) with a number of Bible classes (11:-11:30 This study will be optional. This recommendation is in accord with the interview of the President with the authorities before he left for America a year ago. At that time Dr. Avison recommended that "A break of at least one hour (or more if necessary) be made during the forenoon in the official curriculum and that that time be used for religious exercises and Bible classes suitable for students of all departments." The Faculty proposes with your permission to try this plan.

(3) Other Needs and Changes.

1. The desirability of getting more members of the staff to live on the site is more and more manifest, it being very difficult to secure full attendance at Faculty meetings and regular attendance upon classes. This, of course, would necessitate the building of a number of residences at once. Furthermore, we should contract with each native member of the staff for a term of years at a fixed salary, requiring service for the entire year with the exception of one month's vacation. A summer normal school for teachers of Christian schools, summer religious and social welfare conferences, extension work, preparation of textbooks, all should be part of our program. The members of the Faculty should be so located as to assist in this work.

3. Some change in the grading of teachers should be made. At present

there are three grades, Professor, Associate Professors and Assistants. There should be one more grade, Assistant Professor; A and B grades of each class of professors; and a grade called "Instructors" for those who teach by the hour or for part time.

4. More dormitory accommodation with adequate supervision is urgent. Only students whose homes are in the vicinity of the College or in the city should be allowed to live off the campus. As half our students are married doubtless a number would like to live in the Model Village and ought to do so as soon as houses can be built.

5. Tuition. According to the Board's recommendation tuition rates have been raised to Y24.00 per year and Y6.00 matriculation fee. The laboratory fees have also been raised. Perhaps tuition fees should be increased even more. In spite of the present increase and of larger grants from the Boards we are still facing an annual deficit, while past deficits have accumulated beyond the Y10,000 mark.

6. Korean Cooperation. The recurring deficits naturally bring up the question as to whether it is possible to secure that kind of Korean cooperation that would bring the College financial aid. It is not possible as yet to finance the school on tuition fees and Mission appropriations; nor is it advisable to do so. Perhaps the best example of native cooperation in a Mission school in the Orient is the Canton Christian College, whose plan I commend to the Committee on Korean Cooperation.

Outlook for the coming year.

A week before the date of entrance examinations we have already 34 applications. At most we can admit 130 new students if they are somewhat evenly divided among the departments, as our class rooms will seat from 20 to 20. Our present capacity is about one hundred and fifty students with ten class rooms. By 1922 we may have as many as sixteen classes and will likely have at least twelve, which number by crowding might be accommodated in our present quarters.

Respectfully submitted,

Harry A. Rhodes, Dean.

18. 빌링스 부교장의 이사회 제출 보고서

문서 제목	Chosen Christian College, Report of Vice President to Field Board of Managers
문서 종류	부교장 보고서
제출 시기	1921년 9월 23일
작성 장소	서울
제 출 자	Bliss W. Billings
수 신 자	이사회
페이지 수	1
출 처	Korea Mission Records, 1904~1960, Box 15, Folder 17 (PHS) 2114-5-2: 06 Board of Managers 1915~1922 (UMAH)

자료 소개

부교장인 빌링스가 1921년 9월 23일 열린 이사회 회의 때 제출한 보고서이다. 그는 북경에 간 교장을 대신하여 이 보고서를 제출하였다.

빌링스는 한 페이지 안에서 아래의 사항들을 다루었다.

학교건축, 학생, 교수, 재정운영, 여자대학 설립, 학교 홍보 문제.

내용 요약

건축: 첫 번째 기숙사 건물[핀슨관], 이학관[아펜젤러관], 언더우드관, 선교사 교수 사택 2채를 건축하고 있다. 기숙사는 1층 바닥을 깔았고, 이학관은 기초공사를 끝냈으며, 언더우드관은 기초공사를 하고 있다. 빌링스의 집은 지붕을 덮었고, 피셔의 집은 지붕을 덮고 있다.

학생 · 교수: 학생 수가 크게 늘었고, 교수 인력도 보강되어 앤드류(Thurman Andrew)가 와서 수학을 맡았고, 루카스 건축감독이 3일 전에 도착하였다.

재정: 협력이사회는 대학이사회에 편지를 보내 수입 한도 안에서 지출하고 한국인의 후원을 확보하는 것이 바람직하다는 사실을 지적하였다.

여자대학: 협력이사회가 제안했던 여자대학 설립 문제에 대해 재한 선교사들에게 의견을 물었으나, 캐나다 선교회는 답변을 연기하였고, 북감리회 선교회는 답변하지 않고 있다.

학교 홍보: 북경 의대의 개교식에 참석하러 가는 저명한 의료인들이 가는 도중에 본교를 방문하면서 본교가 선교와 교육 종사자들에게 더 널리 알려지게 되었다.

CHOSEN CHRISTIAN COLLEGE

Report of Vice President to Field Board of Managers
September 23, 1921.

- - - - - - - - - - - - - - - - - - -

Owing to the absence of the President in Peking, it devolves upon me to present a brief report to this meeting.

Since Annual Meeting of the Field Board the principal features in the development of the College have been the getting under way of the first permanent Dormitory, Science Hall and Underwood Hall, and the building of two more residences for foreign teachers. (2) the greatly increased student enrollment; and (3) the further strengthening of the Faculty.

On the two last features, the Dean will report in more detail. The contracts for the various buildings were let at the following figures: all going to the same Contractor, Mr. Mo:--

Underwood Hall	¥102,000
Science Hall	49,500
Dormitory	24,000

As you will see when going over the property, the Dormitory has had the first storey floor laid and the walls of the first storey are going up; Science Hall foundations have been completed and Underwood Hall foundations are under way. The Billings residence has been roofed, and the Fisher house roofing is in progress. The report of the Building Committee will take up these matters in fuller detail.

The Faculty has been strengthened by the arrival of Mr. Thurman Andrew for the Chair of Mathematics, his coming completing the quota of teachers due by the Northern Methodist Mission.

Mr. Lucas arrived three days ago from America and will report in person with special reference to the plans under way for the central heating and lighting plant.

Correspondence from the Secretary of the Cooperating Board in America will be presented, calling the attention of this Board to the advisability of confining expenditures within the limits of assured income, also to the desirability of building up the support from local sources.

The various Missions cooperating with the College were requested on the initiative of the Cooperaing Board to give the Board their judgment as to the advisability of establishing a Women's Department of the College, or the organization of a Union Women's College in Korea. The Canadian Presbyterian Mission took an action which will be reported later. The Northern Presbyterian Mission, not having assumed as yet any jurisdiction in the affairs of the College, it was thought best to defer action by that Mission for another year.

Many prominent medical men and educationists en route to the opening ceremonies in connection with the Peking Union Medical College have visited the College recently, so that the institution is gradually becoming personally known to many men connected with missionary and educational work.

(Signed) B. W. Billings,
Vice President.

19. 로즈 학감의 이사회 제출 보고서

문서 제목	Dean's Report to the Board of Managers
문서 종류	학감 보고서
제출 시기	1921년 9월 23일
작성 장소	서울
제 출 자	Harry A. Rhodes
수 신 자	이사회
페이지 수	3
출 처	Korea Mission Records, 1904~1960, Box 15, Folder 15 (PHS) 2114-5-2: 06 Board of Managers 1915~1922 (UMAH)

자료 소개

로즈 학감이 1921년 9월 23일 열린 이사회 회의에 제출한 보고서이다. PHS와 UMAH에 같은 모양의 문서가 소장되어 있지만, 마지막 서명 부분에서 'Respectfully Submitted Harry A. Rhodes'의 손글씨 모양이 아주 똑같지는 않은 것을 보면, 이 문서는 여러 장을 아래에 받쳐서 타자로 친 후에 서명을 따로 하였던 것이라고 짐작된다.

이 보고서는 항목 분류 없이 아래의 사항들을 설명하고 있다.

학생 현황, 종교교육, 교수, 모범촌 건축.

내용 요약

학생: 학기 초 입학시험에 146명이 입시를 지원했다가 99명이 응시하였다. 5개 과목에서 평균 60점 이상인 학생 34명, 1과목이 60점 미만인 학생 9명, 50점 이상인 학생 18명이 합격하였다. 4명은 무시험으로 입학하였고, 전에 떠났던 학생 9명이 돌아와, 1학년 학생이 총 74명이다. 학생 수는 문과 52명, 상과 48명, 수물과 16명(2학년까지)으로 총 116명이었는데, 5명이 그만두어 현재는 111명이다. 신과, 농과, 응용화학과는 지원자가 적어서 학생을 뽑지 않았다. 입시생 가운데 과목별 점수 미달자가 영어 43%, 일본어 40%, 수학과 물리학 13%였다. 학생들이 전국 각 도의 30개 중등학교에서 왔고, 등록 학생 103명 가운데 장로교인은 31명, 북감리회 교인은 41명, 남감리회 교인은 28명, 조합교회 교인은 1명, 비기

독교인은 2명이다.

종교교육: 학생들에게 선교활동을 하는 스튜어트(Robert Stewart) 박사가 채플 시간에 여러 번 매우 흥미롭게 설교하였지만, 일부 학생들은 전혀 만족하지 않았는데, 이는 소풍 계획 때문이었다. 2교시와 3교시 사이 채플 시간에 그가 설교하고 있는 도중에 도의 검열관이 왔다. 그로 인해 종교의 자유를 위해 학교를 비인가로 돌리는 문제를 심각하게 검토하였다. 두 학기 동안 채플을 주 3회 열었다.

교수: 수물과의 조수인 장세운이 지난주에 미국으로 유학을 떠났고[미국에서 한국 최초로 수학박사 학위를 받았다], 또 한 명은 1월에 떠나기를 희망하고 있다. 일본어 교수는 한 명뿐이고, 교수 부족으로 지리학을 가르치지 못하고 있으며, 다른 과목들도 베커가 돌아오기를 기다리고 있다. 노정일(C. I. Roe)이 최근 미국에서 돌아와 가르치고 있고, 루카스 부부와 앤드류 부부를 맞은 일도 큰 즐거움이 되었다.

모범촌: 한국인과 일본인 교수들의 사택과 모범촌의 일부 주택들을 짓는 일이 전보다 더 시급해졌는데도 덩치가 큰 건축계획을 진행하느라 매우 중요하면서도 작은 것들을 소홀히 하고 있다.

SCOTT Chosen Christian College

Ans'd

FILING DEPT. 1426-2 1 1922 SECRETARIES

DEAN'S REPORT TO THE BOARD OF MANAGERS.
SEPT. 23, 1921.

With the opening of the new school year there were one hundred forty six applications for examination for the first year. But twenty four of these did not report for examination five of them because we could not offer the course for which they had applied. Of the one hundred twenty two who did report for examination, twenty three took only part of their examinations. They became discouraged or took sick I dont know which. Of the ninety nine who took all their examinations, there only thirty four passed according to the conditions laid down, viz., an average of sixty in the five subjects with no mark below forty. Nine others had an average above sixty but had failed in one subject. These we admitted. Also we admitted eigteen others who had an average above fifty and had failed in not more than one subject. Only four were admitted without examination. Nine former students who had dropped out of school returned to take up the work of the first year again.(one of these failed last year) This made a total of seventy four who were entitled to enter the first year classes but of these five did not report for study. Three of our former students returned for the third year's work and two for the second.

Our registration by departments then for this term is as follows: Literary, 1st., 28: 2nd.,13; 3rd.,7; 4th.,4;total,52;
Commercial,1st.,27; 2nd.,15; 3rd.,6; total 48;
Mathematics and Physics, 1st.,14; 2nd.,2; total,16;
total for the three departments, 116. But of these five have already dropped out of school so that we now have (111) one hundred eleven. We could not enter classes in the Biblical, Agricultural, and A Applied Chemistry course because there were not enough applicants.

Remarks upon the entrance examinations may be made as follows. As was the case last year only one third passed according to requirements. Forty three percent failed in English, forty percent in Japanese, and thirty percent in Math.and Physics. Twenty seven percent failed in one subject, twenty five percent in two subjects and fifteen percent in more than two subjects. On the whole the examinations have been too difficult and the whole system of entrance upon examination only, is unsatisfactory.

Out of fifty one examined from thirteen mission schools, thirty four (or 67 %) were admitted, while out of forty examined from twelve non Christian schools, twenty four (or 60%) were admitted. Thirty middle schools and all the thirteen provinces were represented.

As to denominations, out of one hundred three for whom we have records, thirty one are Presbyterians, forty one are Methodist Episcopal, twenty eight are Methodist Episcopal South, one is a Congregationalist, and two are not professing Christians.

Out of ninety nine who took the entrence examinations this year, only one averaged above ninety percent while only three others averaged above eighty percent.

The spring we had the privilege of having Rev. Dr. Robert Stewart, a missionary student evangelist, for an hour each day at the Chapel hour. His talks were powerful, thoroughly Gospel, and intensely interesting. And yet the response on the part of the student body was not entirely satisfactory. This was due perhaps to the fact that their heads were full of the usual Spring excursion that they were planning to take. During one of his talks, the Provincial school inspector dropped in. He left a note of criticism that we were having the Chapel hour between the second and third study hours. How long we will be able to continue this practice remains to be seen. The whole question of being compelled to drag in our religious exercises and Bible study contrary to the law for a registered school is causing us much concern, and the advisability of reverting to the non registered state schould be seriously considered. During these two terms we are trying the plan of having Chapel three days a week. Of course it is better than no Bible study at all but it is not ideal.

In the Chapel service one day I made inquiry as to what religious work is being done by the students. Fiftteen of them are helping regularly each Sunday in churches in the city and in the vacinity of the college, while nine others have helped on occasion during this term. Twelve of those present indicated that they are planning to study for the ministry.

Out of the 111 students who studied at least a part of the time during the Spring term, twenty five have not returned or for one reason or another were not allowed to continue their studies. This is a bad leakage for one term. Nine of these dropped from the Mathematics and Physics Dept. 1st. Yr. Some entered this department because they could not be admitted to the Literary and Commercial Depts and they were dissatisfied, and not qualified. Eight new students were admitted, so that our enrollment stands at ninety four, if they all pay their tuition and other fees.

One of our assistant teachers, Mr. Chang Sei Uon left last week for further study in America. Another hopes to in January. At present we have but one Japanese teacher and only for two days a week. Two hours in Experoise and six hours in History and Geography are not being taught because of the lack of teachers Also severn hours in other subjects are awaiting Mr. Beckers return. Mr. C. l. Roe, recently returned from America is carrying five hours and giving us valuable help in other ways. It is with genuine pleasure that we welcome Mr. and Mrs. Lucas and Mr. and Mrs. Andrew.

The building of Korean and Japanese teachers residences and of some of the model village houses is more urgent than ever. In the midst of our large building projects we are failing to get done many of the smaller things which are very importan if we are to have a well organized well run

- 3 -

school. It may be necessary to get along running somewhat at loose ends for a few years, but certainly the present state of affairs is anything but satisfactory. However there is much to encourage and better days are in the near future.

Respectfully Submitted
Harry A. Rhodes

20. 에비슨 교장의 연전 · 세의전 이사회 연석회의 제출 보고서

문서 제목	Report of President O. R. Avison, Joint Meeting of Boards of Managers of the Severance Union Medical College and Chosen Christian College
문서 종류	교장 보고서
제출 시기	1922년 3월 16일
작성 장소	서울
제 출 자	O. R. Avison
수 신 자	연희전문 이사회와 세브란스의전 이사회
페이지 수	2
출 처	Korea Mission Records, 1904~1960, Box 15, Folder 17 (PHS)

자료 소개

에비슨 교장이 1922년 3월 16일 열린 연희전문 이사회와 세브란스의전 이사회의 연석회의에 제출한 보고서를 보완한 것이다. 연석회의는 총독부가 1922년 2월 제2차 조선교육령을 공포하자 그 대책을 논의하기 위해 열렸다. 양교의 이사들은 이날 오전 9시 30분 에비슨의 집에서 함께 회의한 후, 새로운 교육령에 따라 신청서를 작성하여 학교 인가를 다시 받기로 합의하였다. 그러면서 세브란스의전 측은 그날 오후 2시 30분에, 연희전문 측은 저녁 8시에 따로 이사회 회의를 열어 이 일을 결정하기로 하였다. 그런데 이 보고서의 맨 뒤에 그날 저녁 연희전문 이사회가 결정한 내용이 더해져 있는 것으로 보아 이 보고서는 에비슨이 3월 16일 연석회의 때 제출한 원본을 차후에 증보한 것으로 추정된다. 에비슨이 미국에 보내기 위해 이 증보본을 만들었을 것으로 짐작된다.

양교 교장 에비슨은 이 보고서를 아래와 같이 구성하였다.

회의 개회 이유, 선택할 사항, 양교 교수들의 권고안, 연희전문 이사회의 결정.

내용 요약

회의 이유: 우리는 수년간 총독부를 향해 ① 종교의 자유 제한 철폐, ② 상급과정 설치 권한 부여, ③ 예비(교양)과정 설치 권한 부여, ④ 보다 융통성 있고 큰 교육과정 조정 권한 부여를 요구해왔다. 이제 새 교육령 아래에서 이 모든 것을 실현할 수 있게 되었으므

로 교육령에 대응하는 문제를 더 쉽게 결정하기 위해 이 회의를 열었다.

[1919년 9월 재한 선교사들은 연희전문의 빌링스와 밀러를 대표로 하여 총독부에 종교교육의 자유 허용, 조선어 사용제한 철폐, 조선인에게 일본인과 동등한 교육기회 부여 등을 포함한 7가지 요구 사항을 제출하였다. 그 후 총독부는 1920년 3월 교과목의 제한과 교육 자격을 일부 완화하였고, 1922년 2월 제2차 조선교육령을 공포하였다. 4월부터 시행되는 이 교육령은 조선에서 일본과 동등한 교육을 시행하겠다는 것을 표방하며 교육 연한을 늘렸다. 이때 종교교육이 공식적으로 허용되지 않았지만, 에비슨은 전면적으로 허용될 줄로 알고 있었다. 인가받은 학교의 종교교육은 이듬해 1923년 4월부터 지정학교에 허용되었다. 전면적인 종교교육이 허용되지 않는 것을 알게 된 에비슨은 1920년 4월 미즈노 정무총감을 만나 유감을 표명하였고, 그 자리에서 미즈노의 허가를 받아 이후부터 2교시와 3교시 사이에 주 3회 채플을 열고—학생들의 자발적 선택으로—성경 교육은 신과의 선택과목을 수강하게 하여 오전의 그 시간에 주 2회 시행하는 방법으로 비교적 자유롭게 종교교육을 하였다.]

선택 사항: 양교가 선택할 수 있는 세 가지 방안은 이미 폐기된 이전 법령 아래에서 전문학교로 남는 것, 새 교육령에 따라 인가받은 전문학교가 되고 온전한 종교의 자유를 누리는 것, 비인가 사립학교[각종학교]의 지위로 바꾸는 것이다.

비인가 사립대학으로 만들면, 수준이 낮은 비인가 학교 학생들을 받고, 종교교육이나 교육과정의 조정은 자유롭게 할 수 있어도, 졸업생은 검정고시에 합격하지 않으면 학력을 인정받지 못해 인가받은 상급 학교에 진학하지 못한다. 교육법에 따라 전문학교 인가를 새로 받으면, 관립 · 사립 고등보통학교의 졸업생들을 받고, 예과 과정을 둘 수 있으며, 졸업생들은 법적 지위를 인정받고, 세브란스의전 졸업생들은 총독부의 의료면허시험을 치르지 않고도 위생국에서 인정을 받게 된다. 이전의 전문학교 인가 상태로 남는 경우에는 인가 · 비인가 고등보통학교 학생들을 받고, 예과를 설치하지 못하며, 졸업생은 총독부나 사회에서 열등하게 취급받게 된다.

권고안: 양교 교수들과 조수들은 양교 이사회를 향해 학무국에 즉시 등록 신청을 하는 것에 찬성하라는 권고안을 채택하였다. 양교는 이 일에 필요한 재정적, 인적, 시설 조건들을 이미 갖추고 있다.

연희전문 이사회 결정: [그날 저녁에 열린 연희전문 이사회 연례회의의 회의록에서 해당 부분을 발췌하여 소개하고 있다.] 새 교육령에 따라 학교를 전문학교로 등록해야 한다는 교수회의 권고안을 학감이 연희전문 이사회에 제출하여 그 권고안이 채택되었다.

Dr. O.R. Avison

3/16/22

REPORT OF PRESIDENT O. R. AVISON.

JOINT MEETING OF BOARDS OF MANAGERS OF THE SEVERANCE UNION MEDICAL COLLEGE AND CHOSEN CHRISTIAN COLLEGE.

March 16, 1922

For several years we have desired to secure certain changes in the Educational Ordinance, including the following:

1. Removal of restrictions on Religious Education.
2. Authority to give a more advanced course.
3. Authority to give a preparatory course to fit students better for the regular College course.
4. Greater control over the Curriculum so as to give it more elasticity and greater breadth.

I am able to report to you that all of those desires can now be realized under the New Educational Ordinance.

Probably the most important decision to be arrived at this meeting will be the relation our Colleges are to bear to New Ordinance and, to make decision more easy to arrive at, I will state the three possibilities before us:

1. We may remain as we now are, a Special School (Semmon Gakko) under the superseded regulation, which remains as before except that religious instruction may now be freely given within the Curriculum.
2. We may move forward so as to become a Special School under the new regulations, also with full religious liberty.
3. We may revert to the status of an unregistered private college.

Dealing with these three possibilities in reverse order I would offer the following explanations of each status:

Private College, unregistered:

(a) Entrance requirements - These are under the control of the College and students may be accepted from any lower schools, registered or unregistered.
(b) Preparatory Course - It may have such a course at its discretion.
(c) Curriculum - It may arrange this as it desires.
(d) Its Graduates - Have no recognised standing and no legal standing. Apparently they cannot enter the higher Government schools or registered schools or Colleges without first passing the examination of a Government or registered Higher Common School.

New Special School or College - registered:

(a) Entrance requirements - It can receive as regular students only those who have graduated from regular government or registered Higher Common Schools, but it can receive as Special students those who come to it from any other schools and pass its entrance examinations.
Special Students, however, cannot be regularly graduated unless they first pass the regular examination for graduation from a government or registered Higher Common School and therefore get into the regular line of the Educa-

tional System of the country, but they can take the examinations for graduation and receive a form of certificate, I believe.

(b) Preparatory Course - It may have such a course at its discretion.
(c) Curriculum - It may arrange this practically as it desires, subject to the approval of the Governor General.
(d) Its Graduates - Have full legal standing and have all the opportunities of the country together with the advantage which a ready-made conception that registered schools give a higher grade of education than others give.

We have good reason to believe its graduates will receive recognition from the Sanitary Bureau so that they would not have to take the Government Medical examination for license.

Old Special School or College, registered:

(a) Entrance Requirements - It can receive its students from any registered or non-registered Higher Common School and carry them through to graduation.
(b) Preparatory Course - not permitted.
(c) Curriculum - It can probably secure fair control through special approval by the authorities.
(d) Its Graduates - Must take the Government Medical Examination before entering on practice. They are regarded by the Government and by the general public as inferior and have no chance for Government appointments.

After a careful consideration of the whole subject, a joint meeting of the Faculty and Assistants unanimously adopted a recommendation to the Board of Managers in favor of immediate application to the Educational Bureau for registration under the new ordinance.
I heartily concur in this recommendation.

The factors which enter into such registration are:

1. A Zaidan Hojin must be formed to hold property and administer the affairs of the College. This already exists.
2. A certain amount of Capital Funds and Endowment or guarantee for a certain amount of yearly expenditure must be in the hands of this Zaidin Hojin. These are already provided.
3. A sufficient group of qualified teachers. These are already on hand.
4. Adequate Equipment - We have enough I think to insure granting of our application. Probably suggestions would be made to add certain things as soon as possible.
5. Sufficient Class Rooms and Laboratories - Same remarks as for No. 4.

EXTRACT FROM MINUTES OF ANNUAL MEETING OF THE FIELD BOARD OF MANAGERS, CHOSEN COLLEGE, March 16, 1922

The Dean reported the recommendation of the Faculty that the College should proceed to register as a Semmon Gakko under the new ordinance.
The matter having been thoroughly discussed at the joint session earlier in the day, it was moved by Dr. Noble, seconded by Mr. Wasson, that the recommendation of the Faculty be accepted and steps taken to make application. Carried.

21. 에비슨 교장의 이사회 제출 연례보고서

문서 제목	C. C. C. Report of Preident to Field Board of Managers
문서 종류	교장 보고서
제출 시기	1922년 3월 16일
작성 장소	서울
제 출 자	O. R. Avison
수 신 자	이사회
페이지 수	2 (+ 요약문 1)
출 처	Korea Mission Records, 1904~1960, Box 15, Folder 17 (PHS) 2114-5-2: 06 Board of Managers 1915~1922 (UMAH)

자료 소개

에비슨 교장이 1922년 3월 16일 오후 8시에 열린 대학이사회 연례회의에 제출한 보고서이다. 이 보고서는 2쪽 분량의 원본과 이를 1쪽으로 줄인 요약본, 두 가지가 있다.

이 보고서에서 에비슨 교장은 항목 설정 없이 1921~22년간의 건축 문제와 재정 문제를 주로 거론하였다.

내용 요약

학생 · 교수: 등록생 수가 113명으로 개교 이래로 가장 많아 최고의 한 해를 보냈고, 학년 말에 81명으로 마감하였다. 캐나다장로회만 빼고 다른 모든 협력 선교부들이 파견하는 교수의 쿼터를 다 채우게 되었다. 북감리회의 후원으로 앤드류가 왔다. 그밖에 노정일이 와서 철학을 맡았고, 다카하시가 와서 교수진이 보강되었다.

건축: 학교건축 프로그램이 꾸준히 진행되어 이학관[아펜젤러관], 언더우드관, 첫 번째 기숙사의 건축계약을 지난봄에 체결하였다. 기숙사는 4월 1일 입주할 준비를 끝냈으며, 이학관과 언더우드관은 이번 겨울에 일부를 사용할 수 있게 될 것이다. 빌링스 교수와 피셔 교수의 집을 짓고 있고, 베커의 집은 이번 봄에 건축계약을 맺을 예정이다. 원한경의 집도 건축계약을 할 가능성이 있고, 한국인과 일본인 교수들의 집을 지을 계획을 세우고 있다.

남감리회 선교부가 $17,000을, 캐나다장로회 선교부가 $15,000을, 북감리회 선교부가 $8,000을 보냈다. [1쪽짜리 요약본에는 남감리회와 캐나다장로회 측이 약속한 돈을 모두 보냈다고 기술되어 있다], 충분하지는 않지만, 이 돈을 건축공사에 사용할 것이다. 그래도 협력이사회에 참여하는 선교부들에 학교 발전을 위해 자본금을 더 보내주도록 호소해야 할 것이다. 교수 사택, 모범촌 주택, 운동장, 체육관, 도서관, 박물관, 기숙사들을 지을 기금이 필요하고, 도로, 하수, 급수, 난방, 전기시설 공사를 하기 위해서도 추가기금이 필요하다.

언더우드관과 이학관의 정초식을 지난 10월[10월 5일] 동시에 거행하면서 학교를 처음으로 크게 홍보하였는데, 봉헌식 때 기부자인 존 T. 언더우드를 한국에 오도록 초청한다면 한국 사회의 관심을 높여서 재정 지원을 이끌 수 있을 것이다.

재정: 한 해의 지출을 다 결산하면, 경상예산의 적자가 ￥23,000에서 ￥25,000 사이[요약본에서는 ￥13,000에서 ￥15,000 사이로 기록되어 있다]에 이르렀지만, 미국에서는 적자의 벌충을 위해 건축기금을 사용하지 않게 할 대책을 마련해주지 않고 있다. 남감리회와 캐나다감리회가 일본 고베의 관서학원에는 각각 연 $25,000을 기부하였으나, 우리 학교에는 $3,000, $2.500, $500만을 기부하였다. 총독부도 우리 학교를 향해 전문학교 자격을 유지하려면 경상수입을 늘리라고 요구하고 있는 현재 상황에서는 협력 선교부들이 지급해주는 기금만 가지고 학교를 운영할 수가 없다.

for Scott

Rec'd F. E. B. FILING DEPT. MAY 24 1922 1426-2 SECRETARIES

C. C. C. Mar 1922

Report of President to Field Board of Managers.

In many respects the College has had its best year. Our student enrolment has been the largest in our seven years' history, namely 113 against 96 in 1917. We have finished the year with 81 students in attendance. All of the cooperating Missions excepting the Canadian Presbyterian have maintained their full quota of teachers, Mr. Andrew's coming last autumn filling up the Northern Methodist representation, although he is of course assigned to language study for the present. The teaching staff has been further strengthened by the appointment of Mr. Roe to the chair of Philosophy, and by the engagement of Mr. Y. T. Takahashi.

The building program has gone steadily ahead, contracts for Science Hall, Underwood Hall and the first Dormitory being let last spring. The Dormitory will be ready for occupation on April 1st, and it is possible that parts of Science Hall and Underwood Hall may be in use during the coming winter. Two more foreign residences have been erected, and are being occupied by Messrs. Billings and Fisher. A contract for Mr. Becker's house will be let this spring, and possibly another for Mr. Underwood. We are also planning to build a Japanese teacher's residence and several for Korean teachers.

With the release of the $17,000 from the Southern Methodist Board and $15,000 from the Canadian Presbyterians on account of their $40,000 pledge, we will have received all of the money which has so far been pledged by the various Boards, with the exception of $8,000 from the Northern Methodists who raised their initial pledge of $52,000 to $100,000, $92,000 of which is in course of being paid in. These monies will all be used during the coming building season, but will be insufficient to complete the work that is necessary. We will soon have to face the question of making a new appeal to the cooperating Boards to make further pledges for capital investment in order to complete the development of the institution. These funds will be needed for the housing of our foreign and native teaching staff, model village, athletic field, gymnasium, library and museum building, and for the completion of the dormitory group, which calls for three more dormitories and a central dining hall. Roads, drains, water supply, heating and power plant also require additional funds. One of the dormitories referred to is to be provided by the Canadians.

The simultaneous laying of the cornerstones of Underwood Hall and Science Hall last October was made the occasion of the first big advertising that the College has done, and there was a representative attendance of Korean and Japanese officials, educators and church dignitaries. I suggest that this Board extend an invitation to Mr. John T. Underwood to visit Korea to dedicate the new building which he is providing, and I feel sure that his coming will provide a favorable opportunity for further developing the interest of the Korean community and possibly of building up indigenous financial support. Our efforts should be constantly directed towards the cultivation of that class of the people who can afford to contribute to the support of the College.

Up to February 28th the deficits on current budget which have been accumulating since the first year of the operation of the College amounted to ¥19,372.76, and the salaries and other expenses for February and March have still to be included. The close of the year is likely therefore to see the deficit between ¥23,000 and ¥25,000, but we expect ¥4,000 from the Canadian Mission in lieu of their teacher which will reduce it correspondingly. The fact that no action has yet been taken in North America to reduce the deficit prevents us from having funds to proceed with the

2.

C. C. C.

Report of President to Field Board of Managers

erection of native teachers' residences to the extent needed, and with the development of the foundational work of the site. When it is considered that the two Boards interested in Kwansei Gakuin at Kobe, the Southern Methodist and the Canadian Methodist, contribute $25,000 each annually to that institution, the contributions to our institution of $3,000, $2500 and $500 look very small indeed. Of course, the Kwansei institution has a Middle School in connection; nevertheless the disparity in contributions seems very apparent when the Boards have commissioned us to run an institution of College grade. Furthermore, the government requirements as to current revenue if we remain as a Semmon Gakko will require that our current revenue be made more adequate to the needs of the school, and whether or not we do remain as a Semmon Gakko or revert to some other status past experience has shown that we cannot run the institution with the contributions we are now receiving from the cooperating Boards.

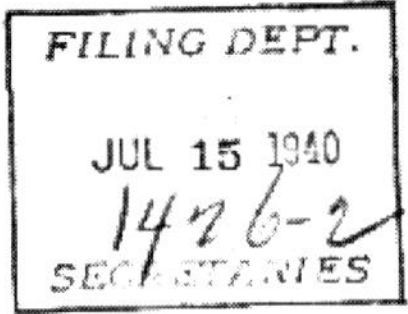

CHOSEN CHRISTIAN COLLEGE - 1921-22.

SUMMARY OF THE PRESIDENT'S REPORT

TO THE FIELD BOARD OF MANAGERS.

The student enrolment for the past year has been the largest in the seven years' history, namely 113, as against 96 in 1917. The year closed with 81 students in attendance.

The Cooperating Missions, with the exception of the Canadian Presbyterian Mission, have maintained the full quota of teachers.

Building Program: Contracts have been let for Science Hall, Underwood Hall and the first Dormitory. Two foreign residences have been completed, and the contract for another foreign residence is to be let this spring, with the possibility of several residences for Japanese and Korean teachers.

All of the monies pledged by the various Boards (with the exception of $8,000. from the Northern Methodist Board) have been received. These monies will all be used during the coming building season, but will be insufficient to complete the entire development as planned. A further appeal will have to be made for the completion of the plans which include the housing of the foreign and native teachers on the staff, a model village, athletic field, gymnasium, library and museum building, three more dormitories and a central dining hall. One of these dormitories is to be provided by the Canadians. Roads, drains, water supply, heating and power plant require additional funds.

The laying of the corner-stones of Underwood and Science Halls last October did much for the advertising of the College among the Japanese and Korean officials, educators, church dignitaries etc. The suggestion was made that a visit from Mr. Underwood at the time of the dedication of Underwood Hall would further the interest of the Korean community in the College.

The close of the year will likely see a deficit of between Yen 13,000. and Yen 15,000. This deficit prevents the erection of native teachers' residences to the extent needed, and also the developing of the foundation work of the site. The Government requirements, if we remain as a Semmon Gakko, will require that our current revenue be made more adequate to the needs of the School, but in any case the Institution cannot be run with the contributions we are now receiving from the Cooperating Boards.

22. 베커 학감의 이사회 제출 연례보고서

문서 제목	Dean's Report for 1921~22
문서 종류	학감 보고서
제출 시기	1922년 3월 16일
작성 장소	서울
제 출 자	A. L. Becker
수 신 자	이사회
페이지 수	10
출 처	Korea Mission Records, 1904~1960, Box 15, Folder 15 (PHS) 2114-5-2: 06 Board of Managers 1915~1922 (UMAH)

자료 소개

베커 학감이 1922년 3월 16일 열린 이사회의 연례회의에 제출한 보고서이다. 그는 1919년 봄부터 미국에서 안식년을 보내고 1921년 가을학기 개학 후 10월에 돌아와 다시 학감이 되었는데, 안식년 기간에 미시간대학에서 물리학 박사학위를 받았다. 이 보고서에는 날짜 표시가 없지만, UMAH 문서에는 페이지마다 오른편 상단에 "3~16-22"라고 필기 되어있다.

베커는 이 보고서를 크게 교수, 학과, 학생의 세 부분으로 구성하였다.

교수 부분: 3개 과의 과장과 교수, 조교수, 강사의 명단, 교수진 보강의 필요성.

학과 부분: 문과 · 수물과 · 상과의 1년간 교육 활동.

학생 부분: 종교교육, 기숙사 운영, 학생등록 현황, 출신 지방, 출신 중등학교, 종교(교파), 졸업생 현황.

내용 요약

교수: 문과 과장은 빌링스, 상과 과장은 백상규, 수물과 과장은 베커이다. 교수진의 인원은 총 23명으로 교수 10명, 조교수 8명, 강사 5명이다. 선교사 교수 8명, 한국인 교수 13명(교수: 백상규, 노정일, 조교수: 송필만, H. R. Rim, 김영환, 원달호, 임용필, S. D. Lee, 김술근, 김원벽, 강사: 김영주, 윤정하, 윤병섭), 일본인 교수 2명이다. 교수들이 과도하게 많은 업무에 시달리고 있으므로 예산을 더 확보하여 교수진을 시급히 보강해야 한다.

학과: 문과는 복음 전도, 저널리즘, 교육 지도자를 양성하기를 희망하고 있는데, 꽤 많은 교수를 영문학 교육에 투입하고 있다. 수물과는 베커가 없는 동안 졸업생 장세운, 임용필, 이원철이 밀러 화학 교수를 도와 봄학기를 이끌었다. 장세운과 이원철이 미국 유학을 떠났고, 임용필은 오는 4월에 떠날 예정인데, 연희전문 교수였던 미시간 대의 루퍼스(W. C. Rufus)가 그들을 도와줄 것이다. 상과에는 완전한 자격을 갖춘 교수가 없고 과장조차 파트타임으로 일하고 있다. 기독교인 실업가와 상업 교사가 양성되기를 희망한다.

학생: 학생들의 종교활동으로 주 5일 동안 오전 10시 40분에 채플을 3회, 성경공부를 2회 시행하고 있다. 교수들이 한 달에 한 번씩 돌아가며 채플을 이끌고 있고, 학생 YMCA가 두 달에 한 번씩 채플을 맡고 있으며, 보통은 외부 강사가 설교하고 있다. 일요일에는 학생들이 흩어지므로 학교에서는 일요 예배가 열리지 않는다.

임시 기숙사에 학생은 평균 40명, 교수는 2명이 있었고, 이들과 근교에서 방을 얻어 사는 학생들은 운동장 근처의 개인 농가에서 식사하였다. 기숙사 건물이 완공되더라도 학생의 2/3 이상은 수용하지 못할 것이므로 또 다른 기숙사 건물과 기혼 학생을 위한 모범촌 주택 몇 채가 절실히 필요하다.

학생 수는 1학년 117명, 2학년 90명, 3학년 79명, 문과 137명, 상과 12명, 수물과 28명인데, 여기에서 43명이 탈락하고, 6명이 재진급하였다. 출신 지역을 보면, 학생들이 함북과 전남 이외의 모든 도에서 왔다. 출신학교를 보면, 122명이 총 34개 중등학교에서 왔고, 평양 광성에서 10명, 송도에서 22명, 배재에서 20명, 관립학교에서 12명이 왔으며, 미션계 학교 출신이 76%, 다른 사립학교 출신이 14%, 관립학교 출신이 10%이었다.

1919년 [제1회] 졸업생은 문과: 김동익, 김한영, 노준탁, 유기준, 전처선, 최치완, 최상현, 홍기원, 상과: 강헌집, 김병석, 김원벽, 김형주, 이범일, 문승찬, 박동걸, 전종린, 정순규, 최순탁, 수물과: 이원철, 임용필, 장세운, 김술근이다. [전에는 1919년 수물과 졸업생 명단에서 보이지 않았던 김술근의 이름이 여기에서 비로소 등장하고 있다.] 1920년 문과 졸업생은 김재련, 박태원이다. 1921년 농과 졸업생은 김희완, 서광진, 송기주이다. (각각의 직업, 해외 유학 사실, 거주지역을 함께 제시하고 있다.) 졸업생들의 다수가 미션계 학교에서 교사로 일하고 있고, 학교 조수, 미국 유학(이원철, 임용필, 장세운), 신문사 업무, 교회 업무, 선교사의 조사, 사업 등을 하고 있으며, 1명(유기준)이 상해 임시정부 요원으로 활동하고 있다. 1922년에는 문과에서만 3명이 졸업할 예정이다.

九九〇一話電

延禧專門學校
CHOSEN CHRISTIAN COLLEGE
朝鮮京城
Seoul, Chosen (Korea)

April meeting
B.D. Trustees

Telephone 1019

\- 1 -

DEAN'S REPORT FOR 1921-22.

Departments in Operation:

Literary Department	B. W. Billings Director.
Commercial Department	S. K. Pack "
Mathematics & Physics Dep't	A. L. Becker "

Teachers:

B. W. Billings,	Prof.	of History and English.
S. K. Pack,	"	of Exonomics and Commerce.
A. L. Becker,	"	of Physics and Astronomy.
E. H. Miller,	"	of Chemistry.
H. A. Rhodes,	"	of Bible and English Literature.
J. E. Fisher,	"	of Education and English.
H. H. Underwood,	"	of Psychology and Ethics.
K. T. Takahashi,	"	of Japanese Language and Lit.
Thurman Andrew,	"	of Mathematics.
C. Y. Roe,	"	of Philosophy.
P. M. Song,	Associate Prof.	Of Com. Law.
H. R. Kim,	" "	of Agriculture.(two terms only) Resigned.
Y. W. Kim,	" "	of Music.
T. H. Yon,	" "	of Commerce.
Y. P. Yim,	Assist. Prof.	of Physics.
S. D. Lee,	" "	of Chemistry.
S. K. Kim,	" "	of Math. & Mechanical Drawing.
W. P. Kim,	" "	of Bookkeeping.
H. T. Owens,	Lecturer	in Short-hand & Typewriting.
Y. C. Kim,	"	in Finance, Money & Com.Practice.
C. H. Yun,	"	in Statistics & Warehouse.
P. S. Youn,	"	in Biology.
K. S. Takahashi,	"	in Ethics & Japa.Language.(two terms only) Resigned.

\- -

Since Jan. all teacher (Except Lecturers) have been devoting at least 25 hours per week to the work of the school and 15 hours of actual teaching has been accepted as the minimum requirement for teachers in full employ of the College. Teachers, doing full work, are requested to consult the College administration before taking on heavy responsibilities outside the school; outside teaching is discouraged. Wherever it is possible we are urging teachers to put the College Work first in their plans.

The members of our present Staff are carrying extra heavy burdens cheerfully and show a great desire to not only make their own teaching efficient but to make the College go. All are agreed that our first objective is the making of Christian Character. There is also a consensus of opinion that there is considerable room for improvement in teaching emthods, in preparation and in sytematic work toward the school objectives. I am confident the next year will be considerable advance in the moral of the teaching force.

九九○一話電

校 學 門 專 禧 延
CHOSEN CHRISTIAN COLLEGE
城 京 鮮 朝
Seoul, Chosen (Korea)

Telephone 1099

Yet the Board must not shut their eyes to the necessity of strengthening the present faculty, if we are to advance in the near future to higher standards and ultimately to the status of a Christian University. The school can not meet the urgent demands of the time unless the Board provides a Budget which will allow of the imployment of a sufficient number of well qualified teachers; unless money is provided the hands of the administration officers are tied and it will be impossible to plan for development. A good faculty will make a good school but a good faculty must be supported by a good budget. Our present budget is inadequate and is smaller than that of most Government Higher Common Schools and even below that of some Mission Higher Common Schools.

Co-operating Missions are expending perhaps four or five times as much on their "High Schools" as they apportion to our College.

Perhaps during the ensuing year we can mark time but the following year whom we can use our new buildings the Board should plan to provide an adequate Budget, otherwise we shall lose the Golden opportunity of the present rage and enthusiasm for Christian Education in Korea.

If we are educationalists or evangelists, in the best sense, we can not neglect the God-given chance of taking a step that will mean much in the rapid development of the Christian church in the East. There must be no sham and what we undertake must bring honor to Christianity.

Dr. Bates of Kwansei Gakuen told us the other day in Chapel that, having visited several Christian Institution in China and elsewhere, we had the best site, the broadest plans and the best prospects for a large Christian school among those he had seen and he congratulated faculty and students on being here when such foundations were being laid.

The rapid development of the school shows clearly that it is the Lord's will that we should have a strong Christian Institution: and this should strengthen our faith and help us to not only plan wisely and largely but to take the necessary steps as they are indicated to us. In a few years many of the students that are crowding the doors of the Preparatory Schools all over Korea will be exerting pressure on us; let us prepare while we may.

THE LITERARY DEPARTMENT. (B. W. Billings)

This department continues to be the one for which there is the greatest demand among the young men of Korea. This is doubtless due in a large measure to the fact that we are working among a people whose ideal for many centuries has been the scholar. Today Korea certainly needs men who are trained in commercial, agricultural and industrial lines and this chool has fortunately been built on such broad lines that we hope to be able to train Christian men who will take their place as leaders in all these various lines. At the same time, we do well to remember that it will always be to this Literary Department that we must look for leaders in evangelism, journalism, and, to a very considerable extent, in educational work as well. Further more this is the one department in which we can hope to train men who can take their place as Citizens of the World. This is because of the fact that through the study of history and literature they are at least introduced to the history and thought-life of the world in which they live.

In this department we have a rather large staff of men engaged in teching English Language and Literatuse including Messrs. Fisher, Miller, Rhodes and Billings. Mr. Takahashi is teaching Japanese and Oriental History and Mr. Billings Occidental History. Mr. T. H. Kim teaches the Chinese.

We are especially pleased with the addition to our staff of C. Y. Roe who returned to Korea after many years of training in Japan and America. He is now teaching Sociology and a class in Philosophy but will take on other work later. Mr. Pack teaches Economics, Mr. Fisher, the History of Education and Pedagogy and Mr. Underwood, Psychology and Ethics and Mr. Rhodes, Logic, Mr. Y. W. Kim who studied ten years in Japan, does most of his music work in this department. The work in Science and Mathematics is naturally carried by the men whose major work is in the scientific department.

Last spring 52 students were enrolled in this department 40 of whom are still with us. The loss of students was preactically all in the first year. Two of the three men who graduate with honors in the present class of ten men are from this depertment.

We have barely made a beginning but we hope in the coming years to see this department develop in such a way that it may train an "Aristocracy of Service" which will really minister to the intellectual and spritual needs of this people.

電話一〇九九

延禧專門學校
CHOSEN CHRISTIAN COLLEGE

Telephone 1099

朝鮮京城
Seoul, Chosen (Korea)

-4-

<u>MATH. & PHYSICS DEP'T</u> (A.L.Becker)

As the Director did not arrive until the Fall term had opened, the work of this Dep't did not get a good send off. Former graduates of this Department, Chang Sei Woon, Yim Yong Pil and Lee Won Chul with the Assistance of Prof. E. H. Miller carried the work in the Spring term. On account of an over-zealous anxiety as to the life of the Department if the regulation ten candidates did not apply for entry, a large proportion of the number received were not fully qualified and at the end of the term were unable to take the examinations. So the number of freshman in the Department were reduced to four the second term and to three in the Spring term. There were only two students in the Sophmore grade but we feel sure what we lack in quanity we make up in quality as these boys are doing fine work, above the average.

Mr. Chang and Mr. Lee left us during the Fall to take up graduate study in America. Mr. Chang entered the Senior class at Lawrence College and will take post-graduate work in Physics at Michigan University next year. Mr. Lee entered Mich. University in Feb. this year; he will specialize in Mathematics; Dr. W. C. Rufus, formerly of our College, now Assoc.Prof. of Astronomy at Mich. has offered to aid these bright young men in their post-graduate work. Mr. Y. P. Yim, who has been my right hand assistant in physics ever since I began work in the C.C.C., will leave the 1st of April for America where he will study for one or two year in De Pauw University and then he too hopes to finish a post-graduate course in Physics and Engineering at Mich. University.

These young men are insired with a desire to prepare themselves for a future position in our College and as we have throughly tested them in every way we feel sure that they will succeed and in the course of a few years return as well qualified teachers, capable of developing this department to the status of a University.

With over 30 applicants for this department already in hand and a prospective faculty for the ensuing year of the Director, E. H. Miller, Mr. Andrew, Mr. S. K. Kim, and a new teacher, (Mr. S. D. Lee, a Korean who has a M.A. from Ohio State for work in Math.) we are hoping to enter a new phase in the work of this dep't. Of course, we will be handicapped until we get the use of our new Science Hall but meanwhile we will do our best in the laboratories of the Temporary Building where we have been during the last year.

The Dep't is undertaking an additional responsibility this year in taking the Entering Class of Severance Medical College two or three days a week in Physics & Chemistry, hoping in this way to open the way for larger Cooperative work between the two institutions.

COMMERCIAL DEPARTMENT (S. K. Pack)

The work of this Dep't has been handicapped by the each of fully qualified teachers. Even the Director could not give more than part time so that a number of Lecturers have carried most of the work. Mr. P. M. Song associate Prof. of Commercial Law has done exceptionally faithful work and has really done much toward getting this dep't thru this year. Mr. Underwood has taught the Commercial English very acceptably.

48 students were enrolled in this department only a few less than that of the Lit.Dep't; this shows the popularity and need of this kind of work. There was a falling off of about 30% during the year, largely in the Freshman grade.

The work of this department during the last year suffered from the lack of room and qualified teachers but the Director and school authorities have plans for gretly improving the work of this Dep't all along the way and hope that next years report will show a long step ahead.

There are seven cadidates for graduation this year and nearly all of these have already been spoken for by Christian Institutions.

We hope to train and send out a fine type of Christian business men and Commercial Teachers.

Year 1921-22

Religious Activities. We have continued the plan of having Chapel three dyas a week and Bible study classes two days a week at 10:40 a.m. each day except Saturdy. The attendance althogub voluntary has been very good-85 percent and above. The Bible classes are held in the class rooms of the school building. The first year students are studying "The Teachings of Jesus", the second year students, Old Testament Characters", the third and fourth students, "The Poetical Books". The teaching has been done mostly by the foreign members of the faculty. Eleven members of the faculty have taken his turn once a month in leading the Chapel services. The Student's Y.M.C.A. have charge of the Chapel service twice a month and usually secure a visiting speaker.

At least one third of the students have regular sunday engagements in some of the churches of the city or in the churches in the vacinity of the college. Some are superintendents of children's S.S., others are teachers, and some preach at the regular Sunday and Wednesday evening services. Two sets of two students each represented the College Y.M.C.A. in making extensive preaching tours in the East and South of Korea during the Summer vacation. Several engaged in evangelistic campaigns during the Winter vaction. Ten or a dozen of the students have been sent two at a time to some of the near country church for Sundays.

Because the teachers and students are scattered and because so many of them have work in the churches, we have not found it possible to hold a regular Sunday service in the College Chapel. Also since there are no lighting facilities as yet, it has not been possible to have night meeting or classes in the Stimson building. The students in the dormitory hold their weekly prayer meeting and on Sunday they all attend the services of the city churches of those in the vicinity of the College. All but one of the students are professing Christinns.

Dormitory. On an average there have been forty students in the temporary dormitory. Two of the teachers also live there. These forty students together with a number who room in private houses in the vacinity run an eating club in the farm house near the athletdc field. The price of board has averaged from nine to eleven yen a month. Mr. S. H. Choi, one of the assistant teachers, acted as dormitory supervisor until Nov. 1st, when he was released to take up editorial work on the Christian Messenger. Since then Mr. Song, one of the Associate Professors in the Commercial Dep't, who lives in the dormitory, has been supervisor. Recently he has had the help of Mr. T. H. Won with the thought that possibly Mr. Won may be capable of acting in the double capacity of dormitory superivisor and athletic director.

Even with the new dormitory finished we will not be able to accommodate more than two thirds of out students. Because of the distance from the city and because of the difficulty of getting room and board in the villages near the college, an additonal dormitoary together with several model village, houses for married students are urgently needed.

STUDENT ENROLLMENT CHOSEN CHRISTIAN COLLEGE
(April 1921 - March 1922)

	1st term	2nd term	3rd term
Literary Department	52	45	40
Commercial Department	48	39	34
Math. & Physics Dep't.	17	6	5
Totals	117	90	79

Dropped out.

	Sickness	Died	Failed in study.	No reason
Literary Dep't.	9	0	0	7
Commercial Dep't.	0	1	2	12
Math.& Physcis Dep't.	1	0	11	0
Totals	10	1	13	19

Total For Year.................... 43.

Students entered 2nd term.

Literary Dep't.	4
Commercial Dep't.	2
Total	6

Districts.

North Pyeng-an	17
South " "	15
Whanghaido	7
Kyengkido	34
North Ham-kyeng	0
South " "	10
Kangwondo	13
North Chungchengdo	2
South "	4
North Chula	6
South "	0
North Kyeng-sang	5
Sough " "	6
North Island	3
Total	122

STUDENTS' HIGH SCHOOL

Name of Schools	Kind of School	No. of Students
Kwangsung High School Pyengyang.....	North. Methodist.................	10
Changyunhakwon Seoul...............	" "	1
Posung High Com. School Seoul........	"Heavenly Church" Native Religion	5
Youngsang Middle School Hamhung....	Canadian Presbyterian...........	5
Songdo High Com. School Songdo.......	Southern Methodist..............	22
Sungduk High Com. School Youngbyen...	Northern "	3
Paichai High Com. School Seoul.......	" "	20
Chang sin High School Masan.........	Australian Presbyterian...........	2
Yungmyung High School Kunsan........	Southern "	2
Yungsil Middle School Kangkei.......	Northern "	1
Singsung Middle School Sunchun......	" "	8
Chungdong High School Seoul.........	Private..........................	3
Keisugn Middle School Taiku.........	Northern Presbyterian...........	1
Kengsung High Common School.........	Publice, Seoul..................	3
Publice Higher Common School Pyengyang	....	2
Yangchung Higher Com. School Seoul...	Private.........................	3
Yungmyung High School Kongju........	Northern Methodist..............	1
Sungsil Middle School Pyengyang.....	" Presbyterian...........	2
John D. Well's School Seoul.........	" "	2
Meiji Middle School Tokyo...........	Private.........................	1
Chungang High Com. School Seoul......	" ....,......................	1
Public Higher Common School Taiku....	....	5
Y.M.C.A. High School Seoul..........	Y.M.C.A.........................	4
Whuimoon High Common School Seoul...	Private.........................	3
Sinhung High School Chunju..........	Soutehrn Presbyterian...........	1
Tongnai High Com. School Fusan.......	Private.........................	2
Pokwang Middle School Wonsan........	Canadian Presbyterian...........	1
Other Schools (5 Public Schools).....	....	5
34 Schools	Total Students..................	122

35 came from Northern Methodist Mission Schools
23 came from Sourthern Methodist Mission Schools
3 Came from Southern Presbyteian Mission Schools
13 came from Northern Presbyterian Missions Schools
5 came from Canadian Presbyterian Mission Schools
2 came from Australian Presbyterian Mission Schools
12 came from Private Schools
4 came from Y.M.C.A.
5 came from "Heavenly Church" School (Native Religion School)
12 came from Public Schools.
Total 122

76% came from Mission Schools
14% came from Other Private Schools
10% came from Government Public Schools.

CHOSEN CHRISTIAN COLLEGE GRADUATES

Nemese	Occupation	Location
1919 A.D.		
Literary Dep't:		
Kim Doug Yik	Died	Seoul
Kim Han Young	Methodist Sunday School Work	Seoul
Noh Chun Tak	Dean's Secretary	C.C.C.
Lyu Ki Chun	Shanghai Official	Shanghai
Chun Chu Sun	Teacher, High School	Kongju
Choi Chi Wan	Teacher, Paiwha Girl's Chool	Seoul
Choi Sang Hun	Christian Messenger (News paper)	Seoul
Hong Ki Won	Teacher, School Seoul	Seoul
Commercial Dep't:		
Kang Hun Chip	Teacher, Sungsil High School	Pyeng-yang
Kim Pyeng Suk	Trader	Soul
Kim Won Pyek	Asst. Teasurer	C.C.C.
Kim Pung Chu	Teacher, Girl's School	Songdo
Yi Pum Yil	Private Writer	Seoul
Moon Sung Cham	Died	Peking
Chun Chong In	Teacher, Chung Chuk Inst	Seoul
Pak Dong Kul	Teacher, High School	Yung-byen
Chung Sun Kyu	In Business	Seoul
Choi Soon Tak	News-paper Agent, Tong-A Ill-PO	Hamhung
Math.& Physics Dep't:		
Lee Won Chul	Studying	Mich.U.S.A.
Yim Yong Pil	Studying	De Pau.U.S.A.
Chang Sei Woon	Studying	Wis.U.S.A.
Kim Sool Kun	Asst.	C.C.C.
1920 A.D.		
Literary Dep't:		
Kim Chai Ryen	Teacher, High School	Hamhung
Pak Tai Won	Died	Taiku
1921 A.D.		
Agricultuge Dep't:		
Kim Hui Wan	Teacher, Masan Chang Sin School	Masan
Su Kwang Chin	Teacher, Ewha Girl's School	Seoul
Song Ki Chu	Teacher, Pokwang High School	Wonsan

九九〇一話電 校學門專禧延 CHOSEN CHRISTIAN COLLEGE Telephone 1099
城京鮮朝
Seoul, Chosen (Korea)

WORK OF GRADUATES

So far the majority of our Graduates have taken position as teacher in Mission schools, and some have entered other phases of Christian Work. Three served for two or more years as Assistants on the Faculty, and have gone to the United States for post-graduate study. One is now in the Univeristy of Michigan, and Arbor; another is in Lawrence College, Wisconsin and another goes to De Pauw University (College).

One is assistant editor of the Christian Messenger, the weekly news paper of the Federal Council; another is secretary to the missionary whose main assignment is Sunday School development. Another graduate is a member of the so called Provisional Government at Shanghai. The following table gives the classification in detail:-

three (3) have died
three (3) have gone to U.S.A. for post-graduate study.
three (3) are employed in the College.
three (2) are in News paper work
two (2) are in Business in Seoul
five (5) are teaching in Christian Schools in Kong-ju, Songdo, Masan, Wonsan, Yeng-byen and Pyeng-yang.
one (1) is in Shanghai
one (1) is in Sunday School Work.
Total...... 27

A number of those who expect to graduate in March have already accepted positions as teachers in Mission Schools. Even the graduates of the Commerce and Agriculture Departments have taken positions as teacher where the salaries offered, from ¥70 to 90 per month, are more attractive at present than the openings in business life or the agricultural calling.

We had applications for teachers far beyond the numbe of graduates; for many of these positions we could not furnish candidates becasue we had no Science Dep't graduates this year and only three graduates of the Literary Dep't, whom we could recommend as qualified for teaching in the high Schools of the Missions.

Even at this stage the College can fairly claim to be of considerable service to the missionary enterprise in furnishing so many teachers and workers to the various lines of mission activety.

23. 에비슨 교장의 북장로회 서울지회 제출 보고서

문서 제목	Chosen Christian College, Report for the Year 1921~22
문서 종류	교장 보고서
제출 시기	1922년 5월 22일
작성 장소	서울
제 출 자	O. R. Avison
수 신 자	이사회
페이지 수	4
출 처	Korea Mission Records, 1904~1960, Box 15, Folder 15 (PHS)

자료 소개

에비슨 교장이 1922년 5월 22일 자로 서울에 있는 북장로교 선교사들에게 제출한 보고서로 추정된다. 이 문서의 일자는 마지막 4쪽 하단에 기재되어 있으나, 제출 대상은 명시되지 않고 있다. 그 대상을 서울 주재 북장로교 선교사들이라고 보는 이유는 이 시기에 이사회가 열린 흔적을 찾을 수 없고, 4쪽에서 에비슨이 "Of the members of our Station"란 표현을 써서 자기 교단의 서울 지역 동료들을 통신의 상대로 지목하고 있기 때문이다. 언더우드도 1915년 9월 4일 그들에게 학교 업무를 보고한 적이 있었고, 에비슨도 이후에 가끔 그들에게 업무 보고를 하였다.

에비슨은 이 보고서에서 아래의 사항들을 다루면서, 베커 학감의 1922년 3월 16일 연례 보고서에 있는 통계를 인용하였다.

2차 조선교육령하의 전문학교 등록 문제, 학생들의 등록현황과 종교, 교수 동향, 재정 상황, 건축 상황, 여자대학 설립 문제, 졸업생 사회활동 현황, 종교교육 상황, 기숙사 상황.

내용 요약

전문학교 등록: 총독부의 새 교육령[2차 조선교육령]으로 일본의 사립 전문학교처럼 종교교육의 자유를 얻고 교육과정의 수준을 높일 수 있게 되었으므로, 이사회가 내린 만장

일치의 결정에 따라 새로운 전문학교 등록 신청서를 작성하여 보냈으나 아직 허가를 받지 않았다.

학생: 1년 전 이사회가 내린 결정으로 입시 통과자가 10명 이상인 과만 개강하게 되어 문과, 상과, 수물과 3개 과만 운영되고 있고, 총 122명이 등록하였다.

학생들이 한국의 13개 도 가운데 11개 도(함북과 전남 제외)에서 왔고, 여러 교파에서 왔으며(무종교도 있음), 미션계 출신이 76%, 다른 사립학교 출신이 14%, 관립학교 출신이 10%이다.

3월에 졸업한 10명 가운데 상과에서 7명, 문과에서 3명이 졸업하였고, 학생 수는 문과 68명, 상과 46명, 수물과 25명이다.

교수: 한 해 동안 교수진이 보강되었는데, 다카하시(K. Takahashi)가 와서 일본어를 가르치고 교장의 자문을 맡고 있고, 일본과 미국에서 유학한 노정일이 왔다. 수물과 졸업생 3명은 미국 유학(각각 Lawrence College, University of Michigan, Depauw University)을 떠났다. 앤드류(Thurman Andrew)가 수물과에 왔고, 베커가 Ph.D. 학위를 받고 지난 10월 돌아와 학감에 복귀하였다.

재정: 재정 상황은 역사상 가장 좋았다. 이는 캐나다장로회에서 교수 대신 ¥4,000을 보냈기 때문이다. 그리하여 적자가 ¥344.02밖에 안 났고, 누적 적자는 ¥14,558.60에 이르렀다.

건축: 교장이 미국에서 1921년 3월에 돌아온 후 언더우드관, 이학관[아펜젤러관], 첫 기숙사, 빌링스·피셔 사택들의 건축공사 계약을 맺었고, 10월 5일 언더우드관과 이학관의 정초식을 함께 거행하였다. 둘 다 겨울 전에 지붕을 덮을 예정이고, 기숙사도 6월 1일까지는 학생들을 입주시킬 예정인데, 루카스가 돌아와 건축 프로그램을 감독하고 있다. 올봄에 베커와 다카하시의 집을 위한 건축계약을 맺었고, 모범촌에 포함될 한국인 교수들을 위한 한옥 6채의 계약을 맺고 2채의 지붕을 덮으려 한다. 남감리회 선교부에서 약속한 $40,000 중에서 $23,000을 받았고, 캐나다장로회 선교회로부터 $15,000을 받았다. 한 해 동안 자본금으로 받은 금액은 총 $87,657.66이지만, 아직 부족하다.

여자대학: 협력이사회가 요청하였던 연합여자대학 설립 문제에 여러 선교회가 찬성하지만, 본교와 연계된 완전히 자율적인 여자학과를 설립한다는 원칙 위에서 찬성하고 있다.

졸업생: 졸업생 37명 가운데 24명이 기독교를 전파하는 일을 하고 있고, 학교(교사, 대학 근무), 신문사(보조 편집인 등), 미국 대학(유학), 상해 임시정부 등에서 활동하고 있다.

(종교교육 및 기숙사 운영에 관해 학감 보고서의 해당 부분을 인용하고 있다.)

Mr Scott

FILING DEPT.
1426-2
JUN 20 19
SECRETARIES

CHOSEN CHRISTIAN COLLEGE

Annual Report for the Year 1921-22 5/31/22

The year just closed has been an eventful one for this College. The changes in the educational law have removed many of the handicaps under which the College has been working. The aim of the government has been to place educational matters in Chosen on the same level as those in Japan. This has resulted in giving us religious liberty as is the case with private Semmon Gakko in Japan. The raising of the educational standards through the whole government system of schools enables us to advance our own curriculum which we have long desired to do.

While the new law gave us the option of reverting to the status of a private institution, the Field Board of Managers after carefully considering the matter from all angles unanimously decided to apply for registration as a new Semmon Gakko, and our application was accordingly sent in but at date of writing the new permit has not been issued.

It was decided over a year ago that hereafter only such departments would be opened for which a minimum of ten students succeeded in passing the entrance examinations. In accordance with this policy only three departments -- Literary, Commercial and Mathematics and Physics -- were carried through the year. A total of 122 students registered for the courses. Of these, 117 were in the spring term, 90 in the fall term, and 79 in the winter term. They came from eleven out of the thirteen provinces of Korea. The following table shows that the large majority came from Mission Academies:

35 came from Northern Methodist Mission Schools
23 came from Southern Methodist Mission Schools
3 came from Southern Presbyterian Mission Schools
13 came from Northern Presbyterian Mission Schools
6 came from Canadian Presbyterian Mission Schools
2 came from Australian Presbyterian Mission Schools
12 came from Private Schools
4 came from Y.M.C.A. School
5 came from "Heavenly Church" School (Native Religion School)
12 came from Public Schools.
Total 122

76% came from Mission Schools
14% came from Other Private Schools
10% came from Government Public Schools.

The Literary Department entered 52 for the spring term and 40 for the final term, while the Commercial Department was a close second with 48 and 34 respectively. The Mathematics and Physics course opened with 17 and closed with 5. Ten were dropped on account of illness, one died, 13 failed in their studies, and 19 left without any reason.

In March, ten men were graduated, seven from the Commercial Department and three from the Literary. Five of these men were snapped up as teachers by Mission Academies, two went into nonmission schools as teachers, and the remaining three went into other pursuits.

The taking in of an entrance class for the present year was delayed owing to the holding of a government examination for the reclassification of students. At our entrance examination, 118 men competed, and 63 were accepted as students. The registration by departments is as follows:

	New students	Old	Total
Literary	29	39	68
Commercial	19	27	46
Mathematics & Physics	15	10	25

making the total registration the largest in our history, or 139. In addition, it has been arranged with the Severance Union Medical College to take their first year students two days a week for instruction in Physics, Chemistry and Biology, which we trust will be but the beginning of a closer cooperation.

The Faculty has been much strengthened during the year by the addition of Mr. K. Takahashi, who takes the Department of Japanese and acts also as adviser, to the President. Mr. C. Y. Roe, who has been trained in Japanese and American universities, joined the staff also. A number of changes were made in the teachers of lower rank. Three of the graduates of the Mathematics and Physics Department who have served the institution as teachers since their graduation, and have incidentally worked as time teachers in Mission Schools in Seoul, went to the United States for postgraduate study. One entered Lawrence College, another the University of Michigan, and the third Depauw University. The foreign personnel was also added to by the coming of Mr. Thurman Andrew, who will be connected with the Department of Mathematics and Physics. After two years of postgraduate work in the University of Michigan we were pleased to welcome back last October Mr. A. L. Becker with his well-earned degree of Ph.D. in Physics who resumed his position as Dean, relieving Mr. Rhodes who had carried the work faithfully during his absence.

Financially, the institution had the best year in its history. Receipts from students were ¥3802.50; from Boards ¥21,740.04, and from other sources ¥3180. Missionary service accounted for ¥33,333.32 in the total income of ¥62,055.86. The expenditures were ¥29,066.56, or a total of ¥62,399.88 including missionary service, leaving a deficit of ¥344.02. The smallness of this deficit compared with former years was due to the fact that the Canadian Mission contributed ¥4,000 in lieu of a teacher. There still remain, however, the accumulated deficits of other years totalling ¥14,558.60 to be cleared away. A higher scale of fees has gone into effect for the new year, so that the income from students from now on should steadily mount.

Progress has also been made in the development of the plant. Shortly after the President's return from America in March, 1921, contracts were let for Underwood Hall, Science Hall, the first Dormitory and residences for Mr. Billings and Mr. Fisher. The two latter were occupied about the beginning of this year. The double ceremony of the laying of the cornerstones of Underwood Hall and Science Hall on October 5th last was made the occasion of much publicity for the institution. Special railroad cars were engaged and a representative company of people of all classes attended. Bishop Welch laid the cornerstone of Science Hall and Mr. H. H. Underwood officiated at Underwood Hall. At date of writing, the second floor of Science Hall is being laid, while Underwood Hall is just slightly behind that stage. Both buildings should be roofed in and well advanced towards completion by the winter. The dormitory is now having the finishing touches put to it, and should be ready for the students by June 1st. Mr. Lucas arrived on the field again in August since which time he has devoted himself to the supervision of the building program.

This spring contracts were let for residences for Dr. Becker and Mr. Takahashi. A start was made in earnest on the Model Village, contracts for six Korean houses for teachers having been let and two of these are now ready for the roof.

During the year $23,000 was received from the Southern Methodist Mission on its $40,000 pledge, and $15,000 from the Canadian Mission. The remaining $17,000 from the Southern Methodist Mission has been promised for this year. The total funds received for capital purposes during the year were ¥87,657.66. Expenditures on capital account totalled ¥130,958.01. The funds in sight, however, are not sufficient for the initial development of the institution, and further grants will soon be required in order that we may utilize the plant that will soon be ready. The buildings still immediately required are a central lighting and power plant, more dormitories and a students' dining hall, a gymnasium, more residences for foreign and native teachers, etc., and the Athletic field should be at once put into good shape.

At the request of the Cooperating Board for Christian Education in Chosen the cooperating Missions were asked for an expression of opinion as to the desirability of having a union Woman's College for Korea. The Missions have endorsed the principle, with a proviso that if it should be organized in connection with this College the Woman's Department should have complete autonomy.

Seven years have passed since the opening of the College, and the graduating roll contains 37 names. A summary of the graduates present activities is presented which shows that 24 of these men have served or are serving the Christian propaganda in Korea:

3 have died
3 have gone to the United States for postgraduate study
3 are employed in the College
3 are in newspaper work (one with the Christian Messenger)
3 are in business in Seoul or Songdo
7 are teaching in Christian Schools in Seoul
9 are teaching in Christian Schools in Kongju, Songdo, Masan, Wonsan, Yengbyen, Pyengyang and Yangchoo.
1 is in Shanghai
1 is in Sunday School work.
2 are teachers in non-mission schools
2 present occupation not reported
Total 37

As there has been much misunderstanding in regard to the religious status of the College, I shall close this report with a quotation from the Dean's report to the Field Board of Managers on the religious activities of the institution. He says:

> "Religious Activities. We have continued the plan of having Chapel three days a week and Bible study classes two days a week at 10:40 a.m. each day except Saturday. The attendance although voluntary has been very good - 86 percent and above. The Bible classes are held in the class rooms of the school building. The first year students are studying '"The Teachings of Jesus"', the second year students, '"Old Testament Characters"', the third and fourth year students, '"The Poetical Books"'. The teaching has been done mostly by the foreign members of the faculty. Eleven members of the faculty have taken their turn once a month in leading the Chapel services. The Student's Y.M.C.A. have charge of the Chapel service twice a month and usually secure a visiting speaker.

"At least one third of the students have regular Sunday engagements in some of the churches of the city or in the churches in the vicinity of the College. Some are superintendents of children's Sunday Schools, others are teachers, and some preach at the regular Sunday and Wednesday evening services. Two sets of two students each represented the College Y.M.C.A. in making extensive preaching tours in the East and South of Korea during the summer vacation. Several engaged in evangelistic campaigns during the Winter vacation. Ten or a dozen of the students have been sent two at a time to some of the near country churches for Sundays.

"Because the teachers and students are scattered and because so many of them have work in the churches, we have not found it possible to hold a regular Sunday service in the College Chapel. Also since there are no lighting facilities as yet, it has not been possible to have night meetings or classes in the Stimson building. The students in the dormitory hold their weekly prayer meeting and on Sunday they all attend the services of the city churches or those in the vicinity of the College. All but one of the students are professing Christians."

Dormitory On an average there have been forty students in the ~~temporary~~ dormitory. Two of the teachers also live there. These forty students together with a number who room in private houses in the vicinity run an eating club in the farm house near the athletic field. The price of board has averaged from nine to eleven yen a month. Mr. S. H. Choi, one of the assistant teachers, acted as dormitory supervisor until November 1st, when he was released to take up editorial work on the Christian Messenger. Since then Mr. Song, one of the Associate Professors in the Commercial Department, who lives in the dormitory, has been supervisor. Recently he has had the help of Mr. T. H. Won with the thought that possibly Mr. Won may be capable of acting in the double capacity of dormitory supervisor and atheletic director.

Even with the new dormitory finished we will not be able to accommodate more than two thirds of our students. Because of the distance from the city and because of the difficulty of getting room and board in the villages near the college, an additional dormitory together with several model village, houses for married students are urgently needed.

Of the members of our Station connected with the College, Mr. Miller had charge of the Chemistry Department besides devoting considerable time to the work of building; Mr. Underwood taught Psychology and Ethics, as well as English in the Commercial Department; and Mr. Rhodes taught English Language and Literature in the Literary Department.

Appended hereto is a copy of the financial statement for the fiscal year.

Respectfully submitted,

President.

May 22nd, 1922.

See Owens - 1197 - 5/13/22

24. 에비슨 교장의 이사회 제출 보고서

문서 제목	Chosen Christian College, Report of President to Field Board of Managers
문서 종류	교장 보고서
제출 시기	1922년 9월 21일
작성 장소	서울
제 출 자	O. R. Avison
수 신 자	이사회
페이지 수	3
출 처	Korea Mission Records, 1904~1960, Box 15, Folder 17 (PHS) 2114-5-2: 06 Board of Managers 1915~1922 (UMAH)

자료 소개

에비슨 교장이 1922년 9월 21일 열린 이사회에 제출한 보고서이다. 이날의 회의는 그때까지 연희전문을 외면하였던 북장로회 한국 선교회가 이사회에 대표를 파견하여 합류하기로 하였던 점에서 특별한 의미가 있었다.

재한 북장로교 선교사들의 공식 조직인 한국선교회는 연희전문의 설립을 반대한 다수파에 장악되어 있었는데, 그들은 1915년 총독부가 사립개정학교규칙을 공포하여 정규 교육과정 안에서 종교교육을 금지한 것을 기독교 탄압으로 규정하고 폐교를 불사하겠다는 의지로 저항하였다. 그러면서 자신들이 세운 숭실 · 신성 · 계명학교 등이 인가를 받지 못한 각종학교로 전락하는 것을 감수하였을 뿐만 아니라 총독부의 교육법에 순응하여 인가를 받은 연희전문과 관계 맺기를 거절하였다. 나아가 뉴욕의 북장로회 선교부와도 크게 충돌하였다. 이는 선교부가 1914년 다른 교단 선교부들과 함께 연희전문(조선기독교대학)의 설립을 결정하고 이 학교를 후원해왔기 때문이었다. 연희전문 측과 소수파는 총독부의 공언, 즉 교육법의 취지는 기독교 탄압에 있지 않다고 한 말을 지렛대로 이용하여 종교교육을 시행할 여지를 확보하려 하였다. 견해차로 인한 갈등은 상당 기간 계속되었으나, 다수파가 마침내 미국 북장로회 총회의 중재에 따라 연희전문의 종교교육 실태를 확인한 후에 대표를 보내 연희전문 이사회 구성에 참여하기로 하였다. 이들은 더 나아가 그들의 학교도 연희전문처럼 총독부의 인가를 받게 하려고 노력하였다, 그리하여 숭실학교의 대학부는 1925년 전문학교가 되었다. 더불어 장로교 선교사들의 의견이 통일됨에 따라 조선 예수교장로회와 남·북감리회 연회들도 학교에 이사를 파견하기로 하였다.

이는 PHS(장로회)와 UMAH(연합감리회)에 내용은 같아도 형태는 약간 다른 문서들이 소장되어 있다. UMAH 문서는 2쪽에 3줄짜리 교정문을 오려 붙인 부분이 있으며, 에비슨의 서명이 비서(오웬스)가 대신 쓴 것 같은 모양을 하고 있다. PHS 문서는 UMAH 문서의 교정문이 본문 안에서 제대로 타이핑되어있는 대신 다른 곳에서 오타를 고치고 있고, 서명이 손글씨가 아닌 타자체로 되어있다. 이런 점에서 두 문서는 동일 인물에 의해 타이핑되었을 수도 있지만, UMAH 문서가 먼저 작성된 것으로 보인다. 이 자료집에서 제시한 것은 복사상태가 더 선명한 PHS 문서이다.

이 보고서는 아래의 사항들에 관해 설명하고 있다.

이사 선출 조건 개편, 건축공사, 교수진.

내용 요약

이사 선출: 북장로회 한국 선교회에서 처음으로 보낸 대표들을 이사로 선출해달라고 이사회에 권고한다. 현재 5명인 한국인 이사의 수를 6명으로 늘리면서, 선출 조건을 개편하여 본교 동창회 대표 1명, 예수교장로회 총회 대표 1명, 남·북감리회 연회 대표 1명씩, 본교 이사회 대표 1명으로 하자고 제안한다. [이후 이 제안대로 되었다.] 일본인 이사의 수(2명)는 일본인 자문의 판단에 따라 늘리지 않기로 하였다.

건축공사: 언더우드관의 건축은 지붕에 목재를 설치하여 타일을 깔 준비를 마쳤고, 이학관[아펜젤러관]은 지붕을 올렸으며, 두 건물 다 1923년에 끝날 예정이지만, 이 건물들을 위해 미국에 주문한 난방과 배관 설비의 운송이 착오로 지연되고 있다. 기숙사 건물은 여름에 완공될 예정이고, 이 건물과 스팀슨관, 이학관, 언더우드관의 현판 작성을 위해 기부자들의 의견을 물을 예정이다. 5번째 외국인 교수 사택의 건축이 거의 끝나 베커가 일주일 내에 입주할 예정이고, 다카하시 교수의 사택과 한국인 교수들 및 강사들의 사택이 모범촌 부지에서 지어지고 있다. 이러한 건축공사와 캠퍼스 부지용 땅의 구매에 기금이 더 많이 필요하다. 캐나다장로회 측이 약속한 $25,000과 북감리회 측이 약속한 채플 건립을 위한 $30,000의 지급을 아직 이행하지 않고 있다.

교수진: 오하이오 주립대에서 수학석사 학위를 받은 이춘호가 와서 9월부터 수물과에서 가르치고 있고, 히치(J. W. Hitch) 남감리회 선교사가 [문과] 교수로 왔다. 그리하여 교수진에 외국인 교수 8명, 일본인 교수 2명, 한국인 교수와 조교수 7명, 조수와 강사 7명이 있다[이름은 밝히지 않고 있다]. 문과, 상과, 수물과를 운영 중인데, 총독부의 인가서는 신과, 농과, 응용화학과의 운영을 승인하고 있으나, 이 과들의 운영은 대학의 재정 수입 상황에 달려 있다. 오랫동안 찾고 있었던 농과 교수를 마침내 확보하였다고 캐나다장로회 선교부가 알려왔으나, 그들이 교수 대신 보낸 돈이 적자를 메꾸는 데에 도움이 되고 농과의 운영 전망이 불확실한 까닭에 보류하라는 전보를 보냈다.

CHOSEN CHRISTIAN COLLEGE

REPORT OF PRESIDENT TO FIELD BOARD OF MANAGERS, September 21, 1922.

This meeting marks an epoch in the history of our College because we have with us for the first time the official nominees of the Northern Presbyterian Mission. I recommendto you their election. We are pleased also because the Southern M. E. Mission has taken up full co-operation by increasing it s contribution to $3000.00 per year and appointing a second missionary professor. They are now entitled to have four members on this Board.

Three out of the four cooperating Missions are now on this basis and the fourth is now contributing the equivalent of the requirement for partial cooperation which entitles them to two members on the Board.

We have had under consideration the problem of strengthening the Korean element on this Board; Hitherto the Board has itself selected the coopted members of whom there are at present 5 Koreans and 2 Japanese. I suggest that we increase the number of Koreans to six and that nominees for these positions be invited from the following bodies:

Alumni Association	1
General Assembly Presbyterian Church	2
Conf. M. E. Church N.	1
" " " S.	1
This Board	1

It is the judgment of our Japanese advisers that we should for the present not change the method of selecting Japanese coopted members.

You will have seen for yourselves the progress that is being made in the construction of the plant. There remains but one storey of the tower of Underwood Hall to be completed, the roof timbers of the structure being practically all in place ready for tiling. The contractor will probably finish most of his work by the close of the present season, and the building may be ready for classes in April 1923. Science Hall is already roofed in and the contractor should finish his work this season on this building also. Some of the subcontracts may be held up to synchronize with the receipt of funds from the Northern Methodist Board as the balance of the grant for Science Hall may not reach the field before June 1923.

There has been a delay through misunderstanding of an order in getting the equipment for those two buildings shipped from the United States so that the installation of the plumbing and heating equipment may not be done until later that next April.

The dormitory was not quite completed for occupation at the opening of the spring term, so that the Agricultural building was used for housing the students as before. During the summer, however, those who attended the summerconference for teachers occupied the Dormitory and the students have taken possession this term. I recommend that this building be considered as the contribution of the Southern Methodist Mission, and that that Mission should be requested to name the building and to suggest a wording for the memorial tablet which will be provided for it in due course.

A suggested wording for the tablet for Stimson Hall will be submitted to you, in English and Chinese characters, which if approved will be sent to America for exedution. The First Methodist Episcopal Church of Pittsfield, Mass., and Mr. J. T. Underwood are being asked to suggest a wording for the tablets for their respective buildings.

~~A suggested wording~~

The fifth foreign residence is almost completed, and will be occupied by the Dean, Dr. Becker, within a week or so. The residence for the Japanese professor, Mr. Takahashi, is well advanced. Six attractive houses, which are intended for the junior teachers or for members of the office staff who should reside on the grounds, have been built in the Model Village. These should be ready for occupancy about the first of Octtober. A contract for additional servants' quarters has also been let. More roads, drains, waterworks, etc., have been constructed during the summer.

The completion of the work now under way will exhaust practically all of the funds that are in immediate prospect. There will be from ¥5000 to ¥7000 left from the Mrs. Russell Sage Legacy towards the building of a small foreign residence. We must undertake next season, if at all possible, theerection of the central heating, lighting and power plant, which is required in order to make the main group of buildings usable during the winter. The funds for Underwood Hall and Science Hall provide for their propertion of the cost on constructing this plant but the remainder will have to come from general funds which are not yet all in sight. The first unit of this plant is estimated to cost $25,000.00.

The only funds pledged for future use are $25,000 by the Canadian Mission, the time of payment of which is indefinite; and the $30,000 earmarked by the Northern Methodist Board for the chapel building. Residences are still required for Mr. Andrew, Mr. Lucas, the Canadian teaching representative, and the second Southern Methodist teacher. Houses are also needed for the Korean professors of the present and future. More funds should be invested in the developmentof the Model Village, the athletic field and gymnasium, and the erection of more dormitories and the dining hall. Funds are urgently xxxxxx wanted to purchase additional land while land values -- which have gohe up greatly since the College site was acquired -- are yet comparitively low. Considerable money must still be spent on the development of the site, its roads, waterworks, drains etc. We hope the Board will devise some means of securing more money for Capital Funds amd more for the Current Budget.

*I recommend that Mr. Hitch be appointed to the Faculty of the College and his department and assignment of work be referred to the Faculty.

Our largest registration of students was during the spring term when 130 paid fees. This term also, 130 are in attendance. Our teaching force has been added to in the person of Mr. Ye Choon Ho, a graduate of Mr. Herman's Boys' School and Ohio Weslegan University and M.A. of Ohio State University in Math., who has joined the Mathematics and Physics Departments from September first. Also Rev. J. W. Hitch who has a fine knowledge of the Korean language, has been assigned to the College by the Southern Methodist Mission raising them to the status of full cooperation. The teaching staff now consists of wight foreign professors, one Japanese professor, three Korean professors and four associate professors. In addition there are 7 junior assistants and lecturers.*

The College at present is operating three departments, Literary, Commercial, and Applied Mathematics and Physics. Its charter permits it tp conduct three more -- Bible, Agriculture and Applied Chemistry. It is the judgment (of the Faculty) that it should be the policy to carry on only the present three departments successfully or until revenue from tuition or other local sources enables the College to carry on a wider program. We can well employ ourselves in the interval in further building up our faculty, developing esprit de corps, and consolidating our position generally.

The Canadian Board has been on the lookout for an agricultural teacher. If the policy just outlined should be followed, an agricultural teacher would not be required for several years to come. The Commercial Department, however, needs reinforcing, and I would strongly recommend to the Canadian Board that it find a man qualified to teach Commercial subjects and so bring this department up to the level of the other two.

In the meantime the money which the Canadian Board is paying in lieu of a teacher is saving us from a large deficit in current budget, and if that Board cares to defer the appointment of a resident teacher until the current budget revenues can be otherwised increased, much embarrassment will be avoided, although we regret the absence from the Staff of a Canadian representative.

(Since writing the above a cable has come saying the Canadian Board has an agriculturist ready to send and asking whether we approve his appointment. This brings the question before us definitely.) It has taken so long for them to find a man and after the arrives it will take so long for him to get the language and gain an inside knowledge of Korean and Japanese agriculture, Korea's need in this line and how best to supplement present Korean methods by American methods that one hesitates to turn the man down if we are sure that he has the qualifications for building up this difficult department.

Furthermore he can be used in the intervening period for supplementing the teaching forse in the already running deaprtments. Our only reason for hesitating is the help of the ¥4000 per year being paid by the Canadian Board in lieu of a teacher's services is giving us in carrying on the work without any great deficit.

I therefore suggest that we cable in reply:-

"Hold agriculturist until you receive our letter."

In speaking of the smallness of our resources, one cheering beam shines through the gloom as you will perceive when I read a quotation from the correspondence from the Pittsfield Church which is building Science Hall (Read promise to support the cost of that Department and pass it around for inspection. Also the latest letter from Mr. Kennedy) I suggest that the Board sendto that Church a word of appreciation.

Respectfully submitted,

(Signed) O. R. Avison

President.

25. 에비슨 교장의 이사회 제출 보고서

문서 제목	Chosen Christian College, Report of President to Field Board of Managers
문서 종류	교장 보고서
제출 시기	1923년 9월 15일
작성 장소	서울
제 출 자	O. R. Avison
수 신 자	이사회
페이지 수	3 (첨부 문서 6쪽 추가)
출 처	Korea Mission Records, 1904~1960, Box 15, Folder 17 (PHS) 2114-5-2: 07 Board of Managers 1923~1927 (UMAH)

자료 소개

에비슨 교장이 1923년 9월 15일 열린 이사회 회의에 제출한 보고서이다. 이 이사회 회의에서 처음으로 한국 예수교장로회 총회 대표 2명, 남 · 북감리회 연회 대표 1명씩, 연희전문 동문회 대표 1명이 이사 자격으로 회의에 참석하여 회의가 2개 언어로 열렸다. 와타나베 판사가 이사직을 사임하였으며, 백상규의 사표가 수리되었고, 이순탁과 유억겸이 교수로, 이순탁이 과장대리로 임명되었다. 이학관의 건축비를 댄 미국 매사추세츠 피츠필드 제일감리교회의 희망에 따라 이 건물을 '아펜젤러관'으로 명명하였다.

그러나 이 보고서는 다른 무엇보다 에비슨이 미국에 가는 문제를 가장 중요하게 다루고 있다. 협력이사회는 그의 미국행을 만류하는 반면 교수들은 그를 반드시 미국에 보내려 하는 다소 기이한 장면이 연출되었다. 이런 논란은 총독부의 2차 조선교육령(1922)과 당시의 민립대학설립 운동과 연계하여 살펴볼 필요가 있다.

이 보고서는 PHS와 UMAH에 똑같은 형태로 소장되어 있으나, PHS 문서에는 이 보고서 뒤에 첨부 문서들이 있다. 이 첨부 문서들은 사실 교장 보고서에 포함된 것이 아니지만, 1923년 당시 학교의 각종 정보를 알려주고 있으므로, 이 자료집에서 함께 제시하기로 한다.

이 보고서는 항목 분류 없이 아래의 사항들을 거론하고 있다.

운영진 변화, 에비슨의 도미 계획, 한국인의 이사회 참석 확대, 별과 설치, 한국인 후원 확보.

내용 요약

운영진 변화: 이사회의 결정에 따라 내가 행정업무에서 놓이게 되었다. [1922년 12월 18일 연전과 세의전 이사회 연석회의에서 결정되어 에비슨은 양교를 위해 대외활동만 하고 행정업무는 부교장과 그 외 임원들에게 맡기게 하였다. 더불어 미국에 가서 후원금을 모금해오게 하였다. 이 결정으로 한동안 베커가 행정을 주도하였고, 이 결정은 1927년 9월 23일 이사회 회의 때 철회되었다.] 부교장인 빌링스도 미국에 가서 베커 학감이 부교장을 맡게 되었다.

에비슨의 도미: 뉴욕 협력이사회는 내게 미국에 가는 계획을 1년 연기하라고 요청하였던 반면, 이사회는 내가 미국으로 가야 한다고 주장하였다. [에비슨은 1924년 3월 출국하였다.]

한국인 이사회 참석: 한국 장 · 감 교회 대표들과 연희전문 동문회 대표가 한국인들과의 협력관계 구축을 위해 이사회의 초청으로 이사 자격을 얻어 이사회에 참석하였다.

별과 설치: 총독부의 새 교육령[1922년]이 우리 대학의 수준을 높이게 하여 학생들을 '본과'와 '별과'로 나누었다. 별과는 인가를 받지 못한 중등학교 출신을 받는데, 감리교 학교들 외에 모든 학교가 비인가 학교에 해당한다. 올봄에 총독의 결정으로 다른 사립학교들도 지정을 받으면 그곳의 졸업생은 고등보통학교 졸업생과 동등한 자격을 인정받게 되고 학교는 성경과목을 교과과정에 넣을 수 있게 되었다. 이제 그곳 졸업생들이 별과에 진학할 필요가 없도록 지정학교로 만드는 일은 선교회들에게 달려 있다. 연희전문이 본과의 입학지원 자격이 없는 학생을 받아들이지 말아야 할지를 이사회가 논의해주기를 바란다.

한국인 후원 확보: 한국인들에게서 재정협력을 얻기 위한 그간의 노력이 별로 성과를 얻지 못하였다. 그래도 한국인들이 세브란스의전에 ¥12,000을 건축비로 기부한 일이 있음을 생각하고 용기를 잃지 말기를 바란다.

(보고서의 다음에 첨부된 문서들은 각 과의 학년별 과목과 수업시수, 교수 명단, 학교의 난제와 고무적 현상, 교수회의 지난해 주요 결정 사항, 학생들의 등록 · 종교 · 출신 지역 현황을 보여주고 있다.)

교수: 문과는 14명(한국인 교수: 노정일, 백남석, 조교수: 김영환, 윤병섭〈생물학〉, 강사:

김도희, 이관용, 정인보), 상과는 5명(한국인 교수: 이순탁, 유억겸, 조교수: 김달호〈K. H. Kim〉, 윤정하), 수물과 6명(한국인 교수: 이춘호, 조교수: Y. C. Kwan, 안재학)이다.

교수회의 지난해 결정 사항: 동양문학을 정규수업으로 편성한다. 학생 상담 교수들을 임명한다. 학생 YMCA 활동으로 매주 1회 토론회와 강연회를 갖는다. 졸업식 때 졸업생이 'caps'[학사모를 뜻하는 듯]를 쓰게 한다. 에비슨 대신 부교장이 교수회를 주재한다. 채플 출석을 수업 출석처럼 산정한다. 불량 학생을 없애기 위해 매 학기말에 1,2학년 학생명단을 교수들이 검토한다. 납부 기한 2일이 지나도록 학비를 내지 않은 학생은 수업을 듣지 못하게 하고 무조건 매일 10전씩 범칙금을 부과한다.

VED

25 1923

WHEELER

CHOSEN CHRISTIAN COLLEGE.

Report of President to Field Board Of Managers

15th September, 1923.

Ans'd 9/25/23 1426

The decision of the Board to relieve the President largely of administrative work was carried into execution and the Vice President being in America, the Acting Vice President , Dean Becker, added these duties to his already onerous ones. I therefore will report chiefly on matters of promotional interest.

At a special meeting of the Field Board of Managers on June 19, 1923 to consider the request of the Cooperating Board that the matter of the President's visit to America be re-considered, the Board again unanimously voted that the visit should be taken. This was reported to the President's Mission which gave unanimous consent to his leaving the field as requested by the Field Board of Managers. This information was cabled to the Presbyterian Board in New York, as the Cooperating Board had made its approval contingent upon that Board's consent. In due time a cable was received from the Presbyterian Board, and later a confirming letter, part of which reads as follows:

PROPOSED RETURN OF DR. O.R. AVISON (Board letter No 631, July 17/23
We received in due time the cable of your Executive Committee dated July 6th............The second part stated that the Mission had given permission to Dr. Avison to return to America and that expenses would be provided outside of Mission funds. As this involved the reconsideration of an action that had formerly been taken by the Board, we had to hold it for the meeting of the Board which was not held until yesterday. The Board then took the following action:

" In reply to a cable from the Executive Committee of the Chosen Mission, regarding the proposed return to America of O.R.Avison, M.D. in the financial interests of the Chosen Christian College and the Severance Union Medical College, the Board voted that the difficulties that were stated in Executive Secretary George T. Scott's letter of April 19 to the Field Board of Managers have been so intensified by subsequent developments that it is inadvisable for Dr. Avison to return at present, and that it would be better for him to postpone his return until next year. A cable was authorized ."

The part of Dr. Scott's letter of April 19th which referred to the subject under consideration was as follows:

" The proposed return of Dr. Avison as indicated in the Minute was carefully and fully discussed. I was instructed to write to the field regarding some of the present restrictions which make very difficult such a campaign as DR. Avison Would Wish to conduct. Most if not all, of the Cooperating Board are now very difinitely limited by their official church bodies in the total amount of money for which they can ever make appeal during a given year, consequently, the amount that can be authorized for appeal for the single institution is extremely small and is terribly discouraging to financial promoters who are now in America to raise money for Missionary institutions. Dr. Williams of Nanking has been trying to secure funds under these handicaps for more than a year and is terribly disappointed. You, of course, realize that the new factor is the limitation of appeal in addition to the limitation of credit for gifts, the latter of which have long existed within the denominations. Our Presbyteroan Board, for instance, and its officers are permitted to appeal for only a very limited amount of property, and with the big Presbyterian deficit which has been reported this week (between $600,000 and $700,000) a larg part of the amount allocated for property will have to be transferred to deficil appeal. Incidentally, the receipts of the Methodist Board for the first five months of the fiscal year are reported to have fallen off 27% and the Canadian Presbyterian Board has been forced to cut its appropriations to the field. Members of the Board consequently feel extremely doubtful as to the wisdom of Dr. Avison's coming at this time, not only becouse he will beforced to campaign under such hampering restrictions, but also becouse we feel that appeal for newpurchase can meet with such little encouragement by the Boards and probably with a reluctant response by the churches. Many members of the Board believe that a special financial campaign should not be begun this year, but other members asked that the matter be not definitely closed and that the Field Board be allowed to reconsider its recommendations and that if the Field Board, in view of the difficulties and the /~~difficulties~~/ general attitude of the Cooperating Board, again requested Dr. Avison to return, that consent would be given.

To say that the difficulties stated in that letter have been "intensified by subsequent developments" is putting the case very mildlyindeed. The financial situation is more ominous than it has ever been before in all the history of the Board. It is painfully evident that unless every possible effort is concentrated on securing the money to clear off the heavy deficit and to cover the large budget for the year, most drastic retrenchments will have to be made. Representatives of other educational institutions who have been trying to raise money in America are quite discouraged. The Home Base Department of the Board feels that under the restrictions which it is compelled by the General Assembly to operate, it could not now give Dr. Avison the cooperation that we would need, and the situation in other Boards is quite as bad as it is in ours, if indeed it is not worse. Some Boards have already cut down their work. In these circumstances the Board believes that it would be the part of wisdomfor Dr. Avison to defer his visit until another year, when we hope the financial skies may be clearer. As a cabled reply was asked by the Executive Committee, it was dispatched immediately after the Board meeting as follows:

> OANUFGUVIR YPAJCOACIP IKKALEJSIR LYEPGUVL R EXEXZYEMAM
> O.R.Avison Board advises /You /to delay leaving the field until next year George T/ Scott explained consitions by letter to H.T.Owens april 19, 1923 Worse than when we lastwrote.

About the same time the Southern Presbyterian Executive Committee in Nashville cabled to Mr. Swinehart, who had been directed by his Mission ~~or~~ to go home on a financial campaign not to go, for similar reasons, so it was decided that it would not be wise for the President to go at this time. I therefore plan to work with all the greater vigor along the lines of interesting the Korean church and people generally in the work of the College.

In order to make the Basis of Korean cooperation more secure, the ield Board invited the following bodies to nominate members in future, instead of having the Board itself coopt all:

Presbyterian General Assembly	2
Conference, Methodist Episcopal Church	1
do do do do South	1
Alumni Association	1
Field Board of Managers	1

The results of these invitations are seen here to-day in the election of:

The new educational ordinance raised the standard of our College and divided our students in "Regular" and "Special", as you already know, "specials" being those coming from any Higher Common School not regularly approved be the Government.

These included all Mission Schools excepting those of the Methodist Episcopal Missions, and made it very difficult for us becouse we naturally prefer to have regularly matriculated students. It was also very hard for students from the unrecognized schools becouse they were greatly handicapped in their relative positions and it was hard on the unrecognized schools becouse their graduates could not be regularly matriculated and they could not easily hold the allegiance of their students.

Last Spring , His Excellency the Governor General, Baron Saito, made it possible for Higher Common Schools outside the regular line to receive government approval and yet retain the Bible in the curriculum and now it is up to the Missions to secure recognition of at least some of their schools so that no students need to came to the College as "specials", It is Therefore a moot question whether the college should from now on refuse to accept students without regular matriculation qualifications. I invite the Board to discuss this question.

The question of Korean cooperation has naturally engaged my attention but so far little visible results have come beyond what has already been reported to you. We may take courage, from the fact that a group of Koreans recently contributed the sum of ¥12,000 to the Severance Union Medical College towards one of its buildings so that the sense of responsibility for the desire to help the work is already manifesting itself and is sure in due time to result in advantage to the Chosen CHristian College.

(Signed) O.R. Avison

President.

1

CHOSEN CHRISTIAN COLLEGE. Appendix II

Literary Dept.-Course of study.

First Year
Bible........................2
Japanese Lit.................2
English......................5
English Special..............3
History, Oriental............2
Civil Government.............2
Biology......................4
Composition, Oriental........2
Occidental History...........3
Chinese Lit..................2
Music........................2
Astronomy Chem...............1
Gymnastics...................1 31

Second Year
Bible........................2
Japanese Lit.................2
English Lit..................5
English Composition..........3
Geology......................3
Occidental History...........3
Psychology...................4
Economics....................3
Chinese Lit..................3
Music........................2
Gymnastics...................1 29

Third Year
Bible........................2
English Lit..................3
Argumentation & Debate.......2
History of Modern World......4
History of Philosophy........3.
Logic........................2
Hist. of Education...........3
Educational Methods..........3
Composition Oriental.........2
Music........................1
Gymnastics...................1 26

Fourth Year
Bible........................2
Public Speaking..............2
English Lit..................3
English and American Hist....5
Educational Psychology.......3
Philosophy...................3
Sociology....................3
Ethics.......................3
Music........................1
Gymnastics...................1 26

Commercial Dept.-Course of study.

First Year
Bible........................2
English......................5
Japanese & Lit...............2
Cevil Government.............2
Music........................2
Chinese Composition..........2
Gymnastics...................1
Economics....................3
Commerce.....................2
Civil Law....................4
Book-keeping.................3
Commercial English...........3 31

Second Year
Bible........................2
English......................5
Finance......................2
Money........................3
History of Commerce..........2
Articles of Commerce.........2
Commercial Geography.........2
Civil Law....................2
Commercial Law...............2
Book-keeping.................2
Commercial English...........3
Gymnastics...................1 28

Third Year
Bible........................2
English......................4
Economic Policy..............2
Insurance....................2
Banking......................2
Business Composition.........2
Commercial Law...............4
Bank Book-keeping............2
Commercial English...........5
Shorthand in English.........1
Gymnastics...................1 27

Fourth Year
Bible........................2
English......................3
Business Mathematics 3
Commercial Practice..........2
Custom. Warehouse. Exchange..2
Buseness Composition.........2
Private International Law....1
Commercial English...........5
Shorthand in English.........2 24
Typerwriting.................1
Gymnastics...................1 24

CHOSEN CHRISTIAN COLLEGE

FACULTY LIST. 1923. - Sept.

Name		Teaching Subjects	Qualified
Literary College	B.W. BILLINGS	Director and Prof. of History	"
	H.H. Underwood		"
	J.E. FIsher	Prof. of English and Education	"
	C.Y. Roe	" " Sociology, Bible, Ethics, Phil.	"
	K.T. Takahoshi.	" " Japanese, Hist, Morals, Civil Gov	"
	J.W. Hitch	" " English, Eng. Literature	"
	Y.W. Kim	Asso. Prof. Of Music	"
	T.H. Kim	Lecturer in Chinese	"
	K.Y. Lee	" " Philosophy, Logic	"
	I.P. Chyeng	" " Chinese	"
	H.A. Rhodes	Prof. of Bible, English	"
	N.S. Paik	" " Education, Psylogy, Eng.Gram.	"
	P.S. Yun	Asso. Prof. of Biology	"
	Kawaku	Lecturer in Exercise	"
Commercial College.	S.T. Lee	Prof. of (STAtistics, History of Com.) (Finance, Insurance, Economics)	"
	U.K. Yu	" " Law	"
	K.H. Kim	Asso. Prof. of Banking, Book-keeping, Eco, Policy, Commerce, Money	"
	C.H. Yun	Asso. Prof. of Commodity, Book-keeping, Ware-house Exchange, Com, Arith. Commercial Geography	"
	R.Katch	Lecturer in Com. Practice	"
Physics and Math. College	A.L. Becker	Director & Prof. of Electrical Eng., Mechanics, Physics, Physics Laboratory	"
	E.H. Miller	Prof. of Physicial Chemistry, Electrical Chemistry, English	"
	C.H. Lee	Prof of Anal., Geometry, Calculus, Astronomy, Algebra, Dif. Equations	"
	Y.C. Kwan	Asso. teacher of Geology, Surveying	"
	C.H. An	Lecturer in Anal, Chmistry	"
	A.E. Lucas	Lecturer in Work-shop, Bible	"

3

Copy

Some Disturbing features during year:-

1. Lack of room (Underwood Hall Unfinished & Science Hall Unfinished)
2. The new Dormitory could not be used during winter becouse of failure to heat.
3. The refusal of Government to recognize the science Ddept. (becouse of lack of qualified teachers) made it impossible to receive new students in this Dept..
4. Shortage of Burget funds meant a severe cutting on the required teaching force, and consequent criticism on the part of the Govenment .Faculty and students.
5. 'Strikes' of students compelled the faculty to suspend 19 students o f the Lit. Sophomores until April 1924.
6. The resignation of Prof. S.K.Paik, who was director of the Com. Dept. and member of the Board. (He had served us efficiently for 9 years)
7. The failure of funds to frovide for necessary equipment.
8. The Building Program could not be carried out as planned.

Some Encouraging Feature.

1. The Registration of the Literary and Commercial Colleges under the new regulations of the Gov. Gen. of Chosen.
2. The adding of two qualified teachers to the Commercial college Faculty namely; Yi Soon Tak and Yu Uok Kyum also the secureng of Mr. N.S.Paik qualified as teacher in the Literary College. In addition we have been able to get Dr. Yi Kwan Young Ph D. as part-time teacher.
3. The loyalty and enthusiasm of practically every member of the Faculty has make the difficulties surmountable and made many definite, forward steps possible.
4. The ability of our treasure Mr. Owens has helped us avoid many dangerous financial shoals.
5. Our music teacher Mr Kim donated a new piano worth Y2200.00.
6. Prof. B.W.Billings D.D. is agion on job after a year of study in U.S.A.

H

CHOSEN CHRISTIAN COLLEGE.

IMPORTANT FACULTY ACTIONS OF THE PAST YEAR.

Nov. 6. 1922.
Rules adapted relating to (1) amount of time teachers are to assume that pupils have for preparing lessons. (2) Monthly grades to be handed in by each teacher . (3) Students who are absent to hand in outline covering work. (4) Students absent 2 weeks or more to take special examination.

Nov. 29. 1922.
Dormitory committee instructed to make arrangements for a physicial visiting the college at stated intervals. Arrangements were made with a Severence Doctor.

Dec. 13. 1922.
(1) New English course adopted . (2) arrangements made for course in Oriental Literature as a part of the regular course.
(3) Faculty advisors appointed for students.
(4) Attendance records to be kept and count the same as a course of study in the general average.

Dec. 13. 1922.
Rules for 'student-body' organisations adapted.

Jan 15. 1923.
(1) Committee appointed to inspekt buildings equipment and students.
(2) One have each week given to students for Y.M.C.A. activities, debates, lectures.
(3) Students permitted to use caps at graduation.
(4) Use of Mr. Underwood Library accepted.
(5) Rules for Students Boarding club adapted.
(6) Dr. Avison resigned as acting chairmant of Faculty and the Acting-Vice President assumed the duties of chairman.

Febrary7. 1923.
Moved to request the Presbyterian Board to grant Mr. H.H.Underwood and extension of one year to his furlough to prepare for his work in C.C.C.March 7th 1923.
'Schem es showing relations of Board trustees, Faculty. student body. committees etc. adapted.

May 2. 1923.
Second year Literary class suspended and allowed to continue work after one week on condition that they fulfil certain requirements.

June 7. 1923.
Rule adapted to count chapel attendance the same as class attendance,

June 18. 1923.
(1) System of demerits approved and committee asked to work out a plan for applying it.
(2) One hour course to have one grade for the whole year instead of one for each term.
(3) At the end of each term names of all Ist 2nd year students to be reviewed by the Faculty for the purfose of eliminating undesirable students.

Sept. 5. 1923.
Students who have not paid their fees within 2 days after scool office not allowed to attend classes and a fine of 10 sen per day to be added to the fee for every day that the student is late in paying regardless off the reason for the delay.

- 5 -

Copy

CHOSEN CHRISTIAN COLLEGE.

ENROLLEMENT.

There was a total enrollement of 131 distributed as follows:-
Literary Dept. Ist., 28; 3rd; 18; 4th, 12 total of 78.
Commercial Dept: Ist. 14. 2nd. 11. 3rd. 12, total of 37.
Science Dept: and 10; 3rd, 3; 4th 3, total of 16.

List of Students who have studied or graduated from
Middle School, Go-Tung School, or other Preparatory Schools.

School Names	Number	Percentage
Middle School graduates	52	39.7%
Go-Tung School graduates	28	21.3%
Middle School (studied)	8	6.2%
Go-Tung School (studied)	18	13.7%
Other Preparatory School Graduates	25	19.1%
Total	131	

(see chart)

Student Church Relations

Church Name	Member	Percentage
Presbyterian	62	47.6%
Northern Methodist	34	26.3%
South Methodist	29	22.3%
"Holiness"	2	1.5%
'Adventist'	1	8. %
No affiliation	3	1.5%
Total	131	

(see chart)

PROVINCES FROM WHICH STUDENTS CAME

Name of Province	Member	Percentage
North Hamhung	5	3.7%
South "	18	13.7%
North Pyenyang	22	16.8%
South "	16	12.2%
Whanghai	8	6.2%
Kyungki	35	26.7%
Kangwon	8	6.2%
North Choongchung	4	3.1%
South Choong Chung	3	2.3%
North Chunna	4	3.1%
South "	0	00.0%
North Kyungsang	2	1.5%
South "	6	4.6%
Total	131	

(see chart)

POINTS WORTHY OF SERIOUS CONSIDERTION BY THE BOARD.

Cop

With
(1) A preperty investment of over 600.000 yen.
(2) A faculty of loyal teachers.
(3) An enthusiastic Christian Body of Students.
(4) Government Recognition.
(5) A College Standard accepted in U.S.A.
(6) A growing Reputation here and Abroad.
(7) A Fine set of Buildings which will accommodate 500 students.

THE TIME IS RIPE FOR A FORWARD MOVEMENT.

Shall we dally with the opportunity of making a definite 'start' (taking in 150 students) in the Spring of 1924. If this start is made, Three things must be done.
(1) The Science College must be registered.
(2) The suggested Budget must be approved.
(3) The Heating & Power plant must be put in.

26. 에비슨 교장의 협력이사회 제출 보고서

문서 제목	Report of Dr. O. R. Avison, President of Severance Union Medical College and Chosen Christian College, to Annual Meeting of Cooperating Board for Christian Education in Chosen
문서 종류	교장 보고서
제출 시기	1925년 4월 10일
작성 장소	New York
제 출 자	O. R. Avison
수 신 자	협력이사회(Cooperating Board)
페이지 수	7
출 처	2114-5-5: 06 Cooperating Board for Christian Education in Chosen Hall, Ernest, 1918~1927 (UMAH) Scan 0801 Cooperating Board for Christian Education in Chosen Minutes-Executive Committee 1912~1928

자료 소개

에비슨 교장이 1925년 4월 10일 뉴욕에서 열린 협력이사회 연례회의에 제출한 보고서이다. 1924년 4월부터 연희전문과 세브란스의전을 위해 벌인 1년간의 모금 활동을 보고하고, 향후 활동에 관해 의견을 제시하며, 두 학교의 현재 상황 설명하고 있다. 그런 가운데 선교사 교수보다 한국인 교수를 쓰는 정책을 양교가 실천하고 있다는 발언을 하고 있다.

이 보고서는 크게 세 부분으로 구성되어 있다.

모금 활동: 교섭 대상과 결과, 필요한 일

학교 현황: 세브란스의전 현황과 모금액 명세, 연희전문 현황과 모금액 명세

종합 결론과 제안: 종합 결론, 제안

내용 요약

◩ 모금 활동

교섭 대상과 결과: 내(에비슨)가 지난[1924년] 3월 한국을 떠나 4월 미국에 도착한 후부터 두 대학의 발전에 필요한 기금을 모금하였다. 오웬스가 1월부터 나를 도왔다. 록펠러

재단, 카네기재단, 커먼웰스 펀드(Commonwealth Fund)와 접촉하였다가 기부를 거절당하였고, 홀 재단(Estate of Charles M. Hall)에서 $50,000, 존 T. 언더우드로부터 $60,000을 받았으며, 존 L. 세브란스 자매로부터 새 병동 건립기금 $100,000과 매년 경상비 $10,000와 부지 건축비 $7,500을 받거나 약속받았다.

필요한 일: 두 학교에 $2,500,000이 필요하다. 6월에 대학원 과정을 마친[뉴욕대 박사 학위 취득] 원한경이 미국에 남아 모금 활동을 돕게 하자는 요청에 대한 투표가 진행되고 있다. 나의 부재 허용 기간 1년도 끝났지만, 반드시 더 연장되어야 한다. 협력이사회가 사업가들을 이사로 받아들여 인력을 보강해야 하고, 캐나다연합교회가 6월에 성립되면 캐나다인 사업가를 더 들일 수 있을 것이다. 남감리회와 남장로회의 사업가들도 이사로 선출해야 하고, 지역별 위원회도 만들어야 한다.

◪ 학교 현황

세브란스의전: 간호부양성소가 세브란스의전처럼 졸업증만 있으면 정부 고시를 치르지 않고 면허를 취득하게 되었다. 의전의 학비를 인상하였고, 졸업생들이 많이 해외로 유학 갔다. 졸업생 김창세가 존스홉킨스대에서 공중보건의 학위를 취득하여 교수로 오게 되었다. 미국 유학생들을 교수로 영입하려 하는데, 그러려면 예산을 많이 늘려야 한다. 한국인들이 격리병동 건축기금 ¥12,000을 기부하여 건축 중인데, 비용이 부족하다. 반버스커크 부교장이 기차역 건너편 대로변의 공터를 임차하는 안을 제출하였다.

(세브란스를 위한 기부자들과 총 $16,929에 달하는 기부금의 명세를 제시하고 있다.)

연희전문: 등록생이 가장 많게 193명이 되었다. 졸업생은 총 114명이 되었고, 이 가운데 사망 4명, 사업 17명, 미션 학교 교사 21명, 다른 학교 교사 10명, 미국 유학 20명, 동양에 있는 대학 유학 10명. 미상 1명이다. 언더우드관과 아펜젤러관을 아직 건축 중이지만 지난 4월부터 쓰고 있다. 남감리회 선교부는 자본금 지급을 완료하였고, 캐나다장로회 선교부는 $15,000만 남기고 있다. 그들이 캐나다연합교회로 재조직되면 훨씬 많은 후원금을 줄 것이다. 첫 번째 한국인 교수 사택의 건축이 진행되고 있다. 교장의 집을 세브란스에서 연희전문으로 옮기는 문제가 제기되고 있으나, 그렇게 하면 케네디 기금 사용 계획에 차질이 생긴다. 채플과 식당이 긴급히 필요하다. 예산이 늘어나 학비를 연 75원으로 인상하였고, 교수 우애회가 한 해 동안 500원을 기부하였다. 남감리회가 노블(Alden Noble)을

교수로 임명하여 생물학을 가르칠 예정이고, 이원철이 미시간대에서, 조병옥이 컬럼비아대에서 Ph.D.를 받아 여름에 교수로 올 예정이며, 캐나다장로회의 스코트(William Scott)를 교수로 초빙하였으나, 현재 허락을 받지 못하고 있다.

1924년 4월의 회의 후에 두 대학이 한국인을 교수로 임명하였거나 임명하려 하고 있다. 그리하여 지난해에 교장이 선교사 교수보다 한국인 교수를 쓰는 정책을 쓰자고 제안했던 것을 실행하고 있다. (세브란스 신임 교수의 담당 과목을 소개하고 있다.) 연희전문에는 수학과 천문학 교수[이원철], 경제학 교수[조병옥]가 부임하고, 프린스턴에서 석사학위를 받고 프린스턴신학교에서 공부 중인 한국인[백낙준]을 금년 아니면 내년에 종교교육 교수로 데려올 예정이다.

(총 $131,041에 달하는 8군데 기부자와 기부금 명세를 제시하고 있다.)

◩ 종합 결론과 제안

종합 결론: 양교의 건축공사를 위해 건축감독이 필요하다. 협력이사회의 회계가 받은 일부 건축비나 시설비는 시급하지 않으므로 은행에 넣어 이자를 받게 하기를 권고한다.

제안: 1. 원한경의 미국 체류를 연장하여 재정 모금을 돕게 할 것. 2. 에비슨의 임무 완수를 위해 부재 기간을 1년 연장할 것. 3. 협력이사회의 이사 수를 늘릴 것. 4. 건축감독을 고용하게 할 것. 5. 지정 기부금들을 은행에 예금하여 이자를 받을 것. 6. 세브란스의전 서남쪽 전면의 땅을 임차하게 할 것.

4-10-25

REPORT OF DR. O. R. AVISON, PRESIDENT OF SEVERANCE UNION MEDICAL COLLEGE AND CHOSEN CHRISTIAN COLLEGE, TO ANNUAL MEETING OF COOPERATING BOARD FOR CHRISTIAN EDUCATION IN CHOSEN, APRIL 10, 1925.

- -

I left Korea last March arriving in the United States in April and have been devoting myself since that time to the securing of funds needed for the development of the two Colleges. Since January, Mr. Owens has been assisting me. I have approached several of the Foundations in recent months. Bishop Welch and I interviewed the Rockefeller Foundation and Dr. Vincent promised to go into the matter and advise me later of their decision. Dr. Keppel of the Carnegie Corporation and the Carnegie Fund informed me that these funds were not available for work in the Orient. I interviewed Mr. Richardson -- Mr. John D. Rockefeller's secretary in charge of gifts -- and received later a reply as follows:

> ...in the light of our policies in such matters it regretfully seems impossible for Mr. Rockefeller, Jr., to take financial interest. After careful thought we came to a clear decision that, for the present at least, Mr. Rockefeller could not wisely assist missionary and other colleges established in foreign lands. We cannot make exception in this instance, and I am, therefore, expressing our regret that Mr. Rockefeller cannot make any contribution to the funds which you are raising.

I have also had a preliminary interview with the assistant Director of the Commonwealth Fund and will later put up a proposition to them; and I have laid our case before Mr. Edward S. Harkness.

From the Estate of Charles M. Hall, a donation of $50,000 for the Endowment of the Chosen Christian College was received, and $60,000 for the same purpose was contributed by Mr. John T. Underwood, the Chairman of this Board. Mrs. F. F. Prentiss and Mr. John L. Severance have given $100,000 for the erection of a new wing to the Hospital, as well as pledging $10,000 a year for five years towards the current budget expenses of the institution: they have also contributed $7500 towards the purchase of land.

The lists of needs of the two institutions call for about two and a half million dollars, a million and a quarter for each. This is a stupendous sum to raise, but with time and effort it can be done. A request is now being voted on by the field authorities to permit Mr. H. H. Underwood to remain on this side for a further period, after he completes his post-graduate work in June, in order to assist in the campaign; and I recommend that this Board concur in the request. As I have also completed one year's absence from the field, a further extension of leave should be authorized. It would also seem advisable to strengthen the personnel of the Board itself by coopting several more business men, well known in New York. The coming into effect of church union in Canada in June will bring a new constituency into relationship with the Colleges, and some Canadian business men might with advantage be added to our membership, and some representative business men of the two Southern churches should be coopted. Furthermore, local or regional committees should be formed in order to diffuse interest.

4-10-25

The two Colleges have had a successful year on the whole although financial conditions have been difficult owing to semi-famine conditions in Korea due to the failure of the harvest last autumn. The northern part of the country was devastated by floods and in the southern part there was failure of crops from drought. I shall report on each institution separately.

SEVERANCE UNION MEDICAL COLLEGE

There is a student registration of 66 of whom only three were non-Christians on admission. There are 27 nurses in the Training School. The Government has extended the same recognition to the Nursing School that it had given to the Medical School the year before, so that our graduate nurses also receive licenses to practice on presentation of their diplomas without taking any government examination. An innovation during the year was the putting of Bible classes (in addition to the chapel service) in the curriculum as part of the required studies. Authority to raise tuition fees from 60 yen to 100 yen per annum was given by the last meeting of the Field Board of Managers. Following the instructions of this Board, insurance to the amount of ¥125,000 has been put on the plant.

An unusual number of our men took postgraduate work during the year. Dr. H. S. Shim has been studying at the Imperial University and was expected to graduate in March of this year with a degree that will entitle him to be recognized as a full professor in the Department of Internal Medicine.
Dr. M. U. Koh took a short course in Surgery at the Peking Union Medical College, and Dr. Paul Choi took a course in Parasitology in the same institution. Dr. S. W. Rhee also took a seminar in Neurology to fit him for carrying the work of that department during the approaching furlough of Dr. McLaren.
Dr. Y. S. Lee of the Surgical staff came to Northwestern University Medical School last fall and was admitted to the senior class. He will on his return to Korea be qualified as a professor in the Department of Surgery. Dr. Y. O. Choi, a graduate, is now studying in Emory University specializing in Physiology, and the son of our Dean, another graduate, is at the same University taking some branches of Internal Medicine in order to fit himself for a professorship in his alma mater. Two resignations occurred in the missionary personnel during the year -- Dr. Frank M. Stites, Jr., of the Department of Internal Medicine, and Dr. Hopkirk of the Department of Roentgenology. Both of these men had rendered able service. A young Korean was sent out last November to succeed Dr. Hopkirk, a Mr. L. K. Jung, who is an X-ray technician graduated as such from the American Army Medical College, and with a long experience with the American army in France and since in a Veterans' Bureau hospital. His recommendations were excellent and reports from the College of his work have been good.
One of our graduates, Dr. Kim Chang Sei, in February secured the degree of Doctor of Public Health from Johns Hopkins University in the School of Hygiene and Public Health, and he will leave for Korea in about a month via Europe to become Professor of Bacteriology, Hygiene and Public Health in our Medical College, thus giving us a permanent head to a department that has had to be carried by time teachers for several years past.

4-10-25

3.

I am also hopeful that Dr. Kim Gay Bong, now Pathologist at St. Joseph's Hospital, Paterson, N.J., will go out in about one year's time to take charge of the Department of Pathology.
We are now negotiating with Mr. M. O. Jung, a laboratory technician in the University of Colorado, trained there for the American Army Medical Bureau to go out in that capacity and supervise laboratory work in Pathology and Bacteriology. We have the finest kind of recommendations from the Professor of that University as to his ability, industry and good character.
One of the most encouraging features at this stage of our growth is the number of capable Korean teachers being added to the staff but it calls for a considerable addition to our budget , each one adding about $2,000 a year for salary, travel and departmental expenses.

It is already within your knowledge that the Koreans turned over to the Hospital a fund of ¥12,000 with whcih to build an Isolation Hospital, promising to supplement it when building operations actually commenced and to find funds for its completion. The first sod was turned by Marquis Pak last March, but the work of construction was deferred as a question arose in our architect's mind as to the proper location. This has now been settled and work is going ahead on the site first selected. Only two-thirds of the building as planned will be erected now, and of that two-thirds only so much as the funds provided will allow. For instance if the money runs out when the first or second storey is completed then the building will be stopped until more funds come in. The contract price for two storeys is ¥18,700 (about $9,000) and the third storey will cost ¥6800 more or $3200. The contract does not cover, heating, wiring, lighting or plumbing or equipment, and the will also be a charge on the Korean contribution.

Thanks to a gift from Mr. Severance for the purchase of land a further addition to our site has been secured as indicated on the map.

Plans for the new hospital wing have been prepared and are now receiving the criticism of the staff. When approved, it is hoped that we may be able to let the contract this spring for the beginning of this building.

I have not yet had time to receive reports for the fiscal year which closed March 31st, but Dr. VanBuskirk has written that he fears that, owing to the famine conditions already alluded to having cut down our earnings and greatly increased our free work, there is likely to be a deficit exceeding our guaranteed resources. If so, this will be the first time that that has occurred. Furthermore, preliminary indications are that the Wholesale Department may not yield a profit this year. The demands of the institution wer so great that for some months past the revolving fund in the hands of Dr. Sutherland have been overdrawn and the field has been unable to make remittances as yet to restore it. Mr. Severance added to the original revolving fund of $5,000 a further $5,000 thus improving the ability of the institution to finance its purchases on this side.

4.

Renewed requests have come from the field through Dr. Van Buskirk, vice president, asking for permission to lease our southwestern frontage so that this vacant lot on the main street of the city, opposite the railway station, may produce some revenue, provided of course that in the judgment of the Field Board a satisfactory lessee can be found.

The growth of our Korean staff is bound to make a big difference in our annual payroll and endowment for current budget funds is our greatest need. A contribution of $50 has been applied to the beginning of an endowment, and I am hoping that the campaign ere it closes will yield considerably more for this purpose. In fact, without more budget funds it will not be possible to operate the new wing which Mr. Severance and Mrs. Prentiss have so generously provided, and for the present we will erect only two storeys and use the balance of the contribution as a temporary endowment to enable us to carry on the added work.

I now report the contributions which have been received for the medical work as follows:

New Hospital wing, from Mrs. B. F. Prentiss and Mr. John L. Severance	$100,000
Current Budget, from above, $10,000 for five years	50,000
Land purchase fund, from Mrs. Prentiss and Mr. Severance	7,500
Scholarship fund, from Mr. Scheide, Titusville	1,000
For Equipping a ward innew wing, from Union Church, Schenectady	132
For Equipping a ward in new wing from Glendale Mission Band	500
For Endowment, from Dr. Charles S. Wood, Washington	50
For Campaign expenses from Mrs. Prentiss	1,500
Various small contributions applied to travel of Dr. C. S. Kim	46
For Endowment from Mrs. A. S. Gray	100
For Endowment from Miss E. W. Stutzer	100
Total - - - - - - - - - - - -	$160,928

CHOSEN CHRISTIAN COLLEGE

Coming to the Chosen Christian College it is a pleasure to report the largest student enrolment we have yet had, namely 193, of whom 46 were non-christians. Dr. Becker writes recently that most of these men have since connected themselves with some church About thirty men were to be graduated last month, bringing our total roll of graduates to about 114. Of these, 4 have died, 17 are in business, 21 are teachers and assistants in Mission schools; 10 are teachers in other schools; 20 are taking post-graduate studies in the United States; 10 are in post-graduate courses in Oriental colleges; and one is unspecified. This mont we expect to enrol 250 in the three departments.

In April last, Underwood Hall and Appenzeller Hall were sufficiently advanced to be occupied for class-room purposes, though not entirely completed. The heating equipment went out last summer and has been installed, the class rooms being removed from Underwood Hal back to Stimson Hall while the work was being done in that building.

5.

J. 1 v. 25

The Southern Methodist Board completed the payment of its pledge of $40,000 to capital funds, leaving now only $25,000 due from the Canadian Church. As the work of reorganization following the church union in Canada will take some time it is likely that we shall have to await progress in that before we receive much from that source but in the end we expect greater support from that body.

Meanwhile some gifts for residences and equipment have been made and the construction of the first house for one of our Korean professors is now going on. The question of whether the President shall contine to reside at Severance as now or move out to the Chosen Christian College site has been raised by the C C C Faculty. The President has put the responsibility for a decision on the authoritie on the field. If the two Faculties and the two Field Boards think this should be done the President is willing to make the move althougt it would not be easy in many regards. If the decision is for the move it would be a question as to whether to apply Mrs. Kennedy's gift of $7,000 for a foreign residence at the College to the erection of a President's home, or to ask Prof. E. H. Miller to turn his home over to the President and erect another but smaller house for Mr. Miller. Mr. Miller has very kindly said he would accede to such a request if it were made. If the President does not move out then the $7,000 can go towards another home for a foreign professor or towards two homes for Korean professors which are very greatly needed, provided, of course, that Mrs. Kennedy would be willing to have her contributio so used.

More funds for capital purposes are urgently needed. A chapel and dining hall should be provided for the rapidly enlarging student body, another dormitory should be built, and above all funds for equipment and current budget should be provided.

Towards increasing revenue the field has advanced tuition fees during the year to ¥ 75 per annum ($37.50) which is more than three times what they were in 1918, and they will be advanced further as fast as possible. A contribution of ¥500 was made during the year by the Association of College Teachers. So that Koreans are comin more and more to see their obligation towards the institution.

The Methodist Board North has appointed Mr. Alden Noble, a secon generation missionary, to the College staff to bring its quota again up to three. He will occupy the chair of Biology, and will arrive on the field this autumn. Two Koreans who have completed their work for the Ph. D degree are ready to return this summer to take positions on the staff of the College. Dr. D. W. Lee gets his Ph. D. in Mathematics and Astronomy from the University of Michigan, and Mr. P. Oakman Chough receives a similar degree in Economics from Columbia The Canadian Mission has been invited by the Field Board to assign Rev. William Scott, M.A. , to the Faculty, but recent correspondence would indicate that that Mission cannot release Mr. Scott at the present time.

Since our last meeting in April 1924 we have therefore appointed or are to appoint this summer the following Koreans to the staffs of the two Colleges, fulfilling in a marked manner the President's statement last year as to the policy of the Colleges to use Korean professors rather than missionary professors as fast as possible.

6.

S. U. M. C. Staff

Professor of Bacteriology, Hygiene & Public Health
X Ray Technician
Laboratory Technician
and for next year we have in view the appointment of a Professor of Pathology

C.C.C. Staff

Professor of Mathematics and Astronomy
Professor of Economics
and we are also negotiating with a Korean graduate of Princeton, an M.A., who is also studying in Princeton Seminary, to go out as Professor in Bible teaching and religious work either this year or next.

I have now to report the following gifts received during the campaign for the Chosen Christian College:

For Endowment, from Mr. John T. Underwood	$ 60,000
For Endowment, from Estate of Charles M. Hall	50,000
For Teacher's residence, from Mrs. Kennedy	7,000
For Teacher's residence, from Mrs. A. F. Schauffler	2,500
From Mr. Henry F. Pope (applied to teacher's home)	250
For Equipment, from Mr. A. C. McKenzie pledge of (paid $1,000, balance $1,000 per annum)	5,000
For Campaign printing account, from Mr. Underwood	5,000
For Campaign expense, from Mr. Underwood	1,291.[illegible]
Total - - - - - - - - - - -	$131,041

The combined total for both Colleges is $291,969

GENERAL:

As there ought to be much construction work going on for the next five years, there should be a reliable man sent out to supervise this work and if the Board will authorize such we will try to find a man for the purpose and a way of financing him. In this connection a communication has been received from Mr. C. P. Wilson who spent several years in Korea as architect for the Standard Oil Company and who married the daughter of one of the missionaries, offering to go out for one, two or three years on a salary of $3600 per year, plus residence and other allowances usually granted missionaries, with ordinary travel expenses for himself and wife from Boston to Seoul and return. The selection of a suitable man might be left to the discretion of the Property Committee of this Board and the President.

Some funds for building or equipment purposes are coming into the hands of the Treasurer of this Board which are not bing immediately called for. I would recommend that such designated funds be put on special deposit either here or on the field and that the interest earned on them be added so that, when they are called for, the special object may receive the increment of interest.

H. 7. 4-10-25

RECOMMENDATIONS:

1. That the necessary extension of leave to Mr. H. H. Underwood to enable him to assist in the financial campaign be approved.

2. That a further absence of one year from the field of Dr. O. R. Avison be authorized if such absence be found necessary to a successful completion of the task.

3. That this Board take steps to add to its membership in order to make it more representative of the whole cooperating constituency.

4. That a supervising architect for construction work be engaged by the President under the advice of the Property Committee of this Board.

5. That the policy of placing funds for designated objects on special deposit until called for so that the special object may receive the benefit of the interest earned be approved.

6. That the request of the Severance authorities for permission to lease the souther-western frontage be approved, provided that the details of the terms of the proposed lease have been approved by the Finance Committee of the Cooperating Board.

O. R. Avison,

President.

27. 베커 부교장의 이사회 제출 보고서

문서 제목	Report of Chosen Christian College
문서 종류	부교장 보고서
제출 시기	1925년 9월 26일
작성 장소	서울
제 출 자	A. L. Becker
수 신 자	이사회
페이지 수	5
출 처	Korea Mission Records, 1904~1960, Box 15, Folder 15 (PHS) 2114-5-2: 07 Board of Managers 1923~1927 (UMAH)

자료 소개

베커 부교장이 1925년 9월 26일 열린 이사회 회의에 제출한 보고서로 추정된다. 이 문서에는 작성자의 서명도, 일자 표기도 없다. 그러나 PHS 문서의 1쪽 오른편 상단에 '1925'라는 필기 표시가 있고, UMAH 문서의 오른편 상단에는 '9-26-25'라는 필기 표시가 있으며, 파일상에서 이 문서가 이날 열린 이사회 회의록 바로 다음 순서에 배치되어있어 그 시기를 짐작하게 한다. 이 문서는 학감 보고서의 형태를 보이지만, 부교장 빌링스가 1923년 안식년을 보내기 위해 미국으로 떠나면서 학감인 베커가 부교장을 맡았으므로, 부교장의 자격으로 이 보고서를 제출하였다고 추정할 수 있다. (이사회의 이날 회의록에는 부교장의 보고서가 제출된 사실만 기록되어 있고, 학감의 보고서가 제출되었다는 기록은 보이지 않는다.) 이날 이사회 회의 때 부학감 유억겸이 학감으로, 수물과와 상과 과장대리 이춘호와 이순탁이 과장으로 임명되었고, 조교수 백남운이 교수로 승급되었다.

이 보고서는 아래의 5가지 항목으로 구성되어 있다.

학과 현황, 학교 임원, 학생 현황, 졸업생 현황, 주목할 일, 교수 명단.

내용 요약

학과: 문과는 빌링스 과장을 포함하여 18명(교수 11명, 조교수 2명, 강사 5명)이 가르치고 있고, 학생 수는 95명이며, 졸업생은 45명이다. 상과는 이순탁 과장대리를 포함하여 9명

(교수 3명, 조교수 4명, 강사 2명)이 가르치고 있고, 컬럼비아대에서 박사학위를 받은 조병옥, 동경상과대학의 백남운, 오하이오 주립대의 홍승국이 교수로 왔으며, 학생은 67명, 졸업생은 52명이다. 수물과는 베커 과장과 이춘호 과장대리를 포함하여 10명(교수 6명, 조교수 1명, 실험실 조수 2명, 강사 1명)이 가르치고 있고, 학생은 49명, 졸업생은 7명이다. 노블 선교사, 교토제국대의 카도와키, 장기원이 교직원[조수]에 합류하였고, 이원철이 올해 미시간대에서 Ph.D.를 받고 내년부터 가르칠 예정이다.

임원: 학교 임원에는 교장 에비슨, 부교장 및 학감 베커, 회계 오웬스, 부학감 유억겸이 있다. [유억겸은 이 보고서가 제출된 후에 학감으로 임명되었다.]

학생: 등록생은 총 211명(문과 95명, 상과 67명, 수물과 49명)이고, 학생들의 종교는 북장로교인 45명, 남장로교인 17명, 호주장로교인 8명, 캐나다장로교인 23명, 북감리교인 50명, 남감리교인 40명, 안식교인 4명이고, 비기독교인 24명이다. 대학 입학 전 학력을 보면, 고등보통학교 졸업생이 32%를 이루고 있다. 출신 지역표에서는 학생들이 제주도만 빼고 전국에서 왔다.

졸업생: 졸업생은 문과 45명, 상과 52명, 수물과 10명, 농과 3명, 총 110명이다. 졸업생들은 현재 미국 유학 20명, 일본 유학 9명, 한국에서 진학 1명, 학교 교사 35명, 교회사역 2명, 사업 5명, 개인사업 15명, 사무직 18명, 편집인 1명, 사망 4명이다.

주목할 일: 학생들이 수적으로나 질적으로 가장 고무적인 모습을 보였고, 운동 분야에서 큰 발전을 이루었다. 춘기 대학 축구대회에서 우승하였고, 테니스코트를 조성하여 9월에 대학 테니스대회를 열었으며, 야구팀이 열심히 훈련하고 있다. 전국 중등학교 체육대회가 9월 23일 8개 학교 151명의 참가로 열려 5,000명이 관람하였다.

교수: (명단을 제시하고 있다.) 한국인 교수는 문과에 이관용 과장대리 · 논리학 및 심리학 교수, 노정일 사회학 교수, 백남석 영어 교수, 김영환 음악 교수, 윤병섭 자연학 조교수, 정인보 한문 조교수, 정인서 동양사 강사, M. H. Hong 문학 강사, 안동원 교육심리학 강사, 홍종숙 성경 강사가 있다. 상과에는 이순탁 과장대리 · 경제학 교수, 유억겸 교수, 김달호 교수, 윤정하 조교수, 백남운 조교수, 조병옥 조교수, 홍승국 조교수, 선우전 강사, 박길용 강사가 있다. 수물과에는 이춘호 과장대리 · 수학 및 천문학 교수, 신제린 조수, 장기원 조수가 있다.

1925

REPORT
of
CHOSEN CHRISTIAN COLLEGE

The College has three Departments in operation, each with a separate faculty, budget and recitation rooms.

The Literary College: Rev. B. W. Billings, D.D. is the Director of this department and there are eleven fully qualified Professors, one Associate Professor, one Assistant Professor and five Lecturers; 18 teachers in all. There are 50 Freshmen, 24 Sophomores, 16 Juniors and 5 Seniors, a total of 95 students enrolled in this department. The graduates of this department now number 45.

The Commercial College: Mr. S. T. Lee is the Acting Director of this department. This department has three year courses (all others have four year courses). There are three fully qualified Professors, four Associate Professors and two Lecturers, nine teachers in all. Dr. P. O. Chough from Columbia University, Mr. N. W. Paik from the Commercial University of Tokyo and Mr. S. K. Hong, a graduate of Ohio State University were added to the staff of this department during the year. There are 32 Freshmen, 25 Sophomores and 10 Seniors, a total of 67 students enrolled in this department. There are 52 graduates.

The Science College: Rev. A. L. Becker, Ph.D. is the Director of this department, but Mr. C. H. Lee as Assistant Director has borne the brunt of the supervision. The Freshman and Sophomore grades only are under the new Registration, so the staff is as yet incomplete and the enrollment relatively small. There are 26 Freshmen, 16 Sophomores and 7 Seniors, a total of 49 students. There are 7 graduates of this lepartment. There are six fully qualified Professors, one Associate 'rofessor and two Laboratory Assistants, as well as one Lecturer. Mr. lden Noble, M.A. Ohio State University, Mr. Katowaki of Kyoto Imperial niversity and Mr. Chang have been added to the staff this year. Mr. . W. Lee, who will probably receive his Ph.D. at the end of the first emester at Michigan University, will probably take up his teaching in his department early next year. The curriculum of this department is argely Mathematics, Physics and Chemistry, but when Mr. Noble gets nto the work, we expect to stress Biological Science also.

COLLEGE OFFICERS

O. R. Avison, M.D., LL.D.	President (Promotional Work, U.S.A.)
A. L. Becker, Ph.D.	Vice President, Dean. (Administrative Work)
H. T. Owens	Treasurer, Business Mgr.
U. K. Yu	Assistant Dean

ENROLLMENT

There was a total enrollment of 211 students distributed as follows:

Class	Lit. Dep't	Com. Dep't	Science Dep't	Total
Freshman	50	32	26	108
Sophomore	34	25	16	65
Junior	16	10	--	26
Senior	5	--	7	12
Total	95	67	49	211

STUDENTS' CHURCH RELATION

CHURCH NAMES	NUMBER	PERCENTAGE
Presbyterian, North	45	21.5 %
" South	17	8.05%
" Australian	8	3.08%
" Canadian	23	10.9 %
Northern Methodist	50	23.7 %
Southern Methodist	40	19.00%
'Adventist'	4	1.9 %
No Affiliation	24	11.37%
Total	211	100 %

List of Students who have studied or graduated from MIDDLE, HIGHER COMMON SCHOOLS, or other PREPARATORY SCHOOLS

SCHOOL NAMES	NUMBER	PERCENTAGE
Middle School Graduates	84	29.9%
Higher Com.School Graduates	68	32.2%
Higher Common School (Studied)	36	18.5%
Middle School (studied)	18	8.5%
Other Prep. School Graduates	2	.9%
Total	211	100%

PROVINCES from which STUDENTS CAME

NAME ofPROVINCE	NUMBER	PERCENTAGE
North Ham-Ktung	13	6.2%
South "	26	12.3%
North Pyeng-An	21	10.0%
South "	22	10.4%
Whang-Hai	10	4.7%
Kyung-Ki	44	20.9%
Kang-Won	10	4.7%
North Choohg-Chung	2	.9%
South "	12	5.7%
North Chulla	8	3.8%
South "	15	7.1%
North Kyung-Sang	12	5.7%
South "	16	7.6%
Total	211	100%

NUMBER of GRADUATES of each DEPT.

Literary Department	45
Commercial Department	52
Math. & Physics Department	10
Agricultural Department	3
Total	110

OCCUPATION of GRADUATES

WORK	NUMBER	PERCENTAGE
Studying in U. S. A.	20	18.2 %
Studying in Japan	9	8.18%
Studying in Korea	1	.9 %
Teacher	35	31.8 %
Church work	2	1.8 %
Business	5	4.5 %
Private work	15	13.6%
Office Work	18	16.4 %
Editor	1	.9 %
Died	4	3.6 %
Total	110	100%

SOME NOTEWORTHY ITEMS

(A) We had a most profitable week of Bible Study during the winter term led by Rev. S. O. Pyun of the Methodist Theological Seminary. Both teachers and pupils got a new spiritual vision.

(B) The enrollment of new students during the year was most encouraging both as to numbers and as to quality. We enrolled quite a number of students who had attained honor rank in their High School courses. The Freshman progress in many subjects, especially in English, can be compared favorably with the Sophomore work. So we are enabled to improve the quantity and quality of our instruction all along the line.

(C) The enthusiasm and loyalty of the faculty have been very marked this year. This has been evinced by their faithful attenddance on classes and the high quality of their instruction. We feel that we have secured a staff that would command respect in any college anywhere and we ought to be proud of them. Nearly all give unselfishly of their time outside of teaching period and show great aptitude in the responsible positions of the Administration. Not only this but they have agreed to raise Y1,450. toward the Budget of the year and the Association of Chosen Christian College Teachers have Y920. in the bank, which is to be used ultimately for some urgent need of the School.

(D) The past year has been a notable advance in College athletics:

(1) The College won the Championship flag and cup in the inter-collegiate football games in the spring.

(2) A fine tennis court has been prövided and the boys have taken up hard-ball tennis. The inter-collegiate tennis tournament was held on our grounds in September. Although our boys did not win, they gave a good account of themselves. Mr. Kilyong Park, a former net star of Ohio State University, is the coach and expects to put up a winning team in another year.

(3) The College has a good baseball team, which is practising hard for the fall games. We beliwve we have a good chance to win out here.

(4) The Third All Korea High School Field Day was pulled off this year on the 23d of September. Eight schools participated and 151 athletes took part. The railroad sent out a special train and about 5,000 people saw the sports. It went off well and testified to the fine co-operation of the Chosen Christian Colleg-e faculty and student body. In fact it was a great advertisement for the College. Mr. U. K. Yu, chairman of the athletic committee, was in charge and showed himself a master hand at this. The faculty contributed about Y200.00 and Mr. Yu raised about Y24.00 among outside friends.

- 5 -

CHOSEN CHRISTIAN COLLEGE

FACULTY LIST. SEPT. 1925

Name	Teaching Subjects	Qualified
Literary Dep't		
B. W. Billings,	Director and Prof. of History	Qualified
K. Y. Lee,	Assistant Director and Prof. of Logic, Psychology and Philosophy.	"
H. H. Underwood,	Prof. of Ethics and Psychology. (on Furlough)	"
H. A. Rhodes,	Prof. of Bible and English.	"
J. E. Fisher,	Prof. of Education and English. (On Furlough)	"
J. W. Hitch,	Prof. of English	"
C. Y. Roe,	Prof. of Sociology, Ethics and Bible. (On Leave of Absence)	"
K. Takahashi,	Prof. of Morals, Japanese and Civil Government	"
N. S. Paik,	Prof. of English	"
M. Hirai,	Prof. of Japanese	"
Y. W. Kim,	Prof. of Music	"
P. S. Yun,	Associate Prof. of Natural Science	Special "
I. P. Chung,	Assistant Prof. of Chinese	" "
I. S. Chung,	Lecturer on Oriental History	" "
M. H. Hong,	Lecturer on Literature.	" "
K. Umezawa,	Lectuerxx on Physical Training	Qualified
T. W. Ahn,	Lecturer on Eduoztional Psychology and Education.	"
C. S. Hong,	Lecturer on Bible	Special "
Commercial Dep't		
S. T. Lee,	Provisional Director and Prof. of Economics	Qualified
U. K. Yu,	Vice Dean and Prof. of Law.	"
K. H. Kim,	Prof. of Banking, Finance and Accounting	"
C. H. Yun,	Associate Prof. of Commercial Practice, Commercial Geography, Com. Arithmetic, Custom House and Warehouse.	Special "
N. W. Paik,	Associate Prof. of Transportation	Qualfieid
P. O. Chough,	Associate Prof. of English and Sociology	"
S. K. Hong,	Associate Prof. of English	Special "
C. Sunwoo,	Lecturer of Commercial Japanese	Qualified
Kilyong Park,	Lecturer on Commercial English and Typewriting.	Special "
Science Dep't		
A. L. Becker,	Director and Prof. of Physics and Electrical Engineering	Qualified
C. H. Lee,	Assistant Director and Prof. of Mathematics and Astronomy	"
T. Tsubakita,	Prof. of Geometry, Surveying, Physics, Thermo-Dynamics, Geology and Minerology	"
A. C. Noble,	Prof. of Biology and English	"
K. Kadowaki,	Associate Prof. of Chemistry Mechanical Drawing and Electro-Chemistry	"
M. Oshima,	Lecturer on Trigonometry	Special "
C. R. Cynn,	Assistant in Physics Laboratory	" "
K. W. Chang,	" in Chemistry Laboratory	" "

28. 베커 부교장의 이사회 제출 보고서

문서 제목	Vice President's Report
문서 종류	부교장 보고서
제출 시기	1926년 6월 5일
작성 장소	서울
제 출 자	A. L. Becker
수 신 자	이사회
페이지 수	2
출 처	Korea Mission Records, 1904~1960, Box 15, Folder 18 (PHS) 2114-5-2: 07 Board of Managers 1923~1927 (UMAH)

자료 소개

부교장 베커가 1926년 6월 5일 열린 이사회 회의에서 제출한 보고서이다. 에비슨 교장이 미국에서 아직 돌아오지 않아 베커가 이날 회의를 주재하였다. 이날 회의에서 연희전문 우애회(교수 클럽)가 곧 안식년을 가질 베커에게 자녀 교육비로 ¥4,000을 기부하기로 한 일이 보고되었고, 최현배가 조교수로 승급되었다. (베커는 이후 안식년 기간에 미국 조지아 공대에서 근무하면서 자녀의 학비 조달을 위해 너 오래 있으려 하였으나, 학교 측의 간곡한 요청과 존 T. 언더우드의 학비 지원으로 2년 만에 돌아왔다.)

이 보고서는 항목 분류 없이 서언에 이어 재정 압박 문제, 교직원에게 당부할 사항, 희망 사항을 다루고 있다.

내용 요약

서언: 11년의 역사를 지닌 학교가 크게 성장하여, 각 교단 선교부가 교수 쿼터를 거의 채우고 있다. [협력이사회의 정관에 의해 각 교단은 학교에 내는 자본금의 규모에 따라 '완전 협력'과 '부분 협력'으로 지위가 나뉘었고 학교에 파송할 교수와 이사의 수의 쿼터를 다르게 할당받았다.] 학생 수도 지난 5년 만에 2배가 되었지만, 빠른 성장에 비례하여 긴장과 심리적 압박도 그만큼 심해졌다.

재정 압박: 총독부와 한국인의 요구에 부응하기 위해 자격 있는 교수를 확보하고 늘어

나는 예산을 조달하는 일이 우리를 압박하였다. 이에 학교 기본재산으로 적자를 벌충하였고, 학비를 몇 차례 인상하였다. 교수들이 돈을 갹출하기까지 하였다. 그런데도 협력이사회의 교단들은 지원금을 올려주지 않았고, 어떤 곳에서는 오히려 축소하였다. 현실적으로는 도서 구입, 시설 보수를 비롯한 모든 방면에서 오히려 지출을 증가할 필요가 발생하였다. 이 문제의 해결책은 미국에서 에비슨이 기본재산 기부금을 더 많이 얻어오고 재학생이 증가하는 데에 있다. 교직원들의 봉급을 올리기는 어려울 것이다. 학생들이 많이 오고 한국인들이 후원해주기를 기대한다.

당부 사항: 교직원들이 대부분 충성스럽고, 열정이 있고, 유능하고, 책임감이 강하지만, 극소수는 온전히 헌신하지 않고 있다.

희망 사항: 부교장의 직무를 내려놓으면서 나는 학교가 앞으로 별문제 없이 운영되기를 희망한다. 그리고 현재 쓰고 있는 자동차를 즉시 처분하고 새 차를 사기를 희망한다. [베커는 자동차에 관한 이 마지막 문장 전체를 대문자로 타이핑하였다.]

VICE PRESIDENT'S REPORT

June 5, 1926.

If we look at our Historical Data we see that we have had a remarkable growth. The institution is only eleven years old, yet it has three well developed Departments (or Colleges) with almost the full quota of qualified teachers. The remarkable growth of the institution is shown in the fact that during the last five years we have nearly doubled our enrollment, our budget, our staff and capital. Of course, such a rapid growth is necessarily caused considerable stress and strain and the necessary adjustments have not been easy. Perhaps it may be questioned as to whether such rapid development has been necessary, but one conversant with the whole educational situation in Korea will realize that these have been 'test' years.

The real test was as to whether we would live or die -- to live meant (1) to meet stiff Government requirements, (2) to meet the Korean demand, if we were to get students: this has meant securing qualified teachers without delay -- as delay would be fatal; and also equipment had to be added. Of course, income from students has increased from ¥3,802, five years ago, to this year's revised estimate of ¥17,545, but this has partially met the imperative need of increased budget. Fortunately, the efforts of our President have provided an increase from endowment but owing to financial stringency the Co-operating Mission Boards have not all increased their apportionments but have tended in some cases to reduce their already small contributions. So, as the Treasurer will report, we are up against a possible deficit this year. The Administration does not want this unbalanced budget, but in spite of long consultations in the Budget Committee in which all phases of the situation were canvassed -- cuts and savings were suggested even where it would be at a definite loss to the growth and future as well as the name of the institution. And even a collection was taken up among the staff to reduce the possible deficit. The truth is that considering all the factors we are operating on an almost irreducible minimum or we would be ashamed to bring a possible deficit to the attention of the Board. But the alternative being worse we are bringing the problem to you. If we had realized from the first the expense connected with running three full-fledged colleges, we might have hesitated taking up the task, but now that we have developed these to almost their complete state, it behooves us to strain every nerve and take no backward step. We are hoping that Dr. Avison may get some additional endowment and that additional students will help us to balance our budget next year without having to make a disastrous cut. It may seem an easy thing to find a saving of at least ¥5,000 in a budget of this size, but when every item is reviewed it will be readily seen that there are weighty reasons for every proposed expenditure; in fact, in almost every direction the sums should be increased for real efficiency. For instance, much more money should be available for Library books, for equipment and for repair and upkeep.

As the sum required for salaries will not increase so rapidly in the future I feel that the larger enrollment (in the next few years) will take care of this increase and allow some surplus for other necessary expenditures. I am sure that as the Koreans begin to realize that this institution embodies much of their hopes and aspirations they will provide a way to a healthy development without an annual deficit to worry the Treasurer and the Administration.

Personnel: I would like to say a few words as to the teaching force and staff. I feel that we have been extremely fortunate in the type of men we have been able to get even under the stress of the rapid expansion. When I see the loyalty, enthusiasm and ability of the most of those entrusted with the heavy responsibilities of developing an institution of this kind, it is wonder how we were able to find in such a short period so many of just the right type who are evidently fitted to carry us through this difficult period. Of course, a few have not yet thrown themselves whole-heartedly into the college work but it is not to be wondered at that a few would find it difficult to adjust themselves. I know that most of our staff have been called to this institution for just this period and I wish to express my faith in them and their ability to help us through to our final goal; that is, an institution which is thoroughly Christian and which will be at the same time an institution of such a grade and such a high standard that the Koreans will be proud to claim it as 'their own'.

As the Vice President lays down his duties there is one thing that he would like to recommend in order that the Administration of the ensuing year may have one less problem.

THAT THE PRESENT AUTO BE DISPOSED OF IMMEDIATELY AND THAT A NEW ONE BE BOUGHT.

Respectfully submitted,

(signed). Arthur L. Becker,
Vice President.

29. 유억겸 학감의 이사회 제출 보고서

문서 제목	Report of Chosen Christian College
문서 종류	학감 보고서
제출 시기	1926년 6월 5일
작성 장소	서울
제 출 자	유억겸
수 신 자	이사회
페이지 수	6
출 처	Korea Mission Records, 1904~1960, Box 15, Folder 15 (PHS) 2114-5-2: 07 Board of Managers 1923~1927 (UMAH)

자료 소개

유억겸 학감이 1926년 6월 5일 열린 이사회 회의에서 제출한 보고서이다. 이 보고서는 제출 시기만 표기하고 제출자의 이름을 표기하지 않은 채, 전년도(1925년 9월 26일)에 제출된 베커의 학감 보고서의 양식을 그대로 따르고 있다. 그런데 6월 5일 자 이사회 회의록에 유억겸은 학감 보고서를 제출하고(회의록 1쪽: "The dean, Mr. U. K. Yu, read his report") 베커는 부교장 보고서를 제출하였다고 하는 기록이 있다. 그러므로 이 보고시는 진넌도에 베커가 제출했던 학감 보고서의 형식에 맞춰서 유억겸이 작성한 것이라고 할 수 있다.

이 보고서는 번호 매김 없이 아래의 9가지 항목으로 구성되어 있는데, 전년도의 학감 보고서와 비교하면, 항목의 순서만 일부 바뀌어 있다.

학과 현황, 학교 임원, 교수 명단, 학생 등급(본과, 별과), 등록생, 학생 출신 지역, 졸업생 수, 졸업생 현황, 학생 종교.

내용 요약

학과: 문과는 빌링스 과장을 포함하여 18명(교수 11명, 조교수 3명, 강사 4명)이 가르치고 있고, 교토제국대학을 졸업한 최현배가 교수진에 더해졌으며, 학생은 75명, 졸업생은 53명이다. 상과는 이순탁 과장을 포함하여 9명(교수 5명, 조교수 3명, 강사 1명)이 가르치고 있고, 학생은 92명, 졸업생은 61명이다. 수물과는 이춘호 과장을 포함하여 교수 6명, 조

교수 2명, 실험실 조수 2명이 가르치고 있고, 올해 수물과를 졸업한 김영성이 교직원에 합류하였으며, 미시간대에서 이달에 Ph.D.를 받게 될 이원철이 가을학기부터 가르칠 예정이다. 학생은 51명, 졸업생은 16명이다.

임원: 에비슨 교장, 베커 부교장, 오웬스 회계·사업 매니저, 유억겸 학감이 있다.

교수: 문과의 교수진은 총 18명이고, 한국인은 10명이다(교수: 이관용〈과장대리〉, 노정일, 백남석, 김영환, 조교수: 윤병섭, 최현배, 정인보, 강사: 정인서, M. H. Hong, 안동원). 상과의 교수진은 총 9명이고, 한국인은 8명이다(교수: 이순탁, 유억겸, 김달호, 조병옥, 백남운, 조교수: 윤정하, 홍승국, 박길용, 강사: 선우전). 수물과의 교수진은 총 9명이고, 한국인은 4명이다(교수: 이춘호, 조교수: 이원철, 조수: 신제린, 김영성).

학생: 본과 학생은 85명, 별과 학생은 149명이다. 등록생은 1학년 106명, 2학년 58명, 3학년 40명, 4학년 14명, 총 218명이다. 학생들은 제주도를 뺀 나머지 전 지역에서 왔다.

졸업생: 졸업생은 총 133명이고, 현재 미국 유학 21명, 일본 유학 8명, 한국에서 진학 2명, 학교 교사 40명, 교회사역 2명, 사업 9명, 개인사업 16명, 사무직 26명, 언론인 4명, 사망 5명이다.

학생 종교: 전체적으로 감리교인이 장로교인보다 많고, 성결교인이 2명, 비기독교인이 35명이다. [학과별, 학년별로 학생들의 소속 교파와 신앙 경력을 분류하고 있다.]

REPORT
OF
CHOSEN CHRISTIAN COLLEGE

June 5, 1926.

The College has three Departments in operation, each with a separate faculty, budget and recitation rooms.

THE LITERARY DEPARTMENT: Rev. B. W. Billings, D. D., is the Director of this Department and there are eleven fully qualified Professors, two Associate Professors, one Assistant Professor, and four Lecturers; 18 teachers in all. Mr. H. P. Choi, a graduate of the Kyoto Imperial University, was added to the staff of this Department during the year. There are 30 Freshmen, 24 Sophomores, 7 Juniors, and 14 Seniors -- a total of 75 enrolled in this Department. The graduates of this Department now number 53.

THE COMMERCIAL DEPARTMENT: Mr. S. T. Lee, Kakushi, is the Director of this Department. This Department alone offers three year courses. There are five fully qualified Professors, three Associate Professors and one Lecturer, nine teachers in all. The enrollment of this Department is as follows: Freshman class, 48; Sophomore class, 22; Junior class, 22; 92 in all. There are 61 graduates.

THE SCIENCE DEPARTMENT: Mr. C. H. Lee, M. A., is the Director of this Department. At present there are only three grades, viz., Freshman, Sophomore and Junior grades. All these grades are being run under the New Registration secured in 1924. There are 28 Freshmen, 12 Sophomores and 11 Juniors -- 51 in all. The graduates of this Department now number 16. There are six fully qualified Professors, two Associate Professors and two laboratory assistants. Mr. C. K. Hahn, M. S., University of Southern California, and Mr. Y. S. Kim, this year's graduate from the Science Department, were added to the staff during the year. Mr. David W. Lee, who will in all proability receive his Ph. D. from the University of Michigan this month will probably take up his teaching in this Department in the fall.

COLLEGE OFFICERS

O. R. Avison, M. D., LL. D.,	President (Promotional work, U. S. A.)
Arthur L. Becker, Ph. D.	Vice President (Administrative Work)
H. T. Owens,	Treasurer and Business Manager.
U. K. Yu, Kakushi,	Dean.

CHOSEN CHRISTIAN COLLEGE
Faculty List. June 5th, 1926.

NAME	RANK SUBJECTS.	QUALIFIED.
Literary Department		
B. W. Billings, Ph. D., M. A., B. D., D. D. (Depauw)	Director and professor, History.	Qualified.
K. Y. Lee. Ph. D. (Zurich)	Asst. Director and Prof., Logic, Psychology and Philosophy.	"
H. H. Underwood, B. A., M. A., Ph. D. (New York)	Professor, Ethics and Psychology. (On Furlough)	"
H. A. Rhodes, B. A., M. A., B. D., D. D.(Grove City)	Professor. Bible and English.	"
J. E. Fisher B. A., M. A. (Columbia)	Professor, English and Education. (On Furlough)	"
J. W. Hitch, LL. B. (University of Georgia)	Professor English	"
C. Y. Roe, B. A., B. D., M. A. (Columbia)	Professor Sociology, Ethics & Bible (On leave of absence)	"
K. Takahashi, (Tokyo Imperial) University)	Professor, Morals and Japanese Civil Government.	"
N. S. Paik, B. A., M. A. (Emory)	Professor. English and Education.	"
Mr. Hirai, Gakushi (Tokyo Imperial)	Professor, Japanese and Japanese Literature	"
Y. M. Kim. Grad. of Tokyo College of Music	Professor. Music.	"
P. S. Yun.(Grad. of Tokyo Imperial)	Associate Professor, Special Natural Sciences.	"
H. P. Choi, Gakushi (Tokyo Imperial)	Associate Professor. Ethics and Philosophy.	"
I. P. Chung.	Assistant Professor. Chinese Literature	" "
I. S. Chung.	Lecturer. Oriental History	" "
M. H. Kong.	Lecturer Literature.	" "
K. Umezawa	Lecturer Physical Training.	" "
T. W. Ahn. B. A., M. A. (Northwestern)	Lecturer Educational Psychology, Education and Bible	Qualified.

2

COMMERCIAL DEPARTMENT

S. T. Lee, Gakushi* (Kyo-to Imperial)	Director& Prof. Economics, Insurance, Statistics and Economic Policy.	Qualified.
U. K. Yu, Gakushi* (Tokyo Imperial)	Dean and Professor, Law.	"
K. H. Kim. (Waseda Gakushi)*	Professor, Banking, Money, Custom & Warehouse and Abacus.	"
P. O. Chough, B. A., M. A., Ph. D. (Columbia)	Professor, English, Sociology and Finance.	"
N. W. Paik, Gakushi* (Tokyo University of Commerce	Professor, Bookkeeping, Sociology History of Commerce and Commerci.	"
C. H. Yun. Grad. of Tokyo Higher Commercial School	Associate Professor, Com. Geography. Com. Arithmetic, Commodity, Exchange and Com. Practice.	(Special Qualified)
S. K. Hong, B. A. (Ohio State)	Associate Prof. English	" "
K. Y. Park, B.Sc. In Bus. Administration (Ohio State)	Associate Professor, Commercial English, Accounting and Type-writing.	" "
J. Shunwoo, (Waseda Gakushi)*	Lecturer, Commercial Japanese and Communication.	" "

3

SCIENCE DEPARTMENT

C. H. Lee, B. A., M.A. (Ohio State)	Director & Professor, Qualified Mathematics & Astronomy.
A. L. Becker, B. A., M. A., Ph.D. (Michigan)	Acting President, and Prof. " Electrical Engineering, Physics, Mechanics and Science English.
E. H. Miller, B. A., D.D. M.A. (Columbia)	Professor, (On furlough) " Bible, English and Chemistry.
T. Tsubakida, B. A. (Stanford)*	Professor. " Geometry, Surveying, Physics, Geology & Mineralogy.
A. E. Noble, B. A., M. A., (Ohio State)	Professor, " Biology and English
K. Kadowaki, Gakushi* (Kyoto Imperial)	Professor, " Chemistry & Drawing.
David Lee, B. A. M. A. (Michigan)	Associate Professor, " Astronomy, Math. and Physics,
C. R. Cynn, Gad. of Chosen Christian College	Assistant, Special Qualified Physics Laboratory.
Y. S. Kim. Gad. of Chosen Christian College	Assistant, " " Chemistry Laboratory.

"Gakushi is equivalent to M. A. in American Universities."

CLASSIFICATION OF STUDENTS.

Regular students.	85	36.4%
Special students.	149	63.6%
TOTAL	234	100.0%

ENROLLMENT.

There was a total enrollment of 218 students distributed as follows:

CLASS.	LIT. DEPT.	COM. DEPT.	SCIENCE DEPT.	TOTAL
Freshman	30 (3)	48(1)	28(1)	106(5)
Sophomore	24 (3)	22(1)	12(3)	58(7)
Junior	7 (3)	22( )	11(1)	40(4)
Senior	14	--	--	14
TOTAL	75	92	51	218

16 students have not yet paid their term fees but some of them partially paid and others promise to pay soon.

PROVINCES FROM WHICH STUDENTS CAME.

NAME OF PROVINCE	NUMBER	PERCENTAGE
North Ham Kyung	14	5.9%
South Ham Kyung	21	8.9%
North Pyeng An	27	11.5%
South Pyeng An	22	9.4%
Whang Hai	18	7.6%
Kyung Ki	66	28.2%
Kang Won	10	4.2%
North Choong Chung	5	2.2%
South Choong Chung	14	6.0%
North Chun La	5	2.2%
South Chun La	12	5.1%
North Kyung Sang	12	5.1%
South Kyung Sang	8	3.4%
TOTAL	234	100.0%

NUMBER OF GRADUATES OF EACH DEPARTMENT

Literary Department	53
Commercial Department	61
Science Department	16
Agricultural Department	3
TOTAL	133

OCCUPATION OF GRADUATES.

WORK	NUMBER	PERCENTAGE
Studying in U. S. A.	21	15.8%
Studying in Japan.	8	6.0%
Studying in Korea.	2	1.5%
Teacher	40	30.0%
Church work	2	1.5%
Business	9	6.8%
Private work	16	12.1%
Office work	26	19.6%
Journalist	4	3.0%
Deceased	5	3.7%
TOTAL	133	100.0%

STUDENTS' CHURCH RELATION. June 1st, 1926.

DEPT.	CLASS.	NO.	PRESBY. MISSIONS.	METHODIST EPISCOPAL.	METHODIST SOUTHERN.	ORIENTAL MISSIONS.	NON-CHRISTIAN.
LITERARY.							
	Fresh.	33.	17.	5.	5.	0.	6
	Sopho.	28.	9.	7.	5.	1.	6
	Junior.	11.	4.	4.	3.	0.	0
	Senior.	14.	5.	4.	4.	1.	0
COMMERCIAL.							
	Frosh.	49.	19.	12.	13.	0.	5
	Sopho.	23.	9.	9.	3.	0.	2
	Senior.	22.	11.	4.	4.	0.	3
SCIENCE.							
	Frosh.	27.	4.	9.	3.	0.	11
	Sopho.	15.	5.	5.	5.	0.	0
	Junior.	12.	5.	4.	1.	0.	2
TOTAL.	10.	234.	80.	63.	43.	2.	35

DEPT.	CLASS.	BAPTIZED.	AUDITORS.	NEW BELIEVERS.	NON-CHRISTIANS.	TOTAL
LITERARY						
	Fresh.	12.	5.	10.	6.	33
	Sopho.	9.	8.	5.	6.	28
	Junior.	7.	1.	3.	0.	11
	Senior.	11.	1.	2.	0.	14
COMMERCIAL						
	Fresh.	16.	6.	22.	5.	49
	Sopho.	8.	3.	10.	2.	23
	Senior.	13.	1.	5.	3.	22
SCIENCE						
	Fresh.	7.	3.	6.	11.	27
	Sopho.	9.	2.	4.	0.	15
	Junior.	6.	3.	1.	2.	12
TOTAL	10	98	33	68	35	234

30. 유억겸 학감의 이사회 제출 보고서

문서 제목	Chosen Christian College, Report of Dean to Field Board of Managers
문서 종류	학감 보고서
제출 시기	1926년 9월 24일
작성 장소	서울
제 출 자	유억겸
수 신 자	이사회
페이지 수	3
출 처	Korea Mission Records, 1904~1960, Box 15, Folder 15 (PHS) 2114-5-2: 07 Board of Managers 1923~1927 (UMAH)

자료 소개

유억겸 학감이 1926년 9월 24일 열린 이사회 회의에서 제출한 보고서이다. 이날 이사회 회의는 에비슨 교장이 주재하였는데, 에비슨은 부교장 베커가 부재하므로 원한경이 교장의 직무를 보좌한다고 공지하였다. 이 회의에서도 이사회는 적자를 해소하는 문제를 주로 논의하였다. 교장이 보고서를 제출하지 않은 것을 양해하고, 그의 귀국을 환영하였으며, 그가 미국에서 한 모금 활동의 성과를 이사회가 기쁘게 여긴다는 것을 의결하였다.

이 보고서는 아래의 4가지 항목으로 구성되어 있다.

등록생, 6.10만세운동, 교수의 도착과 출타, 운동경기.

내용 요약

등록생: 등록생은 총 223명이고, 문과 77명, 상과 94명, 수물과 52명이다. 6·10만세운동으로 등록생 수가 기대에 미치지 못하였다.

6·10만세운동: 학감이 7월에 총독부 학무국에 불려가서 만세운동에 참가한 학생들을 징계하라는 지시를 받았다. 경찰서에 구류된 학생들을 모두 학무국이 정한 수위대로 처벌하되, 문과생 이병립·이석훈·박하균은 퇴학, 문과생 홍명식·김규봉·한일청, 상과생 최현준, 수물과생 이봉진은 무기정학, 문과생 유경상·김세진·박영준, 수물과생 권오상은 4주 정학, 문과생 임병철·송운순·장홍식·김윤근·원종뢰·안태희·박봉래·김영하·

이광준 · 박안근 · 이금산 · 채우병 · 이관희 · 이은택 · 유치려, 상과생 임병철 · 송운순 · 장희창 · 김영소 · 김윤근 · 김낙기 · 김명진 · 김지삼 · 김근배, 수물과생 김영식 · 김영기 · 이석영 · 함창래 · 최창일 · 조대벽 · 박영규는 2주 정학 조치를 하고, 대학과 재단은 학무국에 사과의 글을 제출하라는 지시를 받았다. 또한 이런 일이 또다시 발생하면 연희전문의 설립 인가를 취소시킬 필요가 있을 것이란 경고를 받았다.

교수: 부교장 베커가 안식년을 맞아 6월에 떠났고, 에비슨 교장, 언더우드(원한경) 박사, 이원철 박사가 8월에 돌아왔다.

운동경기: 제4회 전조선 중등학교 육상경기대회가 현재(1926년 9월 24일) 160명이 참가한 가운데 열리고 있고, 이 운동회를 위해 ￥366.00의 후원금이 답지하였다.

DR. BR[illegible], REC'D

Ans'd

CHOSEN CHRISTIAN COLLEGE

Report of Dean to Field Board of Managers

at meeting held September 24th, 1926

ENROLMENT

There was a total enrolment of 223 students distributed as follows at the end of the first term:

Literary Department	77
Commercial Department	94
Science Department	52
Total	223

This failure of enrolment to reach the expectations of the Budget Committee may be partly traced to the June 10th Affair.

JUNE 10th AFFAIR

In July the Dean was summoned to appear before the officials of the Educational Bureau of the Government-General to discuss with them the matter of disciplining those students who were involved in the June 10th Affair. The Educational Bureau gave the following instructions, which all have been duly carried out:

1. To punish all the students held in police custody. Scale of punishment of the students involved in this case as established by the Educational Bureau is as follows:

EXPULSION

Lee Pyung Lip	Literary Second
Lee Suk Hoon	" "
Park Hah Kyun	" "

INDEFINITE SUSPENSION

Hong Myung Sik	Literary First
Kim Kyu Pong	" Second
Han Il Chung	" "
Choi Hyun Choon	Commercial Second
Lee Pong Chin	Science Second

FOUR WEEKS SUSPENSION

Lyu Kyung Sang	Literary	Second
Kim Seh Chin	Literary	First
Park Young Choon	"	"
Kwun Oh Sang	Science	First

TWO WEEKS SUSPENSION

Lim Pyung Chul	Commercial	First
Song Woon Soon	"	"
Kim Young Sik	Science	First
Kim Young Kei	"	"
Lee Suk Young	"	"
Ham Chang Nai	"	Second
Choi Cheng Il	"	Third
Cho Dai Pyuk	"	"
Park Young Kyu	"	"
Chang Hong Sik	Literary	First
Kim Yun Keun	"	"
Won Chong Hoi	"	"
Ahn Tai Heui	"	"
Park Pok Nai	"	"
Kim Young Ha	"	"
Lee Kwang Choon	"	Third
Park Ahn Keun	"	"
Lee Keum San	"	"
Chai Woo Pyung	"	Second
Lee Kwan Heui	"	Fourth
Lee Eun Taik	"	"
Yun Chi Hyun	"	"
Chang Heui Chang	Commercial	Second
Kim Young So	"	"
Kim Yun Keun	"	Third
Kim Nak Keui	"	"
Kim Kyung Chin	"	"
Kim Chi Sam	"	"
Kim Keun Pai	"	"

2. To submit to the Bureau an address of apology by both the College and the Corporation.

The Dean was also given to understand that in the event of another such occurence it may be necessary for the Educational Bureau to withdraw the charter of the Chosen Christian College according to Art. 14 and 16 of the Regulations relating to the private schools.

III. ARRIVALS AND DEPARTURES

Dr. A. L. Becker, Vice President, left on furlough in June.

President Avison and Drs. H. H. Underwood and David Wonchul Lee returned in August.

IV. ATHLETICS

The Fourth All Korea High School Invitation Track and Field Meet is now being held on the College grounds. (September 24th, 1926) This year eight schools have entered the Meet, the number of athletes participating being 160. Contributions for the meet are as follows:

From the College Staff	Y 176.00
" outside Friends	190.00
Total	Y 366.00

Respectfully submitted,

(Signed) U. Kyum Yu
Dean

31. 에비슨 교장의 이사회 제출 보고서

문서 제목	Report of Chosen Christian College
문서 종류	교장 보고서
제출 시기	1927년 5월 25일
작성 장소	서울
제 출 자	O. R. Avison
수 신 자	이사회
페이지 수	3
출 처	2114-5-2: 07 Board of Managers 1923~1927 (UMAH)

자료 소개

에비슨 교장이 1927년 5월 25일 열린 이사회 회의에서 제출한 보고서이다. 이 보고서의 첫머리에 "To Field Board of Managers"라는 문구가 있고 일자 표시와 에비슨 서명이 있으므로, 이 문서가 이날 열린 이사회 회의 때 에비슨이 제출한 보고서인 사실을 알 수 있다. 이날의 회의록은 현재 발견하지 못하였지만, 3월경에 작성된 회계보고서는 1926~27년도가 에비슨이 미국에서 확보한 많은 기본재산 기부금의 수혜를 누린 첫 번째 해라고 기록하고 있다. 이 보고서는 이처럼 학교가 재정 압박에서 벗어나고 있는 상태에서 작성되었다.

에비슨은 이 보고서에서 항목 설정 없이 아래의 사항들을 다루었다.

재정 운영, 기독교인 학생 비율, 총독부 학무국의 교직원 조사, 동양척식회사 및 개인 소유자와의 거래, 적자 해소, 학비 수입, 교수 동향, 9월 이사회 개회 여부, 베커의 귀임 연기 문제.

내용 요약

재정 운영: 3개 과의 학생은 총 228명(신입생 112명)이고, 지난해 재정보고서에서 학비를 낸 학생이 175명가량이었던 것을 고려하면, 예산 대로 운영해도 될 것으로 생각된다. 수입과 지출 예산 안에서 학교를 운영하기를 바란다.

기독교인 학생: 재학생과 졸업생의 기독교인 현황을 비교하면, 기독교인의 비율이 재학생들보다 졸업생들에게서 더 높다.

교직원 조사: 유자격 교수 3명을 2명으로 교체하기로 학교에서 결정한 것을 총독부 학무국이 교수진을 조사한 후에 불허하였으므로 시간제 일본어 교수를 쓸 필요가 생겼다.

토지 거래: 우리는 동양척식회사의 땅을 확보하기 위해 그들과 땅을 교환할 용도로 인근의 논을 사놓았다. 모범촌 진입로의 확보를 위해 철로 북쪽의 땅도 보존할 필요가 있다. 그러므로 학교의 주택 단지 안에 박혀있는 한국인 소유의 한 필지를 사기 위해 지난해 가을에 협상용으로 사놓은 철도 남쪽의 땅을 팔고자 한다. 이 매매를 허가해주도록 이사회에 요청한다.

적자 해소: 내가 존 T. 언더우드와 연락하여 누적된 적자를 해소하는 방안을 논의하였는데, 그 내용은 이사회 연례회의 때 보고하도록 하겠다. 지난 회계연도에 ¥899.96의 소액 흑자가 났던 것은 내가 뉴욕에서의 모금 운동을 위해 책정받은 돈을 쓰지 않고 학교 재정 운영에 돌렸기 때문이다.

학비 수입: 1924~1925년에는 평균 168명의 학생이 1인당 평균 ¥606.59의 학비를 냈고, 1925~1926년에는 평균 179명의 학생이 1인당 평균 ¥704.80의 학비를 냈으며, 1926~27년에는 194.66명의 학생이 1인당 평균 ¥674.64의 학비를 냈다.

교수: 노블(Alden E. Noble)이 미국으로 떠나서 이명혁(컬럼비아대학에서 생물학 전공)이 대신 가르치고 있다. 밀러와 피셔가 가을에 미국에 갈 예정이고, 베커 박사가 가을학기에 돌아올 것으로 예상한다.

이사회 개회: 9월 전에 이사회를 열 필요가 있을 것 같지는 않으나 여름방학 전에 모일 필요가 있다는 의견이 있다면 받아들이겠고, 누가 비판하더라도 달게 받도록 하겠다.

베커 귀임 문제: (추신에서 이 문제를 다루고 있다.) 내가 이 보고서를 작성하는 동안 베커의 편지가 도착하여, 그가 일 년 정도 그곳의 공대에서 가르치면서 경험을 쌓고 자녀 교육비도 해결하려 한다는 사실을 알려주었다. 그러므로 나는 이 소식을 먼저 학교 교육과정위원회와 이사회에 알려야 하고, 그런 후에 그들이 회의한 결과를 베커와 그의 북감리회 한국 선교회와 그의 뉴욕 선교부와 뉴욕 협력이사회에 통지해야 한다. 만일 우리 학교는 그의 체류 연장을 허락하였는데 그의 선교부나 선교회는 반대하는 상황이 벌어진다면, 학교는 예상치 않은 지출을 하게 되는 동시에 공백을 메꾸기 위해 또 다른 교수를 임용해야 하는 문제에 부딪힐 것이다.

R E P O R T

of

CHOSEN CHRISTIAN COLLEGE

May 25, 1927.

TO FIELD BOARD OF MANAGERS:

In transmitting the accompanying financial report for the past fiscal year, I thought it would be well to accompany it by some information in regard to our registration for the new school year.

The various departments have enrolled the following:

	1st year	Other years	Total
Commercial Department	56	43	99
Literary Department	38	39	77
Science Department	18	34	52
	112	116	228

Of the above, about 175 have paid fees to date, and as the unpaid fees are due mainly from old students, we feel we may count upon a registration in accordance with our budget, and therefore we should be able to live within our budgeted income and expenditure.

Dr. Rhodes has made a religious census of the student body and has tabulated the results as follows:

Presbyterian Students	74	32.5 %
Methodist Students	103	45.15%
Other Christian Students	4	1.75%
Nonchristians	47	20.6 %
Total	228	100.00%

In a survey of the graduates of the College, Dr. Rhodes also finds that all but 8% of the 166 constituting the alumni are professing Christians.

Changes in the Faculty have been made as anticipated by the budget and the ad interim votes of the Field Board. The Educational Department, however, has been going over the staff in the light of these changes and the action of the College in dropping three qualified teachers and replacing them by only two does not meet with its approval. We find it necessary therefore to engage a time teacher who can teach the students Japanese translation more acceptably in order to meet the wishes of the Department.

Negotiations have been under way with the Oriental Development Company in relation to securing the land that is needed in the Model Village and residential areas. We have made application for all of the land within the contemplated boundaries of the College that is now still in the hands of the Oriental Development Company, and they have agreed to deed to us what is desired. We propose to exchange the rice fields purchased some years ago for this very purpose in part payment and to pay about Y4,000 yen additional. We shall seek authority from the Board to sell the property south of the railway track (some of which we bought last fall in order to secure pieces north of the track that were necessary to secure an entrance to the Model Village property) and with the proceeds pay the Y4,000 and also purchase a parcel of land in the residential section from a Korean owner with whom we are now negotiating. These land deals will secure to us the major part of the land needed to consolidate our holdings. The other parcels not now in the market represent little islands within our boundaries.

I am also in communication with Mr. J. T. Underwood with reference to a method to dispose of the accumulated budget deficits and hope to have a report on this matter to present to the annual meeting of the Board.

Referring now to the finances of the past year, you will note that there is a small surplus of Y699.96 which has been applied to reduce the accumulated current budget deficits of previous years. This result is due to the release of the funds some Y8,034.03 held in New York for campaign expenses which were not used. The departments generally speaking lived within their budgeted expenditures.

The following table gives an analysis of the paid registration for last year together with some comparative figures for previous years:

Departments	1st term		2nd term		% dec.	3rd term		% dec
	Yen	No	Yen	No		Yen	No	
Commercial Dept.	2350	94	2100	84	10	1875	75	10
Literary "	1925	77	1675	67	13	1437	57	15
Science "	1287	51	1075	43	15	900	36	16
Average decrease per term					12.6%			13.4%
Total	5562	222	4050	194		4212	168	

Average paid enrolment	1926-27	194.66	Average cost	Y674.64
do.	1925-26	179	per	704.80
do.	1924-25	168	Student	606.59

5-26-27

- 3 -

The work of the College is proceeding smoothly. Mr. Aldon D. Noble has returned to America, and is severing his connection with the College. In his place, Mr. Hunter Lee a Korean graduate in Biology from Columbia University is teaching Biology both in Severance Union Medical College and at the Chosen Christian College. We are looking forward to the return of both Prof. E. H. Miller and Prof. J. Earnest Fisher this fall, but in the case of the latter it is reported that he will have to undergo an operation and that there is a possibility that his father's financial affairs may possibly hinder his return. Dr. Becker is also expected back in time to resume his work for the fall term.

From the standpoint of the College administration, there does not seem to be any necessity to call a meeting of the Field Board before September; but if any member of the Board thinks it wise to have a meeting prior to the summer vacation I should be glad to hear from him. I should also be glad to hear any criticism or suggestions that members have to offer.

Very sincerely,

O.R.Avison.

P.S. Since writing the foregoing, a letter has come from Dr. Becker in which he states that he is considering accepting a position for "a year or so" in a School of Technology in order to gain experience that will be useful in making the Science Department of more practical advantage to the needs of Korea, and at the same time helping out the personal problem of educating his family.

This proposition will be considered by the Curriculum Committee and its judgment reported to the Board of Managers whose decision will then be transmitted to Dr. Becker and his Mission and Mission Board and also to the Cooperating Board in New York.

If the final decision is for an extension of his leave of absence we shall have to employ another qualified teacher to cover his work, and as no provision for this was made in the budget, which was made in the full expectation of Dr. Becker's return before September of this year we shall not be able to finance the work unless his Board, or Mission, in granting him permission to remain, will also undertake the additional expense incurred.

32. 에비슨 교장의 북장로회 서울지회 제출 보고서

문서 제목	Chosen Christian College Report to Korea Mission of the presbyterian Church in the U.S.A.
문서 종류	교장 보고서
제출 시기	1927년 6월
작성 장소	서울
제 출 자	O. R. Avison
수 신 자	북장로회 서울 주재 선교사들(Seoul Station, Korea Mission, PCUSA)
페이지 수	8
출 처	Korea Mission Records, 1904~1960, Box 15, Folder 15 (PHS) 2114-5-2: 07 Board of Managers 1923~1927 (UMAH)

자료 소개

에비슨 교장이 1927년 6월 서울 주재 북장로교 선교사들에게 제출한 1926~27년도 학교 운영보고서이다. 제목은 한국선교회를 제출 대상으로 표기하고 있지만, 11월 8일 자 보고서(이 자료집의 33번 문서)에서 에비슨이 밝힌 바에 따르면, 실제로는 한국선교회의 지역 조직인 서울 주재 선교사들에게 제출한 것이다. 제출자의 이름도 이 보고서에서 밝혀져 있지 않지만, 11월 8일 자 보고서를 참고하면, 역시 에비슨이다. 언더우드 때부터 교장들은 때때로 서울에 있는 북장로교 선교사들에게 학교 업무 보고서를 제출하였다. PHS와 UMAH에 있는 문서들은 같은 모양을 하고 있다. UMAH 문서의 오른편 상단에는 "3-3-27"이라고 쓴 손글씨가 있는데, 이 일자가 적힌 이유는 알 수 없다.

에비슨은 이 보고서에서 아래의 사항들을 설명하였다.

학생 현황, 졸업생 수, 졸업생 현황, 학생 종교, 학생 출신 지역, 학교 임원, 교수진, 종교활동, 운동경기, 교지와 자산, 미국에서의 모금 활동, 회계 보고.

내용 요약

학생: 1916~27년 한 학년도 동안 학생 수, 교수 역량, 학생 수준, 재정 증가, 모든 학내 활동에서 또 다른 발전을 이루었다. 학생들이 1924~25년에는 평균 168명이었고, 1925~26년

에는 평균 179명이었으며, 1916~27년에는 평균 194.66명이었다. 종래에는 문과에 학생이 가장 많았지만, 1925년부터는 상과 학생이 가장 많아졌다(문과 77명, 상과 99명, 수물과 52명, 총 228명). 졸업 후 진로 전망, 수물과 운영 중단 사태, 전국의 경제 여건 때문에 그렇게 되었다.

졸업생: 3월 17일 졸업식 때 33명(문과 14명, 상과 17명)이 졸업하여, 졸업생 수가 총 166명(문과 67명, 상과 80명, 수물과 16명, 농과 3명)이 되었다. 졸업생들은 현재 미국 유학 23명, 일본 유학 6명, 한국에서 진학 4명, 연희전문 교수 1명, 학교 교사 56명, 사업 및 사무직 41명, 개인사업 22명, 사망 6명이다.

학생 종교 · 출신지: 등록생 228명에서 장로교인 74명, 감리교인 103명, 비종교인 47명, 기타 4명이다. 학생들이 제주도 외에 전 도에서 왔고, 경기도에서 가장 많이(29%) 왔다.

학교 임원: 교장은 에비슨, 부교장은 베커, 학감은 유억겸이다.

교수: 교수들은 문과에 총 18명이 있고, 한국인은 교수 5명(백낙준, 조병옥, 백남석, 김영환, 최현배)이다. [백낙준은 이때 처음 거명되었고, 조병옥은 상과 교수이지만 사회학을 가르쳐서 거명되었다.] 조교수 2명(정인보, 윤병섭), 강사 2명(정인서, 이운용)이다. 상과에는 총 10명이 있고, 한국인은 교수 4명(이순탁, 유억겸, 백남운, 조병옥), 조교수 3명(박길용, 손봉조, 홍승국), 강사 3명(C. Y. Lee[외국인학교 교사], 오규신, 선우전)이다. 수물과에는 총 8명이 있고, 한국인은 교수 3명(이춘호, 한치관, 이원철[이원철은 1926년 8월에 귀국하여 조교수가 되었다가 이듬해에 정교수가 되었다]), 강사 1명(이명혁)이다.

직급별로 교수는 서양인 7명, 한국인 15명, 일본인 4명이고, 강사는 한국인 7명, 일본인 1명이다. 이 수치는 연희전문이 이미 좋은 동양인 교수들을 확보하고 있음을 보여준다. 밀러와 피셔는 컬럼비아대에서 Ph.D. 학위를 받기 위해 공부하고 있고, 베커 박사는 미시간대에서 물리학을 더 공부하고 있다. 백낙준은 종교교육 교수로 임명되었으나 예일대에서 Ph.D. 학위를 받기 위해 미국에 1년 더 머물도록 허가받았다. 이원철이 미시간대에서 Ph.D.를 받은 후 교수로 합류하였고, 이관용이 사임하여 그의 업무를 나누었으며, 노정일이 더 공부하기 위해 사임하고 미국에 갔다.

종교활동: 학생들에게 성경 공부와 채플에 주 5회 출석하게 하고, 일요일 교회 출석과 교회 활동 상황을 보고하게 하고 있다.

운동경기: 옥외 스포츠 종목에서 우리 대학이 크게 발전하였다. 축구팀이 일본의 최강

팀인 오사카 축구팀과 1 대 1로 비겼고, 일본의 극동올림픽 대표팀을 3 대 2로 이겼으며, 전국 대학별 대회에서 두 번째로 우승하였다. 야구도 전국 대학별 대회에서 두 번째와 세 번째로 우승하여 우승기를 영원히 가져왔다.

교지 · 자산: 존 T. 언더우드의 특별 기부금으로 10에이커가량을 새로 샀다. 교수 사택은 이제까지 선교사 교수용 5채, 한국인 교수용 9채, 일본인 교수용 1채를 지었다. 원한경이 대학교지 곁에 있는 그의 소유지에 집을 짓기 시작하였다.

모금 활동 보고: 내가 건축비와 기본재산을 위한 기부금을 얻기 위해 미국에서 2년간 모금 활동을 하고 지난(1926년) 8월 귀국하였는데, 원한경이 [미국에서] 마지막 1년 동안 이 운동을 도왔고, 그 결과 총 $228,808을 모금하였다.

(마지막 8쪽에서 회계보고서를 첨부하고 있다.)

CHOSEN CHRISTIAN COLLEGE REPORT to the
Korea Mission of the Presbyterian Church in the U.S.A. June 1927

The College Year 1926-27 marked another advance along all lines, number of students, quality of Staff, quality of Students, increase in financial strength &c &c and all connected with the work are grateful to God and much encouraged.

There was a gratifying growth in the student body during the past year as shown by the following table,-

1926-27	Paid Registration	First Term	222
	" "	Second "	194
	" "	Third "	168
			584
		Average	194.66
1925-26	" "	"	179
1924-25	" "	"	168

Up to the year 1925 the Literary Course attracted the greatest number of students, but since then the Commercial Department has had the largest enrolment and the Science Department attracts the smallest number. For instance the enrolment in the three departments this year is as follows,-

Literary	Commercial	Science
77	99	52

The reasons for this are probably various but in general we might explain that the Literary department graduates are as yet given qualification by the Educational Bureau of the Government to teach only one subject after a four years course; the Science Department having had a break in the continuity of its work will not have its first graduation under its improved status until the end of this year, so it has not had a real chance yet to prove specially attractive; the Commercial Department with only a three years course opens up more opportunities to make a living immediately after graduation than the other courses and its graduates are given qualification as teachers in three subjects.

This indicates that the economic condition of the country is affecting the choice of the type of education at this time and that we shall do well to bring our courses into line with the needs of the people by making them as thoroughly practical as possible.

On March 17th, 33 graduated, 14 from the Literary Department and 19 from the Commercial. In March 1928 we shall also have a graduating class from the Science Department.

Most of the graduates have found positions which is encouraging to the students to persevere to the end.

The total number of graduates to date is 166.

A recent investigation by Dr. Rhodes shows that 98% of these are professing Christians.

Graduates by Departments

	No.
Literary Department	67
Commercial Department	80
Science Department	16
Agricultural Department . . . . . (Not now running)	3
Total	166

Occupation of Graduates

Work	No.	Percent
Post Graduates work in U. S. A.	23	13.8
" " " in Japan	6	3.6
" " " in Korea	4	2.4
Teaching in Chosen Christian College	1	0.6
Teaching in Other Schools	56	33.6
Church work	5	3.0
Business and Office Work	41	25.0
Private Work	22	13.2
Journalism	2	1.2
Deceased	6	3.6
	166	100%

Returned from Post Graduate Studies

Name	Degrees	Present Occupation
David Wonchul Lee,	M.A., Ph.D. of Univ. Michigan	Prof. of C. C. C.

The enrolment this year is as follows,-

Literary	77		
Commercial	99		
Science	52	Total	228

Of these 74 are Presbyterians, 32.5%
103 are Methodists, 45.1%
47 are Non-Christian, 20.6%
4 are others, 1.8%

The Faculty recognizes the desirability of restricting the number of non-Christian students in order to conserve the Christian atmosphere of the institution. So far the results have been good from this standpoint as shown by the fact that only 2% of the graduate body, as stated above, does not profess Christianity.

Provinces from which students came

Province	No.	Percent
North Ham Kyung	13	5.7
South " "	24	10.5
North Pyeng Yang	19	8.3
South " "	23	10.0
Whang Hai	16	7.0
Kyung Ki	66	29.0
Kang Won	6	2.8
North Choong Chung	11	4.8
South " "	14	6.0
North Chul La	10	4.3
South " "	9	4.0
North Kyung Sang	11	4.8
South " "	6	2.8
	228	100%

The Faculty of the College is as follows,-

President	O. R. Avison, M.D., LL.D.
Vice-President	A. L. Becker, Ph.D.
Dean	U. K. Yu

Literary Department Director, B. W. Billings

Professor,	History	B.W.Billings, M.A., D.D.(DePauw)
"	Bible & Religion	H.A.Rhodes, M.A., D.D.(Princeton)
"	Bible & Religious Educ'n	L.G.Paik, M.A.,B.A. Studying for Doctorate at Yale
"	Psychology & Educ'al Psych.	H. H. Underwood, Ph.D. (New York)
"	Education	J.E.Fisher, M.A. (Columbia) Studying for doctorate at Columbia
"	English	E.W.Hitch, B.D. (Georgia)
"	Sociology	P.O.Chough, Ph.D. (Columbia)
"	English	N.S.Paik, M.A. (Emory & Colum.)
"	Morals	K. Takahashi (Tokyo Imperial)
"	Music	Y.W.Kim (Coll.of Music, Tokyo)
"	Philosophy	H.P.Choi (Kyoto Imperial)
"	Japanese Language & Lit.	S.Hikaido (Tokyo Imperial)
Asst.Prof.	Chinese	I.P.Chung
" "	Biology & Natural Science	P.S.Yun (" ")
Instructor,	Oriental History	I.S.Chung
"	Drill	K.Umezawa (Normal School)
"	German	O.Y.Lee (Berlin University)

Commercial Department   Director, S. T. Lee

Professor,	Economics	S.T.Lee	(Kyoto Imperial)
"	Civil and Commercial Law	U.K.Yu	(Tokyo Imperial)
"	Commercial History	H.W.Paik	(Commercial Univ.)
"	Finance & Banking	P.O.Chough, Ph.D.	(Columbia)
Asst.Prof.	Commercial English and " Practice	K.Y.Park, A.B.	(Ohio State)
" "	Commercial Geography and Bookkeeping &c.	P.C.Son	(Commercial Univ.)
" "	English	S.K.Hong, A.B.	(Ohio State)
Instructor,	Russian Language	C.Y.Lee	(Foreign Lang.School)
"	Chinese Spoken Language	K.S.Oh	do.
"	Transportation	J.Sunwoo	(Waseda Univ.)

Science Department   Director, C.H.Lee

Professor,	Physics	A.L.Becker, Ph.D.	(Michigan)
"	Mathmatics	C.H.Lee, M.A.	(Ohio State)
"	Mathematics & Geology &c.	T.Tsubakida, A.B.	(Leland Stanford)
"	Chemistry	E.H.Miller, M.A. Candidate for doctorate at Columbia.	(Columbia)
"	Chemistry	K.Kadowaki	(Kyoto Imperial)
"	Electrical Engineering	C.K.Hahn, M.A.	(Southern Calif.)
"	Astronomy & Mathematics	D.W.Lee, Ph.D.	(Michigan)
Instructor,	Biology	M.H.Lee, M.A.	(Columbia)

The present racial ratio in the Faculty is as follows,-

Western 7 Korean 15 Japanese 4
in addition to which there are 7 Korean and 1 Japanese Instructors.

As will be seen 18 of the Korean and 4 of the Japanese have had advanced university work.

This list shows what progress we have made already in the matter of securing a Faculty of well trained Oriental Teachers.

One of our embarrassments during the past year was due to the very effort we are making to secure and keep a Faculty of high attainments.

Prof. E. H. Miller remained a second year after his furlo in order to secure first his M. A. and then his Ph.D. in Chemical Research at Columbia University, New York.

Prof. J. E. Fisher did similarly at the same University to secure a Ph.D. in the realm of Education.

Prof. A. L. Becker, Ph.D., went on early furlo and spent the year in advanced study in Physics at the University of Michigan.

L. Geo. Paik, newly appointed Professor of Religious Education, was allowed to remain an additional year in order to obtain his Ph.D. in the History of Religion and Religious Education from Yale University. But we had some compensations for D. W. Lee, Ph.D., in Mathematics and Astronomy from the University of Michigan rejoined the Faculty as did H. H. Underwood, Ph.D. in Educational Psychology from the University of New York.

The new year sees the loss from our Faculty of Mr. Alden Noble, M.A., Professor of Biology, but in his place we have secured the services of Hunter Lee, M.A. of Columbia University, New York, who will, we hope, prove to be the man who is to lead his people into a due appreciation of the important place Biology is to take in gaining a knowledge of God's methods in the living world.

Mr. J. W. Hitch, B.A., Professor of English, has gone on furlo and there is some uncertainty as to his return.

Dr. A. L. Becker is on furlo and the date of his return is uncertain.

Mr. Hirai, Professor of Japanese Language and Literature resigned at the end of the College year, but his place was at once filled by Rev. S. Nikaido of Tokyo.

Dr. K. Y. Lee resigned at the same time and his work was divided amongst several members of the staff.

Mr. C. Y. Roe resigned during the year, having gone to the U. S. A. for a prolonged stay.

Religious Activities

The study of Bible in the curriculum and chapel attendance five days a week are required. There are eleven Bible classes each reciting two periods a week. Weekly reports as to church attendance and as to actual Christian work done are requested from students.

Over 40 visiting speakers, including eleven from abroad, have spoken at chapel. The latter include Bishop Ainsworth, Robert E. Speer, D.D., Hugh T. Kerr, LL.D., the Lord Bishop of London, Wm. E. Griffis, Litt.D., Dr. W. H. Kilpatrick, Dr. A. Gandier and Dr. James Endicott.

The question may be asked: What contribution has the College made enlisting graduates in the christian ministry? Two of our graduates are in the Presbyterian Theological Seminary at Pyeng Yang; two in the Methodist Seminary at Seoul; and three are in theological schools in U. S. A. Three have already finished their theological course. The number entering the ministry so far is 10.

For many years we have looked forward to making our beautiful campus a resort for summer conferences. Last July a general conference for Christian workers under the auspices of the national council of churches was held, with an attendance of 200 from all parts of the country. The College cooperated in supplying speakers and finances. In addition to prayer and Bible study, there was an hour each on Religion and Science. The church and the young people, The Church and Society, and a Conference hour. So much was it enjoyed that it is planned to have another this summer.

Some friends of the College have underwritten the budget of the Religious Activities department for the next three years which will enable us to plan and carry out a definite program.

ATHLETICS

The coming to the front in athletics of christian schools, both academics and colleges, has been a feature of note this past year. Our college has shown a fine development in outdoor sports as the following summary will show:

April 1926	Football team played the Osaka Soccer Club one of the best in Japan. Score 1 - 1
Fall, 1926	Baseball team won intercollegiate championship for second time. Football team won intercollegiate championship for second time.
April 1927	Defeated Riji Soccer team, the champions of Japan, which represented that country at the last Far Eastern Olympic meet. Score 3-2
June 1927	Baseball team won intercollegiate series for third time, retaining the pennant as a permanent trophy. Baseball Club won the open tournament.

Site & Property

The site was enlarged during the year by the purchase of about 10 acres of land. This purchase was made possible by a special gift of $6,000 from Mr. John T. Underwood.

Residences for two Korean professors were erected out of funds contributed by Mrs. J. S. Kennedy and Mrs. A. F. Scheuffler. Missionary houses now total five and there are 9 homes for Korean and one for Japanese teachers. Dr. H. H. Underwood began the erection of his home of the property which he owns adjoining the College site.

In August last the President returned from a two years' stay in the United States where he had been conducting a campaign for securing building and endowment funds for this College and the Severance Union Medical College. During the last year he had been assisted in this campaign by Dr. H. H. Underwood.

For the Chosen Christian College, the results of the campaign are as follows;

For Endowment in cash and pledges	$ 175,000
For land, Building, etc.	22,750
To be designated later	31,058
	228,808

Respectfully submitted,

(Signed) O. R. Avison
President.

Financial Statement

Capital Account to March 31, 1927:

Northern Presbyterian Contribution	Y463,133.14
" Methodist "	145,913.74
Southern " "	89,810.50
United Church of Canada "	31,000.00
Miscellaneous (Campaign &c.)	73,001.22
Total	802,858.60
Expenditures on Capital a/c	750,473.11
Balance not expended	52,385.49

Summary of Balance:

Cash in Banks	Y 1,887.90	
Accounts Receivable	6,863.38	
Loan to Current Budget, accumulated deficits	24,283.51	
College Book Store Stock	2,594.66	
Loan on a residence	15,407.25	
Suspense Account	1,348.79	52,385.49

Current Receipts
1926-1927

Northern Presbyterian Contribution	Y 10,523.56
" Methodist "	8,742.64
Southern " "	3,938.57
United Church of Canada "	5,000.00
Interest on Endowment	24,145.13
Faculty Contributions	1,000.00
Rents &c.	3,805.47
Tuition	19,271.49
Miscellaneous	1,799.16
	Y 78,226.02

Current Expenditures

Salaries of Teachers	Y49,559.80	
Administration	8,885.77	
Supplies	5,827.83	
Property, Fuel & Miscellaneous . . .	13,052.66	77,326.06
Surplus		899.96

(Missionary service additional calculated at Y54,000)

33. 유억겸 학감의 이사회 제출 보고서

문서 제목	Chosen Christian College, Report of Dean to Field Board of Managers at Board Meeting
문서 종류	학감 보고서
제출 시기	1927년 9월 23일
작성 장소	서울
제 출 자	유억겸
수 신 자	이사회
페이지 수	2
출 처	Korea Mission Records, 1904~1960, Box 15, Folder 15 (PHS) 2114-5-2: 07 Board of Managers 1923~1927 (UMAH)

자료 소개

유억겸 학감이 1927년 9월 23일 열린 이사회 회의에서 제출한 보고서이다. 이날 열린 회의에서 이사회는 도중에 회의를 중단하고 신임 신과 교수 백낙준이 설교하는 채플에 참석한 후에 회의를 재개하였다. 그들은 백낙준이 예일대에서 Ph.D. 학위를 받은 것과 본교 교수로 온 것을 축하하기로 의결하였다. 또한 창천리에 있는 철로 남쪽의 땅을 팔기로 하였고, 교장의 행정업무를 부교장에게 넘기게 하였던 1922년 12월의 결정을 철회하였으며, 원한경을 부교장으로, 조병옥을 이사회 서기로 선출하였고, 조병옥이 이번 가을에 동창회와 우인들이 언더우드 동상을 세울 것이라고 광고하였다. (실제로는 이듬해 4월 동상을 세웠다.)

이 보고서는 아래의 6개 항목으로 구성되어 있다.

I. 학생등록 현황, II. 학생 등급 분류, III. 교수, IV. 운동경기, V. 종교활동,
VI. 아카데미 정신.

내용 요약

I · II. 첫 학기 말에는 등록생이 총 230명이고, 과별로는 문과 77명, 상과 101명, 수물과 52명이며, 학년별로는 1학년 113명, 2학년 50명, 3학년 27명, 4학년 40명이다. 본과의 학생

은 총 114명(문과 37명, 상과 52명, 수물과 25명)이고, 별과의 학생은 116명(문과 40명, 상과 49명, 수물과 27명)이다.

III. 안식년 중인 교수는 히치와 베커이고, 안식년에서 돌아온 교수는 밀러이다. 사임한 교수는 노블, 히라이, 이관용, 윤정하이고, 신임 교수는 손봉조, 최현배, 니카이도, 백낙준, K. Y. Park이다.

IV. 제5회 전조선 중등학교 육상경기대회가 내일(9월 24일) 학교 운동장에서 열려 대략 9개 학교에서 160명가량 참석할 예정이다. 운동장 시설을 개선할 필요가 있다. (1927년 4월, 6월, 9월에 승리를 거둔 축구팀, 야구팀, 테니스팀의 경기 전적을 개관하고 있다.)

V. 로즈 박사의 지도로 다양한 종교활동을 하고 있고, 백낙준이 신과에 합류하였으므로 이 과가 더 발전할 것이다. YMCA 학생들이 전도대를 이남과 이북으로 파송하여 지방에서 복음을 전하게 하였다.

VI. 지난 2년간 아카데미 정신이 크게 고조되어 졸업생들이 교사, 사업가, 유학생으로서 높은 평가를 받으며 좋은 선례를 남기고 있다.

CHOSEN CHRISTIAN COLLEGE

Report of Dean to Field Board of Managers
at Board Meeting held September 23, 1927.

I. ENROLMENT

There was a total enrolment of 230 students distributed as follows at the end of the first term:

Class	Lit. Dept.	Com. Dept.	Science Dept.	Total
Freshman	38	58	17	113
Sophomore	17	24	9	50
Junior	14		13	27
Senior	8	19	13	40
Total	77	101	52	230

II. CLASSIFICATION OF STUDENTS

1. Regular Students.

	Nos	Percentage
Literary Dept.	37	32.45%
Commercial Dept.	52	45.61%
Science Dept.	25	21.93%
	114	100%

2. Special Students

	Nos	Percentage
Literary Dept.	40	34.47
Commercial Dept.	49	42.25
Science Dept.	27	23.28
	116	100%

III.(A) 1. Professors on furlough:
Prof. J. W. Hitch, Lit. Dept. in June 1927
Prof. A. L. Becker Sc. Dept. Who is to stay in America for another year.

2. Professor back from furlough:
Prof. E. H. Miller, Science Dept. In September

(B) Professors resigned
Prof. A. E. Noble, Sc. Dept. in April
Prof. M. Hirai, Lit. " in April
Prof. K. Y. Lee, " " "
Prof. O. H. Yun, Com. " "

(C) New Professors:
Prof. P. C. Sohn, " " in April
Prof. H. P. Choi, Lit. " "
Prof. S. Nikaido, " " "
Prof. George Paik, " " in September

Asst. Prof. K. Y. Park, Com. Dept., resigned in September

- 2 -

IV. ATHLETICS

The Fifth All Korea High School Invitation Track and Field Meet is scheduled for tomorrow on our College grounds.(September 24, 1927) About nine schools will participate and the total number of participants will be about 160. We are looking forward to a great event on the Field.

As to the athletics in our college, our teams have won many honors as the following will show:

April 1927 -- Defeated Rijo Soccer team, the champion of Japan, which represented that country at the last Far Eastern Olympic Meet. Score 3 - 2.

June 1927 -- Baseball Team won intercollegiate series for third time, retaining the pennant as a permanent trophy. Baseball club won the open tornament for the first time.

June 1927 -- Tennis team won intercollegiate series for the first time.

September 1927 -- Defeated the Waseda University soccer team which represented that country in the Far Eastern Olympic Meet by the score of 4-0.

It is urgently necessary that we should have a better athletic grounds for these various athletic activities. Under the present circumstances we are greatly handicapped in various phases. Furthermore we feel very keen for the lack a competent coach.

V. RELIGIOUS ACTIVITES

As to the religious phase of our college, various activities have been conducted under the steadfast leadership of Dr. H. A. Rhodes.

Dr. George Paik has been added to the Biblical Dept. and his service will be invaluable in strengthening that dept. in the future.

During the summer vacation, the student Y.M.C.A. sent out two preaching bands, one to the south and the other to the north, and preached the Gospel to hundreds of people in the rural districts.

VI. ACADEMIC SPIRIT

The academic spirit of our college has been intensified greatly during last few years that our graduates are very well thought of as teachers, businessman, and students or in any other walks of life as the case may be. We are proud of them and their records, which will set for the undergraduates a fine example to follow.

Respectfully submitted,

(Signed) U. K. Yu,
Dean.

34. 에비슨 교장의 북장로회 서울지회 제출 보고서

문서 제목	Chosen Christian College, Report to Seoul Station
문서 종류	교장 보고서
제출 시기	1927년 11월 8일
작성 장소	서울
제 출 자	O. R. Avison
수 신 자	서울 주재 북장로회 선교사들(Seoul Station, Korea Mission, PCUSA)
페이지 수	2
출 처	Korea Mission Records, 1904~1960, Box 15, Folder 18 (PHS)

자료 소개

에비슨 교장이 1927년 11월 8일 서울 주재 북장로교 선교사들에게 제출한 보고서이다. 그가 6월에 그들의 상부 집단인 북장로회 한국 선교회에 보고서를 제출한 일이 있었는데, 이 보고서의 첫 줄에서 6월에 보냈던 보고서가 실제로는 서울 주재 선교사들에게 보낸 것이었음을 밝히고 있다.

에비슨은 이 보고서에서 아래의 사항들을 간략하게 개관하였다.

학생, 교수 동향, 운동경기, 부교장 선출, 본관 진입 계단 공사와 시설 공사,

캠퍼스 부지확보, 언더우드 동상 제막.

내용 요약

학생: 6월에 끝난 첫 학기에 221명(상과 100명, 문과 75명, 수물과 46명)의 학생이 수강하였다. 7월에는 예수교연합공의회가 후원하는 사경회가 대학 캠퍼스에서 성공적으로 열렸고, 9월에 가을학기가 시작되어 210명의 학생이 출석하였다.

교수: 예일대 종교교육과에서 Ph.D.를 받은 백낙준이 신과 교수로 와서 로즈(H. A. Rhodes)와 함께 일하게 되었고, 밀러(E. H. Miller)도 2년 만에 화학 전공으로 Ph.D.를 받고 학교에 돌아왔다.

운동경기: 학생들과 교수들의 사기가 높고, 축구팀과 야구팀이 명성을 유지하고 있다. 축구팀이 올림픽에서 우승한 와세다대 팀을 4대 0으로 이겨 서울에 있는 일본인들에게 학

교의 존재를 알렸고, 전조선 축구대회에서도 우승하였다. 운동경기에서 우승한 것이 학교의 사기를 높이고 학교도 홍보해주고 있다.

부교장: 9월에 열린 대학이사회 회의에서 원한경이 부교장으로 선출되었다.

시설: 여름 동안 본관 건물구역에 진입하는 계단이 완공되어 외관이 크게 좋아졌다. 1년 전 또는 그전에 미국에서 벌였던 모금 활동에서 얻은 기금의 일부 덕분에 전기를 가설하고 식수와 기숙사 용수의 공급시설을 개선하였다. 지역 전기회사와 계약을 맺어 몇 주 내로 건물들과 주택들에 조명을 밝힐 예정이므로 야간에도 대학건물들을 사용할 수 있게 되었다.

캠퍼스 부지: 땅 문제로 거의 8년 동안 벌인 법정 소송이 지난해에 끝났고, 이로 인해 동양척식회사와 일곱 군데의 땅을 사는 일을 타결할 수 있게 되어 211.5에이커의 캠퍼스 부지를 확보하였다. 캠퍼스 부지 곁에 지은 원한경의 주택 공사가 완공되었다.

언더우드 동상: 이번 가을 어느 때에 언더우드 박사를 기리는 동상이 제막될 예정인데, 교수회와 동문회가 그 기금을 마련하였다.

Rev. E. R. Anson

CHOSEN CHRISTIAN COLLEGE

Report to Seoul Station, November 8, 1927.

The last report to the Station was in June. The first term closed that month with a paid enrolment of 221. The Commercial Department led with 100, Literary enrolled 75, and Science 46.

During July a Bible Conference was held on the campus, under the auspices of the National Christian Council and the College, with an attendance of 60, not, however, as large in numbers as that of the year before. It was considered very successful, however, and closed with a decision to hold another conference next year. Various members of the Faculty addressed the Conference, or assisted in its conduct in various ways.

The Fall term opened in September, and the attendance to date is reported as about 210. The most notable addition to the Faculty is Dr. L.George Paik, Ph.D. of Yale in Religious Education. Dr. Paik is assigned to the Bible Department of the College and is associated with Dr. Harry A. Rhodes.

We are also glad to welcome back Mr. and Mrs. E.H. Miller after two years absence from the field and congratulate the former as well as the College upon his having received his Ph.D. in Chemistry during his stay in the homeland.

The Student and Faculty morale is on the whole satisfactory, and the College athletic teams are maintaining their prestige in soccer and baseball. Waseda University's team, which won the soccer championship at the Olympic meet in Shanghai, went down to defeat before our team in September to the tune of 4-0. One of our staff remarked that previous to this time many Japanese in Seoul had never heard of the Chosen Christian College, but they all know now that there is such an institution. In the all-Korea soccer meet held last week, our team once more won the championship. This primacy in athletics is a good advertisement for the College, as well as a means of building up College morale.

At the annual meeting of the Field Board of Managers, in September, Dr. H.H. Underwood was elected Vice President of the College.

During the summer the stairway to the main campus was completed and adds greatly to the appearance of the plant. Some funds which came in from the campaign conducted a year or more ago in the U.S.A., have been made available for certain improvements, such as getting electricity, increasing the water supply, providing bathing facilities for the students in the dormitory, and adding certain conveniences here and there to the plant that have been long desired. A contract for supply of current is being made with the local electric company so that the buildings and houses will be lighted with electricity within a few weeks. In this way the College buildings can be used at night in a way not possible hitherto.

For nearly eight years a land deal in which the College was involved was held up in the courts, due to litigation between the parties to whom the land belonged. This case, however, was settled during the past year, and its completion enabled us to arrange with the Oriental Development Company for the purchase of several tracts of land which were required to round out the site. The College now comprises 211½ acres of land, and the map now exhibited shows our present holdings and what we still hope to acquire.

This year will also mark the completion of Dr. Underwood's residence, which, although not the property of the College, is adjacent to our site. Also a monument is to be unveiled some time this fall to the memory of the late Dr. Horace Grant Underwood, the funds coming from the Faculty and Alumni, and from the admirers of Dr. Underwood at large.

35. 에비슨 교장의 이사회 제출 연례보고서

문서 제목	Chosen Christian College, Annual Report, 1927~1928
문서 종류	교장 보고서
제출 시기	1928년 9월 20일
작성 장소	서울
제 출 자	O. R. Avison
수 신 자	이사회
페이지 수	8
출 처	2114-5-2: 08 Board of Managers 1928~1931 (UMAH)

자료 소개

에비슨 교장이 1928년 9월 20일 열린 이사회 연례회의를 위해 제출한 보고서이다. 이 보고서에 일자 표기가 없지만, 연례회의 제출용인 것이 밝혀져 있으므로, 연례회의가 열렸던 날이 제출일이 된다. (이 보고서의 오른편 상단에 손글씨로 "3-31-28"이라고 쓴 것이 있지만, 이를 작성일로 볼 수는 없다.) 9월 20일 이사회 회의록에는 교장 보고서를 사전에 회람하고 회의 때는 낭독하지 않았다고 기록되어 있다. 이 회의에서 미국에서 돌아온 노블과 베커, 1928년 예루살렘선교대회 참석과 덴마크 농업 시찰을 마치고 돌아온 양주삼과 신흥우가 환영을 받았고, YMCA와 농업문제에 관해 협력할 것과 전년도 흑자의 일부를 학교 자동차 구입에 사용할 것을 의결하였다.

에비슨은 이 보고서에서 아래의 사항들을 설명하였다.

재정, 교수진, 자산, 등록생, 운동경기, 종교활동, 음악, 기숙사, 언더우드 동상.

내용 요약

재정: 1926년 내(에비슨)가 미국에서 돌아온 후, 학교가 적자를 면하기 위해 노력하여 누적 적자를 ¥24,285.94로 줄였다. 1927~28년 예산을 짜면서, 수입을 매우 보수적으로 잡고 지출을 줄인 동시에 로즈 박사의 친구에게 도움을 요청하여 삭감한 금액을 채울 금액을 얻었다. 그렇게 하여 1928년 3월 31일 학년을 끝내면서 상당한 흑자를 보았다. 누적 적자를 줄이기 위해 금년 예산에 ¥1,000을 책정하고, 서점에서 발생한 손실을 만회하기 위

해 ￥500을 책정하며, 북감리회 선교부가 $1,000를 보내준 결과, 적자가 ￥22,223.19로 줄었다.

교수진: 밀러와 피셔가 미국에서 돌아왔고, 백낙준이 합류하였으며, 베커가 9월에 돌아올 예정임을 알려왔다. 한 해 동안 문과 졸업생들을 위해 그들이 역사(동양사와 서양사)와 몇 과목에서 교사 자격을 얻을 수 있게 해주려고 노력하였으나 실패하였다[영어 교사 자격은 이미 얻었다]. 수물과가 학무국의 조사와 시험에서 좋은 점수를 얻어 졸업생에게 세 과목의 교사 자격을 주겠다는 통보를 받았다.

교수진의 최소 2/3 이상은 완전한 교수 자격을 지녀야 할 것을 학무국이 요구하고 있지만, 본교는 유자격 교수가 87%이다. 교수들이 몇 명은 덜 독실해도 모두 기독교인이고, 교수 인원은 총 35명이다. 빌링스가 1928년 3월 말 문과 과장직의 사임을 고집하여 백낙준을 과장으로 임명하였다. 그리하여 교장, 부교장, 회계만 서양인이 맡고 있다. 지금까지 한국인들이 과장과 학감 업무를 잘 수행하였으므로 좋은 결과를 얻을 것으로 기대한다.

자산: 한 해 동안 몇 군데 땅을 사서 학교 진입로와 모범촌을 개발할 수 있게 되었고, 동양척식회사와 땅을 교환하기 위한 오랜 협상을 종결하였으며, 모범촌 부지 안에 있는 한국인 소유의 땅들도 샀다.

모금해온 기금 중의 $6,000로 본관 화강암 계단을 놓았고(뉴욕 한인교회에서 $358을 기부하였다), 스팀슨관에 화장실과 지하의 학생 욕실을 설치하였고, 경성전기회사가 조명시설을 하여 12월부터 야간에만 전기를 쓰고 있다. 사람이 늘면서 물의 수요도 커져서 급수시설을 늘렸는데도 여전히 물이 부족하여 이를 해결하기 위해 노력하고 있다.

등록생: 학생 수가 지난해 봄학기에 220명이었다가 학년말에 185명으로 줄었으나, 전해보다는 10명이 늘었다. 3월에 39명이 졸업하여 졸업생은 총 205명이 되었다. 4월에 시작된 새 학기의 학생 수는 총 271년이고, 과별로는 문과 86명, 상과 123명, 수물과가 43명이다. 학생들의 종교는 장로교 109명, 감리교 112명, 기타 교파 8명, 비기독교 29명(11.24%)이다.

운동경기: 지난 9월 상해 올림픽 우승팀인 와세다대 축구팀을 4대 1로 이겼고, 야구, 축구, 테니스 대회에서 우승하여 많은 트로피를 가져왔으며, 중등학교 육상경기가 10월에 성공적으로 개최되었다. [이날 이사회 회의에서 신기준을 체육주임으로 임명하였다.]

종교활동: 타운센드(W. S. Townsend)가 종교교육을 위한 예산을 공급하였고, 백낙준이 성경을 가르치면서 로즈와 함께 사역하였고, 학생 전도대가 여러 지방에서 전도하였다.

음악: 로즈 교수 부인과 빌링스 교수 부인의 노력으로 좋은 오케스트라와 합창단이 만들어졌고 밴드도 조직하였으며[이 진술은 연희전문 '오케스트라'의 결성을 처음 밝힌 점에서 의미가 있다. 합창단과 밴드는 이미 조직되어 있었다], 세브란스 치과 교수 부츠(Boots)의 부인이 오케스트라를 위해 매주 시간을 내고 있다. 조만간 음악과가 설치되기를 기대한다.

기숙사: 기숙사가 1채뿐이고 66명만을 수용하여, 주변 마을과 서울에서 200명이 기거하고 있으므로, 기숙사가 시급히 더 필요하다. 송치명이 사감을 맡고 있다.

언더우드 동상: 우애회(Friendly Association of the College)가 설립자이자 초대 교장을 기리는 동상 건립 운동을 시작하여 1928년 4월 28일 캠퍼스 중앙에 동상을 세웠다.

CHOSEN CHRISTIAN COLLEGE

ANNUAL REPORT, 1927-1928

The thirteenth year of the College's history finds it still on the upgrade. During the year the student body has grown, the faculty has registered more qualified teachers and greatly needed improvements in the physical property itself have been made. The site has been increased in area.

FINANCES

Many of the years preceding 1926-1927 had ended with a deficit in the budget which at the end of March 1926 had accumulated to the sum of Y25,183.47.

After the President's return in 1926 we set about contriving to avoid a deficit during the fiscal year and on March 31, 1927 we had made such savings in the conduct of the work that we had a surplus of Y898.43.

This was applied to the reduction of the accumulated deficit leaving it at Y24,285.04.

In making the budget for 1927-1928 we kept rigidly to the determination to compute our income very conservatively and hold our expenses down to the estimate. This forced us to cut down the expense budget in several places and the religious work suffered much beyond our wishes. The President made bold to write to a friend of Dr. Rhodes in Pennsylvania who had already helped this work through gifts to him, laying before him the work to be done and the amount needed to do it and he most generously responded by making a pledge for three years which more than covered the cut we had been compelled to make in the budget for the feature of our work.

In finishing the year March 31, 1928 we are happy to report a fair surplus, the exact amount of which is not yet known because we must await the result of enquiries that have been made about a bill presented to us by the Presbyterian Board in New York of which we had no expectation. If payment is shown to be necessary, the surplus will be small but still it will be a surplus.

When the budget for the present year was prepared we inserted in it a sum of Y1,000.00 to be used in diminishing the accumulated deficit and also Y500.00 to repay losses incurred by the bookstore. These amounts will then be returned to the permanent funds from which the original budget money was borrowed. We consider the insertion of these amounts in the budget as an adventure in faith but even so we have much confidence that we shall be able to go through the year without a deficit.

We hope that we have thus established a tradition of careful budgeting that will guide the finance committee throughout the coming years.

The Methodist Episcopal Board sent us a special contribution of $1,000 to be applied to the reduction of the deficit debt which was thus reduced to Y22,223.19. We heartily wish this could be wiped out in toto.

Teaching Staff

Even while we were doing this we improved our teaching staff materially and were able to carry on even though Professors Miller and Fisher, Becker, and Hitch were still in America. During the year Dr. E. H. Miller returned and a new Korean professor from America joined us, viz. Dr. L. G. Paik, while still others, graduates of Japanese Universities, were added. Dr. Fisher rejoined us at the beginning of this school year and Dr. Becker has informed us he will return next September.

During the year we made strenuous efforts to secure from the Educational Bureau the recognition of graduates of the Literary Department as teachers of History (Occidental and Oriental) and some other subjects in addition to English, formerly granted, but we have so far failed to obtain those privileges.

This year, for the first time since the Government's recognition of our Science Department, on the high standard, we had a graduating class in Science and the question of qualification for those graduates as teachers was a very burning one. At our invitation the Educational Bureau sent out three inspectors to examine the status of the equipment, the standing of the teachers and the scholarship of the classes. They spent an entire day doing this, giving written examinations. We were much gratified when they reported that the results of the examinations were excellent, the teachers satisfactory and the equipment good, the graduates would have qualification to teach Mathematics, Physics and Chemistry. They told us they seldom gave qualification to one school for more than one subject, or at most two, but, being so well pleased, they were stretching a point to give us three.

In regard to our teaching Staff, the Bureau required that at least two-thirds of the teachers shall have full qualification. This means that we can carry on with that proportion though it is considered a mark of weakness to have even that proportion non-qualified. This Spring the Government recognized the full qualification of four of those who had been in the unqualified group and gave temporary qualification to five others so that our proportion of qualified teachers is now 87% which is considered very satisfactory.

In regard to Christian standing, all the teachers are rated as Christians though of course some are less stalwart than others. During the year some of them have shown marked growth in Christian character.

- 3 -

The total number on the Staff now is 35. Notable additions to the Staff have been ---

Rev. L. G. Paik, Ph.D., as Associate Professor of Bible with Dr. H. A. Rhodes.
Rev. Nikaido, as Professor of Japanese Language and Literature.
Mr. P. C. Sohn, as Associate Professor in the Commercial Department.
Mr. K. J. Synn, as Associate Professor of Physical Education.
Mr. P. C. Kim, as Associate Professor in the Science Department.

During the year Mr. K. Y. Park resigned as Associate Professor in the Commercial Department.

Dr. B. W. Billings, who has been Director of the Literary Department from the beginning, resigned from this position at the end of March, 1928, although pressed to continue at least one year longer. When it became evident that Dr. Billings would not withdraw his resignation, the President, after conference with the leading teachers, appointed Dr. L. G. Paik as Director so that now each of the three Departments has a Korean Director, and, a Korean being Dean of the Combined Departments, a real test of the capacity of Koreans to organize and conduct educational work is in progress.

This leaves only the offices of President, Vice-President and Treasurer in the hands of Westerners.

As two of the Directorships and the Deanship have already been successfully filled by Koreans during the past few years, there seems to be every reason to expect continued good results. An interesting feature is that the Dean and one of the Directors were educated in Japanese Universities while the other two Directors were educated in American Universities and the result should be to secure the best from both systems of education -- Occidental and Oriental.

CAPITAL DEVELOPMENT

In pursuance of our policy that the College boundaries will extend to the railroad and to the stream on the east, several parcels of land were bought during the year. One of these transactions was the piece between our holdings and the railway property the acquisition of which will enable us to develop the entrance to the College site as well as the Model Village feature. A long differed exchange and purchase from the Oriental Development Company was concluded. Several lots in the Korean Village in the Model Village area were bought. The total area acquired in the year is 11,028 tsubo, while two isolated pieces on the extreme southwestern boundary were exchanged, leaving the net area 9870 tsubo or 8.225 acres. Land transactions totalled ¥7,321.95 in value in the year.

Some $6,000 of Campaign funds were drawn from the Co-operating Board Treasurer in New York for development purposes. This was used as follows:

1. Erection of a granite stairway to the main campus. The main gift for this purpose was $358 from the Korean Church in New York city. The cost of the steps was Y1,762.09. They are a great addition to the whole property giving the campus a dignified approach in place of the former earthen embankment very much in a state of nature.

2. Provision of toilet facilities in Stimson Hall.

3. Provision of a students' bath room in the basement of Stimson Hall, Costing Y1,044.58.

4. Lighting of compound, buildings and residences. Negotiations were successfully concluded with the Keijo Electric Co. for the installation of poles and wire and bringing of their current to the property, after it had been decided that the installing of a plant of our own was greatly beyond our means. The company agreed to stand half the cost of the installation . Early in December the current was switched on and the comfort of the residents has been greatly increased. The installation will cost the College about Y5,000. Only night current is available as yet, so that classes requiring to use electricity must meet at night.

5. As the population increases, pressure on the water supply is greater. Consequently a number of springs were developed, wells constructed and the water supply increased accordingly. There is still a shortage of water, and new developments will have to be made. As chairman of the Property Committee, Prof. C. H. Lee's work is worthy of special mention. He has conducted all of the negotiations for purchasing land and has had charge of the renting of the fields &c.

STUDENT ENROLMENT

There has been a steady, but not large growth in the student body since 1919. The spring term of the past year enrolled 220 students who paid tuition, the fall term enrolment was 208 and the year closed with 185 students in attendance. The average paid tuitions for the three terms was therefore 204-1/3, an increase of ten over the previous year.

The following table shows growth since 1924 in average paid enrolment:

1924-1925	168	1926-1927	194-2/3
1925-1926	179	1927-1928	204-1/3

The student discipline was good. The dean, Mr. U. K. Yu, handled his multifarious duties in a satisfactory way.

In March, a class of 39 was graduated, of whom 8 were from the Literary course, 19 from the Commercial and 12 from Science. The Science men were the first to graduate under the new recognition promised for that course when the freshman class enrolled four years ago. The graduate roll is now 205.

The paid enrolment by courses was as follows:

	1st term	2nd term	3rd term
Literary	75	64	57
Commercial	100	95	85
Science	46	49	43
	221	208	185

In April, a new entrance class was accepted and the tentative enrolment is as follows:

	1st year	2nd year	3rd year	4th year	Total
Literary	40	22	12	12	86
Commercial	63	39	21	--	123
Science	31	11	8	12	62
	134	72	41	24	271

Attendance This accepted enrolment has since shrink to about 258 in actual.

Denominationally, the students are registered as follows:

Presbyterians	109	
Methodists	112	
Others	8	
Total Christians	229	
Non-Christians	29	258

Proportion of Non-Christians 11.2%

Showing the effect of the College on their relation to Christianity of the non-Christian group, the Literary Department has 10, the Commercial Department 12, and the Science Department 7. In classes they run as follows:

1st year	25	3rd year	1
2nd year	3	4th year	0

ATHLETICS

The College maintained its prestige in athletics. The most notable victory was that of the soccer team over Waseda University last September. When the score stood 4-0. The Waseda team had just returned from winning the second place in the championships at the Asiatic Olympic at Shanghai, which fact made the win all the more gratifying.

In addition, the following peninsular championships were won:

Baseball

In June, the all Korea championship. The College holds a championship banner permanently.

Soccer

October -- won the All Korea and the Inter-Collegiate championships.

Tennis

June -- won the intercollegiate series.

A successful field day for middle schools was held in October.

While our football and baseball teams have been bringing many trophies to the College, making us proud of them, we have all felt the need of a type of Physical Education that would promote the health of the whole student body. This year we have been fortunate in securing a thoroughly qualified teacher for this work -- a young Korean, graduate of a College in Shanghai and a noted athlete in that city, who graduated last June from Oberlin College, Ohio, in Physical Education. He is himself a fine specimen of physical manhood, six feet high and correspondingly broad. He has an earnest Christian spirit. It is now up to us to supply him with the money necessary for equipment sufficient for his purpose and that is one of the President's problems.

3-4/5 ...

RELIGIOUS ACTIVITIES

The provision of the budget of this branch of the work by Mr. W. S. Townsend and the Guarantee Liquid Measures Co. of Rochester, PA., has made advance work possible. Dr. Geo. Paik has rendered acceptable service since September in the teaching of Bible, sharing this work with Dr. Harry A. Rhodes. A conference of Christian workers was held in the summer months with an enrolment of 60 paid registrations. Student preaching bands visited numberous centres. The Y. M. C. A. problem as affecting the whole student body was studied, and decision made to put its support on a voluntary basis.

MUSIC

The Musical interests have greatly profited from the efforts put forth by Mrs. Rhodes and Mrs. Billings so that a good orchestra and a very creditable Glee Club have come into being, while at the same time a brass band has been organized and gives promise of fine development.

Mrs. Boots has arranged to give time every week to the orchestra and her efforts are much appreciated. We are all much pleased with this added feature and in due time we expect a real Musical Department will follow and become a part of the College's offering to the culture of the young men.

DORMITORY

The only dormitory accommodation we have is one building housing 66 students, so the surrounding villages and Seoul City house the remainder of our 200 add students. This building was filled to capacity the three terms. The need of more dormitory accommodation is becoming an urgent problem. Mr. C. M. Song supervised the dormitory. The agricultural building which might be used as extra living quarters, and which in fact,was so used before the present dormitory was built, has been used for several years by the primary school which takes care of most of the children of our College community as well as those of the villagers. It is in a rather dilapidated state of repair.

3- 31- 28 RED

- 8 -

STATUE to the LATE Dr. H. G. UNDERWOOD

The Friendly Association of the College started a movement to provide a statue to the memory of its Founder and first President. They gave the opportunity to the friends and admirers of Dr. Underwood to contribute. The project was brought to a successful conclusion on April 28, 1928, when in the presence of a representative assembly three grandsons of the late Dr. Underwood unveiled the statue. Notable tributes to the work and memory of Dr. Underwood were given by Korean leaders. This noteworthy event, shows that the years that have elapsed since his death have not in any way diminished the high regard in which he was held or lessened the alumni's appreciation of the great efforts he made to establish the College.

This monument on its granite pedestal occupies the center of the campus and is an ornament to the whole architectural scheme. The program printed memorabilia and the newspaper reports will be addenda to the filed copy of this report.

The year in retrospect cannot but be a memorable one for the progress it has shown all along the line. While the problems yet to be solved are quite difficult, yet we have faith that one by one they will be surmounted and the College will fulfill the mission which its founders had in view.

O. R. Avison
President

36. 유억겸 학감의 이사회 제출 연례보고서

문서 제목	Chosen Christian College, Report of U. K. Yu, Dean
문서 종류	학감 보고서
제출 시기	1928년 9월 20일
작성 장소	서울
제 출 자	유억겸
수 신 자	이사회
페이지 수	9
출 처	Korea Mission Records, 1904~1960, Box 15, Folder 15 (PHS) 2114-5-2: 08 Board of Managers 1928~1931 (UMAH)

자료 소개

유억겸 학감이 1928년 9월 20일 열린 이사회 연례회의에서 제출한 보고서이다. 이날 회의에서 이 보고서가 낭독되었다.

유업겸은 이 보고서를 아래의 15개 항목으로 구성하였다.

I. 1927~28연도의 학과, II. 교수, III. 강사와 조수, IV. 사무직원, V. 신임과 안식년 교수, VI. 등록생, VII. 학생 등급 분류, VIII. 학생 출신 지역, IX. 학생 종교, X. 졸업생 수, XI. 졸업생 직업, XII. 졸업생의 자격 인정, XIII. 종교활동, XIV. 면학 정신, XV. 운동경기.

내용 요약

I. 본교는 종합대학 체제를 이루고 있다. 문과는 백낙준 과장을 포함하여 16명(교수 11명, 조교수 3명, 강사 2명)이 74명의 학생을 가르치고 있고, 빌링스가 3월에 과장직을 사임하여 백낙준을 대신 임명하였다. 상과는 이순탁 과장을 포함하여 9명(교수 5명, 조교수 1명, 강사 3명)이 106명의 학생을 가르치고 있다. 수물과에서는 이춘호 과장을 포함하여 교수 7명, 강사 3명, 조수 2명이 56명을 가르치고 있고, 베커가 며칠 내로 미국에서 돌아와 가르칠 것이다. 임원은 에비슨 교장, 원한경 부교장, 유억겸 학감, 오웬스 회계 겸 사업매니저이다.

II~V. 교수는 24명, 조교수는 4명, 강사는 8명, 조수는 2명이다. 이 가운데 한국인 교수는 유억겸, 백낙준, 이순탁, 이춘호, 백남석, 김영환, 백남운, 조병옥, 최현배, 이원철, 손봉조, 김봉집이고, 조교수는 윤병섭, 홍승국, 신기준, 정인보이다. 강사는 정인서, 이운용, 신영묵, 김상용, 노동규, 정규창, 이명혁이고, 조수는 신제린, S. T. Ryang이다. [이 명단에서 과의 구분 없이, 이름, 학위, 출신학교, 담당 과목, 교수자격 유무를 제시하고 있다.] 사무직원은 6명이고, 김봉집 교수와 신기준, 가이야 조교수가 새로 왔다. 히치가 안식년을 연장하였고, 피셔, 베커가 복귀하였으며, 한치관, 츠바키다가 사임하였다.

VI~IX. 첫 학기의 학생 수는 총 236명이었는데, 문과 74명, 상과 106명, 수물과 56명이었다. 5월까지 본과 학생은 161명이었고, 별과 학생은 97명이었다. 학생들은 제주도를 제외한 전 도에서 왔다. 학생들의 종교를 보면, 장로교인 109명, 감리교인 112명, 기타 8명, 비기독교인 29명)이고, 기독교인 학생들의 신앙 경력을 보면, 세례교인 115명, 출석 교인 38명, 신입 교인 76명, 비교인 29명이었다.

X~XII. 졸업생은 총 205명(문과 75명, 상과 99명, 수물과 28명, 농과 5명)이고, 현재 미국 유학 34명, 일본 유학 6명, 한국에서 진학 2명, 연희전문 교수 1명, 학교 교사 47명, 교회사역 9명, 사무직 47명, 언론인 3명, 산업 26명, 개인사업 23명, 사망 7명이다. 졸업생들이 고등보통학교와 산업학교의 교사로서 가르칠 자격을 갖는 과목은 문과에서 영어, 조선어, 중국어이고, 상과에서 영어, 상업, 부기이며, 수물과에서 수학, 물리학, 화학이다.

XIII. 로즈와 백낙준이 매일 11개 반에서 주 2시간씩 성경을 필수과목으로 가르치고 있고, 채플 참석과 일요일 교회 출석을 필수적으로 하게 하고 있다. 한 해 동안 46명의 외부 강사가 왔고, 매년 2월에 학생과 교직원이 종교 집회를 갖는다.

XIV. 연희전문 교수들이 이 나라에서 최고 수준에 있고, 계속 연구하고 있으며, 학생들이 교수들의 모범을 따르고 있다. 현재 도서실에 6,047권의 책과 팸플릿이 있는데, 이 대학을 한국문화의 중심지로 만들기를 희망하면서 한국 고서를 수집하고 있다. YMCA 학생들이 팀을 이루어 여름에 지방에서 강연하였고, 하기학교를 열었으며, 대학 합창단, 오케스트라를 조직하여 활동하고 밴드도 발전하고 있는데, 조만간 음악과 설치가 실현되기를 바란다.

XV. 지난해에 운동경기가 역사상 절정에 이르렀다. 1923년부터 매년 전조선 중등학교 육상경기대회를 개최하고, 축구, 야구, 테니스 팀들이 대회에서 우승하였으며, 오벌린대 출신의 신기준 조교수가 체육 교육을 맡고 있다.

CHOSEN CHRISTIAN COLLEGE

REPORT of U. K. Yu, DEAN

To the Field Board of Managers, at the Board meeting held September 20th, 1928.

Gentlemen:

I have the honor to submit the following report concerning the academic phase of the College administration for the College year 1927-28.

Under the wise leadership and patient guidance of President O. R. Avison and the through hearty co-operation and constant prayers of the members of your Board, the College has moved steadily towards the ideals set forth at the foundation of the institution. Several events, to be described later, undoubtedly mark wholesome progress in all departments of the College.

I. THREE DEPARTMENTS of the COLLEGE

The College is organized on a university system and has three separate departments in operation. These departments are separate so far as their internal organizations are concerned with their directors, budget and recitation halls, but they are one in general administration and policy under one Dean.

THE LITERARY DEPARTMENT -- Rev. L. G. Paik, Ph.D., is the Director of the Department and there are 11 full Professors, 2 Associate Professors, 1 Assistant Professor and 2 lecturers; 16 teachers in all. There are 34 Freshmen, 20 Sophomores, 11 Juniors and 9 Seniors, making a total of 74 fully enrolled students in the Department. Dr. B. W. Billings who has helped to build up the institution from the beginning in various ways resigned from the Directorship of the Department last March. His resignation was accepted according to his wish, and in his place Dr. L. G. Paik was appointed to fill the position from the beginning of the present academic year. Dr. Billings, however still remains on the faculty, carrying on a full time schedule in Western History.

THE COMMERCIAL DEPARTMENT -- Mr. S. T. Lee, Gakushi, is the Director of this Department. This Department alone offers a three year course. There are 5 full Professors, 1 Associate Professor and 3 lecturers: 9 teachers in all. The enrolment in the Department is the largest of all three departments. There are 50 Freshmen, 35 Shophomores and 21 Seniors, making a total of 106 in all.

THE SCIENCE DEPARTMENT -- Mr. C. H. Lee, M.A., is the Director of the Department. The faculty of the department is composed of 7 Professors, 3 Lecturers and 2 Assistants. Dr. A. L. Becker who has been on furlough in America will return to us within a few days and will continue his work in this Department. The enrolment of the Department is as follows: 27 Freshmen, 11 Sophomores, 7 Juniors and 11 Seniors, making a total of 56 in all.

One of the most outstanding events in the Department during the year was the Government's recognition of the high standard of the Department's work. After a very thorough examination of the work of department, the Educational Bureau reported, to our great gratification, that the scholarship of our students was excellent, the teachers satisfactory and the equipment good. Furthermore, to graduates of the Department qualification was given to teach Mathematics, Physics and Chemistry in secondary schools.

ADMINISTRATIVE OFFICERS

O. R. Avison, M.D., LL.D., President
H. H. Underwood, Ph.D., Vice President
U. K. Yu, Gakushi, Dean
H. T. Owens, Treasurer and Business Manager.

II. THE FACULTY

O. R. Avison, M.D., LL.D., (Toronto and Wooster)
President of the College (Q)
H. H. Underwood, B.A., M.A., Ph.D., (New York)
Vice-President of the College and Professor of Education, Psychology and English (Q)
U. K. Yu, Gakushi, (Tokyo Imperial)
Dean of the College and Professor of Law (Q)
L. G. Paik, A.B., Th.B., M.A., Ph.D., (Yale)
Director of Literary Department and Professor of Occidental History and Bible (Q)
S. T. Lee, Gakushi, (Kyoto Imperial)
Director of Commercial Department and Professor of Economics, Economic Policy, Insurance, Statistics, and Typewriting. (Q)
C. H. Lee, A.B., M.A., (Ohio State)
Director of Science Department and Professor of Mathematics. (Q)
A. L. Becker, B.A., M.A., Ph.D., (Michigan)
Professor of Physics and Mathematics (Q)
E. H. Miller, B.A., B.D., Ph.D. (Columbia)
Professor of Chemistry nd English (Q)
B.W.Billings, B.A., M.A., D.D. (Depauw)
Professor of Occidental History and English (Q)
H.A.Rhodes, B.A., M.A., B.D., D.D. (Grove City)
Professor of Bible and English (Q)
J. E. Fisher, B.A., M.A., Ph.D. (Columbia)
Professor of Education and English (Q)
J. W. Hitch, LL.B. (University of Georgia)
Professor of English (Q)
K. Takahashi, (Tokyo Imperial)
Professor of Morals and Japanese civil Government (Q)
N. S. Paik, B.S., M.A., (Emory)
Professor of English and Education (Q)
Y.W. Kim, Graduate of Tokyo College of Music
Professor of Music (Q)
N. W. Paik, Gakushi (Tokyo University of Commerce)
Professor of Commerce, Bank Bookkeeping, History of Commerce, Commercial Japanese, Accounting and Social Economics (Q)

P. O. Chough, B.A., M.A., Ph.D. (Columbia)
Professor of Sociology, Banking, Money, Finance and English (Q)

K. Katowaki, Gakushi (Kyoto Imperial)
Professor of Chemistry and Mechanical Drawing (Q)

H. P. Choi, Gakushi (Kyoto Imperial)
Professor of Philosophy, History of Philosophy, Education and Ethics (Q)

D. W. Lee, Graduate of C.C.C., B.A., M.A., Ph.D. (Michigan)
Professor of Mathematics and Astronomy (Q)

S. Nikaido, Gakushi (Tokyo Imperial)
Professor of Japanese, Japanese Literature and Introduction to Literature (Q)

P. C. Son, Gakushi (Tokyo University of Commerce)
Professor of Commercial Arithmatic, Commercial Bookkeeping, Commercial Practice, Exchange, Custom House and Ware House (Q).

P. C. Kim, Gakushi (Waseda University)
Professor of Physics, Electrical Engineering and Shop Work. (Q)

H. Kaiya, Gakushi (Tofuku Imperial)
Professor of Mathematics, Surveying, Physics, Shop Work, Geology and Minerology (Q).

P. S. Yun, Graduate of Tokyo Imperial, Special
Associate Professor of Natural Science S.Q.

S. K. Hong, B.A. (Ohio State)
Associate Professor of English (Q)

K. J. Synn, B.A. (Oberlin)
Associate Professor of Physical Education. S.Q.

I. P. Chung, Assistant Professor of Chinese Literature. S.Q.

Total Profs 28

III. Lecturers and Assistants

J. Shunwoo, (Waseda Gakushi)
Lecturer on Transportation.

I. S. Chung, Lecturer on Oriental History.

O. Y. Lee, (Berlin University)
Lecturer in German

Y. M. Cynn, Graduate of C.C.C., Gakushi (Kyoto Imperial)
Lecturer on Physics (Q)

S. Y. Kim, Gakushi (St. Paul's University)
Lecturer in English (Q)

T. K. Noh, Graduate of C.C.C., Gakushi (Kyoto Imperial)
Lecturer on Commercial Geography (Q)

K. C. Chung, Gakushi (Waseda University)
Lecturer in English & Introduction to Literature (Q)

M. H. Lee, B.A., M.A. (Columbia)
Lecturer on Biology

C. R. Cynn, Graduate of C.C.College
Assistant of Physics Laboratory

S. T. Ryang, Graduate of Yamakuchi High School
Assistant of Chemistry Laboratory.

Total Lecturers 8
" Assts 2

Total Teacher 38

Note: (1) 'Q' signifies Government Qualification
(2) 'Gakushi' is Equivalent to M.A. in American Universities.

IV. Other Officers of Administration

K. W. Pang, Graduate of Government Medical College
College Physician
K. C. Lyu, Graduate of Chosen Christian College
General Office Secretary
W. S. Youn, Graduate of Chosen Christian College
Assistant Treasurer
C. M. Song, Graduate of Chosen Christian College
Superintendent of the Dormitory.
C. K. Kim, Graduate of Choson Christian College
Superintendent of Grounds & Buildings
H. R. Roe, Assistant Librarian.

V. New Professors & Professors on furlough

1. New Professors
   Prof. P. C. Kim, in April 1928.
   Associate Professor K. J. Synn, in April, 1928.
   Professor H. Kaiya, in May, 1928.

2. Professor on Furlough
   J. W. Hitch, Furlough extended one year.

3. Professors returned from furlough
   J. E. Fisher, in April, 1928
   A. L. Becker, in September, 1928.

4. Professors resigned
   C. K. Hahn, in April, 1928.
   T. Tsubakida, in April, 1928.

VI. ENROLMENT

At the end of the first term, there was a total enrolment of 236 students distributed as follows.

Class	Lit.Dept.	Com.Dept.	Sc.Dept	Total
Freshmen	34	50	27	111
Sophomore	20	35	11	66
Junior	11	--	7	18
Senior	9	21	11	41
Total	74	106	56	236

VII. CLASSIFICATION OF STUDENTS

1. Regular Students:

Literary Department	44	
Commercial Department	78	
Science Department	39	161

2. Special Students:

Literary Department	36	
Commercial Department	41	
Science Department	20	97
		258

Note: The number of students given in this and the following tables is based on statistics of May, 1928.

VIII. Provinces from which students come

Provinces	Number	Percentage
North Ham Kyung	27	10.46
South Ham Kyung	10	3.87
North Pyeng An	13	5.03
South Pyeng An	24	9.30
Whang Hai	19	7.36
Kyung Ki	79	30.62
Kang Won	10	3.87
North Choong Chung	7	2.71
South Choong Chung	21	8.13
North Chun La	12	4.65
South Chun La	13	5.03
North Kyung Sang	13	5.03
South Kyung Sang	10	3.87
Total	258	100%

Students come from All parts of Korea

to

Chosen Christian College,

The "Mecca" of

Christian Education in this land.

IX. STUDENTS' CHURCH RELATIONS

Class	Presbyterian	Methodist Episcopal	Southern Methodist	Other Missions	Non Xtians	Total
Literary Department						
Freshmen	15	10	4	1	9	39
Sophomore	6	7	7	0	0	20
Junior	4	5	2	0	1	12
Senior	5	3	2	0	0	10
Commercial Department						
Freshmen	[illegible]	14	6	4	9	58
Sophomore	19	9	8	0	3	39
Senior	12	5	3	1	0	21
Science Department						
Freshmen	10	3	8	1	7	29
Sophomore	3	6	2	0	0	11
Junior	5	1	1	1	0	8
Senior	5	5	1	0	0	11
Total	109	68	44	8	29	258

Department	Class	Baptized	Catechumen	New believers	Non Xtians	Total
Literary	Freshmen	17	4	9	9	39
	Sophomore	14	2	4	0	20
	Junior	8	1	2	1	12
	Senior	4	3	3	0	10
Commercial	Freshmen	17	8	24	9	58
	Sophomore	14	7	15	3	39
	Senior	10	5	6	0	21
Science	Freshmen	16	3	6	7	29
	Sophomore	9	1	3	0	11
	Junior	0	2	1	0	8
	Senior	6	2	6	0	11
	Total	115	38	76	29	259

X. The total number of Graduates from Each Department.

Literary Department 75
Commercial Department 99
Science Department 28
Agricultural Department (not operating) 3

Total 205

XI. OCCUPATION OF GRADUATES

Occupation	Number	Percentage
Studying in U. S. A.	34	16.58
Studying in Japan	6	2.92
Studying in Korea	2	.97
Professor of Chosen Christian College	1	.48
Teachers	47	22.92
Church Work	9	4.39
Office Work	47	22.92
Journalists	3	1.45
Industrial Enterprises	26	12.68
Private Work	23	11.21
Deceased	7	3.41
Total	205	100%

Pastors & those employed in church

XII. GOVERNMENT QUALIFICATIONS

The graduates of the College are given qualification by the Government to teach in private Higher Common Schools and Industrial Schools on the following subjects:

To the graduates of the Literary Dept.	English, Korean and Chinese
To the graduates of the Com. Dept.	English, Commerce and Bookkeeping
To the graduates of the Science Dept.	Mathematics, Physics and Chemistry.

XIII. RELIGIOUS ACTIVITIES

Religious conditions in the College were decidedly good this year. We still maintain the established policy of required Bible study for every student. Drs. H. A. Rhodes and L. G. Paik gave the Bible courses and allied subjects two hours each week in all eleven classes of the College, and students took these studies with receptive attitude and inquiring spirit. Attendance at the Chapel service and the report of church attendance on Sundays are still required. During the past year 46 outside speakers, of whom 19 were foreigners, addressed the student body on various subjects. In spite of the fact that there is no College chapel service on Sundays, students' reports indicate that they take advantage of opportunity of hearing great preachers from various pulpits in the City. As in previous years, we set aside a week during February for devotional services and Conference for students and Staff.

The religious activities of the College are also encouraging. Several bands of our students go out in the neighboring country to preach every Sunday and a still larger number of them give help to churches in the village and in the City in teaching Sunday schools, in music and in preaching. The student Y. M. C. A. is also an effective auxiliary agency to our religious activities. It was separated from the Student Association and became an independent organization with very active members. During the summer a number of teams went out to different localities to preach and to conduct Daily Vacation Bible Schools. Instead of lecturing around different centers as they did in previous years, this summer, they settled down at a center for three to four weeks. These teams returned to the College with very inspiring reports of establishing new churches, restoring of run down churches, making new converts, organizing co-operative guilds and reducing illiteracy among the people.

The annual Church Workers' Conference was held , July 4-11, under the auspices of the Korean Christian National Council with the financial support of the College. There were assembled some 250 Christian workers from all parts of the country in the College buildings, and all the facilities of the College were placed at their disposal. Our teachers had a very large part in administering the Conference.

The Korean Christian Endeavor Society of the Presbyterian Church held its first annual Summer Conference in the College last July. One hundred and thirty young people from all parts of Korea used the College buildings and equipment which we were glad to offer.

XIV. ACADEMIC SPIRIT

We have been making constant efforts to advance the scholastic standing of the institution. It is probably no exaggeration that our faculty is one of the best in the land. Our teachers continue their private studies and research along the lines of their major interest, keeping their own scholarship. Our students follow the good examples set by their teachers and strive for the attainment of high scholarship. In this connection, your careful consideration is invited to the great need of adequate library facilities. There are some 6,407 volumes of books and pamphlets on various subjects in the College Library. Certainly, the present number of accessions of books is but a mere beginning. We are also making efforts to collect the ancient Korean books, hoping to make the College a center of Korean culture.

As did the student Y.M.C.A., the Student Association sent out several teams of student lecturers to the provinces during the summer, to lecture on social, economic and scientific questions. These teams too brought to us very encouraging reports of their activities.

Futhermore, students held three Summer Institutes for poor children in villages near the College. Thus, they have direct contact with the real life of the people, while they also try to share with the people what they know.

The musical activities of the College afford a new opportunity for cultural development of our students. The College Glee Club and Orchestra have already been organized and carry on commendable work. A College band is also being developed. We hope these added features to the College life not only form excellent extra-curricula activities for the students, but also hope to see it developed into a real Musical Department in due time.

XV. ATHLETICS

The prestige that the College had won in athletics was well maintained during the past year. In fact, it was a crowning year in our athletic history. The All Korea High School Track Meet was held at the College Grounds last September, as has been usual every year since 1923. Many secondary schools participated in the competition. As to the athletic records of the College, the enumeration of the following victories will suffice:

Soccer: In September last, the Waseda University Soccer Team which had just returned from winning the second place in the Championship at the Far Eastern Olympics at Shanghai, was defeated by the College team, and the score stood 4-0. Again, in November last, the College Team won the All Korea and Inter-Collegiate Championships in Soccer.

Baseball: In June, 1927, the All Korea Championship was won. The College holds the Championship banner permanently.

Tennis: In June, 1927, the College Team won the Inter-collegiate series.

One of the valued additions to our faculty during the year was Mr. K. J. Synn as Associate Professor in Physical education and Physical Director of the College. Mr. Synn is a graduate of Oberlin College, Ohio, and is a noted athlete. He is now holding an important place in the College life of the students.

Respectfully submitted,

U. K. Yu
U. K. Yu,
Dean.

37. 에비슨 교장의 이사회 제출 연례보고서

문서 제목	Chosen Christian College, 1928~1929 Annual Report
문서 종류	교장 보고서
제출 시기	1929년 9월 20일
작성 장소	서울
제 출 자	O. R. Avison
수 신 자	이사회
페이지 수	5
출 처	Korea Mission Records, 1904~1960, Box 15, Folder 15 (PHS) 2114-5-2: 08 Board of Managers 1928~1931 (UMAH)

자료 소개

에비슨 교장이 1929년 9월 20일 열린 이사회 회의에 제출한 보고서이다. 이 문서도 일자와 제출자를 밝히고 있지 않지만, 1929년도 이사회 회의록들 가운데 연례회의로 규정된 회의가 9월 20일 열렸고, 이날 교장 보고서와 학감 보고서가 다 제출되었는데, 학감 보고서임을 밝힌 문서가 따로 있으므로, 이 문서는 바로 이때 제출된 교장 보고서로 보인다. 이날 열린 회의에서 이사회는 봄학기에 발생한 상과 동맹휴학 사건으로 인해 조병옥을 6개월분 봉급 지급 결정과 함께 해임하였고, 백낙준을 조병옥 대신 이사회 서기로 삼았다. 또한 음악교수 김영환의 사임을 승인하였고, 현제명을 강사로 임명하였다. 이 보고서는 교장이 이날 제출하기는 하였지만, 지난해 9월 20일 회의 때처럼 사전에 회람하였기 때문에 회의 중에 낭독하지는 않았다.

1929년은 연희전문이 역사상 큰 전기를 이룬 해였다. 먼저 에비슨이 미국에서 벌인 모금운동의 성과가 나타나 이 해에 마침내 모든 적자를 해소하였다. 또한 교수회 산하의 학교교육정책에 관한 특별위원회는 종합대학수립제안서를 만들어 1929년 3월 13일 이사회 회의 때 제출하였다. 그 제안서는 기존 3개 과의 발전계획과 음악과, 농과, 종교과의 설치안을 담고 있었다. [이 문서는 연세대 박물관에서 편찬한 『연희전문학교 운영보고서(上)』(선인, 2013)에 수록되어 있다.] 이 해에 3개 학과에 각각 연구실을 설치하였고, 이후에 교수들의 연구 활동이 크게 활발해졌다.

이 보고서는 아래의 사항들을 설명하고 있다.

재정, 등록생, 자산, 교수, 음악, 종교활동, 특별위원회, 농업 사역, 운동경기, 징계, 졸업생.

내용 요약

재정: 내(에비슨)가 미국에서 1924~26년 기간에 벌인 모금 운동의 한 결과로서 이 해에 $200,000을 홀 재단 측으로부터 받았고, 존 T. 언더우드로부터도 $24,000을 기본재산과 자본금으로 받았다. 로드히버(Rodeheaver, 현제명의 미국 유학 후원자)가 봉급을 대어 현제명(Rody Hyun)을 임명하였다. 1927년까지 누적되어온 적자를 줄이려고 노력해오다가 이 해에 받은 기부금들로 인해 적자를 해소하고 새 출발을 할 수 있게 되었다. (이후 건물과 설비 등의 전체 가격과 보유 자본금, 한 해의 수입액과 지출액을 설명하고 있다.)

등록생: 1924~25년도부터 매해 학생이 많아져 5년간 27%가 늘었는데, 전국의 경제 사정과 경성제대가 개교한 사실을 고려하면 이는 기뻐할 일이다.

자산: 모범촌 부지의 땅을 조금 샀고, 철도국과 대학이 함께 진입로의 굴다리를 새로 건설하였다.

교수: 한국인 학감과 과장들이 모두 독실한 기독교인이고, 현제명이 와서 음악을 맡았다.

음악: 현제명이 부임한 후 많은 일이 진행되었는데, 교수회의 음악부가 현제명, 베커 교수 부인과 부츠 교수 부인의 도움으로 합창단, 밴드, 오케스트라를 발전시켰고, 공연도 몇 차례 하였다.

종교활동: 연례적인 봄철 특별집회 주간이 잘 끝났고, 학생들이 인근 교회들과 주일학교들, 지방에서 종교활동을 하고, 야학을 운영하고 있다.

특별위원회: 지난가을 본교의 향후 목적, 방법, 계획을 연구하기 위해 만든 교수회의 특별위원회가 많은 건설적인 제안을 하여, 이사회가 춘기 회의 때 보고서의 많은 사항을 채택하고 나머지는 그 위원회에 돌려보냈다.

농업 사역: 개교 때 개설하였다가 형편상 폐쇄한 농업과를 다시 개설할 수는 없지만, YMCA 농업사업과의 협력 방안을 연구할 위원회를 만들었다.

운동경기: 신기준 교수가 체육 분야를 지도하고 있고, 배구, 육상종목, 씨름(jiu-jitsu)을 도입하였으며, 축구팀이 전국대회 등에서 우승하였다.

징계: 상과의 동맹휴학으로 100명 이상의 학생을 제적하였다.

졸업생: 서울 주재 장로교 선교사들의 미션학교 졸업생 조사 결과를 보면, 연희전문의 졸업생들 가운데 미국 유학 중인 30명을 빼면 거의 60%가 기독교 사역을 하거나 준비하고 있고, 80% 이상이 활발한 기독교인이다.

Appendix I

CHOSEN CHRISTIAN COLLEGE
1928-1929
Annual Report.

The Chosen Christian College is still in its infancy, the present being only the fourteenth year of its history. That history, however, has been one of remarkably rapid and withal sturdy growth. The year on which we are reporting has been noteworthy, though not for as many changes in site and equipment as the previous year.

Finances.

A separate financial report is prepared each year and is available for all who wish a more detailed knowledge of the income and expenditure of the college so that only the more salient facts are presented in this report.

1. Hall Estate Gift.

The largest single gift which the college has received came to us during this year, the receipt of $200,000 at the final settlement of the Hall estate. While received during this year the gift is directly the result of the work done during the campaign in America during 1924-26. The college was already the beneficiary of this estate to the extent of $50,000, making a total of a quarter of a million from this fund. In addition to the increased facilities for work which the additional income will give us, it is most gratifying to know that the trustees of the fund should have considered our college worthy of this gift.

2. Other gifts.

In addition to the Hall estate gift about $14,000 was added to the endowment and $10,000 to other capital funds by gifts from Mr. J. T. Underwood.

Just as the year was closing word was received that the appointment of Mr. Rody Hyun to take charge of the Music in the college had been made possible by the guarantee of his salary for a number of years by Mr. Rodeheaver and his associates.

3. Deficits and Balances.

Due to lean years, over-optimism and other features, a deficit was almost an annual feature up to 1927. At that time the practice was stopped and a small amount set aside in the budget for repayment of the accumulated deficit. It seemed that the process of repayment would be long and weary. This year, however, the income from the new endowment makes it possible to wipe out the accumulated budget deficits, and receipts from campaign pledges make it possible to repay borrowings from capital funds, thus allowing us to start the new year with a clean sheet.

The above would be ample cause for rejoicing but due to favorable exchange, increased budget receipts and eternal vigilance, we actually closed the past financial year with a surplus of ¥ 7,206.53.

4. Financial standing of the college today.

The fixed assets of the college in land, buildings, residences and equipment, etc., represents a total of ¥ 772,311.31 with unexpended capital funds of ¥ 84,026.10. The endowment has reached the sum of $409,000. (This sum is given in dollars and the funds are invested in the United States by the Cooperating Board for Higher Education in Chosen, Inc.) Budget items each year come to almost ¥ 100,000 in actual cash. The budget for the past year was ¥ 136,652.04 of which ¥ 42,000 was computed as the value of the missionary service given by the different Mission representatives on the faculty and staff. Deducting this amount we have cash receipts of ¥ 94,652.04 and expenditures of ¥ 87,445.04. Of this amount almost ¥ 26,000 was received from fees, property, etc., so that approximately 27% of our cash receipts are from the field.

Enrolment

There has been a slow but steady increase in enrolment during the past five years. The average paid enrolment for this period has been as follows:

1924-25 ----- 168
1925-26 ----- 179
1926-27 ----- 194
1927-28 ----- 204
1928-29 ----- 214

or an increase of 27% for the five years. When the financial condition of the country and the opening of the Government University are taken into consideration, this increase is a matter for congratulation.

Property.

Changes in property are not as noticeable as during the previous year. Four small plots in the model village section have been acquired, and a number of valuable and necessary pieces of repair work have been completed. Most noticeable is the new entrance through the tunnel across the railroad station. This work was done jointly by the Railroad Bureau and the college and thanks are due to Mr. Ohara, the Head of the Bureau, for their part in it. The new road to connect up this entrance with the main road to the college buildings is now being constructed.

Faculty.

No changes of note have been made in the faculty during the past year but no report would be complete which did not bear testimony to the faithful work of all members and to the four Koreans in administrative positions. Report was made last year of the fact that the Dean and the Directors of the three departments were all Koreans. All four are church officers and church workers. As already noted the fall term will see the coming of another Korean, Mr. Rody Hyun, to take charge of the music in the college.

Music.

Even before Mr. Hyun's coming much has been done along this line. The Faculty Music Committee, with the aid of Mrs. Rhodes, Mrs.

C.C.C. Annual Report.- 1928-29. page -3-

Becker and Mrs. Boots, has greatly developed the Glee Club, Band and Orchestra, all of which have performed very creditably on several occasions during the year. With Mr. Hyun on our staff we hope to give some real musical training to all the students, special work to those fitted for it and still further develop and perfect the voluntary organizations mentioned above.

Religious Activities.

The usual week of special meetings was held in the spring with very satisfactory results. Two speakers, a Korean and a foreigner, were used and both brought inspiring and helpful messages. Throughout the year a number of the students have carried on religious work in near-by churches and Sunday schools and in unevangelized districts while vacations have been utilized for special preaching bands. A night school and other work has also been conducted by the students. The chapel services have been better and more profitable and the weekly prayer meetings in the dormitory have been well attended and satisfactory. Religious work was one of the matters to which great attention was given by a special Committee of the Faculty and much improvement may be expected from the adoption of the suggestions made by this committee.

Special Committee.

A Special Committee to study objectives, methods and plans for the future was appointed last fall and worked through the year. Many important matters were considered and constructive plans offered. The report was taken up in detail by the Board of Managers at its spring meeting and many of the items adopted, others being referred to special committees. When the report as a whole is acted upon it will probably be made available for general study, many requests having been received that its findings be made public.

Agricultural Work.

When the C.C.C. was first opened, plans for an agricultural course were made and one class graduated. Circumstances made it necessary to close the department and at present we have no plans for reopening a College of Agriculture. The College, does, however, wish to make whatever contribution it can to the needs of the country and a committee has been appointed to study methods of cooperation with the Y.M.C.A. in its agricultural work. At present it looks as though the College would be able to assist by the loan of a building and some farm land with the possibility of some teaching help and other help later. Detailed plans are not yet complete but it is hoped that next year's report will tell not only of the completion of the plans but that they have been put into operation.

Athletics.

Under the present Director of Physical Education, Mr. K. J. Synn, an attempt has been made to place greater emphasis on physical education and development of the whole student body as against the building up of winning teams. Mr. Synn has organized interclass and inter-department contests which have brought out a large number of students who never took part in athletics before. In order to meet different needs and abilities, volley-ball, track and jiu-jitsu have been introduced and pushed, and both tennis and basketball have been given a more prominent place than in former years. The teams have not been neglected for the National Football Championship was won and the Meiji University football team defeated. The dual meet with Pyengyang was held for the first time and won by the C.C.C. This meet was very satisfactory in the sense that a good spirit was shown by both sides and the relations between the two colleges were made more cordial.

Discipline.

The work of the Spical Committee already referred to was largely along the line of theoretical organization but included many details for administration and discipline. All felt that, when the report was once in, the next step was to put some of this theory into practice. This was done with very satisfactory results in several phases, such as collection of fees, and attendance, etc. A certain element in the Commercial Department and in one class in particular had been a matter of concern to the faculty for some time and when opportunity offered an entire class was disciplined. Their dissatisfaction with their treatment made itself apparent in a number of ways. Partly at their instigation the entire Commercial Department petitioned the faculty for certain changes; and in the meantime a member of this class behaved in such a way that it was necessary to expel him, at the same time that four out of five of the requests from the students were refused. This led to a stike and after opportunity had been given for such students as wished to continue their studies to declare their intention to do so, the names of all the striking students, over one hundred, in all, were dropped from the rolls of the college. This seems at present a most unfortunate situation but if through this situation we can re-organize this department, rid ourselves of the undesirable students, establish firmly the fact that insurbordination will in no case be tolerated and begin the department again on a new and better basis, even the regrettable loss of the weaker students who were led or forced into the strike and the other present losses will prove future gains. No violence was shown during the strike and a vacation was declared as the year was almost at an end and study under the disturbed conditions seemed of doubtful value. The support of the faculty has been remarkable and most gratifying.

Graduates.

During the past year Seoul Station made a study of the fruits of our mission schools in Seoul and it is reassuring to turn from temporary insubordination by a few students to the results as shown by this study. At the time of the study there were 197 living graduates. 79 of these, or 40%, are actively engaged in Christian work in Korea, paid and unpaid, and just half of these, 20% of the total graduates, are working in connection with the mission or in its territory. Another 27% are listed as "active Christians" but not as especially engaged in Christian work. 30 of our graduates are studying in the United States

C.C.C. Annual Report - 1928-29. page -5-

and actual study of the names would indicate that at least 25 of the 30 may be counted on to go into Christian work of one sort or another on their return. Counting those studying in Japan and Korea, we can say that almost 60% of our graduates are in Christian work or preparing for it and over 80% are active Christians. The remainder, or a little under 20%, represent those of whom we have lost track and only a small proportion of this 20% need be reckoned as lost from the church.

It is therefore with a deep feeling of gratitude to God for the years that are further in the past as well as for the year that has just closed that we present this report.

38. 유억겸 학감의 이사회 제출 연례보고서

문서 제목	Chosen Christian College, Report of Dean
문서 종류	학감 보고서
제출 시기	1929년 9월 20일
작성 장소	서울
제 출 자	유억겸
수 신 자	이사회
페이지 수	17
출 처	Korea Mission Records, 1904~1960, Box 15, Folder 15 (PHS) 2114-5-2: 08 Board of Managers 1928~1931 (UMAH)

자료 소개

유억겸 학감이 1929년 9월 20일 열린 연례회의에서 제출한 보고서이다. 이날 연례회의가 열린 사실은 회의록으로 확인할 수 있다. 그가 이 회의에 참석하였는데도 보고서는 원한경 부교장이 읽었다.

유억겸은 보고서의 목차를 아래와 같이 구성하면서 분량을 크게 늘렸는데, 특히 동맹휴학에 많은 분량을 할애하였다.

I. 서언, II. 운영진, III. 대학 교무위원회, IV. 대학 예산위원회, V. 교수진, VI. 사무직원, VII. 안식년 중이거나 사임한 교수, VIII. 학과, IX. 종교부, X. 운동경기, XI. 다른 업무들(도서실, 음악, 박물관, 클럽), XII. 등록생과 동맹휴학, XIII. 학생 등급 분류, XIV. 학생 출신 지역, XV. 학생 종교, XVI. 졸업생 수, XVII. 졸업생 직업, XVIII. 졸업생 자격 인정.

내용 요약

I. 교장의 리더십과 이사회, 교무위원회, 교수들의 협력으로 본교가 꾸준히 발전하고 있다.

II~VII. 운영진은 교장(에비슨), 부교장(원한경), 학감(유억겸), 회계 및 사업 매니저(오웬스)이다. 대학 교무위원회(College Council)는 교장, 부교장, 학감, 4개 학과 과장으로 구성되어 있다. 대학 예산위원회는 교장, 부교장, 학감. 과장 4명, 오웬스, 베커로 구성되어 있다. 교수와 조교수는 총 25명(한국인 교수 15명, 조교수 2명)이고, 전임강사는 1명, 강사와 조수는 13명, 사무직원(사감 포함)은 6명이다. 안식년 중인 교수는 히치, 빌링스이고, 사임한 교수는 김영환, 윤병섭, 신기준이다.

VIII. 본교는 종합대학 체제를 이루고 있다. 문과의 과장은 백낙준이고, 17명(교수 10명, 조교수 1명, 전임강사 1명, 강사 5명)이 68명의 학생을 가르치고 있다. 영어 수업 시수를 늘였고, 독일어 과목을 신설하였으며, 학생들이 조선문학을 연구하도록 조선어 과목을 신설하였다. 최현배가 『우리말본』을 출판한 데 이어 정인보가 한국 민요 연구서를 출판할 예정이다. [최현배가 1929년 발행한 『우리말본 첫재매』와 정인보가 1930년 연희전문 문과 교수들의 논문집인 『조선어문연구』(朝鮮語文硏究)에 게재한 「조선문학원류초본」(朝鮮文學源流草本)을 가리키는 것으로 보인다.] 상과의 과장은 이순탁이고, 10명(교수 5명, 조교수 1명, 강사 4명)이 22명의 학생을 가르치고 있다. 중국어 과목을 신설하였고, 상품진열관을 설치하였다. 수물과는 이춘호가 과장이고, 11명(교수 7명, 강사 2명, 조수 2명)이 41명의 학생을 가르치고 있으며, 전기공학, 응용화학, 토목공학, 독어 과목을 신설하였다.

IX. 종교부에서는 로즈와 백낙준이 성경을 가르치고, 송치명이 학생들을 관리하고 있다. 종교학 입문(1학년), 기독교 증거(2학년), 기독교윤리(3학년), 종교철학(4학년) 과목을 신설하였다. 학생들이 몇 개 집단을 이루어 인근 마을과 도시에서 전도하고 가르치고 있으며, YMCA 학생들이 수요일 채플을 월 2회 담당하고 있다.

X. 신기준 체육주임이 사임하였고, 학교에서 제6회 전조선 중등학교 육상경기대회를 개최하였다. 축구, 농구, 테니스 팀들이 대회에서 승리하였으나, 1928년 12월 상해에서 열린 아마추어 축구대회에서는 선수 부상으로 이기지 못하였다. 유도부를 결성하였다.

XI. 도서부장은 피셔이고, 도서실에 컬럼비아대 사범대 학생들의 도서 기증과 개인들의 기증으로 7,000권이 소장되어 있다. 음악부장은 백남석이고, 베커 부인, 로즈 부인, 부츠 부인이 자문하면서 음악교육, 채플, 몇 개 악단을 돕고 있으며, 이번 가을 현제명이 20점 가량의 악기를 가지고 와서 합창단, 오케스트라, 밴드를 재조직하는 한편 귀국 음악회를 준비하고 있다. 박물관은 박물관부를 발족한 지 1년도 안 되었는데, 러들로로부터 도자기들을, 정인보로부터 가문의 유산인 옛 가구를 기증받았고, 다른 기증품도 많이 받았다. 학생 클럽에는 학생회, 연희전문 기독청년회(YMCA), 문과 문우회, 상과 경제연구회, 수물과 수리연구회, 글리클럽(합창단), 오케스트라, 밴드(관악대), 웅변연구구락부가 있고, 우애회

(교직원 클럽)가 있다.

XII. 1929년 6월 8일까지 학생은 총 211명이었고, 문과 59명, 상과 106명, 수물과 26명이었다.

동맹휴학은 다음과 같이 진행되었다. 4월 25일 상과 2학년생이 27일에 소풍 가기를 요구하여 거절당하자 그날 2학년생 모두 등교하지 않았고, 학교에서 이들을 징계하였다. 이에 5월 20일 2학년생들이 로즈 신과 과장, 이순탁 상과 과장의 교체와 홍승국 교수, 정규창 강사의 해임을 포함한 8가지 사항을 요구하였다. 5월 27일 상과생 전체가 똑같이 요구하였고, 사태가 계속되다 소수의 학생만 학교의 지시대로 학업을 계속할 뜻을 밝혀 나머지 학생들을 제적시켰는데, 문과와 수물과에서도 상과에 동조하려는 움직임을 보여 6월 10일 방학하였다. 그 후 동문회가 두 번 제적생의 구제를 요청하였으나 학교에서 거절하였고, 제적생 60명이 개학 후에 반성문을 제출하였으나 학교에서 그해에는 복교시키지 않기로 하여, 9월 7일 현재 상과에 22명(1학년 9명, 2학년 10명, 4학년 3명)이 있다.

XIII~XV. 1929년 9월 7일까지 학생은 총 131명이고 문과 68명, 상과 22명, 수물과 41명이다. 본과는 88명, 별과는 43명이다. 학생들의 출신 지역과 종교는 표를 참고.

XVI~XVIII. 졸업생은 9월 7일까지 총 248명이고, 현재 한국에서 수학 3명, 일본 유학 7명, 미국 유학 32명, 연희전문 교수(교수, 강사) 3명, 연희전문 사무직원 6명, 기독교 학교 교사 38명, 비기독교학교 교사 18명, 교회사역 13명, 사무직 29명, 공무원 15명, 언론인 4명, 산업 31명, 개인사업 39명, 사망 10명이다. 졸업생들은 다음 과목들에서 교사 자격을 인정받고 있다. 문과: 영어, 조선어, 중국어(한문), 상과: 영어, 상업, 부기, 수물과: 수학, 물리학, 화학.

Appendix II

CHOSEN CHRISTIAN COLLEGE

REPORT of the DEAN

I. Introductory Remarks

To the Field Board of Managers at the Board Meeting held September 20th, 1929.

Gentlemen:

I have the honor to summit the following report concerning the academic phase of the College administration for the academic year 1928-29.

Under the wise leadership and patient guidance of President O. R. Avison and through the hearty co-operation and constant prayers of the members of your Board, the members of the College Council, and the faculty, the College has moved steadily towards the objectives set forth at the foundation of the institution. Several events, to be described later, undoubtedly mark wholesome progress in all departments of the College.

II. Administrative Officers

O. R. Avison, M.D., LL.D., President
H. H. Underwood, Ph.D., Vice-President
U. K. Yu, Gakushi, Dean
H. T. Owens, Treasurer and Business Manager

III. College Council

O. R. Avison, M.D., LL.D., President
H. H. Underwood, Ph.D., Vice-President
U. K. Yu, Gakushi, Dean
L. G. Paik, Ph.D., Director of the Literary Department
S. T. Lee, Gakushi, Director of the Commercial Department
C. H. Lee, M.A., Director of the Science Department
H. A. Rhodes, D.D., Director of the Religious Department

IV. College Budget Committee

O. R. Avison, M.D., LL.D., President
H.H.Underwood, Ph.D., Vice-President

U. K. Yu, Gakushi, Dean
L. G. Paik, Ph.D., Director of the Literary Department
S. T. Lee, Gakushi, Director of the Commercial Department.
C. H. Lee, M.A., Director of the Science Department
H. T. Owens, Treasurer & Business Manager.
A. L. Becker, Ph.D., Professor of Physics.

V. Faculty

A. Professors

O. R. Avison, M.D., LL.D., (Toronto and Wooster)
President of the College (Q)

H. H. Underwood, B.A., M.A., Ph.D., (New York)
Vice-President of the College and Professor of Education, Psychology and English (Q)

U. K. Yu, Gakushi, (Tokyo Imperial)
Dean of the College and Professor of Law (Q)

L. G. Paik, A.B., Th.B., M.A., Ph.D., (Yale)
Director of Literary Department and Professor of Occidental History and Bible (Q)

S. T. Lee, Gakushi, (Kyoto Imperial)
Director of Commercial Department and Professor of Economics, Economic Policy, Insurance, Statistics, and Typewriting. (Q)

C. H. Lee, A.B., M.A., (Ohio State)
Director of Science Department and Professor of Mathematics. (Q)

A. L. Becker, B.A., M.A., Ph.D., (Michigan)
Professor of Physics and Mathematics (Q)

E. H. Miller, B.A., B.D., Ph.D. (Columbia)
Professor of Chemistry and English (Q)

B. W. Billings, B.A., M.A., D.D. (Depauw)
Professor of Occidental History and English (Q)

H. A. Rhodes, B.A., M.A., B.D., D.D. (Grove City)
Professor of Bible and English (Q)

J.E.Fisher, B.A., M.A., Ph.D. (Columbia)
Professor of Education and English (Q)

J. W. Hitch, LL.B. (University of Georgia)
Professor of English (Q)

K. Takahashi, (Tokyo Imperial)
Professor of Morals and Japanese Civil Government (Q)

N. S. Paik, B.S., M.A., (Emory)
Professor of English and Education (Q)

N. W. Paik, Gakushi (Tokyo University of Commerce)
Professor of Commerce, Bank Bookkeeping, History of Commerce, Commercial Japanese, Accounting and Social Economics (Q)

P. O. Chough, B. A., M.A., Ph.D. (Columbia)
Professor of Sociology, Banking, Money, Finance and English (Q)

K. Katowaki, Gakushi (Kyoto Imperial)
Professor of Chemistry and Mechanical Drawing (Q)

H. P. Choi, Gakushi (Kyoto Imperial)
Professor of Philosophy, History of Philosophy, Education and Ethics (Q)

D. W. Lee, Graduate of C.C.C., B.A., M.A., Ph.D. (Michigan)
Professor of Mathematics and Astronomy (Q)

S. Nikaido, Gakushi (Tokyo Imperial)
Professor of Japanese, Japanese Literature and Introduction to Literature (Q)

P. C. Son, Gakushi (Tokyo University of Commerce)
Professor of Commercial Arithmetic, Commercial Bookkeeping, Commercial Practice, Exchange, Custom House and Ware House (Q)

P. C. Kim, Gakushi (Waseda University)
Professor of Physics, Electrical Engineering and Shop Work. (Q)

H. Kaiya, Gakushi (Tofuku Imperial)
Professor of Mathematics, Surveying, Physics, Shop Work, Geology and Minerology (Q)

S. K. Hong, B. A. (Ohio State)
Assistant Professor of English (Q)

I. P. Chung, Assistant Professor of Chinese Literature.

B. <u>Instructor</u>

C. M. Hyun, M.Mus. (Gunn School of Music and Dramatic Art, Chicago) Music.

C. <u>Lecturers and Assistants</u>

I. S. Chung, Oriental History

O. Y. Lee, (Berlin University)
German

Y. M. Cynn, Graduate of C.C.C., Gakushi (Kyoto Imperial)
Physics (Q)

S. Y. Kim, Gakushi, (St. Paul's University)
English (Q)

T. K. Noh, Graduate of C.C.C., Gakushi (Kyoto Imperial)
Commercial Geography & Transportation (Q)

K. C. Chung, Gakushi (Waseda University)
English (Q)
M. H. Lee, B.A., M.A., (Columbia)
Biology
K. S. Oh, Graduate of the Government Seoul Foreign Language School.
Chinese Language.
Insup Chung, Gakushi (Waseda)
English and Introduction to Literature (Q)
Y. C. Lee, Oriental History
R. W. Kang, Physical Education
C. R. Cynn, Graduate of C.C.C.
Assistant, Physics Laboratory
Y. S. Kim, Graduate of C.C.C.
Assistant, Chemistry Laboratory.

Note: "Q" Signifies Government Qualification
"Gakushi" is equivalent to M.A. in American Universities.

VI. Office and Administration Staff

K. C. Lyu, Graduate of C.C.C.
General Office Secretary.
W. S. Youn, Graduate of C.C.C.
Assistant Treasurer.
C. M. Song, Graduate of C.C.C.
Dormitory Superintendent.
C. K. Kim, Graduate of C.C.C.
Superintendent of Grounds and Buildings
H. R. Roe, Junior Office Secretary.

K. S. Lyu, Graduate of C.C.C.
Library Secretary.

VII. Professors on Furlough and Resigned

A. Professors on Furlough

J. W. Hitch, Furlough extended one year
B. W. Billings, Furlough

B. Professors Resigned

Y. W. Kim, in April, 1929
P. S. Yun, in April, 1929
K. J. Synn, in August, 1929

VIII. The Three Departments of the College

The College is organized on a university system and has four deparrments but only three are in operation. These departments are separate so far as their internal organization is concerned with their respective directors, budgets and recitation halls, but they are one in general administration and policy under one Dean.

1. The Literary Department

Rev. L. G. Paik, Ph.D., is the Director of the Department and there are 10 full Professors, 1 Assistant Professor, 1 Instructor, and 5 Lecturers; making a total teaching staff of 17 members. There are 26 Freshmen, 22 Sophomores, 9 Juniors, and 11 Seniors, making a total of 68 fully enrolled students in the Department. As to the courses of instruction, several changes have been made in the department: for the betterment of the English Section, the number of hours in English and English Literature have been increased; to make the students better prepared for a further study, German language has been added; and in order to lead the students into the research of Korean literature, Korean language has been added. In addition to the regular class room activities and progress the Department has published Prof. H. P. Choi's book on the Korean language " 우리말본 " and expects to publish Prof. I. P. Chung's Study of Korean Folk Songs.

2. The Commercial Department

Mr. S. T. Lee, Gakushi, is the Director of this Department. This Department alone offers a three year course. There are 5 full Professors, 1 Assistant Professor, and 4 Lecturers; making a total teaching staff of 10 members. Up to the 8th of June the enrolment in this Department was the largest at that time, the strike broke out and now it is the smallest of the 3 Departments, numbering 9 Freshmen, 10 Sophomores, and 3 Seniors, making a total of 22. As to the courses of study, Chinese language has been added for the benefit of those students who may, after graduation, undertake import and export business with the Chinese people. A new feature in this department is the Commercial Museum for the exhibition of samples of different commodities or articles of commercial interest. It is hoped that this will be valuable for the general study of commodities as well as for the department.

3. The Science Department

Mr. C. H. Lee, M.A., is the Director of the Department. The faculty of the Department is composed of 7 Professors, 2 Lecturers, and 2 Assistants, making a total teaching staff of 11 members. The enrolment of the Department is as follows: 14 Freshmen, 13 Sophomores, 5 Juniors, and 9 Seniors, making a total of 41 in all. Laying a special stress on the theoretical work, on the one hand, this Department deems it necessary to pay no less attention to the practical side. To make it perfect, therefore, courses in Electrical Engineering, Applied Chemistry, and Civil Engineering have been added. In addition to these, a course in German language has been added, to enable the students to carry on further study if they so desire.

For the first time in the history of this institution, we have enrolled a post graduate student in the seminar work of Physics under the supervision of Dr. A. L. Becker. The student seems to be doing very satisfactory work.

IX. Religious Department

The Religious Department forms an important part in the College life. There are three well-equipped men in charge of the many sided activities of the Department. Drs. H. A. Rhodes and L. G. Paik give instruction in the Bible and its allied subjects, while Mr. C. M. Song has charge of the Dormitory and student-visiting. During the year, we experimented with a new scheme of religious instruction. In addition to the direct Bible instruction, there was added a lecture course to each class for a term. Subjects for these lectures are Introduction to the Study of Religion, for Freshmen, Christian Evidences, for Sophomore, Christian Ethics, for Juniors and Philosophy of Religion, for Seniors. The experiment has been so successful that we are giving again the same courses of lectures this year. The Bible is holding its own place in the College curriculum, and students study it in very profitable manner. Attendance at the daily Chapel exercises and the report of church attendance on Sundays are still required. As it has been custom for many years, during the past year, many prominent men in Korea and from other lands spoke from the chapel platform. It is regretable that there is no College Church where Sunday services can be held for Students. But our students are attending various churches both in the city and in the country around the College and take the advantage of hearing many great preachers. As in previous years, we set aside a week during the month of February for devotional service and conferences for students and staff Dr. Riddout of Ashbury College and Rev. Suh Sung Hyun led these meetings this year.

Students of the College have been active in religious work during the year. Several bands of them go out in the near by country to preach every Sunday and a large number of them give assistance to churches in the village and in the city in teaching Sunday schools, in music and in preaching. The student Y.M.C.A. has been co-operating with this department in seeing to it that the Christian spirit permeate the student body. It had charge of the Wednesday Chapel hour twice each month. On account of sudden close of the College last June, the Y.M.C.A. could not make plans for its usual summer program for preaching. This was a regret to us all.

The annual Church Workers' Conference was suspended this year due to the delay of securing the permit from the Railway Bureau for special rate of travel and certain unavoidable conflicts of dates. We hope that nothing will hinder our plans for the coming year.

As is indicated elsewhere in this report, the Special Committee of the Faculty has made valuable suggestions for improving and vitalizing the chapel exercises and other phases of the religious activities. We have put certain parts of the recommendation into execution and we find the chapel attendance on the parts of the staff and students has been greatly improved and the quality of service has also been effective. Mention should also be made in this connection that the addition of Mr. Rody C. M. Hyun to the staff of the College is a great asset to the work of this department. His excellent training in evangelistic singing and sacred music is and will continue to be great help for religious life of the College.

X. <u>Athletics</u>

Ever since Mr. K. J. Synn came to this College, the work of the Physical Education department made a surprising degree of progress. But unfortunately he resigned his position here last August and accepted a similar position at the North Eastern University in Mukden, which is to a great loss to our College. In consequence of his resignation the program for the department will have to be somewhat revised until we get a qualified director.

The most noteworthy activities of this department, both in and out of the College during the last academic year are as follows:

1. October, 1928 - The Sixth Annual Field Meet for the Middle School- Eleven schools participated with 130 athletes, breaking old records and making several new ones.

2. October, 1928 - Inter-Departmental Athletic Meet, Commercial Department winning the honor.

3. Soccer:
May, 1928 - Meiji University - 0, C.C.C. - 6
Nov.,1928 - All Korea soccer Tournament, won by the score of 2 - 0
Nov.,1928 - Intercollegiate Soccer Tournament, won by the score of 3 - 0

4. October, 1928 - Pyeng Yang Union Christian College vs. C. C. C., won in all three events: soccer, basket ball and tennis.

5. December, 1928 - The China National Amateur Athletic Federation invited our Soccer Team over to Shanghai with a guarantee of ¥1,500.oo for the travelling expenses, and they played four important games including All Shanghai Foreigners, Shanghai Chinese, United Services and Chinan University, but due to sickness and the fact that one of our team suffered a broken leg, we were not able to win in any of the games. However, our team won a high place of honor in the athletic world, and made it possible to carry the name of C. C. C. beyond the seas.

6. From the Spring of 1928, a Ju-do department has been established under the instruction of Mr. Kang, Rak-Won, the All Ju-do champion of Korea, and is making a wonderful progress. We are expecting to hold a Ju-do match in the near future under the auspices of this department.

7. Spring, 1929 - A base ball game with the Government Medical College in which we were revenged by the score of 4 - 2 for last year's 3 - 1 defeat.

We regret that due to the striking in the Commercial Department, most of the athletic activities have, of necessity, been practically suspended. We are hoping that it will not be long before we can claim not only our former place in athletics but a still higher place.

XI. Other Items of Interest

1. Library - Professor J. E. Fisher is the chairman of the Library Committee. Through his untiring efforts, we have been

able to purchase some of the most needed books lately. The students of Teachers' College, Columbia University repeated their generous gift, and certain private gifts have been made which brings the total number of volumes just under 7,000, an increase of 376 during the year. We are glad of even small advances but feel keenly the needs of more rapid increase in the facilities of the library.

2. Music - Professor N. S. Paik is the Chairman of the Music Committee , with Mrs. A. L. Becker, Mrs. H. A. Rhodes, and Mrs. J. L. Boots in the advisory capacity. In addition to advising on the Committee these ladies have given valued and faithful assistance in the music of the College, at chapel and in the several musical organizations. Last Fall we participated in the Intercollegiate Concert given by Ewha, U. C. C., Severance and C. C. C. by way of cultivating mutual friendship. In this event we won high honor in the musical world. This Fall we have been very fortunate in adding to the department a teacher in the person of Mr. Hyun, Chai-Myung who won the first prize in a musical contest last Spring in Chicago. Mr. Hyun has brought along with him about twenty pieces of musical instruments for use in his work here. He is , at present, working hard in reorganizing the Glee Club, Orchestra and Band. We are expecting to give the musical world of Korea a chance to hear him in the form of Mr. Hyun's "Welcome Home" recital in the near future. In addition to this, we are looking forward to wonderful progress in this department.

3. Museum - One of the special features of the College is the opening and progress of the Museum. Despite the fact that it is less than a year since it was begun the efforts of the Museum Committee have been successful in gathering quite a good collection. Dr. A. I. Ludlow has made very generous gifts of Korai pottery; Prof. I. P. Chung donated two old official chair heir looms in his family, and many other contributions have been received.

4. Clubs and Organizations
- A. C. C. C. Students Association (The Student Body)
- B. C. C. C. Y. M. C. A. (Voluntary organization)
- C. Literary Friends Club (Students of Literary Department)
- D. Economic Research Club (Commercial Department Students)
- E. Science Research Club (Science Department Students)

F. Glee Club
G. Orchestra
H. Band
I. Oratorical Club
(Voluntary, all departments)
J. Friendly Association
(Korean Teaching and Office Staff)

XII. Enrollment and Report on Strike

A. Enrollment

Annual average of the students who paid tuition during the past three years:

1926 - '27 - 194
1927 - '28 - 204
1928 - '29 - 214

Up to June 8, 1929, there was a total enrollment of 211 students distributed as follows:

Class		Lit.Dept.	Com.Dept.	Sc.Dept.	Total
Freshman		29	46	15	90
Sophomore		20	32	10	62
Junior		9	28	4	41
Senior		11		7	18
	Total	69	106	36	211

B. A Report on the Strike of the Students of the Commercial Department

On April 25, 1929, students, representing the second year of the Commercial Department asked the Director to give them permission to have an outing on the 27th, which he refused to do on the ground that the President had spoken of the shortness of the term. Regardless of this, the entire second year class was absent from school on the 27th. The College authorities, in accordance with the decision of the Commercial Department Meeting, the Curriculum and Conduct Committee and the Faculty, announced, on April 30th, that the students of the second year class would be put under probation for the first term, and that they would be marked absent for five days, and 25 hours for the absence on the 27th.

After May 1st the students of the second year class petitioned about three times asking the College to cancel the punishment which request the College rejected.

On May 20th the following petition was made by the entire second year class:

"In the present day of Korea, there are a great many things for which we can not but feel dissatisfied, and we regret to present this petition,

"We have made several requests for the sympathetic consideration in regard to the punishment meted out to us, but our requests have been rejected every time. We, therefore, can not endure it any longer and herewith we are frankly expressing our complaints in order to urge the College authorities for a reconsideration, and are making the following requests not only for our own future but also for all the students of Korea.

1. As to improving the treatment of students: That the system of grading the department of students by each teacher and also the system of rigid marking of absences be discontinued.

2. That the Bible instruction be made scientific and that Dr. H. A. Rhodes, the Bible professor, be discharged.

3. That the directorship of Prof. S. T. Lee be discontined.

4. That Prof. S. K. Hong of Commercial Department be released.

5. That Mr. K. C. Chung, Lecturer in English, also be released.

6. That the tuition be lowered.

7. That the medical fee be abolished.

8. That the former punishment on account of a day's outing be canceled.

"We wish that you would answer us before the end of this month. May 20, 1929.

Signed as from the entire second year class students.

After the presentation of the above petition, the students did not attend the lectures of some of the teachers in question (i.e., Profs. Hong, Chung, Rhodes). The College regarded it as a kind of strike and held a special faculty meeting on May22.

In accordance with the decision of the Faculty Meeting the Second Year Students were remonstrated with for their improper conduct, were given a day's time with no studies (May 23) to think over the whole situation, and were told that they should come to express their repentance before 9:30 A.M., the next day (May 24) or their names be stricken from the Roll as students leaving the College. The third and first year students who had no concern with this case volunteered to help out in the situation as fellow students, and asked the College to postpone the limit of time to noon of May 24th, which was granted. Fortunately the second year students sent representatives to express their repentance within the time set and the matter was brought to an end.

On May 27th a petition came from the entire student body of the Commercial Department which was almost the repetition of the former petition from the second year students. Up to June 5, for nine days the curriculum and conduct committee held four special meetings and presented the case to Faculty Meeting to give careful consideration to the items in the petition. It was decided that the course in typewriting might be made an elective course as requested but the other things in the petition were rejected. On June 6, the students of the Commercial Department were called together in a room, and the President spent about an hour remonstrating with them and answering their questions and he spent another hour with the second year students in order to give them a full and careful answer and make them clearly understand his deep and sincere interest in their welfare.

The students were not satisfied with the above decision and in one class, the students disturbed the lectures of a Bible Professor three times in succession, and the College, according to the rules dealing with such cases, expelled for misbehavior Kim Dong Woon who was one of the leaders.

On June 7th the entire student body of the Commercial Department presented another petition and went on a strike from that day. The Faculty held a special meeting and after discussion decided to follow the former plan and gave the following instructions to them:

"We have received a demand which purports to come from all the students of the Commercial Department.

Those students who adhere to and support this demand are no longer students of the Chosen Christian College and their names shall be stricken from the rolls of the College.

The demand however was presented by certain delegates and is unsigned. We do not wish to do injustice to students who are not in sympathy with such lawless actions.

Therefore

Any such students who wish to make their position in regard to the College clear may do so in writing or in person up to 12 M., Saturday, June 8th and the case of such students will then be considered on their merits."

Up to noon June 8th a few more than ten students expressed their desire to continue their studies and in addition to these there were several who had been absent on account of sickness or other causes. All the others, i.e., 29 in the third year, 28 in the second year, and 41 in the first year, decided to consider themselves as no longer studentsof the College and accordingly the College authorities took action as decided.

From 10:00 A.M., June 8th, some studentsin the Literary and Science Departments were trying to stir up the students in these two departments to strike in order to show their sympathy with the Commercial Students. The College in order to adjust the situation, announced the summer vacation to begin from June 10 and urged the students to go home.

So far as the entire Commercial Students are concerned, from May 27th up to June 8th, they disobeyed the College authorities and continued to hold meetings and make decisions against the College.

From April 30th to June 8th the College authorities did their best to stop this unfortunate affair and they regret that they did not succeed in doing so.

Soon after the strike, the Alumni Association sent in a petition, requesting the College to take back the striking students unconditionally. The President after consulting the different members of the Faculty, replied to the Alumni Association that the students could not be received back at this time. The Alumni Association made a second similar request, and an answer was sent to the effect that the Faculty did not wish to reconsider their decision.

When the fall term opened some sixty of ex-students returned. They held several meetings and finally sent a signed petition to the President stating that all the ex-students were repentant and wished to return to school.

The Faculty again considered the matters and decided, that it would not be wise to receive the ex-students back during this school year.

As is known to every body, the aim of the College is to give higher education to the Korean young men under Christian influence and to produce the proper kind of leaders and workers that this country needs. As you all know, this spring a program was prepared to develop this school into a larger institution with the hope of carrying it out within the next seven years. We are afraid that the strike case of this year may be a hindrance to our effort along this line.

Despite this, it is the firm conviction of the faculty and administrative officers that a strong attitude on the strike question will be of great benefit to the institution and that with this once settled and our position clearly demonstrated, we can then move forward with the other plans.

Without assurance against internal disturbances no real progress can be made.

The number of the students according to departments up to September 7th is as follows:

Class	Lit.Dept.	Com.Dept.	Sc.Dept.	Total
Freshmen	26	9	14	48
Sophomore	22	10	13	45
Junior	9		5	14
Senior	11	3	9	23
Total	68	22	41	131

XIII. Classification of Students

A. Regular Students

Literary Department	47	
Commercial Department	10	
Science Department	31	88

B. Special Students

Literary Departments	21	
Commercial Department	12	
Science Department	10	43
Total		131

XIV. Provinces from which students come

Province	Number	Percentages
North Ham Kyung	2	1.45
South Ham Kyung	11	8.39
North Pyung An	5	3.81
South Pyung An	18	13.74
Whang Hai	7	5.34
Kyung Ki	46	35.11
Kang Won	8	6.10
North Choong Chung	2	1.45
South Choong Chung	6	4.58
North Chun La	10	7.63
South Chun La	4	3.05
North Kyung Sang	6	4.58
South Kyung Sang	6	4.58
Total	131	100%

XV. Students' Church Relations

Class	Presbyterian	Methodist Episcopal	South. Metho.	Other Miss'ns	Non Xtians	Total
Literary Department						
Freshmen	13	4	6	0	3	26
Sophomore	5	10	4	2	1	22
Junior	2	4	5	0	0	9
Senior	6	3	2	0	0	11
계	26	21	15	2	4	68

Class	Presby terian	Methodist Episcopal	South. Metho.	Other Miss'ns	Non Xtians	Total
Commercial Department						
Freshmen	2	2	3	0	2	9
Sophomore	4	3	1	0	2	10
Senior	1	0	2	0	0	3
Science Department						
Freshmen	5	3	1	1	4	14
Sophomore	4	5	2	1	1	13
Junior	2	1	2	0	0	5
Senior	5	4	9	0	0	9
Total	49	39	26	4	13	131

Dept.	Class	Baptized	Catechumen	Believers	Non Xtians	Total
Lit.	Freshmen	12	4	7	3	26
	Sophomore	10	2	7	3	22
	Junior	7	1	1	0	9
	Senior	8	1	2	0	11
Com.	Freshmen	6	0	2	1	9
	Sophomore	6	1	1	2	10
	Senior	1	2	0	0	3
Sc.	Freshmen	6	0	3	5	14
	Sophomore	7	1	3	2	13
	Junior	3	0	2	0	5
	Senior	1	3	5	0	9
	Total	67	15	33	16	131

XVI. The Total number of Graduates from each Department (September 7th, 1929)

Literary Department	85
Commercial Department	120
Science Department	40
Agricultural Department (Not operating)	3
Total	248

XVII. <u>Occupation of Graduates</u> (September 7th, 1929)

Occupation	Number	Percentage
Studying in Korea	3	1.21
Studying in Japan	7	2.82
Studying in U. S. A.	32	12.90
Professor & Lecturer of C.C.C. . . .	3	1.21
Secretaries of C.C.C.	6	2.83
Teacher in Christian Schools	38	15.33
Teacher in Non-Christian Schools . .	18	7.25
Church Work	13	5.24
Office Work	29	11.69
Official	15	6.05
Journalist	4	1.61
Industrial Enterprise	31	12.50
Private work	39	15.73
Deceased	10	3.63
Total	248	100%

XVIII. <u>Government Qualifications</u>

The graudates of the College are given qualification by the Government to teach in Private Higher Common Schools and Industrial Schools on the following subjects:-

To the graduates of Literary Department

English (Korean & Chinese)

To the graduates of the Commercial Department

English, Commerce, and Bookkeeping.

To the graduates of the Science Department

Mathematics, Physics, and Chemistry.

Respectfully submitted,

U. K. Yu

U. K. Yu, Dean

39. 유억겸 학감의 이사회 제출 연례보고서

문서 제목	Chosen Christian College, Report of the Dean
문서 종류	학감 보고서
제출 시기	1930년 10월 2일
작성 장소	서울
제 출 자	유억겸
수 신 자	이사회
페이지 수	14
출 처	Korea Mission Records, 1904~1960, Box 15, Folder 15 (PHS) 2114-5-2: 08 Board of Managers 1928~1931 (UMAH)

자료 소개

유억겸 학감이 1930년 10월 2일 열린 이사회 연례회의에서 제출한 보고서이다. 유억겸이 보고서를 작성하였고, 이 회의에도 참석하였으나, 보고서의 낭독은 원한경 부교장이 하였다. 에비슨 교장은 보고서를 문서로 제출하지 않고 구두로 몇 가지 사항을 언급하였다. (지난해에 취소된 그의 미국 방문을 재가해주도록 요구하였고, 그가 구내의 빌링스 집으로 이사해온 지 8개월이 되었다는 것과 존 T. 언더우드로부터 언더우드관 건축비의 잔액을 모범촌 부지에 필요한 땅의 구입비로 돌리라는 지시를 받았다는 것을 알렸다.) 이날 회의에서 이사회는 에비슨의 70회 생일을 축하하였고, 이재량과 아들들이 제공한 조선왕조실록 구입 기금 ¥6,000을 받기로 하였으며, 정인보를 조교수에서 교수로 승격시켰다. 감리교신학교의 협력사업 요청을 승인하였고, 철로 남쪽 서쪽 산의 띠 모양 땅 1,992평을 철도회사에 기증하기로 하였다.

유억겸은 이 보고서의 목차를 전년도처럼 구성하였으나, VIII에 조력자 항목을 새로 둔 점에서는 차이를 보였다.

I. 서언, II. 운영진, III. 대학 교무위원회, IV. 대학 예산위원회, V. 교수진, VI. 사무직원, VII. 안식년 중이거나 사임한 교수, VIII. 음악교육 조력자, IX. 학과, X. 종교부, XI. 운동경기, XII. 다른 업무들(도서관, 음악, 박물관, 학생 클럽), XIII. 등록생, XIV. 학생 등급 분류, XV. 학생 출신 지역, XVI. 학생 종교, XVII. 졸업생 수, XVIII. 졸업생 직업, XIX.

졸업생 자격 인정.

내용 요약

I. 교장의 리더쉽과 이사회, 교무위원회, 교수들의 협력으로 본교가 꾸준히 발전하고 있다.

II~VIII. 운영진은 교장(에비슨), 부교장(원한경), 학감(유억겸), 회계 및 사업 매니저(오웬스)이다. 대학 교무위원회(College Council)는 교장, 부교장, 학감, 4개 학과 과장으로 구성되어 있다. 대학 예산위원회는 교장, 부교장, 학감, 과장들, 오웬스, 베커로 구성되어 있다. 교수와 조교수는 총 25명(한국인 교수 11명, 조교수 2명)이고, 전임강사는 4명, 강사와 조수는 11명, 사무직원(사감 포함)은 6명이다. 안식년 중인 교수는 이춘호, 히치이고, 사임한 교수는 조병옥이다. 교수 부인 4명이 음악교육을 조력하고 있다.

IX. 본교는 종합대학 체제를 이루고 있다. 문과의 과장은 백낙준이고, 20명(교수 10명, 조교수 2명, 전임강사 2명, 강사 6명)이 64명의 학생을 가르치고 있으며, 언더우드(원한경) 부인이 영어를 가르치고 있다. 연구실을 설치하였고, 조선어와 문학에 관해 연구한 결과를 논문집으로 간행하고 있다. 상과의 과장은 이순탁이고, 11명(교수 5명, 강사 2명, 강사 4명)이 108명의 학생을 가르치고 있다. 본교 출신 최순주(뉴욕대 Ph.D.)가 부임하였고, 상업연구실을 설치하였다. 수물과에서는 베커가 과장을 대리하고, 11명(교수 7명, 강사 2명, 조수 2명)이 40명의 학생을 가르치고 있다. 이춘호가 안식년을 얻어 뉴욕에서 공부하고 있고, 교수들이 매주 연구모임을 갖고 있다.

X. 종교부가 역사상 가장 잘 운영되었다. 한 해 동안 채플 설교의 3/4을 교수들이 맡았고, 1/4을 외부 강사가 맡았다. 현제명은 채플 시간의 음악 순서를 감동적으로 이끌고 있다. 캠퍼스에서 교회들이 하기 수양회를 열었고, 학생들도 많은 교회에서 활발하게 활동하고 있다. 채플실의 혼잡에 대한 대비책을 세워야 한다.

XI. 학생들에게 축구, 럭비, 테니스, 야구, 육상경기, 농구, 유도 종목을 가르쳤다. 9월 23일 제7회 전조선 중등학교 육상경기대회, 6월 21일 제1회 중등학교 유도대회를 개최하였으며, 10월 11일 제1회 중등학교 테니스대회를 개최할 예정이다. 경성의전과의 야구시합에서는 패하였고, 중앙 YMCA 주최 전국야구대회에서는 우승하였다.

XII. 이원용, 이환용, 이희용, 이배용이 도서관에 조선왕조실록 848권의 구입비 ￥6,000을 기부하였고, 교직원 우애회도 연례행사로 ￥100을 기부하였다. 음악이 현제명의 지도와 베커 부인, 로즈 부인, 빌링스 부인의 조력으로 크게 발전하였고, 순회공연 등의 여러 음악회를 개최하였다. 박물관은 귀중한 한국 도자기들을 확보하였고, 오규신 교수가 180점 이상의 옛 화폐와 부적들을 기증하였다. (학생 클럽에 관해 전년도와 같은 목록을 제시하고 있다.)

XIII~XVI. 1930년 5월 10일까지 학생은 총 212명이고 문과 64명, 상과 108명, 수물과 40명이다. 본과는 160명, 별과는 52명이다. 학생은 제주도를 제외한 전 도에서 왔고, 과별 학생 종교 상황은 감리교인이 장로교인보다 더 많고, 비기독교인이 13명이다.

XVII~XIX. 졸업생은 3월 31일까지 총 271명이고, 현재 연희전문 교수 6명, 연희전문 사무직원 5명, 기독교 학교 교사 41명, 교회사역 20명, 신학생 1명, 비기독교 학교 교사 16명, 미국 유학 35명, 일본 유학 3명, 한국에서 진학 4명, 언론인 3명, 문필가 4명, 사무직 26명, 공무원 15명, 산업(공업), 23명, 농업 2명, 개인사업 51명, 사망 16명이다. 졸업생들이 중등학교 교사 자격을 문과 졸업은 영어, 조선어, 중국어(한문)에서, 상과 졸업은 영어, 상업, 부기에서, 수물과 졸업은 수학, 물리학, 화학에서 인정받고 있다.

(1930)

CHOSEN CHRISTIAN COLLEGE

Report of the Dean

I. Introductory Remarks

To the Field Board of Managers at the Board Meeting held October 2nd, 1930.

Gentlemen:

I have the honor to submit the following report concerning the academic phase of the College administration for the academic year 1929-30.

Under the wise leadership and patient guidance of President O. R. Avison and through the hearty co-operation and constant prayers of the members of your Board, the members of the College Council, and the faculty, the College has moved steadily towards the objectives set forth at the foundation of the institution. Several events, to be described later, undoubtedly mark wholesome progress in all departments of the College.

II. Administrative Officers

O. R. Avison, M.D., LL.D., President
H. H. Underwood, Ph.D., Vice-President
U. K. Yu, Gakushi, Dean
H. T. Owens, Treasurer and Business Manager

III. College Council

O. R. Avison, M.D., LL.D., President
H. H. Underwood, Ph.D., Vice-President
U. K. Yu, Gakushi, Dean
L. G. Paik, Ph.D.,
Director of the Literary Department
S. T. Lee, Gakushi,
Director of the Commercial Department
C. H. Lee, M.A.,
Director of the Science Department
H. A. Rhodes, D.D.,
Director of the Religious Department

IV. College Budget Committee

O. R. Avison, M.D., LL.D., President
H. H. Underwood, Ph.D., Vice-President
U. K. Yu, Gakushi, Dean

L. G. Paik, Ph.D.,
Director of the Literary Department
S. T. Lee, Gakushi,
Director of the Commercial Department
C. H. Lee, M.A.,
Director of the Science Department
A. L. Becker, Ph.D.,
Professor of Physics
H. T. Owens,
Treasurer & Business Manager

V. Faculty

A. Professors

O. R. Avison, M.D., LL.D., (Toronto and Wooster)
President of the College (Q)
H. H. Underwood, B.A., M.A., Ph.D., (New York)
Vice-President of the College and Professor of Education, Psychology and English (Q)
U. K. Yu, Gakushi, (Tokyo University)
Dean of the College and Professor of Law (Q)
L. G. Paik, A.B., Th.B., M.A., Ph.D., (Yale)
Director of Literary Department and Professor of Occidental History and Bible (Q)
S. T. Lee, Gakushi, (Kyoto Imperial)
Director of Commercial Department and Professor of Economics, Insurance, Statistics, and Abacus (Q)
C. H. Lee, A. B., M. A., (Ohio State)
Director of Science Department and Professor of Mathematics (Q)
A. L. Becker, B.A., M.A., Ph.D., (Michigan)
Professor of Physics and Mathematics (Q)
E. H. Miller, B.A., B.D., Ph.D. (Columbia)
Professor of Chemistry and English (Q)
B. W. Billings, B.A., M.A., S.T.M., D.D. (Depauw)
Professor of Occidental History, Bible and English (Q)
H. A. Rhodes, B.A., M.A., B.D., D.D. (Grove City)
Professor of Bible and English (Q)
J. E. Fisher, B.A., M.A., Ph.D. (Columbia)
Professor of Education and English (Q)
J. W. Hitch, LL.B. (University of Georgia)
Professor of English (Q)
K. Takahashi, (Tokyo Imperial)
Professor of Morals and Japanese Civil Government (Q)
N. S. Paik, B.S., M.A. (Emory)
Professor of English and Education (Q)

N. W. Paik, Gakushi, (Tokyo University of Commerce) Professor of Commerce, Bank Bookkeeping, History of Commerce, Commercial Japanese, Accounting, and Sociology (Q)

K. Katowaki, Gakushi, (Kyoto Imperial) Professor of Chemistry, Mechanical Drawing (Q)

H. P. Choi, Gakushi, (Kyoto Imperial) Professor of Philosophy, Education, Ethics, and Korean Language (Q)

D. W. Lee, Graduate of C.C.C., B.A., M.A., Ph.D. (Michigan) Professor of Mathematics and Astronomy (Q)

S. Nikaido, Gakushi (Tokyo Imperial) Professor of Japanese, Japanese Literature and Introduction to Literature (Q)

P. C. Son, Gakushi (Tokyo University of Commerce) Professor of Commercial Arithmetic, Commercial Bookkeeping, Exchange, Custom House and Ware House (Q)

P. C. Kim, Gakushi (Waseda University) Professor of Physics, Electrical Engineering, and Mathematics (Q)

H. Kaiya, Gakushi, (Tofuku Imperial) Professor of Mathematics, Surveying, Physics, Civil Engineering, Drawing, Geology, and Minerology (Q)

S. K. Hong, B. A. (Ohio State) Professor of English (Q)

I. P. Chung, Assistant Professor of Chinese Literature and Korean Literature (Q)

C. M. Hyun, M. Mus. (Gunn School of Music and Dramatic Art, Chicago) Assistant Professor of Music (Q)

B. <u>Instructors</u>

T. K. Noh, Graduate of C.C.C., Gakushi (Kyoto Imperial) Commercial Geography, Transportation, Economic Policy and Commercial English (Q)

S. J. Chey, Graduate of C.C.C., B.S., M.B.A., Ph.D. (New York) Commercial Practice, Commercial English and Typewriting (Q)

Mrs. H. H. Underwood, B.A., M.A. (New York) English (Q)

O. Y. Lee, (Berlin University) German

C. Lecturers and Assistants

I. S. Chung, Oriental History

Y. M. Cynn, Graduate of C.C.C., Gakushi (Kyoto Imperial) Physics (Q)
S. Y. Kim, Gakushi, (St. Paul's University) English (Q)
K. C. Chung, Gakushi (Waseda University) English (Q)
M. H. Lee, B.A., M.A., (Columbia) Biology
K. S. Oh, Graduate of the Government Seoul Foreign Language School. Chinese Language
Insup Chung, Gakushi (Waseda University) English and Introduction to Literature (Q)
Y. C. Lee, Oriental History

L. W. Kang, Physical Education

C. R. Cynn, Graduate of C.C.C. Assistant, Physics Laboratory
Y. S. Kim, Graduate of C.C.C. Assistant, Chemistry Laboratory

NOTE: "Q" signifies Government Qualification
"Gakushi" is equivalent to M.A. in American Universities.

VI. Office and Administration Staff

K. C. Lyu, Graduate of C.C.C. General Office Secretary
W. S. Youn, Graduate of C.C.C. Assistant Treasurer
C. M. Song, Graduate of C.C.C. Dormitory Superintendent
C. K. Kim, Graduate of C.C.C. Superintendent of Grounds and Buildings
H. R. Roe, Junior Office Secretary

K. S. Lyu, Graduate of C.C.C. Library Secretary

VII. Professors on Furlough and Retired

A. Professors on Furlough

C. H. Lee, Leave on absence
J. W. Hitch, Furlough extended one year

B. Professors Retired

P. O. Chough, in September, 1929

VIII. Other Assistants in instruction and Music

Mrs. H. A. Rhodes
Mrs. B. W. Billings
Mrs. A. L. Becker
Mrs. J. E. Fisher

IX. The Three Departments of the College

The College is organized on a university system and has four departments but only three are in operation. These departments are separate so far as their internal organization is concerned with their respective directors, budgets and recitation halls, but they are one in general administration and policy under one Dean.

1. The Literary Department

Rev. L. G. Paik, Ph.D., is the Director of the Department and there are 10 full Professors, 2 Assistant Professors, 2 Instructors, and 6 Lecturers; making a total teaching staff of 20 members. There are 26 Freshmen, 15 Sophomores, 14 Juniors, and 9 Seniors; making a total of 64 fully enrolled students in the Department. Dr. B. W. Billings who was on furlough during the last academic year, returned to the College and has resumed his work. While he was in America he engaged studies which were crowned with the degree of Master of Sacred Theology from the Union Theological Seminary in New York. Mrs. H. H. Underwood, M.A., has been giving instructions in English courses in this Department. The Government granted her the Government qualification to teach. A Research Room has been established this year in connection with the Department providing an ample room and facilities to teachers and students to engage in research in subjects taught by the Department. As result of special researches engaged by members of the faculty of the Department, a Research Bulletin dealing with Korean language and literature is being published.

2. The Commercial Department

Mr. S. T. Lee, Gakushi, is the Director of this Department. This Department alone offers a three year course. There are 5 full Professors, 2 Instructors, and 4 Lecturers; making a total teaching staff of 11 members. The enrolment in this Department is the largest of all three Departments; there are 63 Freshmen, 14 Sophomores, and 31 Seniors; making a total of 108 in all. It is gratifying to mention the fact that Mr. S. J. Chey, Ph.D., has been added to the faculty of this Department.

He is our own graduate from the Department. Since his graduation, he engaged studies in many educational institutions in America crowning his painstaking work with the degree of Doctor of Philosophy from the New York University. His old teachers and new friends are happy to welcome him back to his alma matar. In order fecilitate practical education on Commodities, the Commercial Museum has been established and there are already assembled 898 specimens of native and foreign commodities for study and exhibition. The Commercial Research Room is another feature of development of the department. This room provides a convenient room and materials for research on commercial and economic sciences. The members of the faculty of the Department have pledged to contribute one hundredths of their salary every month for development of Research work of the Department. There are already provided with over one hundred volumes of periodicals and newspapers in the Research Room.

3. The Science Department

Dr. A. L. Becker is the Acting Director of the Department. The faculty of the Department is composed of 7 Professors, 2 Lecturers, and 2 Assistants; making a total teaching staff of 11 members. The enrolment of the Department is as follows: 20 Freshmen, 4 Sophomores, 11 Juniors, and 5 Seniors; making a total of 40 in all. During the year, this Department has greatly missed its Director, Mr. C. H. Lee. Mr. Lee is on his sabbatical leave. He went to America at the beginning of the present academic year and is now engaged in further study along his lines of interest in New York. Mr. Lee was the first professor to whom the Sabbatical leave was granted, and his many sided service to the College deserve this honor. During the absence of Mr. Lee, Dr. A. L. Becker, most ably carried on the administrative work in addition to his teaching load. Members of the faculty of the Department have been holding regular meetings once in a week lecturing on special studies they have made. These lectures were open to the College as a whole and many were profited by them and hope this beginning will continue to grow. This Department is also making special efforts for collection and complitation of Scientific Specimens and apparatus, and a room is provided for these collections.

X. Religious Department

In some respects the past year in religious work has been the best in the history of the College. There has been a better atmosphere on the campus, in Bible classes, and in the Chapel service. A large group of students have been active in the churches and during the vacation period.

Of thirty five members of the Staff, twenty nine have led the Chapel service from one to eight times each during the year. They conducted three-fourths of the Chapel services; for the other one-fourth we have had visiting speakers. Some of these were invited by the Students Y. M. C. A. and the Students Association, which two organizations have charge of the service at least twice each month. Mr. Hyun frequently takes the Chapel hour for a program of music which is very much appreciated. All the unpleasant features of the chapel service before the strike have disappeared. Among the visiting speakers were the Rev. A. W. Cooper of Siam, Dr. Y. S. Lee of Severance Hospital, Rev. P. S. Chun, Rev. V. W. Peters, Bishop Ainsworth, Prof. L. W. Chang, Rev. H. H. Bruen, Rev. H. W. Lampe, D.D., Rev. R. M. Hopkins, D.D., Rev. John H. Kerr, D.D., Rev. W. E. Shaw, Rev. J. K. Chung, Dr. K. T. Hah, Mr. David Lee, Rev. S. O. Pyun, Rev. H. W. Oh, Rev. C. C. Kim, Rev. W. F. Bull, Rev. H. Voelkol, Bishop Dunlop, Dr. Boville, Dr. Hugh Cynn, Dr. C. M. Elmore, Dr. Frederick Starr, Mr. D. L. Pierson, and Mr. Hamata.

The Summer Conference for Christian Workers under the auspices of the College and of the National Christian Council, July 4-11, 1930, was very good but because of floods and other conferences, was not as largely attended as the year before. Among the leaders of the conference were the Rev. L. C. Brannan, Rev. E. H. Pai of Chunju, Rev. J. K. Chung, Dr. L. G. Paik, Dr. J. D. VanBuskirk, President Avison, Rev. K. S. Kim of Hamheung, and Rev. S. O. Pyun. The January Conference for the students was well begun under the leadership of Rev. W. F. Bull and Rev. S. O. Pyun, but unfortunately the sympathetic strike of the students over political matters for a few days, made it necessary to close the conference.

Each Sunday an average of forty students are doing active work in as many churches. They teach Sunday School classes, help with the music, and preach at the regular services. During the Summer five groups of students visited different parts of the country, held evangelistic meetings, and daily vacation Bible schools. Some thirty of the students have met regularly Sunday afternoons for conference and prayer. After school closed in June a large number of students remained for a three day conference.

Drs. Rhodes, Paik, and Avison have carried the Bible teaching throughout the year. Dr. Billings also since his return from furlough, teaches one Bible class and has charge of the Chapel service. All the students study the Bible two hours a week in regular courses. The attendance at the Chapel service is exceptionally good. The practice of having the students report each week as to their church attendance has been continued.

With the opening of a new school year in April, 1931, it is altogether probable that our Chapel room will be too small. If so, it will be a serious handicap to the work of the College. It is hoped that the Board of Managers will at once undertake to find some solution of this problem which is facing us.

XI. Athletics

The past has been a dull year in inter-collegiate athletics due to the strike of June,1929. The loss of students plus the disturbed mental attitude of those in attendance made it inadvisable to attempt any inter-collegiate sports.

The usual middle school Field Meet was held on September 23rd, 1929. This was the 7th Annual Meet and 8 schools with about 150 athletes participated.

During this year we have attempted several branches of Physical Training,namely, Soccer and Rugby Football, Tennis, Baseball, Track, Basketball, Judo.

On June 21, 1930, we held our 1st annual middle school Judo Meet in which 4 schools participated.

The annual baseball matches with the Keijo Government Medical College were held in June and resulted in our defeat by 2 out of 3 games.

On September 20th our Basketball team brought home the pennant in the All Korea Basketball Tournament held under the auspices of the Central Y. M. C. A.

This fall the 8th Annual Field Meet was held on September 24th with seven schools and 130 athletes participating.

On October 11th we expect to hold the 1st Annual Middle School Tennis Meet. We hope to make a contribution to the development of athletics and physical training and the spirit of sportsmanship by these middle school meets. We also find them to be of good advertising value for the College.

XII. Other items of interest

1. Library Of the items of special interest in connection with the library the first is the splendid gift of ¥6,000 by Messrs. Won Yong Lee, Whan Yong Lee, Hee Yong Lee and Pai Yong Lee for the purchase of the 848 volumes of the Chronicles

of the Yi Dynasty now being published. This gift was secured for the College largely through the efforts of Mr. S. T. Lee, Director of the Commercial Department.

The Friendly Association composed of the Korean members of the staff are making an annual gift of Y100 for the purchase of valuable old Korean books.

A new departure which proves to be of great help in building up our library is the collection of a fee of one Yen from all new students the proceeds of which are set aside for the library.

2. Music The musical training of the students has progressed very satisfactorily under the leadership of Prof. Rody Hyun and with the assistance of Mrs. A. L. Becker, Mrs. H. A. Rhodes, and Mrs. B. W. Billings has since her return already been of great assistance. A number of successful concerts were held during the year and one or two concert tours during vacation periods, concerts being given in Chairyung, Sariwon, Songdo, Suwon, Chungju, Chunju, Kwangju, Mokpo, Taiku, and Fusan.

Music has also been furnished for other College programs. Over 25% of the students participate in these activities while all enjoy the Chapel singing and music work at that period under Mr. Hyun's leadership.

3. Museum The Museum Committee has secured a large number of valuable portraits of famous Koreans and photos of famous places in Korea which now decorate the College walls. Dr. K. S. Oh has given the College a valuable collection of over 180 Korean coin chains and amulets.

4. Student Help Prof. C. H. Lee, now on Sabbatical leave in America has secured over Y1,300 from Korean friends in America for a Student Help Fund. It is our hope that the growth of this fund may solve this pressing problem.

5. Clubs and Organizations

A. C.C.C. Students Association (The Student Body)

B. C.C.C. Y. M. C. A. (Voluntary organization)

C. Literary Friends Club (Students of Literary Department)

D. Economic Research Club (Commercial Department Students)

E. Science Research Club (Science Department Students)

F. Glee Club

G. Orchestra

H. Band

I. Oratorical Club
(Voluntary, all departments)

J. Friendly Association
(Korean Teaching and Office Staff)

K. Dramatic Club
(Voluntary, all departments)

XIII. Enrolment

Annual average of the students who paid tuition during the past three years:

1927 - 1928	204
1928 - 1929	214
1929 - 1930	142

Up to May 10, 1930, there was a total enrolment of 212 students distributed as follows:

Class	Lit.Dept.	Com.Dept.	Sc.Dept	Total
Freshman	26	63	20	109
Sophomore	15	14	4	33
Junior	14	31	11	56
Senior	9	—	5	14
	64	108	40	212

XIV. Classification of Students

A. Regular Students

Literary Department	43	
Commercial Department	85	
Science Department	32	160

B. Special Students

Literary Department	18	
Commercial Department	26	
Science Department	8	52
		212

XV. Provinces from which students come

Province	Number	Percentage
North Ham Kyung	8	3.8
South Ham Kyung	22	10.4
North Pyung An	7	3.3
South Pyung An	23	10.9
Whang Hai	14	6.6
Kyung Ki	73	34.3
Kang Won	7	3.3
North Choong Chung	5	2.4
South Choong Chung	22	10.4
North Chun La	9	4.2
South Chun La	10	4.7
North Kyung Sang	8	3.8
South Kyung Sang	4	1.9
	212	100%

XVI. Students' Church Relations

Department	Literary				Commercial			Science				Total
Class	1	2	3	4	1	2	3	1	2	3	4	11
Presbyterian Mission	7	7	2	2	18	4	16	4	3	4	2	69
Northern Methodist	7	3	7	3	23	4	6	6	1	3	3	66
Southern Methodist	4	4	3	3	7	4	9	4	0	2	0	40
Other	0	0	2	0	0	0	0	1	0	1	0	4
Non-Christian	5	0	0	1	10	1	0	3	0	0	0	20
No Report	1	1	0	0	7	1	0	2	0	1	0	13
Total	24	15	14	9	65	14	31	20	4	11	5	212

Department	Class	Baptized	Catechumen	New-Believer	Non-Xn	Total
	Freshman	9	2	7	5	23
Literary	Sophomore	8	3	3	0	14
	Junior	10	1	3	0	14
	Senior	8	0	0	1	9
	Freshman	20	5	23	10	58
Commercial	Sophomore	6	1	5	1	13
	Senior	17	9	5	0	31
Science	Freshman	10	2	3	3	18
	Sophomore	3	1	0	0	4
	Junior	6	2	2	0	10
	Senior	3	1	1	0	5
No Report		13 →	—	—	—	—
Total		100 13	27	52	20	212

XVII. The Total Number of Graduates from each Department

(March 31, 1930)

Department	Number	Percentage
Literary	96	35.42
Commercial	123	45.39
Science Department	49	18.08
Agricultural (not operating) . .	3	1.11
Total	271	100%

XVIII. Occupation of Graduates (August 31, 1930)

Occupation	Number	Percentage
Teachers of C. C. C.	6	2.21
Secretaries of C. C. C.	5	1.84
Teacher in Christian Schools	41	15.12
Church Work	20	7.38
Studying in Theological Seminary	1	.36
Teachers in Non-Christian Schools	16	5.90
Studying in U.S.A.	35	12.91
Studying in Japan	3	1.10
Studying in Korea	4	1.47
Journalist	3	1.10

Occupation	Number	Percentage
Literary Work	4	1.47
Office work	26	9.59
Official	15	5.53
Industrial Enterprise	23	8.89
Agriculture	2	.73
Private work	51	18.81
Deceased	16	5.90
Total	271	100 %

XIX. Government Qualifications

The graduates of the College are given qualification by the Government to teach in Private Higher Common Schools and Industrial Schools on the Following subjects:-

To the graduates of Literary Department

English (Korean & Chinese)

To the graduates of the Commercial Department

English, Commerce, and Bookkeeping

To the graduates of the Science Department

Mathematics, Physics, and Chemistry

to the graduates of the Agricultural Department (not operating).

Agriculture

XX. Changes in Regulations and Administration

1. Feeling the disadvantages inherent in a 3 term system the College petitioned the Government and received permission to make the change to a 2 semester system. The semesters are approximately from April to October and October to March.

2. The College has also been given the privilege of giving a Bachelor's degree in each department as Bachelor of Literature or Commercial or Science, or Theology.

3. To secure the best guidance and most individualized treatment of the students a system of student advisors has been put into effect whereby each of the full time teachers has from five to ten students under his direct care and guidance. It is hoped that this will be of great assistance in the spiritual and intellectual guidance of the students.

Respectfully, submitted,

U. K. Yu, Dean

40. 원한경 부교장의 이사회 제출 연례보고서

문서 제목	Chosen Christian College, Annual Report for the fiscal year 1930~1931
문서 종류	부교장 보고서
제출 시기	1931년 9월 25일
작성 장소	서울
제 출 자	H. H. Underwood
수 신 자	이사회
페이지 수	6
출 처	Korea Mission Records, 1904~1960, Box 15, Folder 15 (PHS) 2114-5-2: 08 Board of Managers 1928~1931 (UMAH)

자료 소개

원한경 부교장이 1931년 9월 25일 열린 이사회에서 5월에 도미한 교장을 대신하여 제출한 연례보고서이다. 일자가 명시되지는 않았지만, 연례회의가 9월 25일 열렸기 때문에 이 날이 제출일이다. 이날 회의에서 이사회는 초등학교(연희보명학교) 건립위원회를 만들었고, 연합교회(Union Church)를 세우는 문제를 논의하였으며, 1929년에 신설된 대학 교무위원회의 규정을 고쳐 교수회가 새로운 구성원들을 뽑을 수 있게 하였다. 또한 윤치호가 동서양 서적들과 ¥2,000의 도서기금을 기부하고 남궁억이 한국의 옛 화폐와 옛 우표를 기증한 것에 대해 감사 표시를 하기로 의결하였다.

원한경은 이 보고서에서 아래의 사항들을 간략하게 설명하였다.

교수, 이사회 회의, 협력이사회 회계의 내한 방문, 등록생, 졸업생, 재정, 종교활동, 방과 후 학생 활동, 운동경기, 출판물, 농촌 사역, 자산 상황.

내용 요약

교수: 한 해 동안 학교가 결정적인 발전을 이루었다. 남감리교 선교사 스피델(Speidel)이 히치 대신 부임하였고, 빌링스와 이춘호가 안식년을 끝내고 복귀하였다. 에비슨 교장이 5월에, 유억겸이 7월에 미국에 가서, 부교장이 교장을 대리하고 이춘호가 학감을 대리하고 있다. 상과의 최순주와 노동규가 조교수로 승진하였다.

이사회: 이사회가 지난해 10월 회의 때 임원들을 재선출하였고, 3월 회의 때 정관을 개정하였다.

내한 방문: 뉴욕 협력이사회의 회계 서덜랜드(Geo. F. Surtherland)가 한국을 방문하여 대학을 둘러보고 재정 문제에 관해 소중한 조언을 해주었다.

등록생 · 졸업생: 학생 수가 지난 3월 말에 183명이었다가 새 학기 5월에 256명(문과 74명, 상과 136명, 수물과 46명)이 되었다. 졸업생은 총 314명이다.

재정: 학교 재정에서 지난해 ¥3,700 이상 잔액을 남겨 긴급한 일에 사용하고 있다. 언더우드관 건축기금 잔액 ¥23,000으로 땅을 사고 남은 ¥15,000을 기본재산으로 넘겼다.

종교활동: 에비슨 교장이 모든 과의 4학년 학생에게 성경 강의를 하였다. 채플 예배는 담당자가 빌링스로 바뀌었고, 현제명이 음악으로 봉사하고 있으며, 전체 교수들이 교대로 설교하고 있다. 에비슨이 부활절 날 연합교회(Union Church)를 출발시켜 종교부가 예배를 이끌고 있다. 특별 부흥집회가 2월에 열렸고, 학생들이 주말과 여름방학 때 지원해서 봉사활동을 하고 있다.

방과 후 활동: 방과 후에 현제명이 교수 부인들의 도움을 받아 오케스트라, 밴드, 합창단을 훈련하면서 서울에서 봄가을에 음악회를 열고 지방 순회공연을 하였다. 음악부도 야외 음악회들을 개최하였고, 중등학교 교사들과 교회 지도자들을 위한 하기강습회를 학교에서 개최하였다.

운동경기: 야구, 축구, 육상 선수들이 대회에서 우승하였고, 럭비, 아이스하키, 등반을 새로 시작하였다. 전국 중등학교 대상 유도, 테니스, 육상, 야구 대회들을 개최하였다.

출판물: 문과에서 최현배, 정인보의 연구 논문들을 담은 논문집[『조선어문연구』]을 발행하였고, 중등학교 영어의 표준에 관해 연구하고 있으며, 문과 3학년생들은 영어 연극을 공연하였다. 학생회는 『연희』지를 반년마다 발행하고 있고, YMCA 학생들도 잡지[『시온』]를 발행하고 있으며, 수물과와 상과에서도 연구 논문들을 발표하고 있다.

농촌 사역: 이사회가 4월 회의에서 학교 땅 15에이커가량을 YMCA의 농촌 사역에 쓰게 하기로 의결하였다. 수물과에서도 토양과 비료 등에 관해 특별한 실험을 하고 있다.

자산: 캠퍼스 부지에 관해 별다른 변동은 없었고, 모범촌 일대의 땅을 샀으며, 30,000그루의 나무를 산지에 심었다.

CHOSEN CHRISTIAN COLLEGE

Annual Report for the fiscal year 1930-1931

The past year at the Chosen Christian College has been one of satisfactory uninterrupted study and decided progress but lacking in those startlingly features which are dear to the heart of the reporter.

FACULTY

Mr. Speidel has come to us a representative of the Southern Methodist Mission to take the place of Mr. Hitch. Mr. Speidel has thrown himself into the study of Language with marked success but has also found time for special evangelistic work. He has initiated and carried on a Sunday afternoon service in English in one of the city churches which has attracted a large number of non-Christian students from all over the city. Mrs. Speidel has been most helpful in assisting the other ladies of the Faculty on all the social occasions where their services are in demand. Mr. Speidel is also an accomplished pianist and has done much with his music. He will take up class work at the College this fall as a member of the Commercial Department Faculty.

Dr. B. W. Billings returned from furlough during the summer and has had charge of the daily chapel services in addition to his regular teaching. Mr. C. H. Lee, Director of the Science Department also returned to us from a year of Sabbatical leave in America. In addition to making many valuable contacts and studying a large number of scientific insitutions, Mr. Lee secured pledges for over ¥6,000 for student help and scholarships. This year Professor Takahashi goes to Japan for six months of Sabbatical leave and Prof. U. K. Yu, our Dean, goes to America in July to attend the Y. M. C. A. conferences in Toronto and Cleveland and to spend eight or ten months studying administrative methods on American colleges and universities.

Dr. Avison left us in May to attend the Decennial Conference of the Presbyterian Mission Board and to carry on work for the two colleges in America. His leaving was the occasion for a great series of farewells and the scene at the railway station was a wonderful testimony to the esteem in which he is held by the Korean people. According to the Korean papers over 800 people were on the platform to bid him "bon voyage". At the College the Annual Founders Day Program was combined with a Farewell to Dr. & Mrs. Avison. On this occasion the students and faculty presented to the College a beautifully framed photo of Dr. Avison and he was informed of the creation by Faculty and students of a Memorial Fund of One Thousand Yen the interest on which is to be used to purchase books for the Library these books to form the Avison Collection. To Mrs. Avison was given a beautiful coat of Korean figured silk.

In the absence of Dr. Avison the Vice President, Dr. Underwood, will act in his place and Mr. C. H. Lee will perform the duties of Dean during Prof. Yu's leave. The work of Dr. S. J. Chey and Mr. T. K. Noh was recognized by the Board at the spring meeting and they were promoted to be Assistant professors.

BOARD MEETINGS

The Field Board of Managers met twice during the year once in October for the regular annual meeting and once in March. At the October meeting the election resulted in the reelection of the former officers. The president's report was read and the usual routine business was conducted. The March meeting was necessitated by the need of certain technical changes in the constitution which were unanimously passed. This meeting also reaffirmed the approval formerly given for President Avison's return to America and again gave its approval to the Y. M. C. A. agricultural project which is referred to in this report.

Dr. Geo. F. Sutherland's VISIT

The college was most fortunate in having on the field for a brief visit Dr. Geo. F. Sutherland, Treasurer of the Cooperating Board in New York. Dr. Sutherland thus saw the college for himself and came to understand the situation in a way which will be of great value to us later when questions arise in New York. Dr. Sutherland also brought to us much valuable advice and counsel from his ripe experience in financial matters and a point of view which was and is most helpful.

ENROLLMENT

The average enrollment for the year April, 1930, to March 1931 was 183. The new year brought in a large entering class so that in May, 1931, the enrollment stood at 256, divided as follows: Commerce-136; Literature-74; and Science-46. The class and department figures are as follows:

Year		Departments			
		Literary	Commercial	Science	Total
IV		11	- - -	10	21
III		11	12	4	27
II		20	43	9	72
I		32	81	23	136
	Total	74	136	46	256

GRADUATES

In March 43 were graduated bringing the total number of graduates up to 314. Of this years class, 9 were from the Literary Department, 5 from the Science, and 29 from the Commercial Department. Of these 43, about 30 secured positions at once which seemed a good testimony to the standing of the school as a number of colleges were unable to place even a third of their graduates.

FINANCES

It is with great pleasure that we are again able to report a balance on the budget for the year 1930-31, amounting this time to over ¥3,700. This balance has been assigned to a number of pressing needs which the College had previously been unable to meet.

SPECIAL GIFTS: The balance on the Underwood Hall Fund was reported to Mr. Underwood and he has directed that over ¥23,000 of it shall be used for necessary purchases of land and that most of the remainder (something over ¥15,000) shall be set aside as endowment for the upkeep of Underwood Hall. This amounts to a new gift of almost ¥40,000.

The gift of ¥1,000 as an Avison Memorial Library Fund has already been mentioned, as also the fact that Mr. C. H. Lee secured pledges of over ¥6,000 for student help and scholships. Mr. Lee was also able to secure a reduction on a 40-line Telephone switchboard for the College which amounts to a gift of about ¥2,000.

The first payment of ¥1,000 on the splendid gift of ¥6,000 for the Chronicles of the Yi Dynasty has been received as had the first installment of the books themselves.

RELIGIOUS WORK

The religious work of the College and students includes the regular Bible Classes in all Departments, the daily chapel services, special revival services, the conduct of the newly opened Union Church and the voluntary work of the students on week-ends and during vacations.

The Bible teaching is largely done by Drs. Paik and Rhodes though during the past year Dr. Avison conducted a very inspiring Bible course for the seniors of all departments. Teaching is also done by other members of the faculty.

The chapel services formerly under the charge of Dr. Rhodes are now a part of Dr. Billings' service for the College. Once a week the Student Y. M. C. A. takes charge and secures a speaker from Seoul or elsewhere. A large number of distinguished visitors have given the students an opportunity to listen to a number of prominent men from abroad, and from time to time Mr. Rody Hyun is given the chapel period for a special musical service, special hymns and religious songs being mimeographed for the occasion. The remainder of the time the various teachers take their turn in leading chapel, and the quality of the addresses delivered is of a remarkably high average.

Dr. Avison opened the new Union Church services on Easter Sunday and these services, Sunday School, Sunday morning and evening worship and Wednesday evening prayer service are now in the hands of the Religious Work Committee of the College. The project is a splendid one, of one Union Church to serve the surrounding community and all the educational institutions which may locate in the neighborhood. Like all worthwhile projects it will take hard work to insure success but a good beginning has been made.

In February the usual week of special services was held. This year the meetings were led by the Rev. I. Y. Kim and the Rev. C. S. Chung both of whom brought a very real and vital message to the students and faculty. An innovation for this year were the evening meetings led by Rev. C. S. Chung. So large a proportion of our students live in the city that the student attendance at the evening services was not large but the dormitory students and people from the local villages attended despite the seas of mud and floods of rain which prevailed at that time.

The voluntary religious work on the part of the students is largely in the hands of the student Y. M. C. A. This organization is in a more thriving condition than in years. The usual forms of work are through the D. V. B. S. in the summer and special preaching bands in both the summer and winter vacations. Less spectacular but equally valuable is the service rendered to over 40 churches and Sunday Schools every Sunday in supplying teachers, preachers, music leaders, etc. The Y. M. C. A. also publishes a quarterly magazine, gives plays of a religious character, conducts student Bible classes; and this year is planning to place special emphasis on personal work among the students.

EXTRA-CURRICULAR ACTIVITIES

MUSIC has had a larger part in the life of the College than ever before. Prof. Rody Hyun, assisted by Mrs. A. L. Becker and Mrs. H. A. Rhodes have developed and trained the orchestra, band and chorus till they are beyond the best we had hoped. Spring and Fall concerts were given in Seoul and concert tours to Chungju, Chunju, Mokpo, Kunsan, Kwangju, Taiku, Fusan, Suwon, Sariwon, Chairyung, Pyengyang and other points. The special musical chapel services have already been mentioned. The Music Committee has also arranged hillside vesper services for the Union Church, outdoor concerts on the campus and other musical programs.

This summer a special conference of High School Music Teachers and leaders of church music will be held at the College.

ATHLETICS

The C. C. C. has "come back" in athletics during the last year. We won the basketball championship in three different leagues, won the championship Soccer Banner of the Korea Athletic Association and won the Intercollegiate Track Meet. New departures for the year are Rugby Football, Ice-Hockey and Climbing. The Climbers made their debut by planting a C. C. C. banner on one of the most inaccessible peaks of the famous Samkak San. Rugby has not yet made its formal bow and ice hockey for the first year will be confined to practice on our rink now building.

For middle schools, meets were held in Judo, Tennis, Track and Basketball thus helping to stimulate physical training and athletics all over the country.

PUBLICATIONS

The catalogue promised last year had to be postponed but will appear this year. The Literary Department has published Prof. Choi's work on the Grammar of the Korean Language, Prof. I. P. Chung's paper on Korean Literature and a reprint of Dr. Underwood's Bibliography of Occidental Works on Korea. The Literary Department made a special study of English standards in Middle Schools preparing, giving and scoring English tests for almost 7,000 students in some thirty schools. The scores have been reported to the schools concerned but the more detailed study and report on the tests is not yet ready for publication. Though not a publication, the English play given by the Junior Class of the Literary Department certainly deserves mention as an extra curricular activity. The "Yun Heui" a semi-annual put out by the

- 6 -

Student Association, and the Y. M. C. A. magazine already mentioned, represent the student publications. The Science Department has published two research papers on "The Pine Tree Pest" and on "A New Hand-Spinning Machine". The members of the Commercial Faculty have contributed largely to other periodicals and magazines but have not published any special report this year.

AGRICULTURAL WORK

No direct agricultural work is now being carried out at the College but in accordance with the vote of the Board of Managers at the meeting in April 1930 a tract of about 15 acres has been turned over to the Rural Work department of the Y. M. C. A. for a special agricultural project. In connection with this it is their expectation to erect temporary buildings and open a Farm School for both Men and Women. In this work it is our hope to cooperate through our students and through our staff. The Science Department is also carrying on special tests and experiments with soils, fertilizers, etc.

PROPERTY

No special changes or additions in property are to be reported. The exchanges with the Railway Bureau and the completion of the new suburban line with a "Yun Heui" station have brought us into much better communication with the city and constitute an important step forward in the development of the school. A number of plots in the model village section have been purchased and over 30,000 trees planted on our hillsides. The trees planted are in the main Pine-nut pines, a pine-worm-resisting pine, and a number of larches.

Property, finances, faculty, enrollment, even formal religious work, all may show satisfactory reports and yet we may fail to secure the desired results. For these results depend not on qualification or equipment but on our personal closeness to Christ and our willingness to accept His guidance for ourselves and for those whom it is folly for us to attempt to guide in our own strength or wisdom. While thanking God for His guidance in the past we can but pray for His continued presence with us that this institution may be used as He would have it used.

Respectfully submitted,

Horace H. Underwood

Acting-President

41. 이춘호 학감 대리의 이사회 제출 연례보고서

문서 제목	Chosen Christian College, Report of the Dean
문서 종류	학감 보고서
제출 시기	1931년 9월 25일
작성 장소	서울
제 출 자	이춘호
수 신 자	이사회
페이지 수	14
출 처	Korea Mission Records, 1904~1960, Box 15, Folder 15 (PHS) 2114-5-2: 08 Board of Managers 1928~1931 (UMAH)

자료 소개

이춘호 학감 대리가 1931년 9월 25일 열린 이사회 연례회의에서 제출한 보고서이다. 유억겸 학감이 안식년을 얻어 이 해 7월 미국에 감에 따라 이춘호가 보고서를 작성하였다. 수물과 과장이던 이춘호가 학감직을 대리하게 되자 베커가 수물과 과장직을 대리하였다.

이춘호는 이 보고서의 목차를 아래와 같이 꾸몄다. 유억겸의 보고서와 비슷한 형식으로 작성하였지만, XI에서 도서관을 단독 항목으로 설정하였고, XII에서 운동경기와 다른 업무들을 하나의 항목으로 합쳤다.

I. 서언, II. 운영진, III. 대학 교무위원회, IV. 대학 예산위원회, V. 교수진, VI. 사무직원, VII. 안식년 중인 임원진, VIII. 교육 조력자, IX. 학과 X. 종교부, XI. 도서관, XII. 운동경기 및 다른 업무들(음악, 장학금, 박물관, 학생 클럽), XIII. 등록생, XIV. 본과와 별과, XV. 학생 출신 지역, XVI. 학생 종교, XVII. 졸업생 수, XVIII. 졸업생 직업, XIX. 졸업생의 교사 자격.

내용 요약

I. 에비슨 교장과 유억겸 학감이 미국에 갔다. 교장 대리 원한경의 리더십과 교수들의 협력으로 본교가 꾸준히 발전하고 있다.

II~VIII. 운영진은 교장, 부교장, 학감(부재 중), 회계 및 사업 매니저, 학감 대리(이춘호)

이다. 대학 교무위원회는 에비슨, 원한경, 유억겸, 백낙준, 이순탁, 이춘호, 로즈로 구성되어 있다. 대학 예산위원회는 교장, 부교장, 학감, 과장들, 베커, 오웬스로 구성되어 있다. 교수와 조교수는 총 25명(한국인 교수 11명, 조교수 2명)이고, 전임강사는 4명, 강사와 조수는 11명, 사무직원(사감 포함)은 6명이다. 안식년 중인 교수는 이춘호, 히치이고, 사임한 교수는 조병옥이다. 교수 부인 4명이 교육을 돕고 있다.

IX. 본교는 종합대학 체제를 이루고 있다. 문과는 백낙준 과장을 포함하여 18명(교수 10명, 조교수 1명, 전임강사 2명, 강사 5명)이 72명의 학생을 가르치면서, 논문집과 연구서 논문들을 발행하고, 한국문화와 중등학교 영어교육의 표준 정하기 위해 조사하고 있다. 능력 있는 후원자들이 이 대학을 한국문화연구의 중심지로 만들게 해주기를 바란다. 상과는 이순탁 과장을 포함하여 14명(교수 5명, 조교수 3명, 강사 6명)이 133명의 학생을 가르치고 연구조사를 하고 있다. 상품진열관이 꾸준히 발전하면서 국내외에서 견본들을 모으고 있다. 수물과는 과장대리 베커를 포함하여 13명(교수 7명, 강사 4명, 조수 2명)이 44명의 학생을 가르치고 있다. 이춘호, 신제린, 김영성이 제주도에서 식물과 광물을 조사하였고, 교수와 학생이 과학적 농법과 한옥 건축의 개선책 등을 연구하고 있다.

X. 부활절에 연합교회가 정규 예배를 시작하여, 주일 낮 예배에 평균 70명이 참석하고 있다. 유백희 목사가 담임을 맡고, 백남석이 주일학교를 맡고 있으며, 김정란을 전도부인으로 고용하였다. 학생들이 일요일과 여름방학에 많은 교회를 열심히 돕고 있다.

XI. 도서관이 커져서 전담 직원 2명이 필요하다. 11,500권을 소장하고 있는데, 윤치호 등으로부터 기증받았고, 시설과 예산을 확충하였다.

XII. 중등학교 야구, 테니스, 육상, 유도 대회들을 성공적으로 개최하였고, 학교의 야구팀과 축구팀도 큰 승리를 거두었다. 음악은 음악부의 관리, 현제명의 지도, 선교사 교수 부인들의 조력으로 크게 발전하였고, 현제명과 베커 부인이 격주로 연습시키고 특별 성악반을 지도하였으며, 여러 음악회와 하기강습회를 개최하였다. 학생장학금은 이춘호가 미국에서 ¥6,000을 구해왔고, 미국의 한국친우회가 기금 지급을 약속하였다. 박물관은 남궁억이 12세기 한국 화폐와 광무 연간의 우표를, 이태웅이 산호와 조개 장식품을 기증하였다. 학생 클럽 및 교직원회 명단은 전년도 보고서의 내용과 같다.

XIII~XVI. 학생은 1931년 5월 10일까지 총 250명(문과 72명, 상과 133명, 수물과 45명)이었다. 본과는 211명, 별과는 39명이었고, 학생들이 제주도를 제외한 전 도에서 왔다. (과별 종교 상황은 표를 참고.)

XVII~XIX. 졸업생은 3월 31일까지 총 314명이고, 현재 연전 교수 4명, 연전 사무직원 10명, 다른 기독교 학교 교사 44명, 교회사역 20명, 신학생 2명, 비기독교 학교 교사 14명, 미국 유학 36명, 일본 유학 2명, 언론인 5명, 문필가 4명, 사무직 47명, 공무원 20명, 산업(공업) 26명, 농업 7명, 개인사업 54명, 사망 18명, 의사 1명이다. 졸업생은 중등학교 교사 자격을 문과는 영어, 조선어, 중국어(한문)에서, 상과는 영어, 상업, 부기에서, 수물과는 수학, 물리학, 화학에서 인정받고 있다.

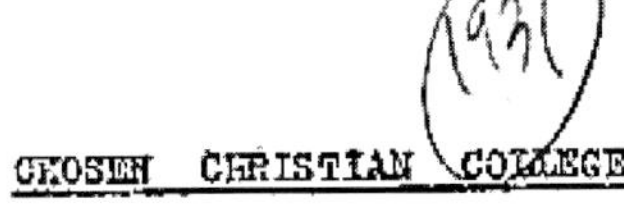

CHOSEN CHRISTIAN COLLEGE

Report of the Dean

I. Introductory Remarks

To the Field Board of Managers at the Board Meeting held September 25th, 1931.

Gentlemen:

I have the honor to submit the following report concerning the academic phase of the College administration for the academic year 1930-31.

During the year the College has greatly missed its President, O. R. Avison, and Dean U. K. Yu. President Avison who is now on furlough went to America at the beginning of the present academic year and is now engaged in the promotion of the interest of our institution in New York. Dean is on his sabbatical leave. He went to America at the end of the present academic year and is now engaged in further study along the line of "Administrative Work" in New York. We all hope that Dr. Avison and Dean Yu may enjoy the months while staying in America and be successful along the lines of their respective endeavors, (which we are sure will be profitable to the College when they return).

Under the leadership of Dr. H. H. Underwood, Acting President, and the hearty cooperation of all members of the faculty the College has moved steadily toward the objectives set forth at the foundation of the institution. Several events to be described later, undoubtedly mark wholesome progress in all departments of the College.

II. Administrative Officers

O. R. Avison, M.D., LL. D., President. (leave on absence)
H. H. Underwood, Ph.D., Vice-President
U. K. Yu, Gakushi, Dean, (leave on absence)
H. T. Owens, Treasurer and Business Manager
C. H. Lee, Acting Dean

III. College Council

O. R. Avison, M.D., LL.D., President (leave on absence)
H. H. Underwood, Ph.D., Vice-President
U. K. Yu, Gakushi, Dean, (leave on absence)
A. L. Becker, Ph.D., Acting Director of the Science Department
L. G. Paik, Ph.D.,
Director of the Liberary Department
S. T. Lee, Gakushi,
Director of the Commercial Department
C. H. Lee, M.A., Acting Dean,
Director of the Science Department
H. A. Rhodes, D.D.,
Director of the Religious Department

V. College Budget Committee

O. R. Avison, M.D., LL.D., President, (leave on absence)
H. H. Underwood, Ph.D., Vice-President
U. K. Yu, Gakushi, Dean, (leave on absence)
L. G. Paik, Ph.D., Director of the Literary Department
S. T. Lee, Gakushi, Director of the Commercial Department
C. H. Lee, M.A. Director of the Science Department
A. L. Becker, Ph.D., Professor of Physics
H. T. Owens, Treasurer & Business Manager

. Faculty

A. Professors

O. R. Avison, M.D., LL.D., (Toronto and Wooster) President of the College, (leave on absence) (Q)
H. H. Underwood, B.A., M.A., Ph.D., (New York) Vice-President of the College and Professor of Education, Psychology and English (Q)
U. K. Yu, Gakushi, (Tokyo University) Dean of the College and Professor of Law (leave on absence) (Q)
L. G. Paik, A.B., Th.B., M.A., Ph.D., (Yale) Director of Literary Department and Professor of Occidental History and Bible (Q)
S. T. Lee, Gakushi, (Kyoto Imperial) Director of Commercial Department and Professor of Economics, Insurance, Statistics, and Abacus (Q)
C. H. Lee, A.B., M.A., (Ohio State) Director of Science Department and Professor of Mathematics (Q)
A. L. Becker, BA., M.A., Ph.D., (Michigan) Professor of Physics and Mathematics (Q)
E. H. Miller, B.A., B.D., M.A., Ph.D. (Columbia) Professor of Chemistry and English (Q)
B. W. Billings, B.ph., B.D., M.A., S.T.M., D.D. (Depauw) Professor of Occidental History, Bible and English (Q)
H. A. Rhodes, B.A., M.A., B.D., D.D. (Grove City) Professor of Bible and English (Q)
J. E. Fisher, B.A., M.A., Ph.D. (Columbia) Professor of Education and English (Q)
J. W. Hitch, LL.B. (University of Georgia) Professor of English, (leave on absence) (Q)
K. Takahashi, (Tokyo Imperial) Professor of Morals and Japanese Civil Government (Q)

N. S. Paik, B.S., M.A. (Emory)
Professor of English and Education (Q)

N. W. Paik, Gakushi, (Tokyo University of Commerce)
Professor of Commerce, Bank Bookkeeping, History of Commerce, Commercial Japanese, Accounting, and Sociology (Q)

K. Katowaki, Gakushi, (Kyoto Imperial)
Professor of Chemistry, Mechanical Drawing (Q)

H. P. Choi, Gakushi, (Kyoto Imperial)
Professor of Philosophy, Education, Ethics, and Korean Language (Q)

D. W. Lee, Graduate of C.C.C., B.A., M.A., Ph.D. (Michigan)
Professor of Mathematics and Astronomy (Q)

S. Nikaido, Gakushi (Tokyo Imperial)
Professor of Japanese, Japanese Literature and Introduction to Literature (Q)

P. C. Son, Gakushi (Tokyo University of Commerce)
Professor of Commercial Arithmetic, Commercial Bookkeeping, Exchange, Custom House and Ware House (Q)

P. C. Kim, Gakushi (Waseda University)
Professor of Physics, Electrical Engineering, and Mathematics (Q)

H. Kaiya, Gakushi, (Tofuku Imperial)
Professor of Mathematics, Surveying, Physics, Civil Engineering, Drawing, Geology, and Minerology (Q)

S. K. Hong, B. A. (Ohio State)
Professor of English (Q)

I. P. Chung, Professor of Chinese Literature and Korean Literature (Q)

C. M. Hyun, M.Mus. (Gunn School of Music and Dramatic Art, Chicago)
Assistant Professor of Music (Q)

T. K. Noh, Graduate of C.C.C., Gakushi (Kyoto Imperial)
Assistant Professor of Commercial Geography, Transportation, Economic Policy and Commercial English (Q)

S. J. Chey, Graduate of C.C.C., B.S., M.B.A., Ph.D. (New York)
Assistant Professor of Commercial Practice, Commercial English and Typewriting (Q)

G. C. Speidel, (M.A.) Assistant Professor of English (Q)

Instructors

Mrs. H. H. Underwood, B.A., M.A. (New York)
English (Q)

O. Y. Lee, (Berlin University)
German

Lecturers and Assistants

I. S. Chung, Oriental History

K. W. Chang, Graduate of C.C.C., Gakushi (Tohoku Imperial)
Mathematics (Q)

M. H. Lee, B.A.,M.A., (Columbia)
Biology
K. S. Oh, Graduate of the Government Seoul Foreign Language School.
Chinese Language
Insup Chung, Gakushi (Waseda University)
English and Introduction to Literature (Q)
Y. C. Lee, Oriental History
K. H. Chung, Gakushi (Tokyo Imperial University)
Instructor in Law (Q)
L. W. Kang, Physical Education
C. R. Cynn, Graduate of C.C.C.
Assistant, Physics Laboratory
Y. S. Kim, Graduate of C.C.C.
Assistant, Chemistry Laboratory

NOTE: "Q" signifies Government Qualification
"Gakushi" is equivalent to M.A. in American Universities

VI. Office and Administration Staff

K. C. Lyu, Graduate of C.C.C.
General Office Secretary
W. S. Youn, Graduate of C.C.C.
Assistant Treasurer
C. M. Song, Graduate of C.C.C.
Dormitory Superintendent
C. K. Kim, Graduate of C.C.C.
Superintendent of Grounds and Buildings
H. R. Roe, Junior Office Secretary
K. S. Lyu, Graduate of C.C.C.
Library Secretary
P. H. Yu, B.A.,M.A.,B.D., (Southern Methodist University)
Student Pastor

VII. College Officers on Furlough

President O. R. Avison, on furlough
Dean U. K. Yu, leave on absence

VIII. Other Assistants in instruction and Music

Mrs. H. A. Rhodes
Mrs. B. W. Billings
Mrs. A. L. Becker
Mrs. J. E. Fisher

IX. The Three Departments of the College

The College is organized on a university system and has four departments but only three are in operation. These departments are separate so far as their internal organization is concerned with their respective directors, budgets and recitation halls, but they are one in general administration and policy under one Dean.

1. Report of the Literary Department

The Literary Department has had another year of progress and improvements. The faculty of the Department is composed with 10 full professors, 1 Assistant Professor, 2 Instructors and 5 Lecturers; making a total teaching staff of 18 members. The Rev. L. G. Paik, Ph.D. is the director of the Department. There has been no change in the faculty except that Mr. K. Takahashi, Professor of Morals and Ethics, was granted leave of absence for six months. He is absent during the first semester and Prof. H. P. Choi and Dr. L. G. Paik are filling his place in the Department. Mr. Takahashi is expected to return from his educational trip to Japan at the beginning of the second semestor to resume his duties. The enrolment of the Department shows a marked tendency of increase. There are 31 Freshmen, 20 Sophomores, 10 Juniors and 11 Seniors making a total of 72 fully enrolled students over against 64 in the last year. Inspite of the prevalent tendency in education toward practical training, the increase evidently indicate the general appreciation of cultural studies on the part of our students. As it was reported previously, as an initial enterprise of the department, there was published a Research Bulletin of 109 pages containing Prof. I. P. Chung's work on the history of the Korean Literature, and Prof. H. P. Choi's studies on Korean Grammar. The book has been well received by scholars in Korea and Japan. Dr. H. H. Underwood's work on the Bibliography of Occidental Works on Korea is being reprinted. This being the first serious work on the subject, it is believed it will mark a notable contribution. While individual teacher carries on his private research in his chosen field, a Study Group has recently been formed for cooperative investigation on the Korean culture. Other similar groups are being formed. It is becoming an established event for the Junior class to give a play in English. The Junior Class of the last year gave Jean Valjean as a class play before the College audience under the direction of Mrs. H. H. Underwood, instructor in English. Under the direction of Dr. Underwood, the Department made a special study of English standards in middle schools in Korea. The preparation of materials for the test, giving of the test to almost 7,000 students in some thirty schools, the scoring of results and making of the pleminary report have already been done. But more detailed study and fuller report has not yet been completed. The Department has been making a special effort for the collection of old Korean books. While these books have already become rare, it is quite expensive to purchase what have been offered to us. However many volumes of valuable books and manuscripts have been added to the collection in the Research Room. Besides these old books on the Korean culture, many recent standard books have been added for general reference. It is earnestly hoped that some generous friend or friends will make the College possible for the making of the College the center for the study of Korean culture.

2. The Commercial Department

Mr. S. T. Lee, Gakushi, is the Director of the Department. This Department alone offers a three year course. The Faculty of the Department is composed of 5 Professors, 3 Assistant Professors and 6 Lecturers; making a total teaching staff of 14 members. The enrolment of this Department is the largest of all three Departments; there are 78 Freshmen, 44 Sophomores and 11 Seniors; making a total of 133 in all. Professor G. C. Speidel from the Southern Methodist Mission has been for the past year studying the Korean language. We are now glad to announce that he has begun teaching classes in this Department from the Fall. Since last July this Department has greatly missed the Dean, Mr. U. K. Yu. Dean Yu is now on his sabbatical leave. He went to America last July and is now engaged in study along the lines of administrative work in New York. During the absence of Mr. Yu, Mr. K. H. Chung, a lecturer, has taken up his teaching in the Department Professor P. C. Son has been ill since last Spring but is making steady progress toward recovery. We are praying that he may recover his health soon and that he will be able to take up all his duties in the near future. During his illness, all his class work has been carried on by lecturers. The Commercial Museum has been growing steadily with additional specimens of native and foreign commodities for study and exhibition. A number of specimens have been secured during the year as gifts from various parts of the country. Commercial Research is another feature of development in the Department. Many teachers during the year have devoted much of their time to this work and have been working on problems which are important to commerce.

3. The Science Department

Dr. A. L. Becker has been the Director of the Department for the past year and carried on the administration work most satisfactorily in addition to his teaching load. He is again appointed as the Acting Director of the Department for the ensuing year as Prof. C. H. Lee has taken up the Dean's work during the absence of Dean U. K. Yu who is now in America. The Faculty of the Department is composed of 7 Professors, 4 Lecturers, and 2 Assistants; making a total teaching staff of 13 members. The enrolment of the Department is as follows: 22 Freshmen, 10 Sophomores 4 Juniors, 9 Seniors; making a total of 45 in all. Prof.C.H.Lee returned to the school last April from America where he spent his Sabbatical Year. He resumed his duties in the College at the beginning of the school year. The members of the Faculty of the Department have been holding meetings, lecturing on special studies they have made. These lectures were open to the College as a whole and many profitted by them. The Department has been also making special efforts for collection and compilation of scientific specimens and apparatus. Last summer Prof. C.H.Lee and Messrs. C.R.Cynn and Y.S.Kim made a trip down to Quelpart and secured a number of valuable Botanical Specimens and minerals. The Department is now taking steps toward solving some of the pressing problems prevailing in Korean farming and in Korean homes. The Chemistry Assistant,Mr.Young Sung Kim, and a Research student have been for sometime making efforts to find a better method of scientific farming. To begin with, they have taken steps toward analyzing soils and studying the character of plants and the problem of fertilizers, which are the essential factors in farming. It is hoped that this experimental work may grow rapidly in scope and quality so that our Department may be of good service to the farmers. Mr.C.R.Cynn, the Physics Assistant, and a research student are asked to investigate the problem of the Korean house architecture and Heating System. First of all they attacked the problem of the hot floor (Ohn Dole) which should be improved to save money and health and the trouble of repairing every two or three years. The general problem of house construction may be treated as soon as the first problem is solved.

X. Religious Department

Since the last meeting of the Board the following religious activities may be reported upon:

The Union Church. Regular services began on Easter Sunday. There has been an average attendance of 70 at the morning service and of 30 at the evening services. The Sunday School also with Mr. N. S. Paik as superintendent has had an average attendance of from 70 to 80. During July and August, the evening services were discontinued.

The proposed plan for the Union Church was approved by the Kyungkui Presbytery of the Presbyterian Church. The matter will be presented to the District Conference of the Methodist Church at their next meeting.

At the Annual Conference of the Methodist Church in Songdo Rev. P. H. Yu (Yu Paik Hui) was assigned to work in the College as student pastor. He also is acting pastor of the Union Church. He is a graduate of the Southern Methodist University of Dallas, Texas, with the degrees B.A.; M.A.; B.D., and has had experience in church work before going to America. He has had special training in rural work.

Up to the present the work of the Union Church has been under the Religious Activities Committee of the College. But it is planned to proceed at once with the completion of the church roll and the selection of a Church Committee according to the proposed plan.

It is very urgent that we proceed at once with the erection of the first unit of a church plant. Plans have been drawn and estimates secured. It is hoped that the erection of this building will be approved by the Board at this meeting.

The Church has employed a very efficient Bible Woman, Miss C. R. Kim (Kim Chung Ran), a graduate of the Methodist Women's Seminary.

Summer Conference. This Conference which is a joint project of the College and the National Christian Council was held July 3-10th. A very good program was arranged including such speakers as Rev. I. Y. Kim, Rev. P. K. Chai, Rev. James K. Chung, Dr. L. G. Paik, Rev. Mr. Pang of the Christian Messenger, and Rev. C. S. Rim. In the evening meetings Mr. F. O. Clark gave several lectures. Mr. C. M. Hyun gave valuable help in music and arranged for an evening concert.

The attendance at the Conference was from 50 to 70 which was small. Other conferences and the financial depression are mentioned as reasons for this.

Students' Religious Work. Forty six students, which is about one-fourth of the student body have been active in helping in from 30 to 40 churches each Sunday. During the summer vacation a larger number of students than usual went out in groups to hold evangelistic meetings and help in Daily Vacation Bible Schools Reports for these are not in yet but the students themselves have come back very enthusiastic over their experiences in this work.

The Bulletin just published gives additional information about the denominational affiliation of the present student body, their church status, and the number of our graduates who are in religious work. In a measure at least we are attaining some of the religious objectives that were in mind when the College was founded.

XI. The Library

In the early days of the life of the College the library did not have the amount of expert attention, and financial support devoted to it that this important feature of the College life deserves. There have been many changes in the personnel of those in charge of the library in the few years that the College has been in existence, and while they have all been faithful in the discharge of their duties, or they understood them, at no time has there been a trained or experienced librarian in charge of this very important department of the College.

Library Assistant. In view of the fact that the library is growing more rapidly in recent years, and in view of the fact that it is taking a larger place in the educational work of the College, we believe that we should have two members of the staff giving their full time to this important work.

Number of volumes. Additions. Our library now has 11,500 volumes including 3000 Chinese and Korean books and about 200, bound and unbound magazines, both oriental and occidental. Since April 1929, when the present librarian took charge, there has been an increase of 1152 volumes by purchase and 1348 by gift, or a total increase of 2500 volumes.

The most notable gift to the library during the past year was received from the Hon. T. H. Yun, LL.D. Dr. Yun gave a valuable collection of oriental and occidental books from his own library. In addition to these books, he also gave ¥2000 to the College and designated that it should go to the Library Fund, and that the interest from it is to be used each year for buying books.

- 9 -

In addition to this gift, collections of books have been received from Dr. O. R. Avison, President of C.C.C., Prof. G. H. Hormoll of Ohio Wesleyan University, Delaware, Ohio, Dr. J. W. Hirst of Severance Union Medical College, and Prof. Benjamin Andrews of Teachers College Columbia University.

The following number of magazines and newspapers are now received in reading room. Magazines: 15 Korean, 30 Japanese, and 30 English. Newspapers: 5 Korean, 3 Japanese and 2 English.

Circulation. The number of books and magazines that have been taken out for reading by teachers and students, in addition to those read in the library, is 2214 volumes, from September 1st, 1930 to July 1st, 1931. This is an average of about 10 volumes per day, for each day the library was open, or eight volumes per person, teacher and students, for the period.

Equipment. Substantial additions have been made to the equipment of the library during the past year. These include reading tables, chairs, book cases, individual reading desks for teachers, catalog card cabinet, pictures, and a magazine rack.

Budget. The past year has seen a substantial increase in the appropriation for the library over the previous years. Even so, all departments are asking for more books and periodicals than can be supplied with our present small budget. This will probably be the case for many years to come, as our needs usually increase faster than our financial resources. However, we wish to impress upon all concerned the great educational importance of the library. In order to keep our present degree of efficiency, and provide for a reasonable growth each year, we should see to it that the library gets a share in any increase in funds available for budgetary purposes which may come to the College.

XII. Athletics

The college athletic activities during the year were quite successful. The High School Tournaments of baseball, tennis, track meet, and judo held under the auspices of our College were carried out with success. The first Annual Middle School Tennis Tournament was held on our campus on the 11th of October, 1930. Eleven schools participated in the tournament.

The Second Annual Middle School Judo Meet was held on the 6th of June of this year. Five schools participated.

The first Annual Middle School Basketball Tournament was held from May 22nd to May 25th of this year. Seven schools participated in the contest.

Our Inter-collegiate Teams of various sports during the year showed marked progress in skill and spirit. The Basketball team played four games during the year winning three of them. When the Kyoto Imperial University Basketball team came to Korea last summer to play a series of games in Seoul, our team was in the tournament. We defeated the visiting team with a marked difference of score. The Football team brought home the championship pennant from the All Korea Football Tournament which was held under the auspices of the Korean Athletic Association in Seoul on Nov. 3rd, 1930.

Through these athletic activities, we hope to make a contribution to the development of athletics and physical training and the spirit of sportsmanship. We also find them to be of good advertising value for the College.

Other items of interest

Music

The musical training of the students during the year has shown marked progress under the good management of the Chairman of the Music Committee and the leadership of Professor Rody Hyun and with the hearty cooperation and assistance of Mrs. A. L. Becker, Mrs. H. A. Rhodes, and Mrs. B. W. Billings. Prof. Hyun and Mrs. Becker gave bi-weekly rehearsals and sometimes arranged special singing classes, which were all well attended by the students. Several concerts were given during the year. Every one of them was well attended and the public seemed to appreciate our good music.

A Summer Music Conference for the music teachers in Middle Schools was held at our college from August 5th-11th, 1931. This conference was the first of its kind ever held in Korea. It was quite successful and 78 students attended.

Student Help

Prof. C. H. Lee who was in America last year has secured a sum of about ¥6,000 in cash and pledges among Korean friends in America for a Student Help Fund. It is hoped that the growth of this fund may solve a pressing problem for many needy students.

The College Museum

The Committee has been very active during the year and securing valuable collections. We are very much pleased to announce the donation of the following articles by Hon. U. C. K. Namkoong in Hong Chun. 1. Old Korean Coins: 71 pieces in all, representing coins made from the 12th century down to the last days of the Yi Dynasty. 2. Old Korean Postage Stamps: 19 pieces in all, stamps made and used from the 2nd year of Kwang Mu to the 8th year of the same reign. Mr. Tai Woong Lee also kindly gave to the college a valuable collections of Red Corals and shell ornaments.

Clubs and Organizations

A. C.C.C. Students Association (The Student Body)

B. C.C.C. Y.M.C.A.
(Voluntary organization)

C. Literary Friends Club
(Students of Literary Department)

D. Economic Research Club
(Commercial Department Students)

E. Science Research Club
(Science Department Students)

F. Glee Club

G. Orchestra

H. Band

I. Oratorical Club
(Voluntary, all departments)

J. Friendly Association
(Korean Teaching and Office Staff)

K. Dramatic Club
(Voluntary, all departments)

XIII. Enrolment

Annual average of the students who paid tuition during the past three years:

1928-1929	214
1929-1930	142
1930-1931	184

Up to May 10, 1931, there was a total enrolment of 250 students distributed as follows:

Class	Lit.Dept.	Com.Dept.	Sc.Dept.	Total
Freshman	31	78	22	131
Sophomore	20	44	10	74
Junior	10	11	4	25
Senior	11		9	20
	72	133	45	250

XIV. Classification of Students

A. Regular Students

Literary Department	58	
Commercial Department	110	
Science Department	43	211

B. Special Students

Literary Department	15	
Commercial Department	22	
Science Department	2	39
		250

XV. Provinces from which students come

Province	Number	Percentage
North Ham Kyung......................	7	2.8
South Ham Kyung......................	23	9.2
North Pyung An.......................	6	2.4
South Pyung An.......................	27	10.8
Whang Hai............................	10	.4
Kyung Ki.............................	101	40.4
Kang Won.............................	8	3.2
North Choong Chung...................	7	2.8
South Choong Chung...................	16	6.4
North Chun La........................	11	4.4
South Chun La........................	12	4.8
North Kyung Sang.....................	14	5.6
South Kyung Sang.....................	8	3.2
	250	100%

XVI. Students' Church Relations

Department	Literary				Commercial			Science				Total
Class	1	2	3	4	1	2	3	1	2	3	4	11
Presbyterian Mission	5	4	5	2	15	12	4	2	3	3	1	56
Korean Methodist	15	12	5	6	32	27	5	15	7	1	6	131
Union Sect.	4	2	0	2	12	1	1	1	0	0	1	24
Other	2	0	0	1	0	0	0	0	0	0	0	3
Non-Christian	5	0	0	0	15	3	0	3	0	0	0	26
No Report	0	2	0	0	4	1	1	1	0	0	1	10
Total	31	20	10	11	78	44	11	22	10	4	9	250

Department	Class	Baptized		Catechumen	New-Believer	Non-In	Total
	Freshman	16		2	8	5	31
Literary	Sophomore	10		3	5	0	18
	Junior	7		0	3	0	10
	Senior	8		1	2	0	11
	Freshman	20		11	28	15	74
Commercial	Sophomore	21		7	12	3	43
	Senior	6		3	1	0	10
	Freshman	15		2	1	3	21
Science	Sophomore	8		1	1	0	10
	Junior	4		0	0	0	4
	Senior	4		3	1	0	8
No Report		___	10	___	___	___	10
	Total	119	10	33	62	26	250

XVII. The Total Number of Graduates from each Department

(March 31, 1931)

Department	Number	Percentage
Literary.................	105	33.4
Commercial..............	152	48.4
Science Department.......	54	17.2
Agricultural (not operating)	3	1.0
Total	314	100%

XVIII. Occupation of Graduates (August 31, 1931)

Occupation	Number	Percentage
Teachers of C.C.C.	4	1.3
Secretaries of C.C.C.	10	3.2
Teacher in Christian Schools...........	44	14.0
Church Work............................	20	6.4
Studying in Theological Seminary........	2	.6
Teachers in Non-Christian Schools.......	14	4.5
Studying in U.S.A.	36	11.5
Studying in Japan......................	2	.6
Journalist.............................	5	1.6
Literary Work..........................	4	1.3
Office work............................	47	15.0
Official...............................	20	6.4
Industrial Enterprise..................	26	8.3
Agriculture............................	7	2.2
Private Work...........................	54	17.1
Deceased...............................	18	5.7
Medical Doctor.........................	1	.3
Total	314	100%

XIX. Government Qualifications

The graduates of the College are given qualification by the Government to teach in Private Higher Common Schools and Industrial Schools on the Following subjects:-

To the graduates of Literary Department

English (Korean & Chinese)

To the graduates of the Commercial Department

English, Commerce, and Bookkeeping

To the graduates of the Science Department

Mathematics, Physics, and Chemistry

To the graduates of the Agricultural Department (not operating)

Agriculture

Respectfully submitted,

C. H. Lee, Acting Dean.

42. 유억겸 학감의 이사회 제출 보고서

문서 제목	Chosen Christian College, Report of the Dean
문서 종류	학감 보고서
제출 시기	1932년 3월 30일
작성 장소	서울
제 출 자	유억겸
수 신 자	이사회
페이지 수	2
출 처	2114-5-3: 01 Board of Managers 1932~1935 (UMAH)

자료 소개

유억겸 학감이 1932년 3월 30일 열린 이사회에 회의에서 제출한 보고서이다. 이날 이사회 회의는 미국에 갔다 돌아온 에비슨 교장이 사회를 보았고, 유억겸 학감도 미국에서 돌아와 참석하였으나, 보고서의 낭독은 백낙준이 대신하였다. 이 회의에서 감리교신학교와의 협력, 중앙 YMCA와의 농촌사업 협력, 교내의 초등학교(연희보명학교) 운영, 연합교회 운영에 관해 의논하였고, 도서들을 기증받은 것에 대해 감사를 표하였으며, 최순주 상과 교수를 부회계로 임명하였다.

유억겸은 이 보고서에서 항목 설정 없이 아래의 사항들을 설명하였다.

유억겸의 미국 활동, 학교 상황, 학생지원 업무.

내용 요약

유억겸의 미국 활동: 교장과 학감의 부재중에서도 모두의 노력으로 학교가 잘 운영되었다. 에비슨이 2월 17일 한국에 돌아왔고, 나(유억겸)도 미국과 캐나다에서 매우 유익한 여행을 하고 3월 2일 집에 돌아왔다. 내가 에비슨과 함께 뉴욕에서 존 T. 언더우드와 협력이사회 이사들과 몇 번 만났고, 유명한 대학들과 도서관과 같은 사회봉사 기관을 많이 방문하였다.

학교 상황: 손봉조 상과 교수가 건강 악화로 사임하였다. 1932년 1월 14일 학교에서 훈

육을 위해 불가피하게 학생회에 해산명령을 내렸다. 학생과 교직원의 부흥회가 1월 18~22일 열렸다. 3월 14일 14회 졸업식이 거행되어 28명이 졸업하였고, 그중 1명이 독일로 유학 갔고, 2명이 미국 유학을 준비하고 있다. 졸업생의 총수는 342명이고, 학생 수는 3월 29일 기준으로 169명(문과 46명, 상과 93명, 수물과 30명)이었다. 동문회보가 3월 9일 처음 발행되었다.

학생지원: 학교에서 3명의 우수학생에게 장학금을 주었고, 미국에 있는 Jhung and Co. 회사가 지난해에 1명분의 학비 장학금을 제공한 데 이어 올해부터 2명분을 제공하기 시작하였다. 미국에 있는 교포들도 이듬해부터 장학금을 주기로 약속하여 다음 학년부터는 총 13명에게 장학금을 지급할 예정이다. 이 외에도 교수회의 학생지원부가 10명 이상을 도우려고 하고 있다.

8-30-32

CHOSEN CHRISTIAN COLLEGE

80 2 H

Report of the Dean

To the Field Board of Managers at the Board Meeting held on Mar. 30,1932

Gentlemen:

I have the honor to submit the following report concerning the College administration for the latter half of the academic year, 1931-32.

It is a great pleasure for me to state the fact that during the past half year under the able management of Acting President Underwood and the Acting Dean C. H. Lee and through the hearty co-operation of the members of the College Council, the members of the Faculty and the Staff, the College has had a very successful year, and has closed the academic year with good results while the President and the Dean were away in America.

Dr. Avison returned to Korea on Feb. 17, and I arrived home on March 2 after a very pleasant and profitable trip in the United States and Canada. Dr. Avison and I had several interviews with Mr. John T. Underwood and several other members of the Co-operating Board while we were in New York City, and we heard many encouraging things from them. I had the great privilege of visiting very many notable institutions of learning as well as organizations for social service; the number of colleges and universities being 102, the number of high schools and public schools being 46; and the number of institutions for social service, including libraries, being 288. Very many of these institutions impressed me deeply, and I hope that we will be able to adopt some of the good things I saw there in educational methods and administration in our College and in this country.

The following notable events happened in the College during the past half year.

(1.) Prof P. C. Son of the Commercial Department resigned on Oct. 18, 1931 on account of poor health.

(2.) The Students Association was ordered to dissolve on January 14, 1932. It was a very unfortunate thing for the College to do, but this step was unavoidable in maintaining the College discipline.

(3.) A revival meeting was held for the students and the Staff of the College from Jan. 18-22, and the meeting was a very profitable one with very helpful messages of Rev. I. K. Chung and Dr. Y. H. Kim.

(4.) The 14th Commencement exercises were held on March 14,1932. There were 28 graduates all told; 11 from the Literary Department; 8 from the Commercial Department; and 9 from the Science Department. Fifteen of these graduates have obtained positions, one has gone to Germany to complete his studies, and two are making plans to go to the United States to continue their studies. The total number of our graduates since the establishment of the College is 342.

(5.) The total number of students on the roll, counted on March 19, 1932, is 169,- 46 in the Literary Department; 93 in the Commercial Department, and 30 in the Science Department.

(6.) The first number of the Alumni Bulletin was issued on March 9 this year, and it is a great pleasure to see this good publication.

(7.) Scholarships. At the regular Board Meeting in September last, an action was taken to request the College Budget Committee to establish 16 tuition scholarships if this could be arranged. The Budget Committee was able to manage to provide for 8 tuition scholarships. The College has hitherto given three tuition scholarships to three honor students, and from last year Jhung and Co. in America, a business firm of Koreans, began to provide for one tuition scholarship. A group of Koreans in America are going to give two tuition scholarships from the next school year. Therefore, there will be 13 scholarships in the College from next school year. Besides the above scholarships, the Student Help Committee of the Faculty are looking after some 10 or more students.

Respectfully submitted,

U. K. Yu,
DEAN

43. 원한경 부교장의 이사회 제출 연례보고서

문서 제목	Chosen Christian College, Annual Report for Year 1931~1932
문서 종류	부교장 보고서
제출 시기	1932년 9월 22일
작성 장소	서울
제 출 자	H. H. Underwood
수 신 자	이사회
페이지 수	6
출 처	Korea Mission Records, 1904~1960, Box 15, Folder 15 (PHS) 2114-5-3: 01 Board of Managers 1932~1935 (UMAH)

자료 소개

원한경 부교장이 1932년 9월 22일 열린 이사회 연례회의에서 제출한 보고서이다. 에비슨 교장이 이 회의의 사회를 보고 있었지만, 부교장이 낸 이 보고서를 기관장 보고서로 인정하였고, 회의가 열리기 전에 회람하였다가 낭독 없이 채택하였다. 이사회는 이날 빌링스의 교수 사임을 승인하였고, 신과 과장 로즈가 떠나게 되면 코엔(R. C. Coen)이 그 직책을 잇게 하였으며, 현제명, 최순주, 노동규를 교수로 승진시켰다. 현제명이 학생 4중창단과 함께 취입한 축음기 음반(1932년)을 제공한 것에 대해 사의를 표하였다.

이 문서는 5쪽 분량의 보고서와 마지막 1쪽의 첨부 문서로 구분된다. 보고서에서 원한경은 아래의 사항들을 설명하였다.

교수진, 에비슨 훈장 수훈, 학생 징계, 등록생, 학교 재정, 졸업생들이 갖는 자격, 종교 사역, 출판물, 과외활동, 연극, 연구실, 운동경기, 자산, 농촌 사역.

내용 요약

교수진: 손봉조 교수의 사임을 지난 10월 승인하였고, 창립 때부터 학교를 섬겨온 빌링스가 감리교신학교 교장을 맡기 위해 4월에 사임하였다. 하경덕(하버드대), 임병혁(시라큐스대), 김창조(뉴멕시코대) 장희창(도쿄상과대학), 요코야마(존스홉킨스대)가 전임강사 또는 강사로 부임하였다.

훈장 수훈: 에비슨이 40년간의 봉직을 인정받아 일본 제국 4등 훈장을 받았다. 그는 오래전에 한국 황제로부터도 훈장을 받았다.

징계: 12월과 1월 학비 감면 청원 건으로 소요가 발생하였으나, 학생들이 자발적으로 이를 해산시켰고, 이후로는 학내 분위기가 매우 좋다.

등록생: 1932년 4월 새 학기의 학생 수는 294명(상과 154명, 문과 90명, 수물과 50명)이었다.

재정: 안식년으로 떠날 예정인 회계 오웬스의 보고에 따르면, 1932년 기본재산은 $419,000이 되었고, ¥3,724.34의 잔액이 남아 재정위원회의 지시에 따라 절실히 필요한 일에 사용하고 있다. (이어서 여러 소액 기부자들의 명단과 금액을 제시하고 있다.)

졸업생: 졸업생들이 일본 본토의 교육부로부터 자격을 더한층 인정받아 5월 31일부로 관공서에 취직하고 공사립 종합대학에 진학할 수 있게 되었다.

종교 사역: 전체 학생이 필수로 주 2시간씩 성경과목을 수강하고, 주 5회 채플에 참석하고 있으며, 매년 특별집회 주간을 갖고 있다. 학생 YMCA와 연합교회(Union Church) 운영도 돕고 있다. 연합교회가 한국 감리회와 장로회에게 공인받았고, 학생들이 그곳의 주일학교를 이끌고 있다. 학생들의 약 85%가 기독교인이다.

출판물: 오랫동안 예고해온 카탈로그를 지난가을 출판하였고, 학생들의 포켓용 다이어리를 오는 봄에 발행할 예정이다. 동문회보 1호가 발행되었다.

과외활동: 현제명의 지도 아래 음악이 두각을 나타내고 있다. 춘추로 서울 공연과 지방 순회공연을 개최하였고, 하기음악강습회를 성공적으로 개최하였으며, 제1회 전조선 중등학교 현상음악대회를 지난 6월 시청에서 개최하였다.

연극: 학생들이 가을에 시청에서 톨스토이의 "어둠의 힘"(Power of Darkness)을 공연하여 신문에서 최고의 공연이란 칭찬을 받았다. 문과 2학년생과 3학년생이 각각 영어연극을 공연하였고, 4학년생도 졸업 전에 한국의 옛 소설을 가지고 공연하였다.

연구실: 과마다 연구실을 두고 특별 주제들에 관해 초청 강연과 토론을 하고 있다.

운동경기: 매우 많은 학생이 한두 개의 팀에 속하여 15종의 운동을 하고 있고, 학내 경기들이 유익한 결과를 내고 있다.

자산: 모범촌 부지 일대에서 약 1,300평을 더 확보하였고, 운동장에 작은 운동 시설을 지었으며, 두 번째 전화기와 교환시설을 설치하였다. 송충이와 전쟁을 벌이고 있다.

농촌 사역: YMCA가 농업학교를 위해 농가, 기숙사, 다른 건물들을 짓고 있는데, 학교에서도 특별위원회를 만들어 협력하고 있다.

(마지막 첨부 문서에서는 앞으로 갖추기를 원하는 학교시설 목록을 제시하고 있다.)

CHOSEN CHRISTIAN COLLEGE

ANNUAL REPORT FOR YEAR 1931-32

An annual report of the complex activities of an institution like a college presents many problems as to where and how the stress or emphasis shall be laid.

Each year presents certain difficulties which must not be forgotten but which should not be overemphasized; each year also brings special blessings for which we would publicly render thanks to our God.

In compliance with many suggestions we are attempting to make this report as brief as possible so we shall not be able to mention as many details, or the work of individuals as fully as we might like.

Faculty. There have been a number of changes, both temporary and permanent, in our faculty. Dr. O. R. Avison and Prof. U. K. Yu, our President and Dean, were both in America for the greater part of the year, while Prof. Takahashi was absent on sick leave and later for special work for about ten months. In October Prof. P. C. Son's resignation was accepted, and, to our deep regret, Dr. B. W. Billings who has served the College since it was founded left us in April to take the Presidency of the Methodist Episcopal Theological Seminary.

Mr. Takahashi returned in December, Dr. Avison and Mr. Yu in March and Dr. E. M. Cable came to us from the M. E. Mission in April. We are glad also to welcome to our staff as instructors or lecturers Dr. K. D. Hah (Harvard), Mr. P. H. Lim (Syracuse U.), Mr. C. C. Kim (U. of N. Mexico), Mr. H. C. Chang (Tokyo Univ. of Commerce), and Dr. Yokoyama (Johns Hopkins) formerly of the Higher Commercial College of Seoul. None of these are as yet on full time but they strengthen our staff greatly and we appreciate their services.

Dr. Avison Decorated. A cause of no small rejoicing was the recognition of Dr. O. R. Avison's forty years of service by the decoration with the 4th degree of the Order of the Sacred Treasure graciously conferred upon him by His Imperial Majesty the Emperor of Japan.

This is the second decoration which has been conferred on Dr. Avison, the first having been graciously granted by His Imperial Majesty the Emperor of Korea many years ago.

Discipline and Spirit. General discontent financial difficulties and a number of other factors centred round a petition for reduced fees and in December and January it looked as though there might be trouble. In the end the students voluntarily disbanded the unwieldy students association, all fees were paid on the dot and since that time the general spirit as exhibited in classroom, chapel and on the campus has been very good.

Enrollment. The enrollment for the year 1931-32 was 214 the largest we have had and the enrollment at the beginning of the new school year in April 1932 was 294 which jams our small assembly room to capacity. The Commercial Department continues to be the favorite with 154 students, Literary next with 90, while in the Science Department the enrollment is 50.

Finances. Mr. H. T. Owens, our Treasurer, leaves on furlough this year. He has served the College most efficiently since 1922 and it is our earnest hope that the way may be opened for him to continue his service for the Lord. He makes some interesting comparisons in his report for the year.

	1922	-	1932
Received for Capital Investment...	359,239	-	880,029
Annual Budget....................	62,055	-	158,738
Student Enrollment...............		-	294
Endowment........................	nil	-	$419,000

Mr. Owens again had the pleasure of reporting a balance for the year, this time of ¥3,724.34 which was used under the direction of the Finance Committee for certain very pressing needs.

Special Gifts. No large special gifts have been received but a number of smaller but most gratifying contributions.

Telephone Switchboard and Day Current........... ¥2,615.00
From Mr. J. T. Underwood

Library Endowment.............................. 2,000.00
From Dr. T. H. Yun

Student Help Fund...................... (approx.) 600.00
From Korean friends in America (about ¥900 previously acknowledged.)

Special library gifts from Korean teachers and others:

700 books from Dr. T. H. Yun
10,000 books from Jung family (South Chulla)
1,700 books from Dr. D. W. Lee
700 books from Mr. T. S. Min

The magnificent gift of the Jung collection only part of which has yet been received deserves an extra report by itself. The collection has been in the making for seven or eight generations and contains many priceless specimens.

We are also very happy to be able to announce that the Carnegie Endowment for International Peace has made our Library a repository for all their publications and are sending us a full set of the publications to date, amounting to about 500 volumes.

Recognition by Department of Education. The standing of the College was further recognized by the permission granted by the Imperial Department of Education, Tokyo, whereby our graduates are qualified for higher civil service positions and are qualified also for entering all Government and private universities, thus being placed on an equal plane with the graduates of the Preparatory Department of these universities. The permission was granted on May 31st and notice of it appeared in the official gazette.

Religious Work. The regular prescribed religious education consists of two hours per week of required Bible study for all classes and five periods a week of chapel. In addition to this the College conducts a week of special Devotional Services each year; a church leaders' conference during the summer and assists in the programs of the Student Y.M.C.A. and of the Union Church.

The Y.M.C.A. takes charge of chapel services once a week, supplies preachers, Sunday School teachers and choir leaders to nearby churches and carries on special preaching services during the summer and winter vacations.

The Union Church has now received the sanction of both the M. E. Conference and the Presbytery and seems ready to begin a career of real community service. Its Sunday School is entirely conducted by students and the recent children's day service packed over 500 into our hall which is crowded with 300.

The year has been characterized by more intensive work among the students themselves and the numbers of those coming out for Christ are encouraging. About 85% of the present student body are Christians.

Publications. The long promised catalogue was published last fall and a students' Pocket Diary is being put out this spring. The first number of the Alumni Bulletin also made its appearance during the year.

Extra-Curricula Activities. Music under the leadership of Prof. Hyun is again to the fore. The deeply spiritual character of his singing at the Presbyterian General Assembly last year made a great impression on all who heard him. Besides the usual Spring and Fall Concerts in Seoul, concert tours brought us in contact with the people of Hungnam, Hamheung, Wonsan, and Anbyun in the north and Fusan and Taiku in the south. The Summer Music Conference was a great success and at the earnest request of those attending will probably be extended to two weeks this year.

In June the College held the first All Korea Middle School Music Contest. Eleven schools, six of which were from points outside of Seoul, participated and the Town Hall was packed to the doors on the night of the contest. The College received much praise for its efforts in thus stimulating musical activity among Korean young people.

Dramatics. The stage has not been neglected. In the fall the students association gave Tolstoy's "Power of Darkness" a strongly religious play to a packed audience in the Town Hall and the local newspapers characterized it as the "best dramatic production ever given in Korea." Later in the year two English plays were given, the Sophomores of the Literary Department giving "A Son of the Yemassee" and the Juniors putting on a very creditable performance of "Hamlet." Just before graduation the Seniors of the same department gave a short Korean play based on an old Korean story. Plans are under way for the construction of an open air theater and the production of out-door plays.

Research and Study Clubs. Special study clubs exist in each of the three departments and lecturers are invited in to speak on special subjects and discussion groups and debates are held from time to time.

Athletics. In the attempt to get as large a number of students as possible into one form or another of athletics we have now fifteen different kinds of organized sports and all students participate to some extent while the regular teams enroll a total about 80 different individuals. The latest team for extra-mural competition is the Ice Hockey team which had a very good initial season, though cut short by the early thaw.

Special attention is also being given to the development of inter-class and inter-department sports with very beneficial results.

Property. No startling changes have been made but about 1,300 tsubo have been acquired in the Model Village section and one well-built house which has been re-modelled for an assistant professor's residence. Two small field houses for athletic equipment etc. have been erected, a second telephone bought and telephone exchange installed and the war on pine worms carried on, as well as a great deal of less noticeable but valuable and costly work done.

Agricultural Work. The national Y.M.C.A. have erected a model farmhouse, a small dormitory and other buildings for the proposed agricultural institute and the College has appointed a special committee to cooperate with them. It is expected that our teachers and students will assist in teaching and running the institution and in other ways give assistance in this very practical work for "dirt farmers."

During the year there have been a number of times when the way was dark financially, in administration, in teaching staff, etc., and yet each time the Lord has led us through the difficulties in a very wonderful way. He has been doing ever since the opening of the College and as we offer thanks for His guidance we can only pray that we may keep close enough to Him to feel His Sounding Hand in all things in all days to come.

Respectfully submitted,

Horace H. Underwood

Horace H. Underwood
Vice-President.

CHOSEN CHRISTIAN COLLEGE

PROPERTY DOCKET 1932

Order of Preference

****

1.	Additional Fund for Library-books and equipment..........	¥ 10,000
2.	Gymnasium building, to serve temporarily as auditorium....	100,000
3.	Endowment Fund..	300,000
4.	Dormitory for unmarried students, one building or several small units..	50,000
5.	Dormitory accommodations for married students at ¥600 per unit..	3,000
6.	Athletic Field improvement..............................	10,000
7.	Agricultural building rehabilitated for use in Y.M.C.A. agricultural project..............................	8,000
8.	Stimson Hall - repairs & changes........................	20,000
9.	Additional residences - 1 foreign ¥15,000; 2 Korean at 7000 14,000	29,000
10.	Applied Science Equipment..............................	5,000
11.	Center Campus grading and stream control................	6,000
12.	Roads & Bridges, improvement and extension..............	5,000
13.	Extension of water supply..............................	11,000
14.	Library Building.......................................	90,000
15.	Primary School project.................................	18,000
16.	Commercial Department Building.........................	60,000
17.	Site Purchase Fund.....................................	4,000
18.	Clock System, Master clock and bells, ...	4,000
19.	Church Building..	40,000
20.	Auditorium Building....................................	150,000
21.	Dining Hall..	45,000
		¥ 968,000

44. 유억겸 학감의 이사회 제출 연례보고서

문서 제목	Chosen Christian College, Report of the Dean
문서 종류	학감 보고서
제출 시기	1932년 9월 22일
작성 장소	서울
제 출 자	유억겸
수 신 자	이사회
페이지 수	20
출 처	Korea Mission Records, 1904~1960, Box 15, Folder 15 (PHS) 2114-5-3: 01 Board of Managers 1932~1935 (UMAH)

자료 소개

유억겸 학감이 1932년 9월 22일 열린 이사회 연례회의에서 제출한 보고서이다. 그가 이 보고서를 작성하였고, 이날 회의에도 참석하였으나, 원한경이 보고서를 대신 요약하여 읽었다. 회의 중에 노블 이사가 이 보고서 덕분에 각 과의 연구 활동에 관해 중요한 내용을 알게 되어 만족한다고 하면서 이사회가 학감을 칭찬하도록 하자고 제안하였다. 에비슨도 학감의 좋은 보고서 작성에 감사한다고 말하고, 이것을 미국에 보내 홍보용으로 활용하면 좋겠다는 의견을 내었다.

유억겸은 예년과 비슷하게 목차를 구성하였다. 그러나 직급별 교직원 명단을 교수진 항목 안에 넣고, 학과 활동, 도서관, 음악 활동을 더 상세히 설명하며, 마지막에 결어를 붙여 더 짜임새 있게 만든 점에서 차이를 보였다.

I. 서언, II. 운영진, III. 대학 교무위원회, IV. 교수진(교수, 전임강사, 강사와 조수, 사무직원, 안식년 중인 임원 · 교수, 파트타임 조력자), V. 학과, VI. 종교활동, VII. 도서관, VIII. 운동경기, IX. 음악, X. 다른 업무들(학생 지원, 박물관, 학생 클럽과 단체), XI. 등록생, XII. 학생 등급 분류, XIII. 학생 출신 지역, XIV. 학생 종교, XV. 졸업생 수, XVI. 졸업생 현황, XVII. 졸업생의 자격 인정, XIII. 결어.

내용 요약

I. 교장과 부교장의 리더십과 교수들의 협력으로 본교가 꾸준히 발전하고 있다.

II~IV. 운영진은 에비슨(교장), 원한경(부교장), 유억겸(학감), 백낙준(문과 과장), 이순탁(상과 과장), 이춘호(수물과 과장), 피셔(교수회 서기), 오웬스(회계 겸 사업매니저, 안식년 중), 최순주(부회계)이다. 교무위원회는 교장, 부교장, 학감, 과장 4인, 베커와 피셔(남·북감리회 선교회 대표)로 구성되어 있다. 교수와 조교수는 총 26명(한국인 교수 11명, 조교수 3명)이고, 전임강사는 2명, 강사와 조수는 19명, 사무직원(사감 포함)은 9명이다. 안식년 중인 교수는 오웬스, 로즈이고, 파트타임 조력자로 교수 부인 4명(2명 안식년)이 있다.

V. 본교는 종합대학 체제를 이루고 있다. 문과는 17명(교수 8명, 조교수 2명, 전임강사 2명, 강사 5명)이 80명의 학생을 가르치고 있다. 문과의 첫 번째 영문출판물로서 원한경의 한국에 관한 서양 문헌 조사연구가 널리 호평을 받고, 교수들이 개별적으로나 학생들과 함께 연구하며, 연구비가 책정되고 있다. 2학년생과 3학년생이 방과 후에 영어연극을 공연하였고, 연극부도 학교에서 공연하였다. 상과는 12명(교수 4명, 조교수 3명, 강사 5명)이 158명의 학생을 가르치고 있다. 상품진열관이 꾸준히 성장하고 있고, 연구조사를 위해 많은 서적, 잡지, 신문을 구비하고, 상업실습실을 운영하고 있으며, 신입생 영어회가 조직되었다. 수물과는 13명(교수 7명, 강사 4명, 조수 2명)이 48명의 학생을 가르치고 있고, 교수들이 초청 강연을 하고 있으며, 광물과 식물, 토양과 비료, 송충이 퇴치법, 한옥 온돌의 문제점을 연구 조사하였다.

VI. 로즈가 미국에 가서 백낙준이 임시로 종교 교육을 맡고 있고, 에비슨이 졸업반 학생들에게 종교철학을 주 1회씩 강의하고 있다. 채플은 유백희 목사가 운영하고, 현제명이 음악 순서를 맡고, 로즈 부인과 베커 부인이 피아노 반주를 하고 있다. (그밖에 학생 신앙지도, 학생 봉사활동, 연합교회 등에 관해 설명하고 있다.)

VII. 도서관은 오전 8시 30분부터 오후 6시까지 개관하고 있고, 전남 지방 정[정봉래] 씨의 가족을 비롯해 여러 곳에서 도서를 기증받았으며, 학교에서도 구입하였다. 전임 직원 2명을 고용하였지만, 소장 서적을 1939년까지 50,000권으로 늘리려면 훈련된 사서들이 필요하다.

VIII. 운동경기도 여러 가지로 성공적이었다. 여러 종목의 스포츠를 감독하는 위원회를 결성하였고, 야구, 테니스, 농구 선수들이 큰 활약을 하였으며, 중등학교 야구, 농구, 씨름 대회를 개최하였다. 운동장을 개선할 필요가 있다.

IX. 음악부가 현제명의 지도 아래 춘·추기 서울 음악회를 열고 지방 순회공연을 하였으며, 전조선 중등학교 현상음악대회와 하기음악강습회를 개최하였다. 현제명과 대학 사중창단이 음반을 취입하였다.

X. 학생지원금이 더 많이 답지하고는 있지만, 학생지원책이 여전히 더 많이 필요하다. (한 해 동안의 박물관 기증품과 기증자 명단을 제시하였고, 클럽과 단체에 관해 전년도와 동일한 내용을 제시하고 있다.)

XI~XIV. 학생 수는 6월 30일까지 총 294명(문과 88명, 상과 158명, 수물과 48명)이다. 본과는 263명, 별과는 31명이다. (출신 지역과 학생 종교 현황은 표를 참고.)

XV~XVII. 졸업생은 342명(문과 110명, 상과 160명, 수물과 63명, 농과 3명)이고, 현재 연전 교수 7명, 연전 직원 12명, 다른 기독교학교 교사 43명, 교회 사역 16명, 신학생 3명, 비기독교학교 교사 13명, 미국 유학 39명, 일본 유학 3명, 은행원 및 회사원 38명, 공무원 28명, 개인사업(상공업) 34명, 농업 4명, 다양한 개인사업 72명, 의사 1명, 사망 21명이다. 졸업생의 교사 자격을 인정하는 과목들은 지난해와 같고, 졸업생이 새롭게 일본의 고등학교, 컬리지, 종합대학 예과의 졸업생과 동등한 자격을 인정받아 시험을 치르지 않고 관공서와 사립 종합대학에 들어갈 수 있게 되었다.

XVIII. 학교가 모든 방면에서 발전하였고, 사회에서 더 널리 인정받으며 총독부와도 잘 지내고 있다. 일리노이 주의 레이크포리스트 대학(Lake Forest College)과 카네기재단과도 좋은 관계를 맺었다. 무엇보다 교수들과 학생들의 연구조사가 크게 활발해져서 몇몇 저서들과 논문들이 발행되었다.

(1932)

CHOSEN CHRISTIAN COLLEGE

Report of the Dean

I. Introductory Remarks

To the Field Board of Managers at the Board Meeting held September 22nd, 1932.

Gentlemen:

I have the honor to submit the following report concerning the academic phase of the College administration for the academic year 1931-32.

Under the leadership of President Avison and Dr. H. H. Underwood, Vice-President, and the hearty cooperation of all members of the faculty the College has moved steadily toward the objectives set forth at the foundation of the institution. Several events to be described later, undoubtedly mark wholesome progress in all departments of the College.

II. Administrative Officers

Oliver R. Avison, M.D., LL.D., President
Horace H. Underwood, M.A., Ph.D., Vice-President
Uck Kyum Yu, Gakushi, Dean
L. George Paik, M.A., Ph.D., Director of the Literary Department
Soon Tak Lee, Gakushi, Director of the Commercial Department
Choon Ho Lee, M.A., Director of the Science Department
James Earnest Fisher, Ph.D., Secretary of the College Faculty
Herbert Thomas Owens, Treasurer and Business Manager (furlough)
Soon Ju Chey, M.B.A., Ph.D., Assistant Treasurer

III. The College Council

O. R. Avison, M.D., LL.D., President
H. H. Underwood, Ph.D., Vice-President
U. K. Yu, Gakushi, Dean
L. G. Paik, Ph.D., Director of the Literary Department
S. T. Lee, Gakushi, Director of the Commercial Department
C. H. Lee, M.A., Director of the Science Department
H. A. Rhodes, D.D., Director of the Religious Department (furlo)
A. L. Becker, D.D., Representative of the M.E.C.Mission
J. E. Fisher, Ph.D., Representative of the M.E.C.S.Mission

IV. **Faculty and Staff**

A. **Professors** 9 American 17 Oriental

O. R. Avison, M.D., LL.D., (Toronto and Wooster)
President of the College

H. H. Underwood, B.A., M.A., Ph.D., (New York)
Vice-President of the College and Professor of Education, Psychology and English

U. K. Yu, Gakushi, (Tokyo Imperial University)
Dean of the College and Professor of Law

L. G. Paik, A.B., Th.B., M.A., Ph.D., (Yale)
Director of Literary Department and Professor of Occidental History and Religion

S. T. Lee, Gakushi, (Kyoto Imperial University)
Director of Commercial Department and Professor of Economics, Insurance, Statistics, and Abacus

C. H. Lee, A.B., M.A., (Ohio State)
Director of Science Department and Professor of Mathematics

A. L. Becker, B.A., M.A., Ph.D., (Michigan)
Professor of Physics and Mathematics

E. H. Miller, B.A., B.D., M.A., Ph.D., (Columbia)
Professor of Chemistry and English

H. A. Rhodes, B.A., M.A., B.D., D.D., (Grove City)
Professor of Bible and English (furlough)

J. E. Fisher, B.A., M.A., Ph.D., (Columbia)
Professor of Education and English

K. Takahashi, (Tokyo Imperial University)
Professor of Morals and Japanese Civil Government

N. S. Paik, B.S., M.A., (Emory)
Professor of English and Education

N. W. Paik, Gakushi, (Tokyo University of Commerce)
Professor of Commerce, Bank Bookkeeping, History of Commerce, Commercial Japanese, Accounting, and Sociology

K. Katowaki, Gakushi, (Kyoto Imperial University)
Professor of Chemistry, Mechanical Drawing

H. P. Choi, Gakushi, (Kyoto Imperial University)
Professor of Philosophy, Education, Ethics, and Korean Language

D. W. Lee, Graduate of C.C.C., B.A., M.A., Ph.D. (Michigan)
Professor of Mathematics and Astronomy

S. Nikaido, Gakushi (Tokyo Imperial University)
Professor of Japanese, Japanese Literature and Introduction to Literature

P. C. Kim, Gakushi, (Waseda University)
Professor of Physics, Electrical Engineering, and Mathematics

H. Kaiya, Gakushi, (Tohoku Imperial University)
Professor of Mathematics, Surveying, Physics, Civil Engineering, Drawing, Geology, and Mineralogy

S. K. Hong, B.A., (Ohio State)
Professor of English

I. P. Chung
Professor of Chinese Literature and Korean Literature

C. M. Hyun, M.Mus., (Gunn School of Music and Dramatic Art)
Assistant Professor of Music

T. K. Roe, Graduate of C.C.C., Gakushi, (Kyoto Imperial Univ.
Assistant Professor of Commercial Geography, Transportation, Economic Policy and Commercial English

S. J. Chey, Graduate of C.C.C., B.S., M.B.A., Ph.D.,(New York
Assistant Professor of Commercial Geography, Commercial Practice, Business English and Typewriting

G. C. Speidel, B.S., M.S., (Virginia)
Assistant Professor of English

E. M. Cable, B.A., M.A., D.D., (Cornell)
Assistant Professor of English, Bible and History

B. Instructors

Mrs. H. H. Underwood, B.A., M.A., (New York)
English

O. Y. Lee, (Berlin University)
German

C. Lecturers and Assistants

I. S. Chung
Oriental History

K. W. Chang, Graduate of C.C.C., Gakushi, (Tohoku Imperial University)
Mathematics

M. H. Lee, B.A., M.A., (Columbia)
Biology

K. S. Oh, Graduate of the Government Seoul Foreign Language School
Chinese Language

Insup Chung, Gakushi, (Waseda University)
English and Introduction to Literature

Y. J. Yi
Oriental History

K. H. Jung, Gakushi, (Tokyo Imperial University)
Commercial Law

L. W. Kang
Physical Education

H. C. Chang, Graduate of C.C.C., Gakushi, (Tokyo University of Commerce)
Commercial Mathematics, Warehouse and Exchange

P. H. Lim, Graduate of C.C.C., B.A., M.A., (Syracuse)
Bookkeeping and Business English
C. C. Kim, Graduate of C.C.C., B.A., M.A., (New Mexico)
Mathematics
K. D. Har, B.A., M.A., Ph.D., (Harvard)
Sociology
T. Yokoyama, B.D., Ph.D., (Johns Hopkins)
English
C. R. Cynn, Graduate of C.C.C.,
Assistant, Physics Laboratory
Y. S. Kim, Graduate of C.C.C.,
Assistant, Chemistry Laboratory
W. Y. Shim, Graduate of C.C.C.,
Assistant, Physical Education
P. D. Kim, Graduate of C.C.C.,
Research Assistant, Literary Department
M. H. Lee, Graduate of C.C.C.,
Research Assistant, Science Department
C. W. Shim, Graduate of C.C.C.,
Research Assistant, Science Department

D. Office and Administration Staff

K. C. Lyu, Graduate of C.C.C.,
Secretary to Administration
W. S. Youn, Graduate of C.C.C.,
Accountant and Cashier
C. M. Song, Graduate of C.C.C.,
Superintendent of the Dormitory
C. K. Kim, Graduate of C.C.C.,
Superintendent of Grounds and Buildings
H. R. Roe
Assistant Secretary to Administration
K. S. Lyu, Graduate of C.C.C.,
Assistant to the Librarian
P. H. Yu, B.A., M.A., B.D., (Southern Methodist)
Student Pastor
K. P. Choy, B.A., (Ohio Wesleyan)
Assistant to the Librarian
S. W. Si-Tu
Stenographer to the President

E. Officers and Professors on Furlough

H. T. Owens
H. A. Rhodes, D.D.

F. Part Time Assistants

Mrs. H. A. Rhodes (furlough)
Mrs. A. L. Becker (furlough)
Mrs. J. E. Fisher
Mrs. E. M. Cable

V. The Three Departments of the College

The College is organized on a university system and has four departments but only three are in operation. These departments are separate so far as their internal organization is concerned with their respective directors, budgets and recitation halls, but they are one in general administration and policy under one Dean.

1. The Literary Department

FACULTY: The Literary Department records another year of steady progress. The Faculty of the department is composed of 8 full professors, 2 assistant professors, 2 instructors and 5 lecturers; making a total teaching staff of 17 members. The department sustains a great loss in the person of Dr. B. W. Billings, who left us in order to accept the call to the Presidency of the Methodist Theological Seminary. However, the department was fortunate in the appointment of the Rev. E. M. Cable, D.D. in place of Dr. Billings. Dr. Cable came to us with many years of experience in the field of education in Korea. He is now teaching courses in English and in the Bible. Dr. K. D. Har, a Doctor of Philosophy from Harvard University, joined the teaching staff as a lecturer in Sociology. T. Yokoyama, Doctor of Philosophy from Johns Hopkins University, is also a new lecturer in English. Professor K. Takahashi, who was on leave of absence returned from a very profitable rest and study in Japan and resumed his duties from last January.

ENROLLMENT: The enrollment of the student in the department indicates another year of increase. There were 90 students at the beginning of the school year. But we have now 8 Seniors, 14 Juniors, 20 Sophomores and 38 Freshmen; making a total of 80 fully enrolled students over against 72 last year. There has been a steady increase in the number of students for the last two years, and we hope this tendency will grow in the years to come.

PUBLICATION: As previously reported Dr. Underwood's work on the Bibliography of Occidental Literature on Korea was published as the first English publication of the department, and it was received with high commendations from scholars in the Occident and the Orient.

RESEARCH WORK: While each individual teacher carries on his private research in his chosen field, study groups also among the teachers are being carried on with sustained interest. From this year a research scholarship was established in the budget of the department and one member of last year's graduating class is now contiming his advanced studies under the direction of the department. We hope to report a satisfactory result of this new work next year.

EXTRA-CURRICULA ACTIVITIES: Extra-Curricula activities among the students in the department have been very profitable to students and to the community. The Sophomore Class, under the direction of Prof. N. S. Paik, gave a play on "A Son of the Yamassee" in English, while the Junior Class, under the direction of Mrs. Underwood, performed "Hamlet" in English. The student Dramatic Club in the department gave as its initial performance 'Ibsen's Lady from the Sea" as an outdoor play before an audience of several thousands in the College campus last spring. The Literary Society, under the guidance of teachers of the department, is also carrying on literary, philosophical and historical studies among the students themselves.

OTHER ITEMS OF INTEREST: The effort to build up a good library of books on Korean culture is still being continued and there are now over 800 volumes in the Research Room. In accordance with the provision in the College budget, three to four students are now receiving scholarship aid, while about 30 students are earning a part of their expenses. A large number are in need of work.

2. The Commercial Department

Mr. S. T. Lee, Gakushi, is the Director of the department. This department is the only one offering a three year course. The faculty of the department is composed of 4 professors, 3 assistant professors and 5 lecturers; making a total teaching staff of 12 members.

The enrollment of this department is the largest of all three departments. There are 70 Freshmen, 47 Sophomores and 41 Seniors; making a total of 158 in all.

Mr. Yu, the Dean, came back from his sabbatical leave last March after studying on commercial education and administrative work in American colleges and is continuing his teaching in this department now. Professor P. C. Son's resignation was accepted at his request last October. Since his resignation, all his class work has been carried on by two lecturers: Mr. P. H. Lim, M.A. and Mr. H. C. Chang, Gakushi, both of whom are graduates of the department. After their graduation Mr. Lim continued his study in America and Mr. Chang in Japan.

The Commercial Museum has been growing steadily with additional specimens of native and foreign commodities. The total numbers of specimens are about 1,300 now. Some of these specimens were secured as gifts from various parts of this country. Professor N. W. Paik is in charge of this work.

As to the Commercial Research work, there are 95 kinds of magazines, 10 daily papers, and 1,012 books. The faculty members and the Senior students have been devoting much of their time to this work and working on important commercial problems.

This department has established Commercial Practice Room and offers the opportunity to the students to do some practical work in the commercial line. Dr. Chey is in charge of this work. The department, also, has begun to study the method of advertising and about 600 pieces of various kind of posters and hand-bills of different countries have been collected.

In the teaching of a modern language for practical use it is increasingly evident that mere class-room work is insufficient to create vital interest or to give satisfactory opportunity for practice. With these ideas in view the Freshman English Society was organized by the students interested in these forms of study. The program includes lectures, stories, dramatic productions, etc. in English with occasional outings and parties at which the use of English is required.

3. The Science Department

Prof. C. H. Lee, M.A., is the director of this department. Prof. Lee resumed his duties as the director of this department last April. We thank Dr. Becker for his good spirit of cooperation in taking up the duties as director of the department while Prof. Lee was serving as the Acting Dean of the College during last school year. The Faculty of the department is composed of 7 professors, 4 lecturers, and 2 assistants; making a total teaching staff of 13 members. We are glad to announce that Mr. Chang Cho Kim was placed on the teaching force of the department from last April. Mr. Kim is a graduate of this department. He continued his studies in Ohio Wesleyan University and in the New Mexico University, and from the latter he received the degree of Master of Science. The present enrollment of students in this department is as follows:- 20 Freshmen, 14 Sophomores, 9 Juniors, 5 Seniors; making a total of 48 in all.

The members of the Faculty of this department have continued to lecture on special investigations they have made and these lectures have and are serving to emphasize to all the importance of Research Work. During the year, and particularly last summer, the department made a good collection of one hundred mineral and about two hundred botanical samples within a radius of four miles of the College besides many others outside.

Under special agricultural research the research assistant, Chai Won Shim, has been vigorously investigating soils and fertilizers. Some of his experimental farming is giving good proof of his theory. Under this Special Research on Mechanical Devices, the research student, Man Hak Lee, has perfected a Pine-Moth Lamp Trap. Last summer the experiment of the College and the Forestry Experiment Station of the Government General proved very successful. When the Experiment Station made its report to the Forestry Bureau it recommended the lamp trap to be adopted as the official implement for catching pine-moths. He also scientifically investigated and experimented with the problem of the "ondol" (hot floor). The results of his experiment were so successful that we are now installing the new system in the teachers' houses of the College. We hope to complete this research within a year and will then make public the result.

VI. Religious Activities

The Religious Activities Department has been under the direction of the Rev. Dr. H. A. Rhodes for many years. As reported elsewhere he has gone to America on furlough and we miss his leadership in this department this year. The Rev. L. G. Paik is temporarily in charge of the work of this department in addition to his duties in the Literary Department, and the Rev. Dr. E. M. Cable, the Rev. P. H. Yu and Mr. C. M. Song are carrying on its many sided activities.

BIBLE TEACHING: This important work is divided among Drs. Cable, Paik and Mr. Yu. President Avison is giving an hour a week in teaching Philosophy of Religion to the three graduating classes.

CHAPEL EXERCISES: The Rev. P. H. Yu has been in charge of the chapel exercises. Members of the College staff take their turn in leading the chapel, while many outside speakers are invited to address the students and the faculty. Mr. C. M. Hyun has charge of the chapel music. This fall we miss the faithful service rendered by Mrs. Rhodes and Mrs. Becker, who took their turns as the chapel pianists.

STUDENT WORK: The student distribution according to their religious affiliation is as follows:- Methodists 156; Presbyterian 86; Holiness 1, and Adventists 2; Federated Church (of the College) 9; and non-Christians 40. This makes the non-Christians 13.6% of the student body. The two-thirds or more of these students are living in boarding houses in the city, while one-third or less are residing in the College dormitory and the nearby villages. The most important and yet most difficult work is that of giving personal guidance to the students in the spiritual needs. Messrs. Yu and Song have given much attention and time to this great need, while the faculty advisors have given helpful personal contacts. Every man in the department is tied up with the teaching work and other duties so that it is very difficult to give much attention to this need.

STUDENTS' RELIGIOUS WORK: Forty-five students have been giving help in from 40 to 45 churches each Sunday. Some of these boys go to distant village churches in order to hold church services. During the summer vacation about 20 students went out in groups to hold evangelistic meetings and conduct Daily Vacation Bible Schools in different places, while a similar number of students went out to preach during the last winter vacation. It is very gratifying to see these students come back with a new happiness which they experienced in sharing with the people what they could give. At the beginning of the school year one hundred and four students indicated their willingness to help in churches.

THE FEDERATED CHURCH: The College Church has been under the direction of the department until the formal organization on the 11th of September. While it was under the department the Sunday morning, Sunday evening and Wednesday evening services were held at the College auditorium every week except two summer months, when only the morning service was continued. There has been an average attendance of 70 at the morning services and at the evening services. The Sunday School also with Prof. N. S. Paik as Superintendent, has had an average attendance of 80 to 100.

The plans for the Federated Church were approved by the Seoul District Conference of the Methodist Church at its meeting last March, and by the Kyunkeui Korean Presbytery of the Presbyterian Church last June. The Federated Church was formally organized by electing an Official Board of six members representing the Methodist and Presbyterian groups. It is hoped that the newly organized church will be well equipped both physically and spiritually to carry on its many sided activities. The Bible woman, Miss Kim Chung Nan, has done very creditable work among the women of the congregation.

CONFERENCES: The Summer Conference for Church Workers was conducted by the College in cooperation with the Korean Christian National Council. It is one of the many ways that the College is rendering some assistance to the church. The Conference was held in the College campus July 6th to 14th. A very good program was arranged including such speakers as Rev. Yun Ha Young, Dr. Song Chang Keun, Rev. H. Appenzeller, Mr. H. Blair, Dr. Hugh Cynn, Dr. Billings, Dr. K. D. Har and others. The attendance at the conference this year was from 50 to 70 which was small. It is regretable that not many of the church workers can take advantage of the opportunity because of the financial depression and other conferences.

The annual evangelistic meeting for the College was held from the 18th to the 22nd of last January. Dr. Kim Young Heui, one of our graduates in Songdo and the Rev. Chung In Kwa led these meetings, and gave us very helpful and inspiring messages.

VII. The Library

This year has marked more progress in the development of the library than any previous year in the history of the College. This statement is true with reference to the number of books acquired, the progress made in cataloguing and the system of keeping records, and the general use made of the library by teachers and students. The reading room has been divided into two sections, one for reading newspapers and magazines and the other for book reading and study. Both sections are usually well filled with students, during the hours that the library is open, i.e. from 8:30 A.M. till 6:00 P.M.

Among the more important gifts to the library during the year, the following are deserving of special mention:-

1. The Jung family of South Chulla presented a collection of 10,000 volumes of Korean and Chinese books. These books have been in process of collection through seven or eight generations, and contain many exceedingly rare and valuable works. That this fine collection should have been turned over to our library, is indeed a source of great satisfaction.

2. Dr. T. H. Yun, who has been a friend and supporter of the College from its establishment, has presented the library with several hundred books in various languages. Also some valuable newspaper and magazine publications covering a very interesting period of Korea's history. In addition to the books Dr. Yun has also donated a fund of ¥2,000.00, the interest of which is to be used in the purchase of books.

3. Dr. D. W. Lee of the Science Department and member of the Board of Managers, this past spring, gave the library a set of old Korean and Chinese books, 1,700 volumes in all. This is a very valuable addition to our growing collection of books of this kind.

4. The Carnegie Endowment for International Peace has made our library the depository in Korea for all their publications. We shall receive copies of all back publications that are still on hand, and all future issues from this important foundation.

5. Mr. T. S. Min, through the solicitation of Prof. S. K. Hong, had donated a set of 700 books on Chinese history.

6. Dr. H. A. Rhodes, before his departure for America, gave us more than a hundred volumes of very useful books. Among them is a voluminous collection of translations from the original writings of the early church fathers.

7. From Dr. H. H. Underwood an encyclopediae of authors and an encyclopedia of Education, also other books.

8. Dr. E. M. Cable has donated 32 volumes of books on history and sets of National Geographic magazine.

9. An interesting addition to the library consists in about 40 copies of the Holy Scriptures in as many different languages. These will be kept on display in a special case in the reading-room. This gift is from the British and Foreign Bible Society.

10. Dr. B. W. Billings gave us some twenty volumes of English books.

11. The Friendly Association, composed of the Korean members of the College Staff, donated some 30 volumes of invaluable Chinese books as its annual gift.

12. The Alumni Association gave the library 22 volumes of books in Japanese.

13. Mr. J. O. Koo has donated 39 volumes of books, some of which are in English.

14. Mr. Taik Sang Chang who has taken interest in the College gave us 11 volumes of good books.

15. Other members of our staff and friends of the College have donated one or more books during the year. While all cannot be mentioned by name, all such gifts are very greatly appreciated.

The total number of books acquired by purchase during the year is 1,016. Those donated are 13,243, most of these are Korean and Chinese.

The adverse exchange rate which has obtained since last winter has prevented the purchase of many books from abroad during the year.

The Library Committee decided on the policy early in the year of confining our purchases as far as possible during this year to books published locally. We have therefore been able to make considerable additions to our collections of modern Japanese and Korean books. We also find that many foreign classical and standard works are being published in English, in Japan with very full notes in Japanese. We have bought a number of such books during the year as they are more satisfactory for the use of the students, than the same books published abroad. We are also trying to secure some of the best of the modern Japanese and Korean publications.

The fluctuation in exchange and consequent effect on the purchase of foreign books and magazines has led the Library Committee to recommend that a part of the library budget be estimated in gold dollars, and kept on deposit with the Board in America to be drawn on for payment of bills there.

Having had two full time workers in the library this year, Mr. K. S. Lyu and Mr. K. P. Choi, our records and catalogues are in far better condition than they have ever been before. A complete card catalogue by authors and by titles, of all our English books has been made. A classified catalogue by subjects, and cross reference cards, are now being made. In addition to Messrs. Lyu and Choi, Mrs. Cable and Mrs. Fisher are now giving voluntary service to the library and are giving valuable assistance with the work of cataloguing, classifying, labeling, recording, etc. Even with the increased help in the work, books are filling up faster than they can be marked and catalogued. A great amount of work must be done in indexing and cataloguing the Korean, Chinese and Japanese books, before they can be conveniently used. When it is remembered that more than 13,000 volumes of these Oriental books have been acquired this year, some idea of the magnitude of our task may be had.

On the recommendation of Dean U. K. Yu a special Library Promotion Committee was appointed this past spring. This Committee is charged with making plans and devising ways and means for increasing the library to the number of 50,000 volumes by the year 1939, and make the library large enough for a university. This Committee is also charged with making plans for maintaining an adequate force of workers to organize and carry on the regular service of the library. A tentative plan for increasing the number of books has been adopted. Even a more difficult problem than securing the required number of books, is that of maintaining an adequate and efficient set of trained library workers. This is absolutely necessary for the successful operation of a modern college or university library.

We should like to suggest that the College look forward to employing in the near future a full time librarian, who should hold a master's or doctor's degree in library science and management.

Such a librarian should hold the rank and receive the salary of a full professor in the Faculty. The time has long since past when the direction of the affairs of the library of a modern higher educational institution can be entrusted to the part time of a teacher who has full time work in other lines, and no special training in library management. At this time when the library is expanding it is urgently needed that we have a trained man in charge to direct its growth and properly integrate the library with the educational work of the whole institution. Problems are arising daily which have to be dealt with in an unsatisfactory and makeshift manner for lack of time and knowledge and skill to deal with them adequately. If we wish this absolutely vital part of our institution to develop properly, and fulfil the true function of a library in a modern college we must have a professionally trained librarian in charge of it.

VIII. Athletics

The College athletic activities in various sports were successful in many respects. The Middle School Tournaments of baseball, basketball, tennis, jujitsu, and field and track held under the auspices of our College were carried out with success.

Sub-Committees have been appointed to supervise the various sports, fifteen in all. A place has been found near Yang-wha-jin for students to practise diving and swimming. A boat with a spring board attached has been bought for this sport. The volley ball ground has recently been put into good condition for playing. Also an old tennis court has been fixed for use of the faculty members.

A basketball game was played with the Waseda University team on April 5th at the Korean Y.M.C.A. Our team lost by the score of 27-32.

Athletic Events:

1. Baseball Meet, C.C.C. and Keijo Medical College.

May 23rd	8-7 (12 innings)	C.C.C. won
May 24th	3-8	C.C.C. lost
June 3rd	8-9	C.C.C. lost

2. Tennis:

May 6th	Osaka R.R. Team vs. C.C.C.	C.C.C. lost
May 14th	Higher Commercial School vs. C.C.C.	C.C.C. won
May 27th	All Taiku Team vs. C.C.C.	C.C.C. lost
May 28th	Taiku Medical College vs. C.C.C.	C.C.C. won
June 18th	Seoul Union Club vs. C.C.C.	won - Score 1-1 doubles 3-1 singles

The Annual Middle School Baseball Meet was held on the 11th of June of this year. Two schools participated. Choong-ang Higher Common School team won in a seventeen innings game.

The Annual Middle School Basketball Meet was held on May 20th and 21st of this year. Eight schools participated in the contest. Hyupsung won the championship.

The Second Annual Middle School Jujitsu Meet was held on June 4th of this year. Six schools took part in the contest. Choong-dong won the championship.

Our College Basketball Team brought home a few days ago the championship pennant they won in the All Korea Basketball Tournament which was held under the auspices of the Korean Y.M.C.A. on September 17th after having defeated the strong U.C.C. team.

One of the urgent needs of the College is the further development of the athletic grounds according to the original plan of the College. Our athletic development has reached such a degree of success that it becomes necessary to have more room. The present upper part of the grounds should be converted into the baseball diamond and the lower part of the now undeveloped grounds should be prepared according to the original plan for track athletics. We trust this all important matter will be given due consideration and such action taken as will make this possible at the earliest moment.

IX. Music

The Music Committee of the College, under the direction of Prof. Hyun, has provided interesting programs throughout the year.

As usual, two regular concerts were held in Seoul and two concert tours were made to the cities of Hungnam, Hamhung, Wonsan, Anbyun, Fusan and Taiku. We estimate that some 12,000 people attended our concerts.

For the first time in Korea, the All Korea Middle School Music contest was held last June at the Town Hall. The responses from both the contestants and the audiences were amazing and delightful. Eleven schools took part in the contest.

The Second Summer Music Conference was held in August for ten days at the College, and in every way it was a better conference than last year's.

Another interesting event was the invitation by the Columbia Graphophone Company to Prof. Hyun and the College Quartette to go to Japan to make records. This invitation was gladly accepted and a number of good records were made including the College songs.

X. Other Items of Interest

1. Student Help

The history of the student help work is practically as long as that of the College but, to our regret, the work can not be said to have been carried on to the fullest extent. It was not because of the fact that there was not any necessity of it but because of the lack of funds. In 1932, however, an amount of ¥600.00 was appropriated and the work was done a little more effectively than before. From that time on to the present the same amount has been appropriated every year and it became a real source of help to nine or ten self-supporting students.

Last July, through the efforts of the Chairman of the Committee, Prof. S. K. Hong, we have been fortunate, to get a pledge of ¥1,000.00 for this work. It is to be paid in at the rate of ¥200.00 every year for five years beginning December, 1932. It is interesting to note that the donor, Mr. Chung Jai Lee, is a very conservative Confucianist but is very much interested in the work of the College.

The Committee had the students fill out a set of questions as to the source of their income and the amount of expenditure. The returns of the questionnaire showed that the average amount of expenditure is about ¥300.00 for 10 months and, as to their income, about 65 per cent of the student body get their means of subsistence and tuition wholly from their parents; about 20 per cent, a partial support from their parents, relatives and friends; and 15 per cent must earn their way entirely themselves. It is clear from the data above that there is a great need of carrying out this work to the fullest extent. The Committee is exerting all its efforts in cooperation with the Property Committee, in securing odd jobs, painting, and places of tutoring, both in and out of the College, for the self-supporting students.

2. Museum

The College Museum has secured some 200 pieces of old Korean art, and has made an interesting collection of ancient Korean coins, some 2,000 pieces in all, some of which have been purchased and others have been donated by different friends of the College. It is to be noted here that the Museum is already in possession of some three thousand yen's worth of ancient Korean coins which were given by Mr. Namkung Uck.

The following are some notable addition to the collections made during the past school year:-

Old Atlas of Korea - Given by President O. R. Avison
Famous Koreans' Correspondence - Given by Mr. T. S. Chang
Ancient Korean Blue Tile - Given by Dr. S. E. Han
Ancient Korean Blue Tile - Given by Mr. C. S. Lee
Ancient Earthen Tile - Given by Mr. Y. K. Keun
Tiles and Boundary Stones - Given by C.C.C. Mountaineeting Party
21½ pairs of Old Korean Shoes - Given by Dr. K. S. Oh

3. Clubs and Organizations

A. C.C.C. Students Association (The Student Body)

B. C.C.C. Y.M.C.A. (Voluntary Organization)

C. Literary Society (Students of Literary Department)

D. Economics Association (Commercial Department Students)

E. Science Club (Science Department Students)

F. Glee Club

G. Orchestra

H. Band

I. Oratorical Club (Voluntary, all departments)

J. Friendly Association (Korean Teaching and Office Staff)

K. Dramatic Club (Voluntary, all departments)

XI. Enrollment

Annual average of the students who paid tuition during the past three years:

1929-1930	142
1930-1931	184
1931-1932	214

Up to June 30th, 1932, there was a total enrollment of 294 students distributed as follows:

Class	Lit. Dept.	Com. Dept.	Sc.Dept.	Total
Freshman	40	70	21	131
Sophomore	25	47	13	85
Junior	15	-	9	24
Senior	8	41	5	54
	88	158	48	294

XII. Classification of Students

A. Regular Students

Literary Department	76	
Commercial Department	142	
Science Department	45	263

B. Special Students

Literary Department	12	
Commercial Department	16	
Science Department	3	31
Total ----------		294

XIII. Provinces from which students come

Province	Number	Percentage
North Ham Kyung	8	2.7
South Ham Kyung	22	7.5
North Pyung An	12	4.0
South Pyung An	37	12.5
Whang Hai	13	4.4
Kyung Ki	117	39.8
Kang Won	12	4.0
North Choong Chung	11	3.9
South Choong Chung	18	6.1
North Chun La	7	2.4
South Chun La	17	5.7
North Kyung Sang	11	3.9
South Kyung Sang	9	3.0
	294	100.%

XIV. Students' Church Relations

Denomination	Literary	Commercial	Science	Total
Presbyterian	25	49	12	86
Methodist	45	79	32	156
Federated Church	4	4	1	9
Other	2	-	1	3
Non-Christian	12	26	2	40
	88	158	48	294

Department	Baptized	Catechumen	New-Believer	Non-Xian	Total
Literary	47	6	23	12	88
Commercial	55	18	59	26	158
Science	32	5	9	2	48
Total	134	29	91	40	294

XV. The Total Number of Graduates from each Department

(March 31, 1932)

Department	Number	Percentage
Literary	116	33.9
Commercial	160	46.8
Science	63	18.4
Agricultural (not operating)	3	0.9
	342	100.%

XVI. Present Status of Graduates (August 31, 1932)

Positions and Occupations	Number	Percentage
Professors in C.C.C.	7	2.0
Non-teaching officers in C.C.C.	12	3.5
Teachers in other Christian Schools	43	12.6
Church Workers	16	4.7
Students in Seminary	3	0.9
Teachers in Non-Christian Schools	13	3.8
Students in U.S.A.	39	11.7
Students in Japan	3	0.9
Journalists	8	2.3
Writers	8	2.3
Employees of banks and business firms	38	11.1
Government Officials	28	8.2
Independent Commercial or Industrial Workers	34	9.9
Agriculturalists	4	1.1
Various lines of independent business	72	21.0
Physician	1	0.3
Deceased	21	6.1
Total --	342	100.%

XVII. Government Qualifications

1. The College has been given the privilege of giving a Bachelor's degree in each department as Bachelor of Literature or Commerce or Science or Theology.

2. The graduates of the College are given qualification by the Government to teach in Private Higher Common Schools and Industrial Schools on the following subjects:-

To the graduate of the Literary Department
English, Korean and Chinese

To the graduates of the Commercial Department
English, Commerce, and Bookkeeping

To the graduates of the Science Department
Mathematics, Physics, and Chemistry

To the graduates of the Agricultural Department
(not operating)
Agriculture

3. In accordance with the ordinance of Imperial Department of Education, No.3, Art. 2, Sec. 4, (Daisho 7th year) this College has been placed on an equal plane with the Japanese Higher Schools, Colleges and the Preparatory Departments of Universities, so that our graduates are exampted from the preliminary examinations for higher civil service positions and are qualified also for entering all Government and private universities.

XVIII. Conclusion

In conclusion we would say that the past year has been one of progress and satisfactory activity in all departments of the College. The relations with the Educational Authorities of the Government have been most pleasant, and on various occasions very strong commendation of our institution has been given by several of the officials. The name of the College is becoming more and more widely known and respected by the general public. The gift to our library of the very valuable Jung collection of books is evidence of the confidence that the scholarly side of Korean life has in the College.

Very satisfying relations have also been established with important foreign colleges and organizations. Lake Forest College in Illinois, U.S.A., has manifested an interest in the College by a contribution of books to the library. The connection that has been established with the Carnegie Endowment is one that promises profitable outcomes to the College and the general public. With these evidences of success and achievement in mind we face the future problems with wholehearted purpose and confidence.

Especially significant is the growth of research work by the staff and students. Several valuable booklets and thesis have been published recently; many kinds of experimental work are being carried on; and plans have been laid for research work along several lines of literary, economic and scientific lines.

Recently a Committee on Diversification of College Activities has been elected to study the means and methods of doing extension work so as to give the general public more opportunity to receive the benefit of educational facilities this institution has in hand.

Respectfully submitted,

U. K. Yu, Dean.

45. 원한경 부교장의 이사회 제출 연례보고서

문서 제목	Chosen Christian College, Annual Report 1932~33
문서 종류	부교장 보고서
제출 시기	1933년
작성 장소	서울
제 출 자	H. H. Underwood
수 신 자	이사회
페이지 수	4
출 처	Korea Mission Records, 1904~1960, Box 15, Folder 15 (PHS)

자료 소개

원한경 부교장이 1933년 이사회에 제출한 연례보고서이다. 작성 시기를 밝히지 않고 제목에서 '1932~33년'이란 시간 범위만 제시하고 있다. 1933년도 이사회 회의록으로 현재 확인되는 것은 2월 14일 자와 10월 4일 자 두 가지인데, 이 보고서에서 1933년 6월의 일이 언급되어 있으므로, 이 문서는 10월 4일 회의 때 제출되었을 것으로 추정해볼 수 있다. 그러나 이날 회의 참석자 명단에 원한경이 없고 그의 보고서를 읽은 기록도 없으므로, 이때 제출되었다는 것을 확정할 수는 없다. 이 회의록에 학감 보고서를 읽었다는 기록도 없다.

원한경은 이 보고서에서 아래의 사항들을 설명하였다.

자산, 등록생, 건강 관리, 운동경기, 학생지원 업무, 도서관, 박물관, 음악, 교수진, 종교 사역, 연합교회.

내용 요약

서언: 환율이 유리해져서 3월 말에 예상 밖으로 ¥38,000의 흑자를 냈지만, 안심할 수 있는 재정 상황은 아니다.

자산: 6월 8일 6,000석의 노천극장 준공식을 거행하였는데, 이런 것은 일본 국내(조선 포함)에서 하나밖에 없다. 400미터 트랙, 야구장, 축구장 등을 포함한 운동장 공사가 4월에 시작되었고, 스팀슨관의 채플실을 800석 이상의 수용공간으로 확장하는 공사가 진행되고 있다.

등록생: 등록생 수가 전년에는 평균 260명이었고, 1933년 학기 초에는 333명이었다. 실용을 강조하는 풍조 속에서도 문과가 꾸준히 성장하였다.

건강 관리: 스미스(R. K. Smith) 의사가 1932년 10월 부임하여 학생들과 교직원의 건강을 관리해왔고, YMCA 사람들도 돌보았다.

운동경기: 축구, 야구, 테니스 시합이 과 대항으로 열렸고, 레슬링, 스케이팅, 씨름(주짓스), 줄다리기 시합이 신입생과 상급 학생 사이에서 열렸다. 농구팀이 전국에서 우승하고 일본에 가서 일본 최강팀과 하와이 대학팀을 이겼다. 아이스하키, 야구, 축구, 테니스 팀들도 학교를 널리 알렸다.

학생지원: 학생지원부는 20~25명의 학생에게 일거리를 주었다.

도서관: 도서관에서 새 책을 사기 위해 많이 노력하여 서적 25,000권, 팸플릿들, 소책자들을 소장하고 있고, 책의 대출이 크게 늘었다. 1939년까지 50,000권을 소장하는 것을 목표로 하고 있다.

(학교 박물관 외에 상품진열관과 과학박물관에 관해서도 설명하고 있다.)

음악: 현제명의 지도로 음악이 대학 생활에서 큰 부분을 차지하고 있다. 8개 도에서 30,000명가량이 음악 공연에 참석하였고, 하기음악강습회에 많은 사람이 참석하였다.

교수진: 로즈의 사임이 승인되고 그 대신 코엔(R. C. Coen)이 임명되었으며, 스피델(G. C. Spiedel)이 사임하고 스나이더(L. H. Snyder)가 임명되었다. 오웬스의 사임이 승인되었고, 이순탁이 안식년을 맞아 4월에 서울을 떠났다. 최현배가 한글문법책의 저술을 마쳐서 곧 발행할 예정이고, 정인섭이 영어교육법 연구를 끝냈으며, 정인보가 한국사와 한국문학 역사책을 개정하고 있다.

종교 사역: 부흥회가 1월에 열렸고, 학생 전도대들이 방학 기간과 일요일에 인근 교회들에서 봉사하고 있다.

연합교회: 뉴욕에서 유학한 장석영 목사가 봄에 연합교회에 부임한 후 교회 출석이 늘었고, 이 이 교회가 이 일대 주민들에게 교육의 중심지가 되고 있다.

CHOSEN CHRISTIAN COLLEGE

ANNUAL REPORT 1932-33

****

It is difficult in a brief report to give a true picture of conditions in a form that will be interesting but not distorted.

This year, 1932-33, was financially the most prosperous that the College has ever had, yet to leave that statement alone would give a false impression since the leanness of 1933 has already eaten up most of the fat of 1932.

Due to the favorable rate of exchange the financial year was closed in March with the unprecedented surplus of ¥38,000. It is this surplus which is helping to save the day for us in 1933 and has given us a number of permanent improvements.

Property. First among these is the open air theater or "bowl" with a seating capacity of about 6000 and perfect acoustics. Work on this was begun by students and teachers who moved a lot of dirt in a short time. The project was found to be too big for this kind of work and was finished by outside labor. It was opened with fitting ceremonies on June 8th with a crowd of over 2,000 in attendance. It is said to be the only one of its kind in the Japanese Empire and it is our hope that many thousands will hear God's work spoken from its stage.

A still larger enterprise, both in area and in cost is the development of the athletic field at a cost of over ¥5,000. A four hundred meter track with a 200 meter straightaway, bleachers, foot-ball field etc. are included in the plan work on which was begun in April. When completed this fall it will be surpassed only by the Keijo Municipal Grounds.

Of more immediate and everyday value is the enlargement of the chapel facilities by the new gallery. This can be extended at need back into the former attic of Stimson Hall to give a total seating capacity of over 800. All three of these projects have been success-fully planned and carried out by the technical knowledge and tireless work of Dr. Miller.

Enrollment. All these facilities and all the work of the College is for the students and the annual enrollment shows a gratifyingly steady growth. Starting 1932 with 294 we averaged about 260 for the year and began 1933 with 333 on our rolls. It is interesting to note a steady growth in the Literary Department which seemed to suffer for a time from the wave of emphasis on "practical" subjects. In 1931 we admitted 31, in 1932 we took 38 and this year 48 were received in this department.

Health Supervision. Probably the most interesting and potentially the most valuable advance made this year or for many years is the medical work done by Dr. R. K. Smith. Dr. Smith came to us in October 1932, being temporarily loaned for this work by the N. Presbyterian Mission. For the first seven months' work Dr. Smith reports 3011 consultations and treatments divided as follows:

Student Physical Examinations	578
Student Consultations and Treatments	606
Faculty (& Family) Office Consultations and Treatments	163
Faculty (& Family) Home Visits	119
Community Visits in Homes	46
Community Examinations, Treatments, etc.	223
Total for College and Community	1735
Attendance at 44 Country Clinics	1276
Total	3011

Quite complete anthropometric measurements were made and data secured on over 400 students the results of which will be published later. In addition to the 44 country clinics held in the fall and winter Dr. Smith is conducting a community clinic for the villages near the College and has given talks on Hygiene not only to our College students but to the Y.M.C.A. folk school conducted jointly by the "Y" and the College and to other groups.

Students and faculty are greatly appreciative of Dr. Smith's work and we hope that his mission will return him to us after his furlough in March of 1934.

Athletics are not always as closely connected with Health as they should be but efforts are being made to see that Dr. Smith's work and that of Athletics shall be better related. The intra-mural sports help in this direction and with this end in view Interdepartmental Sports in football, basketball and tennis have been held as well as contests between the Freshmen and upperclassmen in Wrestling, Skating, Jujitsu and a Tug-of-War.

In events with other institutions we have had our ups and downs. Probably the most brilliant record of the year was that of the basket-ball team which won two Korean Basketball titles, went to Japan and won 6 out of 8 games against the strongest teams in Japan and defeated the strong team which came from the University of Hawaii. Ice Hockey, Baseball, Football and Tennis all brought us renown though not so great as that won in Basketball.

Student Help. A number of students get their "exercise" in paying work under the direction of the Student Help Committee. In addition to securing positions with families both on and off the campus this

Committee has provided work for about 15 students on roads, grounds and other property upkeep and repair work. In addition to this both apple-cider making and the sale of Korean candy were tried out this year. The first was a success giving help to four students and ending the season with a profit. Altogether about twenty to twenty-five students were given work under the direction of the College and positions secured for a large number of others.

Library. Special efforts have been made to push the Library during the year, both in securing new books and in making its service more efficient. Due to this effort the Library now contains about 25,000 bound volumes and almost 4000 unbound pamphlets and booklets. Dr. Fisher and Mr. K. P. Choi have also greatly stimulated the interest in, and use of, the Library by bulletins, placards, exhibitions and lectures so that the number of books taken out per day has been greatly increased. We have set the objective of 50,000 books by 1939 and at the present rate we have hopes of going over the top before that date.

Museum. Closely allied to the Library are the Museums of which we have three: General, Commercial and Scientific. In the General Museum which is chiefly devoted to antiquities our collection of old Korean coins is very valuable and in all lines increases, including many almost priceless specimens, have been made.

In the Commercial Museum special attention has been paid this year to advertising materials such as posters, handbills, etc. and a unique collection of several thousand specimens has already been made.

The Science Museum was the recipient of a splendid gift of over 6000 botanical specimens and Mrs. R. K. Smith has devoted long hours each day to the classification of these specimens. The men in the Science Department are not only grateful to Mrs. Smith but have expressed very strongly their admiration of her ability and the pleasure of working with her.

Music under the direction of Prof. Hyun has played a large part in the life of the College and as a major contribution by the College. Approximately 30,000 people in 8 provinces heard the music clubs perform. Large attendance at the Summer Music Conference and enthusiastic praise from all concerned assured us that this attempt to help church and school music teachers was appreciated.

Faculty. The turnover in the teaching staff each year is remarkably low, but there are some changes. Dr. Rhodes' resignation was finally accepted when it became evident that no persuasions were of avail and we thank the Presbyterian Mission for sending us in Dr. Rhodes' place Mr. R. C. Coen who is to return to Korea in September. Mr. G. C. Speidel of the M. E. Mission South resigned in March and Mr. L. H. Snyder was at once given to us to take his place. The Mission's appreciation of our needs and willingness to send us so experienced and valuable a man as Mr. Snyder is much appreciated. The N. Presbyterian Mission have also sent to us till March 1934 Dr. and Mrs. R. K. Smith whose services have already been referred to in another section. The College reiterates its request that they be assigned to the College on their return from furlough. Mr. H. T. Owens' resignation was at last accepted by the Co-operating Board in New York and it is with deep regret that we lose his valued services. Of the Korean staff Prof. S. T. Lee was sent on a trip of study and investigation around the world leaving Seoul in April and is to return in March 1934. Dr. K. N. Choi, one of our graduates, comes to our Physics Department, from the University of Michigan where he took his doctor's degree in Physics. Other minor changes including the appointment of a number of much needed assistants have been made.

Prof. H. P. Choi has completed his work on the Grammar of the Korean Language which is soon to be published. Mr. Insup Chung is about to publish his book on Methods of Teaching English in Korea. Dr. Underwood has finished a study of Korean ships, ancient and modern, and Prof. I. P. Chung is now revising his History of Korean Literature. No account can be given here of the lectures and addresses made by our professors and teachers but a rough estimate would indicate that their audiences, exclusive of students, would total over 200,000.

Religious Work. A great deal of this is direct evangelistic work in addition to that done under the direction of the Religious Activities Committee. Special meetings were held in January with Dr. Stokes and Dr. Hugh Cynn as the speakers in the morning and Rev. C. M. Cha in the evening. Student preaching bands during vacations and Sunday by Sunday preaching, teaching and musical help in nearby churches is all part of routine work but vital for the very life of the school. Personal work among our own students, prayer meetings, Bible classes, etc. etc. are carried on in campus and nearby churches by student groups.

Union Church. Much of this is now done through the Union Church to which the Rev. S. Y. Chang came as pastor from New York this spring. Attendance is growing, difficulties are being overcome and we believe that this church, so closely connected with the College, though not an integral part of it, has a great part to play in the large educational center which is growing up in this neighborhood.

From Dr. Avison down through the faculty is the conviction that if we fail in our Christian message, if we fail to keep Christ central in everything then we have failed in all.

Your prayers are asked that moment by moment He may be the center of all of our hearts and minds and that we may so show Him forth to Korea.

Respectfully submitted,

Horace H. Underwood
Vice-President

46. 유억겸 부교장 겸 학감의 이사회 제출 연례보고서

문서 제목	Chosen Christian College, Report of the Dean (1934~1935)
문서 종류	학감 보고서
제출 시기	1935년 2월 15일
작성 장소	서울
제 출 자	유억겸
수 신 자	이사회
페이지 수	32
출 처	① Korea Mission Records, 1904~1960, Box 15, Folder 15 (PHS) ① 2114-5-3: 01 Board of Managers 1932~1935 (UMAH) ② 2114-5-4: 02 Underwood, Horace H. (DR.) 1935 (UMAH)

자료 소개

유억겸 부교장 겸 학감이 1935년 2월 15일 열린 이사회 회의에서 제출한 연례보고서이다. 그 전 1934년 2월 17일 열린 연례회의에서 에비슨의 사임이 승인되었고, 부교장 원한경이 교장으로, 학감 유억겸이 부교장으로, 부회계 최순주가 회계로 임명되었다. 원한경은 1934년 10월 12일 3대 교장으로 취임하였고, 유억겸은 그때부터 1939년까지 부교장과 학감을 겸직하였다. 그가 학감 명의로 이 보고서를 제출한 1935년 2월 15일 회의에서 이사회는 초등학교(연희보명학교)의 대학건물 사용 문제와 교수 봉급 문제를 논의하였다. 이 보고서는 PHS와 UMAH에 똑같이 ①번 형태로 소장되어 있으나, UMAH의 ②번 파일 문서에는 마지막 장이 없다.

유억겸은 역대 최대 분량의 보고서를 예년과 비슷하게 아래와 같이 구성하였다.

I. 서언, II. 운영 임원, III. 대학 교무위원회, IV. 대학 예산위원회, V. 명예 교장, VI. 교수진, VII. 3개 학과, VIII. 종교 활동, IX. 도서관, X. 체육 교육, XI. 음악, XII. 다른 사항들, XIII. 학생, XIV. 졸업생, XV. 연구 활동, XVI. 결어.

내용 요약

I. 명예 교장 에비슨과 신임 교장의 리더십과 교직원들의 협력으로 본교가 꾸준히 발전

하고 있다.

II~VI. 운영진은 원한경(교장), 유억겸(부교장, 학감), 백낙준(문과 과장), 이순탁(상과 과장), 이춘호(수물과 과장), 최순주(부회계)이다. 대학 교무위원회는 교장, 부교장, 백낙준, 이순탁, 이춘호, 케이블(신과 과장), 스나이더(남감리회 선교회 대표)로 구성되어 있다. 대학 예산위원회는 교장, 부교장, 과장들, 스나이더, 회계로 구성되어 있다. 에비슨은 명예교장이다. 교수는 20명(한국인 13명) 조교수는 6명(한국인 4명)이고, 전임강사는 5명(한국인 4명), 강사와 조수는 19명(한국인 16명), 사무직원(사감 포함)은 10명, 파트타임 조력자는 4명이다.

VII. 본교는 종합대학 체제를 이루고 있다. 문과는 22명(교수 7명, 조교수 2명, 전임강사 5명, 강사 8명)이 88명의 학생을 가르치고 있다. 오랫동안 가르쳤던 다카하시, 백남석, 피셔, 이윤재 등이 사임하였고, 이묘묵(보스턴대), 갈홍기(시카고대), 손진태(와세다대), 이양하(동경제대), 김두헌(동경제대), 하경덕(하버드대) 등이 그 자리를 채웠다. 상과는 교수와 조교수 9명, 강사 11명, 조수 1명이 171명의 학생을 가르치고 있다. 이순탁이 1934년 4월 직무에 복귀하였으며, 상품진열관이 꾸준히 발전하고 있고, 실용 교육(타자기 11대 보유)을 하고 있다. 수물과는 13명(교수 7명, 조교수 1명, 강사 3명, 조수 2명)이 63명의 학생을 가르치고 있다. 최황(오하이오 주립대)이 새로 부임하였다.

VIII. 성경 교육은 케이블, 갈홍기, 백낙준, 코엔, 장석영이 나누어 맡고 있다. 채플 예배를 위해 다양하게 강사를 구하려고 노력하였고, 교직원들도 이 사역을 열심히 도왔다. 학생들의 25.3%가 비기독교인인데, 장석영과 송치명이 학생들을 돌보고 있고, 학생들은 서울 주변의 여러 교회에서 봉사하고 있다. 3년 차가 된 연합교회를 장석영 목사가 이끌고, 이묘묵이 주일학교를, 김희영 전도부인이 여자 교인들과 아이들을 돌보고 있다. 이화여전이 다음 학년부터 이 사역에 합류하기를 희망한다.

IX. 도서관은 사임한 피셔 대신 이묘묵이 책임을 맡았고. 1935년 1월로 44,633권(정기간행물 5470권)을 소장하고 있는데, 1932년부터 50,000권을 목표로 7개년 도서관 운동(Seven Year Library Campaign)을 벌이던 중 지난해에 2,478권을 확보하였다. (도서 기증자 명단과 소장 문헌의 종류를 제시하고 있다.)

X. 운동을 위한 예산이 축소되었지만, 동문들과 우인들의 지원으로 농구팀을 도쿄에 파견하였다. 야구팀이 경성제대 의학부팀을 이겼을 때는 학생들이 밴드와 함께 거리 행진을

하였다. 농구팀은 도쿄에서 일본챔피언쉽대회에 참가하여 준결승까지 진출하였고, 동경제대 팀을 이겼다, 중앙 YMCA 대회에서는 전승하였다. 9월 24일에는 새로 조성된 400미터 트랙에서 교내 육상경기를 벌였다. 축구팀은 케이프타운에서 온 팀과 경기하여 비겼다. 원한경 교장이 아이스링크를 조성하려 하였으나 당국이 너무 늦게 승인하였다.

XI. 오케스트라 단원은 34명, 합창단원은 40명, 밴드 단원은 26명이고, 현악 4중주단과 남성 사중창단이 있다. 연례 음악회를 서울에서 열었고, 평양에서 목단(Moukden)까지 순회공연을 하였다. 라디오에는 한 해에 26번 출연하였고, 채플과 여러 교회에서 음악 순서를 맡았다. 하기음악강습회, 중등학교 현상음악대회[콩쿨]를 개최하였고, 문과 2학년 이인범에게 장학금을 수여하였다. 교수들과 로드히버[현제명의 미국 유학 후견인]는 악기들과 악보들을 기증하였다. 이 모든 활동은 음악부장 최순주, 현제명, 베커 · 코엔 · 원한경의 부인 등의 덕분에 가능하였다.

XII. 박물관은 적은 예산 때문에 원하는 만큼 구입하지는 못하였지만, 케이블, 정인보, 홍승국을 비롯한 교수들, 학생들, 우인들 덕분에 훌륭한 기증품들을 얻었다. (기증품과 기증자 목록을 제시하고 있다.) 학생지원 업무로 총 24명의 학생을 도왔다. (학생 클럽과 단체를 나열하고 있다.)

XIII. 등록생은 1935년 1월 31일까지 총 324명(문과 88명, 상과 171명, 수물과 65명)이었다. 본과는 298명, 별과는 26명이었다. (출신 지역과 종교는 표를 참조.)

XIV. 졸업생은 455이고, 문과 134명, 상과 242명, 수물과 76명, 농과 3명이다. 현재 연전 교수 10명, 연전 직원 8명, 다른 기독교학교 교사 59명, 교회 사역 23명, 신학생 2명, 비기독교학교 교사 15명, 미국 유학 23명, 일본 유학 13명, 중국 유학 2명, 프랑스 유학 1명, 언론인 10명, 은행원 및 회사원 85명, 공무원 38명, 개인사업(상공업) 55명, 농업 18명, 다양한 개인사업 74명, 의사 1명, 사망 28명이다. 졸업생들은 일본의 고등학교 · 컬리지 · 종합대학 예과 졸업생과 동등한 자격을 인정받아 무시험으로 관공서 취직, 사립 종합대학 진학하게 되었다. (졸업생의 교사 자격 과목은 이전 보고서 내용과 동일하다.)

XV. 문과 교수들은 최고 수준의 학문적 성취를 이루기 위해 노력하고 있다. 신한철, 최현배, 정인보, 백낙준, 케이블, 손진태, 코엔, 이묘묵이 연구 성과를 내고 저서를 출판하였다. 상과의 교수와 학생들도 함께 연구하여 결과를 발표하였다. 백남운, 노동규, 정인섭, 최순주, 스나이더가 책을 집필하고 연구 결과를 발표하였다. 광고 방법 연구와 영어 교사

조사반의 연구도 이루어졌다. 수물과에서는 이만학 학생의 한국 온돌 연구가 3년 만에 끝나서 출판 작업을 하고 있는데, 온돌의 개선에 기여하기를 바란다.

XVI. 학교가 꾸준히 발전하고 있고, 학생들이 한국, 일본, 중국의 약 60개 중등학교에서 왔으며, 졸업생들은 사회의 각 부문에서 성공하고 있다. 교수들은 가르치고 연구하는 일 외에 라디오, 신문, 잡지, 강연장을 통해 이 나라가 나아갈 길을 제시하고 있다. 서민호의 모친, 윤치창, 김희춘이 장학금을 조성해주었고, 도서관과 박물관이 귀중한 서적들과 유물들을 기증받고 있다. 운동팀들도 일본과 한국에서 뛰어난 기록을 세웠고, 교직원들은 세브란스의전 교직원들과 에비슨컵을 놓고 몇 차례 경기를 벌였다. 학생들이 종교활동으로 많은 찬사를 받고 있고, 음악활동으로 대학 안에서만 아니라 전국에서 뛰어난 자리를 차지하였다.

Chosen Christian College

Report of the Dean

(1934 - 1935)

Contents | Page

CHOSEN CHRISTIAN COLLEGE

Report of the Dean

I. Introductory Remarks

To the Field Board of Managers of the Chosen Christian College at the Board Meeting held on February 15th, 1936.

I have the honor to submit the following report concerning the academic phase of the College Administration for the academic year 1934-1935.

Under the leadership of President Avison, who is now President-Emeritus since October 12th, 1934, and of Dr. Underwood, the newly appointed President of the College, and with the hearty co-operation of all members of the Faculty and Staff the College has progressed steadily toward the aims set forth at the foundation of the Institution. The events described in this report will endorse this statement.

II. Administrative Officers.

Horace H. Underwood, M. A., Ph. D., Litt. D., President.
Uok Kyum Yu, Gakushi, Vice-President and Dean.
L. George Paik, M. A., Ph. D., Director of the Literary Department.
Soon Tak Lee, Gakushi, Director of the Commercial Department.
Choon Ho Lee, M. A., Director of the Science Department.
Soon Ju Choy, B. S. E., M. B. A., Ph. D., Treasurer.

III. The College Council.

H. H. Underwood, Ph. D., Litt. D., President
U. K. Yu, Gakushi, Vice-President and Dean.
L. G. Paik, Ph. D., Director of the Literary Department.
S. T. Lee, Gakushi, Director of the Commercial Department.
C. H. Lee, M. A., Director of the Science Department.
E. M. Cable, D. D., Director of the Religious Department and Representative of the M. E. C. Mission.
L. H. Snyder, M. A., Representative of the M. E. C. S. Mission.

IV. The College Budget Committee.

H. H. Underwood, Ph. D., Litt. D., President.
U. K. Yu, Gakushi, Vice-President and Dean.
L. G. Paik, Ph. D. Director of the Literary

S. T. Lee, Gakushi, Director of the Commercial Department.
C. H. Lee, M. A., Director of the Science Department.
A. L. Becker, Ph. D., Representative of the M. E. C. Mission.
L. H. Snyder, M. A., Representative of the M. E. C. S. Mission.
S. J. Chey, Ph. D., Treasurer.

V. The President-Emeritus.

O. R. Avison, M. D., LL. D. (Toronto and Wooster)

VI. Faculty and Staff.

1. Professors.

H. H. Underwood, B. A., M. A., Ph. D. Litt. D., (New York and Mount Union)
President of the College and Professor of Education, Psychology and English.
U. K. Yu, Gakushi, (Tokyo Imperial University)
Vice-President and Dean of the College and Professor of Law.
L. G. Paik, B. A., Th. B., M. A., Ph. D.,(Yale)
Director of the Literary Department and Professor of Occidental History and Religion.
S. T. Lee, Gakushi, (Kyoto Imperial University)
Director of Commercial Department and Professor of Economics, Insurance, Statistics, and Abacus.
C. H. Lee, B. A., M. A., (Ohio State)
Director of Science Department and Professor of Mathematics.
A. L. Becker, B. A., M. A., Ph. D., (Michigan)
Professor of Physics and Mathematics.
E. H. Miller, B. A., B. D., M. A., Ph. D., (Columbia)
Professor of Chemistry and English.
N. W. Paik, Gakushi, (Tokyo University of Commerce)
Professor of Commerce, Bank Bookkeeping, History of Commerce, Commercial Japanese, Accounting and Sociology.

- 3 -

K. Katowaki, Gakushi, (Kyoto Imperial University).
Professor of Chemistry, Mechanical Drawing
(Sabbatical Leave)

H. P. Choi, Gakushi, (Kyoto Imperial University)
Professor of Philosophy, Education, Ethics, and Korean Language.

D. W. Lee, Graduate of C. C. C., B. A., M. A., Ph. D. (Michigan)
Professor of Mathematics and Astronomy.

S. Nikaido, Gakushi (Tokyo Imperial University)
Professor of Japanese, Japanese Literature and Introduction to Literature.

P. C. Kim, Gakushi, (Waseda University)
Professor of Physics, Electrical Engineering, and Mathematics.

H. Kaiya, Gakushi, (Tofuku Imperial University)
Professor of Mathematics, Surveying, Physics, Civil Engineering, Drawing, Geology, and Mineralogy.

S. K. Hong, B. A., (Ohio State)
Professor of English.

I. P. Chung
Professor of Chinese Literature and Korean Literature.

C. M. Hyun, M. Mus., (Gunn School of Music and Dramatic Art)
Professor of Music.

T. K. Roe, Graduate of C. C. C., Gakushi (Kyoto Imperial University)
Professor of Commercial Geography, Transportation, Economic Policy and Commercial English.

S. J. Chey, Graduate of C. C. C., B. S., M. B. A., Ph. D. (New York)
Professor of Commercial Geography, Commercial Practice, Business English and Typewriting.

E. M. Cable, B. S., M. A., D. D., (Cornell)
Professor of English, Bible and History

2. Assistant Professors

O. Y. Lee, (Berlin University)
Assistant Professor of German.

I. S. Jung, Gakushi, (Waseda University)
Assistant Professor of English and Introduction to Literature

P. K. Lim, Graduate of C. C. C., B. A., M. A., (Syracuse)
Assistant Professor of Bookkeeping and Business English.

L. H. Snyder, B. A., M. A., (Princeton)
Assistant Professor of English.

K. N. Choi, Graduate of C. C. C., B. A., M. A., Ph. D., (Michigan)
Assistant Professor of Physics and Mathematics.

R. C. Coen, B. A., B. D., M. A., (Chicago)
Assistant Professor of Bible and English.

3. Instructors.

Mrs. H. H. Underwood, B. A., M. A., (New York)
English.
L. W. Kang,
Physical Education.
K. D. Har, B. A., M. A., Ph. D., (Harvard)
Sociology and Psychology.
S. Y. Chang, B. S., B. D., M. A., (Columbia)
Bible and Religious Education.
M. M. Lee, Graduate of C. C. C., B. A., M. A.,
Ph. D., (Boston)
English.

4. Lecturers and Assistants

I. S. Chung
Oriental History.
K. W. Chang, Graduate of C. C. C., Gakushi, (Tohuku
Imperial University)
Mathematics.
M. H. Lee, B. A., M. A., (Columbia)
Biology.
K. H. Jung, Gakushi, (Tokyo Imperial University)
Commercial Law and Japanese Civil Government.
H. C. Chang, Graduate of C. C. C., Gakushi, (Tokyo
University of Commerce)
Commercial Mathematics, Warehouse and Exchange.
T. Yokoyama, B. A., B. D., Ph. D., (Johns Hopkins)
English.
R. K. Jung, Gakushi, (Keio University)
Finance.
M. E. Cable, B. A., (Cornell)
English.
P. B. Billings, B. A. (Depauw)
English (Leave of absence)
Y. H. Lee, Gakushi, (Tokyo Imperial University)
English
C. T. Son, Gakushi, (Waseda University)
Oriental History.
D. H. Kim, Gakushi, (Tokyo Imperial University)
Morals.
C. N. Kim, Graduate of Paiyoung College.
Chinese Language.
Charles Choi, B. S. in C. E., M. S. in C. E., Ph. D.
(Ohio State)
Chemistry.

H. K. Karl, Graduate of C. C. C., B. D., M. A., Ph. D., (Chicago)
Bible and Education.
C. R. Cynn, Graduate of C. C. C.
Assistant, Physics Laboratory.
Y. S. Kim, Graduate of C. C. C.,
Assistant, Chemistry Laboratory.
M. H. Lee, Graduate of C. C. C.
Research Assistant, Science Department.
K. W. Cho, Graduate of C. C. C.
Assistant, Commercial Department.

5. Office and Administration Staff

Y. S. Koo, M. D., (Emory)
College Physician.
K. C. Lyu, Graduate of C. C. C.
Secretary to Administration.
C. M. Song, Graduate of C. C. C.
Superintendent of the Dormitory.
C. K. Kim, Graduate of C. C. C.
Superintendent of Grounds and Buildings.
H. R. Roe.
Cashier.
K. S. Lyu, Graduate of C. C. C.
Assistant to Librarian.
K. P. Choi, Graduate of C. C. C., B. A., (Ohio Wesleyan)
Assistant to Librarian.
P. Hyen, B. A., (Shanghai)
Accountant
W. Y. Shim, Graduate of C. C. C.
Secretary to Administration.
K. Kaskahlian.
Stenographer to the President.

6. Professor on Furlough

K. Kadowaki, Gakushi.

7. Part Time Assistants

Mrs. A. L. Becker
Mrs. E. H. Miller
Mrs. L. H. Snyder
Mrs. R. C. Coen

VII. The Three Departments of the College.

The College is organized on a university system and has four departments but only three are in operation These departments are separate so far as their internal organization is concerned with their respective directors, budgets and recitation halls, but they are one in general administration and policy under one Dean

1. The Literary Department

Prof. L. G. Paik, Ph. D., is the Director of the Department. The Faculty of the Department is composed of 7 professors, 2 assistant professors, 5 instructors, and 8 lecturers, making a total teaching staff of 22 members. The enrollment of this year in the Department is as follows: 34 Freshmen, 30 Sophomores, 10 Juniors, 14 Seniors, making a total of 88 in all.

The Literary Department records another year of progress. We faced many readjustment problems due to changes made in the faculty and to curtailment of the College budget during the past year. All the changes we made, however, have meant progress rather than retrenchment of our work. All of our hopes and expectations were not fulfilled, but we do not believe that Rome was built in a day. In spite of faculty changes and curtailment of budget, the department made lasting contributions to the advancement of the College and to various fields of learning as the following report will clearly show.

FACULTY: The Department had the largest turn-over of the faculty during the last year. Three Professors of long standing and several instructors resigned from the faculty and new members were invited to fill their places. Prof. K. Takahashi, who was reported of suffering from prolonged illness last year, at last resigned formally last April and moved from the College residence last September. Mr. Takahashi served the College since 1922. He was always a fitting speaker for almost all the Government Holiday ceremonies of the College. He was a faithful and punctilious teacher and a fine Christian gentleman. He taught all the subjects on Morals throughout the curricula of the entire College and made advantageous use of his wide knowledge and practical experience in the Japanese Imperial Diet in teaching his course on Jurisprundence. We were sorry to lose him. We hope and pray that his health may soon be restored for his usefullness. Mr. N. S. Paik who joined the faculty in 1923, also resigned in order to engage in business. Mr. Paik was a good teacher and disciplinarian. He taught foundation courses of English in Freshmen and Sophomores classes for many years. We record with regrets the resignation of Dr. and Mrs. J. E. Fisher from the staff. Dr. Fisher came to the College as a representative of the Southern Methodist Mission in 1919 and served the College continuously except the years of 1925-27 when he engaged in advanced study in Columbia University. He severed his connection with his Mission Board and resigned from the faculty. The Literary Department lost its exclusive claim of Dr. Underwood's service in the department, when he became the President of the College. Mr. Yun Jai Yi, lecturer on the Oriental history, resigned last April. Dr. T. Y. Kim, lecturer on Economics, and Mr. Frank Y. Kim, lecturer on Educational Psychology, severed their connections with the College last September. Mr. Shin Han Chul, a graduate student in the department, left us last October in order to take up an appointment in the Severance Medical College.

While the Department lost the above mentioned members, we made new additions to the teaching staff. We record with much gratification coming of Drs. H. M. Lee and H. K. Karl to the College. They are graduates of the Department and so far only two members out of 136 graduates of the Department, holding the degree of Ph. D. from recognized Universities in America. Dr. Lee received his doctorate from Boston University specializing in History. He lectured on History for some time at Syracuse University from which institution he received his M. A. degree. Beside his excellent training in history, he ably equipped himself with the Library Science. Dr. Lee came to us last April, and most willingly and most ably, he has helped us in the instruction of foundation courses of English, in addition to his regular duties in the College Library. Dr. Karl holds B. D. degree from Garrett Institutê, M. A. from Northwestern University and Ph. D. from Chicago University. While he was a student at the latter University, he served as the pastor of the Korean Church in Chicago and was the President of the Korean Student Federation of North America. He joined the Staff last September and gives course in the history of Education and those in Bible. Mr. Chin T'ai Sohn is another recognized scholar who came to the department last April. Mr. Sohn is a graduate of Waseda University. His major field of research has been in Oriental history and Folk-Lore of the Korean people. He held Japanese Government Research Fellowships for several years. He is an author and editor of several books and was a staff member of the Morrison Library in Tokyo for some time. He is now a lecturer in the Oriental history. Mr. Yang Ha Yi is also a new member in the teaching staff. Mr. Yi is a graduate of Tokyo Imperial University and is a careful and resourceful student. He teaches the language courses in the department of English. Mr. Du Hyun Kim is a new lecturer in the Department. He is also a graduate of Tokyo Imperial University. He has had teaching experience both at Ewha and Buddhist Colleges. He took over Moral courses which Mr. Takahashi had to drop. Dr. K. D. Har took over Dr. T. Y. Kim's course on Economics last September. Mr. Insup Jung kindly has continued the course on Phonetics which Mrs. Fisher dropped when she went to America on furlough last summer. Rev. S. Y. Chang during the second semester, offers a course on Christian Ethics to the Senior class. Dr. Underwood, in addition to his manifold duties, carries on all the courses in Education, since his return from furlough last fall. Mrs. Underwood resumed the teaching of her course in Modern English for the Juniors since last October. These changes at the beginning and in the middle of the year undoubtedly caused a little confusion among the students, but we settled down very quickly and there was no up-set either in instructions or in administration. We are grateful to the teachers and the students for ready adjustment in the situation.

ENROLLMENT: It was reported last year that the student body made a steady growth. We began the year with 46 Freshmen, 33 Sophomores, 10 Juniors, and 14 Seniors making a total of 103. It was the first time that the Department reached one hundred mark. As writing this report, there are 88 students in the Department. This decrease has largerly been due to the economic depression. In spite of the curtailment of the College budget, we awarded scholarships to worthy and needy students in the Department. There are scores of students who are working their way through the College. We expect 14 members in the Senior class will successfully graduate from the Department. This is going to be the second time in the history of the Department that as many as 14 graduate from the Department. We sincerely hope this tendency of steady growth will continue in the years to come. We must not forget to state the fact that quality of the student body has kept pace with the increase of number. We have fine boys with purpose of life and of excellent spirit.

EXTRA CURRICULA ACTIVITIES: The Department aims to provide ample opportunities of extra-curricula activities for wholesome outlet of self-expression of our students. Athletics are always popular with our students. There are two students of the Department on the College Football team. The College Hocky team is almost entirely made up of our students. The famous center-forward of the College Basketball team, which recently won from the Tokyo Imperial University Team, is a member of the Sophomore class. The Department won the second place in the annual inter-departmental athletics. The Department and class hikes and outing always offer a fine opportunity of mutual

- - -

contact not only among students themselves but with teachers as well. Beside athletic activities, Music is another very popular extra-curricula work that a large number of students participate in. The activities of the Music Department have helped our students for their general culture and trained promising musicians in this Department. Drama, being an art that combines the action of athletics and artistic expression of music, has been quite popular among the students of this department. The Drama Club of the Literary Society presented, in the Public Hall, R. C. Sherriff's play on "Journey's End" on the evenings of February first and second last. This was the fourth annual public presentation by that Club. This work is under the strict supervision of competant teachers. Mr. Insup Jung has been the most enthusiastic director of the Drama work. The Junior class is going to observe its annual Junior Night on the 16th of February by presenting two short plays in English: "Man on the Kerb" by Alfred Sutro and "Last Visit of the Unknown Lady" by Sudermann. Dr. E. M. Cable has been bending efforts in training the students. There are four study groups under the direction of teachers. Dr. M. M. Lee has a group of students from the Freshman class and directs the study of English Literature. Mr. Y. H. Yi takes charge of a group which is composed of Sophomore and Freshman students who desire to make additional study of English Literature. Mrs. E. M. Cable has a group on English Coversation. The fourth gr group is a circle of students who are interested in literary productions, and Mr. Yi directs this group. The Department is very grateful to these teachers who are willing to devote extra hours for these students. Beside these group activities, a large number of students participated in the annual intra-mural English Declamation Contest. This year, the first, second, and third places were won by the students of this Department. It is almost impossible to mention all that our students do in church work, such as conducting services, teaching Sunday Schools and providing church music, and radio braadcasting, & etc.

One very important program of the College is establishment of close contact with secondary schools. These schools feed the College with students. The Department inauguarated all Korea Secondary School English Oratorical Contest several years ago. The third Annual Contest was held in the evening of the 17th of November last. Fourteen schools from all parts of the Country participated in the Contest. We are greatly encouraged by remarkable result of this undertaking. We hope great orations and orators will come out of this contest.

GIFTS: This Department was not so fortunate to to receive many large gifts during the past year. We received a tuition scholarship of Y75 from a friend of the College for a worthy student in the Department. Dr. Han Sang Uok through Vice-President Yu generously presented to our Research Room the Complete work of Han Chang Suk. Mr. Suh Chai Keuk presented to us 17 pieces of public papers on the foreign relations of Korea. Mr. S. K. Hong of the College used his good offices in securing this gift. Vice-President Yu donated to the Department Research Room his collections of vernacular daily newspapers for the last ten years. All the daily papers published in the Korean language during the last decade form the collection. These volumes are going to be valuable source of information, and we are very grateful to Mr. Yu for this gift.

NEEDS: The Department has large needs as it grows. We need more equipment for research work. This being a young institution, we do not possess all academic journals. Contributions of such sets as academic journals on History, Philology, Oriental Civilization, Philosophy, Literature, Social Science, and all kinds of publications of learned societies will be most welcome. We need more books on all subjects, especially rare books of and on Korea. We have scholars well equipped to do research work for permanent contribution. It is pity that we can not provide these scholars with needy source materials. We need more scholarships, endowment for professorships, funds for search for and purchase of rare books, publication fund for Research Journal and books, and above all endowment for the work of this Department. Scholarships are in the most urgent need, as our students face desperate situation. It is most discouraging feature in our work when we can not help those worthy students who have to drop because of lack of funds. However, we try to make our motto "No worthy student has to drop out of the school at Chosen Christian College because of lack of funds." We hope our friends will help us to live up to our motto.

2. The Commercial Department

The Commercial Department is the largest department of the College with a faculty of 9 professors and assistant professors, 11 lecturers, one assistant and 171 students (Seniors - 50, Sophomores - 49 and Freshmen 72).

The Director, Prof. S. T. Lee, returned from his tour round the world in February, 1934, inspecting many of the European and American institutions of commerce and collecting numerous materials for teaching purposes. From April 1, 1934, he resumed his chair, discharging the daily duties of his office and of his teaching.

Every now and then he has been asked to make public lectures in Seoul as well as in the country on his observations of the world economic condition. He has published a number of helpful articles in the leading magazines and newspapers on the subjects in which he has been making studies and researches during his tour. He has written a book under the title of "A Tour Around the World". Small as it is, it is full of valuable information for anybody, especially for any prospective traveller who might choose to take the same course as he did.

Commercial Museum

The Commercial Museum has been growing steadily with additional specimens of native and foreign commodities making a total number of 1540. We are proud of the fact that at the present time our museum excells any of its kind in Korea in the number as well as in the variety of the specimens. Prof. N. W. Paik is in charge of the work.

Commercial Practice Work

Along with the theoretical studies of commerce and economics, the practical side of the course is no less important a phase. At the present time there are 11 typewriters for the students to practice on, but we are looking forward to a time when we can complete the equipment for this purpose.

3. The Science Department

Prof. C. H. Lee, M. A., is the Director of the Department. The Faculty of the Department is composed of 7 professors, 1 assistant professor, 3 lecturers, and 2 assistants: making a total teaching staff of 13 members. The enrollment of this year in the Department is as follows: 24 Freshmen, 17 Sophomores, 10 Juniors, 14 Seniors: making a total of 63 in all. A few changes were made during the last year in the teaching staff of the department. Mr. K. Katowaki, Professor in chemistry, was given a six month furlough on account of his health. He went to Kyoto, Japan, last October and since than he made his home there with his family, attending lectures in chemistry at Kyoto Imperial University. We expect him to be back with us at the beginning of this school year. Dr. Charles Choi was added to the teaching staff last September. He is a graduate of Engineering College in Seoul. He went to America and studied in several universities. He received a Master Degree in chemistry from Syracuse University and got a Ph. D. in chemistry from Ohio State University.

VIII. The Religious Activities.

BIBLE TEACHING: The teaching of this subject has been divided among Drs. E. M. Cable, H. K. Karl, L. G. Paik, Rev. R. C. Coen, and Rev. S. Y. Chang. Dr. E. H. Miller has assisted during the year. We are glad to welcome Dr. Karl and already his help has been greatly appreciated by teachers and students. This course has not yet been perfected but we hope to strengthen it materially in the next year or two.

Chapel Exercises: The chapel exercises have been conducted somewhat the same as last year. Much thought and attention has been given to this difficult yet most important phase of our college activities. On the whole, the services have shown marked interest but they are still far from what we hope for them. During the last term we attempted to secure speakers to represent every phase of Christian activity in order to acquaint the students with what Christianity is attempting to do in every phase of human activity. The members of the college staff have given their hearty support to this part of the college work and have been most loyal in doing whatever was asked of them.

Prof. C, M. Hyun has been in charge of the music in ghe chapel services. We all can see a great improvement not only in the singing of the students but also in their appreciation of music. We give two days a month in the chapel services wholly to music and these have been so successful and profitable that I feel we ought to give one day each week to this particular phase of worship.

Student Work: The Student distribution according to their religious affiliation is as follows: Methodists 138; Presbyterians 101; other Christian Denomination 3; non-Christians 82; This makes the non-Christians 25.3% of the student body. We find that 210 students live in the city. This leaves about one third of them in the college dormitory and the villages near the college. We should have more dormitory accomodations in order not to provide better facilities for the students, but in order to properly surpervise them. Rev. S. Y. Chang and Elder C. M. Song devote much of their time and strength to the looking after the students moral welfare. We feel very much the need of a Dean of men who could give his whole time to this all important work.

STUDENT RELIGIOUS WORK: Eighty students have regularly assisted in the various churches in and around the city of Seoul on Sundays, in preaching, teaching in Sunday Schools, assisting in music, and Young Peoples' meetings. During the summer a number of the students went out to assist in the Daily Vacation Bible Schools, and the reports of their summer's work were most interesting and inspiring. As we listened to their thrilling reports we all felt that they were making a real contribution to the work of the Kingdom in Korea. Very few of the regular pastors in Korea are put under more tryingcircumstances and endure as many hardships as these young men. During the Christmas vacation five young men visited five large centers in the south and were, not only able to assist the churches in their evangelistic programs, but in the music of the church and the work of the Young People. As a result of the winter's work the college Y. M. C. A. has published a small volume of folk-songs to be used in the churches among the young folks. I consider it a very constructive piece of work.

We are urging the College Y. M. C. A. to take up certain project work and we sincerely hope that a real beginning will be made in that this year. It is a pleasure to testify that these young men are ready and willing to do anything, go anywhere, and suffer anything for the cause of Christ. Lack of enthusiastic, heroic workers is unknown among the students at the Chosen Christian College.

THE FEDERATED CHURCH: This organization has now entered upon its third year. Rev. S. Y. Chang continues to be the most efficient pastor of the church. The attendance has made some increase during the year. We hope that Ewha College will unite with us in this project from the beginning of next school year.

The Sunday School under the efficient management of Dr. M. M. Lee has made splendid progress and has an attendance of about two hundred. A special feature is the English Bible Classes among the college students.

Miss Kim Hey Young, the Bible woman, has done very effective work among the women and the children of the church.

Special Meetings: Owing to a serious cut in the budget for the Religious activities of the college last year, we were not able to conduct a summer Conference for Church workers. I trust that some means can be provided, either by an endowment or otherwise, to make possible this feature of our work.

The special evangelistic services for the students and Staff of the college were held from January 21-25th. They were conducted by the Rev. Dr. H. K. Ryang, and President Emeritus, Dr. O. R. Avison. The former had charge of the theological side and the latter the apologetical side of the Christian life. We feel that these meetings were very helpful. We were especially gratified to have Dr. O. R. Avison and his addresses upon the vital problems affecting students were deeply appreciated.

Dr. E. M. Cable as chairman of the religious activities is in charge of this work in cooperation with Rev. S. Y. Chung.

IX The College Library.

The loss of Dr. J. E. Fisher from our College must have affected every branch of our College life, yet it is more keenly felt by the Library to which he gave so much time, thought, and energy for a good many years. As Librarian of the College he was succeeded by Dr. M. M. Lee, a graduate of our College, who has received Ph. D. degree in History in Boston University and has had a special training in Syracuse University for this work.

Regardless of the depression the growth of our Library is something phenomenal. The number of total accessions up to January 23, 1935 is 44,633 books of which 5470 is periodicals. The increase of over 12,000 volumes during the last nine months (May 1934- Jan. 23, 1935) is due to the hearty cooperation of the faculty and the staff, yet is largely due to the indefatigable efforts of President Underwood and Vice-President Yu. The former acquired about 1800 books from America, while the latter was instrumental in obtaining the following three valuable donations consisting of 9689 volumes:

(1) The late Rev. P. H. Choi...1641 books, 149 periodicals.

(2) The late Elder I. S. Kim...1184 books 100 periodicals.

(3) The late Baron C. S. Han...6466 books 149 periodicals.

It is estimated that the late Baron C. S. Han collection alone must be worth about twenty thousand Yen.

Aside from this, last year we also secured about 2478 books and 351 periodicals as a result of our Seven Year Library Campaign (began in 1932), aiming at total accessions of 50,000 books in the Library. The names of the donors with the number of books are as follows:

Donors	Books	Periodicals
Dr. O. R. Avison	69	1
Dr. H. H. Underwood	1707	92
Dr. E. M. Cable	99	15
Dr. S. H. Miller		2
Dr. J. E. Fisher	152	150
Dean Yu	35	20
Dr. L. G. Paik	36	17
Prof. N. W. Paik	1	
Prof. S. T. Lee	31	
Prof. S. K. Hong	2	
Prof. K. P. Choi	2	
Prof. C. H. Hyun	1	
Mr. K. H. Jung	41	
Mr. D. H. Kim		1
Mr. L. W. Kang	14	5
Alumni:		
Dr. S. J. Chey	4	21
Dr. H. M. Lee	264	20
Mr. P. K. Lim	6	7
Mr. C. H. Song	6	
Mr. K. S. Lyu	2	
Mr. H. N. Lyu	2	
Total	2478	351

Grand total---2829

The Friendly Association consisting of the Korean staff of the College added 21 more valuable books to its collection, while to the Avison Library M. Courant's "Catalogue des Livros Chinois, Coreens, Japonais" 8 volumes was added.

The total accessions of 44,633 of which 39,163 books are in the following languages:

A. Korean----- 3,143
B. Japanese--- 5,595
C. Chinese---- 21,518
D. Occidental- 8,907

We are also very happy to note the increase of reading interest among our students. The total number of books circulated in 153 days in 1933 (April-Dec.) was 4,763, while during the same length of time in 1934 about 5,802 books of which 658 were in English were borrowed by 4,198 students, showing an increase of 1039 books over last year and making a daily average of 38 books instead of 31 of last year. Even then it only means that every 10 students borrowed one book a day.

If statistics mean anything at all, we may be able to infer the general trend of reading interest of our students from the following table, indicating the nature and number of books the students read during the 153 days (April-Dec. '34) mentioned above:

(1) General works-chiefly reference and periodicals-------1510
(2) Literature------------------1282
(3) Social Science---------------- 940
(4) Science--------------------- 691
(5) Philosophy------------------ 419
(6) History--------------------- 315
(7) Useful Arts----------------- 226
(8) Religious Books------------- 159
(9) Fine Arts------------------- 133
(10) Philology------------------- 127

On account of rapid increase of books and introduction of some improved system we have put two new book shelves into the Reading Room for reference books and two into the Periodical Room. We also have had made two units of new card boxes with 30 drawers for shelf-list cards, 2 units of newspaper stand, two book wagons, and a dictionary stand and some other improvements in the stack

The staff of the Library now consists of three full time workers and two pages of whom one was added last Fall after the departure of Mr. S. H. Pak. Mrs. Cable is also helping us very generously and efficiently with many things. The staff shows a splendid spirit and works very dilligently even without taking vacation.

Despite many limitations and handicaps - lack of funds, space, and staff, etc.- we are progressing slowly but surely. We feel that the most urgent need of our Library is a separate library building where we can accomodate the rapid expansion and where we can place the Departmental Research Rooms so that problems of the library administration will be lessened and that the faculty and students will have better facilities for their research work.

X Physical Education

With the much reduced budget, our athletic activities were accordingly reduced in many ways. We tried our best, however, to keep the various sports going on as usual. Through the financial support by the Alumni and other friends of the College, we were able to send our basketball team to Tokyo last January to participate in the games for the Championship of Japan. A noteworthy event which will interest you most is our victory in baseball games with the Keijo Medical College, which in the past beat us four years in succession. The traditional annual (seventh annual) games were held on June 11th and 15th. On the first day before the game not only our players but all the student body and the faculty were on a nervous tension, being anxious as to the outcome of the games. But the boys fought to the end with a real fighting spirit and proved to be good sportsmen. The enthusiasm and self-control of the "Cheering Section" was another attraction and helped a great deal toward victory.

As soon as the games were over, the student body marched through the streets with the college band at the head, singing college songs and yelling, and finally dispersed in front of the station at 9:30 P. M. It was a real happy event for the college and stimulated college spirit among the students. We were all pleased with the fine spirit of the student body.

On October 2nd, the so-called "Physical Education Day", we had to have another baseball game with the Keijo Medical College team under the auspices of the City Government, for we were selected as the two best college teams to give an exhibition game. We beat them again by the score of 3 to 1.

On November 17th, our basketball team participated in the preliminary contest for championship in Japan under the auspices of the Korea Branch of the Japanese Basketball Association. We won the games and were privileged to go to Tokyo to take part in the games with the selected representative teams from the various parts of Japan. The games and scores were as follows:-

Date	Teams	Scores.
January 9th	Seda-We won	123-15
January 9th	Shiba " "	Forfeited.
January10th	Tokyo Imp.Univ. We lost	73-36

However, though we lost the semi-final game of the tournament, we arranged to have another game with the Tokyo Imperial University team on January 12th and we won this time by the score of 43-42. It was the first time for the said team (which had always been victorious in one-sided games, having held the championship for three years) to get beaten.

During the month of December our Basketball team participated in another set of games for championship under the auspices of the Central Y. M. C. A. and won it for another year. The results were as follows:-

Date	Teams		Scores.
December 12	Whooper	We won	52-22
December 13	S. U. M. C.	We won	72-40
December 14	Keijo Law Col.	We won	61-12
December 15	Samgak	We won	5?-21
December 17	Suri	We won	58-23
December 18	Paikyun(Alumni)	We won	48-24
December 19	Samil	We won	56-27
December 20	Korea	We won	37-28

On September 25th, we had a good game with the visiting team of Manchuria Medical College from Mukden and beat them flat by the score of 94-28.

On the Field-Day, September 24th, all the athletic events were held for the first time on a well-leveled field, the newly made 400-meter Track and Field. On the following day, we held the first annual Intramural Contest between the upperclassmen and freshmen in Track and Field Events, and the upperclassmen won.

On October 29th, the College Football team had a game at Whimoon Ground with the visiting team of "Cape Town", the British Cruiser. The game was well fought and finally came out at 1 to 1, tie.

Since last fall we have set aside every Wednesday Chapel period for holding "Mass Drill" for the Student Body and Staff out in the Outdoor Theatre. Before the mass drill begins a Hymn or College Song is sung and followed by prayer. It was found to be a very good way to develop college spirit without losing spiritual inspiritation.

A fund was secured last fall through the effort of President Underwood to build a good-sized skating-rink, including a hockey field, down south of the newly made field. But on accountof the delay in securing permission from the authorities we failed to start the work before the freezing season. The permission was not given till after Christmas. We will, however, start the work as soon as the Spring comes.

XI. Music

Clubs and Organizations.

Orchestra 34 Members
Glee Club 40 Members
Band 26 Members
String Quartet
Male Quartet.

--20--

Concerts and Concert Tour

As usual two regular concerts were held in Seoul and one Concert Tour was made to the following cities:-

PyengYang　Soonchun
Sinweiju　Antong
Moukden

We estimate that 9,000 people heard us on this tour.

Radio Program on J. O. D. K.

We conducted monthly a thirty minutes Sacred Music program on Sunday evening. Also, programs were given 26 times during the year by the orchestra, Glee Club, String Quartet, Male Quartet and soli.

Co-operation with Religious Activities and other Churches.

The Music Committee has charge of the Chapel Music, Union Church Music, and all of the Music program for the Religious activities.

Ten students were in charge as leaders of the church choirs in town. Twelve students had been in charge as singing teachers of Sunday Schools.

Forty students helped as Church choir members.

The Summer Music Conference.

The fourth Summer Music Conference, which was held at the College from July 30th to August 9th, was initiated by our College and it was very successful. There were eighty students in all, of which 57 were men and 23 women. They came from all over Korea. Some of them came from as far as Tokyo, Kobe, and even from Manchuria. 51 members were registered in singing and the Church Music Course, 17 in Piano, and 7 in Violin.

The duration of the conference for only ten days seems to be too short. Many of the members expressed their wishes to extend it for five days more. However, it will be necessary to have more teachers and more courses which means we will have to have a larger budget to do so.

High School Music Contest.

For the third time in Korea, the all-Korea middle school Music contest was held in June in the Pai Chai Hall. The responses from both the contestants and audience were amazing and delightful. Sixteen Schools (Eleven Boys' Schools and five Girls' Schools) took part in the Contest.

Scholarship.

A Scholarship of ¥75 for a student of music was awarded for the current year to Mr. Lee Inpum, a Literary Sophomore, for his merits in music and high standing in scholarship in the class.

Special Donation of Instruments and Music during the Year.

From Dr. Underwood

Two pianos
Two Violins
Two Banjos
Two Guitars
Two Mandolins
One Crow Violin
82 Phonograph Records.
182 pieces of sheet music.

From Mrs. A. L. Becker.

53 Pieces of Chorus Music.

From Dr. E. M. Cable.

32 Pieces of Quartet Music.

From Columbia Company.

One Electric Phonograph

From Mr. Homer Rodeheaver.

Six Song Books
Eight Pieces Sheet Music

All the above activities concerning music would not have been possible, had it not been for the indefatigable efforts of Dr. S. J. Chey as chairman of the committee, Prof. C. M. Hyun as Director, Mrs. A. L. Becker, Mrs. R. C. Coen and Mrs. H. H. Underwood.

Hopes and Needs.

The music Committee entertains large hopes for its future. We need some special funds for New Instruments, Music Books, Scholarships and for publications.

XII. Other Items of Interest.

1. Museum

Owing to last year's small amount of budget for the Museum, much to our regret we were not able to purchase as much as we wished. However, the good will and generosity of the faculty, students, and friends of our College enabled us to add a fine collection in quality, if not in quantity, to our Museum. The donors and the number of their gifts are as follows:

(1) During his recent trip to Philippines Dr. E. M. Cable secured and brought us,

(A) A spear
(B) A shield
(C) A native weapon (for beheading)
(D) An old Korean Passport.

(2) Prof. I. P. Chung gave us a piece of Stone-Scripture from the wall of the "Wha Am Temple" This object is about one thousand three hundred years and is an old Silla remain

(3) Prof. S. K. Hong was instrumental in acquiring the following objects:

(A) Tai keuk sa do (a dice board based on principles of Tai Keuk.)
(B) So jang do (pictorial explanation of Oriental Philosophy of positive and negative elements.)
(C) Handwriting of "Woo Am" (an old Korean famous Scholar)
(D) Self-Portrait of Kim Po Taik.
(E) An outfit of old Korean ceremonial dress for women.

(4) Dr. S. U. Han

(A) a brass dish
(B) A cane sword

(5) Dr. H. Y. Oh

(A) Two kinds of Manchurian coins.

(6) Dr. Arthur Noble

(A) A Korean hard wood
(B) A canon ball
(C) A Red-Cross copper plate

(7) The late Rev. P. H. Choi

(A) A Korean horsehair hat

(8) Mr. Dong Chul Kim

(A) One "Rin" copper coin

(9) Miss Wambold

A flute from Jerusalem.

If our budget permits us we should like to add portraits of eminent Koreans of the past and autographs and brush paintings of contemporary Koreans to our Museum.
Prof. O. Y. Lee, Curator of the Museum.

2. STUDENT HELP WORK.

During the academic year 1934-35, the Student Help work has been carried on with an appropriation of ¥700.00 In the past years this work had been carried out as a joint affair with the Property Committee. But under an unprecedented condition of things, it was left to be carried out with the appropriated amount only, thereby crippling the work to a large measure. It is true that nearly every branch of the college feels the pressure of the world economic depression, but this work in particular feels the fang of it much more keenly than any others if the demand for help is taken as the index of it.

During the last year, 11 students have been helped out of this fund: 7, by odd jobs; 2, by private tutorship; and 4, by making and selling apple cider, giving a total of 24 students who have come under the sphere of influence of this work, Of this number, some would not have been able to continue their studies, had it not been for the help of this work.

3. Clubs and Organizations.

a. C. C. C. Students Association (The Student Body)

b. C. C. C. Y. M. C. A. (Voluntary Organization)

c. Literary Society (Literary Department Students)

d. Economics Association (Commercial Department Students)

e. Science Club (Science Department Students)

f. Glee Club, Orchestra and Band (Voluntary, all Departments)

g. Oratorical Club (Voluntary, all Departments)

h. Friendly Association (Korean Teaching and Office Staff)

i. Dramatic Club (Voluntary, all Departments)

j. English Club (Voluntary, Commercial Department Students)

XIII. On Students.

1. Enrollment.

Annual average of the students who paid tuition during the past three years:

1931-32----214
1932-33----259
1933-34----304

Up to January 31st, 1935, there was a total enrollment of 324 students distributed as follows:

Class		Lit. Dept.	Com.Dept.	Sc.Dept.	Total
Freshmen		34	72	24	130
Sophomore		30	49	17	96
Junior		10	--	10	20
Senior		14	50	14	78
	Total	88	171	65	324

2. Classification of Students.

Department	Regular	Special	Total	Percentage
	Number of Students			
Literary	79	9	88	27.1%
Commercial	158	13	171	52.8
Science	61	4	65	20.1
	298	26	324	100.0%

3. Provinces from which students come.

Province	Number	Percentage
North Ham Kyung	9	2.8%
South Ham Kyung	22	6.8
North Pyung An	22	6.8
South Pyung An	34	10.5
Whang Hai	25	7.7
Kyung Ki	117	36.1
Kang Won	19	5.9
North Choong Chung	6	1.9
South Choong Chung	16	4.9
North Chun La	11	3.4
South Chun La	12	3.7
North Kyung San	15	4.6
South Kyung San	16	4.9
	324	100.0%

4. Students' Church Relations.

Denomination	No. of Students	Percentage
Presbyterian	101	31.2
Methodist	138	42.6
Other Christian Denominations	3	.9
Non-Christian	82	25.3
Total	324	100.0%

XIV. On Graduates.

1. The Total Number of Graduates from each Department.

(January 31st, 1935.)

Department	Number	Percentage
Literary	134	29.5%
Commercial	242	53.2
Science	76	16.5
Agricultural-(not-operating)	3	.8
	455	100.0%

2. Present Status of Graduates, January 31st, 1935.

Positions and Occupations	Number	Percentage
Teaching Staff in C.C.C.	10	2.18%
Non-Teaching Officers in C.C.C.	8	1.75
Teachers in other Christian Schools	59	12.96
Church Workers	23	5.06
Students in Seminary	2	.43
Teachers in Non-Christian Schools	15	3.30
Students in U.S.A.	23	5.06
Students in Japan	13	2.85
Students in China	2	.43
Student in France	1	.22
Journalists and Writers	10	2.18
Employees of Banks and Business Firms	85	18.68
Government Officials	38	8.35
Independent Commercial or Industrial Workers	55	12.08
Agriculturalists	8	1.75
Various Lines of Independent Business	74	16.26
Physician	1	.22
Deceased	28	6.14
Total	455	100.00%

3. Graduates' privileges conferred by Government.

a. The College has been given the privilege of giving a Bachelor's degree in each Department as Bachelor of Literature or Commerce or Science or Theology.

b. Government qualification for private primary school teachers. (See the Article III of Educational ordinances for private School teachers)

c. The graduates of the College are given qualification by the Government to teach in Private Higher Common Schools and Industrial Schools on the following subjects:-

To the graduates of the Literary Department
English, Korean and Chinese.
To the graduates of the Commercial Department
English, Commerce and Bookkeeping.
To the graduates of the Science Department
Mathematics, Physics and Chemistry.
To the graduates of the Agricultural Department
(not operating) Agriculture.

d. In accordance with the ordinance of Imperial Department of Education, No. 3, Art. 2, Sec. 4 (Daisho the 7th Year) this College has been placed on an equal plane with

The Japanese Higher Schools, Colleges and the Preparatory Departments of Universities, so that our graduates are exempted from the preliminary examinations for higher civil service positions and are qualified also for entering all Government and private universities

e. According to the Imperial Ordinance, No. 261 (Daisho the 2nd Year), the graduates of this college are granted the privilege of ordianry civil official appointment without examination (Ordanance on civil official appointment, Art. 6.)

XV. Research Work

The Research Work of the different lines of studies are as follows:

Literary Department

RESEARCH WORK: Research work is an important part of our program. The faculty have always striven to maintain the highest standards of productive scholarship, besides regular instruction. We made purchases, during the past year, source materials for archaeological, historicel, Philological, Literary and Philosophical works. We had a research assitant in the person of Mr. Shin Han Chul. He has completed his reports on several interesting investigations, though he was not able to complete his entire report on the reign of the King Seijong. Teachers have been aggressive in the pursuit of research work in their chosen field of learning. Mr. H.P. Choi's book on the Korean Grammar for Secondary Schools was first published last April and at once was adopted as textbook by many schools. The second edition was issued last fall and it has been received well. Mr. I.P. Chung's work on Historical Survey on the Spirit of the Korean Race is now appearing on the Dong-A Ilbo. His ripe scholarship and wide range of learning commend respect of all. Thirty installments are already appeared, and we are confident that it is going to be monumental work in the historical literature, when it is completed. Dr. L.G. Paik, at the request of the Presbyterian General Assembly wrote a Jubilee tract. One hundred thousand copies of the tract have been distributed. The same author wrote a booklet on the Life of Rev. H.G. Underwood, D.D., LL.D. at the request of the Presbyterian Board of Christian Training. Two thousand copies have been sold out. Dr. Cable is about to finish the first part of his research on the early America-Korean relations. It will be impossible to mention all the conferences, institutes in which our teachers took parts, and all the lecturers and addresses and short article by our teachers.

Mr. Chin Tai Son, a noted scholar, had about eight articles on the folk-lore of the Korean people; Prof. Coen had four in the Korea Mission Field; and Dr. M.M. Lee had one on "The July Revolution in France."

The Commercial Department

Research Work:

The Commercial Research Work has been carried on through the faculty members. This work facilitates the study and research of the teachers and students alike working on some commercial and economic problems. These results have been published in the leading magazines and newspapers from time to time. There are 70 magazines, 6 newspapers, and 2159 volumes of reference books in the Research Room. Prof. T.K. Roe is in charge of this work.

Prof. N.W. Paik is working on the second volume of his "Social and Economic History of Korea" which he expects to get off the press some time this year. In addition to this, he has published several valuable articles in the leading magazines and newspapers.

Prof. T.K. Roe, Prof. In Sup Jung and Prof. S.J. Chey also have published a number of articles of note in the magazines and newspapers and broadcasted several lectures on various subjects, thereby ringing the good name of Chosen Christian College through the general public as well as educational world of this peninsula. As to Prof. Jung, he represented the College at the meeting "For the advancement of the Teaching of English Language" which was held in Tokyo last October under the auspices of Educational Bureau of Japanese Government, and brought back with him much valuable informations and materials which will be of great help in our English teaching.

Prof. L.H. Snyder has already finished his "A Possible Solution of the War Debt Problem" and is collecting data for his second work " Some Financial Problems on Manchou Kuo".

The Research on Advertisement

The Commercial Department has begun this research work to study the methods of advertising and for reference. 7434 pieces of various kinds of posters, hand bills, folders, labels, enamel and card board signs, newspaper and magazine clippings, and etc. have been collected since April, 1933. Also 26 volumes of books have been secured for study and reference. These have been carefully classified and displayed in the Commercial Practice Room. Mr. P.K. Lim is in charge of the work.

The English Teachers Research Club

Ever since the club became a chartered member of the Institute for Research in English Teaching of the Educational Bureau of Japan, bulletins, periodicals, and publications have been sent to the college and they are being displayed for use in the Commercial Research Room for the time being. The club is devoting much time and effort in planning a unified method of teaching English as a part of this program, phonetics are taught from last year and to verify certain points in phonetics, a phonograph has been served in the department. The club has directed the students to form an English Club of themselves holding meetings with various programs and practicing English is various ways with much interest. Mr. S.K. Hong is the chairman of the Research Club.

Besides the above mentioned features of this department, we are holding an annual prize contest in thesis on some commercial or economic subjects in a way of leading the interest of the students along those lines. Another thing is the extra curriculum lectures of the teaching staff: Every member of the teaching staff is supposed to give a special lecture on his own research or study. This is a semesterial affair and thus far it has been very interesting and instructive to the teachers and students alike. The motive of this is that the teachers are forcing themselves to study and at the same time stir up the inferest of the students along various ways for their special study or as a source of general information.

The Science Department

Mr. Mann Hak Lee, a research student, had devoted himself to the work of research and experimentation on Korean Ohn Dole, Korean Hot Floor, for three years and has just completed his research work. His report is in the press for publication and it will be out within a few weeks. We all hope that his methods of improvement on the Ohn Dole may torn out to be a guiding principle in practice to the public.

An assaying laboratory which is very useful for chemical analysis was equipped last month and is now in full operation. A coal-fired furnace, a single coak-fired furnace, and a weighing balance of high sensibility compose the principal equiptments of the laboratory. Beside our own assaying works for the school we also plan to do assayings for the public and make a charge for the work.

XVI. Conclusion.

The facts mentioned above convince us that our College is progressing steadily year by year toward the high aims of the institution. The students in the College have come from about sixty Middle Schools in Korea, Japan, and China, showing how widely this College is known. Our alumni are working in every walk of life, and they are so loyal to their work and so successful that everywhere they go they exalt the Christian principles of their Alma Mater. The development of our College is in a large measure due to the fine spirit of hearty cooperation among our Faculty and Staff. Aside from their teaching, their sound scholarship and firm conviction expressed through radio, newspapers and magizines, and pulpits play an important role in molding and steering the destiny of this country.

The mission of our College is greatly appreciated and endorsed even by outsiders. The foundation of three new scholarships by the mother of Mr. Shur Min Ho, by Mr. Yun Tchi Chang, and by Kim Hi Choon; donation of valuable books and antiques to the College Library and Museum; and increasing demand for our graduates for banks and other vocations confirm this fact. The generous gifts of our frinds enabled us to heap about fifteen worthy students last year.

In our College athletic activities we emphasise sportsmanship, discipline, and team-work more than anything else. Our teams made a splendid record both in Japan and Korea. We won many games, and even in defeat we came out triumphantly because of our sportsmanship. Our staff also had a series of games with the Severance staff contesting for the Avison Cup and cemented good feelings between the two sister institutions.

The religious activities of our students deserve a great deal of praise and support. They help churches in Seoul and its vicinity in many capacities; and during the Summer and Winter vacations our gospel teams accomplished much in spreading messages of Christ and educating the masses.

Musical activities occupy a prominent position in our College life as well as in the entire country. By the means of an annual tour and Summer conference we are educating our people to appreciate music.

The College Library is expanding and improving rapidly in order to meet the needs of the faculty and students. We are in need of a chapel, a gymnasium, and a library building. Above all a library building is very desparetely needed. ※

In closing, we wish to thank God for His tender mercies and infinite visions. We also feel that this steady progress of our College is largely indebted to the far-sightedness of the Board of Managers, to the leadership of our President, Dr. H H. Underwood, and to the hearty cooperation of the Faculty and the Staff. We are sure that we will make more noticible progress next year, if we go steadily toward the high aims of this institution.

Respectfully submitted,

U. K. Yu

U. K. Yu Dean.

47. 원한경 교장의 이사회 제출 연례보고서

문서 제목	Report of the President to the Chosen Christian College for the Year 1935~36
문서 종류	교장 보고서
제출 시기	1936년 2월 26일
작성 장소	서울
제 출 자	H. H. Underwood
수 신 자	이사회
페이지 수	9
출 처	2114-5-4: 03 Underwood, Horace H. (DR.) 1936 (UMAH)

자료 소개

원한경 교장이 1936년 2월 26일 열린 이사회 연례회의에서 제출한 보고서이다. 이 보고서에 일자가 표기되어 있지는 않지만, 이사회의 이날 회의록에서 원한경이 교장 보고서를 발표한 후 이 보고서 안의 한 제안(뉴욕 협력이사회 이사장이었던 노스(F. M. North)의 죽음을 추도하자는 제안)에 이사들이 호응하였던 것을 확인할 수 있다. 이 회의 때 일본에서 암살당한 사이토를 추모하는 문제와 스팀슨관과 언더우드관의 화재보험을 갱신하는 문제도 논의되었다.

원한경은 이 보고서에서 아래의 주제들을 다루었다.

이사회, 예산, 봉급 규모, 임대료, 교수 사택, 자산, 기증받은 땅, 자산 목록, 구매 업무, 교직원, 교수 승진, 도서관, 음악, 종교 사역, 학생 훈육과 지도, 등록생, 학과, 운동경기, 학교 홍보, 기부금, 동문회.

내용 요약

이사회: 한 해 동안 우리는 학교 기능을 강화하고 유용하게 만들기 위해 노력해왔다.

예산: 1936~37년도 예산이 약간 늘어났지만, 필요한 것이 많아 도서 구입, 음악 활동, 운동경기에 적은 금액만 책정하였다.

봉급: 지난해 채택한 봉급 규모가 이번 해에 적용되어 약간의 변동이 이루어졌지만, 앞으로 다시 개정할 필요가 생길 것이다.

교수 사택: 오래전부터 캠퍼스 안의 사택에서 살았던 교수들에게 갑자기 임대료를 내라고 하는 것은 합당하지 않다. 그들은 대학 예산을 위해 봉급에서 이미 많은 기부를 하였다. 예산 때문에 교수 사택의 신축이 무기한 중지되어 덜 좋은 집들을 사서 유용하게 개조하였다.

자산: 채플실의 천정을 높이고 환기 시설을 하여 수용공간을 넓혔고, 철로 남쪽의 소유지를 ¥85,000에 팔았다. 연희보명학교[초등학교] 건물을 임시 기숙사로 개조할 수 없게 되었다.

기증받은 땅: 땅을 기증받아 기본재산을 늘리려 하는 계획이 강원도 통천에서 어려움에 봉착하였다.

자산: 8월 개학 전에 전체 교직원이 모든 자산에 대한 목록을 작성하였다. 이는 학교 운영의 효율성을 높이기 위해 오래전에 해야 했던 일이었다.

구매 업무: 구매 업무를 맡을 부서를 적절히 조직할 필요가 있다.

교직원: 에비슨 전임 교장이 1935년 12월 한국을 떠났고, 밀러, 케이블, 스나이더가 안식년 중이며, 현제명이 음악 공부[박사학위 취득]를 위해 1년간 나가 있을 예정이다. 1915~17년간에 본교 교수로 있었던 미시간대의 루퍼스(W. C. Rufus)가 6개월간 있으면서 한국 천문학을 연구하고 강의도 하였다. 이묘묵과 하경덕은 조교수가 되었다. 협력이사회의 이사장이었던 북감리회 선교부 총무 노스가 돌아가셨다는 소식이 왔는데, 이사회 회의를 잠시 멈추고 채플에서 추모 예배를 드릴 것을 제안한다.

도서관: 도서관에서 한 해 동안 3,518권을 더하여 사실상 50,000권을 모았고, 이묘묵이 1년 동안 여성 직원 3명을 데리고 도서를 완벽하게 분류하였다. 공간이 부족하여 한문 서적을 상품진열관 뒤에 두었는데, 특별 기부금으로 장소 문제를 해결하였다.

음악: 현제명이 음악 서가를 크게 늘렸으나 여전히 협소하고, 음악실이 도서관 바로 위에 있어서 불편하다. 하기강습회가 7월에 가장 많은 인원과 함께 열렸고, 채플 예배 때 베커 부인, 코엔 부인이 수고[반주]하고 있다.

종교 사역: 학생들이 지방 교회들에서 봉사하였고, YMCA 학생들이 30,000명에게 메시지를 전하였으며, 감리교신학교의 빌링스가 특별집회를 이끌었다.

학생 훈육: 1931년 학생회가 해산된 후 학생들이 오랫동안 계획하여 학생조직을 만들려 하고 있다. 적절한 교육을 위해 필요한 것으로 생각한다.

등록생 · 학과: 등록생이 역사상 가장 많게 400명으로 시작하여 367명(문과 109명, 상과 196명, 수물과 62명)으로 한 해가 끝났다. 백낙준, 이순탁, 이춘호가 교육적으로나 영적으로 전보다 더 효율적으로 일하였다. 학과들에 대해 더 자세히 알려면 학감의 보고서를 참고하라.

운동경기: 운동경기 분야는 올해 대학 역사상 최고의 해를 보냈다. 야구팀이 봄과 가을에 경성제대 팀을 이겼고, 축구팀, 농구팀, 테니스팀은 전국대회에서 우승하였으며, 야구팀이 일본 원정경기에서 승리하였다. 아이스하키팀은 일본에서, 축구팀은 상해에서 패하였다.

학교 홍보: 운동경기가 신문에 보도되고 교수들의 글이 잡지와 신문에 게재되고 있다. 학교에 관한 교수들의 글을 미국에도 보내어 홍보하면 좋을 것 같다.

기부금: 미국에서 무명으로 기부금이 왔고, 15명의 학생에게 장학금을 주었다. 영동에 사는 한국인들이 ￥2,000의 도서기금을 기부하였다.

동문회: 동문회가 1940년 개교 25주년을 대비하여 ￥50,000을 준비하면서 일부를 지급하였다. 본교 출신 갈홍기 교수가 동문회 서기이고, 이원철, 이묘묵, 최순주가 동창회 일을 열심히 하고 있다.

REPORT OF THE PRESIDENT

TO THE

CHOSEN CHRISTIAN COLLEGE

FOR THE YEAR

1935--36

******

Report of the President to the

Chosen Christian College for the year 1935-36

****

Board of Managers

The activities of the year for which I have the honor to report to you today have been varied and manifold, but are not of such a type as to lend themselves readily to presentation in written report, or even in comparative statistics. That much used and much abused phase "report of progress" would probably best summarize the period. We have endeavored to put into execution the suggestions and recommendations which I made last year. We have endeavored to strengthen and make more efficient the operation of the entire College machine from the details of business management and property administration to curricula, classroom procedure and religious activities.

Budget

The task has been made more difficult by our greatly reduced budget of ¥95,866.00, the smallest under which we have operated for many years. The budget which is before you today for the year 1936-37 shows an increase over last year, but is still woefully below our needs for efficient operation, and far short of what we should have if we are to take advantage of the opportunities for service which lie before us. The budget question is covered in the report of the Finance Committee, but I would merely call your attention to a few facts in connection with it. For the purchase of new books for our library the budget only allows about a thousand yen for the year; for research work in the three departments we have been able to allow only about five hundred yen; for music, aside from salaries we have allotted only about a thousand yen, for the expenses of all of our athletic teams, we plan to spend only two thousand yen, which is something like five hundred yen less than the amount to be collected from the students for athletic fees and lastly we are still receiving approximately ¥7,000 from salary contributions from our staff.

Salary Scale

The salary scale adopted last year has been put into operation. Actual trial over a period of years will doubtless show more clearly both its advantages and its short comings and it is probable that it will require revision from time to time in view of actual experience and according to changes in economic conditions. The scale as adopted caused very slight changes for the current year, but it is my understanding that the Board in directing the preparation and adoption of such a scale intended that it should actually be put into operation and we have therefore acted accordingly.

Rents

Closely related to the salary question is that of rental on residences on which I reported last year. The scale then adopted has been put into effect and it is no more than just to state that it has been accepted by the staff in a very fine spirit of loyalty and cooperation. The fact that the scheme is theoretically just and proper, does not make it any more palatable or easy for those who have occupied College houses rent free for a number of years and who now suddenly find themselves required to pay rent on those houses. This is the more true when those same individuals are already making generous contributions from their salaries to the budget of the College.

Residences

As reported last year the construction of any new residences was indefinitely held up on account of the budget situation. We have however done a good deal toward making some of the less desirable houses more useful and have fitted up some of the houses purchased during the year as College residences.

Property

In addition to such remodelling or repairs to residences as that just referred to, the ceiling of our chapel has been raised and ventilators installed to make the galery more useful and to increase its seating capacity. With these changes we shall probably be able to accommodate our estimated student body of about 410 for the coming year, but what we shall do in the following year if the enrollment continues to increase is one of the really major problems which we are facing.

The largest single property item to be reported is the sale of our holdings south of the railway line for a total of about ¥85,000. The proceeds from this sale are being invested in accordance with the directions of the Finance Committee and the estimated income of ¥4,500 from this sum of money is being used to help us out in the budget.

In the general upkeep and supervision of property, the property committee has functioned most efficiently and I take great pleasure in commenting upon the splendid work done by Mr. C. K. Kim, our Superintendent of Buildings and Grounds. I regret to state that it was found impossible to carry out during this year the proposed remodelling of the Po Myung Primary School building as a temporary dormitory. The plan has not been abandoned, but it was found necessary to pospone it for sometime.

Endowment Land

Attention is still being given to the scheme for securing additional endowment in the form of land grants. Especially severe storms coupled with local prejudices caused us some set-backs in connection with the land at Tongchun in Kang Won Province, but I hope to be able to make a more favorable report on this matter next year.

Inventory

The entire staff reported for work a week before the opening of school last August in order to carry out the first steps in the taking

(3)

of a thorough inventory of all our property and the treasurers office has had a special man working on this ever since. This is a thing which should have been done long ago and which should add greatly to the efficient operation of the business end of the College.

Purchasing

Closely connected with the inventory of equipment and materials now on hand is the purchasing of new materials and we are gradually working toward the concentration of all purchasing in the hands of the treasurer. There has been some slight misunderstanding and friction in connection with this new departure and as we have as yet no properly organized Purchasing Department there has been some creaking and groaning as the machinery of the treasurers office has been forced to take on an additional load. All parties concerned however, have worked in a most commendable spirit of cooperation and willingness, both to undertake additional work and to adapt themselves to minor inconveniences for the general good.

Staff

All of this mechanical work as well as the educational functions of the College have only been carried out through the efficient work of the entire staff. No startling changes in personnel have occured during the year with the exception of the departure from Korea of our beloved President Emeritus Dr. O. R. Avison, who left for the Occident in December 1935. His cheery presence; wise advice and inspiring guidance are missed by us all. The staff has also been handicapped by the fact that Dr. E. H. Miller, Dr. E. M. Cable and Prof. L. H. Snyder were all on furlough at the same time. This has imposed additional burdens both on the remaining members of the staff and on the budget in supplying teachers to take their place. Dr. E. W. Koons, principal of the John D. Wells academy has helped out in Bible teaching for the year and the experiment of securing such outside assistance has been most successful, not only from the point of view of the teaching done, but from the closer contact established between the College and a large high school. It is my hope when opportunity offers to bespeak a similar favor from Mr. Appenzeller at Pai Chai and other prominent men in the city. Mr. G. C. Speidel gave us most efficient service almost up to the end of the academic year when the illness of Mrs. Speidel forced him to leave on furlough somewhat earlier than he had anticipated. We look forward to his return to the College and hope that the representatives of his mission on our Board will do everything possible to assure his assignment to this work on his return. While no further furloughs are due during the coming year, Prof. Rody Hyun plans to leave very shortly for a year of intensive study in Music, his expenses being provided through the generousity of Mr. Homer Rodeheaver. We shall greatly miss Prof. Hyun during his absence but expect to receive our reward when he returns, full of new inspiration and with the benefits of a year of study.

While not a member of our staff it has been a great pleasure to have with us for almost six months Prof. W. Carl Rufus of the University of Michigan who was on the faculty of this College from 1915-1917.

Dr. Rufus was doing some research study into ancient Korean Astronomy. The work was done in cooperation with the staff of the Literary Department and will be published as English Publication No. 3 of that Department. Dr. Rufus also lectured to our students on a number of occasions and his presence was most helpful in many ways.

Promotions

I take great pleasure in recommending to the Board of Managers that Dr. M. M. Lee and Dr. K. D. Har be appointed to the rank of Assistant Professor.

Dr. M. M. Lee is known to you all as our Librarian and as a graduate of this College who returned to us in 1934 after securing his Ph.D. degree from Boston University.

Dr. K. D. Har has served for a number of years first as lecturer and then as instructor in the Literary Department. He holds the degree of Ph. D. from Harvard University and is a young man from whom we hope great things. Were our budget conditions more favorable I should be tempted to make further recommendation for promotions, but feel under the circumstances I can not at present recommend additional advances.

The efficient functioning of the College depends of course not only upon the staff here, but on the generous and self-sacrificing work of this Board and its committees, and of the Cooperating Board in New York. It is in this connection that the College has suffered, the severest blow of the year in the death of the Chairman of the Cooperating Board, Dr. Frank Mason North. I can say nothing which will adequately express the sense of loss which we all feel. As soon as the news was received a cable of condolence was dispatched to New York and I am asking that this Board do presently adjourn for a memorial service for Dr. North to be held in the College chapel. A great friend of Korea and of this College has passed to his reward and as we gather in the chapel we can only pray that the inspiration of his life and service may help us all to reconsecrate ourselves to the work of the Kingdom for which he gave himself so unstintedly for so many years. We have not yet been informed as to who has been chosen to fill his place as Chairman of the Cooperating Board, but we are sure that with the membership of the Board as it is, they could not make a bad choice.

Library

Coming back to the work of the College I would report first on the library. During the year that has past the accessions to the library have numbered 3618 thousand volumes, bringing our collection to practically 50,000 volumes. Dr. M. M. Lee's work during his first year as Librarian made it perfectly plain that the most urgent need of the library was proper classification and cataloguing and that the library's rapid growth made this imperative at once if we were not to be so swamped and get so far behind that it would be impossible to ever catch up. Special gifts received during the year made it possible to make a real start along this line by hiring three well educated young women who have been trained by Dr. Lee and who during the year have classified and catalogued over 5000 books. In order to continue this work during the coming year we have deliberately cut the budget for the purchase of books to the absolute minimum trusting largely to gifts both of books and of money to supply our needs in accessions. The crowded conditions of the room occupied by the library made it necessary to move several thousands of the reference books in Chinese into the rear of the Commercial museum and a further special gift made it possible to provide some additional stacks for the greatly increased number of books. The time is not far distant however, when no such shifts and changes will avail in our attempts to find space for the library. Certainly an adequate library building is one of our greatest needs.

Music

Prof. Hyun has gradually been building up quite a music library in addition to his other work and here also the question of space will soon be pressing. The location of the present music room on the floor immediately above the library is not satisfactory either for music or for the library. Adequate provision should be made for this work in which the College has gone so far under the guidance of Prof. Hyun. Perhaps when Mr. Hyun returns from America he will bring with him the much needed music building in which the various parts of our musical program can be adequately carried out. Space does not permit me to report fully, on all that Mr. Hyun and the Music Committee have done, but not only have our concerts been of an exceptionally high standard but the Summer Music Conference held last July was the largest and most successful which we have conducted. In concerts, in chapel music and in special programs Mrs. Becker and Mrs. Coen continue to do a very splendid and very difficult piece of work.

Religious Work

The work in music is not limited to the students who practice and play in College but is carried by them to many thousands of others. In country churches and Sunday Schools, in Daily Vacation Bible School and in Summer work the music forms an intergral of the Religious Work done by our students. Again space does not permit for me to report on this in detail but both during the summer and Christmas vacation the student Y.M.C.A. sent out teams whose work was most successful and worthwhile. A total of some 30,000 people heard their message, the results which can not of course be appraised in statistical terms.

The special week of Religious Services this year was conducted by Dr. B. W. Billings of the Methodist Episcopal Theological Seminary who was for so many years a member of our faculty that we still consider him as our own. These were supplemented by special meetings with the seniors of the three Departments and by personal interviews and conferences. Dr. Billings's message made a deep impression upon the entire student body as was shown both during the meetings and by their comments afterwards. The answers to his request that they state freely problems which were troubling them were most interesting and showed that a surprisingly large portion of the student body realized the vital nature of religious and spiritual problems. We can not be too grateful to Dr. Billings especially as he graciously consented to come to us on very short notice. There are few in Korea who would have come to our rescue as he did and still less who could do so.

(6)

In addition to these special meetings the Religious Committee has given us a particularly high order of chapel speakers and services throughout the year and, the conduct under the Chairmanship of Mr. Coen of the various phases of our Religious Work has been especially fine.

Student Discipline and Guidance

The system of special faculty advisors is beginning to function more satisfactorily and the series of orientation lectures during freshman week was most successful and will in the future be a regular feature of our work.

The students have for sometime felt the need for some form of student organization and after lengthy conference, consultation and study, plans are now under way for the creation of a student organization, to take the place of the students association which was dissolved in 1931. Special pains have been taken to safeguard ourselves against the mistakes of the past and the undesirable features of the old system. It is my firm belief that despite the difficulties and drawbacks some form of student organization is necessary to the proper education of young men toward self-government and self-control.

Enrollment

We opened last April with an enrollment of just over 400, the largest in the history of the College. The usual causes have cut the number down till now at the end of the academic year we have 367 students on our rolls. These are divided between the three Departments as follows: Literary 109, Commercial 196 and Science 62.

The payment of fees has been good with the exception of this present winter term which is always the most difficult time for the students and even in this term, although the payments have not been as prompt as they were in the other two terms, they are now practically all in.

Departments

I will not attempt to deal in detail with the work of the three Departments except to state my belief that the directors, Dr. L. G. Paik, Mr. S. T. Lee, and Mr. C. H. Lee and their respective staff have functioned not only as usual, but with a greater degree of efficiency both educationally and spiritually than ever before, and this despite furloughs, budget shortage and other difficulties. The dean's report gives more detailed information for any who are interested. Students of all three departments unite in the various activities of the College, dramatic, musical, athletic and others.

Athletics

Especially in athletics this year has been a real banner year for the Chosen Christian College. In the spring we won the annual series of baseball games with the Keijo Medical College and beat them again in a post-season game in the fall. At the Annual Athletic Meeting held by the

Chosen Athletic Association we carried off the all Korea Championship in football, basketball and tennis, the first time that any institution has won three pennants in one day. Our basketball team went to Japan and came back as champions of the Japanese Empire. This is the first time that any Korean team has succeeded in winning this honor at least three members of this team will represent Japan at the Olympics. At the same time an All Korea Team largely composed of Chosen Christian College athletes won the Soccer Championship of the Empire and probably two of our students will be on the Japanese team at the Olympic games. Despite the shortage of water and consequence failure of our own rink, our Ice Hockey team defeated all comers in Korea and went to Japan where it suffered its only defeat of the season at the hands of one of the strongest teams in the Japanese Empire. Our football team later made a trip to Shanghai where although it was defeated in two games by strong occidental teams it yet beat the very strong All-China Chinese team. We can not of course hope for such results every year, but coupled with the excellent sportsmanship shown on all occasion they are most gratifying and give the College very fine advertising. The work in Judo and Fencing goes on despite our lack of equipment and has attracted a large number of students till at present they are about 70 who are participating in this very valuable form of athletic training and discipline.

Publicity

In addition to the free advertising from athletics the various activities of the College have been well reported in the Korean press so that scarcely a week goes by without the Chosen Christian College figuring in someway in the press. The Literary work of the members of our staff covers a wide field and articles from their pens appear frequently in the magazines and newspapers of the country.: I have also attempted to see to it that our friends in the home lands should not forget us, and have published and distributed through a carefully selected mailing lists, a thousand copies each of my report to this Board; of Prof. Coens article on Student Evangelism; of Dr. M. M. Lee's article on the Chosen Christian College library and of a brief report of my own on the work of the College. In addition to this I have written over 250 letters to interested friends and possible supporters of the College as well as sending out about 500 special appeals for prayers and for special help. The response has not been large, but is still many times the cost of distribution, having already amounted to about ¥500 in money as well as quite a large number of personal replies indicating interest and the possibility of future support.

Gifts

A special gift of $1300 received from an anonymous friend in the United States last spring was a real life saver in making it possible for us to restore some of the most imperative needs which had been cut. On the field all but about 200 of the accessions to the library have been gifts.

One or two more endowed scholarships have come to us during the year, so that of 15 annual scholarships granted by the College, only three are now a charge upon our budget. The largest single gift received during the year was a donation to the library fund of ¥2000 from a Korean gentleman from the town of Young Dong, secured through the efforts of our treasurer,

(8)

Dr. S. J. Chey. The Vice-President has devoted much time to the cultivation of prospective donors and to a careful survey of ways and means for promotional work in Korea and the Friendly Association of the Chosen Christian College composed of our teachers, provided the salary of a special clerk for this for six months. While it is impossible from the economic conditions and per capita wealth of the Korean people that very large gifts can be secured in Korea, we still feel confident that much can be done along this line.

Alumni

An interesting and encouraging proof that this belief is not ill founded lies in the generous pledge of the Alumni Association to raise a fund of ¥50,000 for our 25th anniversary in 1940. Of this sum something over ¥10,000 has already been pledged and quite a good deal actually paid in. When we remember that the Alumni at present number only about 500 young men and that the vast majority of these are less than ten years out of College the courage and loyalty of the men who have gone out from the Chosen Christian College is evident. Dr. H. K. Karl of our staff who graduated from the Literary Department in 1928 and returned from America last year, is acting as Alumni secretary and has done very fine work in revivifying the Alumni Bulletin and in keeping in touch with the Alumni. Mr. K. C. Lyu of our office staff and one of our first graduates, Dr. W. C. Lee, Dr. M. M. Lee and Dr. S. J. Chey have all been very active in Alumni affairs and have succeeded remarkably in maintaining the interest and loyalty of our widely scattered graduates.

We are at present passing through a rather difficult period of readjustment, of stock taking, of planning and of financial difficulty. The totalitarian theories of government prevalent here as in many other parts of the world do not tend to make this period easier, whatever may be their final effect on education, one of the chief problems which faces us as we emerge from the status of a small and newly established school into that of a large and modern college is that of conserving and maintaining the personal contact, essential to character building; while at the same time seizing upon the advantages and opportunities of greatly increased numbers. Despite the apparent success of mass production in education in both the Occident and the Orient I am more and more convinced that unless we can maintain this personal touch, unless our students continue to be our boys and not our educational cases, we shall probably fail in achieving even the highest aims of secular education and we shall certainly fail in the spiritual values for which the institution was founded. The problem has our keenest attention and is the subject of constant prayer. We appreciate all that the Cooperating bodies and their representatives do for us through this Board, but most of all we ask that we may have your prayers for the achievement of success in the truest sense that all of these young men may come "To know Him whom to know aright is life Eternal".

Respectfully submitted

Horace H. Underwood
President

HHU/DTA

48. 유억겸 부교장 겸 학감의 이사회 제출 연례보고서

문서 제목	Chosen Christian College, Report of the Dean (1935~1936)
문서 종류	학감 보고서
제출 시기	1936년 2월 26일
작성 장소	서울
제 출 자	유억겸
수 신 자	이사회
페이지 수	27
출 처	2114-5-4: 03 Underwood, Horace H. (DR.) 1936 (UMAH)

자료 소개

유억겸 부교장 겸 학감이 1936년 2월 26일 열린 이사회 연례회의에서 제출한 보고서이다. 유억겸이 이 회의에 참석하였지만, 보고서는 백낙준이 읽었다.

유억겸은 이 보고서도 예년의 학감 보고서와 비슷하게 목차를 구성하였다.

I. 서언, II. 운영진 · 교수진, III. 3개 학과, IV. 종교활동, V. 도서관, VI. 체육 교육, VII. 음악, VIII. 다른 사항들, IX. 학생, X. 졸업생, XI. 연구사역, XII. 결어.

내용 요약

I. 원한경 교장의 리더쉽과 교직원들의 협력으로 본교가 꾸준히 발전하고 있다.

II. 운영진은 원한경(교장), 유억겸(부교장, 학감), 백낙준(문과 과장), 이순탁(상과 과장), 이춘호(수물과 과장), 최순주(회계), 이묘묵(도서관장)이다. 대학 교무위원회는 교장, 부교장, 백낙준, 이순탁, 이춘호, 코엔(신과 과장), 베커와 스피델(남 · 북감리회 선교회 대표)로 구성되어 있다. 대학 예산위원회는 원한경, 유억겸, 백낙준, 이순탁, 이춘호, 베커, 스피델, 최순주로 구성되어 있다. 에비슨은 명예 교장이다. 교수는 21명(한국인 13명) 조교수는 6명(한국인 4명)이고, 전임강사는 5명(한국인 4명), 강사와 조수는 22명(한국인 18명), 파트타임 조력자는 4명, 안식년 중인 교수 4명, 사무직원(사감 포함)은 13명이다.

III. 본교는 종합대학 체제를 이루고 있다. 문과는 개정된 교육과정에 따라 동양 문학,

동서양 역사, 독어, 불어, 중국어를 선택과목으로 가르치고 있다. 민원식이 불어를 가르기 시작하였으며, 제4회 대학 영어웅변대회에서 문과의 김성섭이 우승하였다. 상과는 박효삼(메이지대)이 교수로 왔고, 백남운, 정인섭이 신문과 잡지에 연구 논문들을 발표하였으며, 교수들이 여름에 동아일보 후원으로 순회 강연을 하였다. 상품진열관을 확충하고 상업 실습용 비품을 완비하였다. 수물과는 밀러의 부재 속에서 어려움을 이겨냈고, 이원철이 과학박물관을 크게 발전시켰으며, 최규남이 연구실을 맡고 있다.

IV. 코엔이 종교부를 이끌었고 백낙준, 갈홍기, 이묘묵, 장석영이 조력하였으며, 채플 시간과 순서를 조정하였다. 교수들은 매주 수업 시작 전 30분 동안 기도회를 열고 있고, 학생들은 서울 근교의 많은 교회를 돕고 있다. (연합교회와 특별집회에 관해서도 설명하고 있다.)

V. 도서관은 장서의 분량, 운영, 효율성 면에서 큰 발전을 이루었다. 예산 축소로 200권밖에 사지 못하였지만, 많은 기부를 받아 49,325권을 소장하고 있고, 매일 학생 1인당 1.03권이 순환되고 있다. (기부자들과 기부받은 도서들의 목록을 제시하고 있다.)

VI. 체육 교육 분야는 부족한 예산에도 불구하고 기념비적인 성공을 거두었다. 축구, 야구, 농구, 테니스, 아이스하키 대회에서 우승하였고, 농구팀과 아이스하키팀을 도쿄에, 축구팀을 상해에 보냈으며, 농구 선수 3명이 베를린 올림픽 참가팀에 선발되었다. (각종 경기의 전적을 목록으로 나열하고 있다.)

VII. 우리 대학의 음악 활동은 현제명과 긴밀히 연결되어 있다. 한 사람이 어떻게 그처럼 많은 일을 할 수 있는지 때때로 의아하다. 오케스트라 단원은 34명, 합창단원은 42명, 밴드 단원은 30명이고, 현악 4중주단과 남성 사중창단이 있다, 연례 음악회를 서울에서 열었고, 원산에서 웅기까지 순회공연을 하였다. 라디오에도 다양하게 출연하였고, 제5회 하기음악강습회를 개최하였으며, 채플과 여러 교회에서 음악 순서를 맡았다. 제4회 중등학교 현상음악대회(콩쿨)를 개최하였고, 문과 3학년 문학준에게 장학금을 수여하였다. 악기, 음악책, 장학금, 홍보를 위한 특별 기금이 필요하다.

VIII. 박물관을 언더우드관에서 아펜젤러관으로 옮겼고, 기증품들을 받거나 러들로 교수로부터 대여하였다. (입수한 물품들의 목록을 제시하고 있다.) 학생지원업무로 총 ¥780을 조성하여 1936년 1월까지 18명을 도왔다. (학생 클럽들과 단체들의 목록을 제시하고 있다.)

IX. 학생은 1월 31일까지 총 367명(문과 109명, 상과 196명, 수물과 62명)이 등록하였고, 본과는 334명, 별과는 33명이었다. (출신 지역과 종교 현황을 표로 제시하고 있다.)

X. 졸업생은 총 530명이고, 현재 연전 교수 10명, 연전 직원 10명, 다른 기독교학교 교사 65명, 교회 사역 22명, 의학생 1명, 비기독교학교 교사 17명, 미국 유학 23명, 일본 유학 25명, 중국 유학 2명, 영국 유학 1명, 언론인 13명, 은행원 및 회사원 96명, 공무원 43명, 개인사업(상공업) 80명, 농업 28명, 다양한 개인사업[家業] 59명, 의사 1명, 광업 3명, 사망 31명이다. (졸업생이 받는 자격에 관해서는 이전과 같은 내용을 제시하고 있다.)

XI. 연구사역으로 문과에서 최현배가 문법책[『우리말본』, 1937년 간행]을 출간 · 배포할 예정이고, 정인보가 계속 신문에 글[오천년간 조선의 얼]을 연재하고 있으며, 교수들이 잡지와 신문에 많은 글을 발표하고 있다. 상과에서도 교수들과 학생들이 상업과 경제 문제를 연구하여 주요 잡지와 신문에 글을 발표하고 있다. 정인섭이 조선어 음성 훈련을 실험하고 있고, 임병혁이 광고 방법 연구를 이끌고 있다. 수물과에서는 광물분석 실험을 하고 있고, 이원철이 천문학 연구와 강연을 하고 있다. 최규남이 물리학을 연구하고 신문과 잡지에 글을 발표하고 있다. 도서관의 이묘묵도 유럽사에 관한 글을 정간물에 발표하였고, 유경상이 한국 주요 도서서지 사전을 완성하였다.

XII. 결론적으로 학교가 스포츠 활동, 종교 활동, 연전타임스(C.C.C. Times) 창간(1935년 9월), 음악 활동, 도서관 운영 등 여러 방면에서 크게 발전하였다.

Extra Copy

CHOSEN CHRISTIAN COLLEGE
Report of the Dean
(1935--1936)

****

CONTENTS

CHOSEN CHRISTIAN COLLEGE

Report of the Dean

I. Introductory Remarks

To the Field Board of Managers of the Chosen Christian College at the Board Meeting held on February 26th, 1936.

I have the honor to submit the following report concerning the academic phase of the College Administration for the academic year 1935--1936.

Under the leadership of President Underwood, and with the hearty co-operation of all members of the Faculty and Staff the College has progressed steadily toward the aims set forth at the foundation of the Institution. The events described in this report will endorse this statement.

II. Officers of Administration and Instruction

A. Administrative Officers.

Horace H. Underwood, M.A., Ph.D., Litt.D., President.

Uok Kyum Yu, Gakushi, Vice-President and Dean.

L. George Paik, M.A., Ph.D., Director of the Literary Department.

Soon Tak Lee, Gakushi, Director of the Commercial Department.

Choon Ho Lee, M.A., Director of the Science Department.

Soon Ju Chey, B.S.E., M.B.A., Ph.D., Treasurer.

Myo Mook Lee, M.A., Ph.D., Librarian.

B. College Council.

Horace H. Underwood, Ph.D., Litt.D., President.

Uok Kyum Yu, Gakushi, Vice-President and Dean.

L. George Paik, Ph.D., Director of the Literary Department.

Soon Tak Lee, Gakushi, Director of the Commercial Department.

Choon Ho Lee, M.A., Director of the Science Department.

A. L. Becker, Ph.D., Representative of the M. E. C. Mission.

C. C. Speidel, M.S., Representative of the M. E. C. S. Mission.

R. C. Coen, B.D., M.A., Chairman of the Religious Activities Committee.

(2)

C. <u>College Budget Committee.</u>

H. H. Underwood, Ph. D., Litt. D., President.
U. K. Yu, Gakushi, Vice-President and Dean.
L. G. Paik, Ph. D., Director of the Literary Department.
S. T. Lee, Gakushi, Director of the Commercial Department.
C. H. Lee, M. A., Director of the Science Department.
A. L. Becker, Ph. D., Representative of the M. E. Ch. Mission.
G. C. Speidel, M. S., Representative of the M. E. C. S. Mission.
S. J. Chey, Ph. D., Treasurer.

D. <u>President Emeritus.</u>

O. R. Avison, M. D., LL. D. (Toronto and Wooster), residing in the United States of America.

E. <u>Faculty.</u>

(1) <u>Professors. (21)</u>

H. H. Underwood, B. A., M. A., Ph. D., Litt. D., (New York and Mount Union).
[illegible] President of the College and Professor of Education, Psychology and English.

U. K. Yu, Gakushi, (Tokyo Imperial University).
Vice-President and Dean of the College and Professor of Law.

L. G. Paik, B. A., Th. B., M. A., Ph. D., (Yale)
Director of the Literary Department and Professor of Occidental History and Religion.

S. T. Lee, Gakushi, (Kyoto Imperial University).
Director of the Commercial Department and Professor of Economics, Insurance, Statistics, and Abacus.

C. H. Lee, B. A., M. A., (Ohio State).
Director of the Science Department and Professor of Mathematics.

A. L. Becker, B. A., M. A., Ph. D., (Michigan).
Professor of Physics and Mathematics.

E. H. Miller, B. A., B. D., M. A., Ph. D., (Columbia)
Professor of Chemistry, English and Bible. (On furlough)

N. W. Paik, Gakushi, (Tokyo University of Commerce).
Professor of Commerce, Bookkeeping, History of Commerce, Commercial Japanese, Accounting and History of Economics.

K. Kadowaki, Gakushi, (Kyoto Imperial University).
Professor of Chemistry, Mechanical Drawing.

H. P. Choi, Gakushi, (Kyoto Imperial University).
Professor of Philosophy, Education, Ethics, and the Korean Language.

D. W. Lee, Graduate of C. C. C., B. A., M. A., Ph. D., (Michigan)
Professor of Mathematics and Astronomy.

S. Nikaido, Gakushi (Tokyo Imperial University).
Professor of Japanese, Japanese Literature and Introduction to Literature.

(3)

P. C. Kim, Gakushi, (Waseda University).
Professor of Physics, Electrical Engineering, and Mathematics.

H. Kaiya, Gakushi, (Tofuku Imperial University).
Professor of Mathematics, Surveying, Physics, Civil Engineering, Drawing, Geology, Mineralogy, Natural Science and Architecture.

S. K. Hong, B. A., (Ohio State).
Professor of English.

I. P. Chung
Professor of Chinese Literature and Korean Literature.

C. H. Hyun, M. Mus., (Gunn School of Music and Dramatic Art).
Professor of Music.

T. K. Roe, Graduate of C.C.C., Gakushi (Kyoto Imperial University)
Professor of Transportation, Agricultural Economics, and Business English.

S. J. Chey, Graduate of C.C.C., B. S., M. B. A., Ph. D., (New York)
Professor of Commercial Practice, Business English, Typewriting, Advertising, and Foreign Exchange.

E. M. Cable, B. S., M. A., D. D., (Cornell College)
Professor of English, Bible and History. (On furlough)

G. C. Speidel, B. S., M. S., (Virginia)
Professor of English.

(2) Assistant Professors (6)

O. Y. Lee, (Berlin University)
Assistant Professor of German.

I. S. Jung, Gakushi, (Waseda University)
Assistant Professor of English and Introduction to Literature.

P. K. Lim, Graduate of C.C.C., B. A., M. A., (Syracuse).
Assistant Professor of Bookkeeping, Commodities, Business English, Commercial Geography, Marketing and Typewriting.

L. H. Snyder, B. A., M. A., (Princeton).
Assistant Professor of English and Typewriting. (On furlough)

K. N. Choi, Graduate of C.C.C., B. A., M. A., Ph. D., (Michigan)
Assistant Professor of Physics and Mathematics.

R. C. Coen, B. A., B. D., M. A., (Chicago).
Assistant Professor of Bible and English.

(3) Instructors. (5)

Mrs. H. H. Underwood, B. A., M. A., (New York).
English.

L. W. Kang,
Physical Education.

K. D. Hur, B. A., M. A., Ph. D., (Harvard).
Sociology and Psychology.

S. Y. Chang, B. S., B. D., M. A., (Columbia).
Bible and Religious Education.

M. M. Lee, Graduate of C.C.C., B. A., M. A., Ph. D., (Boston).
English.

(4) Lecturers and Assistants. (22)

I. S. Chung
Oriental History.
K. W. Chang, Graduate of C.C.C., Gakushi, (Tohoku Imperial University).
Mathematics.
K. H. Jung, Gakushi, (Tokyo Imperial University).
Commercial Law, Civil Law, and Japanese Civil Government.
H. C. Chang, Graduate of C.C.C., Gakushi, (Tokyo University of Commerce). (Leave of Absence).
Commercial Mathematics, Warehouse and Exchange.
T. Yokoyama, B. A., B. D., Ph. D., (Johns Hopkins)
English.
R. K. Jung, Gakushi, (Keio University).
Finance, Economics and Public Law.
M. D. Cable, B. A., (Cornell) (On furlough).
English
P. B. Billings, B. A. (Depauw).
English (Leave of Absence).
Y. H. Lee, Gakushi, (Tokyo Imperial University).
English
C. T. Son, Gakushi, (Waseda University).
Oriental History.
K. H. Kim, Gakushi, (Tokyo Imperial University).
Morals.
C. N. Kim, Graduate of Paiyoung College.
The Chinese Language.
Charles Choi, B. S. in C. E., M. S. in C. E., Ph. D. (Ohio State).
Chemistry.
H. K. Karl, Graduate of C.C.C., B.D., M.A., Ph. D., (Chicago).
Bible and Education.
E. W. Koons, B. A., B. D., D. D., (Coe)
Bible.
H. S. Park, Gakushi, (Meiji University).
Commercial Mathematics, Economic Affairs, Exchange, Trust, and Business Management.
W. S. Min, B. S., (Nevada).
French.
I. J. Park, B. S. in A. E., (Minnesota) and B. S. in M. E. (Lewis Institute).
Architecture and Drawing.
C. R. Cynn, Graduate of C.C.C.
Assistant, Physics Laboratory.
H. C. Cynn, Graduate of C.C.C.
Assistant, Literary Department.
Y. S. Kim, Graduate of C.C.C.
Assistant, Chemistry Laboratory.
M. H. Lee, Graduate of C.C.C.
Research Assistant, Science Department.

(5) Part Time Assistants. (4)

Mrs. A. L. Becker
Mrs. R. C. Coen
Mrs. E. H. Miller (On furlough).
Mrs. L. H. Snyder (On furlough).

(6) Professors on Furlough. (4)

E. M. Cable, D. D.
L. H. Snyder, M. A.
E. H. Miller, Ph. D.
K. Kadowaki, Gakushi.

F. Office Staff. (13)

Y. S. Koo, M. D., (Emory)
College Physician.
K. C. Lyu, Graduate of C.C.C.
Secretary to Administration.
C. H. Song, Graduate of C.C.C.
Superintendent of Dormitory.
C. K. Kim, Graduate of C.C.C.
Superintendent of Grounds and Buildings.
K. S. Lyu, Graduate of C.C.C.
Assistant to the Librarian.
K. P. Choi, Graduate of C.C.C., B. A., (Ohio Wesleyan).
Assistant, Treasurer's Office.
P. Hyon, B. A., (Shanghai).
Accountant.
W. Y. Shim, Graduate of C.C.C.
Secretary to Administration.
K. W. Yi, Graduate of C.C.C., B. A., M. A., (Michigan).
Cashier.
Miss D. T. Ahn
Stenographer to the President.
Mrs. John Lyu, Graduate of Ewha College
Clerical Assistant of the Library.
Mrs. S. H. Lyu, Graduate of Paiwha,
Clerical Assistant of the Library.
Miss C. N. Choi, Graduate of Ewha College,
Clerical Assistant of the Library.

(6)

III. Three Departments of the College.

The College is organized on a university system and has four Departments, but only three are in operation. These Departments are separate so far as their internal organization is concerned with their respective Directors, budgets and recitation halls, but they are one in general administration and policy under the Dean.

A. Literary Department - Director L. G. Paik, Ph.D.

The Literary Department has had one of the most successful years with a good and wholesome growth in enrollment, a hearty co-operation among the Faculty, and a genial spirit running throughout the whole Department.

The absence of Dr. and Mrs. E. M. Cable, who are now in America on furlough, created a big gap, yet Mr. G. C. Speidel kindly filled it up by taking care of the English Literature course for Juniors. Last year Mr. W. S. Min was added to the Staff, teaching French.

The Department is jubilant over the largest enrollment in the history of the College. The academic year began with an enrollment of 128 last April. There are now 8 Seniors, 29 Juniors, 28 Sophomores and 44 Freshmen making the total of 109. Quality of the student body is excellent and the educational standard of the Department is not impaired by the increased enrollment. Fine spirit has reigned among the students and Faculty throughout the year.

A revised curriculum was put into effect by the beginning of the school year. The main feature on the new curriculum is to offer a room for election to the two upper class students. English Literature, Oriental Literature, Occidental and Oriental History are offered for election. German, French and Chinese are also offered for election. Results seem to be gratifying.

During the absence of Dr. Cable the Fourth Annual Varsity English Oratorical Contest was supervised by Dr. M. M. Lee and Prof. R. C. Coen. There were about 30 students participated in the contest of whom about 20 contestants were the students of the Literary Department; and Sungsup Kim (L.3) and Ha Young Kim (L.2) won the first and third prize respectively.

The Fourth Annual English Oratorical Contest for Secondary Schools was held at the Pai Chai Hall on November 9, 1935. Seven schools including one girl's school participated and had a good contest. The success of this occasion is solely due to Dr. L. G. Paik's indefatigable effort.

The Drama Club, the Senior and Junior classes had very good practices in preparing several plays for presentation. However,

(9)

it was found impossible to produce any one of those during the past year. We hope we will have a better record for the coming year.

B. Commercial Department - Director S. T. Lee, Gakushi.

The Commercial Department is the largest Department of the College with a Faculty of 10 Professors and Assistant Professors, 12 Lecturers, one Assistant, and 196 students. (Seniors 50, Sophomores 66, and Freshmen 80).

Mr. Hyo-Sahm Park has been added to the Faculty from last April on. He is a graduate of the Meiji University, in Tokyo, and where, while doing his post-graduate work for three years, he was given a chair as Lecturer. He is a man of good character and of high scholastic standing and duly deserves the good opinion of the Faculty members as well as that of the students. He is teaching a number of important commercial subjects.

Ever since Mr. L. H. Snyder has gone on his furlough, Mr. G. C. Speidel has been generous enough to come and help us out. We expect Mr. Snyder will come back some time this year and resume his work in the Department.

From the beginning of this academic year, we have newly adopted a system of elective courses of study in the fields of Commerce, Economics, and Law. This will enable the students to make a thorough study of their own inclination as for the theoretical or for the practical phases of their training. The prospects are rather encouraging so far as we have gone this year.

Besides teaching and attending other routine matters in the College, Messrs. T. K. Roe, N. W. Paik, and In-Sup Jung have already published their researches in the important newspapers and magazines no less than a dozen times respectively in this year. This is not all: Messrs. S. T. Lee, N. W. Paik, T. K. Roe, I. S. Jung and D. H. Kim participated in the lecturing tour during the last summer vacation under the auspices of Dong-A Daily Newspaper and their lectures were very well attended to everywhere they were held.

The Faculty members of this Department have been giving extra-curricular lectures, once in every term, for the benefit of the students on some subject of current nature or in a form of report on their researches. These have been very interesting and instructive and were well appreciated by all who had time to attend them. The last one was the sixth of the series.

A brief report on the employment of the 48 graduates last year may not be wholly out of place here. Of this number, 3 are attending universities in Tokyo; 23 are holding responsible positions in various banking houses, manufacturing concerns, government offices, and in the institutions of learning; 11 are either in private business or attending home affairs; and the remaining 11 have not been placed definitely as yet. Inspite of the last number, it is a fairly good record if it is compared with that of other colleges of same standing in the country.

Taking every thing into consideration, we may say that the Commercial Department is holding more than it's own, and, while proud of the present facts, we are looking forward to a better day of this department and consequently greater service to the society.

Commercial Museum

The Commercial Museum has been growing steadily with additional specimens of native and foreign commodities making a total number of 1,598. We are proud of the fact that at the present time our Museum excells any of its kind in Korean Colleges in Korea in the number as well as in the variety of the specimens. Prof. P. K. Lim is in charge of the work.

Commercial Practice Work

Along with the theoretical studies of Commerce and Economics, the practical side of the course is no less important a phase. At the present time there are 11 typewriters for the students to practice on, but we are looking forward to a time when we can complete the equipment for this purpose.

C. Science Department - Director C. H. Lee, M. A.

The Science Department under the directorship of Prof. C. H. Lee, has triumphantly come out itself another year, regardless of hard times.

The Faculty of the Department is composed of 7 Professors, one Assistant Professor, 3 Lectures, and 2 Assistants, making a total of 13 members.

The number of students in the Department is 69: Freshmen 2?, Sophomores 2?, Juniors 13, and Seniors 10.

The Department keenly feels the absence of Dr. E. H. Miller who is on furlough in America. We are looking forward to his return in September.

Prof. Kadowaki returned to the Department from his furlough and resumed his teaching duties at the beginning of the Second Semester of this academic year.

Last spring the Department installed an assaying laboratory with an adequate equipment for the purpose of imparting a profound knowledge of Mineralogy to the students and of encouraging a research work among the Faculty members as well.

The Science Museum under the competent supervision of Dr. D. W. Lee is making a marked progress both in securing more specimens and arranging them. The Botanical collection consisting of 3,350 specimens is one of the best of its kinds throughout the country.

The Science Department Research Room is looked after by Dr. K. N. Choi whose keen vision and scientific mind laid out a thorough plan to develop it. Even at present there are over 770 books easily accessible by the students and teachers.

14. Religious Activities - Chairman, Rev. R. C. Coen, B. D., M. A.

During the absence of Dr. E. M. Cable, Rev. R. C. Coen has acted as Chairman of the Religious Activities Committee. He has been ably assisted by all members of the Committee, especially Drs. L. G. Paik, H. K. Karl, M. M. Lee, and Rev. S. Y. Chang.

BIBLE TEACHING: With Drs. E. M. Cable and E. H. Miller both off the field during the past year, it has been necessary to increase the teaching hours of some of the other Bible teachers, and also to obtain the assistance of Dr. E. W. Koons for one class. The other hours have been carried by Drs. L. G. Paik and H. K. Karl, and Revs. S. Y. Chang and R. C. Coen. No changes were made in the courses of study.

CHAPEL EXERCISES: Believing chapel exercises to be one of the most important activities of the college, we are constantly endeavoring to improve them, and each year shows some success. Two changes have been made during the past year. First, a five minute extension of the rest period between the second hour class and the beginning of the chapel services in order to provide adequate time for closing the class and getting quietly into chapel before the services begin. Second, we have divided the service into two distinct parts, viz; a devotional period of song, scripture reading, and prayer, and a period for an address on some topic of interest and value. These addresses are usually given by members of our own Faculty, but we welcome guest speakers and have been able to have such on an average of two or three times each month. Two services each month are given over to special musical programs under the direction of Professor C. M. Hyun: one service a month is conducted by the College Y.M.C.A. usually with a guest speaker of their own choice; and one service a week, usually on Wednesday, is held outdoors at the Open Air Theatre, where we have devotions and physical exercises.

WORK AMONG FACULTY AND STUDENTS: All during the year a faculty prayer meeting has been conducted on Monday mornings from 9 to 9:30 before school opens.

The most recent check up on the students showed that there were 292 Christians and 75 non-Christian students in the College. As to denominations, the Christian students are distributed as follows: Methodist 144; Presbyterian 135; others 13. The percentage of non-Christians naturally drops as the school year advances due to the fact that many become Christians and that there is a greater tendency for the non-Christians to drop out.

In connection with our care for and influence upon our students our two greatest needs are a well qualified Dean of men and more and better dormitory facilities. At present, we can house only about 60 pupils in our dormitory, and our facilities for caring for those socially and morally are quite inadequate. A few more students live at Sinchon sufficiently near for direct contacts outside school hours, but most (at least 2/3) of our students live in Seoul with all that means in the way of temptations on the one hand and inaccessibility on the other. We have tried, but with little success, to get the cooperation of the city churches and pastors in this difficult task of supervising and helping students who live in Seoul.

In addition to the work done among the students by Rev. S. Y. Chang, the Pastor, and Elder C. M. Song, the dormitory supervisor, much work has been done by other members of the Faculty. The whole student body has been divided up into groups of from 10 to 20, and a teacher put in charge of each group. Those students are his special concern, and it is his business to guide and assist them in any way he can. He meets them individually, or in groups, several times during the year to question and counsel them. This work is new; results differ and are difficult to obtain and tabulate, but all agree that the plan is a good one. We shall continue and strive to perfect it in the future.

Another new feature was began this year by Dr. H. H. Karl. It took the form of a club of some 15 students for the study of religion and the development of their spiritual lives. They have met regularly throughout the year once each week. Once a month a speaker has been invited to address them, but the other times they met with Dr. Karl and studied and discussed religious problems and shared religious convictions and experiences. This year's experience with the Club has proved its value and guarantees its continuance. Whether we shall enlarge this one club, or form other similar clubs and keep them all small for the sake of more intimate contacts and more free expression we do not yet know, but that the work shall be continued and enlarged in some way is certain.

<u>RELIGIOUS WORK BY THE STUDENTS</u>: We are very proud of the religious work our students do, both as to its quantity and quality. Only lack of funds prevents us from doing even more than we do. There are many qualified students willing to serve and many places that need their services but with our limited funds we are unable to render those services.

As it is, about 55 of our pupils assist regularly in many churches in and near Seoul, teaching Sunday School classes, assisting with music and in young peoples' groups, and even preaching. During both the summer and winter vacations, Gospel Teams were sent out by the College Y.M.C.A. These teams, seven in all, consisting of from two to three students each, went to many places far from Seoul where there were either no churches or very weak ones, and worked among the people for a week or ten days teaching and preaching. The work done by these teams has been reported in detail in the "Korea Mission Field", where most of you have read it.

In addition to the work of these teams there was a great amount of work done by individual students while on vacation in their home or neighboring villages. Their work took the form of Daily Vacation Bible Schools, and we know it was extensive and valuable, though we have no statistics concerning it.

A special project has been undertaken by the Y.M.C.A. at Soo Saik a village only 15 minutes ride by train from the College. There is a small church building and a very feeble church organization in this place. Two college students go there every Sunday, and it is their hope to build a strong church there in time. They lead the Sunday School and young peoples' society, preach at the church services, and call from house to house to do personal work. Though the project is only three months old, already there are evidences of success.

THE FEDERATED CHURCH: During this fourth year of the existence of the Federated Church it entered upon a new phase of its life. With the coming of Ewha College to its new home on the campus near the C.C.C., negotiations for uniting these two institutions in the work of the Federated Church were renewed. Though the actual organization has not yet been effected and the plans far from perfected, we have, since the last Sunday in September, been holding the morning services of the church and the Adult Sunday School in the beautiful new chapel of Ewha's Music building, where many of Ewha's staff and pupils unite in the worship and study.

All other activities of the church (Sunday evening and Wednesday night services, the children's Sunday School, etc.) are carried on as formerly at the C.C.C. Rev. S. Y. Chang continues as pastor of the church arranging for speakers and supervising the work in both places, and Miss Kim Hey Young continues her work as Bible Woman among the women and children of the community. Dr. M. N. Lee also remains in charge of the children's Sunday School which continues to prosper.

Just what the final form and the ultimate work of this church may be we do not know, but it is another "noble experiment" which we are trying to work out.

SPECIAL MEETINGS: Our special Evangelistic meetings this year were held from Jan. 20--24th. We devoted the chapel period and the following study period to these services, a total of 1½ hours. Dr. B. W. Billings was our speaker, and he brought us five most helpful messages on the subjects; 1. Why Religion? 2. God. 3. Jesus. 4. The Value of Man. 5. Power for Living. Dr. Billings by his earnestness, his scholarship, his frankness, and his beautiful personality and splendid use of the Korean Language commanded both the interest and respect of the students from the very first hour.

A special feature of the meetings this year was the conferences held with the Senior classes one hour each day during the week. Dr. L. G. Paik met with the Literary Seniors, Dr. H. E. Karl with the Commercial Seniors, and Rev. S. Y. Chang with the Science Seniors.

Each morning the Faculty and the Y.M.C.A. held prayer meetings, also. Dr. Underwood led the Faculty prayers from 9 to 9:30, and the Y.M.C.A. boys used the same room for an hour preceding that. The benefits from all these meetings were both great and lasting.

V. <u>College Library - Librarian, M. M. Lee, Ph. D.</u>

The College Library has witnessed another prosperous year with a great many acquisitions of books and increase of efficiency. On account of the decreased budget the Library has purchased only a couple hundred books all together, but the constant effort of our College Staff - especially of President Underwood and of Vice-President Yu - brought another huge crop of gifts to the Library. The increase of books during the last academic year alone amounts to about 3,618 volumes, while the total accessions are now over 49,325 volumes.

The Library is growing not only in quantity but in quality as well. With the generous endorsement of an additional fund by the President the Library has commenced to classify and catalogue books on up-to-date scientific basis; and for that purpose we have added three women staff, who prove to be very efficient and confirm the general impression that Library routine work is a "She" man's job. Besides we began to purchase essential "tools" for library work such as U. S. Catalogue and A. L. A. Rules, etc. With this equipment we have already classified and catalogued about 5,000 books during the last year. The Oriental books in circulation are thus taken care of; and the staff is now working on the old classics.

The rapid growth naturally requires more room and more staff. There are now seven members on parminent staff working in the Library - Librarian, Assistant to the Librarian, three women Clerical Assistants, and two service boys. We are also looking forward to Mrs. Cable's return who gave so much needed assistance to the Library.

In order to make more room for the books in frequent demands we moved the classics into a part of the Commercial Museum Room, while in the stack proper we put in 8 new book shelves. However, we have to confess that because of the lack of space a majority of our Library books are simply being stored instead of being shelved properly. If the Library keeps up growing in this rate, within a year or two the housing problem of the books will be a grave one, indeed.

There is one more item that calls for an immediate attention - that is, unbound periodicals numbering over 6,800. If we let them accumulate without binding them even in a piece meal fashion each year, we are certainly rearing a white elephant.

We are particularly gratified to note a rapid increase of reading interest among our students. Our open shelf system for all reference materials and periodicals readily quenches their thrust for information, while 1.03 book per student is circulated every day. Even in comparison with the figures of leading Japanese universities our students' reading is at par, if not better. Because 1.87 book per person of Waseda and 1.3 of Meiji include periodicals and reference books as well, while we have them in the open shelves and let them help themselves. If statistics mean anything at all, the general trend of our students' reading comes in the following order:

(1) Literature
(2) General - Chiefly bound periodicals
(3) Sociology and Economics
(4) Science
(5) History
(6) Philosophy
(7) Religion
(8) Useful Arts
(9) Fine Arts
(10) Philology

In a way of encouraging reading among our students we avail of chapel periods for a week and observe the Library Week. Last year (1934-35) we had it in November with the following speakers:

1. Dr. M. M. Lee, "What is Library?"
2. Prof. H. P. Choi, "Han-keul and Library."
3. Prof. I. P. Chung, "History of Library in Korea."

Our Library displayed some of the C.L.S. publications and gave our students an opportunity to get acquainted with them and to buy them. The sale was not very big, but it was worth doing even merely for the purpose of making religious books known to the students.

Our Library is also cooperating with other College and Public libraries throughout Korea, Japan and Manchukuo. The 29th Annual Convention of the Japan Library Association was held at the Keijo Imperial University from October 8 to 10, 1935, at which Dean Yu and Dr. M. M. Lee, Librarian, represented the College.

A good many friends of the College used our Library books last year, of whom Dr. W. Carl Rufus is one, who is a Professor of our College and now a Professor of Astronomy at the University of Michigan. He kindly gave the College a valuable gift, Giles' Chinese-English Dictionary, which is now out of print and is worth 90 yen.

Some of the outstanding gifts to the Library are as follows:

I. Min Yu Dang Collection (through the good offices of Dean Yu and Prof. S. K. Hong)........................ 1,636 vols.
II. General gifts (chiefly from publishers)............ 124
III. Purchase and binding.................................. 224
IV. The result of the Library Campaign................. 1,567

Donors	Books	Periodicals
Dr. O. R. Avison	223	142
Dr. H. H. Underwood	259	
Dr. A. L. Becker	3	
Mr. Snyder	3	24
Dr. E. H. Miller	41	2

(14)

Gifts Continued

Donors	Books	Periodicals
Dean U. K. Yu	233	5
Dr. L. G. Paik	8	2
Prof. S. T. Lee	8	
Prof. C. H. Lee	2	
Dr. K. D. Har	60	
Prof. N. W. Paik	2	
Prof. S. K. Hong	18	
Mr. K. H. Jung	23	
Mr. Insup Jung	1	1
Mr. D. H. Kim		1
Dr. D. W. Lee	4	
Dr. N. M. Lee	378	105
Dr. S. J. Chey	1	28
Dr. H. K. Karl	1	
Mr. P. K. Lim	2	
Mr. K. S. Lyu	2	
Mr. M. H. Lee	2	
Mr. C. H. Song		2
Mr. D. W. Woo	1	

V. The students are also donating books both individually and collectively. The Moon-Wu Club of the Literary Department, for example, has subscribed a drama magazine for the Library and given a considerable number of books on literature and plays. This is really an encouraging feature.

VI. Physical Education - Chairman, D. W. Lee, Ph. D.

Notwithstanding the insufficient budget (reduced almost beyond the limit) our athletic activities were remarkably successful this year. It was really an epoch-making year in the history of our College athletics. We won championships in five different sports - namely, football, baseball, basketball, tennis, and ice hockey. It is a great pleasure to add here that, through the liberal financial aid of the Alumni and other friends of the College, we were able to send the varsity basketball and ice hockey teams to Tokyo to participate in the games for the championship of Japan and to allow the football team to make a trip to Shanghai in January at the invitation of the China National Amateur Athletic Association. As a consequence of winning the championship in the basketball tournament held at Tokyo, three of the varsity players were selected by the Committee representing the Japan Basketball Association to be sent to Berlin for the Olympic games this Summer.

On October 26th our College students participated in the athletic meet held under the auspices of the Korea Athletic Association and won the championship in every sport in which we took part - namely, football, basketball, and tennis.

BASEBALL

In June, 1935, our varsity team defeated the Keijo Medical College team in the eighth annual event by winning two games out of three:

June 14th	We lost	5-0
June 15th	We won	7-6
June 19th	We won	9-7

FOOTBALL

On September 26th our varsity team had a good game with the Union Christian College team at the Municipal Ground and beat them flat by the score of 4-0. They were just on the way back from a football trip to Japan.

The football return from the Shanghai trip is as follows:

January 27th, Shanghai & Hongkong Interport Team	We lost	4-2
January 29th, North China Team	We lost	5-4
February 1st, All Shanghai Team	We won	2-1

BASKETBALL

After having won six games in the Annual Basketball League under the auspices of the Central Y.M.C.A., November 9-27, we received the title for the year.

Severance Union Medical College	We won	76-21
Korea Club	We won	56-21
Posung College	We won	Forfeited
Keijo Law College	We won	79-6
"K" Club	We won	66-19
Samgak	We won	66-23

Early in January the varsity players went to Tokyo and participated in the tournament for the championship of Japan and won the title for the year after having defeated with ease their strong foes, Tokyo Imperial University and Kyoto Imperial University in semi-final and final, respectively.

January 6th, Kwanto Gakuin	We won	52-32
January 6th, Waseda University	We won	36-27
January 7th, Tokyo Imperial University	We won	46-38
January 8th, Kyoto Imperial University	We won	42-22

ICE HOCKEY

The College team won the championship for the season by winning all the games in the Amateur Ice Hockey League of Korea with the following scores:

January 15th, Keijo Imperial University	We won	3-1
January 16th, Yongsan Rail Road Team	We won	6-1

(16)

The scores of the three games we had at Tokyo and Kyoto are as follows:

January 24th	Keio University	We lost	9-3
January 28th	Kyoto Imperial University	Tie	3-3
January 28th	Doshisha University	We won	7-3

During the academic year we hold six kinds of Intramural Athletic Meets for the college student body - namely, jujitsu, swimming, tug o'war, wrestling, skating, and track & field, well distributed throughout the academic year.

In order to encourage and help toward the development of various sports and sportsmanship among the younger generations of Korea, we also hold five different kinds of Annual Athletic Meets for middle schools with success as usual - namely, baseball, basketball, tennis, jujitsu, and track and field.

VII. Music - Chairman, S. J. Chey, Th. D.

Music activities of the College are so closely connected with Prof. Hyun that it would not be an exaggeration to say that in our College he is a music himself. It is sometimes a wonder how one man could do so much. The following skelton report is a part of the activities of the Music Committee.

Clubs and Organizations

Orchestra	34 members
Glee Club	42 members
Band	30 members
String quartet	
Male Voice Quartet	

Concerts and Concert Tours

As usual two regular concerts were held in Seoul and one concert tour was made to the following cities:

Wonsan, Hamheung, Sungjin, Chungjin, Lajin, Oongki. We estimate that 8,000 people heard us on this tour. We gave two outdoor Band concerts during the last year, one at the College Outdoor Theatre and one at the Pagoda Park. We estimate that over 10,000 people enjoyed these concerts.

Radio Programs on J.O.D.K.

We conducted monthly a thirty minutes sacred music program on Sunday evenings, while 22 other programs were furnished by our Orchestra, Glee Club, Band, Quartet and Soli.

The Summer Music Conference

The Fifth Annual Summer Music Conference was held at the College from July 23rd to August 1st under the auspice of our College, and it was very successful. It drew the largest enrollment that we ever had with 88 in all - 41% were students and 30% were teachers, 76% of them were men and 25% were women.

The thirteen provinces were all represented, and some of them came as far as from Manchuria.

Nearly 77% registered in Voice and 20% in Piano. Of course, all of them took several courses. It was interesting to note that quite a number of them had attended the previous conferences.

The duration of the conference for only ten days seemed to be too short. Many of the members expressed their wishes to extend it for five days or a week more. However, it will be necessary to have more teachers and more courses to be included, which means a larger budget.

Co-operation with Religious Activities and Other Churches.

The Music Committee has charge of the chapel music, the Federated church music, and all of the music program for Religious Activities. 12 students were leaders of the church choir in town; 15 students were singing teachers of Sunday Schools; 30 students were church choir members and 3 students were music leaders of the Vacation Gospel Teams.

High School Music Contest

The Fourth Annual All-Korea Middle School Music Contest was held in June at the town hall. 19 high schools took part in the contest.

Scholarship

A Music scholarship of ¥75.00 was awarded for the current year to Mr. Moon Hakjun, a Literary Junior, for his merits in musicianship and high standing in scholarship in the class.

Special Report

The All Korea Music Contest was held in September at the Chosen Ilpo auditorium under the auspices of the Chosen Ilpo. One of our College students took the first prize in Violin and the other boy won the second prize in singing.

Hopes and Needs

This Committee entertains a large hope for its future. We need some special funds for new instruments, music books, scholarships, and funds for publications.

VIII. Other Items of Interest.

A. College Museum - Curator, H. H. Lee, Ph. D.

They say, "Necessity is mother of invention"; and the College Museum proved to be one of the testing cases of this dictum. Last year there was no appropriation for the Museum at all, but it had a good many new treats and additional collections.

The Museum was moved from Underwood Hall and is now located on the top floor of Appenzeller Hall.

The loan collection of Dr. Boots' Korean armors and weapons necessitated us to find something to place and exhibit them in. President Underwood and Dr. H. H. Lee, who is also commissioned to take charge of the Museum, looked round and got hold of 4 or 5 idle wooden lockers and turned them into excellent exhibition cases by installing glasses and applying some varnish to them.

Dr. Ludlow also loaned his precious Korea potteries to the Museum. We had to have a case to place them, and it came-came out of the special gift that President Underwood received from America. The case is all lined with green velvet.

With these new cases we were able to spread out the various objects accumulated during the past. The Museum still needs a great deal of work in classifying and cataloguing its collections.

The gifts to the Museum during the last year are as follows:

1. Dr. Boots's loaned collection of Korean armors and arms consisted of 80 pieces and 3 bundles of arrows.
2. Dr. Ludlow's loaned collection of Koryu potteries, 10 pieces.
3. Mr. C. T. Son, earthen pots, 9 pieces.
4. Ki Yang Pak (through Prof. Hong), scroll 1 piece, letters 3 pieces.
5. Tai Sik Min, Korean brass coins, 153 pieces.
6. Sang Pom Lee (through Dean Yu), Korean painting on fog.
7. Prof. I. P. Chung, Sung Dynasty coins, 2 pieces.
8. H. C. Shin, Korean earthen pot, one piece.
9. Dr. L. G. Paik, Korean gargoyle, one piece.
10. In Whan Pak '34, Johol fossil, one piece.
11. Yung Kiu Min (L 1), Korean spoon and currency, one piece each.
12. T. S. Chang (through Dean Yu), reprints of tombstones.

(19)

B. Student Help Work - Chairman, S. K. Hong, B. A.

During the academic year 1935-1936, the Student Help Work has been begun with an appropriation of ¥600.00 but, feeling that that amount was too insufficient for the work, an increase of ¥180.00 was granted in the course of the year, making a total of ¥780.00. As the present economic depression continues, the demand for help increases every year and so even this amount can not be said to be sufficient by any means if we consider the increasing demand for help.

Up to the end of January, 1936, 18 students have been helped: 12, out of this fund by working on the College campus; 2, by private tutorship; and 4, by odd jobs of various kind. Of this number, some could not have been able to continue their studies, had it not been for the help of this Work.

Mr. Jung-Chai Lee, who had pledged ¥1000.00 for the capital fund of the Student Help Work and had been paying in a few hundred yen every year, just finished his last payment on his pledge. We feel very grateful for his generosity and at the same time hope that his gift of one thousand yen may seed something that will be of real source of help to the needy students in the years to come.

C. Clubs and Organizations.

a. C.C.C. Students Association (The Student Body).
b. C.C.C. Y.M.C.A. (Voluntary Organization).
c. Literary Society (Literary Department Students).
d. Economics Association (Commercial Department Students).
e. Science Club (Science Department Students).
f. Glee Club, Orchestra and Band (Voluntary, all Departments).
g. Oratorical Club (Voluntary, all Departments).
h. Friendly Association (Korean Teaching and Office Staff).
i. Dramatic Club (Voluntary, all Departments).
j. English Club (Voluntary, Commercial Department Students).
k. Religious Research Club (Voluntary, all Departments Students).

IX. Students.

A. Enrollment.

Annual average of the students who paid tuition during the past three years:

1932 - 33 259
1933 - 34 304
1934 - 35 320

Up to January 31st, 1936, there was a total enrollment of 367 students distributed as follows:

Class	Lit.Dept.	Com.Dept.	Sc.Dept.	Total
Freshmen	44	80	22	146
Sophomore	26	66	17	111
Junior	29		13	42
Senior	8	50	10	69
Total	109	196	62	367

B. **Classification of Students.**

Number of Students

Department	Regular	Special	Total	Percentage
Literary	95	14	109	29.70
Commercial	183	13	196	53.41
Science	56	6	62	16.89
	334	33	367	100.00%

C. **Geographical Distribution of Students.**

Province	Number	Percentage
North Ham Kyung	8	2.18
South Ham Kyung	23	6.27
North Pyung An	23	6.27
South Pyung An	43	11.72
Whang Hai	28	7.63
Kyung Ki	135	36.79
Kang Won	17	4.63
North Choong Chung	8	2.18
South Choong Chung	14	3.81
North Chun La	13	3.54
South Chun La	17	4.63
North Kyung San	20	5.45
South Kyung San	18	4.90
Total	367	100.00 %

D. **Students' Church Relations.**

Denomination	No. of Students	Percentage
Presbyterian	135	37.00
Methodist	144	39.00
Other Christian Denominations	13	3.00
Non-Christian	75	20.00
Total	367	100.00 %

X. Graduates.

A. Total Number of Graduates from each Department.

Total Numver of Graduates from each Department. (Continued)

(January 31st, 1936)

Department	Number	Percentage
Literary	147	27.74
Commercial	290	54.71
Science	90	16.99
Agricultural .. (Not Operating)	3	.56
Total	530	100.00%

B. Present Status of Graduates, January 31st, 1936.

Positions and Occupations	Number	Percentage
Teaching Staff in C. C. C.	10	1.88
Non-Teaching Officers in C. C. C.	10	1.88
Teachers in other Christian Schools	65	12.26
Church Workers	22	4.16
Students in Medical	1	.19
Teachers in Non-Christian Schools	17	3.21
Students in U. S. A.	23	4.34
Students in Japan	25	4.72
Students in China	2	.38
Students in England	1	.19
Journalists and Writers	13	2.45
Employees of Banks and Business Firms	96	18.13
Government Officials	43	8.11
Independent Commercial or Industrial Workers	80	15.09
Agriculturalists	28	5.28
Various Lines of Independent Business	59	11.13
Physician	1	.19
Mining	3	.57
Deceased	31	5.85
Total	530	100.00%

C. Graduates' Privileges Conferred by the Government.

a. The College has been given the privilege of giving a Bachelor's degree in each Department as Bachelor of Literature or Commerce or Science or Theology.

b. Government qualification for private primary school teachers (See the Article III of Educational ordinances for private School teachers).

c. The graduates of the College are given qualification by the Government to teach in Private Higher Common Schools and Industrial Schools on the following subjects:

To the graduates of the Literary Department
English, Korean and Chinese.
To the graduates of the Commercial Department
English, Commerce and Bookkeeping.
To the graduates of the Science Department
Mathematics, Physics and Chemistry.
To the graduates of the Agricultural Department
(Not Operating) Agriculture.

d. In accordance with the ordinance of Imperial Department of Education, No. 5, Art. 2, Sec. 4 (Daisho the 7th Year) this College has been placed on an equal plane with the Japanese Higher Schools, Colleges and the Preparatory Departments of Universities, so that our graduates are exempted from the preliminary examinations for higher civil service positions and are qualified also for entering all Government and private universities.

e. According to the Imperial Ordinance, No. 261 (Daisho the 2nd Year), the graduates of this college are granted the privilege of ordinary civil official appointment without examination (Ordinance on civil official appointment, Art. 6.)

XI. <u>Research Work</u>.

The Research Work of different lines of studies by our Faculty and Staff bore the following fruits:

<u>Literary Department</u>

Prof. H. P. Choi has just completed his monumental work on the Korean Grammar. It is going to be a book of over 1,000 pages. The book is in the press and will be out soon.

Prof. I. P. Chung has continued his work on a Survey of the Life of the People and this series has been appearing on one of the leading newspapers of the country.

Numerous articles have been written by Faculty members for the leading Magazines and Newspapers.

The Department wishes to record the research work that Prof. W. Carl Rufus carried on in the Research Room. Prof. Rufus is a well known Astronomer in America. He has held the chair on Astronomy in the University of Michigan for many years. He came to Korea on his sabbatical leave. He used our facilities and completed his research on "Ancient Korean Astronomy" and read the paper before the meeting of the Korea Branch of the Royal Asiatic Society on December 3rd, 1935. This paper will separately issue in a booklet form as a publication of the Department. We hope other scholars in the West will come to us for the purpose of carrying on intellectual cooperation.

We have added during the year over 400 volumes of source material on history, literature, language and philosophy to the collection of the Research Room. Dr. Rufus donated to the Department all the picutes that he used in connection with his study and the original plates of those pictures.

Commercial Department

1. General Research Work

The Commercial Research Work has been carried on through the faculty members. This work facilitates the study and research of the teachers and students alike working on some commercial and economic problems. These results have been published in the leading magazines and newpapers from time to time. There are 20 magazines, 5 newspapers, and 2292 volumes of reference book in the Research Room. Prof. T. K. Roe is in charge of this work.

Mr. Insup Jung has planned an experiment of phonetic training for the first time in Korea and directed the recording of a set of 12 records, under the title of "Educational Record of Korean Language". The materials of them are based on the text books used in primary schools and they are now practically and effectively used in the classrooms of many schools by teachers, at home by parents and their children, and abroad by those interested in phonetics.

2. Research on Advertisement

The Commercial Department has begun this research work to study the methods of advertising and for reference 8,654 pieces of various kinds of posters, handbills, folders, labels, enamel and card board signs, newspaper and magazine clippings, and etc. have been collected since April 1933. Also 26 volumes of books have been secured for study and reference. These have been carefully classified and displayed in the Commercial Practice Room. Mr. P. K. Lim is in charge of the work.

3. The English Teachers Research Club

Ever since the Club became a charted member of the Institute for Research in English Teaching of the Educational Bureau of Japan, bulletins, periodicals, and publications have been sent to the College and they are being displayed for use in the Commercial Research Room for the time being. The Club is devoting much time and effort in planning a unified method of teaching English as a part of this program. Phonetics is taught from last year and, to verify certain points in phonetics, a phonograph has been secured in the Department. The Club has directed the students to form an English Club of themselves holding meetings with various programs and practicing English in various ways with much interest. Prof. S. K. Hong is the Chairman of the Research Club.

(24)

Besides the above mentioned features of this Department, we are holding an annual prize contest in thesis or grades on Commercial, Economic, and English subjects in a way of leading the interest of the students along those lines.

Science Department

An assaying laboratory which is very useful for chemical analysis was equipped last year and is now in full operation. A coal-fired furnace, a single coke-fired furnace, and a weighing balance of high sensibility compose the principal equipments of the laboratory. Beside our own assaying works for the school we are also doing assayings for the public and charge for the work.

Dr. D. W. Lee made an intensive research work in Astronomy and gave a series of lectures on that subject.

Dr. K. K. Choi also did a good deal of painsticking research and contributed a number of learned articles on Physics to the leading newspapers and magazines.

Library

In addition to the teaching work in the Literary Department and the work in the Library, Dr. M. M. Lee contributed about 10 articles, chiefly relating to European History, to the leading periodicals of the country.

Mr. K. S. Lyu has just completed a Biographical Dictionary of 5000 eminent Koreans, which will be published by the Han Sung Publishers in the near future. We are eagerly looking forward to it.

XII. Conclusion.

The data given above make us believe that our College is steadily progressing towards the high aims of the institution. The students of the College have come from 68 Middle Schools in Korea, Japan, and China, proving that this College is widely known in the Orient. In order to live up to this reputation and to elevate the College standing still higher we revised the curricula of the three Departments in April, 1935. The chief asset of the new curricula is laying in the provision of Elective System in the Junior and Senior years.

Our graduates are working in every walk of life and they are so loyal to their works and so successful that everywhere they go they exalt the Christian principles of their Alma Mater. There are about 50 graduates of our College pursuing a higher education in 12 different universities.

The progress of our College is in a large measure due to the fine spirit of hearty cooperation among our Faculty and Staff. Aside from their teaching, their sound scholarship and firm conviction expressed through the means of radio, newspapers and magazines, and pulpits, play an important role in molding and steering the destiny of this country.

The mission of our College is greatly appreciated and supported by outsiders in various ways. An increasing demand for our graduates for bank positions and other vocations and generous donations of valuable books and antiques to College Library and Museum all confirm this fact. Moreover, two new scholarships were added last year. The Paik Woon Chun Commercial Scholarship Fund of 1500 yen is founded by his three sons of whom one is a graduate of our College. The Yun Ki Ik and Yun Kang Hyun Science Scholarship yielding 100 yen annually is also given to us. There are 15 worthy and needy students who are getting the benefits of these and other scholarships.

The College has witnessed an epoch making year in sports. Our teams invaded China and Japan and won championships in five major games. After having captured the much coveted Basketball Championship of Japan, three members of our team are picked to be sent to Berlin for the Olympic games. Our ice hockey team representing Korea was also sent to Tokyo and Kyoto, while the soccer team went to Shanghai at the invitation of the China National Amateur Athletic Federation and demonstrated its skill and speed.

Our College Staff also had a series of games with the Severance Staff contesting for the Avison Cup and cemented good feelings between the two sister institutions.

The religious activities of our students deserve a great deal of praise and support. They help churches in Seoul and its vicinities in many capacities; and during the Summer and Winter vacations our Gospel Teams accomplished much in spreading messages of Christ and educating the masses.

The three Department students cooperated and issued the first number of the C.C.C. Times in September, 1935. This paper embodies all the fine features of modern journalism; and we are quite confident that it reflects and accentuates a harmonious student life on the campus.

Musical activities occupy a prominent position in our College life as well as in the entire country. By the means of an annual tour and Summer Conference we are educating our people to appreciate music.

The College Library is expanding and improving very rapidly and playing an important part in enriching our College life. Amongst all our desparate needs a library building is the most imperative one.

(26)

In closing, we return thanks and glory to our Lord for His guidance, tender mercies and infinite visions bestowed upon this institution. We are certain that this remarkable progress of our College is largely indebted to the far-sightedness of the Board of Managers, to the able leadership of our President, Dr. Horace H. Underwood, and to the hearty cooperation of the Faculty and the entire Staff. Assured by this success of the past year, if we strive still harder, we will certainly make a still more marked progress next year.

Respectfully submitted,

U. K. Yu, Dean

49. 원한경 교장의 이사회 제출 보고서

문서 제목	President's Report 1936~1937
문서 종류	교장 보고서
제출 시기	1937년 2월 19일 (추정)
작성 장소	서울
제 출 자	H. H. Underwood
수 신 자	이사회
페이지 수	8
출 처	2114-5-4: 04 Underwood, Horace H. (DR.) 1937 Sep. to Dec. (UMAH)

자료 소개

원한경 교장이 1937년 2월 19일 열린 이사회 회의에서 제출한 보고서로 보인다. 일자가 표기되어 있지 않고, 1937년도의 이사회 회의록들이 발견되지 않아, 제출일을 확정하기 어려우나, 본문에서 원한경이 며칠 전에 게일의 사망(1937년 1월 31일) 소식을 들었다고 언급한 것을 미루어 이즈음에 작성하였을 것으로 추측할 수 있다. 그런데 이 해(1937년)에 학감이 제출한 보고서(목차 49번)의 제출 일자가 2월 19일이므로, 이 보고서도 이날 제출 되었다고 할 수 있다.

원한경은 이 보고서에서 아래의 사항들을 설명하였다.

죽음(에비슨 부인과 게일 선교사), 교직원, 교수 승급과 부임, 종교 사역, 학생 훈육과 지도, 등록생, 자산, 도서관, 음악, 운동경기, 예산, 대학 홍보, 동문회.

내용 요약

죽음: 명예 교장 에비슨의 부인[Jennie B. Avison]이 가을[9월 15일]에 별세하여 대학 채플에서 추도예배를 열었고, 에비슨에게 조사(弔辭)를 보냈다. 서울에서 북장로회 선교사로 활동했던 게일(James S. Gale)의 별세 소식을 며칠 전에 들었다. 그는 본교의 설립을 위해 노력하였고, 도서를 기부하였다. [게일은 1916년 이사회에서 임명한 'committee of name of the college'의 위원장으로서 '연희'를 교명으로 정하는 일을 주관하였다.]

교직원: 케이블, 밀러, 스나이더가 안식년에서 돌아왔으나, 스피델은 복귀가 불투명하다. 현제명이 미국에서 음악박사 학위를 받고 며칠 내로 도착할 예정이다. 정인섭도 코펜하겐 국제언어학자대회에 참석하고 귀국하는 중에 있다. 현정주[사무직원]가 베를린 올림픽에 참가하였고, 부교장 유억겸이 YMCA 국제대회 참석차 인도에 갔다. 백낙준이 북장로회 선교 백주년 기념행사 참석을 위해 미국에 가는 것을 학교에서 허락하였고, 유경상[사서]도 도서관학 공부를 위해 시라큐스대학에 가게 해주었다.

교수 승급 · 부임: 스나이더와 코엔을 교수로 승급시켰고, 신제린 조수와 김용운 조수를 강사로 승급시켰다. 박용학 목사가 부임하여 학생들의 신앙지도를 맡았다.

종교 사역: 케이블, 장석영, 코엔, 갈홍기, 송치명이 종교 사역에 직접적인 책임을 지고 있다. 종교사역부가 채플 예배, 학생 · 교수 기도회, 일요일 교회 사역, 방학 중 학생 전도대 활동, 연합교회 협력, 연례 특별집회를 이끌고 있다.

학생 훈육: 학생 훈육과 지도의 표준을 마련하여 출석, 교실 훈육, 기숙사 관리 등을 더 철저히 해야 하고, 학생들의 자율을 중시하면서 모든 학생을 최소한 연 1회 상담하는 상담제도를 유지해야 한다.

등록생: 지난해에는 학생 수가 450명(문과 146명, 상과 224명, 수물과 80명)으로 시작하였다가 지금 400명이 되었지만, 그래도 많이 늘어난 셈이었다. 학생이 늘어남에 따라 훈육의 필요성이 커지고 있다.

자산: 학생 수가 증가하여 교직원과 시설도 늘어나고, 채플, 기숙사, 식당이 비좁아졌다. 언더우드관, 아펜젤러관, 몇몇 사택의 난방시설을 고치는 일이 시급하고, 학교 땅에 울타리를 두를 필요가 있다.

도서관: 도서관에 52,000권의 장서를 보유하고 있고, 이묘묵이 도서 분류와 목록화 작업을 계속하며 질서를 잡아가고 있다.

음악: 음악 수준이 높아졌고 방과 후에 활동하는 학생이 늘었으며, 순회공연, 하기음악강습회, 중등학교 현상음악대회의 수준도 높아졌다. 현제명 대신 박경호가 음악을 가르쳤고, 남녀 선교사들도 도왔다. 현제명은 미국에서 음악 장학금, 피아노 등의 악기들을 확보하였고, 음악관 건축비를 약정받았다.

운동경기: 운동경기에 참가하는 학생의 수가 늘어나고 있지만, 체육 교육을 위한 비용과 사람을 구하지 못하고 있다.

예산: 지난해에 수입이 증가하여 이번 해에 가장 절실히 필요한 항목의 지출을 할 수 있게 되었다. 교직원들이 또다시 ¥3,500가량을 기부하였는데, 봉급에서 돈을 갹출하는 것이 부적절한 일인데도 해결책을 마련하지 못하고 있다.

대학 홍보: 예산에 대학 홍보비가 없지만, 교수들이 개인적으로 한 해 동안 글을 발표하고 인쇄물을 배포해왔다. 홍보 활동을 계속하여 미국, 캐나다, 한국에 학교를 널리 알리기를 희망한다.

동문회: 동문회가 동문회보를 발행하여 배포하면서 한국에서 학교 홍보를 잘해주고 있다. 우리 학교에서 근무하는 동문으로 회계 최순주, 도서관장 이묘묵, 수물과 교수 이원철 박사와 최규남 박사, 상과 교수 노동규와 임병혁, 문과 교수 갈홍기 박사, 현금출납계원 이계원, 건축감독 김치각, 기숙사 사감 송치명, 수물과 조수 김영성과 신제린, 사무직의 손재명과 심운영, 그밖에 장기원, 장희창, 유경상, 신한철 등 총 17명[이 이름들을 세면 18명이다]이 있다.

12/31/37 ?
Chosen Christian College

n/p

President's Report

1936 -- 1937

The annual report of the President to the Board of Managers is I presume intended more to furnish them with some idea of the tendencies and trends of the institution and of its general condition and progress than to supply detailed and statistical statements of that progress. For this reason it is, exceedingly difficult to present such a report in any effective way. In addition to this general statement of conditions and progress there are frequently events and specific items which merit inclusion despite the fact that they form a part of the report from other officers of the institution. I shall endeavor, therefore to mention only a few of the incidents and events of the year referring you for the remainder to the reports from the Dean, the Treasurer, the Chairman of the Property Committee and the Financial Committee.

Deaths

It is my sad duty to make formal report of two deaths among those intimately connected for many years with our College. Mrs. O. R. Avison the beloved wife of President Emeritus Avison, passed away last fall in America; a memorial service was held in the College Chapel and appropriate messages of condolence was sent to Dr. Avison. While not officially connected with the College, Mrs. Avison was known to many among both faculty and students as "Mother Avison" and her passing was felt by us all with a deep sense of personal loss as well as sincere sympathy to her bereaved husband.

A few days ago came the word of the passing of Dr. James S. Gale who was one of the charter members of this Board and who gave freely of his time and efforts to the College in its early days as well as making valued contributions to its library. I would suggest that the Board take this opportunity of formally expressing its sympathy to both Dr. Avison and to Mrs. Gale.

Staff

When I reported last year our occidental staff was much depleted by furloughs and it is a great pleasure to report the return in good health of Dr. and Mrs. Cable, Dr. and Mrs. Miller and Prof. and Mrs. Snyder. Prof. Speidel is still away and we do not yet know whether he will be returning to us or not. A number of other members of our faculty and staff have travelled abroad during the year and while we greatly missed their services we rejoice in the opportunities afforded them for study and for observation of modern practice in other lands.

Prof. C. M. Hyun went to the United States and after a period of study received the degree of Doctor of Music from the Chicago Conservatory of Music, Chicago, Illinois. Prof. Hyun then travelled quite extensively making contacts and winning friends for the College. He sailed from New York in December to return to Korea via Europe and should arrive here within a few days.

Prof. In Sup Jung went to Copenhagen to attend the International Linguists' Conference after which he visited authorities on modern language teachining in Berlin, Paris and London, returning to Korea via the Suez Canal.

Mr. C. C. Hyen attended the Olympic games in Berlin and also visited and consulted with certain authorities in Soccer Football in England, being sent by the Korea Football Association.

Early in December the Vice-President, Mr. Yu loft to attend the International Y. M. C. A. Convention at Mysore, India from which trip he returned on February 15th.

In addition to these journeys already made, we have been asked to grant leave of absence to Dr. L. G. Paik to assist at the Centenary celebration of the Presbyterian Board of Foreign Missions, in America and for Mr. K. S. Lyu of the Library staff to study Library Science at Syracuse University. Such travel is inspiring to the traveller and in most cases the benefits are transmitted directly to the students and the College as a whole. Despite the difficulties entailed by the temporary absence of important members of the staff I am convinced of the value of such travel.

Promotions and Additions

I take great pleasure in recommending to the Board of Managers that Mr. R. C. Coen and Mr. L. H. Snyder be appointed to the rank of Professors. Both of these men and their long service to Korea and to the College are well known to this Board. Prof. L. H. Snyder was for some years Principal of the Songdo Higher Common School, while Prof. R. C. Coen served on two occasions as acting principal of John D. Wells School in Seoul. Their services have been sincerely appreciated by the College and this recommendation would have been made at an earlier date except for circumstances quite unrelated to the esteem in which they are held.

I make no other recommendations for promotion this year, but would announce the fact that I have promoted Mr. C. R. Cynn and Mr. Y. S. Kim from the position of Laboratory Assistants to the rank of Instructors.

-5-

I am also happy to announce that the Religious Work of the College has been strengthened by the coming of Mr. Yong Hak Pak to do personal work among the student body. Mr. Pak's services are contributed to us by the First Methodist Church, South; of Dallas, Texas; through the Korean Methodist Church. We are deeply grateful to the Church in America which provides the salary and to Dr. Ryang and to the Korean Methodist Church for their consent in this assignment to the Chosen Christian College. We hope that this is a distinct forward step in our attempt to personally reach each and all of the young men studying in the College.

Religious Work

Mention of Mr. Pak brings us to a consideration of the Religious Work of the College. It is my belief that the past year has seen a strengthening of the conviction that we must succeed in the work of this Department or fail in every Department. Dr. E. M. Cable, Mr. S. Y. Chang, Mr. R. C. Coen, Dr. H. K. Karl and Mr. C. M. Song are those who are more directly responsible for the success of this work while a number of others on the faculty have served faithfully on the Religious Work Committee. The conduct of the daily services, student and faculty prayer meeting, Sunday work in the churches, vacation student preaching bands, our share in the Federated Church and the conduct of the annual special religious services are all under the general direction of this Committee. Time fails to analyze and report on the details on all of this. Some has been very successful, some moderately so and some has shown quite discouraging results.

For our special meetings this year, the Rev. P. K. Chai of Pyengyang came to us and delivered a series of most helpful addresses which were greatly appreciated by the students and faculty. At the same time that these meetings were carried on, Dr. L. G. Paik, Dr. H. K. Karl and Rev. S. Y. Chang met the Seniors of each Department for an hour a day immediately before the general meeting. We have no adequate measuring stick for the results of such meetings, but it is my impression that the services were successful this year. I cannot close this section without referring briefly to the extremely fine work done by our students during the both summer and winter vacations. I personally visited some of the work and came away feeling very proud of the spirit in which it was done and of the good sense and general efficiency shown.

Student Discipline and Gudiance

In regard to general student discipline and gudiance I feel that we still have a long ways to go before we reach the standard which we would like to achieve. It is encouraging however, to report to you that the whole faculty realizes this fact and that we are endeavoring to tighten up on attendance, class room discipline, dormitory control and all the phases of this important side of education. I would not have you understand from the above that our students are an undisciplined and ill-behaved group of young men. In the main I am well pleased with them and have had numerous occasions to be truly proud of their self-control. Furthermore, I would beg you to remember that we are anxious to teach self-control, rather than, secure temporary results by strict supervision. The latter course would be much easier, but the values of self-control and self-discipline are too great to be thrown away for the sake of more temporary results. In this connection, we are continuing the system of student advisors and I am attempting to arrange for personal interviews, at least, once a year with all of the students. During the past year I was unable to carry this out but I did meet personally in my office every member of the Freshmen classes and quite a number of the Seniors. I have reasons to believe that these personal chats with our students were well worth the time involved. I hope during the coming year to arrange some plan of periodic conference both with the class monitors and with the class counsellors.

Enrollment

Some of the above problems of discipline are directly due to increased enrollment which for some years past has shown a very considerable growth; last year reaching 450 at the beginning of the year and despite losses due to failures, hard times, etc., our enrollment still stands at over 400. This years graduating class of 101 is the largest in the history of the College. This growth is shared to a certain degree by all three Departments, though the difficult four years grind in the Science Department discourages many. Both the Literary and the Commercial Department however, have had large increase. The Departmental enrollment at the beginning of the year being as follows: Literary, 146; Commercial, 224 and Science, 80. The Director and faculty of each Department are cognizant of the increased problems and responsibility resulting from the increasing number of students and are endeavoring to handle the situation efficiently and without sacrificing the values of personal contact and personal attention to the needs of each student.

Property

A detailed report from the Property Committee is before you but I must call your attention to the problems under this heading which face us as a result as an increase in student body. The seating capacity of our present chapel room will probably be inadequate from the beginning of the new school year in April. It will certainly be too small to hold the student body by April of 1938. A few years ago we could say that we had dormitory accommodations for one-quarter of our students; for the year 1937-38, we shall have accommodations for only about one-eighth of the students. The dining hall is inadequate. The wear and tear upon buildings and furniture is greatly increased. Increased students mean increased staff and should mean increased accommodation for them in offices in residences, offices and office furniture. The problem is acute and a speedy increase in our facilities is imperative.

Other immediate and extremely pressing needs are the complete or partial renovation of the heating plants in Underwood Hall, Science Hall and in several of the residences. In this connection, the College is extremely grateful to the Southern Methodist Church for the extensive repairs made without cost to the College, on the residence occupied by Prof. L. H. Snyder. The actual care of the Property has been well supervised by the Property Committee and under the direct supervision of the Superintendent of Building and Grounds, Mr. C. K. Kim, whose indefatigable and efficient work does not often receive the recognition which it merits. The inclusion of the College property within the city limits and consequent increase of traffic through our property as well as danger of encroachment made it necessary to begin the fencing of our grounds. Cement posts have been made and as soon as the ground melts a portion of the fencing will be done in the places where it is most necessary.

Library

Among the property items, the need of which is being more and more felt is the Library. Our collection now has gone over 52,000 volumes, has overflowed into the Commercial Museum and threatens to shortly burst even these bounds. Dr. M. M. Lee, our Librarian has continued his efficient work in the classification and cataloguing of the books and is rapidly bringing order out of chaos. I could write at length on the needs and work of the Library as on the work of many of our Departments, but I feel that the concentration during the last two years of our efforts on the classification of our books and on special efforts to stimulate their use are one of the things which we can report as real progress in a period when material progress is not so evident.

Music

Another Department in which continued progress has been made and where we look for still greater things is the Music Work under the direction of Prof. C. M. Hyun and the Music Committee. Year by year, the music standards have been raised and the number of students taking part in this valuable extra-curricula activity have increased. Concert tours, the Summer Music Conference and the Annual High School Music Contest have each year set higher and higher standards. During the absence of Prof. Hyun, Mr. K. H. Park of Ewha came to our assistance and to him and to the Ewha faculty for their gracious consent to his assistance in this work we are deeply grateful. For the Summer Music Conference, Mr. W. J. Anderson came and gave us very splendid assistance for which we are also grateful. No report of the music would be complete without acknowlodgement of the work of Mrs. R. C. Coen and Mrs. A. L. Becker. Throughout the year, Mrs. Coen plays for our chapel services and the faithful conduct of this work is no small task. Mrs. Becker has served as our accompanist for many years and despite ill health and many other difficulties has gone on Music Tours, playing in cold halls, and has practicing untold hours. With Prof. Hyun's return from America, we look forward to a year of renewed vigor with new plans and new developments. Prof. Hyun not only made many valuable contacts in

America, but secured for the College the gift of three scholarships for Music students, a number of pianos and musical instruments and a pledge for a Music Building from a wealthy and generous friend in Chicago. We understand that the money is to be paid sometime within the next two years, so that no immediate construction is intended.

Athletics

The results of our athletic teams have been made known to you through the newspapers and are also included in the Dean's report. I will merely say that it is a great satisfaction to have an ever increasing number of students actually participating in athletics and it is our plan and hope to still further stimulate this participation till all of the students are taking part in some form of healthful athletics. The Inter-Departmental games and contests between new and old students all help along this line. A qualified director of physical education is greatly needed but at present neither the money nor the man is in view so we continue to depend upon the faithful work of the various teachers to whom are assigned the direction of the respective teams and activities.

Budget

Athletics and the cost of their support brings us at once to the Budget which is in your hands. We are grateful for the relative increase over last year which has made possible a beginning toward some of the most necessary expenditures. I am most happy to report that we were able to reduce the staff contributions by one-half and would again express my gratitude to the staff for their loyal support in this and in many other ways. We are still however, accepting from our staff contributions amounting to approximately ¥3,500 and this from salaries which are in many cases quite inadequate. The alarming rise in the cost of living makes the condition of the lower salary men extremely difficult. Young men whose education and position requires them to maintain a relatively high standard find it almost impossible to make ends meet on a salary of ¥80, ¥90 or ¥100 per month. At present however, I do not see any hope of offering them any immediate relief. You will also note that we have continued to carry out the provisions of the salary scale. The budget as it is before you has been submitted to the Finance Committee first in its tentative and later in its final form. I should like to express thanks to the Finance Committee who have met several times during the year and have advised and directed the Administration on important financial questions. I must also express my appreciation of the very fine work done by the Treasurer, Dr. S. J. Choy and his staff.

Publicity

An item which has no place in the budget but which should have one is Publicity. I have during the year published and distributed some letters and leaflets, copies of some of which are before you today. I feel convinced that more should be done along this line and hope that means may be found during the coming year to continue and enlarge the work of making the Chosen Christian College known to the public both in the United States and Canada and here in Korea.

Alumni

In Korea a certain part of this publicity work has been well assumed by the Alumni Association. They are now employing Mr. T. H. Pak as a full time Alumni Secretary. They publish a quarterly Alumni Bulletin which many of you doubtless see and which goes directly to all of our Alumni and indirectly into the hands of many others. I feel that the contribution made by our Alumni both to the country as a whole and to the College is probably not fully realized. The roll of our graduates who have done and are doing distinguish work in various line of endeavor in Korea is most gratifying. Here in our own College, we have Dr. S. J. Chey, Treasurer; Dr. M. M. Lee, Librarian; Dr. D. W. Lee and Dr. K. N. Choi, Professors in Science Department; Mr. T. K. Roe and Mr. P. K. Lim, Professors in the Commercial Department; Dr. H. K. Karl who is doing very splendid work in the Literary Department and the Religious Work in the College; Mr. K. W. Yi in the Treasurers office; Mr. C. K. Kim, Superintendent of Buildings and Grounds; Mr. C. M. Song, Dormitory Superintendent, Mr. Y. S. Kim and Mr. C. R. Cynn in the Science Department and Mr. C. M. Sohn and Mr. W. Y. Shim in the general office, as well as Messrs. K. W. Chang, H. C. Chang, K. S. Lyu and H. C. Cynn - altogether seventeen. These men are all here because they have proved their worth. Many if not all of them are serving the College for less than they might be receiving elsewhere. We are proud and grateful to them.

I cannot close this report without also mentioning with heartfelt appreciation, the work of the administrative offices and the other members of the faculty and staff. It is of course usuall to do this in a formal and matter of course way, but I would like to assure the Board that I do it from a very real sense of appreciation of faithful, self-sacrificing service, of a high degree of harmony and cooperation and of their unremitting devotion to difficult and delicate tasks. Practically all of our faculty and staff also hold important positions and carry heavy burdens in the general work of the church and Korean society, the Y.M.C.A., Christian Literature Society, Severance Board, many church offices, rural work, etc., as well as much valuable research work are represented by the contributions which our staff is making to the cause of Christianity in general.

I regret that I cannot report to you new buildings, increased endowment, new forms of work begun, but I rejoice that I can say that the faculty and staff which I have the honor to represent are placing renewed emphasis on spiritual questions; that they are planning and working constructively for the better development of self-control among our students; that they are endeavoring to improve the educational methods and means; that we are awake to the necessity for properly utilizing our library facilities and for developing the Korean natural gifts along musical lines that we realize that a strong healthy body of students is more important than winning teams; and that we are more and more conscious of the necessity of making Christ first in everything. This is I believe a report of progress and of success, it is one for which I may claim no special credit except as I am one of the faculty and the one to whom the honor of making this report is delegated.

Respectfully submitted,

Horace H. Underwood

Horace H. Underwood
President

50. 유억겸 부교장 겸 학감의 이사회 제출 보고서

문서 제목	Chosen Christian College, Report of the Dean 1936~1937
문서 종류	학감 보고서
제출 시기	1937년 2월 19일
작성 장소	서울
제 출 자	유억겸
수 신 자	이사회
페이지 수	23
출 처	2114-5-4: 04 Underwood, Horace H. (DR.) 1937 Jan. to Aug. (UMAH) 2114-5-4: 04 Underwood, Horace H. (DR.) 1937 Sep. to Dec. (UMAH)

자료 소개

유억겸 부교장 겸 학감이 1937년 2월 19일 열린 이사회 회의에서 제출한 학감 보고서이다. 회의록을 현재 찾지 못하고 있으나, 이날의 회의는 관례상 연례회의였을 것으로 추정된다.

이 보고서도 목차가 예년처럼 구성되어 있으나, 결어 앞의 연구사역 항목은 없어졌다. I. 서언, II. 운영진과 교수진, III. 3개 학과, IV. 종교활동, V. 도서관, VI. 체육 교육, VII. 음악부, VIII. 다른 사항들, IX. 학생, X. 졸업생, XI. 결어.

내용 요약

I. 원한경 교장의 리더쉽과 교직원들의 협력으로 대학이 설립목표를 향해 크게 나아갔다.

II. 에비슨은 명예 교장이다. 운영진은 원한경(교장), 유억겸(부교장, 학감), 백낙준(문과 과장), 이순탁(상과 과장), 이춘호(수물과 과장), 최순주(회계), 이묘묵(도서관장)이다. 대학 교무위원회는 교장, 부교장, 백낙준, 이순탁, 이춘호, 케이블과 스나이더(남·북감리회 선교회 대표)로 구성되어 있다. 대학 예산위원회는 원한경, 유억겸, 백낙준, 이순탁, 이춘호, 베커, 스나이더, 최순주로 구성되어 있다. 교수는 21명(한국인 13명) 조교수는 8명(한국인 6명)이고, 전임강사는 8명(한국인 6명), 강사와 조수는 19명(한국인 16명), 파트타임 조력자는 4명, 안식년 중인 교수 2명, 사무직원(사감 포함)은 14명이다.

III. 본교는 종합대학 체제를 이루고 있다. 문과에서는 안식년 중인 현제명 대신 이화여전의 박경호가 음악을 가르치고 있고, 우메사와가 신입생 체육교육 강사로 왔으며, 정인섭이 떠나 있는 동안(유럽 학술대회 참가) 이묘묵, 하경덕, 이양하, 정인보가 대신 가르쳤다. 방과 후에 4학년생 대상의 미술 강의가 있고 문과만의 운동팀들이 활동하고 있다. 문과생들은 각종 음악 활동, 연극부 공연, 영어웅변대회 참가, 중등학교 영어웅변대회 개최 등의 활동을 하고 있다. 교수들은 연구실에 총 1,945권을 갖추고 있고, 한국문화를 특별히 강조하고 있다. 최현배가 문법책[『우리말본』]을 출판하였고, 김두헌, 손진태, 정인보, 신한철이 연구결과를 발표하였다. 상과에서는 육지수(동경제대) 등이 교수로 왔고, 정인섭이 코펜하겐 국제언어학자대회에서 논문을 발표하였다. 상품진열관을 운영하고 상업 실습용 비품을 완비하였다. 교수들이 연구결과를 신문과 잡지에 발표하고 있고, 광고방법을 연구하고 있다. 수물과에서는 교수들이 매월 모여 근대과학의 문제들과 과학교육의 발전을 논의해왔다. 스나이더가 과학박물관에 동물 표본들을 구비하였다.

IV. 학생들이 채플 예배에 잘 참석하고 있고, 1월에 특별집회가 열렸다. 종교교육을 위해 모든 학생을 기숙사에 수용할 필요가 있다.

V. 도서관이 50,000권을 소장하려는 목표를 초과하여 2월 기준으로 50,107권을 소장하게 되었다. 동문회가 학교 설립일에 모교 방문 행사를 열었을 때 참고자료실에서 희귀서적들을 전시하였다.

VI. 운동경기로 또다시 성공적인 한 해를 기록하였다. 축구, 야구, 테니스, 농구 대회에서 우승하였고, 아이스하키팀이 신설된 대학 아이스링크에서 훈련하고 한국 대표로 뽑혀 일본 챔피언십 대회에 참가하였다. 씨름은 연보전에서 아깝게 패하였고, 펜싱 클럽도 열심히 훈련하였다.

VII. 정례적인 서울 음악회와 지방 순회음악회를 개최하였다. 오케스트라와 합창단이 라디오에 출연하여 연주하였고, 제6회 하기음악강습회와 제5회 중등학교 현상음악대회[콩쿨]를 개최하였다. 현제명이 미국에 가서 박사학위를 취득하였고(6월), 장학금을 확보하고 음악관 건축기금 기부를 약속 받았다. 현제명이 없는 동안 박경호와 베커 부인이 가르쳤다.

VIII. 박물관이 150점을 새로 기증받았는데, 그중 130점을 문과 2년생 민영규를 비롯한 학생들이 기증하였다. 학생지원을 위해 ¥600의 충당금을 집행하였고, 21명의 근로학생이 학비의 절반을 벌었다. (학생 클럽들과 조직들의 목록을 제시하고 있다.)

IX. 등록생은 총 406명(문과 125명, 상과 215명, 수물과 66명)이고, 본과는 373명, 별과는 28명이다(1월 30일까지). (출신 지역과 종교 현황은 표를 참고.)

X. 졸업생은 총 599명이고, 현재 연전 교수 9명, 연전 직원 8명, 다른 기독교학교 교사 68명, 교회 사역 12명, 의학생 2명, 비기독교학교 교사 20명, 미국 유학 20명, 일본 유학 26명, 언론인 15명, 은행원 및 회사원 46명, 공무원 36명, 개인사업(상공업) 57명, 농업 3명, 다양한 개인사업[家業] 236명, 의사 1명, 광업 4명, 사망 36명이다. 졸업생이 갖는 자격은 이전 보고서와 같다.

XI. 이 학년도에 학생들이 가장 많이 왔고, 교수들이 학문연구로 학교와 사회에 크게 공헌하였으며, 학교가 모든 면에서 크게 발전하였다.

12/31

802

TRANSFERRED

CHOSEN CHRISTIAN COLLEGE

Report of the Dean

1936--1937

****

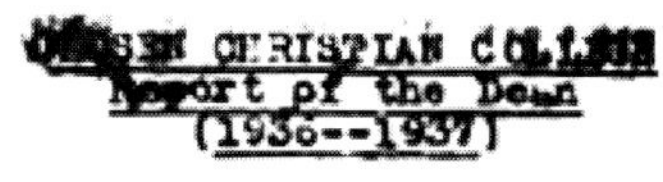
CHOSEN CHRISTIAN COLLEGE
Report of the Dean
(1936--1937)

****

CONTENTS

CHOSEN CHRISTIAN COLLEGE

Report of the Dean

I. Introductory Remarks

To the Field Board of Managers of the Chosen Christian College at the Board Meeting held on February 19th, 1937:

I have the honor to submit the following report concerning the academic phase of the College Administration for the academic year 1936-1937.

The College has made a marked progress during the academic year 1936-1937 toward the high aims set forth at the foundation of the Institution under the far-sighted leadership of President Underwood and with the hearty co-operation of all members of the Faculty and Staff.

I should like to express my appreciation to President Underwood and Prof. C. H. Lee and others who assisted my work during my absence.

II. Officers of Administration and Instruction

A. President Emeritus.

O. R. Avison, M.D., LL.D. (Toronto and Wooster), residing in the United States of America.

B. Administrative Officers.

Horace H. Underwood, M.A., Ph.D., Litt.D., President.

Uck Kyum Yu, Gakushi, Vice-President and Dean.

L. George Paik, M.A., Ph.D., Director of the Literary Dept.

Soon Tak Lee, Gakushi, Director of the Commercial Dept.

Choon Ho Lee, M.A., Director of the Science Dept.

Soon Ju Chey, B.S.E., M.B.A., Ph.D., Treasurer.

Kyo Mook Lee, M.A., Ph.D., Librarian.

C. College Council.

Horace H. Underwood, Ph.D., Litt.D., President.

Uck Kyum Yu, Gakushi, Vice-President and Dean.

C. College Council. (Continued)

L. George Paik, Ph.D., Director of the Literary Dept.

Soon Tak Lee, Gakushi, Director of the Commercial Dept.

Choon Ho Lee, M.A., Director of the Science Dept.

E. M. Cable, D.D., Representative of the M. E. C. Mission.

L. H. Snyder, M.A., Representative of the M. E. C. S. Mission.

D. College Budget Committee.

H. H. Underwood, Ph.D., Litt.D., President.

U. K. Yu, Gakushi, Vice-President and Dean.

L. G. Paik, Ph.D., Director of the Literary Dept.

S. T. Lee, Gakushi, Director of the Commercial Dept.

C. H. Lee, M.A., Director of the Science Dept.

A. L. Becker, Ph.D., Representative of the M. E. C. Mission.

L. H. Snyder, M.A., Representative of the M. E. C. S. Mission.

S. J. Chey, Ph.D., Treasurer.

E. Faculty.

(1) Professors. (21)

H. H. Underwood, B.A., M.A., Ph.D., Litt.D., (New York and Mount Union).
President of the College and Professor of Education, Psychology and English.

U. K. Yu, Gakushi, (Tokyo Imperial University).
Vice-President and Dean of the College and Professor of Law.

L. G. Paik, B.A., Th.B., M.A., Ph.D., (Yale)
Director of the Literary Department and Professor of Occidental History and Religion.

S. T. Lee, Gakushi, (Kyoto Imperial University).
Director of the Commercial Department and Professor of Economics, Insurance, Statistics, and Abacus.

C. H. Lee, B.A., M.A., (Ohio State).
Director of the Science Department and Professor of Mathematics.

A. L. Becker, B.A., M.A., Ph.D., (Michigan).
Professor of Physics and Mathematics.

E. H. Miller, B.A., B.D., M.A., Ph.D., (Columbia)
Professor of Chemistry, English and Bible.

-3-

V. Faculty.

(1) Professors. (21) (Continued)

N. W. Paik, Gakushi, (Tokyo University of Commerce).
Professor of Commerce, Bookkeeping, History of Commerce, Commercial Japanese, Accounting and History of Economics.

K. Kadowaki, Gakushi, (Kyoto Imperial University).
Professor of Chemistry, Mechanical Drawing.

H. P. Choi, Gakushi, (Kyoto Imperial University).
Professor of Philosophy, Education, Ethics, and the Korean Language.

D. W. Lee, Graduate of C.C.C., B.A., M.A., Ph.D., (Michigan).
Professor of Mathematics and Astronomy.

S. Nikaido, Gakushi (Tokyo Imperial University).
Professor of Japanese, Japanese Literature and Introduction to Literature.

P. C. Kim, Gakushi, (Waseda University).
Professor of Physics, Electrical Engineering, and Mathematics.

H. Kaiya, Gakushi, (Tohoku Imperial University).
Professor of Mathematics, Surveying, Physics, Civil Engineering, Drawing, Geology, Mineralogy, Natural Science and Architecture.

S. K. Hong, B.A., (Ohio State).
Professor of English.

I. P. Chung
Professor of Chinese Literature and Korean Literature.

C. M. Hyun, D.Mus., (Gunn School of Music and Dramatic Art).
Professor of Music.

T. K. Roe, Graduate of C.C.C., Gakushi (Kyoto Imperial University).
Professor of Transportation, Agricultural Economics, and Business English.

S. J. Chey, Graduate of C.C.C., B.S., M.B.A., Ph.D., (New York)
Professor of Commercial Practice, Business English, Typewriting, Advertising, and Foreign Exchange.

E. M. Cable, B.S., M.A., D.D., (Cornell College)
Professor of English, Bible and History.

G. C. Speidel, B.S., M.S., (Virginia) (On furlough)
Professor of English.

(2) Assistant Professors (6)

O. Y. Lou, (Berlin University)
Assistant Professor of German.

I. S. Jung, Gakushi, (Waseda University)
Assistant Professor of English and Introduction to Literature.

P. K. Lim, Graduate of C.C.C., B.A., M.A., (Syracuse).
Assistant Professor of Bookkeeping, Commodities, Business English, Commercial Geography, Marketing and Typewriting.

(2) Assistant Professors (8) (Continued)

L. H. Snyder, B.A., M.A., (Princeton).
Assistant Professor of English and Typewriting.
K. N. Choi, Graduate of C.C.C., B.A., M.A., Ph.D., (Michigan)
Assistant Professor of Physics and Mathematics.
R. C. Coen, B.A., B.D., M.A., (Chicago)
Assistant Professor of Bible and English.
K. D. Hor, B.S., M.A., Ph.D., (Harvard).
Assistant Professor of Sociology, Psychology and English.
M. H. Lee, Graduate of C.C.C., B.A., M.A., Ph.D., (Boston)
Assistant Professor of English.

(3) Instructors. (8)

Mrs. H. H. Underwood, B.A., M.A., (New York).
English
L. W. Kang
Physical Education.
S. Y. Chang, B.S., B.D., M.A., (Columbia)
Bible and Religious Education.
H. K. Karl, Graduate of C.C.C., B.D., M.A., Ph.D., (Chicago)
Bible and Philosophy.
K. B. Jung, Gakushi, (Tokyo Imperial University)
Commercial Law, Civil Law, and Japanese Civil Government.
Y. H. Lee, Gakushi, (Tokyo Imperial University)
English
C. N. Kim, Graduate of Paiyoung College
The Chinese Language.
Mrs. E. M. Cable, B.A., (Cornell)
English.

(4) Lecturers and Assistants. (19)

K. W. Chang, Graduate of C.C.C., Gakushi, (Tofuku Imperial University).
Mathematics.
H. C. Chang, Graduate of C.C.C., Gakushi, (Tokyo University of Commerce). (Leave of Absence).
T. Yokoyama, B.A., B.D., Ph.D., (John Hopkins)
English
R. K. Jung, Gakushi, (Keio University).
Finance, Economics and Public Law.
P. B. Billings, B.A. (Depauw).
English. (Leave of Absence).
C. T. Son, Gakushi, (Waseda University).
Oriental History.
D. H. Kim, Gakushi, (Tokyo Imperial University).
Morals.
H. S. Park, Gakushi, (Meiji University).
Commercial Mathematics, Economic Affairs, Exchange, Trust and Business Management.
I. J. Park, B.S. in A. E., (Minnesota) and B.S. in M.E. (Lewis Institute).
Architecture and Drawing.

-5-

(4) Lecturers and Assistants (19) (Continued)

W. S. Min, B.S., (Nevada)
French
C. S. Ryuk, Gakushi, (Tokyo Imperial University)
Economics, Commerce, and German.
H. S. Ryu, Gakushi, (Waseda University)
Chemistry.
R. W. Kim, (Keijo Imperial University)
English
K. Woomesawa,
Physical Education.
K. H. Pak, B.S., (Cincinati Conservatory)
Music.
C. R. Cynn, Graduate of C.C.C.
Assistant, Physics Laboratory.
H. C. Cynn, Graduate of C.C.C.
Assistant, Literary Department.
Y. S. Kim, Graduate of C.C.C.
Assistant, Chemistry Laboratory.
Y. H. Pak, B.A., M.A. (Texas Christian College and Southern Methodist University)
Secretary of the Religious Department.

(5) Part Time Assistants. (4)

Mrs. A. L. Becker
Mrs. R. C. Coen
Mrs. E. H. Miller
Mrs. L. H. Snyder

(6) Professors on Furlough. (2)

G. C. Speidel, B.S., M.S.
C. M. Hyun, D. Mus.

F. Office Staff. (14)

Y. S. Koo, M.D., (Emory)
College Physican.
C.M. Sohn, Graduate of C.C.C.
Secretary to Administration.
C. M. Song, Graduate of C.C.C.
Superintendent of Dormitory.
C. K. Kim, Graduate of C.C.C.
Superintendent of Grounds and Buildings.
K. S. Lyu, Graduate of C.C.C.
Assistant to the Librarian.
P. Hyen, B.A., (Shanghai)
Accountant.
W. Y. Shim, Graduate of C.C.C.
Secretary to Administration.
K. W. Yi, Graduate of C.C.C., B.A., M.A., (Michigan).
Cashier.

F. Office Staff. (14) (Continued)

Miss D. P. Ahn,
Stenographer to the President.
Mrs. S. H. Lyu, Graduate of [illegible]
Clerical Assistant of the Library.
Miss D. P. Chang,
Assistant to the Cashier.
Miss K. J. Kim, Graduate of Ewha College
Clerical Assistant of the Library.
Miss S. N. You, Graduate of Ewha College
Clerical Assistant of the Library.
Y. S. Lee, Graduate of C.C.C.
Assistant in Music.

III. Three Departments of the College.

The College is organized on a university system and has four Departments, but only three are in operation. These Departments are separate so far as their internal organization is concerned with their respective Directors, budgets and recitation halls, but they are one in general administration and policy under one Dean.

A. Literary Department - Director L. G. Paik, Ph.D.

The Literary Department had one of the most successful years last year with the largest enrollment and graduating class and with the fine spirit of cooperation among the faculty.

FACULTY: Dr. and Mrs. E. M. Cable returned from furlo.
Mr. G. C. Speidel left on furlo.
Dr. Hyun on furlo.
Mr. Kyong Ho Pak of Ewha gave instruction in Music during the absence of Dr. Hyun.
Mr. Moomosawa, new instructor for Physical Education for Freshmen.
While Mr. Insub Jung was away, Drs. H. M. Lee, K. D. Har and Messrs. I. P. Chung, and Y. H. Lee shared burdens of class instruction.

STUDENTS:
Largest enrollment in the history of the College.
For the first time the Department took in the maximum number of 50 to the Freshmen Class.
Began the year 145 in roll. As the report is written, there are 38 Freshmen, 32 Sophomores, 25 Juniors and 29 Seniors, making the total of 124.
Gradual and wholesome growth of the Department is seen and good discipline is maintained. Efforts are kept up for personal attention to every student.

EXTRA-CURRICULA ACTIVITIES:

A. Extra-Curricula Course: Esthetics for Seniors for one hour per week for three months, for general information on the subject by Mr. Y. S. Ko, Curator of the Songdo Municipal Museum and an Instructor in Ewha.

B. Athletics: 3 students of the Department in the College Football team, 2 in the Basketball team and 3 in the Hockey team. One of the Seniors in the Basketball team went to Berlin as a member of the Basketball team sent by Japan. These athletes had the advantage of travels aboard and good discipline in training. General physical education for the entire student body is carried on.

C. Music: 19 boys are in various branch of Musical activities of the College. These boys have had advantage of travels and good training in music.

D. Drama: The Drama Club presented Ibsen's play on "Little Eyolf" on the evening of the 11th of December, before a packed audience.

E. English Oratorical Contest: Out of 22 boys participated in the Intra-mural English Oratorical Contest, 14 were from the Literary Department, Hahn Pyo Wook (L.3) won the first prize and Kim Sungsup (L.4) won the third prize in the final contest. Thanks are due to Drs. Cable and M. M. Lee for this successful work.

F. Friendly Association Essay Contest: Dramatization of an old Korean story, Life of Shim Chung and Hahn Sang Chik (L.2) won the first prize.

G. Contests promoted by out-side organizations: Chosun Ilbo: Han Sang Chik, (L.3) won the 2nd prize in Drama Contest. Maii-Il Shinpo: Cho Pung Yen (L.3) won honorable mention in story contest and his story is being published in the said paper. Chung-Ang Shinpo: Ye Sang Hyun (L.2) won the first prize in Poetry contest.

SECONDARY SCHOOL CONTACTS: The Fifth Annual English Oratorical Contest for Secondary Schools were held in the Pai Chai auditorium on the evening of November 14th, 1936. 9 schools participated, 7 boys' and 2 girls' schools.

RESEARCH WORK:

A. Source Materials in the Research Room: Total accessions since the last report amounts to 225 volumes of history, literature philosophy etc. Total accessions 1,945 - Special emphasis on Korean culture.

B. Published work by our staff: Completion and publication of Prof. Choi's work on Korean Grammar, a book of over 1,200 pages. It took a whole year for printing. A monumental work in the field.

Publication of Dr. W. Carl Rufus's research on Korean Astronomy as the No.3 of the English Publication of the Department. Dr. Rufus made it possible for the publication. Thanks are due to him.

Mr. D. H. Kim, an Instructor, published his study on Mourning Apparels; Mr. Chin Tai Son, another Instructor, on Believes and Theories of Spirits among the Chinese.

Numerous articles by our staff appeared on magazines and newspapers.

Dr. Cable's work on United States and Korean Relations from 1866 to 1871 has been completed and read before the Korea Branch of the Royal Asiatic Society. We look forward to publishing this interesting work based on original documents.

Prof. I. P. Chung's work on Korean history, which were running for more than a year and half on the Dong-A-Ilpo, came to a stop, when the Paper was suppressed last August. We regret it.

Mr. Han Chul Shin, an Assistant, has kept up his study on the history of the Formitive Period of the Yi Dynasty.

3. Commercial Department - Director S. T. Lee, Gakushi

The Commercial Department is the largest department of the College with a faculty of 10 professors and assistant professors, 16 lecturers, 1 assistant, and 215 students (Seniors 59, Sophomores 71, Freshmen 85).

Messrs. Ryong-Whan Kim and Chi-Shu Lyuk have been added to the faculty from last April on. Mr. Kim is a graduate of the Keijo Imperial University and has taught 6 years at the Chuncho Public Higher Common School. He is teaching English. Mr. Lyuk is a graduate of the Tokyo Imperial University and was a graduate student of the University for 3 years. He is teaching a number of commercial subjects. He is also lecturing at the Preparatory School of the Keijo Imperial University. Mr. L. H. Snyder came back last fall from his furlough and has resumed his work in the department. He is giving his extra time in teaching short-hand to those students who wish to take it as an extra work. He has also organized a a special class for Freshmen whose examination grades on English Conversation are below average. He has recently written a thesis on "Currency Reform in Manchukuo and the Central Bank of Manchou 1932-35" and presented before Dr. E. W. Kemmerer's Class, Modern Currency Reforms, Graduate School, Princeton, University.

Prof. In-Sup Jung made a trip to Europe last summer to attend the 4th International Linguists' Conference which was held at Copenhagen, Denmark, from August 6th to September 1st. His report to the said Conference were "The Romanization of Korean", "A comparative Study of Phonetics in English, Japanese, Korean as the Foundation of English Teaching in Korea", and "Best Modern Korean Poems". He visited important cities in Europe and Educational Institutes and met prominent scholars and writers. He returned to the College in October with many valuable information and materials.

The faculty members of this department have been giving extra-curricula lectures, once in every semester, for the benefit of the students on some subject of current nature or in a form of report on their researches. These have been very interesting and instructive and were well appreciated by all who attended them.

A brief report on employment of the 50 graduates of last year may not be wholly out of place here. Of this number, 4 are attending universities in Tokyo; 20 out of 27 who applied for position are holding responsible positions in various banking house, manufacturing concerns, government offices, and in the institutions of learning, 19 are either in private business or attending home affairs; and the remaining 7 have not been placed definitely as yet. Inspite of the last number, it is fairly good record if it is compared with that of other colleges of same standing in the country.

Taking every thing into consideration, we may say that the Commercial Department is holding more than its own, and, while proud of its present facts, we are looking forward to a better day of this department and consequently greater service to the society.

Commercial Museum

The Commercial Museum has been growing steadily with additional specimens of native and foreign commodities making a total number of 1610. We are proud of the fact that at the present time our Museum excells any of its kind in Korean colleges in Korea in the number as well as in the variety of the specimens. Prof. P. K. Lim is in charge of the work.

Commercial Practice Work

Along with the theoretical studies of Commerce and Economics, the practical side of the course is no less important a phase. At the present time, there are 11 typewriters for the students to practice on, but we are looking forward to a time when we can complete the equipment for this purpose. Furthermore, a special course on shorthand has been giving since last fall for those who take it as an extra curriculum work. Prof. L. H. Snyder is in charge of this work.

General Research Work

The Commercial Research Work has been carried on through the faculty members. This work facilitates the study and research of the teachers and students alike working on some commercial and economic problems. These results have been published in the leading newspapers and magazines from time to time. There are 30 magazines, 4 newspapers, and 2500 volumes of reference books in the Research Room. Prof. T. K. Roe is in charge of this work.

Research on Advertisement

The Commercial Department has begun this research work to study the method of advertising and for reference. Nearly 10,000 pieces of various kinds of posters, handbills, folders, labels, enamel and card signs, newspaper and magazine advertisement clippings, etc., have been collected since April, 1933. Also quite a number of books have been secured for study and reference. These have been carefully classified and displayed in the Commercial Practice Room. Prof. P. K. Lim is in charge of this work.

The English Teachers' Research Club

Ever since the Club became a chartered member of the Institute for Research of English Teaching of the Educational Bureau of Japan, bulletins, periodicals, and other publications have been sent to the College, and they are being displayed for use in one of the teacher's rooms for the time being. The Club is devoting much time and effort in planning a unified method of teaching English as a part of this program. Phonetics is taught from two years ago, and to verify points in phonetics, a phonograph has been secured in the department. The Club has directed the students to form an English Club of themselves holding meetings with various programs and practicing English in various ways with much interest. Prof. S. K. Hong is the Chairman of this Club.

Besides the above mentioned features of this department, we are holding an annual prize contest in thesis or grades on Commercial, Economic, and English Subjects in a way of leading the interest of the students along these lines.

C. Science Department - Director, C. H. Lee, M.A.

The Science Department has made definite progress during the past year in spite of the reduced budget. The teachers have been loyal and enthusiastic even though they have had to carry heavy loads in their regular work and have had many extra outside assignments.

The Faculty of this Department consists of 7 Professors, one Assistant Professor, 3 Lecturers and 2 Assistants making a total of 13 members.

The number of students in this Department is 72 an increase over last year. There are 26 Freshmen, 16 Sophomores, 17 Juniors and 13 Seniors.

The new Architectural Engineering (Construction) Courses have received the enthusiatic support of the students in the upper classes. Giving optional courses in the Junior and Senior years has helped advance the scholarship in all the grades. Also the chance of getting "jobs", for the graduates seem much better and this helps in the total enrollment; more applicants and more "hang on" during the whole four years.

One thing that has helped the "spirit-de-corps" of our Department Staff has been the Science Club to which all the members of the staff belonged. This Club has had regular monthly meetings at the homes of the various members and some modern Scientific problem has been presented at each meeting in well prepared papers. In addition, problems dealing with the practical development of Scientific Education in the Department have been well talked over. Also there have been social meetings to which the wives have been invited.

There has been no serious sickness among the personnel of the Department and the return of Dr. E. H. Miller, last September has considerably strengthened the morale of the Chemistry teaching staff.

Prof. Snyder is trying to build up the Science Museum by furnishing specimens of rare birds and animals. He is working in touch with specialists in America as well as in Korea.

IV. Religious Activities - Chairman, E. M. Cable, D.D.

The Rekigious activities Department has been very busy during the year trying to improve the religious atmosphere and activities of the college campus and in carrying on special religious work not only in the churches in and around the city of Seoul, but in different parts of the country, especially during the summer and Christmas recesses.

The chapel services have been well attended and on the whole have been quite successful but we feel that there is yet much to be desired along this line. The department has in mind some changes to be made next year. We have been favored with some prominent speakers among visitors passing through Korea. However, most of our chapel services have been conducted by our own faculty. We are finding it more and more difficult to secure Korean speakers among the clergymen of the city.

Our Special Services in January this year were conducted by the Reverend Chai Pil Keun of Pyengyang and were most helpful and inspiring. Rev. P. K. Chai is a forceful, clear, intellectual, spiritual and practical speaker. The interest in his messages was clearly demonstrated by the fact that the attendance was as good the day he finished as when he began. He held the students and faculty as none of our recent speakers have done. We feel sure his utterances will bear much fruit in the lives of the faculty and students.

The students during the Summer recess, in addition to visiting a number of places and preaching, did some real good project work. We shall urge that more of this be done this next year. The opportunity for such work is becoming more and more apparent in the Suburbs of Seoul, and the adjacent villages that the churches of the city are not touching.

We were glad to secure the help of Mr. Y. H. Pak, from Texas Christian College, to act as Secretary of the Department. His time will be entirely given up to work among the students, both religious and social. This is what we have long desired and hoped for. We are sure his presence and help will result in more effective work among the students this coming year.

The department feels that a new dormitory and a dining room are very essential to the success of our religious and social work activities among the students. We would like to have the Freshman class all housed in the dormitories. If we can begin with them under our supervision and direction we feel that we can set quite a different stamp upon the student body.

However, we also feel that more than equipment and students a Christian faculty is necessary to make a Christian college. We could have all these and without the latter our institution would be a complete failure to build Christian character. We hope to urge a special campaign this coming year to increase the religious interest and enthusiasm among the faculty and then the students.

V. College Library - Librarian, M. M. Lee, Ph.D.

The academic year 1936-37 is the year of fulfillment for the Library, for the much coveted goal of toal accessions of fifty thousand books is reached and even passed. The Library is now boasting of possessing 50,107 volumes (Feb. 12) and is now working for another object.

During the last year, the Library put much stress upon giving proper cares to the books - classfying, cataloguing, filling cards and shelving books in right places, etc. Mr. K. S. Lyu and three women staff with the aid of Mrs. E. M. Cable and the Librarian took care of over 12,300 old classical books. However, acquisition of books is rather small in number, amounting to about 800 volumes of which 192 were purchased.

Among the outstanding gifts nearly 300 volumes by President Underwood, 189 volumes brought from America by Dr. Miller and 150 volumes of Mrs. Charles Leonard, Troy, Pa., should be mentioned. The students also manifest their interests in the Library by contributing books and periodicals individually or collectively. A half dozen students of present Literary third class students, for example, presented 137 readable books to the Library. Moreover, Mr. Bok Hun Song, father of a student in Commercial Department, donated 2,000 Yen through Dr. S. J. Chey, to the Library to purchase books.

The Library handles annually about 148 kinds of periodicals of which 40 are in the Occidental languages. On account of the lack of appropriation unbound periodicals are being accumulated.

Proper caring coupled with rapid expansion necessitated more stacks; and 4 new stacks were installed in the stack room proper and a long side wall book-shelves were built in the Commercial Museum.

The Library week was observed on the first week of February and had the following speakers:

President Underwood, "Books and Library"
Prof. I. P. Chung, "Books of Korea"
Dr. H. M. Lee, "A Phase of American Policy in the Far East"

It is very gratifying to see that the students swarm to the card boxes, news and magazine racks and charging desk, looking for something new and demanding for reference materials of which some were as serious as the Chronicles of the Yi Dynasty. Taking just one month, the month of May, 1936, the following reference books were taken out by the students:

Literature	527	Natural Science	91
General	405	Philosophy	64
Economics	148	Religion	61
Social Science	147	Philology	48
History	100	Fine Arts	4

As a way of cementing the relations between Alumni and Alma Mater the College observed a Home Coming Day on the Founder's Day, and the Library had an exhibition of some rare books in the Reference Room.

The College Library is in need of a good many things, yet the following needs are very desparate:

(A) A fund of 3,000 Yen to purchase certain books which students in general read most such as, literature, etc.

(B) A fund of 1,000 Yen to bind newspapers and magazines.

(C) More space for expansion.

(D) The library building.

VI. Physical Education - Chairman, U. K. Yu, Gakushi.

This is another successful year of athletic activities of the College. We won championships in three different sports during the fall championship games namely, football, basketball, and tennis. During last summer vacation, our football team made a very successful trip to the northern part of Korea, and tennis team to the western part of Korea and as far as to Dairen. Our basketball and ice-hockey teams participated the All Japan National Championship Games which were held in Tokyo in January this year.

Both football and Jujitsu teams of our College began their annual intercollegiate contest last fall with the Union Christian College and the Posung College respectively.

Baseball

Our annual dual meet with the Keijo Medical College has been suspended temporarily by the wish of the Medical College; however, we are still a member of the College Baseball League.

Football

Our football team is the holder of the All Korea Championship and has done many important games throughout the year.

Basketball

Our basketball team is almost a non-defeating one. 19 out of 23 major games throughout the year were to our victory, and it has won 3 important championship titles during the year. As our team had been the holder of All Japan Basketball Championship for the year of 1936, it made a trip again to Tokyo in January this year to participate in the All Japan National Basketball Championship Games. But to our regret we lost the first game to the Kyoto University by the difference of only 1 point. Moreover, our College provided three best players to the Japan Basketball team to the Olympic game.

-16-

Tennis

Our Tennis Team had been a member of the Korea Student Soft Ball Tennis League, but had to withdraw from it last year on account of the other league members insisting having Sunday games. During the summer vacation the team made a trip to the western part of Korea and Manchuria, and won three games out of five.

Our team also won the Championship Game under the auspices of Korea Athletic Association by defeating Posung College.

Ice-Hockey

Inspite of the fact that the condition of the ice during the early part of the season was not good, the team did constant practice on our new College Ice-Hockey Rink which has been in use from this season. Our team was selected from the Korea Ice-Hockey League and sent to Tokyo to participate in the All Japan Ice-Hockey Championship Games.

Jujitsu and Fencing

Our Jujitsu and Fencing Club has been considerably active this year. It had special training during the summer as well as during the winter. Our Jujitsu dual meet with the Posung College started last year, and we lost it by the slight difference of 1 point.

During the academic year, we held different kinds of intramural Athletic Meets and Interdepartmental Meets for the College student body in football, tennis, basketball, jujitsu, tug-of-war, wrestling, swimming, skating, and track and field, well distributed throughout the academic year.

In order to encourage and help toward the development of various sports and sportsmanship among the younger generations of Korea, we also held five different kinds of Annual Athletic Meets for middle schools with success as well, namely, baseball, basketball, tennis, jujitsu, and track and field.

VII. Music Committee - Chairman, S. J. Chey, Ph.D.

Concert and Concert Tour

Two regular concerts were held in Seoul and one concert tour was made in the following places: Sinwiju, Pyengyang, Seriwon, Chairyung, Sinchon and Haiju. We estimate that over 10,000 people heard us on our tour.

Radio program was broadcasted on the J.O.D.K. During the last year 18 radio programs were furnished by the College Orchestra and by the members of the Glee Club. Especially we put our efforts to broadcast sacred music on Sunday evenings.

The Summer Music Conference

The Sixth Summer Music Conference was held in the College from July 18th to August 8th. There were 70 members registered, of whom a majority were teachers in secondary schools and students from other distant schools.

For the fifth time in Korea the All Korea Middle School Music Contest was held on June 13th last, and 16 schools participated.

Prof. Hyun went to America to study and to make connections with Music organizations. We are happy to report that he received his doctorate from the Music Conservatory in Chicago last June. After that, he worked for the College and informed us that he had secured four new scholarships and four pianos and other musical instruments. He also secured a promise of a fund for the erection of our future Music Building. He broadcasted many times over the radio and several solo concerts were held in cities like Philadelphia and New York. He is now on his way home via Europe and expects to arrive here in March.

In the absence of Prof. Hyun, Prof. K. H. Park of Ewha College has taken the responsibility of conducting the Music. His service is satisfactory. It is not necessary to mention the worthy services given by Mrs. Becker from the beginning of the Music Work in this College up to today. Without her sacrifical service the music work for last year could not have been carried on successfully. The assistance of Mr. W. J. Anderson during the Summer Music Conference was also very much appreciated by us all.

VIII. Other Items of Interest.

A. College Museum - Curator, M. M. Lee, Ph.D.

The College Museum is growing chiefly through the gifts of the friends of the College. Even last year with no budget over 150 new articles were added to the Museum. One encouraging thing is that even our students realize the important mission of our College Museum and make special efforts in building up the Museum. Out of 150 newly added objects over 130 came from the student donors, and Mr. Yung Kiu Min, a Sophomore of Literary Department, presented a fine collection of Silla and Koryu pottery consisted of 128 pieces.

Under the auspicious of the Museum, Mrs. Crane's water colors were exhibited, and a large number of students and faculty attended and appreciated them.

Being in its infant stage the Museum needs both increasing assessments and giving proper cares to the things already in possession. Without a huge sum and a great deal of efforts the College could put up a respectable museum with the articles at hand.

3. Student Help Work - Chairman, S. K. Hong

During the Academic year 1936-37, the Student Help Work has been carried on with an appropriation of ¥600.00. Small as it is, an appropriation of this nature is not to be found in any other institution of learning in Korea; it is like a flake of snow in a glowing fire (as the old Korean saying is), if we consider the increasing demand for help among the students; yet it means a great deal, for some of the needy students could not have been able to continue their studies, had it not been for the help of this work.

Through the instrumentality of this work, it has been possible for 21 students to earn about a half or a part of their school expenses: 13 were given work on the college campus, athletic field, and in the library; 3, by private tutorship; and 5, by odd jobs of various kind.

We are looking forward to a time when the appropriation of this work may be doubled or tripled, or still better, some plan may be worked out by which we may be able to meet all the demandfor help of those students who may not have the necessary means but have good heart and spirit for higher education for the benefit of their own and for the glory of God.

C. Clubs and Organizations.

a. C.C.C. Students Association (The Student Body).
b. C.C.C. Y.M.C.A. (Voluntary Organization).
c. Literary Society (Literary Department Students).
d. Economics Association (Commercial Department Students).
e. Science Club (Science Department Students).
f. Glee Club, Orchestra and Band (Voluntary, all Depts.).
g. Oratorical Club (Voluntary, all Departments).
h. Friendly Association (Korean Teaching and Office Staff).
i. Dramatic Club (Voluntary, all Departments).
j. English Club (Voluntary, Commercial Department Students).
k. Religious Research Club (Voluntary, all Departments' Students).

IX. Students.

A. Enrollment.

Annual average of the students who paid tuition during the past three years:

1932 - 33 259
1933 - 34 304
1934 - 35 320
1935 - 36 394

Up to January 30th, 1937, there was a total enrollment of 406 students distributed as follows:

Class	Lit.Dept.	Com.Dept.	Sc.Dept.	Total
Freshmen	38	85	22	145
Sophomore	33	71	14	118
Junior	25		17	42
Senior	29	59	13	101
Total	125	215	66	406

B. Classification of Students.

Number of Students

Department	Regular	Special	Total	Percentage
Literary	111	14	125	30.79
Commercial	203	12	215	52.95
Science	64	2	66	16.26
	378	28	406	100.00%

C. Geographical Distribution of Students.

Province	Number	Percentage
North Ham Kyung	9	2.22
South Ham Kyung	20	4.93
North Pyung An	28	6.90
South Pyung An	46	11.33
Whang Hai	36	8.87
Kyung Ki	149	36.70
Kang Won	19	4.68
North Choong Chung	10	2.44
South Choong Chung	18	4.43
North Chun La	14	3.45
South Chun La	17	4.19
North Kyung San	23	5.67
South Kyung San	17	4.19
Total	406	100.00%

D. Students' Church Relations.

Denomination	No. of Students		Percentage
Presbyterian......................	155	....	38.18
Methodist.........................	164	....	40.39
Other Christian Denominations......	10	....	2.46
Non-Christian......................	77	....	18.97
Total	406		100.00%

X. Graduates.

A. Total Number of Graduates from each Department.

(January 31st, 1937)

Department	Number		Percentage
Literary......................	156	....	36.04
Commercial....................	340	....	56.76
Science.......................	100	....	16.70
Agricultural (Not Operating)...	3	....	0.50
Total	599		100.00%

B. Present Status of Graduates, January 31st, 1937.

Positions and Occupations	Number		Percentage
Teaching Staff in C.C.C...............	9	....	1.49
Non-Teaching Officers in C.C.C........	8	....	1.34
Teachers in other Christian Schools...	68	....	11.35
Church Workers........................	12	....	2.00
Students in Medical...................	2	....	.33
Teachers in Non-Christian Schools.....	20	....	3.34
Students in U.S.A.....................	20	....	3.34
Students in Japan.....................	26	....	4.34
Journalists and Writers...............	15	....	2.50
Employees of Banks and Business Firms.	46	....	7.68
Government Officials..................	36	....	6.01
Independent Commercial or Industrial Workers........................	57	....	9.52
Agriculturalists......................	3	....	.50
Various Lines of Independent Business.	236	....	39.41
Physician.............................	1	....	.17
Mining................................	4	....	.67
Deceased..............................	36	....	6.01
Total	599		100.00%

C. Graduates' Privileges Conferred by the Government.

a. The College has been given the privilege of giving a Bachelor's degree in each Department as Bachelor of Literature or Commerce or Science or Theology.

b. Government qualification for private primary school teachers (See the Article III of Educational ordinances for private school teachers).

c. The graduates of the College are given qualification by the Government to teach in Private Higher Common Schools and Industrial Schools on the following subjects:

To the graduates of the Literary Department.
English, Korean and Chinese.
To the graduates of the Commercial Department.
English, Commerce and Bookkeeping.
To the graduates of the Science Department.
Mathematics, Physics and Chemistry.
To the graduates of the Agricultural Department.
(Not Operating) Agriculture.

d. In accordance with the ordinance of Imperial Department of Education, No. 3, Art. 2, Sec. 4 (Daisho the 7th Year) this College has been placed on an equal plane with the Japanese Higher Schools, Colleges and the Preparatory Departments of Universities, so that our graduates are exempted from the preliminary examinations for higher civil service positions and are qualified also for entering all Government and private universities.

e. According to the Imperial Ordinance, No. 261 (Daisho the 2nd Year), the graduates of this College are granted the privilege of ordinary civil official appointment without examination (Ordinance on civil official appointment, Art. 6.)

XI. Conclusion.

The College had one of the most successful years with the largest enrollment of students, representing every Province of Korea and all the leading secondary schools in Korea, Japan and China.

-21-

Our learned faculty are not only elevating the scholastic standing of the college, but are also making a good many noted contributions to the general public by various means.

The Alumni, student gospel team, athletic teams and music tour made good impressions wherever they went and put their college on the map.

The College Library is growing in size and improving in its efficiency, playing an important role in enriching our college life.

We cannot help feeling that the college is making a remarkable progress in every respect. This progress is chiefly indebted to the wisdom of the Board of Managers, to the splendid leadership of President Underwood, and to the hearty cooperation of the Faculty and Staff.

In closing we wish to thank God for His infinite mercies bestowed upon this College.

Respectfully submitted,

U. K. Yu, Dean

51. 원한경 교장의 북장로회 한국 선교회 제출 보고서

문서 제목	Report of Chosen Christian College to Chosen Mission of Presbyterian Church in U. S. A.
문서 종류	교장 보고서 (추정)
제출 시기	1938년 2월 초 (추정)
작성 장소	서울
제 출 자	H. H. Underwood (추정)
수 신 자	북장로회 한국 선교회(Korea Mission, PCUSA)
페이지 수	3
출 처	Korea Mission Records, 1904~1960, Box 15, Folder 18 (PHS)

자료 소개

1938년 2월 초에 원한경 교장(추정)이 북장로회 한국 선교회에 제출한 보고서이다. 이 보고서에 제출 시기와 제출자가 표기되어 있지는 않지만, 본문의 내용으로 추측해볼 수 있다. 제출 시기는 본문에서 존 T. 언더우드가 1937년 7월 사망한 일과 연희전문의 연례 특별 종교집회가 '지난주'에 열린 사실이 언급된 것으로 짐작할 수 있다. 이 해의 연례 집회는 유억겸 학감의 보고서(목차 51번)에서 1월 25~29일 열렸던 것으로 기술되어 있다. 그러므로 이 보고서의 작성 시기는 1월 29일의 다음 주중인 2월 초가 된다. 제출자는 본문에서 원한경의 미국 활동이 꽤 구체적으로 설명되어있는 점에서 원한경 교장일 가능성이 크다. 그는 7월경에 도미하여 2월 초에 돌아왔다.

보고서의 전반적인 논조와 마지막 장의 주장은 이 보고서의 작성 의도를 밝히 드러내고 있다. 그것은 본교가 종교교육을 충실히 수행하고 있으므로 선교사들의 비판이 부당하다고 항의하는 것이다. 연희전문이 무슨 일 때문에 비판을 받았는지는 본문에서 밝히고 있지 않지만, 숭실전문이 1938년 3월에 자진 폐교한 사실에 비추어보면, 신사참배 문제와 관련되었을 가능성이 크다.

이 보고서의 제출자는 여기에서 아래의 사항들을 다루었다.

학교의 인력 변동, 교장의 미국 출타, 종교 사역, 학생, 도서관, 운동경기, 교수 동향, 학교에 대한 비판.

내용 요약

학내 변동: 지난해는 개교 이래로 종교교육을 하기에 가장 힘들었던 해였다. 정치 상황, 질병, 출타로 학감과 과장들에 변동이 생겼고, 13명 이상의 교수가 일시적으로 자리를 비웠다. 교장도 미국에 가서 6개월 이상 자리를 비웠다.

교장 출타: 7월 2일에 별세한 존 T. 언더우드께서 생전에 $300,000.00 이상을 희사해주신 것에 대해 감사를 표한다. 원한경 박사는 미국에서 본교와 세브란스의전 재정 지원 문제를 협력이사회와 논의하였다.

종교 사역: 어려움 속에서도 교수들과 학생들이 하나님을 더욱 의지하고 영적 가치를 높이 추구하였다. 채플 예배, 1월에 열린 특별집회, 개별 신앙지도, 교수회의 월요일 기도회, 학생 전도대 활동 등을 충실히 수행하였다. 모든 교직원이 기독교인이고, 한국인 목사가 4명, 장로교회 장로가 2명이고, 나머지는 대부분 교회 임원, 주일학교 교사, 열성적인 교인이다.

학생: 학생들은 지원자 369명 가운데 170명을 선발하였고, 103명을 졸업시켰으며, 새 학기의 학생 수는 475명으로 설립 이래 가장 많다.

도서관: 도서관의 장서가 52,000권을 넘고, 도서관 직원 1명이 시라큐스대학에서 도서관학을 공부하고 있다.

운동경기: 운동경기와 체육 수업을 통해 많은 학생이 건강을 지키고 있다.

교수: 최현배와 백남운의 책들이 호평을 받고 있다. 백낙준은 미국, 영국에서 학교를 알리고 있는데, 원래는 올봄에 돌아와야 했지만, 여러 이유에서 안식년을 연장해주었다. [동우회사건으로 귀국하지 못하였다.]

학교 비판: 학교를 향한 비판들은 부당하고 사실에 대한 무지에서 비롯되었다. 학교가 선교사들에게는 비판받지만, 한국 기독교인들에게는 신뢰받는 것을 실감하면서 위로를 느낀다.

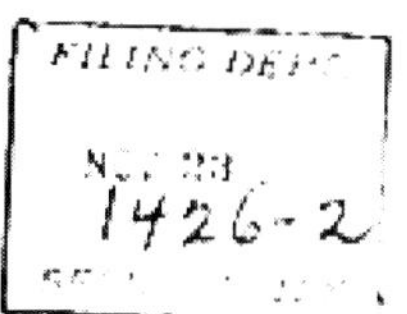

Report of Chosen Christian College
to
Chosen Mission
of
Presbyterian Church in U. S. A.

The past year has been a difficult and eventful one for the College. The conduct of the regular teaching work has been maintained, but with more difficulty than in almost any year since the College was opened in 1915. Political circumstances sickness, leave of absence have struck heavily in our midst and at the time of writing this report we find changes in the offices of the Dean, the Directors of all three Departments and the Treasurer, while just at present time no less than 13 of our regular staff are absent for one reason or another. In addition to those who are now away, the President, Dr. Underwood was away in the United States for little over six months and Mrs. Underwood was prevented by sickness from doing any teaching for six months and even now is doing only a part of what she formerly did.

Many of these absences were or are temporary, but on July 2nd, 1937, the College suffered an irreparable loss in the passing of Mr. John T. Underwood who was not only a generous financial benefactor, but a strong friend and wise guide. Mr. Underwood remembered the College in his will with a generous gift of $300,000.00 bringing his total benefactions to C.C.C. over $500,000.00. An appropriate memorial service was held at the college and we believe it would have been very gratifying to Mr. Underwood's family to see how deeply moved by gratitude and sympathy were those people who had never seen him but who have felt his generosity and love.

Dr. Underwood's visit to the United States for the purpose of consulting with the officers of the Cooperating Board in New York and arranging for the early initiation of a special financial effort for this college and for the Severance Union Medical College. Mr. B. L. Swinehart who has been so successful in everything which he has under taken was engaged by the Cooperating Board as Executive Secretary and opened an office for his work at 150 Fifth Avenue, New York City. Health reasons made it necessary for Mr. Swinehart to take time out for recuperation, but it is his intention to continue the prosecution of this work, and there are many reasons for hoping that despite the difficulties of the times that he will meet success.

During this year the bequest of Miss Norton of Norwich, Connecticut amounting to $15,000.00 was also paid over and the Finance Committee of the Cooperating Board under the wise guidance of Mr. Harry Wood, as Chairman has spent much time on the problem of making our endowment funds more productive. Dr. Underwood found wide spread interest in the work of the Colleges and a very sympathetic attitude on the part of the Secretaries of the various Cooperating Boards. At the meeting held in New York in December all of the Boards except the Southern Presbyterian were represented and evinced keen interest in the problems connected in the future conduct of the institution.

The stress and difficulties of the present time have in certain ways proved a real blessing, for faculty and students have come more and more to realize their dependence upon God and the need for close communion with Him and for the cultivation of those spiritual values which are too often pushed aside by the material necessities of the moment. Our Chapel services have never been on so high a place or so valuable to all as during this year.

The usual special evangelistic services were held during the last week in January under the leadership of the Rev. Y. Y. Lee of Pyengyang and all those privileged to attend felt that Mr. Lee brought to the College a real and very dynamic blessing.

No report on the Religious Work of the College would be complete without mention of the service of Mr. Y. H. Park who has done personal visitation among all of our students. Scattered as many of them are over the city, this work has been very difficult and correspondingly valuable and needy. He has been able to secure better and more appropriate lodgings, to give warning, advice, health service, and to carry a real spiritual message. Mr. Park's services are given to the College by the First Methodist Church of Dallas, Texas and certainly during the past year it has been a contribution for which we were grateful and of which the church may well be proud.

The Monday morning faculty prayer meeting has been well attended and many of our teachers who are anxious and worried over many things have found comfort and strength in these meetings. The usual evangelistic bands went out to different parts of the country during the summer and winter vacations and so far as this type of service can be evaluated their work was efficient and much appreciated. Present conditions make it doubtful whether this particular type of work can be carried on during the coming summer but we plan to urge on each student the necessity and responsibility of personal evangelistic work and if the difficulties facing the work of organized bands can bring our students to a keener realization of those personal responsibilities which cannot be shifted to a band or organization we will have occasion to thank God for the difficulties which have awakened us in this way.

The College is first and last a Christian College and its life, purpose and work must be Christ-centered. At the present time, all of the regular teaching faculty and staff of the College are Christians. Fair are ordained ministers, (not counting missionaries); two are Presbyterian Elders and most of the rest are officers, Sunday School Teachers; and active Church workers. It is fortunate that the leaders in the College both occidental and oriental realize the necessity for maintaining and showing forth the Christian character of the school. Dr. R. K. Cable, Mr. H. C. Owen, Rev. C. Y. Chang, Elder C. M. Jang of the Religious Work Department, the other foreign missionaries and such men as Dr. L. G. Paik, Dr. K. I. Lee, the Dean Prof. C. H. Lee, Rev. H. K. Karl, Dr. Rody Hyun and others of the leading figures in the life of the College are keenly conscience of the privileges and responsibilities of the College mission.

The students for whom the College is conducted are of a remarkably high type which is made possible by the good name and standing of the College. This attracts each year a large number of applicants and enables us to select by competitive examination, the best out of this group. This year we received a total of 170 out of 360 applicants. In March we graduated 103 young men bringing the total graduates up to a little over 800. The new students taken in in April raised our enrollment to 475 which is the highest point that we have reached since the founding of the College. These are students divided between the Departments as follows; Literary 156; Commercial 237; Science 82. Religiously, about 80% of the total enrollment are Christians and these are fairly equally divided between Presbyterians and Methodists. As might be hoped and expected if the clergy is really awake to the need for Christian education we have a large number of minister's sons. Many of the well known Pastors of both the Presbyterian and Methodist churches send their sons here.

It seems probable that as a mission you are more interested in the essential spirit and direct religious work of the institution than in the other manifold activities and phases of its work, but they merit at least honorable mention.

The Library has prospered and now holds a total of over 52,000 volumes. One of our assistant from the Library is now studying Library Science in Syracuse University and we hope to make our work still more efficient when he returns.

Athletics with their ups and downs have been carried on in a number of lines and a large proportion of our students have received healthful training through these sports as well as through the regular physical exercises of the College.

Profs. H. P. Choi and N. W. Paik were each the author of books which have been very well received and which we hope will prove to be permanent contribution to their respective spheres of study.

Dr. L. G. Paik represented not only the College, but the Presbyterian Church of Korea at the last General Assembly and before many churches and group in America. He also attended the conferences in Edinburgh and Oxford last summer and worthily represented Korea and this College. Dr. Paik would have normally returned to Korea this Spring, but for variety of reasons it was deemed best to grant him another years furlough for further study in the United States.

The College has come in for its share and perhaps more than its share of criticism and attack. We believe much of this to have been unjustified and through ignorance of the facts. It has been discouraging and difficult at times to bear such bitter criticism and to hear the Christian character of our faculty and staff so unjustly impugned. Under this criticism from missionaries, it has been a comfort to realize the trust and confidence placed in the College by the Korean Christians, as a whole and to receive written and spoken testimonies of this confidence from so many leaders of the Korean church.

But far beyond and above human words of comfort, we find our help and strength in the Lord. We can only pray that in a very real way He may guide this College through the difficulties of the present period so that it may continue its work for the Glory of Him, Whose we are and Whom we serve.

52. 유억겸 부교장 겸 학감의 이사회 제출 연례보고서

문서 제목	Chosen Christian College, Report of the Dean 1937~1938
문서 종류	학감 보고서
제출 시기	1938년 2월 25일
작성 장소	서울
제 출 자	유억겸
수 신 자	이사회
페이지 수	23
출 처	2114-5-4: 06 Underwood, Horace H. (DR.) 1938 (UMAH)

자료 소개

유억겸 부교장 겸 학감이 1938년 2월 25일 열린 이사회 회의에서 제출한 학감 보고서이다. 이 회의는 원한경이 미국에서 돌아온 지 며칠이 지나지 않았던 때에 열렸다. 이사회는 이날 원한경 교장이 미국에서 모금 활동을 하고 미국 북장로회 선교부로부터 협력 지속을 확인받은 것에 대해 감사를 표하였다. 또한 세브란스의전과의 연합을 원칙적으로 승인하면서 그 가능성을 연구해보기로 하였다. 이 회의 때 원한경 교장도 보고서를 제출하였지만, 교장 보고서는 찾지 못하고 있다.

유억겸은 이 보고서의 목차를 지난해와 똑같이 구성하였다.

I. 서언, II. 운영진과 교수진, III. 3개 학과, IV. 종교 활동, V. 도서관, VI. 체육 교육, VII. 음악 활동, VIII. 다른 사항들, IX. 학생, X. 졸업생, XI. 결어.

내용 요약

I. 원한경 교장이 미국에 가서 내(유억겸)가 교장을 대리하였고, 이춘호가 학감을 대리하였다. 보고서는 내가 내지만, 모든 업무는 이춘호가 관장하고 있음을 여러분에게 알린다.

II. 에비슨이 명예 교장이다. 운영진은 원한경(교장), 유억겸(부교장, 학감), 백낙준(문과 과장, 부재), 최현배(문과 과장대리), 이순탁(상과 과장), 이춘호(수물과 과장), 최순주(회계)이다. 대학 교무위원회는 교장, 부교장, 백낙준, 이순탁, 이춘호, 케이블과 스나이더(남・북감리회 선교회 대표)로 구성되어 있다. 대학 예산위원회는 원한경, 유억겸, 백낙준, 최현배, 이순탁, 이춘호, 베커, 스나이더, 최순주로 구성되어 있다. 교수는 21명(한국인 12명), 조교수는 4명(모두 한국인), 전임강사는 10명(한국인 8명), 강사와 조수는 17명(한국인 16명), 파트타임 조력자는 4명(교수 부인)이다. 현재 부재한 교수는 3명(스피델, 백낙준, 정인보), 사임한 교수는 5명(카도와키, 현제명, 하경덕, 이묘묵, 갈홍기)[한국인 교수들은 동우회사건 연루자들이다], 사무직원은 14명(사감 포함)이다.

III. 본교는 종합대학 체제를 이루고 있다. 문과는 교수들의 출타, 병가(정인보), 사임으로 많은 공백이 생겼다. 현제명 대신 박경호가 음악을 가르치고, 최현배가 10월 초 도쿄 철학학회에 참석하였다. 엄중한 상황에서 4학년의 과외활동 외에 모든 대외 행사와 과외활동이 취소되었다. 상과는 이순탁과 최순주가 7월과 8월 도쿄에서 학회들에 참석하였다. 백남운은 8월에 도쿄에 다녀왔고, 11월에 한국사회경제사 책[『조선봉건사회경제사상』]을 출판하였다. (이어 상품진열관 운영, 상업 실습 교육, 교수와 학생 연구, 광고방법 연구, 영어교육법 통합 연구에 관해 설명하고 있다.) 수물과에서는 12년간 근무했던 카도와키가 사임하였다. 교수들이 매월 모여 발표와 토의를 하고 있다. 교수와 학생들이 함께 연구하여 기회가 있는 대로 잡지들과 신문들에 글을 발표하며, 연구자료들을 수집하고 있다. 과학박물관이 최근의 기증품들로 인해 크게 발전하였다.

IV. 비상한 상황에서 채플 운영에 매우 조심하였으나 많은 학생이 참석하였다. 특별집회가 열렸고, 학생들이 하기 전도와 봉사활동을 하였으며, 박용학이 모든 학생의 집과 하숙집을 방문하고 보고서를 작성하여 기숙사의 필요성을 입증하였다.

V. 이묘묵이 7월 도서관장직을 사임하여 노동규가 대리하였고, 케이블 교수 부인이 영어 서적을 분류하였다. 1937년 동안 분류한 장서는 11,577권이고, 총 44,950권을 등록하였으며, 52,000권을 소장하고 있다. (윤치호 등의 도서 기증자 명단을 제시하고 있다.)

VI. 운동경기 분야에서 매우 성공적인 한 해를 보내어, 축구, 농구, 테니스, 아이스하키, 스피드 스케이팅 경기에서 우승하였다.

VII. 외부 음악 활동을 모두 중단하였지만, 제6회 중등학교 현상음악대회는 5월에 개최하였다. 박경호가 현제명 대신 가르쳤고, 베커 부인이 도왔다.

VIII. 박물관은 홍승국 등으로부터 기증품을 받고 45점을 사서 총 979점의 예술품과

3,151점의 주화를 소장하고 있다. 학생지원을 위해 ￥600의 충당금을 집행하여 19명의 근로학생에게 학비를 지원하였다. 국내외에서 답지한 장학기금으로 36명에게 장학금을 지급하였는데, 이 가운데 3명이 성적 장학금을 받았다. (학생 클럽과 단체의 목록을 제시하고 있다.)

IX. 등록생은 1월 31일까지 총 417명(문과 122명, 상과 221명, 수물과 74명)이었고, 본과는 390명, 별과는 28명이었다. (출신 지역과 종교 현황은 표를 참고.)

X. 졸업생은 총 698명이고, 졸업생 현황은 연전 교수 8명, 연전 직원 8명, 다른 기독교학교 교사 70명, 교회 사역 10명, 의학생 2명, 비기독교학교 교사 32명, 미국 · 독일 유학 17명, 일본 유학 39명, 언론인 11명, 은행원 및 회사원 150명, 공무원 59명, 개인사업(상공업) 99명, 농업 5명, 다양한 개인사업[家業] 145명, 의사 1명, 광업 3명, 사망 39명이다. 졸업생이 갖는 자격은 이전 보고서와 같다.

XI. 최현배와 백남운이 저서를 출판하여 불멸의 명성을 얻었다. 이순탁과 최순주가 도쿄 국제학술대회에 참석하였고, 이원철이 도쿄에서 중등학교 수학에 관한 연구 결과를 발표하였으며, 백낙준이 미국과 영국에서 주요 대회들에 참석하였다. 학생들이 가장 많이 등록하여 본교가 대중에게 중요한 교육기관으로 널리 인정받고 있다.

Appendix II

CHOSEN CHRISTIAN COLLEGE

Report of the Dean

1937---1938

*****

CHOSEN CHRISTIAN COLLEGE
Report of the Dean
(1937—1938)

****

CONTENTS

CHOSEN CHRISTIAN COLLEGE

Report of the Dean

I. Introductory Remarks:

To the Field Board of Managers of the Chosen Christian College at the Board Meeting held on February 25th, 1938:

I have the honor of submitting to you the following report concerning the academic phase of the College Administration for the academic year 1937-1938.

As you all know very well, since President Underwood was called away by the Board of Foreign Missions of the Presbyterian Church in the U.S.A. and by the death of his uncle, the late Mr. John T. Underwood in America, the College administrative offices had to be somewhat rearranged to meet the administrative business of the college. Thereupon the Vice-President had to take charge of the office of Acting President and Mr. C. H. Lee, the Director of the Science Department, the office of Acting Dean. Under these changes, however, everything has been operating very nicely without any serious blunder, through the Grace of God, the backing of the Executive Committee of the Board, the College Council, the cooperation of the Directors, the Treasurer's office, and the staff members.

While I submit this report, I wish to inform you that Mr. C. H. Lee has acted as a man of the time, for he managed to carry everything through the hard times with his untiring effort and intelligence for the period of six months.

II. Officers of Administration and Instruction

A. President Emeritus.

O. R. Avison, M.D., LL.D. (Toronto and Wooster), residing in the United States of America.

B. Administrative Officers.

Horace H. Underwood, M.A., Ph.D., Litt.D., President.

Uck Kyum Yu, Gakushi, Vice-President and Dean.

L. George Paik, M.A., Ph.D., Director of the Literary Dept. (On leave of Absence).

Hyun Pai Choi, Gakushi, Acting Director of the Literary Department.

Soon Tak Lee, Gakushi, Director of the Commercial Department.

Choon Ho Lee, M.A., Director of the Science Department.

Soon Ju Chey, B.S.E., M.B.A., Ph.D., Treasurer.

Tong Kyu Roo, Gakushi, Acting Librarian.

C. College Council.

Horace H. Underwood, Ph.D., Litt.D., President.

Uok Kyum Yu, Gakushi, Vice-President and Dean.

L. George Paik, Ph.D., Director of the Literary Department.
(On Leave of Absence).

Hyun Pai Choi, Gakushi, Acting Director of the Literary Department.

Soon Tak Lee, Gakushi, Director of the Commercial Department.

Choon Ho Lee, M.A., Director of the Science Department.

E. M. Cable, D.D., Representative of the M. E. C. Mission.

L. H. Snyder, M.A., Representative of the M. E. C. S. Mission.

D. College Budget Committee.

Horace H. Underwood, Ph.D., Litt.D., President.

Uok Kyum Yu, Gakushi, Vice-President and Dean.

L. George Paik, Ph.D., Director of the Literary Department.
(On leave of Absence).

Hyun Pai Choi, Gakushi, Acting Director of the Literary Department.

Soon Tak Lee, Gakushi, Director of the Commercial Department.

Choon Ho Lee, M.A., Director of the Science Department.

A. L. Becker, Ph.D., Representative of the M. E. C. Mission.

L. H. Snyder, M.A., Representative of the M. E. C. S. Mission.

S. J. Chey, Ph.D., Treasurer.

E. Faculty.

(1) Professors. (21)

H. H. Underwood, B.A., M.A., Ph.D., Litt.D., (New York and Mount Union).
President of the College and Professor of Education, Psychology and English.

U. K. Yu, Gakushi, (Tokyo Imperial University).
Vice-President and Dean of the College and Professor of Law.

-3-

E. Faculty. (Continued)

L. G. Paik, B.A., Th.B., M.A., Ph.D., (Yale)
Director of the Literary Department and Professor of Occidental History and Religion. (On leave of Absence).

S. T. Lee, Gakushi, (Kyoto Imperial University).
Director of the Commercial Department and Professor of Economics, Insurance, Statistics, and Abacus.

C. H. Lee, B.A., M.A., (Ohio State).
Director of the Science Department and Professor of Mathematics.

A. L. Becker, B.A., M.A., Ph.D., (Michigan).
Professor of Physics and Mathematics.

E. H. Miller, B.A., B.D., M.A., Ph.D., (Columbia)
Professor of Chemistry, English and Bible.

N. W. Paik, Gakushi, (Tokyo University of Commerce).
Professor of Commerce, Bookkeeping, History of Commerce, Accounting, Oriental Economics and History.

H. P. Choi, Gakushi, (Kyoto Imperial University).
Professor of Philosophy, Education, Ethics, Logic and the Korean Language. Acting Director of the Literary Department.

D. W. Lee, Graduate of C.C.C., B.A., M.A., Ph.D., (Michigan).
Professor of Mathematics and Astronomy.

S. Nikaido, Gakushi (Tokyo Imperial University).
Professor of Japanese, Japanese Literature and Introduction to Literature.

P. C. Kim, Gakushi, (Waseda University).
Professor of Physics, Electrical Engineering, and Mathematics.

H. Kaiya, Gakushi, (Tofuku Imperial University).
Professor of Mathematics, Surveying, Physics, Civil Engineering, Drawing, Geology, Mineralogy, Natural Science and Architecture.

S. K. Hong, B.A., (Ohio State).
Professor of English.

I. P. Chung,
Professor of Chinese Literature and Korean Literature.

T. K. Roo, Graduate of C.C.C., Gakushi (Kyoto Imperial University).
Professor of Transportation, Economic Policy, Money, Banking, Agricultural Economy and Business English, and Acting Librarian of the College.

S. J. Chey, Graduate of C.C.C., B.S., M.B.A., Ph.D., (New York)
Professor of Commerce, Commercial Practice, Business English, Typewriting, Advertising, Foreign Exchange and Treasurer of the College.

E. M. Cablo, B.S., M.A., D.D., (Cornell College)
Professor of English, Bible and History.

G. C. Speidel, B.S., M.S., (Virginia) (On leave of Absence).
Professor of English.

E. Faculty. (Continued)

L. H. Snyder, B.A., M.A., (Princeton).
Professor of English and Typewriting.
E. C. Chen, B.A., B.D., M.A., (Chicago)
Professor of Bible and English.

(2) Assistant Professors. (4)

O. Y. Lee, (Berlin University)
Assistant Professor of German.
Y. S. Jung, Gakushi, (Waseda University)
Assistant Professor of English, Phonetics, Introduction to Literature, and English Literature.
P. K. Lim, Graduate of C.C.C., B.A., M.A., (Syracuse).
Assistant Professor of Bank Bookkeeping, Commodities, and Business English.
K. N. Choi. Graduate of C.C.C., B.A., M.A., Ph.D., (Michigan)
Assistant Professor of Physics and Mathematics.

(3) Instructors. (10)

Mrs H. H. Underwood, B.A., M.A., (New York).
English
L. W. Kang,
Physical Education.
S. Y. Chang, B.S., B.D., M.A., (Columbia)
Bible and Religious Education.
K. H. Jung, Gakushi, (Tokyo Imperial University)
Jurisprudence, and Civil, Commercial and Special Laws.
Y. H. Lee, Gakushi, (Tokyo Imperial University)
English and English Literature.
C. N. Kim, Graduate of Paiyoung College.
The Chinese Language.
Mrs. E. M. Cable, B.A., (Cornell)
English.
H. S. Park, Gakushi (Meiji University)
Commercial Mathematics, Exchange, Economic Affairs, Trust and Business Management.
R. K. Kim, Gakushi (Keijo Imperial University).
English.
H. S. Ryu, Gakushi (Waseda University)
Chemistry.

(4) Lecturers and Assistants. (17)

K. W. Chang, Graduate of C.C.C., Gakushi, (Tofuku Imperial University).
Mathematics.
H. C. Chang, Graduate of C.C.C., Gakushi, (Tokyo University of Commerce). (On leave of Absence).
T. Yokoyama, B.A., B.D., Ph.D., (Johns Hopkins).
English

(4) Lecturers and Assistants (Continued)

L. K. Jung, Gakushi, (Keio University).
Finance, Economics and Public Law.
P. S. Billings, B.A. (Depauw).
English. (On leave of Absence).
C. T. Son, Gakushi, (Wasoda University).
Oriental History.
D. H. Kim, Gakushi, (Tokyo Imperial University).
Morals.
I. J. Park, B.S. in A.E., (Minnesota) and B.S. in M.E. (Lewis Institute).
Architecture, Construction and Drawing.
T. S. Kim, B.S., (Nevada)
French
C. S. Ryuk, Gakushi, (Tokyo Imperial University)
Marketing, Commercial Geography, Custom House, Japanese Commercial Letter Writing and German.
K. Takesawa.
Physical Education.
K. H. Pak, B.S., (Cincinnati Conservatory)
Music.
S. K. Lee, Gakushi (Wasada University)
Occidental History.
C. R. Cynn, Graduate of C.C.C.
Assistant, Physics Laboratory.
Y. S. Kim, Graduate of C.C.C.
Assistant, Chemistry Laboratory.
H. C. Cynn, Graduate of C.C.C.
Assistant, Literary Department.
Y. H. Pak, B.A., M.A. (Southwestern University) and Southern Methodist University).
Secretary of the Religious Department.

(5) Part Time Assistants. (4)

Mrs. A. L. Becker
Mrs. R. C. Coen
Mrs. E. H. Miller
Mrs. L. H. Snyder

(6) Professors on Leave of Absence. (3)

G. C. Speidel, B.S., M.S.
L. G. Paik, Th.B., M.A., Ph.D.
I. P. Chyung.

(7) Professors and Instructors Resigned. (5)

K. Kadowaki, Gakushi
C. M. Hyun, D. Mus.
K. D. Har, Ph.D.
K. M. Lee, Ph.D.
H. K. Karl, Ph.D.

F. Office Staff. (14)

Byron Koo, M.D., (Emory)
College Physician.
C. M. Sohn, Graduate of C.C.C.
Secretary to Administration.
C. M. Song, Graduate of C.C.C.
Superintendent of Dormitory
C. K. Kim, Graduate of C.C.C.
Superintendent of Grounds and Buildings.
K. S. Lyu, Graduate of C.C.C.
Assistant to the Librarian. (On leave of Absence).
P. Hyun, B.A., (Shanghai)
Accountant.
W. Y. Shim, Graduate of C.C.C.
Secretary to Administration.
K. W. Yi, Graduate of C.C.C., B.A., M.A., (Michigan).
Cashier.
P. S. Kim, B.A., (C.C.C.)
Clerical Assistant in the Library.
Miss D. T. Ahn,
Stenographer to the President.
Mrs. S. E. Lyu, Graduate of Daiwha.
Clerical Assistant of the Library.
Miss D. H. Whang,
Assistant to the Cashier.
Miss S. H. You, Graduate of Ewha College.
Clerical Assistant of the Library.
C. [illegible]. Whang,
Clerical Assistant in the Library.

III. Three Departments of the College.

The College is organized on a university system and has four Departments, but only three are in operation. These Departments are separate so far as their internal organization is concerned with their respective Directors, budgets and recitation halls, but they are one in general administration and policy under one Dean.

A. Literary Department - Acting Director, H. P. Choi, Gakushi

Last year, the Literary Department had one of the most eventful years in its history. In the first place, Dr. L. G. Paik, the Director of the Department went to U.S.A., and has been away all through the year. In addition to this, many Professors suddenly resigned and another Professor was obliged to take a long rest because of ill health. Even though all the members of the faculty shared the burdens of teaching doing their best, still there were so many vacancies that there was no way to escape completely from the troubles, and I am very sorry to report that studies and instructions for the students were not carried out satisfactorily, because of the above mentioned difficulties. But we thank God, that with the spirit of cooperation of the faculty and by God's help, we have been able to get through the difficulties to some degree.

Dr. Underwood stopped teaching from September because of his trip to U.S.A.

Dr. L. G. Paik went to U.S.A. to be present at the Centennial Celebration of the Board of Foreign Missions of the Presbyterian Church in U.S.A.

Mr. I. P. Chung was given a rest from September because of ill health.

Mrs. Underwood stopped teaching about the middle of October because of ill health.

The following members of the teaching staff tendered their resignations last September, which were accepted at that time: Drs. C. M. Hyun, K. D. Har, M. M. Lee, and H. K. Earl.

Mr. K. H. Park gave instructions in Music from September in place of Dr. Rody Hyun.

Mr. Sun Keun Lee taught in Occidental History from September which Dr. M. M. Lee was teaching during the absence of Dr. Paik.

Several new Lecturers were invited to fill the vacancies, and the courses which could not be provided even after the new Lecturers came, were divided among the faculty.

Mr. H. P. Choi represented the College at the Philosophical conference held in Tokyo under the auspieces of the Department of Education, in the first part of October, 1937.

We began the year with 130 students on the roll. At the time of this report, there are 40 Freshmen, 29 Sophomores, 30 Juniors and 23 Seniors making a total of 122.

Extra-Curricula Activities

In view of the critical situation, such activities as Music, Drama, English Oratorical Contest, and the Oratorical Contest for the secondary schools were given up. Only the extra-curricula course for Seniors were given as before, (Esthetics, Korean Literature and Journalism).

General Research Work

Materials in the Research Room: The total accession of books amounted to 2,083 - special emphasis on Korean Cultures. Three kinds of Newspapers and four kinds of Magazines.

As a result of nearly twenty year's work, Mr. H. P. Choi has published a book of 1282 pages on Korean grammar and language. Of all the publications, he has made in the past, this volume commands a special note among his works.

Every one of the teachers has been so busy in sharing the extra burdens that there was not any special research work produced by our staff, but several short essays and articles appeared on magazines and newspapers.

B. Commercial Department - Director, S. T. Lee, Gakushi

The Commercial Department is the largest department of the College with a faculty of 8 Professors and Assistant Professors, 4 Instructors, 10 Lecturers, 1 Assistant, and 221 Students. (Seniors 64, Sophomores 69, and Freshmen 88).

Professors S. T. Lee and S. J. Choy, representing the College, attended the Seventh World's Education Conference which was held in Tokyo from July 31st to August 9th and brought back to the College many valuable materials for reference and they also attended the Fourth Commercial English Association meeting which was also held in Tokyo from July 28th to 30th and secured many worthwhile materials for teaching Commercial English in the Department. Professor N. W. Paik took a trip to Tokyo from August 13th to 31st to complete his work on "Social and Economic History of Korea", which was finally published in November last. This is his second volume of over 800 pages, as his first volume, bearing the same title, was published a few years ago. There are many valuable source materials contained in the book, and it is the result of many years' painstaking work. It is widely circulated and commands a high reputation.

The faculty members of this department have been giving extra-curricula lectures, once in every semester, for the benefit of the students on some subject of current nature or in a form of report on their researches. These have been very interesting and instructive and were well appreciated by all who attended them.

A brief report on employment of the 57 graduates of last year may not be wholly out of place here. Of this number, 2 are attending universities in Tokyo; 22 out of 35 who applied for positions are holding responsible positions in various banking houses, manufacturing concerns, government offices, and in the institutions of learning, 20 are either in private business or attending home affairs; and the remaining 13 have not been placed definitely as yet. In spite of the last number, it is a fairly good record if it is compared with that of other colleges of the same standing in the country.

Taking every thing into consideration, we may say that the Commercial Department is holding more than its own, and, while proud of its present facts, we are looking forward to a better day of this department and consequently greater service to the society.

Commercial Museum

The Commercial Museum has been growing steadily with additional specimens of native and foreign commodities making a total number of 2821. We are proud of the fact that at the present time our Museum excells any of its kind in Korean colleges in Korea in the number as well as in the variety of the specimens. Prof. P. K. Lim is in charge of the work.

Commercial Practice Work

Along with the theoretical studies of Commerce and Economics, the practical side of the course is no less important a phase. At the present time, there are 11 typewriters for the students to practice on, but we are looking forward to a time when we can complete the equipment for this purpose. Furthermore, a special course on Shorthand has been given since the year of 1936 for those who take it as an extra curriculum work. Prof. L. H. Snyder is in charge of this work.

General Research Work

The Commercial Research Work has been carried on through the faculty members. This work facilitates the study and research of the teachers and students alike working on some commercial and economic problems. These results have been published in the leading newspapers and magazines from time to time. There are 59 Magazines, 6 Newspapers, and 2850 Volumes of Reference Books in the Research Room. Prof. T. K. Roo is in charge of this work.

Research on Advertisement

The Commercial Department has begun research work to study the method of advertising and for reference. Nearly 10,584 pieces of various kinds of posters, handbills, folders, labels, enamel and card signs, newspaper and magazine advertisement clippings, etc., have been collected since April, 1933. Also quite a number of books have been secured for study and reference. These have been carefully classified and displayed in the Commercial practice room. Prof. P. K. Lim is in charge of this work.

English Teachers' Research Club

Ever since the Club became a chartered member of the Institute for Research of English Teaching of the Educational Bureau of Japan, bulletins, periodicals, and other publications have been sent to the College, and they are being displayed for use in one of the teacher's rooms for the time being. About 2000 various valuable kinds of books and materials have been secured, some by purchase and some by donation, and displayed in one of the teachers' rooms. The Club is devoting much time and effort in planning a unified method of teaching English as a part of this program. Phonetics is taught from two years ago, and to verify points in phonetics, a phonograph has been secured in the department. The Club has directed the students to form an English Club of themselves holding meetings with various programs and practicing English in various ways with much interest. Profs. S. K. Hong and Insup Jung are in charge of this Club.

Besides the above mentioned features of this department, we are holding an annual prize contest in thesis or grades on Commercial, Economic, and English subjects in a way of leading the interest of the students along these lines.

C. Science Department - Director, C. H. Lee, M. A.

The faculty of the Science Department have done their best to carry out the work of the department assigned to them during the past year. I am glad to say that the teachers have been loyal to the college and to their work and enthusiastic even though they have had to carry heavy loads in their regular work. Prof. K. Kadowaki in Chemistry resigned from the college last May and accepted the offer of a position in an artificial silk factory in Japan proper. He had been with us in the college for 12 years. The department lost a good teacher and the staff of the college all felt sorry for his leaving. Because it was difficult to get a teacher in his place, Mr. H. S. Lyu in the Department was asked to carry on two men's work during the past year. We appreciate very much his spirit of cooperation with the college. We are in need of a permanent teacher in the place of Mr. Kadowaki, but it is not easy at all nowadays to get a proper man who studied Chemistry. However, we are now negotiating with one of our graduates who studied Chemistry in one of the Imperial Universities in Japan proper.

The faculty of this department for the present year consists of 6 Professors, 1 Assistant Professor, 1 full-time Instructor, 2 Lecturers, and 2 Assistants, making a total of 12 members.

The number of students in this department is 74, which shows an increase of 8 over that of last year. There are 23 Freshmen, 19 Sophomores, 15 Juniors and 17 Seniors in the department.

The Seniors who are to graduate in March will be placed as follows: 3 are planning to enter the Engineering Colleges of the Kyoto Imperial University, 3 have positions promised in the Government Railway, 3 in private construction firms, 2 in mining companies, 4 to the Government Civil Engineering Departments, 1 to the Government Hygienic Department and 1 as a teacher to a Middle School.

Teachers' Science Club

The Science Club of this department-staff has had as usual regular monthly meetings at the homes of the members. Some scientific problem has been presented at each meeting by one of the members and a general discussion of the topic usually takes place. Such a gathering tends to create friendship among the members as well as to give each member something new and afresh.

Science Research Work

The Science Research Work has been carried on through the faculty members and the students of this department. Any study or research outside of the regular curriculum of the department is carried on through this Research Work and the results have been published from time to time in the various magazines and newspapers.

To facilitate the research work, books on natural science and various materials and specimens have been collected and placed on the shelves for reference. There are 911 volumes of books, of which 278 volumes are in the occidental languages and 632 volumes in the oriental languages; and 3 kinds of magazines in the oriental language. Dr. K. N. Choi is in charge of this work.

Science Museum

The Science Museum has been greatly increased by the recent donations. Prof. L. H. Snyder of our college donated many rare specimens of birds; and Mr. Joo Myung Seuk of Song-Do Higher Common School gave a complete set of specimens of butterflies that are found in Korea. The later specimens are 202 in kind and 437 in number of pieces. These new additions bring the total of biological as well as mineral specimens and scientific specimens up to 5811. The Science Museum is in charge of Dr. D. W. Lee.

IV. Religious Activities - Chairman, E. M. Cable, D.D.

This department has had a very busy year on the campus. No opportunity has been neglected to develop and strengthen the religious influence and interest in the college both among the students and faculty.

Owing to the unusual conditions which faced us at the beginning of the year we have had to be very careful in the conducting of the chapel exercises. However, I feel that the chapel services have been the best we have had for a long time. This has been largely due to the fact that we have been compelled to have only religious matters discussed and further that our own faculty members have had charge of them. We have had very few speakers from the outside. This has been a most helpful and interesting development for both faculty and students. The attendance at the chapel services has been very good until this last term. The change of the chapel hour from the second period to the hour before the opening of school has accounted for this, especially during the winter months, as many of the students come late.

The special services this year were held from January 25th to the 29th inclusive. Two study periods in the forenoon were given up to this under the leadership of Rev. Y. Y. Lee of Pyengyang. His messages were strictly religious and inspiring. At the close of the meetings the students were asked to sign cards expressing their purpose to become Christians and those who were Christians to pledge themselves to more active Christian service and living. The results were very encouraging.

During the summer recess three bands of our students went out to different parts of the country to do evangelistic and social service work. Their reports were most inspiring. I sincerely hope that the students will do more of this work, especially project work along this line.

The work of Mr. Y. H. Pak, Religious Secretary, has been most successful. He has done a very fine piece of work with the student body. He was able to visit all the students in their homes and boarding houses. His report anent this is most enlightening and thought provoking. This report stresses, more eloquent than any words, the pressing need for more dormitories if we are going to really help our students. In addition to this work Mr. Pak has done much social work among the students. I am hoping that this year he will be able to supplement this work with a more definite religious program. I feel that Mr. Pak is doing a piece of work that the college cannot afford to be without and I hope that every member of the faculty will co-operate with him in every way possible.

Once more I urge the need for a dormitory to care for our Freshman class. The first year to most of these young men is the crucial year. The conditions under which most of them live in the city is most detrimental to their moral and religious life. If we cannot influence them this first year there is little hope of doing much for them the remaining years. Along with this urgent need of the dormitory is the need of a Dining Hall to supplement our social and religious activities.

I feel that we have made a real advance in religious interest among the members of the faculty as well as the students and I hope that this year will see a still greater interest. The college stands, first of all, for the development of moral and Christian character in its students. If the college fails here, especially in this needy hour, it fails at every other point and there is no valid argument for the continuance of the college. We cannot afford to engage in purely secular education. In this great task we must all have a share.

V. College Library - Acting Librarian, T. K. Roo, Gakushi

The academic year 1937-1938 has been one of the most difficult years in the history of the college library, for Dr. M. M. Lee, the Librarian, resigned and Mr. T. K. Roe was placed in charge of the Library, as Acting Librarian in July, 1937. Mr. K. S. Lyu, assistant to the Librarian took his leave of absence for a year and a half, from April 1937 to August, 1938 to make a research in library science in America. Mr. P. S. Kim, class of 1937, was placed in the Library as a Clerical Assistant, and Mr. C. Y. Whang, graduate of a Commercial Middle School, was engaged as an assistant. Therefore the staff of the Library consists of Mr. T. K. Roe, Acting Librarian; Mr. P. S. Kim, Clerical Assistant; Mr. C. Y. Whang, Mrs. K. S. Lyu, Clerk, and Miss S. M. You, Clerk.

In addition to these regular members of the staff, Mrs. E. M. Cable gave us a great deal of her valuable time in classifying some of the English books.

During 1937, 11,577 volumes of books were classified and registered and now the grand total of the registered books is 44,950 volumes.

We have made a thorough inventory recently of the books, magazines, and newspapers that were not yet classified and registered and found them to be 5,161 volumes of books, 8,535 volumes of magazines and 162 volumes of newspapers. When these are bound and registered, we shall have 52,000 volumes of books in the Library.

During the period of ten months, (February, 1937 - January, 1938) we have purchased 522 volumes of books and received 2,030 volumes, of which the most valuable are those of the Rev. J. S. Ryang, consisting of 498 books and 1,664 volumes of magazines. It has been decided to keep these separately as the Paik-Sa-Dang Collection.

Honorable T. H. Yun gave us 63 volumes of books and 46 volumes of magazines to be added to the T. H. Yun's Collection.

A number of foreign friends of the college made some valuable donations in books: Mrs. C. Leonard, 144 volumes; Miss Edith Phillipson, 47 volumes; Dr. A. L. Ludlow, 52 volumes; and Mr. Gerald Bonwick, 41 volumes. Some of these cannot be obtained even at a high price out here in the Orient.

Many of the staff members of the college made some precious gifts; Dr. H. H. Underwood, 133 volumes; Dr. K. D. Har, while he was a member of the staff, 40 volumes; Mr. C. M. Song, 39 volumes; Mr. K. H. Jung, 30 volumes; Mr. T. K. Roe, 24 volumes; Mr. U. K. Yu, 20 volumes; and Mr. S. T. Lee, 17 volumes.

Some of the students' associations and Alumni members did their share; Economics Association, 156 volumes; late Mr. Hong No Lee, class of 1938, 33 volumes; and/the late Mr. Do Chip Kim, Literary Senior, 2? volumes.

We certainly appreciate these donations and are glad that the Library is getting richer and richer in books day by day, but what encourages us most is the fact that the students are making the most use of these valuable books: from April to July, 1937, 797 students checked out 1,083 volumes; from September to December, 1937, 1,327 students checked out 1,762 volumes.

Magazines and newspapers are being provided in the general reading room and we feel the necessity of a larger reading room very much more keenly than we did before.

In a view to increase the number of books and to encourage the students in the use of the library, two important plans were proposed by the Library Committee to the faculty which adopted the same.

1. To launch a campaign to secure books to the extent of 100,000 volumes by 1945.

   In order to arrange the campaign, the organization of a special committee was suggested.

2. To establish a Students' Library.

   This library corresponds to a students' reserved library for their use chiefly.

   In order to establish and enlarge this library, it was thought necessary to charge a small fee to the Freshman as well as to the upper classman.

It is the sense of the Library Committee that if we succeed in this campaign we shall realize our goal for securing 100,000 volumes of books by 1945 in the C. C. C. Library.

VI. Physical Education - Chairman, D. W. Lee, Ph.D.

This has been a very successful year in the athletic activities of the College. We have won championships in five different sports, namely, football, basketball, tennis, ice hockey and speed skating. The limited budget, the high prices of sporting goods and the present world situation all have affected our athletic activities to a great extent, but we have made every effort to meet the situation and make the year a successful one.

Football

Our football team won the title of championship in two different occasions: one in the All Korea Athletic Meet held under the auspices of the Korean Athletic Association, and the other in the Chosen Students Football League consisting of the Keijo Imperial University and other government colleges.

Basketball

Our basketball team is also the holder of the championship title both in spring and fall; in June, we won the championship in the games held under the auspices of the Korean Basketball Association, and in November, we won in the contest held by the Korea Branch of the Japan Basketball Association.

On April 29, we had a game with the visiting Waseda University Team of Tokyo, the championship holder of the Empire, and won the game by the score of 57 to 31.

Tennis

Although we have on our team at present the best players in Korea, we had to forfeit many games on account of the Sunday schedule and this spoiled the spirit of the players. However, two of our students managed to win the championship in Tokyo last fall.

Winter Sports

As we did not have good ice on our home rink this winter, we made a temporary rink at Kwangnaru outside the East Gate (about 30 li from the city) so that the boys could practice during the winter vacation. We won the championship in the games held under the auspices of the Chosen Shrine.

In January our speed skaters won the championship in the Chosen Students Ice Sports League games.

During the past year we had our usual Intramural Athletic meets in football, baseball, tennis, jujitsu, fencing, wrestling, swimming, skating, tug o' war, and track and field. These "meets" are planned to develop athletic spirit in our student body and this year we were encouraged by the enthusiastic way in which most of the students took part in the various contests.

In order to encourage and help toward the development of various sports and sportsmanship among the high school boys of Korea, we also held five different kinds of Annual Athletic Meets with our usual success, namely; baseball, basketball, jujitsu, tennis, and track and field.

VII. Musical Activities - Chairman, S. T. Chey, Ph D

The report on the musical activities for the last year is rather short. On account of the present circumstances, the music committee has decided to stop for the time being all the outside activities. In addition to this, Dr. C. H. Pyun tendered his resignation. However, we gave the Sixth All Korea Middle School Music Contest on May 19th, 1937 and six schools participated in it.

During the absence of Dr. C. H. Hyun, Mr. Kyung Ho Park has taken the responsibility of conducting our music. He spends the forenoons at the college, besides giving practice in Orchestra and Chorus once a week. He has a class of Harmony for those students who elect the course. There are now 20 students in the Harmony class.

We wish to record again the worthy service given by Mrs. A. L. Becker from the beginning of the music work of this college up to the present date. Without her sacrifical service, the music work for the last years could not have been carried on successfully.

Also, a word of appreciation is due to Mrs. R. C. Coen, who plays music for our chapel services everyday.

VIII. Other Items of Interest.

A. College Museum   Acting Curator, T. K. Roe, Gakushi

In the academic year 1937-1938, our museum has received some valuable additions, in spite of the small budget. Mr. S. K. Hong, Mr. Young Ho Pyen, Dr. J. L. Boots and the late Dr. J. S. Gale have made valuable donations, of which a cap and gown of the late Dr. J. S. Gale is the most precious. We have also bought 46 pieces of earthenwares, bricks, tiles, and other remains of Lolang Era and Kokuryu period excavated in Pyungyang districts. The present number of articles is 879, in addition to 3,151 pieces of coins.

B. Student Help Work - Chairman, S. K. Hong, B. A.

During the academic year 1937-1938, the Student Help Work has been carried on with an appropriation of ¥600.00. Small as it is, an appropriation of this nature is not to be found in any other institution of learning in Korea; it is like a flake of snow in a glowing fire (as the Old Korean saying is), if we consider the increasing demand for help among the students; yet it meets a great deal, for some of the needy students could not have been able to continue their studies, had it not been for the help of this work.

Through the instrumentality of this work, it has been possible for 19 students to earn about a half or a part of their school expenses; 12 were given work on the college campus, athletic field, and in the library and museum; 3 by private tutorship; and 5 by odd jobs of verious kind.

We are looking forward to a time when the appropriation of this work may be doubled or tripled, or still better, some plan may be worked out by which we may be able to meet all the demand for help of those students who may not have the necessary means, but have good heart and spirit for higher education for the benefit of their own and for the glory of God.

C. Scholarships.

It has been seriously considered every year by the college as well as in the meetings of the Board of Managers as to how scholarships may be provided for the worthy students. As a result of this, we have been very fortunate to arouse the sympathy of Mr. Chong Ik Lee whose generosity was expressed in the permanent scholarship fund of ¥1,500.00 and Mr. Byung Gap Cho for a permanent fund of ¥20,000.00 in addition to Mr. Chong Sun Kim's annual sum of ¥300.00 for 10 years beginning from 1936 and all those that are continuing. Beside these, there are generous persons of all nationalities who help some of our students from time to time such as the Lafayette Avenue Church and Mr. J. H. Mack. At the present time, the college is providing 36 scholarships including those 3 that are granted by the college for the highest grades above 90. Fortunate as we are in this respect, we are not going to stop here and feel satisfied, but shall exert ourselves all the more for a greater result.

D. Clubs and Organizations.

a. C.C.C. Students Association (The Student Body), (not functioning)
b. C.C.C. Y.M.C.A. (Voluntary Organization).
c. Literary Society (Literary Department Students).
d. Economics Association (Commercial Department Students).
e. Science Club (Science Department Students).
f. Glee Club, Orchestra and Band (Voluntary, all Depts.).
g. Oratorical Club (Voluntary, all Depts.).
h. Friendly Association (Korean Teaching and Office Staff).
i. Dramatic Club (Voluntary, all Depts.).
j. English Club (Voluntary, Commercial Department Students).
k. Religious Research Club (Voluntary, all Depts.).

IX. Students.

A. Enrollment.

Annual average of the students who paid tuition during the past three years:

1934 - 35 320
1935 - 36 394
1936 - 37 417

Up to January 31st, 1938, there was a total enrollment of 417 students distributed as follows:

Class	Lit. Dept.	Com. Dept.	Sc. Dept.	Total
Freshman	40	88	23	151
Sophomore	29	69	19	117
Junior	30		15	45
Senior	23	64	17	104
	122	221	74	417

B. Classification of Students.

Number of Students

Department	Regular	Special	Total	Percentage
Literary	105	17	122	29.26
Commercial	215	6	221	53.00
Science	70	4	74	17.74
	390	27	417	100.00%

C. Geographical Distribution of Students.

Province	Number	Percentage
North Ham Kyung	8	1.92
South Han Kyung	19	4.56
North Pyung An	32	7.67
South Pyung An	50	11.99
Whang Hai	37	8.87
Kyung Ki	160	38.37
Kang Won	17	4.08
North Choong Chung	8	1.92
South Choong Chung	20	4.79
North Chun La	13	3.12
South Chun La	22	5.27
North Kyung Sang	16	3.84
South Kyung Sang	15	3.60
Total	417	100.00%

D. Students' Church Relations.

Denominations	No. of Students	Percentage
Presbyterian	139	33.33
Methodist	153	33.69
Other Christian Denominations	51	12.23
Non-Christian	74	17.75
Total	417	100.00%

X. Graduates.

A. Total Number of Graduates from Each Department.

(January 31st, 1938)

Department	Number	Percentage
Literary......................................	184	26.34
Commercial..................................	3[illegible]9	56.98
Science.......................................	1[illegible]	16.37
Agricultural (Not Operating).............	3	.41
Total......................................	69[illegible]	100.00%

B. Present Status of Graduates, January 31st, 1938.

Positions and Occupations	Number	Percentage
Teaching Staff in C.C.C..................	[illegible]	1.14
Non-Teaching Officers in C.C.C...........	[illegible]	1.14
Teachers in Other Christian Schools......	70	10.02
Church Workers............................	10	1.43
Teachers in Non-Christian Schools........	32	4.58
Students in Medical.......................	2	.29
Students in U.S.A. and Germany...........	17	2.43
Students in Japan proper..................	39	5.58
Journalists and Writers...................	11	1.57
Employees in Banks and Business Firms....	150	21.46
Government Officials......................	5[illegible]	8.44
Independent Commercial or Industrial Workers	9[illegible]	14.07
Agriculturalists..........................	5	.71
Various Lines of Independent Business....	145	20.75
Physician.................................	[illegible]	.14
Mining....................................	[illegible]	.43
Deceased..................................	39	5.58
Total................................	698	100.00%

C. Graduates' Privileges Conferred by the Government.

a. The College has been granted the privilege of confering a Bachelor's degree in each Department as Bachelor of Literature or Commerce or Science or Theology.

b. Government qualification for private primary school teachers (See Article I of the Educational Ordinance for private school teachers).

c. The graduates of the College are granted qualification by the Government to teach in Private Higher Common Schools on the following subjects: (See Article III of the Educational Ordinance for private school teachers.)

To the graduates of the Literary Department:
English, and (Korean).
To the graduates of the Commercial Department:
English, Commerce, and Bookkeeping.
To the graduates of the Science Department:
Mathematics, Physics, and Chemistry.
To the graduates of the Agricultural Department:
(Not Operating) Agriculture.

d. The graduates of the College are also granted qualification by the Government to teach all the subjects taught in the Professional Schools: Technical, Agricultural, Commercial, Veterinary, Nautical, and other vocational schools. (See Article IV of the Educational Ordinance for private school teachers.)

e. In accordance with the Ordinance of the Imperial Department of Education, No.3, Art.2, Sec.4 (Daisho the 7th Year) this College has been placed on an equal plane with the Higher Schools, Colleges, and the Preparatory Departments of Universities in Japan proper, so that our graduates are exempted from the preliminary examinations for Higher Civil Service positions and are qualified also for entering all Government and private universities.

f. According to the Imperial Ordinance, No.261 (Daisho the 2nd Year), the graduates of this College are granted the privilege of ordinary Civil Official appointment without examination (Ordinance on Civil Official Appointment, Art.6.)

XI. Conclusion.

As a summary of my report, I wish to call your attention to the following points:

1. Profs. H. P. Choi and N. W. Paik made an imperishable name in the world of publication by publishing a book each.

2. Profs. S. T. Lee and S. J. Chey represented the college at the Seventh World Educational Conference and at the Fourth Annual Conference for Research in Commercial English in Japan, both held in Tokyo.

3. Prof. D. W. Lee represented the college at the Nineteenth Annual Conference for the Middle School Mathematics held in Tokyo.

4. Prof. L. G. Paik went to America on leave of absence to attend the Centennial Celebration of the Board of Foreign Missions of the Presbyterian Church in U.S.A.; Edinburgh Conference, in Edinburgh, England; and Oxford Conference, in Oxford, England.

5. President Underwood has been to America on the invitation of the Cooperating Board and the North Presbyterian Mission and pressed the necessity of the continuation of educational work in Korea. While he was there he helped in the reorganization of the Cooperating Board in America and made it possible to appoint Capt. Swinehart as the Executive Secretary of the Board. Wherever he went, he took every opportunity to speak a word in behalf of the college and made the name of C.C.C. known all over the country. He also condoled his Aunt, the wife of the late Mr. John T. Underwood and Mrs. James, the only daughter of the deceased gentleman.

6. The college had one of the most successful years with the largest enrollment of students, representing every province in Korea and coming from 75 leading secondary schools in the Orient.

From this fact alone, we can realize clearly what an important role this college plays as an educational institution. The larger measure this college plays in such a role, the greater becomes the recognition of the general public. And so the increasing endowment fund, the scholarship funds, and the valuable gifts in books may all be considered as tokens of the recognition of the merits of this college by the general public.

Lastly, I am glad to say that in this extraordinary time of the China incident, we have been one in Christ and have heartily cooperated in carrying everything through without any serious blunder. However, we cannot help feeling that the progress of the college is chiefly due to the wisdom of the Board of Managers, to the splendid leadership of President Underwood, and to the hearty cooperation of the Faculty and Staff.

In closing, I thank God for His infinite mercy, love, and care for this college.

Respectfully submitted,

U. K. Yu, Dean

53. 이묘묵 학감 대리의 이사회 제출 연례보고서

문서 제목	Chosen Christian College, Report of the Dean 1938~1939
문서 종류	학감 보고서
제출 시기	1939년 2월 20일
작성 장소	서울
제 출 자	이묘묵
수 신 자	H. H. Underwood, 이사회
페이지 수	23
출 처	2114-5-4: 06 Underwood, Horace H. (DR.) 1938 (UMAH) 2114-5-4: 07 Underwood, Horace H. (DR.) 1939 Jan. to Feb. (UMAH)

자료 소개

학감 대리 이묘묵이 1939년 2월 23일 열리는 이사회를 앞두고 2월 20일 원한경 교장에게 보낸 학감 보고서이다. 유억겸 부교장 겸 학감이 1938년 흥업구락부사건으로 체포되어 사임하자 1937년에 먼저 동우회사건으로 체포되었다가 풀려난 이묘묵이 학감을 대리하였다. 수물과 과장 이춘호도 이 사건으로 체포되어 사임하였고, 상과 과장 이순탁도 1938년 경제연구회사건으로 체포되어 사임하였다. 이묘묵은 1939년 이사회 회의 개회 전에 원한경에게 학감 보고서를 미리 보냈고, 원한경은 이를 이사들에게 미리 회람시킨 후 회의 때 낭독 없이 이묘묵에게 질문만 하게 하였다. 이날 베커가 부교장으로 선출되었고, 백낙준의 미국 체류를 가을학기 전까지로 연장해주었다. 이양하, 박효삼, 정래길, 유한상이 조교수로 승급되었고, 1940년 개교 25주년 행사를 준비하는 위원회가 만들어졌다.

이 문서는 표지(1쪽), 원한경에게 보낸 편지(2쪽), 보고서(3~23쪽)로 대별 된다. 편지에서는 이묘묵이 혼란 속에서도 대학은 설립자가 세운 목표를 향해 나아가고 있다고 진술하였다. 보고서에서는 예년처럼 목차를 구성하면서, 서언과 결어 항목을 없앴다.

I. 운영진과 교수진, II. 3개 학과, III. 종교활동, IV. 도서관, V. 체육 교육,

VI. 음악 활동, VII. 다른 사항들, VIII. 학생, IX. 졸업생.

내용 요약

I. 에비슨은 명예 교장이다. 운영진은 원한경(교장), 이묘묵(학감 대리), 백낙준(문과 과장, 부재), 하경덕(문과 과장대리), 임병혁(상과 과장대리), 최규남(수물과 과장대리), 최순주(회계), 이묘묵(도서관장, 박물관장)이다. 대학 교무위원회는 원한경, 이묘묵, 백낙준(부재), 하경덕, 임병혁, 최규남, 케이블 · 스나이더(남 · 북감리회 선교회 대표), 최순주로 구성되어 있다. 대학 예산위원회는 원한경, 이묘묵, 백낙준(부재), 하경덕, 임병혁, 최규남, 베커, 스나이더, 최순주로 구성되어 있다. 교수는 17명(한국인 10명), 조교수는 1명(갈홍기), 전임강사는 12명(한국인 8명), 강사와 조수는 28명(한국인 21명), 파트타임 조력자는 4명(선교사 교수 부인)이다. 현재 부재한 교수는 2명(백낙준, 정인보), 사임한 교수는 12명(유억겸, 이춘호, 홍승국, 최현배, 이원철, 최순주, 장석영, 정광현, 이순탁, 백남운, 노동규, 가이야)[가이야 외에는 흥업구락부사건과 경제연구회사건 연루자들], 사무직원은 14명(사감 포함)이다.

II. 문과는 과장 백낙준이 1937년 5월 미국에 가서 돌아오지 않았고, 최현배가 1938년 7월까지 과장을 대리한 후 8월 25일 사임하였고, 정인보도 없어서 조선어, 조선문학을 가르칠 교수가 없다. 1937년 8월 사임한 현제명, 하경덕, 이묘묵, 갈홍기가 6월 10일 돌아왔으나, 현제명이 12월 다시 떠났고, 이묘묵이 9월 임시 학감이 되었다. 상과는 백남운이 4~9월 병가를 가졌고, 최순주가 4~8월 동경제대에서 연구하였으며, 임병혁, 박효삼 교수와 강사 3명이 수업을 이끌었다. 홍승국이 1~7월에 과장을 대리한 후 8월에 사임하였고, 최순주가 9월에 도쿄에서 돌아왔다가 곧 사임하였으며, 임병혁이 과장대리로 임명되었고, 정광현도 사임하였다. 수물과는 이춘호 과장이 4월부터 학감을 겸직하다 9월 사임하여 이원철이 여름에 과장을 대리하였고, 그 후 베커에 이어 최규남이 10월부터 과장대리가 되었으며, 이원철이 10월 사임하였다.

III. 채플 예배, 특별집회, 학생들의 하기 봉사활동이 수행되었고, 박용학이 학생들의 집을 순방하였다. 장석영이 복귀하기를 바란다.

IV. 도서관에 있는 총 53,048권의 장서에서 17,040권이 서양 서적이다. 한 해 동안 683권을 샀고, 1,211권을 기증받았다.

V. 이원철의 사임으로 이운용이 체육부를 맡았다. 테니스, 축구, 농구, 자전거, 아이스

하키 경기에서 좋은 성적을 거두었다.

VI. 음악 활동이 축소되었지만, 그런 상황에서도 연례 추기 음악회를 열었고, 대구지방 순회공연을 하였다. 박경호가 가르쳤고, 베커 부인이 도왔다.

VII. 언더우드관 2층의 박물관에 있는 4,000~5,000점을 적절히 분류 · 전시하지 못하고 있지만, 인물 초상화에는 모두 액자를 끼웠다.

9명의 근로학생을 도왔고, 2명에게 성적 장학금을 주고, 25명에게 장학금을 주었다. (장학금 기부자와 수령자 명단, 학생 클럽과 단체의 목록을 제시하고 있다.)

VIII. 학생은 총 455명(문과 141명, 상과 238명, 수물과 76명)이 등록하였고, 본과는 425명, 별과는 30명이다(1월 31일까지). (출신 지역 현황은 표를 참고.)

IX. 졸업생은 총 802명이고, 현재 연전 교수 9명, 연전 직원 8명, 다른 기독교학교 교사 73명, 교회 사역 10명, 비기독교학교 교사 32명, 의학생 2명, 미국 · 독일 유학 30명, 일본 유학 52명, 언론인 12명, 은행원 및 회사원 183명, 공무원 69명, 개인사업(상공업) 102명, 농업 5명, 다양한 개인사업[家業] 175명, 의사 1명, 광업 3명, 사망 39명이다. 졸업생이 갖는 자격은 이전 보고서의 내용과 같다.

CHOSEN CHRISTIAN COLLEGE

Report of the Dean

1938---1939

*****

Chosen Christian College
Seoul, Korea

February 20, 1939

Dr. Horace H. Underwood, Ph.D., Litt.D.
Chosen Christian College
Seoul, Korea

My dear President Underwood:-

The academic year of 1938 - 1939 has been one of the most difficult and trying years in the annals of the Chosen Christian College. During the last year the College lost eleven of its best teachers and experienced administrators. Without any exaggeration the College put in almost all of its energy and time in filling up the vacancies and in maintaining morale among the staff and students.

We are fully convinced that it is Providence and your invincible and sagacious stewardship that led our College safely through this stormy channel. Neither can we forget the hearty and self-forgetful cooperation of our faculty and staff and the most encouraging and sympathetic attitude taken by the educational authorities of the Government-General.

Even in the midst of this upset the College has made headway towards the high aims set by its founder. I, hereby, have the honor of submitting to you the following report as a token of our appreciation and as a testimony of your vigorous leadership.

Respectfully submitted by,

Hyo-Mook Lee
Acting Dean.

CHOSEN CHRISTIAN COLLEGE
Report of the Dean
(1938-1939)

CONTENTS

I. Officers of Administration and Instruction.

A. President Emeritus.

O. R. Avison, M.D., LL.D. (Toronto and Wooster), residing in U.S.A.

B. Officers of Administration.

Horace H. Underwood, M.A., Ph.D., Litt.D., President.
Myo-Mook Lee, M.A., Ph.D., Acting Dean.
L. George Paik, M.A., Ph.D., Director of the Literary Department.
(On Leave of Absence).
Kyung Duk Har, M.A., Ph.D., Acting Director of Literary Department.
Pyung Hyuk Lim, M.A., Acting Director of Commercial Department.
Kyu Nam Choi, M.A., Ph.D., Acting Director of Science Department.
Soon Ju Chey, M.B.A., Ph.D., Treasurer.
Myo-Mook Lee, M.A., Ph.D., Librarian and Curator.

C. College Council.

Horace H. Underwood, Ph.D., Litt.D., President.
Myo-Mook Lee, M.A., Ph.D., Acting Dean.
L. George Paik, Ph.D., Director of the Literary Department. (On Leave of Absence).
Kyung Duk Har, M.A., Ph.D., Acting Director of the Literary Department.
Pyung Hyuk Lim, M.A., Acting Director of the Commercial Department.
Kyu Nam Choi, M.A., Ph.D., Acting Director of the Science Department.
E. M. Cable, D.D., Representative of the M.E.C. Mission.
L. H. Snyder, M.A., Representative of the M.E.C. Mission, South.
Soon Ju Chey, M.B.A., Ph.D., Treasurer.
Myo-Mook Lee, M.A., Ph.D., Librarian.

D. College Budget Committee.

Horace H. Underwood, Ph.D., Litt.D., President.
Myo-Mook Lee, M.A., Ph.D., Acting Dean.
L. George Paik, Ph.D., Acting Director of the Literary Department.
(On Leave of Absence).
Kyung Duk Har, Ph.D., Acting Director of the Literary Department.
Pyung Hyuk Lim, M.A., Acting Director of the Commercial Department.
Kyu Nam Choi, Ph.D., Acting Director of the Science Department.
A. L. Becker, Ph.D., Representative of the M.E.C. Mission.
L. H. Snyder, M.A., Representative of the M.E.C. Mission, South.
S. J. Chey, Ph.D., Treasurer.

F. Faculty.

(1). Professors. (17)

H. H. Underwood, B.A., M.A., Ph.D., Litt.D., (New York University and Mount Union). President of the College and Professor of Education, Psychology and English, 1915 ---

I. Faculty.

(1) Professors. (Continued)

Myo-Mook Lee, C.C.C. Graduate, M.A., Ph.D. (Syracuse, Harvard, Boston). Acting Dean, Librarian, and Professor of Western History and English, 1934 ---

L. George Paik, B.A., Th.B., M.A., Ph.D., (Yale). Director of the Literary Department and Professor of Occidental History and Religion, 1927 --- (On Leave of Absence).

Kyung Duk Har, M.A., Ph.D., (Harvard). Acting Director of the Literary Department and Professor of Sociology and English, 1932 ---

Pyung Hyuck Kim, C.C.C. Graduate, B.A., M.A., (Syracuse). Acting Director of the Commercial Department and Professor of Bank Bookkeeping, Commodities, and Business English, 1932 ---

Kyu Nam Choi, C.C.C. Graduate, B.A., M.A., Ph.D., (Michigan). Acting Director of the Science Department and Professor of Physics and Mathematics, 1933 ---

A. L. Becker, B.A., M.A., Ph.D., (Michigan). Professor of Physics and Mathematics, 1915 ---

E. H. Miller, B.A., B.D., M.A., Ph.D., (Columbia). Professor of Chemistry, English and Bible, 1915 ---

S. Nikaido, Gakushi, (Tokyo Imperial University). Professor of Japanese, Japanese Literature and Introduction to Literature, 1927 ---

Pong Chip Kim, Gakushi, (Waseda University). Professor of Physics, Electrical Engineering, and Mathematics, 1927 ---

In Po Chung, Professor of Chinese Literature and Korean Literature, 1922 ---

Rody Cheymyung Hyun, M.Mus., D.Mus., (Gunn and Chicago Conservatory). Professor of Music, 1929 ---

E. M. Cable, B.S., M.A., D.D., (Cornell College). Professor of English, Bible and History, 1932 ---

L. H. Snyder, B.A., M.A., (Princeton). Professor of English and Typewriting, 1933 ---

R. C. Coen, B.A., B.D., M.A., (Chicago). Professor of Bible and English, 1933 ---

Ounn Yong Lee, (Berlin University). Professor of German, 1926 ---

E. Faculty.

(1). Professors. (Continued)

Insub Jung, Gakushi, (Waseda University). Professor of English, Phonetics, Introduction to Literature, and English Literature, 1929 ----

(2). Assistant Professor. (1)

Hong Kee Karl, B.D., M.A., Ph.D., (Chicago). Assistant Professor of Philosophy of Religion and Bible, 1934 ---

(3). Instructors. (12)

Mrs. H. H. Underwood, B.A., M.A., (New York University). English, 1918 ---

Lak Won Kang, Physical Education, 1927 ---

Yang Ha Lee, Gakushi, (Tokyo Imperial University). English and English Literature, 1935 ---

Chung Nok Kim, Graduate of Paiyoung College. The Chinese Language, 1934 ---

Mrs. E. M. Cable, B.A., (Cornell). English, 1932 ---

Hyo Sam Park, Gakushi, (Meiji University). Commercial Mathematics, Exchange, Economic Affairs, Trust and Business Management, 1937 ---

Ryong Whan Kim, Gakushi, (Keijo Imperial University). English, 1937 ---

Lai Kil Chung, Gakushi, (Keio). Public Law, Finance, and Economics, 1933 ---

Han Sung Ryu, Gakushi (Waseda University). Chemistry, 1936 ---

Hyung Kon Ko, Gakushi, (Keijo). Philosophy and Ethics, 1938 ---

In Suk Han, C.C.C. Graduate, Gakushi, (Tohoku). Physics and Mathematics, 1938 ---

Sun Gi Gim, C.C.C. Graduate, M.A., (London). English and Phonetics, 1938 ---

(4). Lecturers and Assistants. (28)

Ki Won Chang, C.C.C. Graduate, Gakushi, (Tohoku Imperial University). Mathematics, 1930 ---

-4-

I. Faculty. (Continued)

(4). Lecturers and Assistants.

Hoo Chang Chen, C.C.T. Graduate, Gakushi, (Tokyo University of Commerce). Bookkeeping, Statistics, Money, 1932, 1938 ---

T. Yokoyama, B.A., B.D., Ph.D., (Johns Hopkins). English, 1932 ---

P. B. Billings, B.A., (Depauw). English. (On Leave of Absence).

Chin Tai Son, Gakushi (Waseda University). Oriental History, 1934 ---

Doo Houn Kim, Gakushi, (Tokyo Imperial University). Morals, 1934 ---

James Injun Park, B.S. in A.E., (Minnesota) and B.S. in M.E. (Lewis Institute). Architecture, Construction and Drawing, 1935

Won Sik Min, B.A., (Nevada). French, 1936 ---

Chi Soo Ryuk, Gakushi, (Tokyo Imperial University) Marketing, Commercial Geography, Custom House, Japanese Commercial Letter Writing and German, 1936 ---

K. Woomesawa, Physical Education, 1937 ---

Kyung Ho Pak, B.S., (Cincinnati Conservatory). Music, 1935, 1938 ---

Tai Sik Min, Gakushi, (Keijo Imperial University). Chinese Classics, 1938 ---

K. Ogawa, (Tokyo Tech.). Civil Engineering, 1938 ---

K. Matsunami, Gakushi, (Kyoto Imperial University). Law, 1938 ---

Tong Kil Pak, Gakushi (Tohoku Imperial University). Mineralogy, 1938 ---

Kui Won Yi, M.A., (Michigan). Science English, 1938 ---

In Mok Jung, Gakushi, (Meiji University). Abacus, Insurance, 1938 ---

Pyung Kuk Ko, Gakushi, (Tokyo Imperial University). Law, 1938 ---

S. Toyoshima, Gakushi, (Tokyo Imperial University). Law, 1938 ---

Sang Hoon Lee, Gakushi, (Tokyo Commercial College). Commercial Practice, 1938 ---

Kouk Chai Pak, Gakushi, (Kyoto Imperial University). Commerce, 1938 ---

S. Kida, Gakushi, (Tokyo Imperial University). National History, 1938 ---

-5-

E. Faculty. (Continued)

(4). Lecturers and Assistants.

Young Sum Yang, Gakushi, (Rikkyo). Western History, 1938 ---

Kyung Ok Chung, B.D., M.A., (Northwestern). Bible, 1938 ---

Cho Rin Cynn, C.C.C. Graduate, Assistant, Physics Laboratory, 1924 ---

Young Sung Kim, C.C.C. Graduate, Assistant, Physics Laboratory, 1926 ---

Kun Chul Cynn, C.C.C. Graduate, Assistant, Literary Department, 1933 ---

Yong Kuk Pak, B.A., M.A., (Southwestern University and Southern Methodist University). Secretary of the Religious Department, 1936 ---

(5) Part Time Assistants. (4)

Mrs. A. L. Becker.
Mrs. R. C. Coen.
Mrs. E. H. Miller.
Mrs. L. L. Snyder.

(6). Professors on Leave of Absence. (2)

L. G. Paik, Th.B., M.A., Ph.D.
I. P. Chung.

(7). Professors and Instructors Resigned. (12)

U. K. Yu
C. H. Yoo
S. K. Hong
H. P. Choi
D. W. Lee
S. J. Choy
S. Y. Chang
K. H. Jung
S. T. Lee
N. W. Paik
T. K. Roe
K. Kaiyo

F. Office Staff. (14)

Suk Young Whang, B.D., M.A., Student Pastor.

F. Office Staff. (Continued)

Byron Koo, M.D., (Emory). C.C.C. Graduate. College Physician.

Chai Kyung Sohn, C.C.C. Graduate, Secretary to Administration.

Chi Myung Song, C.C.C. Graduate. Superintendent of Dormitory.

Chi Hak Kim, C.C.C. Graduate, Superintendent of Grounds and Buildings.

Kyung Sang Lyu, C.C.C. Graduate, Assistant to the Librarian. (On Leave of Absence.)

Paul Hyon, B.A., (Shanghai). Accountant.

Woon Yong Shim, C.C.C. Graduate, Secretary to Administration.

Kei Won Yi, C.C.C. Graduate, B.A., M.A. (Michigan). Cashier.

P[illegible] Sur Kim, B.A. (C.C.C.). Clerical Assistant in the Library.

Miss Lori Thelma Ahn, Stenographer to the President.

Mrs. Sang Hoo Lyu, Graduate of P[illegible]wha, Clerical Assistant of the Library.

Miss Duk Hoo Whang, Assistant to the Cashier.

Chai Yun Whang, Clerical Assistant in the Library.

II. Three Departments of the College.

A. Literary Department - Acting Director, Kyung Duk Har, Ph.D.

The difficulties which began the year before last were partly removed last June on the return of the four members of the faculty who had resigned. In addition, two new full-time teachers as well as several part-time teachers joined the faculty. With this re-enforcement we have managed to run the Department.

Dr. L. G. Paik, Director of the Department, who went to America in May 1937, to attend the Centennial Celebration of the Presbyterian Board of Foreign Missions, did not return. In his place Prof. H. P. Choi continued to act as Director till July 6, 1938, and on August 25th he tendered his resignation which was accepted. Since his resignation his Education courses have been conducted by Dr. H. K. Karl; but his Korean Language courses have been left vacant, owing to the difficulty of obtaining the Government permit for new teachers.

Prof. I. P. Chung has continued to be on leave of absence throughout the academic year because of serious illness. His Chinese Classics courses have been conducted by Mr. T. S. Min of Pai Chai Middle School from May 13; but the Korean Literature courses have been left vacant.

A. Literary Department - (Continued).

On June 10, Drs. C. M. Hyun, K. D. Har, M. M. Lee, and H. K. Karl, who had resigned in August, 1937, returned to College and resumed their respective work. Dr. Hyun continued active till the early part of December when he was again in difficulty and had to stay away, indefinitely from the College. From July 14, when Professor H. P. Choi could no longer continue his work, Dr. K. D. Har has acted as Director of the Department. Dr. M. M. Lee became Dean of the College pro tempore in September.

Two full-time instructors joined the faculty from the early part of the academic year: Messrs. Koh and Gim. Mr. H. K. Koh, Gakushi, of the Keijo Imperial University, took up the courses of Morals, Logic, Psychology, and Philosophy, from April 6; and Mr. S. G. Gim, M.A., of London University, took up the courses in English from April 20.

In September, Assistant Prof. S. Y. Chang tendered his resignation which was accepted; and his Bible courses were temporarily given to the Rev. K. O. Chung who began teaching from December 6.

Mrs. H. H. Underwood, who had been kind enough to help the Department, released her course in the Junior English Conversation in the second semester, in order to help the Commercial Department where her presence was more urgently needed.

Mr. S. K. Lee, who had been teaching Occidental history since September, 1937, resigned on October 6, 1938, in order to look after his new business in Manchukuo. His place was filled by Mr. N. C. Yang, Gakushi, of St. Paul's University, Tokyo, from December 3.

At the suggestion of the Bureau of Education, Japanese National History was added to the curriculum at the beginning of the second semester; and Prof. Kita of the Preparatory School for the Keijo Imperial University began his lectures, 2 hours a week, from December 1. At the same time, in order to make this change possible, the Oriental History course was shorten 1 to 8 hours a week.

The Department began the year with 158 students on the roll: 50 Freshmen, 37 Sophomores; 36 Juniors, and 35 Seniors. At present there are 44 Freshmen; 30 Sophomores; 34 Juniors; and 33 Seniors, making a total of 141.

EXTRA-CURRICULUM ACTIVITIES

In view of the critical situation which still continued, the annual Dramatic Play, the All Korea Middle School English Oratorical Contest, and the extra-curriculum course in Journalism were given up. But the Varsity English Oratorical Contest was held with great success on December 9, preceded by a two weeks' preliminary contest in which sixty-six students participated. The first prize was won by a Freshman of our Department.

A. Literary Department - (Continued)

GENERAL RESEARCH WORK

Materials in the Research Room: Up to the present 76 volumes of new books have been purchased, and 32 volumes received as gifts. Three kinds of newspapers and four kinds of periodicals have been provided in the Research Room. However, in September, 27 volumes of the books purchased in the preceding years were removed.

The total Collection in the Research Room is made up of the following books:

Oriental Books..................................	2,048
Occidental Books..................................	185
Pamphlets and Periodicals........................	156

Publications: The year has been eventful throughout, keeping all the members of the Department busy. But, still many of us found leisure to do creative writing. The works of Dr. E. M. Cable and Mr. D. H. Kim deserve to be specially mentioned: the former produced a notable book, "The United States - Korean Relations, 1866-1871," together with his article on "Foreign Names in Korea"; and the latter another notable book, "An Outline of Ethics," together with his five interesting short essays which appeared in various periodicals. Other members of the Department contributed 45 articles to the leading newspapers and magazines in the city.

B. Commercial Department - Acting Director, Pyung Hyuk Lim, M.A.

The Commercial Department is the largest Department of the College with a faculty of 6 Professors, 1 Assistant Professor, 7 Instructors, and 11 Lecturers, making a total of 25 members. The enrollment of this Department is as follows:

Seniors..................	68
Sophomores..............	84
Freshmen................	86
Total.......	238

Professor N. Y. Paik was given a six months leave of absence from April to September on account of his poor health. Professor S. J. Choy was away for five months from April to August for special study in the Tokyo Imperial University. During the absence of these two Professors, all the work has been carried on by Professor P. H. Lim, Mr. H. S. Park, and three other Lecturers.

The present fiscal year has been the most difficult and trying year in the history of the Department. During the whole year, we had to carry on the work without the services of Director S. T. Lee, Professors N. Y. Paik, T. L. Roo, S. J. Choy, and Mr. K. H. Jung. To our regret, Director S. T. Lee, Professors N. Y. Paik, T. L. Roe, and Mr. K. H. Jung resigned

B. Commercial Department - (Continued).

in January. During the absence of Director S. T. Lee, Professor S. K. Hong was appointed as Acting Director of the Department. He held this position until July and resigned in August. Professor S. J. Chey succeeded Professor Hong, when he returned in September from his study in Tokyo. He, however, resigned in the same month. Professor P. K. Lim was appointed as the third Acting Director of the Department and has been carrying on the work. Assistant Professor Rev. S. Y. Chang also resigned in September.

On account of the absence and resignation of many teachers during the year, 8 new teachers and Mrs. Ethel Underwood have been added to the Department staff. Even among the newly added teachers; in January, Mr. K. C. Kim resigned, and Mr. P. C. Chang has been teaching extra hours to make up the vacant periods.

Professor L. H. Snyder has been giving extra time in shorthand to those students who wish to take it as an extra work.

A brief report on the employment of the 84 graduates of last year may not be out of place here. Of this number, 8 are attending universities in Japan Proper and one in the United States. 38 out of 49 who applied for positions are holding responsible positions in various banks, companies, manufacturing concerns, government offices, and in the institutions of learning; 4 are either in private business or attending family affairs; and the remaining 7 have not been placed definitely as yet.

COMMERCIAL MUSEUM

The Commercial Museum has been growing steadily with additional specimens of native and foreign commodities, making a total number of 1,828. We are proud of the fact that at the present time our Museum excells any of its kind in colleges in Korea in number as well as in variety of the specimens. Professor P. K. Lim is in charge of the Museum.

COMMERCIAL PRACTICE WORK

Along with the theoretical studies of Commerce and Economics, the practical side of the course is no less important. At the present time, there are 11 typewriters for the students to practice on. Furthermore, a special course in shorthand is offered for those students who take it as extra curricula work. Professor L. H. Snyder is in charge of this work.

GENERAL RESEARCH WORK

The Commercial Research Work has been carried on through the faculty members. This work facilitates the study and research of the teachers and students alike working on various commercial and economic problems. These results have been published in the leading newspapers and magazines from time to time. There are 61 different magazines, 5 newspapers, and 2976 volumes of reference books in the Research Room. Mr. L. K. Jung is in charge of this work.

B. Commercial Department - (Continued)

RESEARCH ON ADVERTISEMENT

The Commercial Department has begun this Research Work, to study the method of advertising and for reference. Nearly 11,035 pieces of various kinds of posters, handbills, folders, labels, enamel and card signs, etc. have been collected. These have been carefully classified and displayed in the Commercial Practice Room and also in one of the teacher's rooms. Prof. P. K. Kim is in charge of this work.

THE ENGLISH TEACHER'S RESEARCH CLUB

Ever since the Club became a chartered member of the Institute for Research of English Teaching of the Educational Bureau of Japan, bulletins, periodicals, and other publications have been sent to the College, and they are being displayed for use in one of the teacher's rooms for the time being. The Club is devoting much time and effort to plan a unified method of teaching English as a part of this program. It has directed the students in the organization of an English Club of themselves, holding meetings with various programs and practicing English in various ways. Prof. I. S. Jung is in charge of this club.

C. Science Department - Acting Director, Kyu Nam Choi, Ph.D.

The faculty members of the Science Department have done their best to carry out the work of the Department assigned to them during the past year. They have been loyal to the College and to their work and enthusiastic even though they have had to carry heavy loads in their regular work. In last April, Prof. C. H. Lee, who had been working as Director of this Department for more than 15 years was promoted to the position of the Dean of the College. Prof. D. W. Lee was appointed as his successor. A new teacher, Mr. I. S. Han, Gakushi, Tohoku Imperial University, who is one of our Science graduates and specialized in Physics and Mathematics, has been added to our staff from last April. Prof. H. Kaiya, teacher of Civil Engineering, resigned last July and accepted the offer of a position in the Boin Mining Company in Seoul. He had been with us in the College for 12 years. Prof. K. Ogawa, who has been teaching at Higher Technical College in Seoul for the last 20 years, was appointed as a new Lecturer in Civil Engineering and Surveying from last September. At the same time, Mr. C. K. Park, also a teacher of the Higher Technical College in Seoul, was appointed as a time teacher in Geology and Mineralogy. To our regret, Dean C. H. Lee resigned from the College last September and Prof. D. W. Lee was appointed as an Acting Dean during the summer. Prof. A. L. Becker who had taken up the directorship resigned from this position and Prof. K. N. Choi has been in charge of the Science Department as Acting Director from last October. It was a matter of great regret that Prof. D. W. Lee also resigned from the College in October. Mr. K. W. Chang from Ewha College has been appointed as a time teacher in Mathematics from October.

The faculty of this Department for the present year consists of 4 Professors, 2 full-time Instructors, 4 Lecturers and 2 Assistants making a total of 12 members.

C. Science Department - (Continued)

The enrollment of this Department for this year is as follows:

Seniors........................	15
Juniors........................	19
Sophomores.....................	17
Freshman.......................	25
Total..............	76

The Seniors who are to graduate in March will be placed as follows: 3 are planning to enter the Engineering Colleges of the Kyoto Imperial University, 5 have positions promised in the Government-Railway, 1 in Tai-Dong Mining Firm, 1 in the Fusan Customs House, 1 in the Keijo Radio Company and 4 as teachers to various middle schools.

TEACHERS' SCIENCE CLUB

The Science Club of this Department staff has had (as usual) regular monthly meetings at the homes of the members. Some scientific problems have been presented at each meeting by one of the members and a general discussion of the topic usually takes place. Such a gathering tends to create friendship among the members as well as to give each member something new and fresh.

SCIENCE RESEARCH WORK

The Science Research Work has been carried on by the faculty members and the students of the Department; and the results have been published from time to time in the various magazines and newspapers.

To facilitate the research work, books on natural science and various materials and specimens have been collected and placed on the shelves. There are 997 volumes of books, of which 285 volumes are in the occidental languages and 712 volumes in the oriental languages; and 6 kinds of magazines in the oriental language. Dr. K. N. Choi is in charge of this work.

SCIENCE MUSEUM

The Science Museum has been greatly increased by the recent donations. Prof. L. H. Snyder of our College donated many rare specimens of birds; and Mr. Joo Myung Souk of Song-Do Middle School gave a complete set of specimens of butterflies of Korea. The latter specimens are 202 in kind and 437 in number of pieces.

During the past summer the College prepared a moth proof case for the preservation of bird skins, and 66 specimens representing 53 species and 28 families were prepared by one of the students. These specimens, representing many of common birds and a few rare ones found in Korea and preserved in the form of partial taxidermy, are available to those who wish to examine and study them. A list of these 66 specimens with the scientific names both in English and Japanese and a complete data, giving sex, date, and place where found was attached and is filed in the Science Department.

C. Science Department - (Continued)

Each specimen were donated to the College by Prof. L. H. Snyder. It is hoped that within the coming year additional specimens will be secured so that 100 different species are represented. These new additions bring the total of biological as well as mineral specimens and scientific specimens up to 5,877.

III. Religious Activities Department - Chairman, E. M. Cable, D.D.

The unusual conditions that the College confronted a year ago affected somewhat the religious activities in the College. However, the work has been very successful. Outside of all the patriotic and national services, all of our chapel services have been of a religious nature. These services were largely conducted by Faculty members. Only a few times have we been privileged to have speakers from abroad. The attendance at the chapel services continues to be encouraging. The change of the train service from the fall term on has made it impossible for all the students to be on time when the chapel was held the first hour. However, from the winter term on the hour of chapel has been changed to the second period and the attendance has been very good.

The Special Services this year were held from February 13th to 18th. Rev. Yun, In Koo, had charge of them. He is one of the rising young Christian scholars of Korea, as well as one of the most prominent preachers. He was educated both in Korea and abroad and is well qualified to meet student problems both intellectually and spiritually. Each day before the meeting with the students he conducted the Faculty Prayer Meeting with great benefit and blessing to all. In addition to his general meeting with the student body he conducted special services in the senior class of each Department and had one day for interview with students without respect to class. Rev. Yun did a great service for the College and was an inspiration and blessing to both students and faculty.

During the summer recess a band of students representing the Y.M.C.A. of the College and Rev. S. Y. Chang visited Ki Rin Island on the Western Coast of Korea, where our College student Gospel Teams had founded the first church and spent two or more weeks in evangelistic and social work. They reported a very successful and interesting work. Our effort along this line has been somewhat curtailed owing to the present situation.

Mr. Y. H. Pak, our Religious Secretary, has been very successful in his student visitation work. He has one of the most difficult and thankless tasks of anyone connected with the College, but at the same time one of the most urgent and important. Our students are residing in an area ranging from a half a mile to several miles radius of the College. During the year Mr. Pak has called upon these students in their homes and boarding houses and in addition to discovering the circumstances connected with their homes and boarding houses, to render very necessary and helpful service.

A careful study of the map he has prepared showing the location of the students is very enlightening and stresses more eloquently than words the

III. Religious Activities Department - (Continued)

urgent and pressing need of dormitories for the College. As urgent as are the needs for a new Library, Gymnasium or College Chapel, none of these takes precedence of dormitories. Without these we cannot shield, direct and guide our ever growing student body.

During part of the year we have been deprived of the services of Rev. S. Y. Chang, but hope to have him back soon. During the last term Rev. K. O. Chyung, who is one of the rising scholars of Korea and is in much demand as a teacher and speaker has been substituting.

The success of the religious activities is due to all the members of the Religious Activities Department and to the members of the Faculty for their most hearty co-operation during these very strenuous times. We hope that the same cooperation may continue throughout the coming year.

IV. College Library - Librarian, Hyo-Kook Lee, Ph.D.

The Library is perhaps one of the few integral parts of the College which is the least affected by the turmoil of the last year.

The main Library alone boasts of total accessions of 53,048 volumes, of which 17,040 books are in the occidental languages. The Library is also handling a large number of current periodicals consisting of the following:

Magazines:

Oriental...... 54 (of which 11 gifts)
Occidental.... 37 (of which 3 gifts)

Newspapers:

Oriental...... 13 (of which 6 gifts)
Occidental.... 1

During the last year 683 books were purchased and 1,211 books were given to the Library. In order to encourage the students to study the library began to build up a large collection of reference materials solely for their own use; and the College will put in over 900 Yen annually in order to re-enforce the Study Reference Library. The College also took much pains in collecting and circulating the books dealing with the clarification of the conception of the state and with the present China incident.

Aside from quantity, the library staff worked hard on improving the filing system of cards in order to facilitate the use of the books. The long coveted division of cards into Japanese, Korean and occidental languages has been begun and within the near future the dream will be fulfilled.

Much care was given to periodicals, and useful ones were bound and placed properly for reference use. Last year alone 393 volumes of magazines and 19 volumes of newspapers were bound.

IV. College Library - (Continued)

Adding the books more up to date and improving the use of library produced an immediate and eloquent result - namely, an increase of circulation. About 1,024 books were circulated each month; and the nature of the books in the order of demand is as follows:

(1) Literature; (2) History; (3) Sociology and Social Science; (4) Philosophy; (5) General Books including Periodicals; (6) Books on Religion; (7) Philology; (8) Science; (9) Useful Science; (10) Fine Arts; (11) Biography; (12) Travels.

The Library gave up 588 books chiefly dealing with radical thoughts. The Library is going to purchase a considerable number of books in Japanese in order to commemorate the 2600th anniversary of the foundation of Japan.

The College Library is very fortunate in having a congenial group of staff. Dr. Hong Kee Karl has been a great help in looking after the library, while Librarian M. M. Lee was mostly away in the Dean's office. Mrs. Cable has been also a faithful helper to the library, despite her heavy teaching load. There are Mr. P. S. Kimm, Mrs. S. H. Lyu, and Mr. C. Y. Whang to who the credit of carrying out the routine work should be given.

Crisis or no crisis, the library is steadily growing both in quantity and quality. Some more trained workers are needed; and, moreover, a separate library building is absolutely indispensable.

V. Physical Education - Chairman, Oumn Yong Lee.

The same old story of resignation and filling up the vacancies is repeated even in this phase of the College life. Dr. D. W. Lee resigned last September and Prof. O. Y. Lee was appointed to succeed him. Despite the psychological effect of the hard time and the rise of prices of sport goods, the College lived up to its high reputation of sportsmanship and added a splendid chapter to the annals of the College sports. This success is chiefly due to the indefatigable spirit of the men who were in charge of the various sports and to the hearty cooperation and team work of the players. The athletic reputation of the Chosen Christian College players are such that without their participation no All-Japan or All-Korea Team could be held. Giving only a few high lights of the athletic activities of the College:

(1). Tennis: The College Tennis Team retained its championship at the Jinzu Contest. Furthermore, under the auspices of the All-Korea Team, our College Tennis Team invaded Japan Proper and won victories at the All-Japan High School and College Tennis Championship Meets.

(2). Football: At the Three Regional Contest, which began last year, a number of our undergraduates and graduate members were chosen to membership of the All-Korea Team. They played an important role in the games won at the Koshien Ground, Osaka.

V. Physical Education - (Continued)

(3). Basketball: As in the preceding years the College Basketball Team played at the All-Japan Championship Meet. Unfortunately our team lost the game, but made a very fine impression. Several of our undergraduate players joined the All-Japan Basketball Team and went to Manila, Philippine Islands.

(4). Bicycle: The Bicycle division was established last year. The Team represented our College at Tokyo and established several new records and won individual championship at the Jinzu Contest.

(5). Ice Hockey: The team members themselves assumed considerable financial burden of the purchase of equipment. They made a good showing during the winter sport season. Several of them were on the All-Korea Team and participated in the contest between Japan, Choson, and Manchukuo, which was held at Antung. Our team was also invited to Heijo, Kaijo, and other places where it demonstrated its skill. Its service to the sporting circles of the Peninsula was considerable.

The activities of other sports also showed a marked progress. We can only regret that, owing to the sudden rise of prices of goods and the outbreak of the unexpected events, our budget could not enable us to carry our activities to full fruition. It is hoped that in the future, we may have an adequate budget to improve the equipment of the various Departments, to stimulate the Inter-Departmental athletic activities in the College, and to enable our teams to participate in the various over-seas athletic meets. With these means we hope to develop athletic skill and to promote health.

VI. Musical Activities - Chairman, C. M. Hyun, Mus. D.

The report on the musical activities for the year is rather short, for, on account of the present circumstances, the outside activities have been very few. Mr. Kyung Ho Park has been kind enough to take the responsibility of teaching and conducting our music during the absence of Dr. Hyun.

Our annual fall concert was held at the Citizen's Hall in October, and it was a great success. Dr. Hyun and the students made a special music trip to Taikyu in the fall; and they have also broadcasted special programs from time to time through the Central Broadcasting Station in Seoul.

We wish to record again the worthy service given by Mrs. A. L. Becker from the beginning of the music work of this College up to the present time. Without her sacrificial service, the music work for the year could not have been carried on successfully. Great thanks are also due to Mrs. R. C. Coen, who plays music for our chapel services every day.

VII. Other Items of Interest.

A. College Museum - Curator, Myo-Mook Lee, Ph.D.

The College Museum is one of the most fascinating, yet the least known places on the campus. The museum possesses four or five thousand interesting and valuable objects chiefly given by the staff and friends of the College. At present they are simply dumped in the sunny room on the second floor of the Underwood Hall; and they are neither classified nor exhibited properly. Even as they are, our College Museum is something unique. We need a trained Curator; and a wider space is needed to house them.

Last year a thorough inventory was made; and the old precious Korean portrait paintings were all framed. Prof. Insub Jung and others gave a good many interesting objects.

We hope to have the students get better acquainted with the museum next year.

B. Student Help Work - Chairman, Hong Koo Karl, Ph.D.

Prof. S. K. Hong, who had been heading this committee for years and looked after the needy students with so much affection, resigned last September; and in his place Dr. Karl is now doing the work. The appropriation for this work was 780 Yen by which 9 students were given the opportunity to earn a part of their school expenses.

The Student Help Committee does more than this. It is also an Employment Bureau through which a good many students secure odd jobs and private tutorship.

C. Scholarships.

The endowments and donations of scholarship funds by the friends of the College seem to be one of the most encouraging factors. In addition to two honor students, Kang Yo Han (L 4) and Kang Young Houn (C 2), twenty five students get the benefit of the following scholarships:

Donors	Recipients	Amount
Yun Chi Chang	Kang Pil Ju (C 3)	¥ 75.00
Lee Won Yoh	Cho Hyo Won (C 2)	75.00
Kim Hi Jun	Kim Tai Jun (C 2)	75.00
Paik Won Chun	Pak Young Sang (C 2)	75.00
Yun Bang Hyun	Lim Chang Soo (S 4)	75.00
Koreans in U.S.A.	Han Hyung Koun (S 2)	75.00
E. M. Cable	Pak Chang Hai (L 4)	75.00
Glen Olden Church	Chang Yun Sup (L 3)	75.00
Paul E. Burbank	Kim Dai Sung (L 4)	75.00

VII. Other Items of Interest. (Continued)

C. Scholarships.

Donors	Recipients	Amount
Kim Chong Sun	Dyun Hyo Chin (L 2)	¥75.00
	Kim Tai Chin (C 3)	75.00
	Chang Hi Sun (C 3)	75.00
	Pak Chung Ki (C 3)	75.00
Cho Pyung Kap	Lim Koun Su (L 4)	75.00
	Kim Jun Suo (L 3)	75.00
	Loo Yong Hi (L 3)	75.00
	Chung Hi Suk (L 2)	75.00
	Choi Eun Sup (C 2)	75.00
	Kim Young Whan (L 4)	50.00
	Kim Soung Yun (L 3)	50.00
	Kim Dong Won (C 2)	50.00
	Chung Kui Whan (S 3)	50.00
	Pak Yong Up (C 3)	75.00
Yun Chang Hyun	Hyun Sook Chul (L 4)	75.00
Loo Chung Ik	Pak Woo Chul (C 2)	75.00

D. Clubs and Organizations.

a. C.C.C. Students Association. (The Student Body).(not functioning).
b. C.C.C. Y.M.C.A. (Voluntary Organization).
c. Literary Society. (Literary Department Students).
d. Commercial Department Students Society.
e. Science Club. (Science Department Students).
f. Glee Club, Orchestra and Band (Voluntary, all Departments).
g. Oratorical Club.(Voluntary, all Departments).
h. Dramatic Club. (Voluntary, all Departments).
i. English Club. (Voluntary, Commercial Department Students).
j. Religious Research Club. (Voluntary, all Departments).

VIII. Students.

A. Enrollment.

Annual average of the students who paid tuition during the past three years:

1935 - 36 320
1936 - 37 394
1937 - 38 417

- 4 -

VIII. Students. (Continued)

A. Enrollment.

Up to January 31st, 1939, there was a total enrollment of 455 students distributed as follows:

Class	Lit. Dept.	Com. Dept.	Sci. Dept.	Total
Freshman	44	86	25	155
Sophomore	30	84	17	131
Junior	34		19	53
Senior	33	68	15	[illegible]
	141	238	76	455

B. Classification of Students.

Department	Regular	Special	Total	Percentage
	Number of Students			
Literary	120	21	141	30.99
Commercial	232	6	238	52.31
Science	73	3	76	16.70
	425	30	455	100.00%

C. Geographical Distribution of Students.

Province	Number	Percentage
North Ham Kyung	10	2.20
South Ham Kyung	12	2.64
North Pyung An	36	7.91
South Pyung An	57	12.52
Whang Hai	42	9.23
Kyung Ki	175	38.46
Kang Won	15	3.30
North Choong Chung	13	2.86
South Choong Chung	27	5.93
North Chun La	16	3.51
South Chun La	19	4.18
North Kyung Sang	19	4.18
South Kyung Sang	14	3.06
	455	100.00%

IX. Graduates.

A. Total Number of Graduates from Each Department.

(January 31st, 1938)

Department	Number	Percentage
Literary	207	25.81
Commercial	462	57.61
Science	130	16.21
Agricultural (Not Operating)	3	.37
Total	802	100.00%

IX. Graduates. (Continued)

B. Present Status of Graduates, January 31st, 1939.

Positions and Occupations	Number	Percentage
Teaching Staff in C.C.C.	9	1.11
Non-Teaching Officers in C.C.C.	8	.99
Teachers in Other Christian Schools	73	9.01
Church Workers	10	1.23
Teachers in Non-Christian Schools	40	4.94
Students in Medical	2	.25
Students in U.S.A. and Germany	30	3.70
Students in Japan Proper	52	6.42
Journalists and Writers	12	1.53
Employees in Banks and Business Firms	183	22.58
Government Officials	69	8.52
Independent Commercial or Industrial Workers	102	12.59
Agriculturalists	5	.62
Various Lines of Independent Business	175	20.60
Physician	1	.12
Mining	3	.37
Deceased	39	4.80
Total	302	100.00%

C. Graduates' Privileges Conferred by the Government.

a. The College has been granted the privilege of conferring a Bachelor's degree in each Department as Bachelor of Literature or Commerce or Science or Theology.

b. Government qualification for private primary school teachers. (See Article I of the Educational Ordinance for private school teachers).

c. The graduates of the College are granted qualification by the Government to teach in Private Higher Common Schools on the following subjects; (See Article III of the Educational Ordinance for private school teachers.)

To the graduates of the Literary Department:
English, and (Korean).
To the graduates of the Commercial Department:
English, Commerce, and Bookkeeping.
To the graduates of the Science Department:
Mathematics, Physics, and Chemistry.
To the graduates of the Agricultural Department:
(Not Operating). Agriculture.

d. The graduates of the College are also granted qualification by the Government to teach all the subjects taught in the Professional Schools: Technical, Agricultural, Commercial, Veterinary, Nautical, and other vocational schools. (See Article IV of the Educational Ordinance for private school teachers.)

XI. Graduates. (Continued)

C. Graduates' Privileges conferred by the Government.

e. In accordance with the Ordinance of the Imperial Department of Education, No.3, Art.9, Sec.4 (Daisho 7th Year) this college has been placed on an equal plane with the Higher Schools, Colleges, and the Preparatory Departments of Universities in Japan Proper, so that our graduates are exempted from the preliminary examinations for Higher Civil Service positions and are qualified also for entering all Government and private universities.

f. According to the Imperial Ordinance, No. 261 (Daisho 2nd Year), the graduates of this College are granted the privilege of ordinary Civil Official appointment without examination (Ordinance on Civil Official Appointment, Art. 6).

54. 원한경 교장의 이사회 제출 연례보고서

문서 제목	Report to the Board of Managers of Chosen Christian College
문서 종류	교장 보고서
제출 시기	1939년 2월 23일
작성 장소	서울
제 출 자	H. H. Underwood
수 신 자	이사회
페이지 수	7
출 처	2114-5-4: 07 Underwood, Horace H. (DR.) 1939 Jan. to Feb. (UMAH)

자료 소개

원한경 교장이 1939년 2월 23일 열린 이사회 연례회의에서 제출한 보고서이다. 이 보고서는 이전과는 매우 다른 분위기를 드러내고 있다. 1937년 이후 검거 선풍으로 인한 학교 교수진의 극심한 변동은 이묘묵이 학감 보고서[목차 52번]에서 어느 정도 설명하였다. 그런데 이 일은 학교가 당면한 심각한 일들의 하나에 불과하였다. 연희전문은 신사참배 문제와 관련하여 그때까지 양대 후원 세력이었던 ① 장로교 선교사들, ② 한국 교회와 사회로부터 학교의 존폐를 선택하라는 상반된 압력을 받고 있었다. 선교사들은 폐교를, 한국 사회는 유지를 요구하였다. 이 보고서는 그러한 상황에서 작성되었다.

원한경은 이 보고서에서 아래의 사항들에 관해 설명하였다.

중진급 교수들의 대거 사임, 주요 보직들의 잦은 교체, 신진 교수들의 중용, 북장로회 측의 관계 절연 통첩, 세브란스의전 교장직 제안, 오긍선 세의전 교장의 기독교 학교 통합 제안, 일본인 교수 영입 노력, 회계업무 담당자 변동과 교직원 봉급 조정안, 존 T. 언더우드 유산 유치의 어려움, 학생 훈육의 필요성과 각 분야 학생 활동.

내용 요약

교수 동향: 내(원한경)가 학교에 몸담은 24년 기간과 교장으로 지낸 5년 기간은 힘든 일의 연속이었다. 가장 큰 어려움은 기강이 해이해지는 시기를 맞은 것이지만, 한 해 동안

잘 지켜왔다. 정인보, 백낙준, 이순탁, 백남운, 노동규 등 13명 이상의 중진 교수들을 여러 사유로 잃은 것도 큰 어려움이었다. 이춘호, 최현배, 홍승국, 이원철, 장석영, 최순주, 현제명 등이 학교 측의 요청으로 복직을 허가받았으나, 현제명이 또다시 체포되었다. 빈번한 보직 교체 속에서 이묘묵, 최규남, 하경덕, 임병혁 등의 젊은 교수들이 운영의 책임을 지게 되었다.

관계 절연: 북장로회 한국 선교회가 7월 평양에서 모여 연희전문학교에서의 철수를 결정하고 소속 선교사들에게 1939년 3월까지 이사회와 교수진에서 떠나도록 권고하였다. 뉴욕의 북장로회 선교부도 1941년 3월 말까지 대학에서 철수할 것을 결정하였다는 통지문을 1939년 1월 13(?)일 보내왔다. 이에 학교에서 만장일치의 결정으로 선교회에 항의 서한을 보냈고, 뉴욕 선교부에도 유감을 표명하는 문제를 논의하고 있다.

세의전 교장직 제안: 세브란스에서 내게 교장직을 제안하여 내가 수용할 뜻을 밝혔고, 실행위원회도 1938년 3월 17일 이 일을 승인하였으나, 세브란스 운영진의 반발과 총독부 학무당국의 의심을 사서 11월 10일 세브란스 이사회에 사임을 통보하였다. 내가 세브란스의 상황을 바르게 판단하지 못하여 물의가 빚어진 것에 대해 본교 이사회에 사과한다.

오긍선 제안: 오긍선 세브란스의전 교장이 몇 주 전에 만나기를 요청하고 연합 문제를 제기하였다. 나는 연합의 원칙에는 찬성하나 현실적인 여건에서는 어떠한 계획도 세울 수 없다고 말하였고, 오긍선은 두 대학만 아니라 다른 기독교 학교들까지 연합하여 교육의 중심지를 만들자고 제안하였다. 이 대화가 신문에 보도되면서 많은 오해가 발생하였다.

일본인 교수: 일본인 교수 2명마저 사임하였다. 기독교인 일본인 교수를 얻기 위해 초가을에 도쿄에 가서 대학설립 때 도움을 주었던 현 교육부 수장 세키야를 만나고 여러 곳을 다니면서 몇 사람을 구하였다. 귀국 후에는 오가와를 얻었는데, 그를 교수로 임명해주기를 요청한다.

회계업무: 최순주가 9월에 사임하여 스나이더가 회계업무를 맡았는데, 지출이 급격히 늘어나고 있던 때에 ¥4,000의 특별 기부금을 확보해왔다. 봉급 조정 문제는 다음 해에 검토하고 전임강사의 봉급만 가족 부양을 위해 ¥80에서 ¥100으로 인상하는 것이 좋으리라고 생각한다.

언더우드의 유산: 존 T. 언더우드의 유산에서 학교 자본금을 얻기를 원하지만, 뉴욕 협력이사회의 [실행 총무] 스와인하트가 몸이 아파서 일을 처리하지 못하고 있다.

학생: 신학기에 174명을 선발하여 등록생이 총 478명(문과 158명, 상 238명, 수물과 82명)이 되었다. 3월 13일에는 이들 중에서 116명이 졸업할 것으로 예상된다. 교수의 부재, 새 학년의 시작, 혼란한 대학 상황 속에서 학생들의 기율을 유지해주기를 당부한다.

지난여름 학생들이 서해 기린도 교회에서 봉사활동을 하였고, 주일 오후에 시내 교회에서 봉사활동을 하였다. 운동경기도 경제적인 여건과 국내 상황 때문에 축소되었다. 윤인구 목사가 이끈 연례 특별집회가 방금 끝났다.

Appendix I

Report to the Board of Managers

of

Chosen Christian College

February 23, 1939

Gentlemen:-

This is the fifth annual report which I have had the honor of presenting to you and this is the 24th year of my connection with the College. Neither during the five years of my administration nor at any time during my connection to the College do I recollect a year which has been so full of difficulties and dangers to the College. All the more, therefore, do I feel the deepest gratitude to God who has guided us through the year, and, under God, to the faithful and fearless service of the various members of our teaching and administrative staff.

On account of these difficulties I confess with regret that I have no startling accomplishments to report and no great achievements to record. But the daily work of the College has been carried on. Our Chapel services have been maintained at a high standard. More personal visitation of the students has been done than in the past. While there have been times when there was a slump in morale, on the whole, I think, that both morale and discipline have been fairly maintained throughout the year. The greatest of our difficulties has been the loss or absence for long periods of no less than 13 of the senior members of our staff. Prof. I. F. Chung has been away on account of health for the entire year, Dr. Paik has not returned from America. The absences of these two men alone would have been seriously felt, but at the very beginning of the year Prof. S. T. Lee, Director of the Commercial Department, Prof. N. W. Paik, and Prof. T. K. Rho, were arrested and after a lengthy investigation by the police have been indicted on charges of propagating communism. These three gentlemen presented their resignation under date of December 28, 1938 and the resignation were accepted.

In May, Mr. C. C. Hyen of the treasurer's office and Prof. C. H. Lee who had shortly before been appointed Dean were arrested. Following this the Vice-President, Prof. U. K. Yu; Prof. H. P. Choi, Acting Director of the Literary Department; and Prof. S. K. Hong, Acting Director of the Commercial Department were arrested in July. In September, Prof. D. W. Lee at that time Acting Dean; Rev. S. Y. Chai and Prof. S. J. Choy, Treasurer of the College, were also arrested. These gentlemen were charged with having connections with movements for Korean nationalism and all of them presented their resignations.

As in the somewhat similar case in the previous year, the College of course, had no desire to retain on its staff men who might be guilty of the charges brought against these men. I am happy to say that the care and direction of the Sh'sho Kwansatsu Sho (Parole Board), six of these men have been cleared of the stigma formerly attaching to them and an application has been made to the Educational Department for teaching permits for Messrs. C. H. Lee; H. P. Choi; S. K. Hong; D. W. Lee; S. Y. Chang and S. J. Choy. By the kind permission of the authorities, Rev. S. Y. Chang has been permitted to assume certain religious duties in the College although not yet teaching and Dr. S. J. Chey has received permission to again act as Treasurer. In addition to this, Mr. C. C. Hyen was on unconditionally released in September. I must also regretfully report the fact that Dr. Rody Hyun was arrested in December on an entirely different charge and his case is now before the procurator. The loss of these teachers naturally cast a gloom over both the faculty and students; upset the teaching schedules and brought upon the College heavy expenses, as both the men detained by the police and their substitutes had to be paid. However, while there were periods when this or that class was interrupted, in the main, teaching of all classes has gone forward and substitute teachers have been secured. The Government-General Educational officials have been most kind and helpful, especially in securing substitute teachers as well as in many other ways. At the present time, Judge M. Toyoshima of the Court of Appeal; Mr. S. Kido of the Preparatory School of the Keijo Imperial University; Mr. K. Matsunami of Keijo Law College are each giving several periods a week to assist us and for this we are very grateful. During this whole period, we have leaned heavily upon Mr. Nima and Mr. [illegible] of our [illegible] Board of Managers and it is impossible to tell you either how much they have done for us or how grateful we are to them.

On our own staff, the very splendid group of younger teachers have risen to the occasion and have ably shouldered the responsibilities placed upon them. Even yet, we do not know just how our staff will be composed during the coming year and I have therefore made temporary appointments which may be changed as circumstances change. I must assure you, however, that Dr. M. M. Lee as Acting Dean, Dr. K. N. Choi, Dr. K. D. Har, and Mr. P. K. Lim as Acting Departmental Directors have given splendid and untiring service. To suddenly assume these offices at any time is difficult but to be required to take over under the circumstances of last year, was doubly difficult and the greater portion of credit should be given to these men and to the others who held these offices during these time.

As Dean, Dr. C. H. Lee succeeded Prof. U. K. Yu; Dr. D. W. Lee followed Mr. C. L. Lee and in September, Dr. M. M. Lee undertook the work, being the fourth to hold that position since the Board met last. In the Science Department, Dr. D. W. Lee took Mr. C. Y. Lee's place and was then followed by Dr. K. N. Choi. In the Literary Department, Prof. H. P. Choi acted in Dr. Paik's place and Dr. K. D. Har took Prof. H. P. Choi's place when it became vacant. In the Commercial Department, Mr. J. K. Hong served during the first period of Mr. S. T. Lee's detention. Dr. S. J. Chey served for a short time after Mr. S. K. Hong left us and then Prof. P. K. Lim took over. The loss of the older men and the assumption of the responsibility taken over by the younger men made necessary and desirable several promotions. I, therefore, on September 30th secured by circular vote your approval for the appointment of Dr. M. M. Lee; Dr. K. D. Har; Dr. K. N. Choi; Mr. P. K. Lim; Mr. I. S. Jung; and Mr. C. Y. Lee as full professors and Dr. H. K. Karl as Assistant Professor. You having previously approved the re-appointment of Dr. C. M. Hyun as Professor and Dr. M. M. Lee, Dr. K. D. Har as Assistant Professors and Dr. H. K. Karl as Instructor. The difficulties of the year however have not been confined to the personell losses referred to in the above.

The Chosen Mission of the Presbyterian Church in U.S.A. met in Pyeng Yang in July and in pursuance of its policy of withdrawal from educational work passed the following action:

> "Withdrawal from Chosen Christian College. Recommend that we withdraw our Mission representatives from the Board of Managers and the Staff of the Chosen Christian College in March, 1939."

This was formally transmitted to me by the Chairman of the Mission, Executive Committee under date of January 17, 1939, together with the information that the Board in New York had cabled as follows.

> "Board voted date withdrawal colleges end of March 1941."

Dr. Rhodes also on the same date informs me of the following supplementary action:

> "Work in connection with secular schools. Recommend that no member of the Mission be permitted to occupy a position of control, administration, or full time teaching in any institution of secular education from which the Mission withdraws. Nevertheless, this action shall not prevent the members of the Mission from engaging in part time Bible teaching or other religious activities in any school."

A protest against these actions were signed by more than 70 members of the Mission and sent to the Board in New York on July and it is at least possible that this protest as well as the representations made by Dr. Armstrong of the United Church of Canada may have influenced the Board to delay their withdrawal until 1941.

This action by the Presbyterian Mission which has had so large a part in the conduct of the College since its foundation was much regretted by us all and a number felt that it would be desirable for the Board of Managers to express its gratitude for the part which they had played, our regret at their withdrawal and our hope that some plan for continuance might be arrived at. Those favoring this idea conferred with me as to the modus operandi. There seemed to be no by-laws of this Board as to the initiation and procedure in regard to a circular vote and it also seemed both difficult and unnecessary to call a special meeting. After consultation with Dr. A. L. Becker who has served both as Acting President and Vice-President and is the senior member of this Board, it seemed proper to initiate it under the form of a motion made by one member and seconded by another. The resolution was therefore moved by Mr. Shin Pong Cho and seconded by Dr. A. L. Becker and circulated under date of July 11th, 1938. The action was passed but I must report that a letter protesting against the procedure was received from [illegible] which letter should presumably be taken as a negative vote. With this exception all the replies received were unanimously in favor of the action. It was, therefore, forwarded to the Presbyterian Board of Foreign Missions.

The action as sent expressed to the Presbyterian Board our regret at their withdrawal, our hope that a plan already suggested by some members of the Mission might be approved and our gratitude for their past cooperation. It is quite possible that in the lack of by-laws on the subject, I was out of order in in presenting such an action for circular vote. It is also quite possible for this body to either censure me for the irregularity of the procedure or to reverse the action taken at that time. I must, however, take issue on the question of the propriety of the action. This body has previously asked other churches or groups to join in cooperation with us. We have in the past presented appeals to certain Missions when they reduced their representation on the faculty and when they reduced the appropriation previously made. Surely, it is not inappropriate to express our thanks for past cooperation, our regret at the action which would separate them from us and our hope that some plan for continued cooperation might be arrived at. For the College Board to take action on something which concerned only the Mission would certainly be highly inappropriate. This action directly affects the College and most intimately concerns us. The action offers no criticism, but an earnest regret; it urges, it could not in any sense constrain or nullify. I cannot therefore see any impropriety in a respectfully worded request that they continue the cooperation which we have enjoyed for the past 24 years.

Still another matter which has caused me some embarrassment and may possibly have affected the College was the election of myself as president of the Severance Union Medical College. At the time of the election, it seemed as though I might be able to be of some service to that institution and that with a slight reorganization of administration in this College, the cause of Christ and the best interest of both colleges could be served. The Executive Committee met on March 17th and after very full and free discussion voted to approve my acceptance of the Presidency. However, it soon developed that this action was unwelcome to the administration at Severance and it later became apparent that the Government-General Educational authorities were very doubtful as to the wisdom of permitting one individual to serve as president of the two colleges. During the spring and summer, while we were awaiting some action from the Educational Department, the situation in this College became such that I would have found it very difficult to take over any additional work. I, therefore, sent in my resignation as president to the Severance Board on November 10th, 1938. This was accepted by the Board and was so reported to the Educational authorities. I wish to express my regret to this Board for any embarrassment which I may have caused the College by my failure to correctly estimate the situation at Severance.

The question of the possible union of this institution and Severance is still talked of and has recently been given some publicity in the newspapers. Dr. K. S. Oh asked for a conference with me some weeks ago and again broached this question. I replied that I was still in favor of the principle of union, but that I would be unwilling to sacrifice the exceedingly favorable constitution graciously granted to this College and could not, therefore, favor any plan unless it could be consummated under the provisions of the existing charter. I also informed Dr. Oh that I doubted if the present was an auspicious time to push for such a union. In the course of the conversation, he talked of a possible educational center under which should be grouped not only Severance and the Chosen Christian College, but other Christian institutions. As reported in the newspapers, this conversation has given rise to considerable misunderstanding. Actually, I told Dr. Oh that anything beyond the union of our two colleges, was a matter for future consideration and dependent upon the desires of any institutions to be concerned and that in my mind no direct steps could be taken at the present time, however, ideally desirable, such a plan might seem. Dr. Oh stated that their Board of

5

Assessors would probably present to you some action on the question of union and I told him that any such action would of course receive your careful and prayerful consideration.

The loss of so many teachers and the resignation for other reasons of two of our Japanese professors made it imperative to secure for the institution the assistance of some capable Christian Japanese. I, therefore, asked for a meeting of the Executive Committee on September 12th and with their approval went to Japan in an attempt to secure such help.

Both in Tokyo and in the early fall before going to Tokyo, the Honorable Mr. Seikiya, head of the Educational Department, when this College was founded, was of great assistance and I cannot find words to express our gratitude to him for his untiring interest in and assistance to the College. I visited Shimonoseki, Fukuoka, Kobe, Kyoto, Yokohama, and Tokyo, but was unable at the time to secure any one who would fulfill the requirements which we had laid down. However, I think, the trip was worthwhile in the connections established with educators and educational institutions and I was able to get a line on a number of men. We have been active in correspondence and investigating ever since my return and I expect at the opening of the new College year to have at least one if not two of these men serving on our staff. In addition to men from Japan, I report with great pleasure that we have been fortunate in securing the service of Mr. K. Ogawa, who was formerly connected with the Higher Technical College of this city. Mr. Ogawa is a Christian and a man of very fine personality. He came to us in the fall as a part-time teacher and soon made a place for himself both among the teachers and students. You will notice that I have recommended him to you for appointment as a Professor

It is my hope to continue the work of strengthening our faculty by the addition of teachers from Japan Proper until we have a more adequate representation of such teachers.

Our Treasurer, Dr. S. J. Choy was on leave of absence in Japan from April to August and as above reported, resigned in September. Mr. L. E. Snyder, therefore, took over the duties of the Treasurer's office and carried on most satisfactorily. This was not at all easy as Mr. Snyder is carrying what most men would call a full assignment in his own Mission. In addition to the routine work in the treasurer's office Mr. Snyder was able to secure from anonymous sources, special gifts amounting to over ¥4,000. You may perhaps imagine how welcome this was in a year when we have watched the expenditures rapidly climbing skyward. I must also add a very strong word of praise for Mr. K. H. Yi, the assistant in the treasurer's office who has had to carry the heaviest burden of this office almost alone througout the year. With Dr. Choy in Japan, Mr. Hyon away and Miss Chang sick, he has carried an unbelievable heavy burden.

For the coming year, we have prepared and present to you today a balanced Budget. This was done partly by a fortunate increase in the endowment income, and partly by the strictest economy and also by an increase in such supplementary fees as Library, Physical Education, Dormitory and the like, though it seemed unwise at present to ask the Educational Department for permission to increase the tuition fees. I must, also report with great gratitude a slightly increased appropriation from the Methodist Episcopal Board. The amount of increase is not startlingly large, but in a day when withdrawals, cuts, and retrenchment seems to be the rule, this action is refreshingly encouraging.

In view of the financial difficulties and the uncertainty as to how our staff will be constituted and also on account of the press of other affairs, it has been impossible to complete the work of revising the salary scale during this year. I must beg your consideration for this failure and ask that you allow the Committee to continue its work during the coming year. This does not mean that no work has been done. Dr. L. N. Choi and Mr. Y. H. Lee, faculty representatives of this Committee have both submitted elaborate and carefully thought out plans. It is questionable, however, until more adequate endowment is provided whether we can contemplate the more adequate salary rates which are recommended in the higher brackets of the scale.

That educational qualification, experience and years of faithful service should be properly rewarded is agreed by all, but it is useless and misleading to recommend rewards which is beyond our powers to give. For the present year and pending the revision of the scale, I have taken two arbitrary actions for which I have secured the approval of your Finance Committee. I have raised the salaries of full-time Instructors from ¥80 to ¥100 as it seems impossible for young men with growing families and with a high standard of living forced upon them by their positions to make ends meet on ¥80 a month. At the other end of the scale, I have temporarily held up all salary raises for the higher salaried men even when indicated by the present salary scale. I have no desire to discriminate against these men all of whom are my personal friends and valued colleagues, but felt that at least for the time being such action was imperative.

Reference to financial matters brings me to a consideration of the Cooperating Board in New York and their work in our behalf. The Finance Committee of that Board has been very active, they have cleared out certain properties which were a liability rather than an asset and have regretfully written this off as a loss. On the other hand with the advice of Mr. Reed, the President of the Board, they have made a careful re-investment and are continuing the study of how best to invest both the Underwood bequest and other funds which have been temporarily idle. This promises increased income, but no safe investment scheme can provide adequate income from the present endowment. We must secure additional capital funds. This work in its turn has been greatly held up both by the continued ill health of Capt. Swinehart and by the uncertainty as to the future cooperation of certain Boards. A recent letter from Capt. Swinehart states that his health is much better and that he still hopes to be able to be of help and assistance to us. I, myself, believe that it is imperative that someone should undertake the work of at least of maintaining the interest of the present friends of the institution. I hope and believe that the Cooperating Board in New York will find means to do this.

Lastly, I must say a word for our students. We admitted 194 new students at the opening of the College year bringing our enrollment to a total of 478 which were divided between the different Departments as follows: Literary Department 158; Commercial Department 238; and the Science Department 82. Considering the national emergency as well as the present situation in the College, I think, the enrollment has held very well. We find ourselves at present with an enrollment of 455 of whom 116 are expected to graduate on March 13. As stated in the earlier of the report, the absence of old teachers, coming of the new, and the disturbed conditions of the College, have permitted a certain relaxation in the conduct of the students, but in the main the spirit and discipline have well been maintained in the College.

The students last summer continued the island work established in Korrindo in the Yellow Sea. For the first time they were accompanied by the Rev. S. Y. Chang, Professor of Bible and Student Pastor. On reaching the island they found a group of young people waiting for baptism, as no Pastor had visited the island for almost five years. It was very impressive to be present at this service and see the fruits of the students effort.

Other student work has been more or less interrupted and certain forms hav of necessity been suspended, but a large number of our students continue, as in the past, to render very valuable service Sunday after Sunday in the churches of the city, its suburbs and the nearby country.

Athletics also have been reduced on account of the necessity for economy and on account of the situation throughout the whole country. However, our teams have conducted themselves in a manner to bring honor to the College both in the events which they have won and in the events where they have lost.

We have just completed the annual special religious services which were lead by the Rev. In Koo Yun from Masan. Mr. Yun has been greatly blessed in this work in the past and while it is always impossible by material and numerical standards, I feel sure that his work has greatly helped us all and that we will continue to reap of its fruits in the future.

In closing, I think, I have reasons to believe that the coming year will see us in a much better position in many ways than in the past. The restoration of a number of the previous teachers, the coming of new and well qualified teachers from Japan Proper and a greater realization of the necessity for more careful supervision along many lines promise well.

God has very wonderfully blessed this institution since its founding and I firmly believe that He will continue to bless the efforts which we are putting forth to train Christian young men to take their place in the nation and in the world.

We thank you all for your time and effort which you so generously give to the work of this Institution and would beg that you continue to be earnest in prayer for the College.

Yours very respectfully,

Horace H. Underwood

Horace H. Underwood
President

55. 이묘묵 학감의 이사회 제출 연례보고서

문서 제목	Chosen Christian College, Report of the Dean 1939~1940
문서 종류	학감 보고서
제출 시기	1940년 2월 20일
작성 장소	서울
제 출 자	이묘묵
수 신 자	H. H. Underwood, 이사회
페이지 수	22
출 처	2114-5-4: 09 Underwood, Horace H. (DR.) 1940 (UMAH)

자료 소개

이묘묵 학감이 1940년 2월 23일 열린 이사회 연례회의를 위해 2월 20일 자로 원한경 교장에게 미리 보낸 보고서이다. 이묘묵은 지난해에도 보고서를 회의일 전에 원한경 교장에게 보냈다. 그때는 회의에 참석하였어도 보고서를 읽지 않았으나, 이번에는 구두로 교육과정 변경과 교수진의 변동에 대해 보고하였다. [이 교육과정 변경은 1937년 중일전쟁 발발, 1938년 조선인에 대한 육군지원병 제도 시행, 3차 조선교육령을 통한 조선어교육 금지 등으로 일제가 황국신민화정책을 강화하던 상황에서 이루어졌다.] 이사회는 이날 백낙준과 신과 과장 코엔의 사임을 승인하였고, 장기원을 교수로 임명하였으며, 고형곤, 장희창, 김정록, 고병국, 한인석을 전임강사에서 조교수로 승급시켰다. 또한 이 해에 맞이하는 개교 25주년의 행사를 포기하고 동문회와 함께 모금행사를 하기로 하였다.

이 문서는 표지(1쪽), 원한경에게 보낸 편지(2~3쪽), 보고서(4~22쪽)로 대별 된다. 보고서는 지난해처럼 목차를 구성하면서, 박물관만 도서관 항목으로 옮기고 있다.

I. 운영진과 교수진, II. 3개 학과, III. 종교활동, IV. 도서관과 박물관, V. 체육 교육, VI. 음악 활동, VII. 다른 사항들, VIII. 학생, IX. 졸업생.

내용 요약

◪ 원한경에게 보내는 편지

이 보고서는 본교가 극히 힘든 시련의 해에 이룬 영적 승리에 대한 신실한 기록이다.

총독부 학무국의 제안에 따라 변경되는 교육과정은 7가지 특징을 띠고 있다. ① 1939년 9월부터 주 1시간 군사교련 시행, ② 문과의 조선어 과목(주 5시간) 폐지, ③ 일본문화: 전교생 주 1시간 수강, ④ 일본사: 신입생은 주 2시간, 문과 2학년은 2시간 추가 수강, ⑤ 중국어: 문과 4시간, 상과 6시간, 수물과 4시간 수강, ⑥ 수물과 신입생 30명에서 40명으로 증원[수물과는 이후에 '이과'로 개칭되었다], ⑦ 독일어: 수물과 6시간 필수 수강.

마츠모토(松本卓夫) 교수가 새로 오고 원일한[H. G. Underwood, 원한경의 아들]이 교수로 온 것은 큰 행운이다.

◪ 보고서

I. 에비슨이 명예 교장이다. 운영진은 원한경(교장), 베커(부교장), 이묘묵(학감 겸 도서관장), 하경덕(문과 과장대리), 임병혁(상과 과장대리), 최규남(수물과 과장대리), 최순주(회계)이다. 대학 교무위원회는 원한경, 베커, 이묘묵, 하경덕, 임병혁, 최규남, 케이블 · 스나이더, 최순주로 구성되어 있다. 대학 예산위원회는 원한경, 베커, 이묘묵, 하경덕, 임병혁, 최규남, 케이블, 스나이더, 최순주로 구성되어 있다. 교수는 19명(한국인 9명), 조교수는 5명(모두 한국인), 전임강사는 15명(한국인 13명), 강사와 조수는 14명(한국인 12명), 파트타임 조력자는 4명, 부재 교수는 3명(베커, 정인보, 현제명), 사임한 교수는 11명(김광진, 양능점(Yang Neung Chum), 스피델, 쿤스, 빌링스, 박극채, 김용환, 최황, 백낙준, 우메사와, 김영성), 사무직원은 13명(사감 포함)이다.

II. 본교는 종합대학 체제를 이루고 있다. 문과에서는 과장 백낙준이 8월에 귀국한 후 곧 사임하였고, 정인보가 오랜 병가 끝에 임시 사임 명단에 올랐다. 민태식이 중국 문학을 맡았고, 교련 수업을 하고 있다. 상과에서는 신태환(전임강사), 김효록(강사) 등이 새로 왔고, 상품진열관 운영, 상업 실습 교육, 광고방법 연구, 영어교육 연구를 수행하였다. 수물과에서는 오가와, 장기원이 교수가 되었고, 베커가 6월 안식년으로 떠났으며, 이효순이 부임하였다. 교수들의 월례회가 계속 열렸고, 수물과연구실, 과학박물관이 운영되었다.

III. 채플 예배는 주 4회 시행되었고, 학생들의 방학 기간 교회 봉사활동, 일요일 교회활동, 연희전문과 이화여전 학생들의 연합교회 참석, 교수 기도회가 잘 수행되었다.

VI. 도서관은 개교 25주년과 일본 개국 2,600주년 기념으로 기금을 모아 일본책 865권을 샀고, 511권을 기증받았다. (잡지와 신문의 소장 현황과 직원 상황을 설명하고 있다.) 박물관은 분류작업을 하고 있다.

V. 올해에도 모든 팀이 대회에 참가하였고, 여러 팀이 우승하였으며, 조선을 대표하여 만주국, 북중국 팀들과 친선경기를 가졌다. 일부 팀은 전국 순회 경기와 일본 원정경기를 가졌다. (테니스, 축구, 농구, 자전거, 유도, 육상, 아이스하키의 전적을 설명하고 있다.)

VI. 음악 활동은 축소되었고, 박경호가 계속 가르치고 있다. 그런 가운데 17회 추기 음악회를 시청에서 열었다.

VII. 학생지원 업무로서 9명의 근로학생을 도왔고, 2명에게 성적 장학금을, 25명에게 장학금을 주었다. (장학금 기부자와 수령자 명단을 제시하고 있다. 학생 클럽 및 단체의 목록을 제시하고 있다.)

VIII. 학생은 1월 31일까지 총 435명(문과 121명, 상과 235명, 수물과 79명)이 등록하였고, 본과는 410명, 별과는 25명이었다. (출신 지역 현황을 표로 제시하고 있다.)

IX. 졸업생은 총 918명이고, 현재 연전 교수 12명, 연전 직원 10명, 다른 기독교학교 교사 47명, 교회 사역 9명, 비기독교학교 교사 110명, 의학생 3명, 미국 · 독일 유학 26명, 일본 유학 53명, 언론인 13명, 은행원 및 회사원 145명, 공무원 72명, 개인사업(상공업) 179명, 농업 5명, 다양한 개인사업[家業] 186명, 의사 1명, 광업 4명, 사망 43명이다. 졸업생이 갖는 자격은 이전 보고서 내용과 같다.

802

CHOSEN CHRISTIAN COLLEGE

Report of the Dean

1939 - 1940

****
**
*

February 20, 1940

Dr. Horace H. Underwood, Ph.D., Litt. D.
Office of the President
Chosen Christian College
Seoul, Korea

My dear President Underwood:-

Once more I have the honor of submitting to you an annual report chiefly dealing with the academic phase of the College for the year 1939-1940, which marks the 25th anniversary of our College.

This report, however, contains nothing either spectacular or boastful. Neither do I expect you to find anything new in it, for you have been steering the institution and have kept in touch with everything going on on the campus. If this report has any merit or any distinction at all, it is a faithful record of one of the most difficult and trying years that our College ever went through and it is also a true picture of a spiritual victory over greedy and selfish aggrandizement.

This spiritual victory, which is after all a true realization of the noble aims set by the founder of our College, is brought about by your assiduous patience and the undivided support of the Directors of the three Departments. For your constant encouragement and utmost confidence in me and for the hearty cooperation of the other administrators and the whole staff, I have no words to express my gratitude.

Neither am I forgetful in acknowledging our indebtedness to the government authorities and army officers. Through the good offices of the Army Headquarters in Choson, our senior students were admitted to the armory to work during the summer labor period. And our curricula revision was kindly suggested and constantly helped by the educational authorities of the Government-General.

The outstanding changes of the curricula are as follows:

(1) Military Drill, an hour per week, was introduced to the College in September, 1939;

(2) The Korean Language course, 5 hours per week, are entirely dropped from the Literary Department curriculum;

(3) Japanese Culture (Nippon Gaku), an hour per week, is added to each class throughout all Departments;

(4) National History, 2 hours to each Freshman Class and 2 more hours to the Sophomore Class of the Literary Department are added;

(5) The Chinese Language is put on the required list:- 4 hours in the Literary Department, 6 hours in the Commercial Department, and 4 hours in the Science Department;

-2-

(6) The number of the Science Freshman Class is increased from 30 to 40; and

(7) German, 6 hours, is required in the Science Department.

The application for the revision of the curricula is still in the hands of the Government authorities; and we hope to have the new schedule be in force beginning with coming April.

I cannot help feeling that we were very fortunate in securing such a fine group of teachers last year, who are all very upright Christians. We are also looking forward to the coming of Dr. Takuo Matsumoto, a splendid Christian leader and an accomplished scholar on the New Testament and of Mr. Horace Grant Underwood, a young man whose name itself carries a deep affection among the Koreans and of whom everything great could be expected. He is a third generation member of the Underwood family, who has consecrated himself to the cause of Korea and of Koreans.

Respectfully submitted by

Myo-Mook Lee
Dean

CHOSEN CHRISTIAN COLLEGE
Report of the Dean
(1939-1940)

CONTENTS

I. Officers of Administration and Instruction.

A. President Emeritus.

O. R. Avison, M.D., LL.D. (Toronto and Wooster), residing in U.S.A.

B. Officers of Administration.

Horace H. Underwood, M.A., Ph.D., Litt.D., President
A. L. Becker, M.A., Ph.D., Vice-President (On furlough)
Myo-Mook Lee, M.A., Ph.D., Dean and Librarian
Kyung Duk Har, M.A., Ph.D., Acting Director of Literary Department
Pyung Hyuk Lim, M.A., Acting Director of Commercial Department
Kyu Nam Choi, M.A., Ph.D., Acting Director of Science Department
Soon Ju Choy, M.B.A., Ph.D., Treasurer

C. College Council.

Horace H. Underwood, Ph.D., Litt.D., President
A. L. Becker, M.A., Ph.D., Vice-President (On furlough)
Myo-Mook Lee, M.A., Ph.D., Dean and Librarian
Kyung Duk Har, M.A., Ph.D., Acting Director of the Literary Department
Pyung Hyuk Lim, M.A., Acting Director of the Commercial Department
Kyu Nam Choi, M.A., Ph.D., Acting Director of the Science Department
E. M. Cable, D.D., Representative of the M.E.C. Mission
L. H. Snyder, M.A., Representative of the M.E.C. Mission, South
Soon Ju Choy, M.B.A., Ph.D., Treasurer

D. College Budget Committee.

Horace H. Underwood, Ph.D., Litt.D., President
A. L. Becker, M.A., Ph.D., Vice-President (On furlough)
Myo-Mook Lee, M.A., Ph.D., Dean and Librarian
Kyung Duk Har, Ph.D., Acting Director of the Literary Department
Pyung Hyuk Lim, M.A., Acting Director of the Commercial Department
Kyu Nam Choi, Ph.D., Acting Director of the Science Department
E. M. Cable, D.D., Representative of the M.E.C. Mission
L. H. Snyder, M.A., Representative of the M.E.C. Mission, South
S. J. Choy, Ph.D., Treasurer

F. Faculty.

(1) Professors (19)

H. H. Underwood, B.A., M.A., Ph.D., Litt.D., (New York University and Mount Union). President of the College and Professor of Education, Psychology and English, 1915 ----.

A. L. Becker, B.A., M.A., Ph.D., (Michigan). Vice-President of the College, Professor of Physics and Mathematics, 1915 ---- (On furlough)

(1) Professors (Continued)

Myo-Mook Lee, C.C.C. Graduate, M.A., Ph.D., (Syracuse, Harvard, Boston). Dean, Librarian, and Professor of Western History and English, 1934 ----

Kyung Duk Har, M.A., Ph.D., (Harvard). Acting Director of the Literary Department and Professor of English, 1932 ----

Pyung Hyuck Lim, C.C.C. Graduate, B.A., M.A., (Syracuse). Acting Director of the Commercial Department and Professor of Bank Bookkeeping, Commodities, and Business English, 1932 ----

Kyu Nam Choi, C.C.C. Graduate, M.A., Ph.D., (Michigan). Acting Director of the Science Department and Professor of Physics and Mathematics, 1933 ----

E. H. Miller, B.D., M.A., Ph.D., (Columbia). Professor of Chemistry, English and Bible, 1915 ----

C. Nikaido, Gakushi, (Tokyo Imperial University). Professor of Japanese, Japanese Literature and Introduction to Literature, 1927 ---

Bong Chip Kim, Gakushi, (Waseda University). Professor of Physics and Electrical Engineering, 1927 ----

In Po Chung, Professor of Chinese Literature and Korean Literature, 1922 ---- (On Leave of Absence)

Rody Cheymyung Hyun, M.Mus., D.Mus., (Gunn and Chicago Conservatory). Professor of Music, 1929 ---- (On Leave of Absence)

E. M. Cable, B.S., M.A., D.D., (Cornell College).. Professor of English, Bible and History, 1932 ----

L. H. Snyder, B.A., M.A., (Princeton). Professor of English and Typewriting, 1933 ----

R. C. Coen, B.A., B.D., M.A., (Chicago). Professor of Bible and English, 1933 ----

Ounn Yong Lee, (Berlin University). Professor of German, 1926 ----

Insub Jung, Gakushi, (Waseda University). Professor of English, Phonetics, Introduction to Literature, and English Literature, 1929 ----

K. Ogawa, (Tokyo Tech.), Civil Engineering, 1938 ----

Ki Won Chang, C.C.C. Graduate, Gakushi (Tohoku University), Mathematics, 1930 ----

Capt. Chang Ha Pak, (Professorial) Military Training, 1939 ----

-3-

(2) Assistant Professors. (5)

Hong Kee Karl, B.D., M.A., Ph.D., (Chicago). Assistant Professor of Philosophy of Religion and Bible, 1934 ----

Yang Ha Lee, Gakushi, (Tokyo Imperial University). English and English Literature, 1934 ----

Hyo Sam Pak, Gakushi, (Meiji University). Commercial Mathematics and Exchange, 1937 ----

Lai Kil Chung, Gakushi, (Keio University). Public Law, Finance, Economics, and Sociology, 1933 ----

Han Sang Ryu, Gakushi, (Waseda University). Chemistry, 1936 ----

(3) Instructors and Full-Time Lecturers. (15)

Mrs. H. H. Underwood, B.A., M.A., (New York University). English, 1918 ----

Lak Won Kang, Physical Education, 1927 ----

Chung Nok Kim, Graduate of Paiyoung College. The Chinese Language, 1934 ----

Mrs. E. M. Cable, B.A., (Cornell College). English, 1932 ----

Hyung Kon Ko, Gakushi, (Keijo University). Philosophy and Ethics, 1938 ----

In Suk Han, C.C.C. Graduate, Gakushi, (Tohoku University). Physics and Mathematics, 1938 ----

Sun Gi Gim, C.C.C. Graduate, M.A., (London). English and Phonetics, 1938 ----

Hee Chang Chang, C.C.C. Graduate, Gakushi, (Tokyo College of Commerce). Bookkeeping, Statistics, Money, 1932, 1938 ----

Pyung Kuk Ko, Gakushi, (Tokyo Imperial University). Law, 1938 ----

Tai Sik Min, Gakushi, (Keijo Imperial University). Chinese Classics, 1938 ----

Hyo Rok Kim, Gakushi, (Kobe Commercial College). Marketing, Principles of Commerce and Banking, 1939 ----

Eui Sul Cho, C.C.C. Graduate, Gakushi, (Tohoku Imperial University). Western History, 1939 ----

Ji Soo Ryuk, Gakushi, (Tokyo Imperial University). History of Economics, Commercial Geography, 1936 ----

Sang Hyun Pak, C.C.C. Graduate, Gakushi, (Kyushu Imperial University). Education, Psychology, Logic, 1939 ----

Tai Whan Shin, Gakushi, (Tokyo Commercial College). Economics, Commerce, 1939 ----

(4) Lecturers and Assistants. (14)

T. Yokoyama, B.A., B.D., Ph.D., (Johns Hopkins). English 1932 ----

Chin Tai Sohn, Gakushi, (Waseda University). Oriental History, 1934 ----

James Injun Park, B.S. in A.E., (Minnesota) and B.S. in M.E.,(Lewis Institute) Architecture, Construction, and Drawing, 1936 ----

Won Sik Min, B.A., (Nevada). French, 1936 ----

Kyung Ho Pak, B.S., (Cincinnati Conservatory). Music, 1936, 1938 ----

Tong Kil Pak, Gakushi, (Tohoku Imperial University). Mineralogy, 1938 ----

Kei Won Yi, M.A., (Michigan). Science English, 1938 -----

Sang Hoon Lee, Gakushi, (Tokyo Commercial College). Commercial Practice, 1938 ----

S. Kida, Gakushi, (Tokyo Imperial University). National History, 1938 ----

Chi Chung Kim, Gakushi, (Tokyo Imperial University). Mathematics, 1939 ----

Hyo Soon Lee, Graduate of Kyoto Imperial University, Civil Engineering, 1939 ---

Che Rin Cynn, C.C.C. Graduate, Assistant, Physics Laboratory, 1924 ----

Yong Hak Pak, B.A., M.A., (Southwestern University and Southern Methodist University). Secretary of the Religious Department, 1936 ----

Koo Cho Lee, C.C.C. Graduate, Assistant, Literary Department, 1939 ----

(5) Part-Time Assistants. (4)

Mrs. A. L. Becker (On furlough)
Mrs. R. C. Coen
Mrs. E. H. Miller
Mrs. L. H. Snyder

(6) Professors on Leave of Absence. (3)

A. L. Becker, M.A., Ph.D., Vice-President
I. P. Chung
Rody C. Hyun, M.Mus., D.Mus.

(7) Faculty and Staff Resigned. (11)

Kim Kwang Jin
Yang Neung Chum
G. C. Speidel
E. W. Koons
Paul Billings
Pak Keuk Chai
Kim Rong Whan
Charles Choi
L. G. Paik
K. Yonezawa
Young Sung Kim

F. Office Staff. (13)

Suk Young Chang, B.D., M.A., Student Pastor.

Chai Myung Sohn, C.C.C. Graduate, Secretary to Administration.

Chi Myung Song, C.C.C. Graduate, Superintendent of Dormitory.

Chi Kak Kim, C.C.C. Graduate, Superintendent of Grounds and Buildings.

Han Chul Shin, C.C.C. Graduate, Assistant to the Librarian.

Paul Hyen, B.A., (Shanghai). Accountant.

Yoon Yong Shim, C.C.C. Graduate, Secretary to Administration.

Kei Won Yi, C.C.C. Graduate, B.A., M.A., (Michigan). Cashier.

Pyung Sur Kimm, B.A. (C.C.C.). Clerical Assistant in the Library.

Miss Dora T. Ahn, Stenographer to the President.

Mrs. Sang Hoo Lyu, Graduate of Paiwha, Clerical Assistant of the Library.

Miss Duk Hee Whang, Assistant to the Cashier.

Sang Ik Nam, Assistant Secretary to the Administration.

II. The Three Departments of the College.

The College is organized on a university system and has four departments, but only three are in operation. These departments are separate so far as their internal organization is concerned with their respective directors, budgets, and recitation halls, but they are one in general administration and policy under one Dean.

A. Literary Department - Acting Director, Kyung-Duk Har, Ph.D.

There are 6 Professors, 2 Assistant Professors, 3 Instructors, and 5 Lecturers in the Literary Department.

The enrollment of the Department is as follows:

Freshman..................	42
Sophomore.................	29
Junior....................	21
Senior....................	29
	121

President Dr. Underwood took up the Senior English Composition course from the beginning of the academic year.

Dr. L. G. Paik, who went to America in May, 1937, returned to Korea in August. Immeditately after his return he tendored his resignation which was accepted. Dr. K. D. Bar has continued and is still continuing to act as Director of the Department.

Prof. I. P. Chung was placed on the list of temporary retirement on account of his long and serious illness. His Chinese Classics courses have been conducted by Mr. T. S. Min, Gakushi, of the Keijo Imperial University, who became a full-time Instructor in April, 1939. But the Korean Literature courses together with the Korean Language courses have been left vacant owing to unavoidable circumstances.

Two other full-time Instructors joined the teaching staff from the early part of the academic year: Messrs. Cho and Park. Mr. E. S. Cho, Gakushi, of the Tofuku Imperial University, took up the courses in Occidental History from April; and Mr. S. H. Park, Gakushi, of the Kyushu Imperial University, took up the courses of Psychology, Logic, and Education.

At the suggestion of the Government educational authorities, Military Drill, an hour a week for all classes, was added to the curriculum from September 1, and Captain C. H. Park was put in charge of the work. Also, the circumstances during the last several years led to a careful reconsideration of the present curriculum. A tentative curriculum was drafted in November and presented to the Bureau of Education for permission to adopt it. The most salient feature of the proposed curriculum is the addition of a new course in the History of the Japanese Culture, an hour a week for all classes, and the omission of the Korean Language courses. (See the attached sheet).

Mr. H. C. Cynn, Assistant for many years, was promoted and transfered to the Library, and in his stead Mr. K. C. Lee, a graduate of our College, took up the work from September 1.

Extra-Curriculum Activities

Owing to unavoidable circumstances, the annual Dramatic Play and the All-Korea Middle School English Oratorical Contest were discontinued. But the Varsity English Oratorical Contest was held with great success on December 15, preceded by preliminary contests in which about fifty students participated. The second and third prizes were won by students of the Department. The annual special lecture on Journalism was revised, and Dr. Hoon Koo Lee, Vice-President of the Chosen Dail News Company delivered a lecture on February 16th.

General Research Work

Materials in the Research Room: Up to the present 22 volumes of new books and magazines have been purchased, and 49 volumes received as gifts. One newspaper and three periodicals have been provided in the Research Room. The total collection in the Research Room consists of the following books:

Oriental Books.............. 1,916
Occidental Books............ 268
Pamphlets and Periodicals... 387
Total.... 2,571

Publications: About fifteen articles of interest have been contributed during the year by members of the Literary Department to various magazines and newspapers.

B. Commercial Department - Acting Director, Pyung-byuk K. Lim, M.A.

The Commercial Department is the largest Department of the College with a faculty of 3 Professors, 2 Assistant Professors, 4 Instructors, and 15 Lecturers, making a total of 24 members. The enrollment of this Department is as follows:

Seniors..................... 81
Sophomores.................. 72
Freshmen.................... 83
236

The following teachers have been added to the Department:

Mr. T. W. Shin, Lecturer; graduate of the Tokio University of Commerce. Mr. Shin teaches a number of Commercial subjects.

Mr. H. R. Kim, Instructor; graduate of the Kobe University of Commerce. Mr. Kim taught a number of years at the Soong-in Commercial School, Pyeng Yang. He teaches a number of Commercial subjects.

Mr. S. G. Gim, Instructor of the Literary Department, has been helping out in teaching English in the Commercial Department.

A brief report on the employment of the 68 graduates of last year may not be out of place here. Of this number 8 are attending universities in Japan Proper, 9 are teaching in the middle schools, 13 have positions in companies, 10 in various banking institutions, 7 in government offices, 11 are in private business, and the remaining 10 are attending family affairs.

Commercial Museum

The Commercial Museum has been growing steadily with additional specimens of native and foreign commodities, making a total number of 1,828. Mr. T. W. Shin is in charge of this work.

Commercial Practice Room

Along with the theoretical studies of Commerce and Economics, the practical side of the course is no less important. At the present time, there are 11 typewriters for the students to practice on. Furthermore, a special course in shorthand is offered for those students who take it as an extra curricula work. Professor L. H. Snyder is in charge of this work.

Commercial Research Work

The Commercial Research Work has been carried on by the faculty members. Their results have been published in the leading newspapers and magazines from time to time. There are 60 different magazines, 6 newspapers, and 2,906 volumes of reference books in the Research Room. Professor L. K. Jung is in charge of this work.

Research on Advertisement

The Commercial Department has begun this research work to study the method of advertising and for reference. Nearly 12,000 pieces of various kinds of posters, handbills, folders, labels, enamel and card signs, etc. have been collected. These have been carefully classified and displayed in the Commercial Practice Room and also in one of the teacher's rooms. Mr. Hyo Rok Kim is in charge of this work.

English Teachers' Research Club

Ever since the Club became a chartered member of the Institute for Research of English Teaching of the Educational Bureau of Japan, bulletins, periodicals, and other publications have been sent to the College, and they are being displayed for use in one of the teacher's rooms for the time being. The Club is devoting much time and effort to plan a unified method of teaching English as a part of this program. It has directed the students in the organization of an English Club of themselves, holding meetings with various programs and practising English in various ways. Professor I. S. Jung is in charge of this work.

C. Science Department - Acting Director, Kyu Nam, Choi, Ph.D.

The faculty of this Department for present year consists of 5 Professors, 1 Assistant Professor, 1 Instructor, 5 Lecturers and 2 Assistant making a total of 14 members.

The enrollment of this Department for this year is as follows:

Seniors..................	18
Juniors..................	16
Sophomores..............	23
Freshmen................	22
	79

The faculty members of the Science Department have done their utmost in carrying out the work assigned to them during the past year. They have been loyal to the college and to their work and enthusiastic, even though they had to carry heavy teaching loads. In last April Mr. K. Ogawa was promoted as a Professor in Architecture. He is a good Christian and very valuable member in the Department. Dr. A. L. Becker went back to America on his furlough last June. We are looking forward to his coming this fall. Last September Mr. K. J. Chang, who had been teaching ten years at Ewha College, was appointed as a Professor in Mathematics. He is one of the Science Graduates in 1925 and is doing an excellent work. His fine spirit and whole hearted cooperation is very much appreciated. A new Survey teacher, Mr. H. S. Lee, who graduated from Kyoto Imperial University, has been added to the staff last September. In spite of being so busy, Mrs. H. H. Underwood has been teaching English Conversation. The Department appreciates very much her good work and fine influence upon the students.

Mr. Y. S. Kim, Chemistry Laboratory Assistant, resigned from the College last November, and he is now undertaking a rubber shoes store in Pyongyang.

The Seniors who are to graduate in March will be placed as follows: 2 are planning to enter the Engineering Colleges of the Kyoto Imperial University, 7 have positions promised in the Government-Railway, 1 in Hwasun Firm, and 6 as teachers to various middle schools.

Teachers' Science Club

The Science Club of the Department staff had regular monthly meetings at the homes of the members. Some scientific problems were presented at each meeting by one of the members and a general discussion usually took place. Such a gathering tends to create friendship among the members as well as to give each member something new and fresh.

Science Research Work

The Science Research Work has been carried on by the faculty members and the students of the Department; and the results have been published from time to time in the various magazines and newspapers.

To facilitate the research work books on natural science and various materials and specimens were collected and placed on the shelves. There are 1104 volumes of books, of which 329 volumes are in the occidental languages and 776 volumes in the oriental languages. There are also 6 kinds of magazines in the oriental languages. Dr. K. N. Choi is in charge of this work.

Science Museum

The Science Museum has been greatly increased by the recent donations. Prof. L. H. Snyder donated many rare specimens of birds; and Mr. Joo Myung Souk of the Song-Do Middle School gave a complete set of specimens of butterflies of Korea. The latter specimens are 202 in kind and 437 in number of pieces.

A few years ago the College prepared a moth proof case for the preservation of bird skins and 66 specimens. A student of the Department trained in taxidermy stuffed 74 species and 22 families of birds during the past year. Those specimens, representing many of common birds and a few rare ones found in Korea, are available to those who wish to examine and study them. A list of those 66 specimens with the scientific names both in English and Japanese and a complete data, giving sex, date, and place where found, was made and is kept in the Science Department. All of the specimens were donated to the College by Prof. L. H. Snyder. It is hoped that within the coming year additional specimens could be secured in order to make our collection something unique and useful. The Science Museum now roofs 5,898 specimens of birds, botanical, and mineral things.

III. Religious Activities Committee - Chairman, E. M. Cable, D.D.

The cardinal aim of our College was and still is to develop Christian character and to offer high scholastic training. Thus, the policy of the College is to have all its Professors and staff not merely nominal but active Christians.

The chapel services during the year have been well attended and a more intelligent and appreciative interest has been manifested. Four services are held in the chapel each week and one Mass Drill in the Outdoor Theatre in which both Faculty and students participate. Most of the chapel services have been conducted by members of the Faculty. During the year we have had a few prominent Christian leaders from abroad who have spoken to the students.

The students have a very active Y.M.C.A. with a large membership. During the summer and winter vacations they send out evangelistic bands to different parts of the country. The last three years this work has been directed into regular project work which has been most helpful to the students as well as to the Christian Church. Islands off the western coast of Korea have been selected to which the students have gone and through their efforts Christian groups have been organized. The reports of these students upon their return are most interesting and inspiring.

The Yuenhei Federated Church is more and more making itself felt in the spiritual life of the students of both Yunhei and Ewha Colleges. Its worship services are most inspriring as well as impressive. If the College had more dormitory accommodations we could have a much larger attendance at this services. One of the most pressing needs of the College is new dormitories.

The Special Services were held this year from February 5th to 9th and Rev. Kim Chong Pil of Songdo took charge of them. It is the purpose of the College to press upon the students at this time the claim of Jesus Christ. Many of our young men made decisions to live Christian lives during these meetings.

Rev. S. Y. Chang has been acting as religious advisor during the last semester with very good results. Not being allowed to teach all his time is given to conferences with the students, visiting those who are sick or in special need of aid. The first report handed to me was most interesting and I am pleased to give a summary of it here hoping that it will be helpful to all the readers of this report.

At the beginning of the year 467 students were enrolled; 140 in the Literary Department; 248 in the Commercial Department; and 87 in the Science Department; a total of 467. Out of this number the total baptized Christians were 143, Catechumens 21 and new believers 144. The church affiliation is: Methodists 179, Presbyterians 123, other denominations 8 and 153 non-Christians.

The College has a Faculty Prayer-Meeting which has been very well attended this last year. These meetings are led by members of the faculty and it is our sincere desire that we may soon have all the members of the faculty taking part in this meeting.

The students are expected to attend the churches in and outside of the city to promote their faith and render assistance to these churches in the Sunday Schools and in church music.

The percentage of non-Christians this year is about 30%, smaller than the previous year. We hope by the end of this year that even this figure will be very greatly reduced.

Our Bible instruction remains the same as last year. This is Prof. B. C. Coen's last term with us and we greatly regret his leaving. His influence and teaching have been a great asset to the Religious Activities Department as well as to the whole College. We are glad to know that Dr. Matsumoto, one of the outstand New Testament scholars in Japan, is to be with us from the beginning of the new year and we feel sure his presence and work will be a great help to the College.

Mr. Y. H. Pak who has been giving his time to the student work has been requisitioned by the College for other service and is no longer able to give any time to the student visitation work. We are very sorry to lose Mr. Pak, but are glad that he is still to serve the College in another capacity.

IV. The College Library - Librarian, Myo-Mook Lee, Ph.D.

The year 1940 marks the 25th anniversary of our College and the 2600th year of the foundation of the Japanese Empire. In memory of this happy occasion the College planned to raise money in order to buy books for the Library. Everybody in the College contributed generously, and a fund mounting to about 4,500 yen was raised. With this the College purchased 865 books chiefly in the line of Japanese Culture, and the collection of these books is known as the 2600th year collection. The friends both abroad and at home also gave 511 books to the College library during the last year, which makes an addition of 1,376 volumes to the library.

The exact number of the total accessions is not known, but roughly speaking there are 50,718 volumes of which 17,099 are in the occidental languages.

The library is also handling a large number of periodicals, consisting of the following:

Magazines:............................ 172 kinds
Oriental.......... 113 (of which 68 gifts)
Occidental........ 59 (of which 25 gifts)

Newspapers:.......................... 34 kinds
Oriental.......... 32 (of which 22 gifts)
Occidental........ 2 (of which 1 gift)

Handling and circulating these heterogeneous periodicals and the rapid increase of books demand a good many hands - especially skillful hands. Ever since Mr. Kyung Sang Lyu's departure from the library and the appointment of Librarian, Dr. Myo-Mook Lee, as Dean of the College, the Library has been short of hands. In addition, Mr. Chei Yun Whang resigned in order to take up a better position in Manchuria. Regardless of this handicap, Mr. Pyung Sur Kim and Mrs. Sang Hee Lyu did a splendid piece of work in carrying on the library. They did more than this. They filed the cards of Oriental books and are in the midst of making subject heading cards of the Occidental books.

Much care was given to the periodicals. In spite of exorbitant price of binding, 289 volumes of magazines and 10 volumes of newspapers were bound last year.

The College regrets the loss of Mr. Kyung Sang Lyu's service as a staff of the library. After having served in the College Library over seven long years, he wished to take up Library Science. The College, therefore, extended its good offices in securing a scholarship in the School of Library Science, Syracuse University, Syracuse, New York, and gave him a leave of absence. He graduated from the school with the degree of B.L.S. yet he wanted to change his line from Library Science to Philosophy. In September 1939 much hoped return of Mr. Lyu failed to take place and the College decided to transfer Mr. Han Chul Shin from the Literary Department to the Library. He took charge of the Library very efficiently until his father's serious illness called him back to his home.

Adding the books more up to date and improving the use of library produces an immediate and eloquent result:- namely, an increase of circulation. About 637 books were circulated each month; and the nature of the books in the order of demand is as follows:

1. Literature
2. Sociology and Social Science
3. Philosophy
4. Travels
5. Fine Arts
6. Philology
7. General Books including Periodicals
8. Science
9. Books on Religion
10. Useful Science
11. Biography
12. History

The Library needs a great number of things: - more funds, some more adequately trained workers, and more bookshelves, etc. Above all the Library needs a separate Library Building. Even now the whole upper floor of the Underwood Hall is over-flooded with books. A large number of books are dumped on the floor, thus being damaged by moisture.

The College Museum - Head, Eui Sul Cho, Gakushi

The College Museum is one of the most fascinating, yet the least known place on the campus. The Museum possesses four or five thousand interesting and valuable objects chiefly given by the staff and friends of the College. After a good many migrations from one building to another the Museum is now stationed in the sunny room on the second floor of the Underwood Hall.

In order to make a good use of it, Mr. Eui Sul Cho is working hard on classification and exhibition. We hope to find a more spacious room to spread out the objects. Once the accessioning and classification is completed, a large number of exhibition cases will be in demand.

Mr. Cho wishes to put the Museum on the College map so that everybody would get better acquainted with it.

V. Physical Education - Chairman, O. Y. Lee

This year, too, all of our College teams participated in the annual athletic competitions and secured a number of championships. What is more, in sportsmanship and athletic skill, our College teams surpassed all others. We are proud to say that our College teams represented Chosen at the friendly games with the Manchukuo, and later with the North-China team both of which visited the country. Some of our College teams toured North Chosen, while others toured South, exerting wholesome influence on the local athletic circles. Of a still grater significance was the invasion of our College teams into Tokyo, which brought us not only re-known, but also the acquaintance with the most recent developments of strategy and tactics. A bright future is opening before us. During the year we had to face a number of difficulties, owing to the inadequacy of funds and the rising prices of goods. But often the students helped out by their cheerful assumption of the expenses in part in buying the tools. We also owe thanks to our graduates whose cooperation was much appreciated in the maintenance of morale among the undergraduate athletes as well as in their Tokyo trips.

A brief summary of the activities of the several sections during the year is attached below:

Tennis: We obtained championship at the National Shrine Annual Meet, both in group contest and in individual. At the All-Japan-Student Meet we lost unexpectedly at the final game, owing to the excessive fatigue caused by the long journey to Tokyo. But we secured the first place in the Student Tennis Records of the year. During the summer we toured South Chosen, holding matches in seven cities, and won everywhere except in one, namely in Taiku.

Football: The All Yun-Houi Team fought bravely at the All-Japan Championship Meet held at Tokyo, although unfortunately beaten at the final game, the team received praises for fine play. The Varsity Football Team toured North Chosen in the summer with good results. Many of the Varsity Football Team members represented Chosen at the friendly games of All-Chosen vs. North China, and All-Chosen vs. Manchukuo.

Basket-Ball: The Varsity Team won at the National Shrine Annual Meet; but was defeated by the Canadian Team, 26:23, owing to inexperience in international contest. Many of the Varsity Team members represented Chosen at the friendly games of All-Chosen vs. North China and All-Chosen vs. Manchukuo. The Varsity Basket-Ball Team also played at the All-Japan Championship Meet held at Tokyo and was unfortunately beaten.

Bicycle: Though only recently formed, the Bicycle Team was victorious in nearly all the amateur contests. They also represented Chosen at the All-Japan Championship Meet held at Tokyo, where they made a new record.

Judo: The Judo Team fought at the Student League games, and though beaten at the final it was the first time that our team was able to carry the game to the final. The All Yun-Houi Judo Team also toured West Chosen and left a fine record.

Track: 8 men participated in the Student League Meet for the first time this year, scored 16 points and was ranked the 9th.

Ice-Hockey: The Varsity Team achieved an overwhelming victory at the National Shrine Annual Meet and represented Chosen at the friendly game of All-Chosen vs. Manchukuo. The Varsity Team also participated in the All-Japan Championship Meet held at Tokyo where though beaten by the victor of this year, the team was greatly strengthened by this experience, so much so that it faces the future with bright prospects. Besides these, all the annual athletic performances were carried out with great success.

VI. Musical Activities - Chairman, K. N. Choi, Ph.D.

The report on the musical activities for the year is rather short, for on account of the present circumstances the outside activities have been very few. Mr. Kyung Ho Park has been kind enough to take the responsibility of teaching and conducting our music during the absence of Dr. Rody Hyun. The 17th Fall Concert was held at the Citizen's Hall on November 30th and it was a great success. The College Glee Club have broadcasted Special Program from time to time through the Central Broadcasting Station in Seoul. Many thanks are due to Mrs. R. C. Coon, who plays music for our Chapel service every day.

VII. Other Items of Interest

A. Student Help Committee - Chairman, Hong Ki Karl, Ph.D.

Among the student body of 470 there are a good many students earning their ways through College. The Student Help Committee has found out that about 60 boys are self-supporting, of whom one-third are helped either directly or indirectly by the Committee.

This Committee is very fortunate to have a warm hearted, sympathetic, and capable man as its Chairman. There are also a great number of staff who are keenly interested in the welfare of the needy students.

The number of needy students is increasing on account of the drought last year, while the committee has only 780 yen as its annual appropriation. Small as the sum is, with this fund, 9 needy and worthy students have been helped - 3 working indoors, while 6 boys working outdoors. There are also a numerous students working at private homes as tutors.

The Committee wishes that the academic year 1940-1941 would be a still better and more helpful one to the needy and worthy students.

B. Scholarships

Source	Recipient		Amount
College................	Kang Yung Heum	(C.3)	¥75.00
College................	Yun Chung Sup	(S.4)	75.00
Yun Tchi Chang.........	Lee Chong Koo	(C.2)	75.00
Lee Won Yo.............	Cho Pyung Eui	(L.3)	75.00
Kim Hi Jun.............	Pak Yung Dai	(C.2)	75.00
Paik Won Chun..........	Cho Hyo Won	(C.3)	75.00
Yun Bang Hyun..........	Pak Chung Ki	(S.4)	75.00
Friends in U.S.A.......	Han Hyung Koum	(S.3)	75.00
E. M. Cable............	Lee Yun Sam	(L.4)	90.00
Paul E. Burbank........	Choi Pong Chul	(L.2)	75.00
Kim Chong Sun..........	Chun Hyo Jin	(L.3)	75.00
	Rha Ik Jin	(C.2)	75.00
	Lee Tai Heup	(C.2)	75.00
	Lee Chang Kyun	(S.1)	75.00
Cho Pyung Kap..........	Lee Yong Hi	(L.4)	75.00
	Kim Chong Lim	(L.4)	75.00

B. Scholarships (Continued)

Source	Recipient		Amount
Cho Pyung Kop & Sung Chai...	Min Nam Ki	(C.2)	.........460.00
Cho Pyung Kap & Mook Cho....	Kim Chun Suk	(C.2)	.........460.00
	Lee Chai Hang	(C.2)	.... 75.00
	Kang Chong Sam	(C.1)	.... 75.00
	Cho Chun Pong	(S.1)	.... 75.00
Lee Chung Chai..............	Cho Jin Oh	(C.3)	.... 75.00
Lee Chong Ik................	Cho Kook Hyung	(L.3)	.... 75.00
College.....................	Sur Yong Kil	(L.3)	.... 75.00
College.....................	Pak Do Soo	(L.1)	.... 75.00
Yun Chang Hyun..............	Chung Kiu Wha	(S.4)	.... 75.00
	Kim Sang Kul	(S.4)	.... 75.00
Anonymous...................	Kim Chang Ho	(L.4)	.... 75.00
Pyung Wha Dang Drug Store...	Kim Dong Won	(L.3)	.........120.00
	Han Sang Tai	(L.4)	.........120.00

C. Clubs and Organizations

a. C.C.C. Y.M.C.A. (Voluntary Organization)
b. Literary Society. (Literary Department Students)
c. Commercial Department Students Society
d. Science Club. (Science Department Students)
e. Glee Club, Orchestra and Band. (Voluntary, all Departments)
f. English Club. (Voluntary, Commercial Department Students)
g. Religious Research Club. (Voluntary, all Departments)

VIII. Students

A. Enrollment

Annual average of the students who paid tuition during the past four years:

1936--1937	394
1937--1938	417
1938--1939	455
1939--1940	471

Up to January 31st, 1940, there was a total enrollment of 435 students distributed as follows:

Class	Lit. Dept.	Com. Dept.	Sci. Dept.	Total
Freshman...........	42	82	22	146
Sophomore..........	29	72	23	124
Junior.............	21		16	37
Senior.............	29	81	18	128
Total.....	121	235	79	435

B. Classification of Students

Department	Regular	Special	Total	Percentage
	Number of Students			
Literary	102	19	121	27.82
Commercial	231	4	235	54.02
Science	77	2	79	18.16
	410	25	435	100.00%

C. Geographical Distribution of Students

Province	Number	Percentage
North Ham Kyung	7	1.61
South Ham Kyung	8	1.84
North Pyung An	30	6.90
South Pyung An	63	14.48
Hwang Hai	46	10.57
Kyung Ki	165	37.93
Kang Won	14	3.22
North Choong Chung	9	2.07
South Choong Chung	34	7.81
North Chun La	15	3.45
South Chun La	11	2.53
North Kyung Sang	19	4.37
South Kyung Sang	14	3.22
	435	100.00%

IX. Graduates

A. Total Number of Graduates from each Department

(January 31st, 1939)

Department	Number	Percentage
Literary	240	26.14
Commercial	530	57.73
Science	145	15.80
Agricultural (Not Operating)	3	.33
	918	100.00%

B. Present Status of Graduates, January 31st, 1940

Positions and Occupation	Number	Percentage
Teaching Staff in C.C.C.	12	1.31
Non-Teaching Officers in C.C.C.	10	1.09
Teachers in Other Christian Schools	47	5.11
Church Workers	9	.98
Teachers in Non-Christian Schools	110	11.98
Students in Medical	3	.33
Students in U.S.A. and Germany	26	2.84
Students in Japan Proper	53	5.78
Journalists and Writers	13	1.41
Employees in Banks and Business Firms	145	15.79
Government Officials	72	7.85
Independent Commercial or Industrial Workers	179	19.49
Agriculturalists	5	.55
Various Lines of Independent Business	186	20.26
Physician	1	.10
Mining	4	.44
Deceased	43	4.69
Total	918	100.00%

C. Graduates' Privileges Conferred by the Government

a. The College has been granted the privilege of conferring a Bachelor's degree in each Department as Bachelor of Literature or Commerce or Science or Theology.

b. Government qualification for private primary school teachers. (See Article I of the Educational Ordinance for private school teachers.)

c. The graduates of the College are granted qualification by the Government to teach in Private Higher Common Schools on the following subjects: (See Article III of the Educational Ordinance for private school teachers).

To the graduates of the Literary Department:
English, and (Korean).
To the graduates of the Commercial Department:
English, Commerce, and Bookkeeping.
To the graduates of the Science Department:
Mathematics, Physics, and Chemistry.
To the graduates of the Agricultural Department:
(Not Operating). Agriculture.

d. The graduates of the College are also granted qualification by the Government to teach all the subjects taught in the Professional Schools: Technical, Agricultural, Commercial, Veterinary, Nautical, and other vocational schools. (See Article IV of the Educational Ordinance for private school teachers).

e. In accordance with the Ordinance of the Imperial Department of Education, No. 3, Art. 2, Sec. 4 (Daisho 7th Year) this College has been placed on an equal plane with the Higher Schools, Colleges, and the Preparatory Departments of Universities in Japan Proper, so that our graduates are exempted from the preliminary examinations for Higher Civil Service positions and are qualified also for entering all Government and private universities.

f. According to the Imperial Ordinance, No. 261 (Daisho 2nd Year), the graduates of this College are granted the privilege of ordinary Civil Official appointment without examination (Ordinance on Civil Official Appointment, Art. 6).

56. 원한경 교장의 이사회 제출 연례보고서

문서 제목	Report of the President to the Board of Managers of Chosen Christian College
문서 종류	교장 보고서
제출 시기	1940년 2월 23일
작성 장소	서울
제 출 자	H. H. Underwood
수 신 자	이사회
페이지 수	8
출 처	2114-5-4: 09 Underwood, Horace H. (DR.) 1940 (UMAH)

자료 소개

원한경 교장이 1940년 2월 23일 열린 이사회 연례회의에 제출한 보고서이다. 지난해 교장 보고서에 이어 이 보고서도 황국신민화 교육정책 강행과 학교 존폐 논란의 영향으로 음울한 기조를 띠고 있다.

원한경은 이 보고서에서 아래의 사항들에 관해 설명하였다.

25주년 기념행사, 봉급 인상, 교수, 특별 기부금, 예산, 교육과정, 식당 건물, 기숙사, 학생, 운동경기, 종교 교육, 격려.

내용 요약

25주년 기념행사: 25년 전 이달에 아버지 언더우드의 집에서 많은 모임이 열리고 본교의 개교가 최종 결정되었다. 지금의 여건에서는 25주년 기념행사를 우리가 바라는 대로 여는 것이 지혜롭지 않을 듯하므로, 5월에 조촐하게 몇 가지 행사를 열면 좋을 것 같다.

봉급: 학생과 교수의 작은 집단으로 시작했던 학교가 거의 천 명의 졸업생을 내고, $450,000의 기본재산을 보유하게 되었다. 그러나 정치적 상황 때문에 해외에 자금지원을 요청하기 어려워 전면적인 물가 상승으로 인한 봉급 인상의 필요에 대처하기 힘들어졌다.

교수: 신과를 맡았던 북장로회 소속의 코엔이 아쉽게도 사임하였고, 북장로회 한국 선교회가 코엔 대신 모우리(E. M. Mowry)를 임명하여 1940~41년까지 있게 하였다. [한국 선

교회는 1939년 3월 말에는 이 학교와의 관계를 끊겠다고 선언하였으나, 그들의 본국 선교부는 1941년 3월 말까지 후원할 것을 결정하였다. 그러므로 선교부의 쿼터로 모우리가 오게 되었던 것 같다.] 일본인 마츠모토(드류신학교)와 이화여전의 교수인 장기원(도호쿠제대) 동문이 지난가을 연전으로 왔다. 그를 교수로 임명해주도록 추천한다.

특별 기부금: 전년도 학교 재정에서 약간의 흑자를 남긴 이유는 첫째로 환율이 유리해졌고, 둘째로 이름 모를 여러 사람이 특별 기부금을 보냈으며, 셋째로 돌아오지 않은 교수들로 인해 예산에 책정된 봉급이 나가지 않았기 때문이었다. (특별 기부금 기부자들의 명단과 금액과 사용처를 나열하고 있다.)

예산: 교직원에게 인상해서 지급해야 할 1년분 봉급이 거의 ¥150,000에 달한다. 그런데 환율이 유리해졌고 협력이사회도 $2,000을 더 보낼 것을 통보해왔다.

교육과정: 총독부 학무당국의 '조언과 제안'으로 각 과의 교육과정을 바꿀 계획인데, 교수회가 재검토하고 실행위원회가 승인하면 학무당국에 제출할 예정이다. 교육과정의 가장 큰 변화는 총독부의 요망에 따라 군사교련을 시작한 것이다. 일본문화 과목을 신설하고 일본사와 중국어 시간을 늘리는 대신 영어 시간은 줄였으며, 수물과의 학생 수를 늘렸다.

식당: 날씨만 좋으면 식당[한경관] 건축을 재개할 것인데, 지난해 이사회에서 1층만 올리고 본 층은 나중에 올리도록 허가를 받았다.

기숙사: 학생들이 시내에서 기숙하는 환경이 매우 부적합하여 온돌로 난방하는 1층짜리 기숙사를 한두 채 지어야 하고, 서울에 집이 없는 신입생을 모두 수용하려면 ¥40,000 이상이 들 것이다. 이사회가 이 문제를 검토해주기를 바란다.

학생: 등록생이 470명으로 시작해서 436명(상과 235명, 문과 121명, 수물과 80명)으로 줄었다. 이 중에서 128명이 졸업하면 졸업생이 총 1,046명이 될 것이다. 학생들의 기풍이 좋지만, 불안정하고 염려하는 모습도 보인다.

운동경기: 학생들의 일요일 운동경기 참가가 우려를 사고 있는데, 총독부가 주관하는 전국대회 참가가 형식상 강제로 하는 것은 아니어도 실제로는 빠질 수 없는 까닭에 내가 한중일 미션계 학교들에 의견을 구하여 답장을 받았다. 이사회에 결의안 초안(기독교 안식일 준수가 본 대학의 정책임을 확인한다는 내용)을 제출하니 승인해주기를 바란다.

종교교육: 케이블이 종교사역부를 이끌어왔으나 마츠모토 교수가 왔으므로 그에게 부

서를 맡기는 것이 바람직하다는 결론을 냈다. 채플 예배, 교수 기도회, 성경 교육, 특별집회, 연합교회가 여러 사람의 수고로 중단없이 잘 수행되어왔다. (학생 YMCA 활동, 하기방학 섬[기린도] 교회 봉사활동, 특별집회에 관해 설명하고 있다.)

격려: 이 대학이 신실하게 사역해온 것을 자랑스럽게 여겨도 된다. 총독부가 앞으로 어떤 새 정책으로 영향을 줄지 모르지만, 지난 25년간 해온 것처럼 어려움을 이겨나가도록 하자.

TRANSFERRED 802

Report of the President
to the
Board of Managers
of
Chosen Christian College

February 23, 1940

****

Gentlemen:-

Twenty-five years ago this month my father's home was the scene of much activity and many meetings and conferences as the final arrangements were made for the formal opening of the Chosen Christian College in the rooms secured in the Central Y.M.C.A. of Seoul. The circumstances of the day here in Chosen make it unwise for us to attempt to celebrate our 25th anniversary as we would perhaps have wished. At present, our plans call for the publication of small souvenir booklets in English and in the vernacular; for a ceremony and an open-air concert at the College; for some athletic events; and for a series of lectures to be given to our students by certain selected men. The celebration will take place sometime in May, when we can be reasonably sure that weather conditions will permit us to use our open-air theatre. We sincerely hope that you will be present with us in joy and in thanksgiving to God.

The College of 25 years ago was little more than a small collection of students and teachers gathered in a few rented rooms. To-day you meet as the governing Board of that College with almost a thousand graduates; with 450 students; with property worth several million yen and an endowment of over ¥450,000.00. We would be both ungrateful and dull of perception if we allowed the difficulties and anxieties of the present period to make us forget the past 25 years or to make us doubt the power of Him who has lead and guided us thus far.

On the other hand, we would be foolish and I would be remiss in my duty, if I failed to recognize and report to you on the difficulties and dangers of our present situation. The political situation in the Far-East has made the solicitation of funds from abroad almost impossible. The high hopes we had built upon the activities of Capt. Swinehart have been dashed. The rising cost of everything from pencils and paper to coal and wood swells our Maintenance Budget to alarming proportions. This same rise in prices makes the salaries which we deemed relatively adequate, now quite inadequate for the living expenses of our faithful teachers. The uncertainty not only as to our future, but as to our neighbors, and even as to our friends produces a nervous tension which is a prolific source of trouble. Added to all this are the various and sometimes inconsistent demands made upon us by over-zealous individuals in various positions both official and unofficial. All these have made the year a difficult one and I have often felt my own inadequacy to meet the demands of my position. It would, in fact, have been impossible to go on except for the loyal support of the majority of our staff, and the kindly help and advice given me by many of you and by many friends of the College. The Salary question and certain necessary promotions have brought some discontent and dissatisfaction among those not promoted. There have been days when the strain of misunderstanding has almost reached the breaking point, but we have come through safely and I am happy to say that I think some of the causes of misunderstanding have been removed or are in process of removal. The Board will realize that it is impossible to suddenly replace 12 or 14 Professors of high standing, especially, when one does not know whether these replacements are to be permanent or temporary. There have at times resulted confusion and mistakes for which I am fully ready to take responsibility for which I wish to apologize. In the main the staff has been patient and has made allowances for the difficulties with which we have met. For those who will make such allowances and who are ready to struggle through this period with us I am indeed thankful to God. If there be any who are unwilling to be patient who are unwilling to endure hardship and unwilling to make allowances for circumstances we will probably be better off if they leave us altogether.

Faculty:

A matter of deep regret to me and, I feel sure, to all of you, is the resignation of Prof. R. C. Coen from our staff. Prof. Coen handed me his resignation last Spring to take effect on March 21st of this year. It is a decision which he has arrived at after long and careful thought and which he feels cannot be changed. Mr. Coen is a member of my own Mission and his coming to the College was largely due to my urging upon him the value to the opportunity here. He has been not only my colleague, but my friend, and I consider his going to be a serious loss to the institution. As President of the College, I wish to recommend to the Board the following resolution:

"Recommend that this Board express its sincere regret at the resignation of Prof. R. C. Coen from the Faculty of the Chosen Christian College and that we further express to him and to Mrs. Coen our deep appreciation of the valuable services which both of them have rendered since their appointment to the College in 1933. Mr. Coen was appointed an Instructor on our staff in the Fall of 1933. By action of this Board, he became Assistant Professor in 1934, and Professor in 1937. During the seven years of his service, he has carried very heavy schedules in both English and Bible, as well as, a large amount of committee and other work, serving as Secretary of the Faculty since 1937. In addition to the formal work of teaching and committees, Mr. and Mrs. Coen have made their home a spiritual center for many of the students, and there are now many of our graduates who throughout their lives will thank God that Mr. Coen was their teacher, and more than teacher, their guide to a closer and more intimate knowledge of Jesus Christ. Mrs. Coen, in addition to much social activity and work among the wives and families of our staff, has carried the burden of our Chapel Music for the last five or six years. This is a work which brings neither applause nor glory, but it means much in the religious life of the College. It would be conservative to estimate that Mrs. Coen has played our Chapel hymns, on at least 800 or a 1,000 days. The Board of Managers pray that in whatever line of work they may be called God's richest blessings may go with Prof. and Mrs. Coen."

Closely connected with Mr. Coen's resignation is the relationship between this College and the Mission and Board of the Presbyterian Church in the U.S.A. At its last annual meeting the Mission voted to assign Dr. E. M. Mowry to the College to take Mr. Coen's place for the year 1940-1941. Since that time Dr. Mowry's health has become such that his physician informs me that it will be impossible for him to fill this assignment. I, therefore, took up the question with Mr. Crothers, Chairman of the Mission's Executive Committee asking him to fill the vacancy. He informs me that this will not be possible and I have, therefore, written to the Presbyterian Board asking them to follow the usual precedent by providing us with an additional appropriation of ¥4,000 in lieu of a teacher.

As to the relationship between this College and the Presbyterian Church in the U.S.A. after 1941, we can only hope and pray that some way may be found by which a connection either direct or indirect may be continued, but at present, there are no visible signs of any change in the decision to withdraw after March 31st, 1941.

While dealing with changes on our Faculty, I take great pleasure in announcing to you that arrangements have been completed for Dr. T. Matsumoto of the Aoyama Gakuin to come to this College in April of this year. Dr. Matsumoto is a graduate of Drew Theological Seminary and holds degrees from the University of Pennsylvania, and from the Ohio Wesleyan University. He is a man of deep spiritual thought and life and he comes to us at considerable sacrifice and with a real missionary spirit. In the recommendations made for promotions, I am recommending that you appoint Dr. Matsumoto to the rank of Professor.

I am also happy to announce the coming to our Faculty family of Mr. Kee Won Chang. Mr. Chang graduated from this College in 1925, studied at Tohoku University and for ten years served as a Professor in Ewha College. Last Fall, he came back to this Alma Mater and I am recommending to you his appointment as Professor in the Chosen Christian College.

I have also taken up both with Dr. Wasson and Dr. Moore the question of possible re-enforcements for this College, and I found both of these friends very sympathetic to our needs. There is nothing definite which I can report at present except to say that I was much encouraged both by the letter of Dr. Wasson and by the personal conference which I had with Bishop Moore when he was here. It is to be hoped that such re-enforcement may be sent without delay, especially, in view of the fact, that so far as we know at present, the withdrawal of the Presbyterian Mission from cooperation will be consumated in March of 1941.

As to re-enforcement in the form of re-instatement of former teachers, we are still in the dark and can only hope and pray that some at least of these men who are so badly needed may be restored to us by the generous and far-sighted policy of the government.

Finances:

I have already referred briefly to some of our finaicial problems. To be more specific, we have come through the year without a deficit and will probably finish the year with a small surplus. This has been accomplished through a variety of factors. In the first place, the exchange rate has been more favorable than we had estimated in making our budget. In the second place, we have been fortunate enough to receive a number of anonymous special gifts for current expenses which have meant a great deal to us. In the third place, there has been a forced economy due to the non-return of certain teachers whose salaries had been budgeted. Lastly, the Treasurer, the Dean, and the Heads of Departments and Committees are to be complimented on the strict economy which has been exercised in all branches.

Special Gifts:

In addition to the above mentioned anonymous special gifts the College has received a number of others which I report to you with very sincere gratitude.

1. From Mr. Shi Chong Kang, Commercial, 1933; ¥1,000 for Library Fund as a memorial to his Uncle. (Mr. Kang expects to continue this gift every year for some years.)

2. From Mr. Chung Kyu Lee, Commercial, 1931; ¥500 toward the 25th Anniversary expenses and also a pledge to give ¥500 annually for two scholarships.

3. From Mr. Young Ho Kim, Literary, 1927; ¥75 per annum for tuition scholarship for a student in the Literary Department.

4. From Miss E. Stutzer, ¥200 for Emergency Medical Fund.

5. From Mr. Man Hi Choi, Commercial, 1935; ¥75 annually to a Commercial student who writes the best essay on Foreign Trade.

I would recommend that this Board instruct the Secretary to write a suitable letter of thanks to each of these people.

Budget:

For the coming year we present to you a balanced budget. The inclusion again this year of budget allowances, both for teachers who are with us and for teachers who may be with us, together with the necessary increases for those in the lower brackets of our salary scale have raised the total of our estimated expenses for the year to almost ¥150,000; the highest level which it has ever reached. To meet this on the income side, there is of course the relatively favorable exchange and we are also fortunate in that Dr. Sutherland reports that for this year we may expect increased income of about $2,000. The nature of this additional sum is not clear and we must not look upon it as a permanent increase on which we may definitely count for future years. We also hope that we may look forward to at least some income from some special gifts during the coming year.

Curriculum:

Changes in staff and increases in our budget are not the only changes to be reported for the year. Under the advice and suggestion of the Government Educational Department the faculty has had under consideration various changes in the curricula of our Departments. These were submitted to your Executive Committee which asked that certain changes be made. After reconsideration by the faculty they were again submitted to the Executive Committee which approved them. Application was then made to the educational authorities. Here again, certain minor changes were asked and as these in no way conflicted with the suggestions from the Executive Committee they were incorporated in the final application, permission for which will doubtless be received ere long. To any who are interested, we shall be happy to furnish a detailed statement as to the new curricula in each of the Departments. I will merely mention briefly the major changes.

The greatest innovation was made last September when in compliance with the desires of the Government, we began military training in the College. We were fortunate in securing for our Military Instructor, Capt. Chang Ha Pak, who was for many years instructor in this subject at the Central High School. Capt. Pak's family are Christians and he is himself an attendant at Christian services though not an avowed Christian. From the point of view of discipline, I think that his coming has done a great deal to bring about greater care and attention to these matters on the part of the students and it is our hope that we may realize the best features of such training in the College. Other changes are the addition of courses in Japanese Culture; increased hours in Japanese History; some increase in the study of the Chinese spoken language; and some decrease in the amount of English required. In some ways, most important, is the proposed increase in the number of students in the Science Department where we are asking to be permitted to accept an entering class of 40.

Dining Hall:

On the campus you may see the walls of our new Dining Hall on which work will be resumed as soon as the weather permits. This was approved by the Board last year and provides for the erection of only the ground floor of this building, the main floors to be added later when it is possible to secure the necessary structural steel and other materials. The building will not only solve many of the present difficulties in regard to the noon meal, but will provide in the rear section a place for Judo and these provisions in turn will release for us no less than 5 large rooms in the basement of Underwood Hall, thus making possible shifts and readjustment to more adequately care for the increased enrollment in the Commercial and Science Departments as well as providing rooms for other features which are much crowded at present.

Dormitory:

The Dormitory question has been again raised during the year. The thought being that in view of the highly unsatisfactory condition of student lodgings in the city, we should set aside funds and erect one or more units of relatively low-cost single-story dormitories to be heated by the Korean "ondol". These buildings could be built of stone and roofed in a style similar to our other building. It is thought that they could be located along the hillside and among the pine trees and that they would not conflict with the architectural scheme of the College. They would provide accommodations for many more students. Estimates for such units - each to house about 25 students - vary from ¥15,000 each up. The need for such dormitory accommodations is undoubtedly great and I am frank to say that I would sincerely tell any prospective donor that I consider this our first and most important need. It is, however, a debateable question whether we should use or borrow such funds as our so-called Special Land Fund for the erection of such buildings or not. To house all of the Freshman Class whose homes are not in Seoul, would require in addition to our present dormitory at least two such units and I do not believe that we could hope to erect the two for less than a total cost of ¥40,000. I am, therefore, not prepared to definitely recommend to you that we borrow this amount from any of our permanent funds, but it is a question well worth your consideration, as there is no doubt whatsoever as to the need and value of housing our students on our own site.

Student Body:

The student enrollment for the past year began with 470 and has gradually dropped until at the present time we have 436 students of whom 235 are in the Commercial Department; 121 in the Literary Department; and 80 in the Science Department. Of this total we expect to graduate 128 on March 11th, 1940, which will bring the total graduates of the College to 1,046. The general discipline and the spirit among the students has been good, though they also show signs of the feeling of restlessness and anxiety which effects us all at this time.

Athletics:

In student athletics has arisen the question of participation by our students in Sunday athletics. You are doubtless aware of the fact, that the present Chosen Athletic Association, which is the guiding and directing body in all athletics for the country, is a government project and that the government considers physical education of its subjects to be one of the most important features in its program. Technically, no school is compelled to participate in any special form of athletics or to take part in any of the general athletic meets or events which are held. But under the present system participation in individual games without participation in the meets is almost impossible and it has been clearly indicated that no institution would be permitted to withdraw entirely from the general program of athletics as instituted and conducted by the government. This has meant that on several occasions our students have unavoidably participated in such events on Sundays, on which day many of these meets are scheduled. The question is a difficult one and yet, I think, we must recognize the fact that among large bodies of Christians such participation is not considered wrong. This appears to be true in practically all branches of the Christian church both in Japan and China. A member of this Board brought the question to me and in order to have adequate data to present to you I wrote to a large number of Christian educational institutions and to Christian workers and found that such participation in athletic events is either openly approved or permitted in practically all Christian institutions, in China, Korea, and Japan. Answers came to me from Meiji Gakuin; Aoyama Gakuin; Kwansei Gakuin; Yengching University; the Ewha College for women; Severance Union Medical College; the Songdo Middle School; the Pai Chai Middle School; and the Middle Schools conducted by the Canadian Mission in Hamboung as well as from many other schools. In view of all the circumstances I would beg to submit to you for your approval the following resolution:

> "This Board reaffirms its belief in the necessity and value of preserving the Lord's day as a day of worship and for the development of the spiritual side of life. We, therefore, recommend that the policy of this College be to refrain from participation in public athletic meets on Sunday and that every effort be made to continue to hold up a high ideal of the proper observance of the Christian Sabbath. We recommend that when questions arise either in connection with the government program of physical education or in regard to other public and national activities the President take such course as seems necessary.

I have stated this in this form because I feel that we may and must affirm our belief in the spiritual value of the day, and may yet acknowledge that there are divergent opinions as to specific activities and that our policy in these matters may be guided by the policy of the Christians with whom we are working. I can assure you that all my own prejudices and feeling are in favor of a stricter rather than of a more lax observance of the Lord's Day. But on the other hand, I do not see how under the present system of government or indeed under any system of government we can refuse to allow a government to require its own nationals to participate in such activities. It becomes still more impossible when we realize that the Christian nationals themselves do not hold the same views on this subject as do we. We and other bodies of Christians are at times required to participate in processions, to meet or to bid farewell to dignitaries, or to gather for special addresses and meetings on Sunday. All of these, I regret, but see no way in which such activities can be avoided. It, therefore, seemed wise to me that any minute or resolution which we might take on this subject should be worded as a positive affirmation rather than in a negative form.

Religious Program:

It is a relief to turn from such troubulous questions to the religious program of the College. This is carried on under the direction of the Religious Wrok Committee of which Dr. E. M. Cable has been Chairman for a number of years. Before going further, I would like to refer to a detail of our religious program which I think worthy of mention. When Dr. T. Matsumoto was invited to join our Faculty it was felt desirable that he should be given a position which would enable us to more fully utilize his talents and abilities and which would at the same time give him a place on the Administrative Council of the College. In talking this over with Dr. Cable, we came to the conclusion that this could most fittingly be done by making Dr. Matsumoto, Chairman of the Religious Work Committee. While agreeing with the idea, I only agreed and consented to it because I felt confident that whether as Chairman or as member of a committee, we could count fully upon Dr. Cable's cooperation and his interest and zeal in this primary objective of our work. Dr. Cable has given efficient and valuable service in this capacity for many years and I would like to recommend to you for your approval the following resolution:

> "Recommend that this Board express to Dr. Cable our very sincere appreciation of his efficient work as Chairman of the Religious Activities Committee of the Chosen Christian College and our appreciation of the vision and of the generous spirit with which he relinquishes this position in favor of another. It is the Board's sincere hope and belief that as a member of this committee, Dr. Cable will continue to give to this work the interest and missionary zeal which he has shown throughout the more than 41 years of his work in Korea."

During the past year the program of Religious Work within the College has gone on successfully without interruption, and has, I believe, been very efficient. The formal religious work consists in the conduct of our Chapel services; faculty prayer meetings; Bible teaching; special religious services; and in our cooperation in the work of the Federated Church. All this has been done, and been done in the main on a high spiritual plane. In addition to this work, the Religious Work Department through Mr. Y. H. Park and the Rev. S. Y. Chang has done a great deal both in visitation and personal interviews. Dr. E. M. Cable, Mr. R. C. Coen, Dr. H. K. Karl and others have all cooperated efficiently and lovingly in these varied forms of work. The Religious Work

-8-

Committee also supervises the Student Y. M. C. A. activities and despite the necessary curtailment of this work, I am happy to report that the summer island projects were successfully carried out, Mr. S. Y. Chang and Dr. H. K. Karl accompanying the students. A separate account of this has been published in the "Korea Mission Field", as the work was most interesting and inspiring. There has been no interference or difficulty experienced in any part of this religious program.

The week of special religious service was conducted this year by the Rev. Chong Pil Kim of Songdo, whose oldest son is a graduate of this College and is now in Drew Theological Seminary. Students and teachers alike were much helped by Rev. Kim's daily messages in Chapel, by the morning prayer meetings which he conducted and by the special week of prayer meetings held in preparation for these meetings.

We sometimes hear this or that work described as a "faith" enterprise. I think, we may be proud to describe the work of this College as a "faith" enterprise. We have no assurances from year to year as to the amount of our endowment income from the United States. We do not know what vicissitudes in local conditions may decrease or increase in our income from tuition. We do not know, now less than two months from the opening of the new year, what teachers we will have on our staff on April 1st. We do not know what effect new policies of government may have upon our entire work. Despite all these difficulties, we carry on and have carried on for 25 years. Even if we had no other grounds for faith, we might well look back over the past and say that we "believe for the very work's sake", and once more thank God who has brought us thus far.

Yours very respectfully,

Horace H. Underwood

Horace H. Underwood
President

HHU/DTA

57. 원한경 교장의 이사회 제출 연례보고서

문서 제목	Report of the President to the Board of Managers of Chosen Christian College
문서 종류	교장 보고서
제출 시기	1941년 2월 25일
작성 장소	서울
제 출 자	H. H. Underwood
수 신 자	이사회
페이지 수	6
출 처	2114-5-5: 01 Underwood, Horace H. (DR.) 1941~1944 (UMAH)

자료 소개

원한경 교장은 1941년 2월 25일 마지막으로 이사회 회의를 주재하면서 이 보고를 제출하였다. 이 회의에는 1940년 11월에 본진과 함께 철수하지 않고 잔류한 연희전문 관련 선교사들과 윤치호, 양주삼, 유형기 등의 한인 목사들이 참석하였다. 잔류 선교사들은 주한 미국 총영사의 철수 요청과 본국 선교부들의 철수 지시에도 불구하고 떠나지 않았다. 이 날 이사회는 원한경의 사임서를 수리하고 그를 명예교장과 이사로 선출하였으며, 윤치호를 교장으로, 마츠모토를 부교장으로 선출하였다. 또한 대학에 거액을 기부했던 김성권에게 윤치호와 양주삼을 시켜 감사를 표하게 하였다.

참고로 북장로회 선교부는 1941년 3월 말까지만 후원하기로 하였지만, 뉴욕 협력이사회의 나머지 선교부들(남 · 북감리회, 캐나다장로회)은 후원 관계를 유지하였다. 따라서 협력이사회는 존속하였지만, 후원금을 학교 계좌로 보내는 것이 위험해져서 학교 계좌가 아닌 '학교 관계자', 곧 회계 최순주의 계좌로 송금하는 방법을 사용하려 하였다. 그러나 미국 정부의 미국 내 일본자산 동결과 동양으로의 송금 중지(필요한 경우에 요청하면 허가) 결정에 이은 미국 은행들의 회피로 송금이 중단되었다.

원한경은 이 보고서에서 아래의 사항들에 관해 설명하였다.

교장직 사임 과정, 교수진, 북장로회 협력 중단, 이사회 구성원, 1940년 개교 25주년 기념행사, 신과, 종교 사역, 식당 건물과 기숙사 건축, 특별 기부금, 재정, 예산.

내용 요약

사임 과정: 총독부가 일본 국민에 의한 학교 운영을 바라기 때문에 내(원한경)가 지난 가을 학무국에 가서 사임 의사를 밝혔고, 학무국장 시오바라[鹽原時三郎]는 이 학교가 기독교 정신으로 운영될 필요가 있다고 하며 윤치호에게 교장직을 승계할 것을 제안하였다. 이는 내가 바라는 바이므로 기뻐하면서 윤치호가 이날 회의에서 선출되도록 사임서를 제출한다. [원한경은 일제의 압력으로 사임하게 된 내막을 미국 도착 후 이 자료집의 60번 보고서에서 더 자세히 설명하였다.]

교수진: 수물과의 유한상 조교수, 상과의 김정록 조교수, 사무직원 몇 명이 사임하였다. 베커와 케이블이 떠난 것은 아쉽지만, 유억겸이 돌아올 수 있게 되어 기쁘다.

북장로회 협력 중단: 미국 북장로회 선교부가 협력을 중단하는 시점[1941년 3월 말]이 이르게 되어 유감이지만, 1940년 9월에 선교부가 최종적으로 내린 결정을 보면, 이 대학에 개인적으로 계속 참여하는 것은 용인하는 것처럼 보인다.

이사회: 운영진이 교체되어 이사회의 정관을 개정할 여지가 생겼다. 이사회에서 내국인을 다수로 만들어 학교가 외국기관으로 분류되지 않게 할 필요가 있다. 케이블의 사임과 장로교 선교회의 철수로 외국인 이사가 줄었으므로, 이 문제로 비판받지 않게 될 것이다.

개교기념행사: 개교 25주년과 일본 개국[황기] 2600주년이 지난해(1940년)에 겹쳐서 간소하게 개교기념행사를 진행하였다. 소책자를 2개 언어로 발행하였고, 오전에 간단한 기념식과 학생 운동경기를 열었으며, 오후에 노천극장에서 동문회가 윤치호, 존 T. 언더우드, 에비슨, 세키야, 베커, 밀러, 원한경에게 각각 은컵을 증정하였다. 저녁에 원한경의 집에서 만찬을 가진 후, 노천극장에서 음악회를 열었고, 그 주간에 몇 차례 강연회를 열었다. 교수들과 학생들이 학교의 눈부신 역사에 감동하여 장래에 더 큰 성취를 이루도록 분투할 마음을 갖게 되었을 것이다.

신과: 신과의 복설이 바람직해 보이지만, 그 일은 새 교장에게 맡기는 것이 지혜로울 듯하다.

종교 사역: 어려움 속에서도 종교 사역을 수행하여, 한 해 평균 250회의 예배를 열었고, 평균 80시간 성경 교육을 하였다. 많은 교수가 여러 곳에서 종교 사역을 하였고, 나도 50~60번 설교하였다. 학생들이 주일학교, 성가대에서 봉사하였고, 전도대들이 하기 봉사를 하였으

며, 일본 감리교회 사메지마 목사가 학교 특별집회를 인도하였다.

식당 · 기숙사: 식당 건물[한경관]은 초가을에 완공되었으나 기숙사는 건축허가를 받지 못하고 있다.

특별 기부금: 김성권이 1940년 12월 24일 ¥50,000 상당의 땅을 기증하여 거기에서 매년 ¥20,000~40,000의 수입을 얻게 해주었고, 상과 동문 이정규가 ¥10,000을 기부하였다. (그 밖의 기부 명단을 제시하고 있다.)

재정: 물가 인상으로 생활고가 심해져서 긴급급여를 만들어 월급이 150원 이상인 교직원에게는 10원을, 150원 미만인 교직원에게는 20원을 더 지급하였다. 예상 밖의 기부들 덕분에 지출 증가에도 불구하고 큰 적자를 내지 않았다.

예산: 예산을 정하는 일은 교수의 승급, 부임, 사임 등을 고려해야 하므로 신임 운영진에게 맡기고, 교수 승급 문제도 새 교장에게 맡기도록 하겠다.

지난 7년간 이사들이 나에게 보여준 신뢰와 후원에 감사한다. 내가 가능성을 살리지 못한 것에 대해 깊은 실패감을 느낀다.

TRANSFERRED

882

Report of the President
to the
Board of Managers
of
Chosen Christian College

February 25, 1941

****

Gentlemen:-

The Empire has completed the 2600th year of its history and is in the midst of perfecting the new structure from which so much is hoped. Not only all subjects of Japan but all friends of Japan sincerely hope that the nation may indeed have both a new structure and a new birth followed by a new life based on a deeper realization and knowledge of the presence and power of God whom to know aright is life eternal. This new structure calls for many changes, for new policy and new departures. Each individual must do his part for the highest and deepest good of the nation which has so large a part to play both in Asia and in the world.

In the educational sphere the policy of the government demands that educational institutions shall be under the administration of nationals. Consistently with this policy I called upon the Director of the Educational Bureau last fall and stated my complete willingness to resign my position as president of this College provided I could be assured that the institution which had been handed down from Dr. H. G. Underwood to Dr. O. R. Avison and then to me would be conducted according to the Christian ideals and spirit under which it was founded. I am happy to say that Mr. Shihobara expressed his full agreement with the necessity of maintaining the Christian spirit and the character of the institution. After some weeks of consideration, Mr. Shihobara suggested to me the name of our honored friend, Dr. T. H. Yun, as my possible successor. I was, of course, overjoyed to think that so happy a result might be achieved and it is my earnest hope that the Board will agree with this opinion and elect Dr. Yun at this meeting. I have, therefore, prepared my resignation which I shall submit to the Board today and which is conditioned only on the selection of Dr. Yun or someone who, like him, may be counted upon to carry on the Christian traditions of the College. It is my hope to continue as a teacher of this institution and to render any services that are in my power and that are consistent with the national policy. This statement might perhaps have been reserved until the actual presentation of my resignation but for the fact that it affects other sections of this report and is necessary for your understanding of certain omissions in the report.

Faculty:

Turning from my own relation with the College to the faculty as a whole, I have to report the resignation from our staff of Assistant Professor Han Sang Ryu of the Science Department and Assistant Professor Chung Nok Kim of the Commercial Department. In addition to this, I regretfully report that Mr. Paul Hyen who served for many years in the Treasurer's office left us to go into business and that Mr. W. Y. Shim of the general office also resigned to go into business. I must also report that the withdrawals of foreign missionaries have already deprived us of the services of Dr. A. L. Becker and Dr. and Mrs. E. M. Cable as well

-2-

as the assistance in extra curricula activities which was given to us by Mrs. E. H. Miller. It is needless to say that we deeply regret their going and the circumstances which made it seem necessary. Our prayers go with them for their success wherever they are and for their early return to the College if it be God's will. I have already taken the liberty of writing to the Methodist Board of Foreign Missions urging that they plan either for the early return of these teachers or for the sending to Korea of others to take their place. When and in what degree such restoration may be possible we cannot at present tell.

It gives me great joy to report that our application for a teaching permit for Mr. U. K. Yu was granted on February 15th thus restoring to us the services of Mr. Yu of which we have been deprived for more than two years. I feel sure that Mr. Yu will prove a tower of strength to the new administration as he did to the old. The new administration will continue with renewed strength our efforts for the restoration of other teachers still absent and it is our earnest hope that before too great a lapse of time the College may again enjoy their services.

Withdrawal of Presbyterian Mission:

The end of this year brings us to the date set by the Presbyterian Board of Foreign Missions for its withdrawal from cooperation in the work of this College. All who are acquainted with the history of this College and the large part which this Board played in that history will see this withdrawal with deep regret. As I understand the action taken by the Board this means that the Mission will no longer nominate representatives on this Board of Managers; that the Presbyterian Board of Foreign Missions will discontinue the subsidy hitherto given to the College, and that members of this Mission may no longer occupy "positions of administration and control" in the College. The final action of the Board on this question taken in September 1940 seems to indicate that members of the Mission may continue to serve the College in teaching or in religious work. It would also appear from the precedent recently established in the case of the Union Christian Hospital in Pyengyang that individuals may serve on the Board of Managers as individuals but not as representative members. Should this Board, therefore, care to elect from among the members of the Presbyterian Mission certain individuals it would seem that they might serve though not as representing the Presbyterian Mission or Board. As a member of that Mission I continue to hope that the day may come when conditions are such that this church will renew its cooperation in the institution for which it has done so much.

Membership of the Board:

It seems probable that among the tasks before the new administration will be that of revising certain features of our constitution. Among other sections the size of the Board and hence its constituent membership may well be taken up. Even before this, however, it was brought to my attention that it was essential that the Board should have a majority of nationals in order to avoid classification as a foreign incorporation. I, therefore, consulted with Dr. Cable before he left last fall and Dr. E. M. Cable presented to me his resignation from this Board thus at once reducing the foreign membership to a minority. It seemed plain that this step should be taken at once and while I regretted to have Dr. Cable resign he was generous enough to do so with great good will so as to make

-3-

plain as early as possible the national status of the institution. The Presbyterian withdrawal and any reductions that are made in the size of the Board will probably further reduce this minority to a place where no criticism may be expected on this score.

The 25th Anniversary Celebration in 1940:

As you all know it was the 2600th year of the Empire and the 25th year of the College. The institution loyally and whole heartedly cooperated in the various forms of celebration for this 2600th year at the same time that we rejoiced over our own completion of a quarter of a century. Our celebration was held rather quietly as seemed appropriate to the spirit of the times. Booklets, in the national language and also in English were published to remind our friends of this happy occassion and to give its celebration permanent record. After brief ceremonies in the College quadrangle in the morning, athletic events were held for our students, followed in the afternoon by an impressive ceremony at the open air amphi-theatro. At this time the Alumni Association graciously presented silver cups and certificates of service for Dr. L. H. Yu; Mr. John T. Underwood; Dr. O. R. Avison; Hon. T. Sekiya; Dr. A. L. Becker; Dr. E. H. Miller and myself. The special guests at the ceremony were then entertained at dinner at our home after which an open air concert was held in the evening. Several lecturers were brought to the College during that week to lecture to our students and I feel sure that the faculty, students and public were again impressed with the splendid history of the College and that all were inspired to strive toward greater things in the future.

Theological Department:

It had been our hope that we might find it possible to open our Theological Department this spring, but with general conditions as they are and with the coming of the new administration to the College it seemed to me unwise to take such a step and inappropriate for me on the eve of retirement to commit the new administration to so serious an undertaking. I continue to hope that without too long delay this may be accomplished. The difficulties which have beset both of the existing seminaries, and other conditions both in and out of the College would make it seem desirable to attempt the revival of this Department but it is one of the many questions which I must leave to be settled under the wise direction of the new president and of the Board.

Religious Work:

Once again I find myself at a loss how to express in a few lines something of the volume of religious work carried on by students and professors, even during this past year when such work has been carried out under difficulties. I can but remind you that this College conducts some 250 religious services per year; that our 450 students each receive approximately 80 hours of Bible instruction or a total of some 36,000 pupil hours of teaching, and that in addition to this many of the members of the faculty take a leading part in religious work in many places. Dr. T. Matsumoto, for instance, has led special meetings in Chinampo, Taiku, and in Jinsen. I, myself, have spoken 50 or 60 times during the course of the year and many of the other teachers have similar records. Still again the weekly contribution of our students in Sunday Schools, choirs, and in other forms of Christian work mounts up to an astonishing total. Last, but by no means least, are our summer preaching bands and the special week of religious services. Two teams

-4-

consisting of two students and one teacher each went out this summer; one to an island near Jinsen and another to an island off the coast of Whang Hai Province. Both brought back thrilling stories and a record of splendid service rendered. Our special week of services was led this year by the Rev. Samejima of the Keijo Methodist Church and I feel sure that Mr. Samejima's spiritual and yet scholarly addresses brought a great blessing to both the students and faculty.

Dining Hall and Dormitory:

When you met here last year I pointed out to you the walls of our new dining hall then under construction. This was completed in the early fall and has been in use ever since to our great satisfaction and joy. The hoped for dormitory has not yet materialized both on account of the difficulty in securing the permits from the many different bureaus and departments concerned and because in view of the present difficult conditions it hardly seemed wise to begin such an undertaking at present. The need remains as great as ever and perhaps the new administration may find means to carry out this long hoped for addition to our campus.

Special Gifts:

Such financial difficulties are always with us, but if we continue to enjoy the confidence of the people of this Peninsula it is quite possible that these difficulties may be wiped away by generous special gifts. It is with the greatest joy that I have the honor to report the magnificent gift made by Mr. Sung Kwon Kim. Mr. Kim on December 24th, 1940, promised to give to the College land to the value of approximately ¥500,000.00 the annual income from which is estimated to yield from ¥20,000.00 to ¥40,000.00. Mr. Kim made this gift quite unconditionally, the income to be used for the current expenses of the College. The Executive Committee is recommending to you that in partial acknowledgement of this generosity and so as to conserve for the College Mr. Kim's interest and help we should elect as coopted members of the Board one or two suitable Christians suggested by Mr. Kim as his representatives. It gives me great pleasure to personally endorse this recommendation of the Committee. I am also more than happy to announce the gift of ¥10,000.00 by Mr. Chung Kyu Lee a graduate of the Commercial Department of this College just ten years ago in 1931. This is the largest single gift to be received from an alumnus to date and I would remind you that only last year Mr. Lee gave ¥500.00 toward the 25th anniversary expenses as well as ¥600 annually for two scholarships. In addition to this, we have received a number of anonymous gifts for the current expenses of the College. Other special gifts during the year have been:

Name of Donor	Purpose	Amount
Kim Choo Yun	Gymnasium	1,000.00
Friends in America	Religious Work	868.00
Miss E. Stutzer	Medical Fund	200.00
Lee Chung Kyu	Scholarship	600.00
Kim Chong Sun	Scholarship	300.00
Lee Chung Hwa	Scholarship	225.00
Yun Pang Hyun	Scholarship	200.00
Kim Young Ho	Scholarship	75.00
Yun Tchi Chang	Scholarship	75.00

-5-

In addition to these monetary gifts Bishop Cecil Cooper of the English Church Mission turned over to the College the splendid Trollope Collection of oriental books amounting to some 10,000 volumes as well as the Landis Library of occidental works on the orient. The conditions on which these are loaned us makes this really a gift rather than a loan. Both of these collections are in their own way priceless. The Trollope collection represents the careful and scholarly selection made by the Bishop during his many years in Korea and contains volumes which could not now be purchased at any price. The Landis collection is undoubtedly the finest collection of occidental works on Korea anywhere in existence. All of these gifts as well as smaller donations of $5.00 and $10.00 sent to help a needy student or for special religious work are deeply appreciated and we feel sure that the donors would be amply satisfied if they could but see even a part of the results achieved.

Finances:

The year has been a difficult one both for the College and for the teachers. The unprecedent rise in prices has made living very difficult and last spring it became evident that it was almost impossible for our staff to live on the salaries given them. After careful study of the question both on the side of what should be done and what could be done we made a Special Emergency Allowance by which all those receiving salaries of over ¥150 would receive a special monthly allowance of ¥10, while those receiving salaries of less than ¥150 would receive ¥20 a month. The total expenditure for this allowance for the academic year has been about ¥10,000.00. With other expenses increasing we would barily have gotten through the year without an appalling deficit had it not been for stringent economy and care on the part of all officers as well as by virtue of unexpected gifts and income. As it is we hope to close the year with at worst only a small deficit.

Budget:

For the coming year I presented to the Joint Meeting of the Executive and Finance Committees an incomplete or tentative budget. It is presented in this form because so large portion of the budget depends upon teaching salaries which in turn may vary very widely as changes are made in the faculty. Promotions, additions to the staff, resignations from the staff, all of these questions should be decided by the new president and the new administration, yet until they are decided it is impossible to in any way accurately prepare a budget for the coming year. We have, therefore, estimated the income, have added an item for the president's salary and with one or two other minor changes have merely re-submitted the budget in effect during the past year. This will, of course, require early action on the part of the new administration and this and other matters are the basis of recommendations which come to you from the Executive Committee looking toward a special meeting of the Board early in the new school year.

The above statement as to the budget will make clear to you the reason why I do not recommend certain members for promotion of the faculty. You will, of course, understand that there are a number of men fully worthy of promotion both from the rank of Instructor to that of Assistant Professor and from Assistant Professor to that of full Professor, but here again it seems to me that the new president should be given a free hand.

-6-

In closing this my last report as president I cannot refrain from expressing to the Board my deep gratitude for the honor they have done me, the confidence that they have shown me and the support that they have given me during the past seven years. It has been a great honor and a great responsibility. I feel deeply my failure to live up to its possibilities.

With renewed gratitude to the Board and to our God in whose name the work of the College is done.

Respectfully submitted,

Horace H. Underwood

Horace H. Underwood
President

HHU:DA

58. 원한경 교장의 이사회 제출 사임서

문서 제목	Resignation of Horace H. Underwood, President, Presented to Board of Managers, Chosen Christian College
문서 종류	교장 사임서
제출 시기	1941년 2월 25일
작성 장소	서울
제 출 자	H. H. Underwood
수 신 자	이사회
페이지 수	3
출 처	2114-5-5: 01 Underwood, Horace H. (DR.) 1941~1944 (UMAH)

자료 소개

원한경 교장이 1941년 2월 25일 열린 이사회 연례회의에 낸 사임서이다. 원한경이 사임하기까지의 과정은 같은 날 제출한 교장 보고서에서도 간략히 설명되었다. 그는 이 회의를 주재하면서 사임서를 제출하였고, 이사회는 이를 수리하고, 그를 명예 교장과 이사로, 윤치호를 후임 교장으로 선출하였다. 그 후 원한경은 일본의 진주만 공습 다음 날인 1941년 12월 8일 체포되어 구금되었다가 1942년 5월 31일 풀려나 다음날 미국으로 송환되었다. 일제는 1942년 8월 학교 재산을 적산으로 규정하여 몰수하고 학교에 일본인 교장을 두게 하였으며, 1944년 5월 학교를 경성공업전문학교로 만들었다.

원한경은 이 사임서에서 아래의 사항들을 언급하였다.

사임 과정 설명, 교직원에 대한 감사와 치하, 재임 기간 재산관리 총평, 이후의 학교 운영에 대한 당부.

내용 요약

사임 과정: 총독부와 일본 정부가 사립학교들까지 일본 정부의 교육기관으로 간주하면서 일본인이 운영하기를 원하고 있으므로, 내가 1940년 가을에 학무국에 출두하여 사임 의사를 밝혔다. 학무국장이 윤치호를 후임자로 지명하여 이 대학이 기독교적 성격을 유지할 수 있게 해주었고, 이에 내가 그 제안을 기쁘게 받아들였다. 이사회의 승인을 받아 3월

10일 졸업식과 4월 1일 새 학기 시작 사이에 사임이 발효되도록 사임서를 제출한다.

감사 · 치하: 이 대학이 윤치호, 이사회, 동문회와 같이 굳건한 사람들에 의해 뒷받침되고 있어서 기뻐하고, 교장으로 있는 동안 함께 수고해준 교직원들에게 감사한다. 학감으로 활동한 유억겸 · 이춘호 · 이원철 · 이묘묵, 수물과 과장 이춘호 · 이원철 · 최규남, 문과 과장 백낙준 · 최현배 · 하경덕, 상과 과장 이순탁 · 홍승국 · 임병혁 · 장희창이 급변하는 상황과 주위의 질시와 오해를 무릅쓰고 수고해준 데 대해 감사한다. 특히 이묘묵이 많은 비판, 비방, 공격 속에서도 성실하게 봉사한 것을 치하한다. 최순주가 1938년 가을부터 가르칠 수 없게 되었으나 회계업무는 계속 맡게 되어 많은 돈을 절약하게 해주었다. 운동부, 종교부, 음악부 등 각 부서의 부장들에게도 감사한다.

자산관리: 내가 교장으로 재직한 7년 동안 미국에서 $65,000을, 국내에서 ￥520,000을 대학의 기본재산으로 받았다. 학비만 아니라 다른 재원들도 많이 늘었고, 시설들과 삼림도 크게 개선되었지만, 간신히 살아남을 정도로만 이끌어왔다.

당부: 이사들께 후임 교장을 도와주기를 당부한다. 학무국장도 기독교적 성격을 보존할 필요가 있음을 인정하였다. 채플 예배, 성경 교육, 종교행사 참석의 의무화 등으로 인해 반기독교 세력으로부터 공격을 받을지라도 기독교 교수를 확보하는 일과 대학의 기독교적 성격을 굳게 지켜주기를 당부한다. 내가 이 학교에서 계속 가르칠 수 있기를 희망한다. 임원을 교체하는 시기에 도움이 되도록 내가 이곳에 머물러 있기 위해 7월로 예정된 안식년을 1년 연기해달라고 선교회에 요청하였다.

한국인을 교장으로 세운 것을 보게 되어 기쁘다. 25년간 이 대학을 안전하게 이끄신 하나님께서 앞으로도 인도해주기를 바란다.

Resignation of
Horace H. Underwood, President
Presented to
Board of Managers
Chosen Christian College

February 25, 1941

Dear Sirs:-

As you are all aware the present policy both of the Government-General of Chosen and of the government in Japan Proper regards even private educational institutions as an integral part of the government organs of education and therefore demands that all such institutions shall be under the administration of subjects of the Empire. Realizing this fact, last fall, I called upon Mr. Shihobara the Director of the Educational Bureau of the Government-General of Chosen and expressed to him my perfect willingness to resign my position in accordance with this policy; if and when a suitable successor could be found. I pointed out to Mr. Shihobara that my connection with the institution and my responsibility for it was such that I could not lightly lay it aside or see it undertaken by one who might not understand its historic position as an essentially Christian institution. I was gratified to find that Mr. Shihobara expressed full agreement with me as to the necessity of maintaining the Christian character of the institution and of seeing it placed under strong Christian leadership. Some weeks later, Mr. Shihobara did me the honor to ask my opinion concerning Dr. T. H. Yun as my possible successor. I was, of course, delighted with the possibility of the College passing under such leadership and I assured Mr. Shihobara that if Dr. Yun were elected by the Board and his election confirmed by the Government-General I would be very happy to turn over to his capable hands the administration of the College.

I, therefore, at this time wish to formally offer to this Board my resignation; conditioned only on the election by the Board and appointment by the educational authorities of Dr. Yun, or of some other strong Christian character, who may be expected to preserve and strengthen the Christian character of the institution. With the Boards consent I would make my resignation to take affect at such a time between commencement on March 10th and the opening of College on April 1st as may be most convenient for the parties concerned.

In laying down these responsibilities I do so with very mixed feelings. There is joy in the knowledge that I may be succeeded by such a man as Dr. Yun and that the College itself has the stalwart backing of such a body of Christian men as are gathered in this Board and as are found in our Alumni Association. There is sincere gratitude to God for the blessing of this opportunity to serve the institution in this position for a few years. There is gratitude to the members of this Board both individually and to the various bodies which you represent. There is also very sincere gratitude to the men who have served with me, who have faithfully helped me and who have frequently taken the blame for my mistakes. Since I assumed office in 1934, we have lost almost 40 members from our faculty and staff. Nearly all of these were men whom we regretted to see go and who for longer or shorter periods had served the College faithfully. Mr. U. K. Yu; Mr. C. H. Lee; Dr. D. W. Lee; and Dr. M. M. Lee; have all held the difficult position of Dean and all have had to suffer for my mistakes. Especially difficult has the position been for Dr. M. M. Lee, who despite bitter criticism and violent attacks has given patient and yet whole-hearted service even when he was most misunderstood and when the most malicious slanders were circulated about him. In the Science Department, Mr. C. H. Lee; Dr. D. W. Lee; and Dr. K. N. Choi have served as departmental heads under me. In the Literary Department, Dr. L. G. Paik; Mr. H. P. Choi; and Dr. K. D. Harr in the Commercial Department, Mr. S. T. Lee; Mr. S. K. Hong; Mr. P. K. Lim; and Mr. H. C. Chang have carried the director's burden. In all of these offices the later incumbents came to their positions with a depleted staff from which the oldest and most experienced members had been taken and in a period of transition and of tension. Their own promotion was relatively sudden and brought with it jealousy and misunderstanding. They are quite properly resigning these positions so as to leave the decks clear for the new administration. At present, some of them are still under fire but it is my sincere conviction that the time will come when not only I, but all will realize the debt which the College owes to these men who during the last two years have carried uncomplainingly so heavy a burden.

Dr. S. J. Choy although unable since the fall of 1938 to hold a teaching position has fortunately been allowed to continue his work as Treasurer. His report today tells something of the decade during which he has held this important position. He has saved thousands of yen and made thousands of yen for the College. With a small staff and under many difficulties he has accomplished an outstanding piece of work. There are many others to whom I owe thanks. Mr. O. Y. Lee who has capably headed the Athletic Committee; Pastor Chang whose religious work has meant so much to us; Dr. E. M. Cable and later Dr. T. Matsumoto in the Religious Work Committee; Dr. Eody Hyun in the Music Department; Mr. I. S. Jung who has done so much as Chairman of the Public Occassion Committee; Capt. C. H. Pak who has greatly improved the discipline of the College; Dr. E. H. Miller of the Property Committee; Mr. Chi Kak Kim who carries the chief burden of seeing that our buildings are heated that they have water and light; that they are repaired and cared for; and so on, until I might list almost all of the members of our faculty and staff.

With these feelings of joy and gratitude there is mingled a very sincere regret that I personally have not measured up more adequately to the demands of the position. In these seven years the College has received endowment gifts of over $65,000.00 in the United States and of about ¥520,000.00 in Chosen. Our student body has almost doubled. Our receipts, not only from tuition, but from other sources from the field have greatly increased. Dr. Choy's report tells more in detail of the improvement of the site, of water development, of building decoration, athletic field development, planting of trees, increase in equipment and progress in many ways. I can, however, claim little or no credit for any of this and I see now many places where I have woefully failed. I can say honestly that I have done my best and I feel a great sense of satisfaction that however poorly the ship has been steered it has still survived, the storms of the last four years, until I may turn it over into the hands of a more capable commander.

I would earnestly beg that the Board give every assistance and support to my successor in the difficult task before him. We have been assured by the Director of the Educational Bureau that he recognizes the necessity for preserv

-3-

ing the Christian character of the institution. On the other hand, there are in this country as in every country both anti-Christian forces and groups which while not actively anti-Christian see no value in Christianity. It will not be easy to hold fast to those things which while invisible are most precious. Specious arguements will be produced by which compulsory chapel, Bible instruction, religious exercises, the need of Christian teachers and other features will be attacked one by one. These arguements are most dangerous because it is true that the Christian character of the institution does not depend on any single one of these or on their formal application. Yet, we all realize that as these are attacked the danger to the deeper values increases.

My membership on this Board at present depends upon my position as president, but I hope to continue to serve the institution as a teacher or in any other capacity that the members of the Board and the new administration in the College may desire. In view of the large withdrawals among the missionary forces I have asked the Executive Committee of our Mission to postpone my furlough for one year with the hope that my presence might be of some help in this transitional period. If this permission is not granted, I shall take my regular furlough in July and hope to return to serve at the disposal of the Board and the new president.

It will be a great joy to me to see a Korean installed as president of the College and I pray for him, for you, and for the institution that God, who has brought us safely through 25 years of splendid work for the youth of Korea may continue to guide and control the destinies of the institution through servants whom He may chose and who look to Him in all things.

Respectfully submitted,

Horace H. Underwood

Horace H. Underwood, President

HHU/DA

59. 원한경 전임 교장의 협력이사회 제출 첫 번째 경과보고서

문서 제목	Report of Horace H. Underwood to the Cooperating Board for Christian Education in Chosen
문서 종류	교장 보고서
제출 시기	1942년 11월 17일
작성 장소	뉴욕 (추정)
제 출 자	H. H. Underwood
수 신 자	미국 협력이사회 관계자
페이지 수	6
출 처	2114-5-5: 01 Underwood, Horace H. (DR.) 1941~1944 (UMAH)

자료 소개

원한경 전임 교장이 일경에게 체포되었다가 풀려나 미국으로 송환된 후 1942년 11월 17일 자로 협력이사회에 제출한 첫 번째 경과보고서이다. 그가 1942년 12월 23일 자로 협력이사회의 회계인 서덜랜드(George F. Sutherland)에게 쓴 편지를 보면, 이 보고서는 협력이사회 사람들과 가진 점심 모임에서 제출되었다(이 문서는 p.52에 사진자료로 제시되어 있다). 그런 점에서 작성 장소는 협력이사회의 사무실이 있는 뉴욕으로 보인다.

이 보고서에서 원한경은 교장직 사임서를 제출한 후부터 송환 전까지 겪은 일들을 아래의 소제목들로 묶어서 설명하고, 그가 들은 방콕의 일화를 소개하며 마무리하였다.

사임서 제출 후 교장직 수행, 새 운영진, 1941년 3월 이후의 활동, 재정, 10월 이사회 특별회의, 1941년 7월부터 12월까지, 12월 8일부터 6월 1일까지.

내용 요약

교장직 수행: 나(원한경)는 1941년 2월 25일 교장 보고서에서 사임 의사를 밝혔고, 그 후 3월(3월 10일)에 열린 졸업식 때까지 교장직을 수행하였다. 102명이 졸업하여, 졸업생은 총 1143명이 되었다.

새 운영진: 졸업식을 거행한 지 얼마 안 되어 윤치호 교장과 마츠모토 부교장이 별다른 취임식 없이 부임하였는데, 윤치호가 학감 직을 없애고 5개 부서를 두었고, 유억겸이 학

교 운영을 사실상 주도하였다. 원한경과 같은 날 사임한 학감과 과장들의 자리를 총독부가 일본에서 공부한 사람들로만 채우기를 원하여 교직원들이 분개하였다. 이전에는 학교에서 선교사의 수업 시간 외에는 일어로 수업하면서도 채플 등 종교행사와 이사회 · 교수회 회의는 한국말로 하고, 회의록만 영어로 작성하였으며, 캠퍼스에서는 일상적으로 조선어를 사용하였지만, 오직 일어만 사용하게 하였다.

사임 후 활동: 나는 사임한 후에 명예 교장과 이사회 이사가 되었고, 성경과 영문학을 가르치면서 조선어로 수업하였으며, 학교 업무에 관해 조언하였다. 교수들과 학생들도 나와 내 가족을 전보다 더 친절히 대해주었다.

재정: 미국에서 7월에 취한 자산동결 결정으로 해외 자금의 도입이 완전히 중단되었다. 윤치호가 6월에 연 이사회의 특별회의에서 은행으로부터의 거액 차용, 학비 인상, 후원회 조직, 특별 모금 계획을 승인받았다. 캠퍼스의 일부 부지 매각계획도 제시하였다가 많은 반대를 받았다.

이사회 특별회의: 10월에 이사회의 특별회의가 소집되어 경찰 3명과 특별경찰 3명이 착석한 가운데 중요한 일들을 결정하였다. 추가로 대출받는 것을 불허하였고, 거액을 기부한 김성권을 대리할 이사를 선출하였으며, 한국을 떠난 서양인 이사의 자격을 영구히 박탈하였다. 문과와 수물과를 3년제로 축소하고[본래는 4년제] 교육과정도 많이 바꾸기로 하여 이를 내가 크게 반대하였다. 이런 결정에 대해 총독부의 허가가 나지 않아 교육과정이 예전처럼 운영되고 있다.

1941년 7~12월: 1941년 7월 말부터 1달간 군대의 기차 이동이 예정되어 있어서 방학이 일찍 시작되었는데, 군인들이 북쪽으로 가는 것을 보고 러시아를 치려는 것으로 추측하였다. 교수들과 학생들이 나를 만나러 왔으나 경찰과 총독부 관리들에게 오해를 사지 않도록 조심하였다. 대학교회에는 12월 7일 마지막으로 참석하였다.

12월 8일~이듬해 6월: 나는 12월 9일[원문의 '9일'은 8일로 수정되어야 한다] 전쟁이 발발했다는 소식을 오전에 전화로 듣고 대학에 가서 두 시간 강의한 후, 오후 4시쯤 경찰에 체포되었다. 내 아들도 9시경에 체포되어 10일 후에 만났다. 체포된 후부터 학생들과 오가와 교수가 자주 집에 와서 생필품들을 주었고, 마츠모토는 수시로, 교수들은 저녁 시간에 찾아왔다. 나는 4월 10~16일 풀려났다가 다시 구금되어 5월 31일 풀려났다. 그 후부터 6월 1일 떠나기 전까지 이춘호, 최순주, 이묘묵, 하경덕, 유억겸이 와서 이 학교를 기독교

대학으로 유지하도록 모든 노력을 다하겠다고 서약하였고, 내게 돌아올 것과 미국 협력이사회와의 협력관계를 갱신할 것을 요청하였다. 떠나는 날에 세브란스의전 교장 오긍선의 아들 오한영을 만나 오긍선이 사임하고 후임이 선출되었다는 소식을 들었고, 오긍선과 다른 교수들이 전쟁이 끝나면 더글라스 에비슨(D. B. Avison), 나(원한경), 다른 선교사들이 돌아오기를 바라고 있으며, 오긍선이 세브란스병원과 의전의 기독교 성격을 유지시킬 뜻을 품고 있음을 협력이사회에 전해주기를 바란다는 말을 들었다.

크리스마스 이브 때 일본 군복을 입은 청년이 방콕 YMCA에 와서 서울에서 온 반하트(Barnhart, YMCA 간사)와 나를 찾은 후, 자리에 앉아 같이 캐롤을 부르고 떠났는데, 반하트의 비서가 내일 다시 오라고 하자 그 청년이 자기는 연희전문 학생인데 오늘 밤 전선으로 떠나므로 반하트를 천국에서 만나게 될 것이라고 말하였다. 그 청년은 본인도 미워하고 태국인들도 미워하는 일본의 군복을 입고 태국의 기독교인들과 함께 크리스마스 노래를 부르며 신앙을 나타내었다.

802

REPORT OF HORACE H. UNDERWOOD

to the

COOPERATING BOARD FOR CHRISTIAN EDUCATION IN CHOSEN

November 17, 1942

My last report as President of the Chosen Christian College was made on February 25, 1941. In that report I presented to the Board of Managers in Chosen my resignation, and the material of that report was intended to bring those who read it up to date as far as the events leading up to and including my resignation and the election of Dr. Yun as president of the college.

Although my resignation was presented on February 25th it was arranged that I should carry on until after graduation. I, therefore, had the pleasure of once more presenting the diplomas to a graduating class at the Chosen Christian College and at the same time of making to them and to the friends gathered at the time of Commencement in March 1941 a farewell address. One hundred and two young men graduated in the class of '41, bringing the total of our graduates to 1143. I do not have before me the complete statistics as to their employment but even if I had them, could not give you a true picture of the influence which these young men have had and are having throughout the Korean peninsula, and even in Japan proper and in Manchuria.

The New Administration

Shortly after the graduation ceremonies Dr. Yun and Dr. Matsumoto took over without any special inaugural ceremonies. The demands of the government and of the situation made it necessary for them to make a number of changes both in the formal organization of the institution and in other ways. The rising cost of living made it necessary to raise salaries although the extent of these raises seemed to me to verge on real danger. This raise of salaries was accompanied by other expenditures, some of which were demanded by the government and others which could hardly be avoided in view of the situation within the college. To illustrate;- The government requirements for anti-air raid precautions cost us several thousand Yen while the appointment of some of the former faculty members, who had been under arrest and were not yet allowed to hold teaching positions, to various forms of office and administrative work added greatly to the overhead expenditures without in any way relieving the teaching situation.

The government quite obviously expected rather sweeping changes to be made and Dr. Yun and his assistants drew up a new scheme of administrative organization doing away with the former position of Dean and setting up four or five so-called divisions such as Educational - Religious - Student Discipline et cetera. This seemed to satisfy the authorities and did no real harm as it was clearly understood from the beginning that under whatever name, Mr. U. K. Yu would be the real head of the institution and the administrator of its internal affairs. A certain amount of misunderstanding and feeling was however aroused by his attempt to subordinate the Treasurer's position to that of the other administrative officers of the college. The Treasurer maintained, and correctly so, that the Treasurer was appointed by the Board of Managers and that it was the intention of the Board that he should supervise the administrative expenditures as the agent of the Board. He successfully maintained the argument, at least in theory, up to the time when I left Korea in the summer of 1942, but an unfortunate amount of friction was engendered in the process.

When I resigned not only the Dean but the heads of the three departments also resigned with me. In view of the government's attitude toward American trained men, the administration saw fit to accept their resignations and to appoint in their place from our staff graduates of Japanese universities. As this happened to mean the appointment of less capable men, it also was a cause of considerable feeling and resentment within the staff. The new administration also had to take on itself the unpleasant task of carrying out the government's policy in regard to the use of the Japanese language. In passing, I may remark that in Korea it is a serious offense to refer to this as "Japanese" as if it were another language. It must always be referred to as "the national language". For many years all of our teaching with the exception of the courses taught by the foreign missionaries had been in Japanese, but we had conducted our chapel exercises in Korean on the ground that religious services throughout the country were still conducted in Korean. Furthermore on the campus and in the college offices Korean was quite largely used, the staff being very glad to avail itself of the excuse that I and the other Occidental professors did not understand Japanese. Thus our faculty meetings were conducted in Korean, essential questions being interpreted into Japanese and English whenever necessary. The faculty minutes, the minutes of the Board of Managers and all other such minutes and papers were kept in English and the English version was considered as the official one. This was all changed now, all business was conducted in Japanese and the records so kept. Except when conversing with me all discussions and conversation in college offices, classrooms and on the campus were now held in Japanese, and signs urging on the students "complete use of national language" were posted in prominent places in all college buildings. The government required that additional courses in national history and "national culture" be given at once, and Japanese part time teachers of these courses were secured, beginning their work with the opening of the new term in April 1941. A committee was further appointed to study the curricula of the three departments or schools with a view to shortening the science and arts courses and bringing them more "in line with the national spirit".

Horace H. Underwood's Position after March 1941

My own position after 1941 is perhaps significant of the goodwill and friendship of the new administration and the entire staff. The Board of Managers, the faculty and the staff organization all passed very kind resolutions on my resignation, and the faculty joined in presenting me a beautiful inlaid tray with the main buildings of the college done in mother-of-pearl inlay work. I was made president emeritus, and a member of the Board of Managers as well as continuing as a full voting member of the faculty. I took on a schedule of teaching including three courses in Bible and two in English literature. I was allowed to continue teaching in Korean and suffered no interference or criticism in the subject matter of my lectures, although such topics as "The Social Teachings of the New Testament" which was my course with the seniors in the science department might easily have been open to criticism had anyone cared to make trouble. Mrs. Underwood and my son both continued to carry full schedules in the teaching of English. Dr. Yun and Dr. Matsumoto and Mr. Yu were all very considerate in calling me into consultation on various questions that came up, and I am happy to say that on several occasions I was able to be of assistance to them. My strong opposition to certain proposals gave them both the moral backing and the excuse which they needed in order to avoid doing certain things which I feel sure were distasteful to them. I also continued to assist the Treasurer in the handling of such drafts as came from America and in the clearing up of the funds which had been deposited with the United Missions Treasurer in Shanghai. This was a rather delicate matter as we were sailing very close to the wind legally and I did not wish to involve any of my Korean associates in legal difficulties. We managed in one way or another to get the bulk of those funds transferred to our account in Seoul without doing anything which the authorities of the Government-General Finance Department could take hold of as a charge against us. Mrs. Underwood and my son and I were much touched and pleased by the kindness and consideration of the faculty and students who went out of their way to be even more helpful and more kind than previously. When the College Annual was published in April 1941 with my picture, a large number of additional copies of the picture were printed and eagerly bought by practically all the students and faculty, and for some days I was kept busy autographing those pictures. The graduates in each of the three departments made us very beautiful farewell presents and the memory of these kindnesses will always remain with us although we, of course, were unable to bring those or other such souvenirs from Korea with us.

Finances

I regret that I cannot furnish the Cooperating Board with any clear picture of the financial situation in the college even up to the time of the outbreak of war, as we were not allowed to bring any such papers with us. I have already referred to increased expenditures, and the Board will realize that the freezing regulations enacted by the United States in July completely cut off further income from abroad. As the endowment income from the United States amounted to from 50,000 to 70,000 Yen out of a total budget of approximately 150,000, the difficulties caused by the sudden loss of this income can well be imagined. A special meeting of the Board of Managers was held in June at which the Administration was authorized to make quite large loans from the local banks. Both Mr. Scott and I felt it our duty to say a word of warning against the policy of incurring such indebtedness but we did not feel it wise to vote against the measure which was introduced by Dr. Yun and for which Mr. Yu made a lengthy plea. The Administration had certain plans for meeting the shortages caused by increased expenditures and decreased income. Briefly, the plans were along three lines:

(1) The increase of student fees.

(2) The organization of an association to be called "the Supporters or Patrons of the Chosen Christian College".

The members were to be of several classes and to pay annual or lump sums for the support of the institution. It was believed that with the college's name and reputation it would be possible to secure a large number who would enroll themselves at 10, 25, 50 and 100 Yen per annum to support the institution.

(3) A special campaign to raise large funds for the college.

The fourth suggestion which was hinted at but which met with much opposition in the Board meeting involved the sale of part of the present site. In regard to the above plans a considerable increase can be secured by increased fees and increased enrollment. If the Administration can secure government permission to enroll as many as 600 instead of the 450 odd now in the college, and if they are allowed to raise the fees to a more adequate figure, it is quite true that the receipts can be very largely increased. This, however, will by no means be adequate and I have small faith in the financial success of the proposed Association of Supporters although it may have good propaganda and advertising value. What can be done in the way of a special financial campaign will depend largely on the government's attitude and action, and on how well the new Administration can "sell" themselves and their program to the small group of really wealthy men in the country. A last possibility is that Mr. S. K. Kim who gave to the college property amounting to about 500,000 Yen may be persuaded to still further underwrite the current budget of the institution. Unfortunately, there is a feeling that he might demand a disproportionate control of the institution and Dr. Yun and Mr. Yu look on this with what seems to me unnecessary alarm. This attitude is known to Mr. Kim and naturally does not make him inclined to financially support their administration. However, I believe that the guarantee of the institution's finances will probably be found in the interest and generosity of Mr. Kim whatever readjustments may be necessary between him and the administration of the college to make this effective.

October Board Meeting

In October a special meeting of the Board of Managers was called and merits a brief notice here on account of the significance of a number both of the things done and not done. In the first place this meeting refused to permit further loans to be made for the current support of the college, and directed the Administration to find other means of carrying the expenses. In the second place two new members of the Board of Managers were elected to more or less represent Mr. S.K. Kim, the large donor previously referred to. Mr. Kim was not a Christian and could not therefore himself serve on the Board of Managers. The suggestion that two Christians who were satisfactory to Mr. Kim should be elected as his representatives had been made at the February meeting but had been quite strongly opposed by the new Administration. It was significant both of the financial situation and of better understandings that at this meeting these gentlemen were received by a unanimous vote.

A third significant action was the decision that Occidental members of the Board who had left Korea had ipso facto ceased to be members of the Board. I strongly protested this action and urged that they be considered as members of the Board until the expiration of their term. I was listened to with great courtesy and consideration but Mr. Oda put the matter as clearly as he dared when he said that perhaps Dr. Underwood did not understand all the factors involved. Inasmuch as there were present at the meeting three representatives of the gendarmerie and three from the special police I think I understood these factors quite well but felt it my duty to make the protest although I had no doubt as to the outcome of the vote. This meeting of the Board of Managers also recommended that the science and literary courses be shortened to three years each and that a number of changes within the curricula should also be made. This action also I protested but it was passed over my protest. It was rather interesting to me to learn later that when these recommendations went to the Government-General educational authorities, the requested changes were not permitted so that up to June 1942 the same courses have been taught as reported to you some years ago.

While the permanent shortening of the courses was turned down by the Government-General, it later required as a temporary war measure a shortening of the course by which the students who would normally have graduated in March 1942 were given their diplomas in December 1941, and those who were to graduate in March 1943 would be given diplomas at the end of September 1942. This however was merely a temporary measure and involved more intensive teaching rather than a theoretical shortening of the whole course.

July to December 1942

It is perhaps best after speaking of the October meeting of the Board to go back and very briefly mention the events between the close of school in July and the outbreak of the war on December 8th. School was closed early for ourselves and all schools and the students sent home preparatory to the taking over of the railways for troop transport for about a month from the end of July until about the end of August. During this period large military forces with full equipment passed through Korea on their way north leading many of us to suppose that Japan would strike at Russia. By the time college opened again in September normal passenger traffic had been almost completely restored and after some trouble leaving the beach where we had spent the summer, we got back to Seoul to take up again our work. It was a period of tension and suspicion but one during which we had many quite happy contacts with faculty and students. The students were conducting a series of early morning prayer meetings and asked me to lead those for two weeks. Those morning hours with a group of from twenty-five to fifty earnest young men will long live in my memory, and I feel sure that we were all greatly blessed by this morning watch. Faculty members continued to come and see us but it was necessary to be extremely tactful and not give any ground for misunderstanding either to the police, the Government-General officials or to other members of the faculty. Mrs. Underwood and my daughter-in-law met with the faculty women though less frequently than in the past. She was able to be of assistance in a number of ways and especially at the time when Dr. Matsumoto entertained the officials of the educational department. It was not considered wise for us to be in evidence but Mrs. Underwood arranged to have the entire meal for some twenty-five people cooked at our house, taken a mile and a half to Dr. Matsumoto's residence where our cook and house-boy with some outside assistance served the dinner. Of course, table linen, silver, china and glass ware also had to be provided as a Japanese household does not include those items. Later when it was decided to graduate the students in December we arranged to give our usual graduation dinner, breaking the class up into four groups, thus making four dinners with about thirty-five (including the necessary faculty members) at each dinner. By this time the war tension had become so great that we gravely doubted if we would get through the series before war broke. However, we were permitted the great pleasure of having them all to dinner which was a farewell in more senses than we then realized. On December 7th we attended our last church service at the college church where we had the great pleasure of seeing quite a number of our seniors received into the church.

December 8 to June 1

On the morning of December 9th we received a telephone message from the city telling us that war had broken out. I went over to the college and met my first two classes, making it more of a farewell than a teaching period. In the afternoon about four o'clock I was arrested by the gendarmerie and at eight o'clock my son was arrested and taken to the internment center where I met him ten days later. Mrs. Underwood, my daughter-in-law and Dick and Grace remained at home and were treated very generously by the local police officer who gave them permission to go into the city whenever it was really necessary. We were all much touched by the generosity of our students who, soon after my arrest, sent a delegation to tell Mrs. Underwood that if she was in financial difficulties the student body would undertake the support of our family for as long as might be necessary. Professor Ogawa, a Japanese Christian, called regularly every week or ten days up to the time we left Korea to see if Mrs. Underwood needed anything, and usually to bring a present of sugar, flour, rice or something that he thought she might be needing. Dr. Matsumoto called quite frequently at the home and the Korean members of the faculty, though naturally not so free to show their feelings as the Japanese, came at night to see Mrs. Underwood. We were released for six days from April 10 to April 16 when it was expected that the exchange ship would be sailing at the end of April. During that period and on May 31st and June 1st before we left Korea, I met among others Professor C. H. Lee, formerly head of the science department, Dr. S. J. Choy, college treasurer, Dr. M. M. Lee, formerly Dean, Dr. Har, formerly head of the literary department and Mr. U. K. Yu. All of these gentlemen not only gave me assurances of their own personal regard but, more important, solemnly pledged their best efforts to maintain the institution as a Christian college and to stand by so that when a better day came they could recover whatever values in policy and practice had been temporarily lost. They all urged my own return and asked that the Cooperating Board in America, as representing the cooperating Christian churches in America, should look forward to a day when cooperation might be renewed and might be more fruitful than in the past. I was greatly encouraged to learn that up to that time (June 1st) chapel was being continued and Bible classes were being regularly taught in all departments. I was grieved but not greatly surprised to learn that the difficulties of the situation and the suspicion of the police, expressed in many forms of petty pressure, had so discouraged Dr. Matsumoto that he had resigned from the college staff at the end of the school year in March and had returned to Japan to take a position in a school at Hiroshima. We are grateful to him for what he did and only wish that he could have continued his contribution as a Christian scholar and educator during those difficult days. On the day when I left Seoul I met Dr. H. Y. Oh, the son of Dr. K. S. Oh, president of Severance Union Medical College. He told me that his father had resigned and that Dr. Y. C. Lee had been selected to take his place as president. However, this action had not yet received the approval of the Government-General and I cannot tell you whether it was finally carried out or not. What I do wish to bring to you is a message from Dr. Oh. He asked me to tell you that his father and the other members of the faculty hoped that both Dr. D. B. Avison and I would return to Korea together with other missionaries after the war, and he also asked that we assure the Cooperating Board of Dr. Oh's intentions to so far as possible maintain the Christian character both of the Severance Union Medical College and of Severance hospital.

It is my belief that the men now in the two colleges will be able to preserve for the future at least the essential characteristics and bases of the institutions on which in a future day they and we may build even better than we have in the past but if that be not so, I think we have little to regret. The police told Dr. Koons that in twenty-five years he had put a "crook" in the minds of the Korean students which it would take the government three hundred years to straighten out. I think that the same can be said for the young men who have attended the Severance Union Medical College, and the Chosen Christian College. Including the rush-graduates of 1941 and 1942, the Chosen Christian College has now sent out almost 1,400 young men. Their lives lived and to be lived more than justify the investment of money and time, of tears and prayers which have gone into these institutions.

On Christmas Eve a young man in the uniform of a Japanese soldier appeared at the Y.M.C.A. in Bangkok. He asked for Mr. Barnhart formerly of Seoul, Korea, and asked about me. They were singing Christmas carols and he sat down and sang with them for a little while. When he got up to leave, Mr. Barnhart's secretary asked him if he would not drop in again the next day. He told her that he was a Korean, a graduate of the Chosen Christian College in Seoul, and rather sadly yet with a smile said, "Tonight at midnight we leave for the front. Tell Mr. Barnhart that I will meet him in heaven". To me the episode is deeply significant. A Korean boy thousands of miles from home in a uniform which he hated and which was hated by the people of Thailand, yet meeting the young people of Thailand in Christian fellowship in the singing of Christmas carols expressive of their mutual loyalty to one leader and Saviour and going out into the night sustained by the Christian faith which had become his in college.

---

60. 원한경 전임 교장의 선교관계자 대상 두 번째 경과보고서

문서 제목	Personal Report of Horace H. Underwood, Seoul, Korea 1940~1942 to Presbyterian Board of Foreign Missions
문서 종류	교장 보고서
제출 시기	1942년 겨울
작성 장소	미국
제 출 자	H. H. Underwood
수 신 자	미국 북장로회 선교부 관계자
페이지 수	13
출 처	2114-5-5: 01 Underwood, Horace H. (DR.) 1941~1944 (UMAH)

자료 소개

원한경 전임 교장이 1942년 겨울에 미국에서 다수의 선교관계자에게 보낸 두 번째 경과보고서이다. 이 보고서는 수신자가 다른데도 이것과 첫 번째 경과보고서(차례 58번)의 발행비 및 우편 발송비를 협력이사회에서 지급하였다. 첫 번째 경과보고서의 내용 해제에서 소개된, 원한경이 뉴욕 북장로회 선교부의 용지에 써서 1942년 12월 23일 자로 협력이사회 회계 서덜랜드에게 보낸 편지에 의하면, 그는 첫 번째 보고서를 협력이사회 관계자들에게 제출한 후 이 두 번째 보고서를 써서 많은 곳에 보내고 답장을 받았다. 그러므로 그가 이 두 번째 보고서를 쓴 곳은 뉴욕이고, 그 시기는 첫 번째 보고서의 제출일인 11월 17일 이후와 12월 23일 자 편지의 발송일 이전의 어느 때로 추정할 수 있다.

원한경은 이 보고서에서 연희전문의 전임 교장이자 마지막에 철수한 선교사들의 한 명으로서 겪은 일들을, 아래의 소제목들을 붙여, 설명하였다.

연희전문학교, 안식년 연기, 강의, YMCA, 피어선성경학원, 여학교, 예수교서회, 서대문(교회), 지방 교회들, 자산 처리계획, 인물들, 결혼식, 여름, 졸업, 선전포고, 체포, 수용소, 가족, 송별, 출발과 여정, 미래.

내용 요약

서언: 한국에 맨 처음 교육선교사로 왔던 언더우드(H. G. Underwood)의 후손(원한경 가

족)이 마지막에 철수하는 선교사들과 함께 이 나라를 떠났다. 1940년 11월 16일 마리포사호(S. S. Mariposa)로 먼저 떠난 선교사들과 합류하지 않고 남았다가 마지막에 철수한 이들의 이야기는 선교역사의 중요한 부분을 이룰 것이다.

연희전문학교: 총독부가 1940년 9월부터 원한경의 자발적 사퇴를 유도함에 따라 12월 양자 간 거래로 6가지 합의에 이르렀다. 그것은 원한경이 사임한 후 명예 교장과 이사가 되고, 윤치호가 교장이, 마츠모토가 부교장이 되며, 유억겸이 윤치호를 보필하면서 사실상 수장이 된다는 것이었다. 또한 성경교육과 이사회 정관의 기독교 조항을 유지하고, 이사회에서 외국인을 소수로 만든다는 것이었다. 그리하여 3월 10일 졸업식 때 내가 고별연설을 하였고, 그 후 윤치호, 마츠모토, 유억겸이 운영진을 일본 유학 출신 일색으로 바꾸려 하고, 캠퍼스에서 일본어만 쓰게 하며, 성경 시간을 축소하고, 기독교에 맞지 않는 데도 총독부가 좋아하는 사람을 임명하려 하여, 내가 항의하였다.

안식년 연기: 내가 안식년을 1년 미루어 머물러 있는 동안, 총독부가 언론탄압, 조선어 사용 금지, 지원병 제도, 창씨개명 등을 진행하였다. 종교를 불문하고 한국사회의 거의 모든 집단이 나를 찾아왔다.

강의: 나는 교장직을 사임한 후, 학교에서 성경과 영문학을 가르쳤고, 아내[Ethel Van Wagner Underwood]와 아들[원일한, Horace G. Underwood]도 계속 학생을 가르쳤다.

YMCA: 전국 YMCA는 선교사 철수 이전에 외국 회원들과의 관계를 단절하였고, 나는 1940년부터 YMCA와의 관계를 단절하였다.

피어선성경학원: 내가 이사장으로 있는 피어선성경학원의 운영권을 장악하려는 시도가 있었고, 경찰이 내 집에서 이 학교와 관련된 문서를 모두 압수해갔다.

여학교: 내가 설립자로 있는 여학교의 폐교원을 냈으나 학무국이 승인하지 않았고, 새 학무국장이 내게 설립자 자격을 포기하고 운영책임을 재단에 넘기도록 요구하여 내가 서명하였다.

예수교서회: 마리포사 호의 철수 후에 남은 북장로회 선교사 3명이 교파 연합기관인 예수교서회를 책임지게 되었는데, 자산에 대한 권한은 선교사가 유지하고 사업권만 한국인들에게 넘기려 하였으나, 그곳의 대표인 양주삼 전 감리회 총리사가 극심한 반외세로 돌변하고, 총독부가 1942년 4, 5월경 그곳 자산을 적산으로 정하고 양주삼을 관리인으로 임명하였다.

서대문교회: 1941년 경찰이 서대문교회[새문안교회]에서 미국인이 설교하는 것을 금지하여 내 부친이 설립하고 내가 24년간 일요일마다 설교한 교회를 나가지 못하게 되었다.

지방 교회들: 서대문교회와 연계된 서부 구역의 지방 교회 교인들이 나를 찾아와 마리포사 호로 가지 않고 남아주어서 감사하다고 말하였다.

자산 처리계획: 서울 외국인학교, 유니온교회, 소래 해변과 화진포의 자산 등을 자산관리인에게 맡기거나, 안전한 곳에 두거나, 임대하였다.

인물들: 외국인학교에서 가르치는 원한경의 부인과 다른 여자 선교사들이 3월 26일 경찰에 체포되었다가 1주일 후에 풀려났다.

결혼식: 내 아들(원일한)이 7월 10일 성공회 성당에서 결혼식을 올렸고, 시내 식당에서 450명 이상의 한국인들을 초청하여 잔치를 열었다.

여름: 아들의 결혼식 후에 내가 해변으로 휴가를 떠났으나, 경찰에게 계속 감시, 수색, 압류를 당하였고, 서울에 돌아올 때도 감시를 받았다.

졸업: 총독부의 결정으로 졸업식이 12월 말에 열리게 되어[이때 윤동주와 송몽규가 졸업하였다] 과별로 졸업생들을 나누어 초대하여 만찬을 가졌고, 12월 6일 결혼기념일을 맞았으며, 12월 7일 대학교회에 가서 졸업생들에게 세례를 주었다.

선전포고: 월요일 오전에 전쟁 발발 소식을 들은 후, 아들 부부가 짐을 싸서 내 집에 왔고, 나는 학교에 가서 학생들과 작별 인사를 하고 돌아와 아들 짐을 나르다 오후 4시에 경찰에게 연행되었다.

체포: 경찰서로 끌려가 동료 선교사, 다른 외국인들과 한 방에 구류되어 밤낮 감시받고 간첩 행위를 했는지 취조당하였다.

수용소: 10일 후 감리교신학교 건물로 이송되어 아들과 합류하였고, 그곳에서는 가족이 보낸 음식을 먹었으며, 세 번 가족과 면회하였다. 밀러는 12월 27일 용산 경찰서 유치장으로 이송되어 5월 25일까지 있었다고 설명하였다.

가족: 내 가족은 집에 억류되어 있다가 나중에 경찰에게 알리고 시내에 외출하는 것을 허락받았다. 학생들과 일본인 교수가 가족에게 생필품을 가져다주었고, 많은 사람이 몰래 와서 위로하였다. 나는 4월 10일부터 16일까지 풀려났다가 다시 구금되었고, 5월 31일 오전에 풀려나 다음 날 저녁에 떠났다.

송별: 나의 석방 소식을 듣고 매우 많은 사람이 찾아와 작별 인사를 하였고, 짐을 들고

갈 만큼만 싸게 하여 양가의 유물, 부모가 한국 왕실로부터 받은 선물들, 귀중한 사진들, 한국 관련 서적들을 모두 남겨두고 떠났다.

출발과 여정: 일행이 기차로 출발하여 고베, 도쿄, 요코하마, 홍콩, 사이공, 순다해협, 로렌소 마르케스[현재 모잠비크 수도 마푸투]를 거쳐 미국에 도착하였다.

미래: 불확실성 속에서도 확실한 10가지 사실들이 있다. 그것은 한국에 복음이 필요한 2천만 명의 비기독교인이 있고, 많은 기독교인과 교회가 있고, 한국에 돌아가기를 원하는 숙련된 선교사들이 있다는 점 등이다. 상황이 좋아지면 해야 할 6가지 일들이 있다. 그것은 선교부가 한국 복귀 희망자들을 파악하고 그중 소수를 먼저 한국에 보내되 우리 부부를 1차로 보낼 집단에 넣어줄 것 등이다. 나는 다시 옛날로 돌아간다 해도 잔류하기로 했던 결정을 바꾸지 않을 것이다. 부디 한국에 가게 되기를 바란다.

PERSONAL REPORT OF HORACE H. UNDERWOOD, SEOUL, KOREA
1940 - 1942
to
PRESBYTERIAN BOARD OF FOREIGN MISSIONS

A little more than 57 years after Dr. H. G. Underwood landed in Korea as the first educational missionary, the second and third generation Underwoods were evacuated with the last group of missionaries to leave the country. Eighteen regular and two short term missionaries, two missionary children and one member of the Japan mission, altogether twenty-three individuals under our Presbyterian Board, were on that train. With us were Roman Catholic Maryknoll fathers and sisters, four United Church of Canada workers, two Anglican priests, four Southern Presbyterians, a half dozen or so business people and the British Consular staff.

It was quite a reunion since all had been interned or confined to their homes incommunicado since the day war was declared. Some had suffered severely, some less, all had suffered from loneliness, anxiety, and from the oppressive sense of utter isolation and helplessness. Each of these missionaries have a report to make, a story to tell to the Board and Church which helped them to hold on till the end. While these reports will have little that is startling or sensational, taken together they make a significant chapter in missionary history and a chapter which rightly interpreted promises much for the future.

For all this group the past two or three years are divided into "A.M." or ante "Mariposa" and "P.M." or post "Mariposa". The ante-Mariposa period has already been fully reported, but enters into these reports as a prologue to the final drama. When the "Mariposa" had sailed, the remaining members of the mission looked about to see how under the handicaps of reduced members, growing suspicion, and increasing restrictions, the remnant might best serve the cause. How best might we serve the Korean church, conserve for the future the material interests of mission and board and preserve unspotted the essential values of our Christian message?

CHOSEN CHRISTIAN COLLEGE

For myself these problems were most immediate in the college. For some time past we had been undergoing a process of Japanizing or nationalization which was disturbing but inevitable and not necessarily inconsistent with the Christian character of the college. Military training was made a required subject by the government, but we secured a Christian Korean military instructor. Courses on the spirit and culture of Japan were put into the curriculum and we tried to show in Bible course and chapel how man's highest ideals are found in Christianity and withal a Saviour to help us achieve these ideals. It was clear that the government felt that we needed much reforming.

Early in September 1940 it was plainly intimated to me that the government considered that such an institution should have a national and not an alien at its head. Japanese officialdom never likes to take responsibility, especially for any unpopular policy or action. The system is to bring about "voluntary" action by persuasion, force or trickery. The government itself had twice honoured my service in the country by public citation. The college was founded by my father and the second and third generation of our family were working in it. In thirty years of work, backed by my father's name and history, I had become fairly well-known in Korea. My attitude since I became president had given them no excuse for now demanding my resignation. I was, therefore, in a very good position to make a favourable bargain, for I was sure they would make many concessions to secure my voluntary withdrawal.

From September till the end of November the bargaining went on - largely through third parties so as to save face. Finally early in December we arrived at the following general terms:

1. I, to resign, but to become President Emeritus and retain a seat on the Board of Managers.
2. Dr. T. H. Yun (probably the most prominent Korean Christian) to be President.
3. Dr. Matsumoto, head of our religious department, to be Vice President.
4. Our former Vice President, Mr. U. K. Yu, to be allowed to work with Dr. Yun and to be the real head of the college.
5. Bible teaching and the Christian provisions of the charter to be preserved.
6. The alien membership on the Board of Managers to be reduced to a minority.

This constituted, on its face at least, an almost ideal arrangement and one under which I was quite willing to resign. The danger lay not in the new president, but in the value of the promises made and the possibility that Dr. Yun might be forced to step out to make room for a non-Christian Japanese. We would but do our best and, as always, leave the future to God.

The government attitude solved for me the difficult question of my relation to our mission, and since the way was no longer open to serve the college as its president we rejoiced that we were not required to make the sacrifice of resigning from the mission and thus severing ties which were rooted in so many years. The College Board of Managers met in February and approved the program I had laid out. At the same time it passed some very kind resolutions in regard to my own services. It further arranged that I should continue in office till after graduation. Therefore on March 10th, 1941, it was once more my privilege to give the diplomas to another group of my boys, this time 129 in all. Despite the fears of some as to how the government would regard it, we obstinately held to our usual graduation procedure with prayer, scripture and benediction, and I made my farewell address in Korean. With coming events casting so gloomy a shadow before them the ceremony was one which deeply stirred the emotions of all present.

Previous to graduation we entertained the graduates at dinner as has been our custom for many years. These dinners have been a great joy and most of our 1200 graduates have thus been at our table at least once.

Immediately after graduation Dr. Yun, Dr. Matsumoto and Mr. Yu prepared a program of changes in administration, personnel, curricula and procedure and did me the honour of calling me into conference with them. It was plain that, not only I, but American-trained Koreans must give place to Japanese trained men in administrative positions; it was also plain that not only in class-rooms, but in chapel, offices, and campus the Japanese language must be used exclusively. However, there were cases both in appointments and in curricula where I ventured to protest strongly certain changes. Among these were a reduction in Bible teaching hours and the appointment of a man favoured by the government but ill-fitted from a Christian point of view. Dr. Yun graciously accepted the changes I proposed and strengthened by my protest was able to get the necessary government consent.

FURLOUGH POSTPONED

Realizing some of the problems which would face the new administration and the terrible shortage of workers in mission and station, Mrs. Underwood and I applied through the Mission Executive Committee for permission to postpone our furlough one year. This was finally granted and made it possible for us to be with our Korean friends through these difficult months. We can never be sufficiently grateful for the privilege. Students and teachers, college Board members, church workers, Y.M.C.A. men and Y.W.C.A. women, country church leaders and laymen, non-Christian friends, newspaper men, old graduates, people of almost every group in Korean society have visited us, some like Nicodemus by night, some by the back door and many openly. In a year when the last of the Korean newspapers was suppressed; when Korean ceased to be taught even in primary schools; when "volunteers" for the army were secured by methods far from voluntary, and when even their family names were taken from the Korean people that they might be given Japanese names - in such a year it was a privilege for us to stay. Perhaps it was a help to our friends to take them by the hand, to say a few words of comfort and to promise that we would at least "stand-by" till forcibly ejected. Sometimes, as in the Christian Literature Society, the missionaries' presence prevented (for the time at least) the loss of the institution to non-Christian forces. Sometimes, as in the college, a word of protest was able to preserve essential Christian work. Sometimes, as in the famous case of the Women's Day of Prayer, American women took the blame and saved their Korean sisters from responsibility and imprisonment; often there was active service rendered, as in class-room teaching or in hospital work.

TEACHING

After my resignation as president my routine college work was chiefly that of teaching. I had a most interesting course on the Social Teaching of the New Testament with the seniors in the Science Department as well as a course, based on Dr. H. H. Horne's book "Jesus our Standard", which I gave to the Literary and Commercial juniors. In addition to these courses I taught English literature to the Literary juniors and seniors. Both of these courses gave plenty of opportunity to speak for and of Christ, and to show the power of the religion which has so deeply coloured all the best literature in the English language. Mrs. Underwood also taught several courses in English, as did my son; but with them as with me this teaching was far from being all their work. We like to believe that personal contacts outside of the class-room with students and teachers, faculty wives and staff members; that student prayer meetings and small social gatherings - that these impalpables counted for much.

In the case of my son, in addition to the work done, the mere coming to Korea of Dr. Underwood's grandson, his trip to Tokyo to study Japanese and his wedding in the city where his grandfather and grandmother were married made a deep impression, not only in Christian circles, but in non-Christian society.

Outside the college as well as in it, the story of these months is one of steadily narrowing spheres of work.

Y. M. C. A.

Even before the "Mariposa" sailed the National Y.M.C.A. Board was forced to pass an action abolishing all foreign membership and consequently foreign membership on the Board. Not long after this action it became plain that it was best for Mr. Barnhart, the American Y.M.C.A. secretary, to take his furlough. I maintained such contact as was possible with the Korean and Japanese "Y" secretaries and organization but practically speaking 1940 saw the close of 29 years of connection with the Y.M.C.A.

PIERSON MEMORIAL BIBLE SCHOOL

Still another institution for which I had a share of responsibility was the Pierson Memorial Bible School. My direct relation to this school began when Dr. Rhodes and Mr. Anderson went on furlough and I became chief director. The mission policy and the wishes of Mr. Pierson prevented the opening of the school under the conditions laid down by the government. The previous charter had been forfeited and we were in the process of securing a new one. Strangely enough, the courts had recognized the directors, but no one seemed to know whether these directors, elected after the charter was forfeited, really owned the property or not. As time went on the terms of some of these directors expired and while we met and reelected them it was still more doubtful whether we had a right to elect anyone. Propositions to purchase the property, to lease parts of it etc., etc. came from many sources and each had to be considered (especially the leases) with regard to the bearing that such a deal would have on the whole future status of the property. Certain groups seemed to consider the time ripe for an attempt to seize control by shady methods. Eventually most of the property was rented and the income from rents paid all expenses for upkeep and taxes and left a fair balance. The propositions for sale were rejected; first because the real estate ceiling fixed by the government was too low to make a sale worthwhile; second, it was felt that even if this limit could be raised, money held in the bank in Korea in the name of an alien would be even less secure than real estate. When war was declared the gendarmerie officers searched our house and among other papers seized all those pertaining to the Pierson Memorial Bible School. The Managing director employed by the Board (the Rev. Kum Ho Kim) was retained by the government and later was appointed as custodian of the property. There is thus at least a chance to recover title or compensation after the war.

GIRL'S SCHOOL

Closer to my heart, through years of connection, was our Seoul Girl's School. Its work and problem took more of my time than anything else outside the college and certainly gave me more heart- and headaches. Yet the problem remained vexed, unsolved, anomalous and highly embarrassing up to the very end. One of the last cables sent to the Board before the declaration of war dealt with still another proposition in regard to the school. The Board's request for permission to close the school was presented to the government early in the year (1941); but despite repeated demands we could get no official reply from them. Actually, they were determined not to permit the closure of the school, but were most reluctant to go on record as forcing aliens to continue it, nor were they willing to take the responsibility for seizing alien property and turning it over to non-Christian parties. Finally, in November, the Director of the Department in the presence of witnesses "strongly advised me to withdraw the application to close". I replied "If you give it back to me I can only accept it." He hesitated a moment, as my statement threw the responsibility back on him, but passed the papers across the desk to me saying "Take them." I replied "I have no authority to ask for these, but receive them because you give them." He then went on to give a tentative and unofficial consent to the transfer of the school to Christian parties if the Board would consent. This was the proposition cabled the Board late in November. Officially I was still the "founder" and the legally responsible representative of the school. Before any reply was received from New York war broke out and the Director of the Educational Department was changed. The new Director refused to recognize the claims of the Christian who had offered to take over the school. Finally, early in March 1942 the officials sent asking that I resign as "sollipja" in favour of the Mission Zaidan Hojin (Incorporation). After consultation with the other Mission members interned with me I consented and on March 25th signed the papers whereby I ceased to be "sollipja" and the Incorporated body assumed the responsibility. This appeared to be not only unavoidable, but a measure which would tend to safeguard the Mission property interests.

CHRISTIAN LITERATURE SOCIETY

Obviously, as missionaries left, heavier burdens fell on those who remained and as other Missions withdrew the responsibility for union institutions fell on our Mission. Especially was this true in the Christian Literature Society when at the last only Dr. Koons, Dr. Miller and I remained of the former trustees in Seoul. The problem of the Society early became acute. In the last days of the "A.M." period a group of nationals, apparently acting on suggestions from the authorities, made a request or virtual command that the society and its property be transferred to national control. A few prominent names were attached to the request, but the character of the group and of the request was such as to preclude giving it serious consideration. A meeting of the Trustees was held, at which a vague and innocuous motion was passed promising to give further consideration to the whole question of national representation. The general sentiment of an informal caucus of the trustees was that the interests of the society would be best conserved by maintaining the Occidental control rather than by any measures which would give ownership of the property into the hands of a group which might be dominated by extreme right wing elements, either official or unofficial.

Considerable fencing went on in the early fall, with the remaining occidental members of the Executive Committee in a most embarrassing and difficult position. We were determined not to surrender the valuable property rights, yet it seemed probable that the forces working to eliminate alien control would go to great lengths to secure their ends, unless some compromise were effected. The situation was further complicated by the fact that two or three Methodist members, who had not left on the "Mariposa", were due to leave soon, reducing the Foreign representation to a bare fifty percent or even a minority. We therefore "organized" a group of Korean Christians and drew up a proposition to turn over to them the management of the Society business for a period of three years, the title to the property to remain with the incorporated body as now constituted. The police (indirectly) required some revisions in the nominations for the group of managers; but the plan of a group constituted of a majority of trustworthy Korean Christians and headed by Dr. J. S. Ryang, formerly General Superintendent of the Korean Methodist Church, stood, and the agreement went into effect on May 1st, 1941. The arrangement was far from perfect. Some of the "directors" added to our original slate of nominations were neither satisfactory nor congenial, either to Dr. Ryang or to the Executive Committee of the Incorporation. Certain misunderstandings arose between Dr. Miller, Chief Director of the Incorporation, and Dr. Ryang, Managing Director of the new body. Dr. Ryang, to protect himself and his associates in a very difficult position, took a strongly anti-foreign position which both hurt and embarrassed his former friends. After war was declared, while we were interned, we received by registered mail two calls for meetings of the Executive Committee which, of course, we could not attend. What actions may have been taken at such "rump" meetings we do not know. Still later, in April or May, 1942, the government decided that the Christian Literature Society property was Enemy Alien and appointed Dr. Ryang as the custodian. Lastly, just before we were evacuated, Dr. Koons met Dr. Ryang, who assured him that as far as he and his group was concerned they considered the agreement begun May 1st, 1941, as binding.

WEST GATE

Only a few blocks from the Christian Literature Society building is the West Gate Presbyterian Church, of which my father was the first pastor and founder, and where I was ordained an elder in 1918. I have served on its session from that date on and I have preached in its pulpit on an average of one Sunday a month for twenty four years. In June of 1941 I was called to a meeting of the session at which, with tears in his eyes, the pastor told me that there would be grave difficulties with the police if an American were allowed to use the pulpit, and that the police thought I ought to sever my connections with the church. Pastor and session, however, refused to consider an actual break in our relations, but were obviously much relieved when I said I would absent myself from the church and would not expect any further invitations to occupy the pulpit. Since that time my connection has been entirely "sub rosa", but has included such messages of love, friendship and hope of future work as have warmed our hearts.

COUNTRY GROUPS

From the hive of the West Gate Church many suburban and country groups have swarmed, and most of the rural work of what is called the West District in Seoul Station territory is connected with the former mother church. It used to be my joy to visit these rural churches several times a year. Recently the press of affairs in connection with the college and other city work, and the growing suspicion of the police as to any excursions outside the city practically stopped my visitation of country churches for at least six months "A.M.", though a few visits, usually by invitation, were made. In September of 1940 I attended a mass outdoor service of five or six churches about fifty miles from Seoul, and preached in the same district in January, 1941. In May of '41 Miss Delmarter, Mrs. Underwood and I accepted a most cordial invitation to a wedding in a country church about twenty miles from Seoul and in early July I preached in the suburbs of Seoul.

Contacts, however, did not depend on sermons and all through the "P.M." period right up to June 1st, 1942, the day when we left Seoul, we had visitors who came both to give and receive such comfort as we could exchange. Especially just at the time the "Mariposa" left our visitors and the anxious queries were many. "Are you going too?" "Why are so many leaving?" "Oh, dear, how can we endure when all our American friends and leaders are gone?" "Even if you are locked in your houses we can look at your windows and know that you are still here and praying for us." One man and his wife came one hundred and fifty miles to see us when it was first reported that all missionaries were leaving. All through the period from November, 1940 to December 8th, 1941 there was hardly a day when such visitors did not come or send messages thanking us for staying on.

In some cases we could be of real practical assistance, but altogether aside from such help given I think that all the missionaries who remained in Korea were made to feel that the moral and spiritual effect was worth many times the personal loss or inconvenience suffered.

COMMUNITY PROJECTS

Upon those of us who remained there devolved the duty of trying to save for the future what could be saved in community projects. The Seoul Foreign Church; the Seoul Foreign School, where missionary children have been and we hope will be taught; the Seoul Cemetary Association and the little plot where lie our dead; the Seoul Union - our recreational centre; the summer resort properties at Sorai Beach and Whachinpo; the valuable records and library of the Korea Branch of the Royal Asiatic Society -- all were worth saving if possible. The first impulse of the evacuation by the "Mariposa" was "Scrap everything", "Sell out", "You can't take it with you." To some this seemed unwise and unnecessary. In all these things, as in all branches of missionary work, we look forward to a day when God will permit us (or others) to go on, and it seemed a duty to try to save what we could. The Royal Asiatic Society Library is in good hands; Sorai Beach property is registered with the mission property under a Christian custodian; Seoul Union Church records are placed in reasonable safety; the Seoul Union property titles are recognized and the property rented for five years; the Seoul Foreign School is rented and a satisfactory custodian appointed; the Cemetery property was left in charge of the Russian and French Consulates.

These accomplishments - such as they are - may prove useless after all. They are not to be "credited" to any individual, certainly not the writer, but they were part of the task attempted by the whole group - part of the reason for which they stayed in Korea. We pray God these and other earnest prayerful efforts of those months may in God's good time bear fruit - perhaps even a hundred-fold.

PERSONAL

So much - perhaps too much - for a more formal report on the work from November, 1940 to December, 1941. Any such report must be read in the light of the individual's personal experiences and reactions, so perhaps some space should be given to a more personal record.

As soon as the "Mariposa" left all our personal arrangements for community life had to be revised. The Seoul Foreign School found itself with a baker's dozen or so of pupils and no teachers. Dr. Koons, as principal, and I, as Chairman of the School Association (my part being largely that of approving his work), found teachers (more teachers than pupils), rearranged schedules and fees, and kept the school going till the morning of December 8th. Dr. Koons, Mrs. Koons, Horace and Joan, Dr. Miller and my wife were among the many who each taught a little. The Union Church moved to the upper room of our recreation center and other adjustments were made. We grew accustomed to not being allowed to go outside the city without reporting to the police; we learned that not even the weather was a safe topic for letters, and that any reference to shortages, to prices, or even to social conditions might land you in jail under the Military Secrets Act. Re-adjustments made, things went on rather quietly, though with a tense atmosphere, till the Women's Day of Prayer case. For us in Seoul it broke with the arrest of Mrs. Underwood, Mrs. Koons, Miss Delmarter, Miss Hartness and Mrs. Genso, and the searching of our homes by the police on the morning of March 26th. I was sick in bed and saw only the officers that entered the sickroom. There is little doubt that the whole case was "made" on the flimsiest of grounds so as to have a handle against a large number of missionaries and against missions in general. Mrs. Underwood and the ladies in Seoul were allowed to return home each night, were not struck or insulted, though subjected to severe and frequently rude police grilling. The police seized (almost at random) part of my correspondence files, old books, some church records over forty years old, and a souvenir album made by my mother when a school girl (about 1870)! After about a week of questioning, my wife was released, called in once again about the end of April and finally dismissed. I also was called in to "explain" certain of my correspondence, after which most of the papers and books seized were returned to me. The "case", both then in the arrest and treatment of Miss Butts and the entirely unwarranted arrest and detention of Mr. H. E. Blair, as well as in its later developments again showed the attitude of the police toward Christian missionaries in Korea. However, most of those then on the field had few illusions on this subject and were not greatly surprised or alarmed.

WEDDING

For us the next event and the great event of the year was the engagement and marriage of our son Horace to Miss Joan Davidson, a childhood playmate. They were married in the Church of England pro-Cathedral on July tenth. After the wedding a lovely reception for occidental friends was held at the home of the bride's parents. Partly from gratitude and appreciation of our many Korean friends, both

and partly as a public demonstration of the friendly relations still maintaining between Americans and Koreans, we arranged for a Korean wedding feast at the largest restaurant in town. I think that the attendance of Korean friends, both at the church and at the dinner, astonished the police. Over four hundred and fifty prominent Korean men and women sat down at the long, low Korean tables. The whole spirit was one of love and friendship, and the fact that many of the guests had known the groom's grandparents, added much to the emotional feeling of the occasion. It was most gratifying to see how many were willing to publically show their friendship for an American boy and his English bride. To us the joy of a new daughter, the happiness for our son, and gratitude for our friends' love and kindness was only tempered by the thought of many dear friends who had left.

SUMMER

Shortly after the wedding, and while the bride and groom were on their honeymoon in Peking, we went to the beach. While there the "freezing" order went into effect and large troop movements took place. Joan and Horace barely got back from Peking after an exciting trip on trains which started when they pleased and went only as long as they pleased, to dump the passengers out for waits of unknown duration. At the beach we found ourselves almost prisoners. We might not leave the beach either by boat or car except with police permission and escort. We were quizzed and those individuals who did leave the beach were searched with the greatest thoroughness - fountain pen caps probed for papers, trouser cuffs, eye glass cases - everything. Cameras were sealed, some books and photographs seized. When it came time for us to leave we were told we could not go for another two weeks. I immediately telegraphed the Foreign Affairs Section in Seoul and got quick action. Of our trip with police escort all the way, of the auto-breakdown, of hasty repairs in the boiling sun, of a broken spring, a night in a Japanese inn, of a series of punctures and our arrival in Seoul about 2 a.m. of the second night - 38 hours for a 7 hour trip - I will not tell in detail.

We went back to our teaching and routine work, but to all of us it was just a question of "when?" Soon after our return the principals in the Women's Day of Prayer were gotten out of the country, some to get safely to the United States and some to land in Manila and horrors which will not be fully known till the end of the war. Those last departures reduced the mission to the number now on the "Gripsholm" as I write.

GRADUATION

The government decided to shorten the school year by three months and graduate students at the end of December. Once again we planned our graduation dinner. Already it looked as though war might come any moment. We had the Commercial Seniors in two installments of 35 each on November 20th and 21st. Safely over. Next the Literary Seniors on December 2nd, also safe. Science boys on December 3rd. No war yet. We were much touched that each of these groups of students broke precedent by giving us beautiful farewell gifts.

December 6th was our 25th wedding anniversary. On that morning our twin sons in Princeton Seminary called us on the telephone to give us their good wishes and love! How precious that three minutes conversation seemed through the following months! That night my son and daughter gave us a Wedding Dinner. Sunday we attended the college church (our last Korean church service) where a number of our graduatdes were baptised. Sunday afternoon I preached to our little group at Seoul Foreign Church.

WAR DECLARED

Monday morning after the children had gone to school a friend phoned from the city that war had begun! We sent a servant to bring the children home and I went to my classes as usual. To each class I made a brief speech of farewell and good wishes and, after warm handshakes with the boys who pressed round me, went home. Jean and Horace came over from their house to ours with their suitcases right after lunch. Our local policeman called to say we'd better stay quietly at home, I decided that Horace, Dick and I would take the car andgot some more of Horace and Jean's things from their house across the campus. While there a car drove up with three gendarmes and announced that they had come to take me into "protective custody" for a few days. I asked and got permission to go home, change my clothes and get a blanket. They took our radio and I left our home about 4 p.m. December 8th, to see my wife and children again on January 29th and our home on April 10th.

ARREST

I was taken to the gendarmerie headquarters and put in a room where I found Mr. Reiner, of our mission, and Mr. A. W. Taylor, an American business man. I was given some bread and jam for supper and then questioned till 1:30 a.m. They then searched me and took from me everything in my pockets except my handkerchief and sent me to bed. We had small iron cots and I had a blanket I had brought from home as well as the heavy army blankets provided by the gendarmes. The next morning Miss Astrid Pederson, a Russian girl of Norwegian citizenship, was brought in from another room and was with us from then on.

We were under armed guard night and day and were escorted even to the toilet by our guards. We were not allowed anything to read nor were we allowed to talk to each other. We of course had no knowledge as to what had happened to our families or to the rest of the community. We were called out at the convenience of the inquisitors and grilled sometimes for four or five hours at a time. The inquiries took five main lines:

1. Our relationship with the United States Consul, an attempt to prove that the Consulate was a center of espionage and we the agents.
2. Radio, to prove illegal use of short wave radio.
3. Foreign exchange - to get evidence of criminal violations of the Foreign Exchange Law.
4. Photographs - a search both for technical violation of the law as well as use of photography in espionage.
5. Questions or rather accusations attacking missionary life.

The language was usually abusive and insulting and the whole aim was plainly to "make" a criminal case against us. We were told that we might be shot with impunity. Expecting early American victories we feared that we might feel the weight of reprisal and vengeance. It is only fair to say that we were not struck or maltreated, were kept warm enough and given enough food. It was a low grade of Japanese food served cold and in dirty dishes by a filthy little boy from the kitchen. I should also say that the chief examiner, Captain Fuda, was almost uniformly courteous.

INTERNMENT

After ten days of great mental distress as to our families and ourselves we were allowed to shave for the first time, were put in a car and taken to the

Methodist Episcopal Theological Seminary. Here I found my son and other male members of our community. Altogether there were one woman and twelve men prisoners. With us there were usually two policeman and one gendarme. Sometimes four policemen and two gendarmes, usually sixteen in the room which was about 25 x 25. Here we were fairly comfortable. We slept on wooden cots with bedding and food sent from home. We were allowed relative freedom in the building, though only the one room was heated. Each day we were allowed half-an-hour of exercise outdoors. All food and parcels coming in were carefully examined and the empty containers searched on the way out. Almost without exception the guards used insulting and abusive language and some of them took pains to make themselves obnoxious. The police officer in charge of the "camp" was a Korean educated in a mission school and did his best for us. However he was only at the camp about an hour a day and sometimes several days would elapse between his visits. Meanwhile we were utterly at the mercy of the particular policemen and gendarmes who happened to be on duty.

On December 27th Dr. E. H. Miller was removed to the Ryengsan Police Detention cells and remained there till May 25th. How a man of his age and weak health survived five months under such conditions and such treatment none but a merciful God can know. However it should be remembered that Dr. Miller's treatment was after all only that which hundreds of our Korean Christians have endured and to which any one living under the Japanese government is liable at anytime without any possibility of redress.

January 29th was a red-letter day for us all! Our families were allowed to visit us for a half hour interview in the presence of guards and interpreters. That same day a Hungarian, a white Russian and the Norwegian girl were released.

We settled back for another dreary spell. We received Japanese newspapers which of course gave nothing but Japanese victories and slanders against the allies. A little news leaked in through subterranean channels, but in the main we knew nothing, even of the health of our families. Now that we were allowed to have books most of us turned, of course, to the Bible and to all came a new and richer comfort from God's word and a deeper sense of God's presence. Other books were sent in and games, parchisi, halma, etc. together with language study helped to pass the time. With guards clumping in and out, the refractory stove being stoked and loud conversation among the men on guard there was never any quiet and some suffered a good deal from lack of sleep.

On March 3rd we were granted another interview with our families and on March 5th the two American business men were released. This left only the missionaries and the lone British prisoner. We missionaries were apparently kept because of our wide Korean contacts and the fear lest we might communicate with the Koreans.

FAMILIES

Meanwhile our family was kept at home at first, but later allowed to make necessary visits in the city, reporting each time to the police. They saw no signs of animosity on the streets. Grace (12) began in February to go to and from her music lesson in the city, three miles from our house. Mrs. Underwood received many evidences of love and sympathy from our friends. She was especially touched by a call from a representative of the college students. He came to ask if she had sufficient funds to go on with and said that the boys would raise a fund to provide for the family if necessary! Others called with presents of rice and other supplies and to offer help in any way possible. One Japanese Christian professor called regularly once a month, always with some present of butter or coffee or eggs.

Many others came secretly to offer comfort or help. Fortunately we had a secret "hoard" of cash, and before that was exhausted provision was made for drawing from the bank sufficient for specified needs each month. Our house was searched four times and books, papers, cameras, films, photographs, radios and my hunting guns taken. Some of my books were later returned, but some 7000 feet of movie film, mostly pictures of our home and children, were confiscated and burned. Early in April we were told that an exchange had been arranged and that the ship would sail about April 20th. We were therefore released, very unexpectedly, on April 10th to pack. What a joyful reunion it was in the home I had never expected to see again! Six happy days were spent together; days tinged with the sadness of what was possibly even probably, a last farewell to our home and the accumulated souvenirs of fifty-seven blessed years in Korea. Then, on April 16th, we were told that the ship's sailing was delayed and we were taken back to concentration camp. During this second period came the arrest of Mr. Reiner and Dr. Koons by the Ryongsan police and their torture under investigation. At last, on May 25th, we saw Koons, Reiner and Miller coming up the path! How deeply we thanked God for their deliverance from that awful place. Finally, on the morning of May 31st, we were released to leave the next evening.

FAREWELLS

The news that we were home leaked out, and how many people risked arrest to come and see us, wish us good-bye and beg us to come back soon.

Mrs. Underwood had done most of the heavy work, but the two days were filled to bursting with callers, farewells, final storage, final packing, and last minute arrangements with the official custodian. We were allowed such jewelry as we wore, family portrait photographs, only such baggage as we could carry. With clothes for the tropics and southern hemisphere winter, on a three months journey, there was not much "extra" we could take. Therefore everything we own is still in Korea; family heirlooms from both sides of the family, souvenirs of my father's and mother's association with the Korean Royal family, precious photographs, my unique library on Korea - everything. But after all, they are only things and before the "Mariposa" sailed we had made our decision that they should not count.

We had family prayers for the last time with our faithful servants who had stayed by under real difficulty and danger. Kimsi, the children's nurse, who has carried all our children in her arms, came to the edge of the hill for a tearful farewell.

DEPARTURE AND JOURNEY

The train with people we had not seen for six months; my son's father-in-law sick and carried on a stretcher; the curious glances of the people as we were herded on board; the whistle, and we pulled out on the strangest leave-taking of my life. We arrived at Kobe on June 3rd to hear of another delay. We were herded into two floors of a large building and kept in Kobe two weeks. On June 16th we left for Tokyo and Yokohama, on the 17th we actually boarded the steamer, "Asama Maru". "We're off!" But no, more delays, some hitch in the negotiations. Till June 25th we lay in Yokohama Bay, wondering if we were going back to concentration. Without warning we sailed at 1:20 A.M. on the morning of the 25th. June 29th - HongKong and a new crowd of half starved refugees who had been through the horror of the siege. July 3rd - Saigon and more passengers, many now from Thailand and our own mission. Then through the mine-fields to anchorage fifty miles from Singapore on July 6th. Here we lay for three days, finally sailing on the 9th. We passed through Sunda Straits into the Indian Ocean on the 11th and saw the masts of a sunken vessel projecting above the waves. Finally, on July 22nd, we came into Lorenco Marques. Twenty or more freighters were anchored in the harbor and as we came in they broke out their flags - American and British on most of them! How we cheered.

On the 24th we transferred to this ship, free for the first time from Japanese rule! On the 26th the "Asama" and the "Conte Verdi" sailed with the Japanese for Japan, and on the afternoon of the 23th we sailed for America! We are not there yet. There are plenty of floating mines and submarines between here and New York and as 1600 passengers and 300 of the crew mill on the deck for the pre-arranged boat drill at 11 A.M. we cannot help but wonder what would happen in a real alarm, at 11 P.M. with a high sea running. Then we remember that He who stilled the waves on Galilee can still them on the Atlantic and that as Sir Humphrey Gilbert said, "We are as near to Heaven on the sea as on the land." If it be God's will, we shall soon be in America.

THE FUTURE

And the future? So much is shrouded in uncertainty, and so dark is the present, that many feel that "finis" has been written on the missionary enterprise; it is said that we must take a realistic view. But no view which does not embrace the Power of God can be called realistic, and it is not for His servants to cry "quit" till He Himself writes "Finis" in glorious letters.

It is still true that we cannot build on uncertainties, so let us see what are, humanly speaking, the certainties of the future as regards Korea.

1. The need for the Gospel message to 20,000,000 non-Christians will still exist.
2. There will still be a large body of Korean Christians friendly to America and American missionaries and anxious for help, as well as a warm welcome from non-Christian Korean society.
3. There will still be an organization of Christians, whether a United Christian Church or a Presbyterian Church.
4. After retirement, illness, personal disqualification, etc. is taken into account, there will still be a nucleus of the present group of experienced missionaries anxious and able to return to Korea.
5. The action of the General Assembly makes it certain that there will be reinforcements ready when needed.
6. The economic condition of Korea makes it practically certain that the Koreans will need financial aid.
7. The educational condition of the church makes it certain that they will need leadership aid.
8. Under whatever government the country may be, there will be greater need of disinterested Christian work to heal wounds than ever before.
9. There will be something, great or small, to be salvaged from the Board's property investments, as a start for new work.
10. However restrictive of Christian work the government attitude may be, there will be some form of international contacts and some way by which Christian missionaries can make their influence felt. It has been done in Turkey, Mexico, and other countries and can be done again.

SUGGESTIONS

If these be certainties, as we believe them to be I would suggest:

1. That the Board proceed at once to ascertain who of the present Choson Missionaries are able and willing to return to Choson. In determining who can return, the Board should take into account the factors of personal acceptability as well as health and other conditions.
2. That as soon after peace as possible a small party out of the above group should be sent to Korea. Such a party should include some women and at least one doctor. If necessary, the excuse of looking after the salvage of property could be used to gain entry even before other direct missionary work was possible.
3. That this group contact the Korean Church and Korean Christians and ascertain their attitude and that of the Government, and in consultation with Korean Christians, study the forms of work best suited to the new conditions.
4. That the Board be prepared to return to the field the remainder of the group selected under section one as soon as advice be received from the survey party.
5. That the Board be prepared to strongly reinforce the mission and give it adequate support so as to fully capitalize the pro-American, pro-Christian reaction from present conditions, which will surely come if given any opportunity.
6. I would beg for myself and my wife the privilege of being in the first group to return.

As a family we have lost much by this last stay in Korea, but we have gained infinitely more. Even in the dark days in the gendarmerie prison I would not, if I could, have turned the calendar back and changed our decision to stay. We are grateful to the Board and the Church which made it possible for us to go to Korea and stay there. We pray that God may open the door so that we may perhaps go back "to build the old waste places, raise up the foundation of many generations, repair the breach and restore the paths to dwell in" in Korea.

▎찾 아 보 기 ▎

ㄱ

ㄴ

ㅂ

ㅅ

ㅇ

ㅈ

ㅊ

ㅋ

ㅌ

ㅍ

ㅎ

기타

편찬자 소개

▌연세대학교 국학연구원 연세학풍연구소

연세학풍연구소는 연세 역사 속에서 축적된 연세정신, 연세 학풍, 학문적 성과 등을 정리하고, 한국의 근대 학술, 고등교육의 역사와 성격을 살펴보기 위해 설립되었다. 일제 강점하 민족교육을 통해 천명된 "동서고근 사상의 화충(和衷)"의 학풍을 계승, 재창조하는 "연세학"의 정립을 지향한다. 〈연세학풍연구총서〉, 〈연세사료총서〉를 간행하고 있다.

▌자료 수집 · 설명 | 문백란

전남대학교 사학과, 연세대학교 대학원(문학박사)에서 수학하였으며, 현재 연세학풍연구소 전문연구원으로 활동하고 있다. 「언더우드와 에비슨의 신앙관 비교」 등의 논문들을 썼고, 본 연구소에서 간행한 『연 · 세전 교장 에비슨 자료집』(Ⅰ)과 (Ⅲ)~(Ⅴ)를 번역하였다.

▌감수 | 김도형

서울대학교 국사학과, 연세대학교 대학원(문학박사)에서 수학하였으며, 연세대학교 교수, 한국사연구회 회장, 한국사연구단체협의회 회장, 한국대학박물관협회 회장, 동북아역사재단 이사장 등을 역임하였다. 『민족문화와 대학: 연희전문학교의 학풍과 학문』과 『근대한국의 문명전환과 개혁론: 유교비판과 변통』을 비롯한 다수의 논저가 있다.